THE TOUGALOO NINE

From *Prophets for a New Day*, by Margaret Walker, 1970

JOEL (partial)

Joel, that young prophet . . .
Joel is a do-something man
Joel is a young man of action
He is the sit-in suffering without shame
He is the man marching in the streets
And praying on the steps
Filling the jails with song, with singing that is sweet
Joel is the power-wire of living, flaming truth
Joel is the lighted torch of sacrificing youth
Crying, "We shall overcome!"
Crying, "We are not afraid!"
Crying, "We do not fear to die!"
Joel is the torch of truth towering high above the temples
Above the spires and steeples of the synagogues and sanctuaries
Lighting the nation with the fire of revelation
Lighting the nation with the everlasting flame of truth
Joel is our burning-hearted youth.
Speak on, Joel, your harsh and bitter words of burning Truth.

From *This Is My Century: New and Collected Poems*, by Margaret Walker. ©1989 by Margaret Walker Alexander. Reprinted by permission of University of Georgia Press.

THE
TOUGALOO

The Jackson Library Sit-In
at the Crossroads of
Civil War and Civil Rights

NINE

M. J. O'Brien

UNIVERSITY PRESS OF MISSISSIPPI / JACKSON

The University Press of Mississippi is the scholarly publishing agency of the Mississippi Institutions of Higher Learning: Alcorn State University, Delta State University, Jackson State University, Mississippi State University, Mississippi University for Women, Mississippi Valley State University, University of Mississippi, and University of Southern Mississippi.

www.upress.state.ms.us

Designed by Peter D. Halverson

The University Press of Mississippi is a member of the Association of University Presses.

Publisher: University Press of Mississippi, Jackson, USA
Authorised GPSR Safety Representative: Easy Access System Europe – Mustamäe tee 50, 10621 Tallinn, Estonia, gpsr.requests@easproject.com

Library of Congress Cataloging-in-Publication Data

Names: O'Brien, M. J., 1951– author | Thompson, Bennie, 1948– writer of foreword
Title: The Tougaloo Nine : the Jackson Library sit-in at the crossroads of civil war and civil rights / M. J. O'Brien, Bennie Thompson.
Description: Jackson : University Press of Mississippi, 2025. | Includes bibliographical references and index.
Identifiers: LCCN 2025030750 (print) | LCCN 2025030751 (ebook) | ISBN 9781496856036 hardback | ISBN 9781496859808 epub | ISBN 9781496859815 epub | ISBN 9781496859822 pdf | ISBN 9781496859839 pdf
Subjects: LCSH: Tougaloo College—History | Jackson State College—History | Civil rights movements—Mississippi—History—20th century | African American student movements—Mississippi—History—20th century | Civil rights demonstrations—Mississippi—History—20th century | African Americans—Civil rights—Mississippi—History—20th century | African Americans—Segregation—Mississippi—History—20th century | Public libraries—Mississippi—20th century | Mississippi—Race relations—History—20th century | BISAC: HISTORY / African American & Black | SOCIAL SCIENCE / Activism & Social Justice
Classification: LCC E185.93.M6 O26 2025 (print) | LCC E185.93.M6 (ebook) | DDC 305.896/073097620904—dc23/eng/20250825
LC record available at https://lccn.loc.gov/2025030750
LC ebook record available at https://lccn.loc.gov/2025030751

British Library Cataloging-in-Publication Data available

CONTENTS

PART VI—AFTERSHOCKS

PART VII—LEAVING THE NEST

PART VIII—WHERE THIS STORY ENDS

FOREWORD

CONGRESSMAN BENNIE THOMPSON

WHEN I REFLECT ON MY JOURNEY FROM THE SMALL TOWN OF BOLTON, Mississippi, to the halls of Congress, I often think of the remarkable individuals whose courage and conviction paved the way for my own path. Among them, the Tougaloo Nine stand out as a beacon of bravery and resilience. Their story, captured by M. J. O'Brien so poignantly in *The Tougaloo Nine: The Jackson Library Sit-In at the Crossroads of Civil War and Civil Rights*, is not merely a chapter in our history but a living testament to the transformative power of unwavering dedication to justice.

As a student at Tougaloo College, I was deeply moved by the legacy of the Tougaloo Nine. The sit-in they orchestrated in 1961 was not just an act of defiance but a profound assertion of dignity and rights in the face of entrenched segregation and systemic oppression. Their commitment to challenging the status quo, to standing up for their principles in the face of adversity, served as a powerful source of inspiration for me and countless others.

In those formative years, I learned that true change demands more than just a passive hope for a better future—it requires active, courageous engagement. The Tougaloo Nine's bravery in the library sit-in was a masterclass in this very principle. Their steadfast resolve in demanding equality and justice was a guiding light, illuminating the path for young activists like me who sought to contribute meaningfully to the civil rights movement.

Their actions inspired me to become more than just an observer of history. They motivated me to take up the mantle of leadership, to fight for civil rights and social justice with the same fervor and determination that they demonstrated. The courage of the Tougaloo Nine became a personal call to action, pushing me to embrace the role of public service and ultimately to serve as a congressman dedicated to continuing their legacy of fighting for the marginalized and the oppressed.

This book captures the essence of their struggle and triumph, offering readers a chance to understand the historical significance of their actions and the profound impact they have had on shaping the trajectory of the civil rights movement. *The Tougaloo Nine* is more than a recounting of events; it is a celebration of the spirit that drives us to seek justice and equality.

As you delve into the pages of this remarkable work, may you be inspired by the courage of the Tougaloo Nine, just as I was. Their story is a powerful reminder that the fight for freedom is an ongoing journey, and it is our collective duty to carry forward their legacy with the same determination and hope.

INTRODUCTION

THE TOUGALOO NINE IS A PREQUEL, OF SORTS, TO MY FIRST WORK OF nonfiction, *We Shall Not Be Moved*. It tells a more complete story of how the indigenous movement for civil rights in Jackson, Mississippi, began. While *We Shall Not Be Moved* focused on what might be considered one of the most dramatic student-led sit-ins to occur in Mississippi—the Jackson Woolworth's sit-in of 1963—*The Tougaloo Nine* focuses on what most historians consider the first student-led sit-in within the Magnolia State's capital city in 1961. Typical of any prequel, many of the same characters from the earlier work play leading parts: Medgar Evers still occupies a central role as the state's lead NAACP representative; Ross Barnett still occupies the Governor's Mansion on Capitol Street, as does Allen Thompson the mayor's office at City Hall; Dan Beittel has just become president of Tougaloo College, and Professor Ernst Borinski, two years younger and a little less bald, consistently encourages his students at Tougaloo to think creatively about how to change their status as second-class citizens.

The prequel form also allows for new, unfamiliar faces and forces to appear, helping to understand what comes later in the narrative. Chief among these will be Reverend John Dee Mangram, Tougaloo's chaplain from 1950 to 1961. Heretofore a somewhat unsung and underrepresented force among Tougaloo's storied progressive past, Mangram now takes a central role, though much remains to be discovered about his life and legacy. Here too, the reader will find a more full-blown exploration of the twin-headed hydra of racial suppression: The Citizens' Council and the Mississippi Sovereignty Commission. These radically conservative organizations and their leaders receive a broader exploration here. In addition, through sheer serendipity (or was it expert planning?) the execution of the Tougaloo Nine library sit-in will overlap Mississippi's over-the-top celebration of the centenary of the state's entry into the Civil War, thus the book's subtitle (*at the Crossroads of Civil War and Civil Rights*).

Most importantly, *The Tougaloo Nine* explores the lives of those nine brave Tougaloo students who decisively dared to be the first to publicly break the city's strict segregation codes by entering a "Whites-only" library, sitting down, and starting to read.

THE TOUGALOO NINE

PROLOGUE

WHEN HE WAS ELEVEN YEARS OLD, JOSEPH JACKSON JR. WATCHED POWER-lessly as his beloved mother was beaten to the dusty, graveled ground by a burly bus driver. It happened in the little Delta town of Clarksdale, Mississippi, as the Jacksons were returning from an extended visit with family further south. Joseph's mother had meekly approached the driver with a question just before the bus was scheduled to pull out after a brief pit stop at the Greyhound station. The youth didn't know exactly what transpired between the two adults—only that almost instantaneously the bus driver raised his hand and smacked his mother across the mouth; she then fell to the stones. No one came to their aid; indeed, no one uttered a word of either protest or concern. Young Jackson rushed to his mother's side, saw blood coming from her mouth, and hurriedly helped her up and onto the bus as the driver jumped into his seat and prepared to pull off. The shock of that moment stayed with Jackson for the rest of his life.

Joseph Jackson and his mother never talked about the incident—neither as she recovered on the bus ride home to Memphis nor in the years that followed. It was too alarming and painful even to speak of. But for Jackson, it was an awakening to the harsh and horrifying reality of what it meant to be Black in the White-ruled world of the Deep South. It was a moment he would brood over. It fueled his anger at the unjust social system that confronted him daily. It eventually caused him to stand up to such cruelty, such barbarism, by getting involved in the burgeoning civil rights movement in Mississippi a dozen years later.

Not every member of the Tougaloo Nine—the group Joseph Jackson would join—had such a visceral experience of Southern racism to fuel their protest. But each had enough run-ins with Jim Crow practices to know that they were not willing to live in such an unbalanced and cruel society. Something had to change. Their shabbier neighborhoods, their fewer job opportunities, and even society's lower expectations of them pushed them to challenge the status quo.

This book tells the story of these nine activists who took some of the first deliberately public steps to challenge and rectify the established social order in the deepest Deep South state of Mississippi. And they did it, incredibly, at the very time when the White South was caught up in the frenzy of celebrating its cherished and oh-so-tragic Lost Cause traditions during the centenary commemoration of the Civil War—the very mythology that arose from and fueled their White-supremacist ideology. This clash of cultures—one harking back to a romanticized, unjust past; the other looking forward to a more equitable future—constitutes the underlying theme of this book. It provides, in miniature, an example of the conflicting visions of America playing out across this nation during the turbulent overlapping years of both the Civil War Centennial and the emerging student-led civil rights movement.

Throughout this book, the reader will meet personalities such as Medgar Evers and Ross Barnett—both on the cusp of playing outsized roles on the national stage. But presented for the first time are heretofore unheralded individuals such as Joseph Jackson Jr. and his cohort, who would keep pushing against America's then-status-quo ethos of laissez-faire segregation until things began to change.

In his landmark exploration of the nation's mid-twentieth-century race problem, social engineer Gunnar Myrdal wrote that "America is continuously struggling for its soul."[1] This book offers a microcosmic look at how that struggle began playing out in Deep South Jackson, Mississippi.

Part I

THE SETUP

Chapter 1

AMERICA'S DILEMMA

IN 1937, THE YEAR OF JOSEPH JACKSON JR.'S BIRTH, THE CARNEGIE CORporation invited the Swedish economist and social scientist Gunnar Myrdal to perform a comprehensive study on America's "Negro problem." The dashing, forty-year-old Myrdal, who would later win the Nobel Memorial Prize in Economics, had visited the United States just once, at the beginning of the Great Depression, under the auspices of a Spelman Fund fellowship. Myrdal's relative inexperience with American customs and mores was seen as an advantage by the Carnegie leadership. Frederick Paul "F. P." Keppel, Carnegie's president at the time, explained that "it appeared wise to seek as the responsible head of the undertaking someone who could approach his task with a fresh mind, uninfluenced by traditional attitudes or by earlier conclusions."[1]

Myrdal may have been only one of many scholars considered by Keppel to lead the study—there were two dozen suggestions on a compiled list of luminaries, with Myrdal dead last—but his selection turned out to be a prescient one. Born in 1898 in a tiny rural village in central Sweden, Myrdal earned a law degree and a doctorate in economics from the University of Stockholm, where he would later teach. His early exposure to America aroused in him a deep appreciation for the country's foundational eighteenth-century Enlightenment values of freedom and equality—something he would use to great effect in the Carnegie study.[2]

The idea for the study came from one of the Carnegie Corporation's board members, Newton D. Baker, a progressive politician who had had the distinction of serving as Woodrow Wilson's secretary of war during America's involvement in World War I. Baker previously oversaw the city of Cleveland as its mayor at a time when that metropolis was experiencing a significant increase in its Black population at the start of what would come to be known as "The Great Migration"—Black citizens fleeing the Jim Crow South for what they hoped would be more opportunity and freedom in the North. Interestingly, Baker's father had served as a Confederate cavalryman during the Civil War, though most of his West Virginia family had been for the Union. Nevertheless, Baker expressed to the Carnegie Board his deep concern over the growing racial issues developing throughout the country and urged them to undertake a comprehensive study if for no other reason than to ensure that the philanthropic organization was spending its money wisely in attempting to assist Black Americans and their institutions. "We agreed with him further," Keppel recalled, "in believing that the gathering and digestion of the material might well have a usefulness far beyond our own needs"—an understatement, as it would turn out.[3]

Myrdal, with boundless energy and a seemingly open-ended budget, put together one of the most impressive teams ever assembled to tackle a single American social issue. These included, to name just a few, future United Nations undersecretary and Nobel Peace Prize–winner Ralph Bunche; American sociologist E. Franklin Frazier; poet and Black cultural scholar Sterling Brown; sociologist and future president of Fisk University Charles S. Johnson; psychologist Kenneth Clark; education expert Doxey Wilkerson; sociologist and statistician Dorothy S. Thomas; and anthropologists Ruth Landes and Melville Herskovits. In all, some seventy-five experts from various fields joined the team during the report's development.[4]

When it finally arrived in January 1944 during the dark days of World War II, *An American Dilemma: The Negro Problem and Modern Democracy* was met with polite but somewhat tepid reviews by the popular press of the day. It would take time for the book's power to take hold. In its brief review, *Time* magazine observed that "Dr. Myrdal drew conclusions that will make US citizens either nod or squirm." The nodders, apparently, would be those who thought it was about time America's moral hypocrisy was exposed—fighting overseas to protect democracy and end fascism while at home denying 10 percent of its own citizens their democratic rights to "life, liberty and the pursuit of happiness." Those squirming, presumably, would be everyone else.[5]

This apt soundbite analysis got to the heart of Myrdal's bedrock observation that when it came to the treatment of its nearly 13 million Negro citizens, America was not living up to its stated ideals—its "America Creed"—as put forth in the Declaration of Independence, the Preamble to the Constitution, and the Bill of Rights. Unless and until this changed, America, particularly White America, would have an ongoing crisis of conscience trying to match its soaring national rhetoric with its less-than-honorable practices—thus, America's dilemma.[6]

Published in two volumes, *An America Dilemma* totaled more than one thousand pages in length, with almost five hundred additional pages of appendices, notes, and an index. This double doorstop of a book delved into every conceivable aspect of Black life in America. Conducted during the birth and early childhood years of the Tougaloo Nine participants, this exhaustive study lays out in striking detail the world they were entering—a world where everything seemed stacked against them. From limited access to schools, to jobs, to social and economic opportunity, *An American Dilemma* relentlessly points out how the reality of African American life stood in stark contrast to the nation's democratic ideals of equality and justice.[7]

And it was the majority race that Myrdal was holding accountable. "The Negro problem is a white man's problem," Myrdal bluntly states at the start. "Practically all the economic, social, and political power is held by whites. The Negroes do not have by far anything approaching a tenth of the things worth having in America."[8] The solution, he claimed, was simple—though admittedly its implementation would be fraught. America needed to start living up to its high ideals. "From the point of view of the American Creed the status accorded the Negro in America represents nothing more and nothing less than a century-long lag of public morals," Myrdal declared. "The Negro in America has not yet been given the elemental civil and political rights of formal democracy, including a fair opportunity to earn his living. . . . And this anachronism constitutes the contemporary 'problem' both to Negroes and to whites. If those rights were respected, many other pressing social problems would, of course, remain. . . . But there would no longer be a *Negro* problem."[9]

Myrdal believed that this fundamental disconnect between America's stated lofty "values" and its failure to implement them fully was creating a crisis of conscience that would inevitably lead to a dramatic change of course. Indeed, Myrdal's thorough analysis presages all of the nation's progress on civil rights during the next quarter century. One can even hear echoes of Myrdal in Martin Luther King Jr.'s 1963 March on Washington speech nearly twenty years later: "I have a dream that one day this nation will rise up and live out the true meaning of its *creed*: 'We hold these truths to be self-evident, that all men are created equal.'"[10] Just as King would later do, Myrdal points out the huge divide between America's stated beliefs and its lagging execution. And that "century-long lag" is one of the themes of this book—the contrast between the state of Mississippi's stuck-in-the-past celebration of its mythic Confederate heritage versus the Tougaloo Nine's insistence that it was time instead for the state—and by inference, the nation—to turn the page and start a new chapter.

After complimenting Americans for their extraordinary form of government and the way that every American seems to have imbibed the country's originating ethos, Myrdal gets down to the business at hand. He spends eleven chapters in a section called "Economics"—his specialty—demonstrating how America's Black citizens are getting a raw deal. By every measure, African Americans are not just being left out, but they are forcibly being kept out of achieving anything close to the American Dream. He tackles topics such as "Negro Poverty," "Economic Exploitation," "Discrimination in Public Service," and "The Self-Perpetuating Color Bar." There are tables and charts—even maps—on everything from birth rates to employment comparisons to eating habits, each of which demonstrates how Black citizens end up on the losing end of the measurements.

Ralph Bunche, perhaps Myrdal's most important collaborator, supplied him with extensive background research in four lengthy studies on Black leadership, political status, achievement, and "betterment" organizations. Myrdal used this invaluable intel and wove it through this vast and detailed work.[11]

When the book was finally released in early 1944, having been delayed by various issues related to World War II, including limited paper supply, *An American Dilemma* received mixed reviews from the academic establishment. But the audience Myrdal was most interested in—White political decision-makers and Black thought leaders—proved effusive. Chief among these was W. E. B. Du Bois, the grand old man of Black scholarship. The notoriously prickly Du Bois did not, in this case, withhold his praise. "Never before in American history has a scholar so completely covered this field," Du Bois wrote. "The work is monumental." He also noted that "Myrdal does not gag at facts" and marveled that "He does not appease the South." The eminent Black influencer—who by then had been railing about these same issues for nearly half a century—seemed to realize that *An American Dilemma* would have a major impact upon American society. He also rightly predicted that the study would come in for "sharp attack." "What have ideals to do with science?" Du Bois imagined hidebound American sociologists asking. "Everything," he replied, "if Science is Truth."[12]

Well-regarded theologian Reinhold Niebuhr also offered high praise for *An American Dilemma*, suggesting that "every thoughtful student of American life ought not only read but possess" a copy. Other liberal theologians followed suit. Even some liberal Southern scholars initially praised Myrdal's work while at the same time questioning some of his observations and conclusions.[13]

RANKING PREJUDICE

One brilliant observation, somewhat comical in retrospect, that Myrdal lays out in detail in *An American Dilemma* could only have been developed by an outsider—someone not entangled by the seemingly impossible Gordian knot of American race prejudice. Myrdal attempts to put the race issue into a sort of unified theory. Early in the book, in a chapter titled "Facets of the Negro Problem," he posits his formula for why the conundrum was so complex; he calls this "The White Man's Rank Order of Discriminations." Myrdal suggests that there is an order, a ranking system from highest to lowest, of the excuses that White Americans offer for not allowing Black citizens equality in society. And although Myrdal notes that these rankings, these predispositions, seem to occur more prominently in the South, he also acknowledges that things, "on the whole [are] not greatly divergent" in the North. He records that this order held "nearly unanimously" in all of the interactions he had while conducting his field research during 1938 and 1939.

Here is Myrdal's ranking system, listing White rationale for resisting social and political equality for Blacks, from those of highest concern to lowest:

Rank 1: Highest in this order stands the bar against intermarriage and sexual intercourse involving white women.

Rank 2: Next come the several etiquettes and discriminations, which specifically concern behavior in personal relations. (These are the barriers against dancing, bathing, eating, drinking together, and social intercourse generally; peculiar rules as to handshaking, the hat lifting, use of titles, house entrance to be used, social forms when meeting on streets and in work, and so forth. These patterns are sometimes referred to as the denial of "social equality" in the narrow meaning of the term.)

Rank 3: Thereafter follow the segregations and discriminations in use of public facilities such as schools, churches and means of conveyance.

Rank 4: Next comes political disfranchisement.

Rank 5: Thereafter come discrimination in law courts, by the police, and by other public servants.

Rank 6: Finally come the discriminations in securing land, credit, jobs, or other means of earning a living, and discriminations in public relief and other social welfare activities.[14]

Myrdal clarifies what may be obvious to those familiar with the intimate dance of segregation: that "the rank order is very apparently determined by the factors of sex and social status, so that the closer the association of a type of interracial behavior is to the sexual and social intercourse on an equalitarian basis, the higher it ranks among the forbidden things."

Most interesting about Myrdal's observation is that this generally unspoken White ranking system on why Black equality must be forbidden is in the *exact opposite order* of the issues most important to Black people! He states emphatically—and the italics are his—"*[T]he Negro's own rank order is just about parallel, but inverse, to that of the white man.*" In other words, for Black Americans—at least those that Myrdal had a chance to interview—having access to good jobs, fairness in the justice system, and the ability to vote are much more important than having sex with a White partner or dancing with or having a meal with a White person. The claim brings to mind Martin Luther King Jr.'s often-repeated quip, "The basic aim of the Negro is to be the white man's brother, not his brother-in-law."[15]

Whether or not Myrdal's sociological observations on White-Black interactions hold up in the light of modern scholarship seems inconsequential for this discussion.[16] What Myrdal did in the early 1940s was to call attention, as objectively as he could, to Black America's plight and to reflect those findings back to the country holding itself up as a beacon of democracy. In chapter after chapter, Myrdal details how America's Black citizens are being discriminated against—cheated out of jobs, disenfranchised from the voting booth, kept from even the most basic interactions with society—eating and drinking in public restaurants, staying at hotels, visiting libraries and public parks. Relentlessly, Myrdal and his researchers point out how Blacks are being barred from full participation in the public economy, from fair and affordable housing, even from basic health care. *An American Dilemma* was as damning a portrait of race relations as had ever been presented since the Civil War, and it shook the political and intellectual centers of American life. Historian of the South C. Vann Woodward later acknowledged: "It is noteworthy that the first writer to succeed significantly in removing the scales from native whites' eyes was a foreigner, the Swedish scholar Gunnar Myrdal, author of *An American Dilemma*."[17]

TO SECURE THESE RIGHTS

The findings of *An American Dilemma* are said to have influenced President Harry Truman's decision in 1946 to create the President's Committee on Civil Rights to develop recommendations for "more adequate and effective means and procedures for the protection of the civil rights of the people of the United States." *To Secure These Rights*, the commission's report, came out a year later and proposed substantive changes to laws and policies at the national as well as state and local levels to ensure a more robust legal underpinning of civil rights protections.[18]

Scholars also suggest that *An American Dilemma* helped ensure the desegregation of the US military in 1948. *To Secure These Rights* had recommended a number of policy and legislative initiatives using, though uncredited, Myrdal's three primary reasons—morality, economy, and international reputation—as their rationale. A key policy recommendation was "to end immediately all discrimination and segregation based on race, color, creed, or national origin, in . . . all branches of the Armed Services." During his tough

1948 presidential campaign, Truman did just that, announcing his Executive Order 9981 in July of that year. One of those entrusted to implement that order was Stuart Symington, the first secretary of the US Air Force, who would later go on to become a US senator from Missouri and a contender for the 1960 Democratic presidential nomination. His unflinching implementation of Truman's executive order became a model for the other branches of the military. Symington would later write that it was something he had read in Myrdal's work—a quote from George Bernard Shaw's *Man and Superman* (a footnote in *An American Dilemma*)—that stuck in his craw and caused him to see the "Negro problem" in a new light. "[It] went something like this": Symington recorded, "First the American white man makes the negro clean his shoes, then criticizes him for being a bootblack."[19]

Apparently, many White men in positions of power were having similar epiphanies. In 1947, Hubert Humphrey, then-mayor of Minneapolis, delivered an impassioned speech about fair employment that was classic Myrdal: "Our conscience in America has become corroded and encrusted with a bitter feeling of guilt because we profess a belief in justice and equality of opportunity, but we practice injustice and discrimination." Humphrey had read *An American Dilemma* prior to running for office. Later, in his 1948 speech at the Democratic National Convention calling on the consciences of all gathered delegates for a stronger civil rights plank in the party's platform, Humphrey electrified the progressives in the room. The speech pushed him onto the national stage, particularly after his "minority report" on civil rights passed in a close vote on the convention floor.[20]

Certainly, the most enduring reference to *An American Dilemma* came in the form of a footnote in the landmark 1954 school desegregation case *Brown v. Board of Education*, the case that more than any other had an accelerating effect on the movement for civil rights in America. In fact, references to Myrdal's masterpiece in American civil rights court cases started six years earlier in *Shelly v. Kraemer* (1948), a landmark restrictive housing covenant case, and continued through *Henderson v. United States* (1950), outlawing segregation in interstate forms of transportation, and *Sweatt v. Painter* (1950) and *McLaurin v. Oklahoma State* (1950), two cases requiring that graduate schools begin accepting qualified Black applicants. Myrdal's text had quickly entered into the canon of essential documents of the twentieth century.[21] Indeed, one prominent scholar, University of Chicago sociologist Ernest Burgess, would later uniquely praise Myrdal's work: "The combination of knowledge of the facts and its value-orientation has made *An American Dilemma* the most powerful instrument of action in the field of race relations since Harriet Beecher Stowe's *Uncle Tom's Cabin*." Comparing *An American* Dilemma to another foundational text pointing out racism in the land of the free suggests that Myrdal's study was having as much impact on American race relations as Stowe's narrative had on the push to end slavery in the United States.[22]

Many came to see *An American Dilemma* as a prophetic document that predicted for the quarter century following its publication—from 1944 to 1969—all that would transpire in race relations in the United States, up to and including the Civil Rights Act of 1964, the Voting Rights Act of 1965, and the Fair Housing Act of 1968. In fact, in 1964, the influential *Saturday Review* magazine asked a small sampling of some of its most esteemed readers, "What books published during the past four decades most significantly altered the direction of our society?" *An American Dilemma* appeared second on the list, following only John Maynard Keynes's groundbreaking book on economics *The General Theory of Employment, Interest and Money*.[23]

By commissioning *An American Dilemma* and publishing its unvarnished findings, the Carnegie Corporation, unwittingly, had hit upon a winning strategy to push America out of its laissez faire attitude toward the treatment of its Black citizens. For anyone paying attention, it became clear that the country's go-slow/status quo approach to race relations would no longer fly, particularly with increased international scrutiny. Landing as it did "during the most anxious months" of World War II, as Myrdal later wrote, the study also placed in stark relief America's international reputation as a bellwether of freedom with its domestic practice of imprisoning in poverty and severe social deprivation a full one-tenth of its own citizens.[24]

Having acknowledged *An American Dilemma*'s crucial impact on American life, one must also observe that it certainly is not a perfect document. There are cringeworthy passages, particularly those decrying the pathologies of African American culture. These and other aspects of the study created a cottage industry of social and political scientists publishing critiques and criticisms of Myrdal, his techniques, his observations, and his findings. "To be sure," one historian observed, "by 1969, no significant part of the hallowed study had gone uncontested."[25] Despite its imperfections, however, *An American Dilemma* offers a compelling and clear analysis of the country's racial problem at a point in time when for most Americans it was so intractable as to defy solution. Even the modern scholar of race Ibram X. Kendi, while acknowledging *An American Dilemma*'s faults, pays his respects to the work, calling its appearance in 1944 "a landmark manifesto for the coming civil rights movement." In addition, journalist Isabel Wilkerson references Myrdal's work in her groundbreaking 2020 book, *Caste*, saying that *An American Dilemma* is "still considered perhaps the most comprehensive study of race in America."[26]

Yet, as historian Oscar Handlin observed in a twenty-year retrospective of the work, Myrdal's study took as its overall thesis the impact of discrimination on the Black community and on the nation as a whole.[27] As such, it is essentially a grievance document, pointing out all the problems experienced by Black Americans. It therefore misses important sustaining realities in Black life at the time. What cannot be quantified by Myrdal and his army of social scientists—what does *not* come across in *An American Dilemma*—is the incredible persistence, the enduring hope, even the heightened expectation that each successive generation of Black Americans has for themselves and their children: that the American Dream, if not exactly tangible for themselves, is within reach for the next generation. As evidenced in the upcoming profiles of the Tougaloo Nine demonstrators, in nearly every case a cocoon of hope and expectation is woven around them from birth, it seems, which appears impenetrable during their early formative years. They don't know they're poor; they don't have a sense of the risks they run; they aren't privy to the statistics about life expectancy or future livelihood based on current circumstances. They are shielded for a time from the troubling world that awaits them.

Given the harsh data that Myrdal presented right at the time of their birth, the Tougaloo Nine will far exceed any predictions that might have been made about their potential futures. In addition, what is not to be undervalued in this analysis is the Black institutions that predate the lives of these nine soon-to-be freedom fighters. Chief among these are the Black churches that fostered a spirit of endurance, if not rebellion; the National Association for the Advancement of Colored People (NAACP), which pushed the envelope further through constitutionally acceptable resistance and legal challenges to unjust laws and practices; and the Historically Black Colleges and Universities (HBCUs), which provided a cultural embrace of Blackness while holding their African American charges to a strict ethos of academic and moral rigor.

For this narrative, the most important of these institutions will be one particular HBCU—Tougaloo College located just outside of Jackson, Mississippi—and both the local branch and the national headquarters of the NAACP, which will provide significant encouragement and legal support for the Tougaloo students once they take their historic steps into the sacrosanct "Whites-only" library.

First, however, some appreciation for the local social and political milieu into which the Tougaloo Nine will insert themselves is required. For that, it is necessary to enter the complex maze of Deep South society in *Mississippi, USA*.

Chapter 2

MISSISSIPPI, USA

IN 1961—THE SAME YEAR THE TOUGALOO NINE MADE THEIR BELLWETHER push for racial equality—an enterprising television broadcasting team out of Oklahoma developed a documentary about the political forces shaping the nearby Magnolia State. The editorial focus on Mississippi came not because of any in-state disruptions but because Freedom Riders from outside of the state decided to push the point that it was about time Mississippi, and by extension the rest of the Deep South, began to act like they were part of the United States of America rather than their own sovereign region. The program was called *Mississippi, USA*.[1]

Although a relic of its time—all grainy black-and-white newsreel and a formal, formulaic script and announcer—this thirty-minute short provides deep insight into the personalities, the organizations, and the issues that the state was wrestling with: How far can any individual state go in defending its rights against an encroaching, overarching federalism? How far can organizations go in advocating for their members' interests? And perhaps most importantly, how can people of various ethnic and racial backgrounds find common ground to ensure that all are treated equally?

Mississippi, USA introduces some of the key individuals and organizations that will enliven this volume and provides priceless videographic evidence of the world into which the Tougaloo Nine inserted themselves. Among the personalities presented are Ross Barnett, then governor of Mississippi and a key figure in the states-rights movement at the time; William Simmons, low-key leader of and spokesperson for the Citizens' Council, a dues-paying group of White residents fearful of losing their near-dictatorial power within the state; and Medgar Evers, head of the statewide arm of the NAACP, a national, multiracial coalition of activists working hard to move America toward a more just and equitable society for all. The footage of all three is priceless, as are the clips of downtown Jackson as it looked near the beginning of that eventful decade when the Tougaloo Nine strode into history.

Simmons is the first to appear, announced as "the Secretary of the Jackson Citizens' Council." That may have been his official title, but the man was much more. Born, bred, and educated in Mississippi, Simmons traveled widely in his early years, even serving a stint with the US State Department during World War II. The son of a wealthy banker, Simmons found his own path to riches through his involvement with the oil industry in Louisiana before settling in Jackson in 1954. There he became deeply involved with the states' rights and prosegregation movements. He eventually became a full-time employee of the Citizens' Councils of America—a group with a reach across the South—and publisher of the organization's monthly newspaper *The Citizens' Council* (1955–1961) and later, its monthly magazine *The Citizen* (1961–1989). The "Racists' Strategist" as the *New York Times* dubbed him, Simmons also ran the Jackson-based Citizens' Council *Forum*—a weekly series of TV and radio programs that promoted the council's arch-segregationist and states-rights philosophies. Once described as "Dixieland apartheid's number-one organization man," Simmons served as the mouthpiece for the Citizens' Council movement, most especially at the council's then-headquarters in Mississippi's capital city of Jackson.[2]

"The South has a large 'nigra' population," Simmons says in his opening comments in the documentary. "In our state, it's about 42 percent of the total. And anyone with two eyes in his head and roughly normal vision can look around him and see that there's a vast and permanent difference between the White and Colored people that . . . would forever prohibit them in terms of equality in the same society."

As the lead administrator and publicity man for the Citizens' Council, Simmons spread its virulent gospel of White supremacy throughout the South and beyond, but he didn't create the organization. That was left to some Mississippi Delta farmers, businessmen, and civic leaders in the immediate wake of the 1954 unanimous US Supreme Court *Brown v. Board of Education* decision, which called for the desegregation of America's public schools, thus signaling an end to racial segregation in American public life. By 1961, largely in response to the successes of the emerging civil rights movement, Citizens' Council groups across the South reportedly had developed a combined membership base of a quarter-million people, about eighty thousand of whom lived in Mississippi.[3] When the headquarters for the group moved from the Delta town of Greenwood to the capital city of Jackson in 1960, Simmons, an able promoter and polished public speaker, became the primary spokesman for the group, which catered not to poor, lower-class Whites but to the upper crust.

As Mississippi newspaperman (and later aide to US president Jimmy Carter) Hodding Carter III noted in a 1961 piece for *The New York Times*, "It is difficult to explain to an outsider just how powerful a force this white-supremacy group has become. Perhaps the hardest point to grasp is that the Citizens Council in Mississippi—no matter how dubious its aims, repugnant its methods, or despicable its philosophy—is not made up of hooded figures meeting furtively in back alleys. The leadership is drawn not from the pool hall but from the country club. Its membership generally exhibits the attitudes of the middle and upper classes rather than of the poor white."[4]

William Simmons may have been one of the biggest beneficiaries of the Citizens' Council's rise to power. While managing the various council organizations, Simmons gained the ear of Mississippi's new governor, Ross Barnett, and reportedly became an unofficial member of his cabinet, sitting in on high-level meetings, accompanying Barnett on out of town speaking engagements, and even writing some of his most prosegregation booster- ism speeches. Indeed, Barnett owed a great deal of his electoral success to Simmons and to the membership of the Association of Citizens' Councils of Mississippi.

ROLLING WITH ROSS

Much is made of the ascendance of Ross Barnett to the Governor's Mansion in 1960, and with good reason. Barnett was a caricature of all the South- ern bigot stereotypes portrayed in the Northern press. He was blustery; he developed phrases not heard before in the English language; he grabbed headlines and had a way of tripping himself up in the most awkward—and sometimes dangerous—ways. During a 1959 gubernatorial campaign stop, Barnett accidentally backed into a slowly rotating airplane propeller and was severely injured. (Robert Kennedy would later cite this incident as reason to believe that Barnett had a screw loose.) But Barnett was an accurate reflection of the society he represented.[5]

In 1959, Mississippi—like most of the South—was reeling from the ramifications of the *Brown* decision on school integration and the impact of civil rights activism that it had unleashed. Every one of Mississippi's neighboring states had gone through—or were about to go through—some major disruption to the racial compact that had held for nearly a century. In Alabama, there had been the successful Montgomery bus boycott. In Arkansas, there had been the Little Rock High School integration crisis. Louisiana was about to be placed under a court order to begin integrat- ing its public schools. And Tennessee's Black college students had already begun to meet regularly to discuss nonviolent resistance tactics to White oppression and would go on to lead the student sit-in movement once it erupted in North Carolina in February 1960. Mississippi was one of the few states where no significant civil rights disturbances had broken its staunch segregationist veneer. Most of Mississippi's voting (i.e., White) residents wanted to keep things that way.

Even with all the surrounding civil rights disturbances, the staunchly segregationist Barnett was not necessarily Mississippians' first choice to lead their state through the civil rights landmines of the early 1960s. As journalist Curtis Wilkie describes it, Barnett was something of a "worst of all worlds" choice that was made possible as a result of political chicanery by one of the state's highest elected officials. The Democratic primary initially had only two candidates, the hardline segregationist Barnett, from the state's senior Senator James Eastland branch of the party, and "moderate" segregationist lieutenant governor Carroll Gartin from the probusiness junior Senator John Stennis wing. Eastland nursed a grudge against Gartin ever since Gartin ran against him during his 1954 reelection bid for the US Senate. During that campaign, and despite Eastland's well-known rabid segregationist past, Gartin tried to blame the *Brown* decision on Eastland's ineffectiveness. The gambit failed, and Eastland vowed to "send Gartin to political oblivion." He did so by encouraging a third candidate, a progressive, into the race. By doing so, Eastland was able to siphon off enough votes from the shoo-in Gartin to force a runoff between Gartin and Barnett—no man having won by a clear majority. Barnett ran away with the runoff, beating a weakened Gartin by nearly nine percentage points. Barnett went on to garner all of the votes for governor, as there was no Republican opposition.[6]

Ross Robert Barnett had an interesting back story. Born in 1898 on a small farm near the Choctaw enclave of Standing Pine, near Carthage, Mississippi, he was the tenth and youngest child of a Confederate veteran, thus making him the last major political figure in the state with such a direct link to the Civil War. Barnett relished retelling the family lore about his father's martial exploits, from having a horse shot out from under him at the Battle of Shiloh just north of the Mississippi state line in Tennessee to surviving the siege of Vicksburg and walking the one hundred or so miles home afterward. "He was a symbol of the South," Barnett's publicity manager, Erle Johnston, would later write of his boss, "with the red blood of his Confederate soldier father running through his veins."[7] The stories were meant to demonstrate the persistence, loyalty, and doggedness of the Barnett line as well to highlight his lineage to the defenders of Southern Way of Life.

Barnett's tales of his own youth were equally compelling. As a youngster, he plowed the ground for six cents an hour then graduated to cutting hair for ten cents a head. As he got older, Barnett held a series of odd jobs while working his way through both high school and college: barber, janitor, logger, kitchenware and insurance salesman.

Most biographies suggest that Barnett fought in World War I as a member of the US Army before entering Mississippi College. In fact, Barnett admitted in a 1981 interview that he had only served in the Student Army Training

Corps and had never actually been called up for active duty. "I would've gone in about thirty days to France if the Armistice had not been signed," he demurred. Nonetheless, the boy from Standing Pine was determined to make something of himself. After graduating from Mississippi College in 1922, Barnett set his sights on studying law to further both his economic and political aims. He enrolled in the University of Mississippi's School of Law, where he was elected class president and became a standout on the school's debating team. After graduating in 1926, Barnett went on to develop a highly successful law practice in Jackson. From 1943 through 1944, the future governor served as the head of the Mississippi Bar Association. This was no Foghorn Leghorn cartoonish clown that the national media would make him out to be: Barnett was a highly successful trial lawyer and well liked by his colleagues.[8]

In 1951, Barnett entered politics by running for governor, hoping to reach the top rung without jumping through any lower hoops. Ultimately unsuccessful—finishing fourth in a crowded field of eight—Barnett tried again in 1955, again finishing fourth with 21 percent of the vote. Since Mississippi governors are barred from serving two consecutive terms, it was not uncommon for aspiring candidates to run more than once to get the needed name recognition and exposure statewide. This strategy ultimately worked for Barnett in 1959 as he made abundantly clear where he stood on the race issue when he ran for the state's highest office for the third time. "I am a vigorous segregationist," he would repeatedly say on the campaign trail. "I will work to maintain our heritage, our customs, constitutional government, rights of the states, and segregation of the races." Those phrases may not have resonated in 1951 or 1955, but they were Barnett's winning slogans in 1959, and he became governor elect of the Magnolia State.[9]

Barnett turned sixty-two just days after assuming the governorship in January 1960 and stuck to his campaign promises, which aligned perfectly with the White Southern agenda. Barnett did his best to unite the Democratic Party of Mississippi by offering something for both wings: He made no bones about his support for segregation, but he merged his racist rants with a message of economic empowerment and the promise to bring jobs and industry into the state like no other state leader had ever done—albeit primarily for the benefit of his White constituents. Even the popular public historian Walter Lord gave Barnett his props: "Whatever might be said of Ross Barnett on racial matters," Lord wrote in his review of Mississippi's troubled racial history, *The Past That Would Not Die*, "he was a bear on getting business, and his administration featured an all-out drive to bring new industry into the state."[10]

Yet, another reason for Barnett's trouncing of Gartin in the decisive second Democratic primary was, as then-US Congressman from Mississippi Frank Smith would later recount, Barnett won the wholehearted support of the Citizens' Councils of Mississippi. "In 1959, the Citizens Council assumed a strong control over state politics," Smith wrote in his autobiography, "electing Governor Ross Barnett and a legislature ready to do his bidding."[11] In fact, Barnett's first public appearance after winning election was to acknowledge the debt he owed to the Citizens' Councils of Mississippi by appearing at one of its meetings in Jackson with William Simmons by his side. There he vowed to maintain the state's segregated school system, even promising to go to jail before he would allow for "mixing" in the school—or anywhere else, for that matter. He also urged all in the assembled crowd to join the organization. "I am proud that I have been a Citizens' Council member since the Council's early days," he told his audience of nearly one thousand. "I hope that every white Mississippian will join with me in becoming a member of this fine organization."[12]

A second bulwark of segregation—unique to the state—that Barnett used effectively to keep a lid on dissent was the Mississippi State Sovereignty Commission, a tax-supported arm of government created by his predecessor to serve as "a permanent authority for the maintenance of segregation." Charged with investigative, advisory, and public-relations functions, the commission became a vast spying agency, keeping tabs on anyone within Mississippi's borders who might be suspected of attempting to challenge the "sovereign" state's segregation laws and practices. The commission received about $125,000 per year from the state legislature and employed former FBI agents and policemen to investigate and write detailed reports about all manner of activities going on within the state that could be construed in any way as challenging Mississippi's racial status quo. Together, the Citizens' Council and the State Sovereignty Commission formed an unholy alliance to suppress dissent and promote separation of the races, which Barnett would effectively exploit.[13] Both groups, however, would court unwanted scrutiny in the wake of the Tougaloo Nine protest.

In *Mississippi, USA*, Barnett mostly rails against the Freedom Riders who had just arrived on the scene and who, he asserts, "are willfully intending to violate the law and stir up strife." He doesn't mention that Black students within his state are already making moves to shift the balance from equality (and prosperity) for Whites to equality for All. The program's narrator, however, notes in passing that "Negro college students have attempted to use the White library" but suggests that the sit-in "drew no positive support from the rest of the Negro community."[14]

This statement is made as a way of introducing a third important personality in Mississippi's racial politics—Medgar Evers, statewide field secretary for the NAACP. Evers admits to a certain amount of reluctance on the part of Mississippi Blacks to step out and claim their freedom. "Certainly, there has not been the aggressiveness on the part of Negroes as there has been in other states," he says, "but this is coming into the fore now, especially with the younger people." That was pure Medgar Evers, always putting his faith in the younger generation to lead the way—and giving credit where credit was due.

MEDGAR WILEY EVERS

Volumes have been written about the life and legacy of Medgar Wiley Evers, activist son of Mississippi. In those pages, one can read reams about Evers's full-throttled resistance to his native state's deeply ingrained practices of racial terror as encoded into the White Southern psyche. Here, a brief summary of his deep commitment to racial justice will have to suffice.[15]

Evers was born in 1925 into Mississippi Jim Crow segregation in the small town of Decatur, which served as the seat of Newton County. Thus, Medgar and his older brother, Charles, who would also make his name as a civil rights pioneer in the state, were affronted daily by the town square's Confederate monument located on the county courthouse grounds, just as in nearly every other county seat in the Southland. It may have been partly because of this constant visual reminder of their subordinate social status that the Evers brothers became ardent antisegregationists and worked for most of their lives for the uplift of their hard-pressed people. Their antipathy toward the status quo was also reinforced by the ten-mile walk to the Negro Newton High School that Charles and Medgar had to make daily as teens since no school bus service was provided to Black children at the time, as well as the fact that a perfectly appointed high school for Whites was not far from their home.[16]

The Evers brothers did their patriotic duty in World War II—Medgar in the European theater, Charles, in the Pacific—and, in the words of W. E. B. Du Bois, they "returned fighting."[17] Having helped destroy racist enemies abroad, they, along with many of their Black Southern compatriots, began to fight even harder to win their freedoms at home.

Medgar was the early standout. Shy, quiet, bookish, something of an outdoorsman—he loved to fish and hunt—this determined Magnolia State freedom fighter found national attention when he decided to attempt to integrate the University of Mississippi Law School in 1954. Rejected on a technicality, he urged the NAACP to take up his cause. Realizing those long odds, NAACP leaders Roy Wilkins and Thurgood Marshall demurred and instead decided to hire this intense, gregarious veteran to become the storied civil rights group's first full-time paid staffer in the great and sovereign state of Mississippi. The US Supreme Court had just reached its landmark *Brown* decision earlier that year, and the two men—Wilkins as NAACP executive secretary and Marshall as head of its legal team—knew that a steady hand would be needed to press for change in Mississippi now that a way had been opened up. Their instincts would prove to be spot on.[18]

The organization's presence, let alone its effectiveness, in the state had been spotty at best until Evers came on board. The NAACP traces its beginning back to an original "Call" sent out in 1909—on the centennial of "the great Emancipator" Abraham Lincoln's birth—by a group of well-off and influential White reformers and prominent Black activists seeking to ensure for "each and every citizen, irrespective of color, the equality of opportunity and equality before the law." It took a full year before this informal group of interested advocates "organized a permanent body to be known as the National Association for the Advancement of Colored People" and another year before the group was officially incorporated. By 1912, three branches of the association had formed in some of America's largest cities—New York, Chicago, and Boston. By 1914, twenty-four branches had been organized with a combined membership of three thousand.[19]

Not surprisingly, the NAACP's expansion into the South was slow going. This was due largely to the repressive racial environment that punished any aberration from the expected norms of Jim Crow Southern practices. But NAACP rules also hampered growth. To apply for branch membership in the national association, a local group needed at least fifty members—a high hurdle for freedom-seeking people of color in the South, who often had to meet in secret even to discuss such matters. In addition, individual membership cost one dollar per year, something out of reach of many Southern Blacks, who then were mostly relegated to the lowest economic strata. In Mississippi, a group of enterprising Black citizens formed the state's first branch in Vicksburg in 1918; the all-Black town of Mound Bayou petitioned for membership the following year. Three other branches followed suit during the 1920s: Jackson, Natchez, and Meridian. All five, however, fell in and out of compliance during the ensuing two decades, often because their leaders were identified and driven out of the state. By 1944, the indomitable Ella Baker, then serving as the NAACP's director of branches, reported "with regret" that there were only 129 dues-paying members within the entire Magnolia State.[20]

It wasn't until after World War II that the NAACP took hold in Mississippi, primarily in Jackson, where, as historian John Dittmer notes, "living in the state's capital and largest city afforded black activists a degree of protection." Even with that, Dittmer reports, the Jackson activists "took precaution, seldom meeting in the same place twice in succession."²¹ Some of the early Jackson stalwarts—postman John Dixon, attorney Jack Young, educator William Bender, and entrepreneurs A. M. E. Logan, Mary Cox and R. L. T. Smith—would pave the way for the student activism of the 1960s; most would still be around to provide financial, legal, and moral support to the Tougaloo Nine.

By 1946, thanks to this concerted effort to form branches in the war's immediate aftermath, the NAACP's growth in Mississippi warranted the creation of a state apparatus—called the Mississippi State Conference—to help coordinate the activity of local branches within the state, to lobby on behalf of people of color within the state legislature (as much as that might be possible), and to reach across state lines and collaborate with other NAACP statewide organizations as well as other like-minded, freedom-loving regional groups such as the Southern Regional Council. Even so, at least until 1957, some members of the NAACP staff, including those working in the South, were referring to Mississippi as the organization's "lost cause." Historian Neil McMillan concluded that "in no other state was white opposition [to the NAACP] as violent or pervasive."²²

TOXIC REALITY

This was the reality that Medgar Evers stepped into when he agreed to become the NAACP's first statewide field secretary in Mississippi, where fear reigned and where violence often was the first and immediate response to any challenge to the established order. From December 1954 through mid-June 1963, Evers's herculean commitment to this organization and to its cause would become the stuff of legend. It would also cost him his life. For those eight-and-a-half years, though, Medgar Evers created his legacy daily by sallying forth from his homestead in Jackson into the grotesque racialized landscape that comprised his statewide territory. Each day he would involve himself in—and report back to the NAACP headquarters in New York—the details of every racial crime within the state's borders, starting with the most notorious racial outrage of the century—the horrific 1955 murder, née lynching, of a fourteen-year-old boy from Chicago, Emmett Till. But Till's was only one of a too-long list of names and stories that haunted Evers's nightmares. The lesser known but equally egregious tales of Mack Charles Parker, Lamar Smith, George and Herbert Lee, Clyde Kennard, Roman Ducksworth—and countless more—were just as troubling, all absorbed into the consciousness of this stolid, solitary man.

Evers's wife, Myrlie, who served for many of those years as his office secretary (and who in time would find her own heroic voice), summed up her husband's daily trauma this way: "If the years were stamped with the names of the murdered, the months were inked with those of the beaten and the maimed. Affidavits testifying to the routine cruelty of white Mississippians toward Negroes piled up in Medgar's files. Each represented an hour, a day, a week of Medgar's life in a surrealist version of Hell."[23]

Despite it all, Medgar Evers continued to keep his focus on the goal—freedom at all costs. His special focus was on the young. He knew that they were inheriting a world not of their own making—and not the one he would have wished for them. But he also knew that they, more so than their parents, were in a position to rise up against the Mississippi madness and fight back against the White-supremacist insanity. Throughout the 1950s, Evers urged each local branch of the NAACP to form a Youth Council—young people in their teens, often the children of the adult members—who would meet monthly with an adult advisor and, just like their elders, plan activities, educate themselves on racial issues, and experiment with ways to challenge racial barriers.

Many of the Tougaloo Nine had some connection to Evers even before they set foot on the campus of Tougaloo College, mostly through participation in their local NAACP Youth Councils. All were deeply influenced by Evers's example of activism and worked to prepare themselves to step out on their own should he just say the word.

During the second clip of Medgar Evers in the *Mississippi, USA* newscast, he is at a lectern speaking at a meeting of more than one hundred Black citizens, encouraging them to continue to fight for their civil rights. At these public meetings, police, the local press, and even Sovereignty Commission spies would comingle with the faithful, attempting to put a damper on their enthusiasm and keeping a record of every damning critique of the Mississippi apartheid system. Evers didn't care; he spoke his mind freely. "Here in Mississippi," he declares, "all of you know that your tax dollar and mine is taken from us not because we give it willingly, but it's taken from us unwillingly, and it's given to the Citizens' Council; it's given to the Sovereignty Commission. . . . And why is it given? This money is given to keep you and I second-class citizens here in this great country. Why do I say that? I say that because you and I are helping to pay . . . for the maintenance of segregation!"

Evers's reference to the White-supremacist group and the state spying agency was no accident. Both groups were under attack in the White press for their lackluster performance during the Tougaloo Nine incident. Evers was pressing his advantage and advertising to the broader world the crazy-making inconsistencies that Black citizens were forced to live with in their home state.

In his third and final appearance in the program, Evers is asked if integration will ever be accepted in Mississippi. "I think it will be accepted," Evers states matter-of-factly. "I don't know just how long [it will take], but I think it will be accepted."

In typical journalistic "point/counterpoint" style, Evers's final comments are contrasted with those of the Citizen's Council's William Simmons, who suggests that the outcome of the integration battle will be "a question of leadership" and frames the question within the concept of state's rights parlance. "I think the ultimate result of this conflict of authority between the federal and state sovereignty is something that has not been resolved," he concludes.

The narrator has the final word, noting that until now, Mississippians have "followed where their leaders have led. Should these leaders falter, if in the future they should appear to be losing the fight against integration—and some outside the state believe, of course, this is inevitable—then Mississippi will seek other means of dealing with its problems. There are no alternatives. Some [states] may have moderate opinions or groups of citizens for compromise, but not Mississippi, USA." The credits then roll as the Confederate hymn "Dixie" plays jauntily in the background until fadeout.

This, then, is the chilling environment in which the Tougaloo Nine made their decision to act, with the authority of the state and a powerful regional hate group fully aligned against their taking even the smallest step to challenge the status quo. Each of them had their own reasons to push against this oppressive dominant culture to see what might happen. And they had only the reassurances of Medgar Evers and the NAACP on their side, along with the encouragement of a small cadre of educators from their private, historically Black Tougaloo College.

Chapter 3

THE OASIS

IN 1961, THE SAME YEAR AS THE TOUGALOO NINE LIBRARY SIT-IN, A FIRST-term student at the college wrote the following about her future alma mater: "Tougaloo Southern Christian College is often referred to (among liberal elements, that is) as 'The Oasis.' It is the one place in Mississippi where people of all colors, nationalities, and religious persuasions live and work together as people." Later in her essay, this perceptive newcomer observed, "The only remarkable thing about Tougaloo is that it exists at all—in Mississippi. . . . Tougaloo IS 'The Oasis.'"[1]

Tougaloo College was, indeed, a world apart from the rest of Mississippi. Established in 1869 by the Christian abolitionist American Missionary Association (AMA) in the aftermath of the Civil War, Tougaloo would go on to become one of the most highly regarded higher educational institutions for Black youth in the state. Initially dubbed Tougaloo University—a lofty aspiration that would later be scaled back to Tougaloo College in 1916—the AMA's most enduring foray into college education in Mississippi joined the likes of other AMA schools established in the South at about the same time. These included Atlanta University (now Clark Atlanta University) of Georgia (1865); Fisk University of Nashville, Tennessee (1866); Talladega College of Alabama (1867); Hampton Institute of Virginia (1868); and Straight University (now Dillard University) of New Orleans, Louisiana (1869).

The push to provide education to recently freed Blacks in the South became the AMA's passionate mission once freedom for the enslaved had been won. In fact, it might be said that no organization, not even the federal Freedman's Bureau, provided more funding, more recruits, nor more missionary zeal than the American Missionary Association did in the aftermath of the Civil War to ensure that the formerly enslaved received a proper education undergirded by Christian values.[2] Besides colleges, the AMA established more than five hundred elementary and high schools throughout the South. And though the AMA invited people of all races to enroll in their schools—and some poor whites did so early on—very quickly after the demise of Reconstruction, their schools became education mills for freed Black children and youth.

The AMA's strategy was as brilliant as it was simple: educate as many Black youth as possible and then have them continue the process through the generations to come. Thus, Tougaloo and its sister institutions in neighboring states became what might now be called "Teacher Colleges," training large percentages of elementary and high school teachers for their respective locales. In fact, within twenty years of its founding, Tougaloo's well-trained teachers were in high demand, not only in Mississippi but also in nearby Louisiana and Arkansas.[3] Education, however, was useless without opportunity, so in the early days, the AMA also included training in agriculture and the technical trades so that Black men, mostly, could apply what they had learned in practical ways after graduation and be ensured a modicum of economic security and independence outside of their higher learning bastions' hallowed gates.

The land that encompasses Tougaloo College had been, not surprisingly, a cotton plantation owned by one John Boddie, a planter with more than two thousand acres of tillable land. Boddie's story survives through the annals of history primarily because the AMA purchased what had once been his pride and joy.

Boddie is said to have had a sizeable number of enslaved people who worked his plantation and ensured his wealth. Those same slaves built an attractive and spacious plantation home on the highest point of Boddie's land, ostensibly to house Boddie and his soon-to-be bride. When the marriage was called off—some say because the youthful woman couldn't stomach the way Boddie treated his slaves—the man was heartsick. Indeed, "the Mansion" as it would come to be known, was built specifically to his fiancée's specifications, with a commanding upper-floor cupola so that on a clear day she could see all the way to downtown Jackson, about nine miles due south. It is said that, perhaps out of spite, the Mansion was then used by Boddie "to store his cotton and the cupola to observe, not Jackson, but the progress of his field hands."[4]

The Mansion and the plantation survived the Civil War unscathed, but Boddie, like most of his fellow Southerners, was ruined. In addition, without free labor, the plantation proved unprofitable. "Boddie sold the place to pay his debts," Tougaloo's historians observe. Then the new owner almost lost his recently purchased prize over unpaid taxes. He offered the entire two thousand acres to the AMA at a fire-sale price of $15,000. But the AMA leaders dithered, and the place fell into the hands of a land developer. The AMA ended up paying $10,500 for just the Mansion and the five hundred acres that surrounded it. Nevertheless, the racial uplift organization would go on to build an impressive, if rustic, legacy of Christian goodwill and Northern resistance to enduring Southern racism.[5]

During the ensuing ninety-plus years between its founding and the Tougaloo Nine insurrection, the college would go through extraordinary ups and downs, variously ignored, and then miraculously aided by the AMA administrators and their financial backers.[6] Additionally, Tougaloo was often referred to by its sister colleges in patronizing terms during its early years. "Poor little Tougaloo," they would say; "our country cousin" and "our poor relation" were other endearments.[7] Despite the institution's limited means, Tougaloo would somehow survive, to the general frustration and outright outrage of Mississippi's White power structure. In fact, as historian Maria Lowe points out, Tougaloo's remote rural setting would serve as a protection, of sorts, from those who would wish it harm. And although most institutions within the state could be threatened with economic reprisals should they not tow the segregationist line, Tougaloo's array of Northern funders and foundation support provided immunity from such financial blackmail.[8]

Things weren't always troublesome between the college and the politicians, however. Initially, Tougaloo received funding from the federal Freedman's Bureau as well as from the Mississippi legislature to supplement the AMA's often scanty support. (Famously, the AMA rarely saw a project it didn't like and thus ended up with too few resources spread across too many projects.)

PROUD LEGACY

Tougaloo distinguished itself during those years in impressive ways. Three separate "schools" were created: a "normal" school (essentially a high school for training future teachers); a "model" school (a grade school for teachers-in-training to develop their skills while educating the next generation of students); and a "plantation" school for teaching the basics of agricultural production and animal husbandry. The schools developed a reputation for quality, and its teachers and administrators were known for their zeal and their desire to "light the fires of freedom and righteousness" within their students.[9]

As the schools developed, Tougaloo was able to accept more and more students, not only from the nearby community but from all parts of the state of Mississippi. In fact, by the turn of the century, of all the AMA's projects, only Fisk University bested Tougaloo in the number of boarders it could handle. It was about that time, too, that Tougaloo achieved its goal of becoming a full-blown college. In 1897, Tougaloo opened its doors to its first college applicants and in 1901, minted its first bachelor-of-arts-degree student.

That same year saw the dedication of Tougaloo's first (and still-standing) chapel, with its commanding bell tower that called faculty and students alike to daily prayer and twice-weekly church services. It must be remembered that the AMA was, above all, a Christian missionary society and that seven of Tougaloo's first nine leaders were men of the cloth who carried the title of *Reverend*. One of these, Reverend Frank G. Woodworth, had the distinction of having served the longest of any Tougaloo president (1887–1912) and, honoring his career-spanning dedication to Tougaloo's survival, the chapel bears his name: Woodworth Chapel.[10]

During these early days of the college, life at Tougaloo was rigorous. All students were expected to contribute daily to the physical upkeep of the institution as part of their tuition. This could include working in the laundry, cleaning the dormitories, or laboring in the fields. Some students rose at 4:00 a.m. to begin preparations for breakfast. The rest of the campus slept in until 5:00 a.m., when all were expected to rise and tend to their chores, which might mean kindling fires throughout the campus—the Mansion itself boasted fourteen fireplaces!—milking the cows, collecting the eggs laid overnight by the chickens, or mopping the floors. After breakfast and daily devotionals, classes commenced at 9:00 a.m. sharp, starting with Bible study. After a day full of classwork, recreation, and community service, dinner was served. Study hall and evening prayer followed. Lamps were extinguished at 10:00 p.m. It was a no-nonsense existence. Even the slightest rule infraction could meet with harsh punishment—hours of extra work in the fields or, in more serious cases, expulsion.

One early innovation pioneered by AMA schools was the introduction of night classes. The daily operation of the campus required many more hands than the AMA could afford to pay. So those youth who could not afford even the meager monthly tuition were invited to become full-time workers, who could then attend evening classes to ensure they, too, could benefit from the academic environment in which they lived and worked. (One of the Tougaloo Nine would benefit from this practice.)

Tougaloo was not without its controversies, even early on. Despite the missionary zeal of its staff, the idea of social or academic equality with those they served—essentially the formerly enslaved and their children—was anathema to many of the White AMA workers, particularly the women. Early suggestions that some talented graduates should stay on as teachers and work side-by-side with the Northern AMA recruits met with strong objections from some of the staff. It wasn't until the 1920s and the influence of the Harlem Renaissance that the hiring of Black teachers and administrators became a common occurrence.

This, too, was not without its risks. Tougaloo College had to operate and survive within the narrow strictures of the political realities of Mississippi's ever-shifting racial codes. In its earliest days during the period of Reconstruction, it was not out of the ordinary for Blacks and Whites—particularly Northern Whites—to interact freely and without barriers to race and caste. However, as Reconstruction came to a close, and White Southerners took hold of the reins of political power, Jim Crow segregation and a strict White supremacy ethos began to dominate the Southern landscape. It is a testament to both Tougaloo's adroit handling of these racial realities and to Mississippi's (often grudging) willingness to tolerate such a radical experiment within its borders that the college not only survived but thrived. Indeed, the Mississippi legislature provided funding to Tougaloo beginning with its Reconstruction government in 1870 and extending nearly every year for the next twenty years until the notorious Mississippi 1890 constitution created the strict racial codes that would endure until federal legislation swept them away in the mid-1960s.

Of course, Tougaloo needed the endorsement by the state to operate. Tougaloo received its charter from the Mississippi legislature in 1871. Interestingly, race is not referenced anywhere in that incorporating document. And in fact, Tougaloo's very first graduating high school class in 1879 included a young White woman, Luella Miner, the daughter of Tougaloo's then business manager and treasurer.[11] Tougaloo's charter, however, caused the AMA some difficulty when, in 1877, some members of the Tougaloo Board of Trustees objected to the heavy-handed nature of the AMA's authoritarian, top-down approach to appointments of administrators and staff. The state charter gave the school's Board of Trustees the power "upon nomination of the AMA" to appoint the school's president and professors. This practice was contrary to the AMA's typical approach, and in the early years, the association dismissed as a mere formality the board's approval of staffing decisions.

But the Tougaloo Board of Trustees was made up of both state and AMA appointees. The government of Mississippi (at that time, multi-racial) had appointed several high-level Black officials to the post, including then Mississippi secretary of state James Hill. Hill, along with Tougaloo's White chairman of the board, Colonel J. L. Power, was advocating for Black teachers to join the ranks of Tougaloo's professional staff because they were well qualified and because such appointments might provide inspiration for aspiring Black students. The AMA would have none of it, and as a result, Tougaloo lost its state funding for two years until the impasse could be finessed. (In this case, the state backed down, agreeing in 1878 to waive the right to appoint board members and instead, selecting a "visiting committee" to keep tabs on Tougaloo and how it spent its state-allocated funds.)[12]

This rather benign settlement of differences between the State of Mississippi and the AMA contrasted sharply with various efforts in ensuing years for state officials to interfere with the nature of Tougaloo's multiethnic make-up and its flouting of Jim Crow practices. In 1916, for instance, the Mississippi House of Representatives introduced a bill that would make it "unlawful for any person to serve as a teacher in a school attended by pupils

of a different race than that of the teacher." This would have forced Tougaloo
(and, by extension, the AMA) to end its multicultural experiment in the Deep
South state. One of Tougaloo's highly influential White trustees, Episcopalian
Bishop Theodore Bratton—he would later serve as chaplain to the United
Confederate Veterans—was able to quietly exercise his influence and have the
bill defeated.[13] During the civil rights era of the 1960s, additional challenges
to Tougaloo's charter would be mounted, but each time outside pressure
would be brought to either drop the challenge or significantly weaken the
threatening legislation so as to make it inapplicable.[14]

ACCREDITATION CRISIS

But it wasn't just state legislative efforts that could derail Tougaloo's mission.
State and regional accreditation authorities also had sway over the college's
survival. Tougaloo prided itself in having been the first "Negro" school in
the state to have won accreditation for its normal school once the accrediting
organization, the Southern Association of Colleges and Secondary Schools,
opened up its process to Black schools in 1931. The college also won accreditation soon thereafter. (Interesting, particularly for the story that follows,
Tougaloo's library came under scrutiny [as did teachers' low salaries] and
needed to be upgraded before the Southern association would green light
accreditation for the college.) The accreditation designation provided significant benefit to Tougaloo graduates, who became eligible to apply to graduate
schools that would not have considered them previously. In addition, graduates with at least eighteen hours of education credits qualified immediately for
a state teacher's license—without further testing—which was valid for life.[15]

   In the early 1950s—at the dawn of the modern civil rights era—as court
cases leading to the 1954 landmark *Brown v. Board of Education* decision
were making their way through the lower courts, influential White Southern
educators turned their gazes once again toward Tougaloo and other schools
like it. At a December 1951 meeting of the Southern Association of Colleges
and Secondary Schools, it was decided that all schools would be accredited
on the same basis, no matter if they served predominately White or Black
students. (Previously there had been a separate, lower bar for accreditation
of Black schools.) This action put Tougaloo at risk of not meeting the new
criteria. Four "deficiencies" were noted which would have to be improved
to meet the new standards, which would go into effect in the fall of 1952.

   Again, Tougaloo's library was found to be insufficiently funded. Tougaloo
had no endowment to speak of, putting it at significant economic disadvantage. Faculty salaries ranked among the lowest of any Black college in the

region. And the ratio of professors with doctorates fell below the 50 percent threshold required to qualify for full accreditation. The combination of these factors put Tougaloo in an untenable position, and it lost its accredited status for about eighteen months while each hurdle was tackled. With the AMA's help, as well as that of various foundations, which had by then become crucial to Tougaloo's survival, the college won back its coveted accreditation in the autumn of 1953, thus causing only one cadre of graduates to matriculate without the desired accreditation designation.[16]

Despite these challenges, which can sometimes seem like installments of the early twentieth-century cliffhanging film serial *The Perils of Pauline*, Tougaloo enjoyed great success in attracting top-echelon students from throughout the state of Mississippi. It did, indeed, become an "oasis," what historian Lowe describes as an "oppositional free space"—the one place in the state where a Black student could feel totally free: free of the dehumanizing effects of segregation, free to explore fully one's heritage and birthright, free to aspire to whatever heights one's spirit could soar. The school's mascot became an eaglet—a majestic young bird that would eventually fly high after a period of growth and development within mother Tougaloo's nest.[17]

In 1954, just after the accreditation crisis had passed, Tougaloo merged with the Disciples of Christ–sponsored Southern Christian Institute in order to strengthen its financial standing (the Institute had a substantial endowment) and to expand its religious studies program. In the wake of the merger, the school became known as *Tougaloo Southern Christian College*—a moniker that lasted less than a decade. In 1962, the name reverted back to *Tougaloo College*.[18]

The college attracted extraordinary talent, as well, both in its teaching pool and in its guest lecturers and visiting professors. The likes of George Washington Carver—an early visitor—as well as Harlem Renaissance literary stars Langston Hughes, Countee Cullen, and James Wheldon Johnson graced the halls of Tougaloo's increasingly modernized buildings for lectures and moderated discussions, not only about race but also about the arts and the place of the African diaspora in American society. In later years, statesman Ralph Bunche and societal firebrand and race prophet James Baldwin would visit the campus on the strength of Tougaloo's growing reputation for excellence and with the help of crucial foundation funding.[19]

RENEWED VITALITY

By the late 1950s, Tougaloo was *the* place to be if you were a young, up-and-coming go getter who wanted the best education a "Negro" could find in Mississippi. Once the 1952/1953 accreditation crisis was over, Tougaloo's ranks swelled, and youth who had high achievement on their minds flocked to the campus to see what the fuss was all about. It was these students, the post-*Brown* breakthrough generation, who would put Tougaloo on the map and would find ways to make a difference, not just within the world of Black society but also within American society as a whole.

To usher in this renaissance, the AMA appointed Dr. Samuel Kincheloe as president of the college in 1956. The scholarly Kincheloe is often overlooked by those who study Tougaloo's history, but his imprint is everywhere. It was Kincheloe who began to liberalize and equalize the administration of Tougaloo. Starting with his inaugural Presidential Address, Kincheloe laid out what he viewed as the "Basic Assumptions of the Christian College." Tying religious and scientific principles to the issue of race, Kincheloe declared: "There is one creation of man and that mankind is a biological unity." And "Language, religion and learning vary according to conditioning and not according to race." And "[A]ny theory that Negroes are intellectually inferior to whites is scientifically unjustified." He also observed that "[t]he great prophetic messages of religion have come out of sensitive souls in the presence of great human need." Echoing Myrdal, Kincheloe continued, "We, here in the heart of Mississippi and of the Old South, are in the presence of one of the greatest problems of mankind—namely human relations." Kincheloe then boldly proclaimed to anyone who might be listening that "the Christian college . . . recognizes the unity of mankind."[20]

Kincheloe's background had well prepared him for the challenges of building up a multicultural institution in the center of the Deep South. After earning a bachelor's degree from Iowa's Drake University, he focused his attention on sociology, gaining both a master's degree and a doctorate from the famed University of Chicago. He then turned to teaching, researching, and writing while at the same time studying for the ministry in the Congregational church. He taught for decades in various capacities at the University of Chicago, focusing mostly on the sociology of religion. He directed a number of church-affiliated research organizations and, most relevant for this discussion, served as president of the University of Chicago Settlement, a vast social-welfare organization initiated at the suggestion of social pioneer Jane Addams at the turn of the century to help facilitate the integration of various immigrant Europeans and migrant Black citizens into the surrounding neighborhoods of the university.[21]

Kincheloe may have been suggested for the job as Tougaloo's leader by one of his former students, Dr. Philip Widenhouse, then serving as the chairman of the Tougaloo Board of Trustees. Kincheloe brought to Tougaloo a deep understanding of the problems facing America and an adept analysis of current events. He typically infused his remarks to the Tougaloo board with his perception of public education in the South and how the issues of racial segregation and the draconian efforts by the Citizens' Councils to maintain it at all costs affected the society at large and Mississippi's public educational institutions in particular. Kincheloe admitted that given then-current conditions, Tougaloo "has a difficult time in relating itself to the white citizens of Mississippi"—something the AMA insisted upon in order to maintain its schools' viability in a hostile Southern racialized climate. Nevertheless, he pushed back hard against the prevailing sentiment that Black students were somehow inferior to Whites. "We do not dare to let it be assumed that we accept the proposition of white supremacy and of racial inferiority," he proclaimed to his board trustees. "We do not dare to work under false assumptions. If we should, we would betray the entire history of the American Missionary Association and the United Christian Missionary Society."[22]

During his tenure at Tougaloo, Kincheloe grew the student population from an anemic 305 souls in January 1956 to more than 520 by April 1960, a bit more than the school's full capacity at the time.[23] He also regularly pointed out Tougaloo's physical needs. "The building and grounds look better than they actually are," he alerted the board. The water system—a perennial problem—was failing; old dorms and classroom buildings needed shoring up; and gas was leaking from below ground and escaping though discolored patches of grass in the center of campus! Kincheloe worked hard not only to raise awareness of these issues but also to raise funds to rectify them. And he oversaw the construction of a new science building—one that would eventually carry his name—a single bright note on a list of mostly troubled infrastructure projects.[24]

But Kincheloe was much more than a brick-and-mortar president; he was a social philosopher, as well. It was Kincheloe, who, during his second year as president, uttered the radical statement: "We think of the work of our college as liberal and liberating." He would later be the first president to allow the formation of a college branch of the NAACP on campus. This occurrence, in 1959, established the chief organizational structure that would support the students who planned the library sit-in eighteen months later.[25]

By then, however, Kincheloe would be gone. He had found that he preferred teaching students to the day-to-day business of running a college. When he was offered a teaching position at the newly formed Interdenominational Theological Center in Atlanta, he jumped at the chance, leaving Tougaloo at the end of the 1959/1960 school year. Though his sudden departure would leave the school in a bit of a quandary, Kincheloe had established the philosophical underpinning for how Tougaloo might ardently push back against the coming battle with the arch segregationists who had just taken power.

Part II

INTRODUCING
THE TOUGALOO NINE

Chapter 4

THE MEMPHIS CONTINGENT

JUST AS TOUGALOO COLLEGE WAS HITTING ITS STRIDE, THE STUDENTS who would come to be known collectively as "The Tougaloo Nine" were finding their way to this Southern oasis. Each emerged from unique circumstances, of course, yet the Nine were all equal in the degree to which they were undervalued by the culture at large, making their eventual agency all the more surprising to the White world they dared to challenge. Their early life stories—divided into the three geographic regions from which they hailed—provide a window into the post–World War II Southern Black America from which they emerged.[1]

THE MEMPHIS CONTINGENT

There's an old trope that pokes fun at the Magnolia State and it goes something like this: "Mississippi has three great cities: Memphis, New Orleans, and Birmingham." (*drumroll*)

Memphis, certainly, comes by its reputation honestly if the stories of our cast of characters is any form of evidence. Three of the Jackson library demonstrators came from Memphis—Tennessee's southwestern outpost, that claims as its borders both the state and the river named Mississippi. And the families of two of these three—Joseph Jackson and Ethel Sawyer—emigrated to the River City from rural Mississippi to escape the harsh cruelty that the Magnolia State routinely visited upon its Black citizens. The family of the third student from Memphis, James Bradford, experienced similar privations closer to home in rural Tennessee (and later in Memphis proper). All three would emerge from their time at Tougaloo College more enlightened than when they arrived. One would even make the tiny town of Tougaloo his lifelong home.

JOSEPH JACKSON JR.

Born on April 14, 1937, Joseph Jackson Jr. claims the spot of the eldest member of the Tougaloo Nine. From all accounts, he was a man on the move. By age twenty-one, Joseph Jackson was married with two children and was serving as pastor of a small church. At twenty-three, he entered Tougaloo College on a music scholarship. He could sing. Man, could he sing! His rich tenor voice got him recognized early on. In fact, by 1953, when he entered Booker T. Washington High School, Jackson had earned a place with the locally renowned WDIA Teen Town Singers—a group that regularly appeared on Memphis's (and the South's) first all-Black radio station.[2]

Joseph would continue his career in music throughout high school and, after a series of complex life choices, would be recruited by Tougaloo's legendary music director, Ariel "Pops" Lovelace, into Tougaloo's esteemed college choir and its rarified Schola Cantorum. (In total, five members the Tougaloo Nine sang for Pops and had obtained music scholarships; for some, it was the only way they managed to attend college at all.)

But Joseph Jackson's sparkling tenor voice, his amiable disposition, and his religious inclination concealed a troubled childhood. Joseph Sr. was a "functioning alcoholic" who would regularly get drunk on the weekends and beat his wife—something that deeply troubled his young son. As an only child, Joseph Jr. grew close to his mother, Beatrice, and found his father "distant" and often uncommunicative. Beatrice, on the other hand, had a light about her. And like her son, Beatrice loved to sing—mostly gospel tunes around the house and at nearby St. Matthew Missionary Baptist Church, where she was a member of the choir.

When the younger Joe was eleven years old, he witnessed violence of another sort visited upon his mother, a public beating that shocked him into realizing the vast discrepancy between Blacks and Whites in American society. Both of Joseph's parents had grown up in and around Belzoni, Mississippi, a Delta town situated along the Yazoo River—a major Delta artery.[3] Joseph and his mom would regularly travel by bus to visit her family there. One summer, as they were returning to Memphis, the bus stopped in Clarksdale for a quick pitstop and to pick up additional passengers. As Joe Jr. and Beatrice headed back toward the bus, she said something to the White bus driver. Suddenly, the driver turned and smacked her to the ground. Young Joseph was stunned. He stooped to help Beatrice, now bleeding from the mouth and prostrate on the gravel ground. "That really was the beginning of feeling, *feeling* the challenges of racism," Jackson would later say.

It was only then that his eyes were opened to the unfairness of the entire system that he had grown up with. "You become socialized, and so you don't question," he later reflected. "When you would get on the bus, just like a trained dog, you knew your place. You would head straight to the back." Although Joseph and Beatrice never talked about the incident, and she never told Joe Sr. about it when they returned home, for young Joseph Jackson, the bus beating would remain a defining event of his long life. He would often relive it in his mind's eye, and he marked his interest in the civil rights movement from that sharp awakening.

In school, Joseph was a high achiever. He attended LaRose Elementary and Junior High, and then Booker T. Washington High School. Elected class president in his junior year at Booker T., Jackson held membership in the National Honor Society and was recognized as one of the "Who's Who in American High Schools." The school's motto, "We Lead, and Others Follow," was a phrase Joseph took to heart. By senior year, he was serving on the Student Council—as chaplain.

Joseph attributes his spirituality to the training he was required to attend as a youth. Beatrice was a church lady, and she dragged her only child to church every Sunday. Because she sang in the choir, Beatrice had to be separated from her son during church services. Early on, she let him know, "Joe, Junior! As I march up to the choir stand, I want you sitting on the front pew so I can see where you are!" He'd be under his mother's watchful eye all Sunday, from the 11:00 a.m. service straight through to the one at 3:00 p.m. Then came the Baptist Youth Training program and finally the 8:00 p.m. evening service. This rigorous religious training would become Joe Jackson's saving grace as he navigated life's vicissitudes. "That spiritual underpinning has always been my inner-directedness—a positive direction in thought as opposed to the negative," he later observed. "My religious experiences have always been my guide."

Jackson also began to see how Black preachers were perceived by the larger society. "I realized that the ministers were always the spokesmen. They were always in the forefront." By the end of high school, he felt a strong pull toward the ministry.

But he also had started to realize that he had a great voice. He sang in the glee club for all four years at Booker T. Washington thanks, in part, to his discovery at age thirteen of the great operatic American tenor Mario Lanza. During his junior year, Joe entered the amateur night competition held weekly at the Beale Street Palace Theater. Though he didn't win, a talent scout found him a regular weekly gig at the celebrated Plantation Inn night club just across the Mississippi River in West Memphis, Arkansas. There he came to the attention of music impresario and record producer Willie Mitchell, who a decade later would groom famed R&B singer Al Green for stardom. Mitchell helped Jackson tighten up his performance style, expand his repertoire, and find additional gigs to earn much-needed spending money.

By his senior year, Joseph was being scouted by Black college choral directors, including Pops Lovelace. Upon graduating from high school in the spring of 1957, Jackson was offered a music scholarship to Arkansas Agricultural, Mechanical, and Normal College (Arkansas AM&N) at Pine Bluff, where Pops was then serving as musical director. During his first year at Arkansas, life, you might say, intervened. While home on Spring Break, Joseph learned that his girlfriend, Clara Wallace, was pregnant. He returned to Pine Bluff to complete the spring semester and then dropped out to marry Clara and get a job to support his new family. Joseph went through a series of jobs—production-line worker in an automotive assembly plant, hospital porter, stock-room clerk, and finally pharmacy clerk. His daughter, Glenis Marie Jackson, was born in October 1958. At the end of the following year, Clara would give birth to a son, Joseph Jackson III.

Meanwhile, Joe continued his education at S. A. Owen Junior College—a Baptist-affiliated school in Memphis (later merged with the older HBCU LeMoyne College to become LeMoyne-Owen College)—where he began studying for the ministry. During this time, though raised in the Baptist tradition, Joe was lured by his former high school principal to become a member of the Mississippi Boulevard Christian Church, an affiliate of the Disciples of Christ denomination. Joe liked the reasoned, dispassionate approach to the gospel that the Disciples of Christ offered, a stark contrast to the emotionalism that he experienced during his Baptist upbringing.

By January 1959, Joseph was ordained and began serving as junior pastor of a small Disciples of Christ church, Riverview Christian Church, on the outskirts of Memphis—a heady experience for a twenty-one-year-old. After two years at Riverside, all the while working full time, Jackson felt the need to further his education. He appealed to the church elders for a ministerial scholarship. The church agreed to send him to its nearest affiliated school, Tougaloo Southern Christian College.

Coincidentally, Pops Lovelace had accepted the job as head of the music department at Tougaloo and was looking to shore up his tenor section. Pops tracked down his former star tenor and offered him a partial music scholarship if he would consider coming to Tougaloo. Destiny seemed to be calling. In the fall of 1960, with Joe's finances falling into place, Clara agreed to stay in Memphis with their two children while he headed to Tougaloo to attempt to complete his ministerial and musical education. The brief eighteen months he would spend there would set the foundation on which he would build the rest of his life.

ETHEL SAWYER

If Joe Jackson's awakening to the racial culture of the South was violent and demeaning, Ethel Sawyer's was comedic and uplifting. Ethel was born in Mississippi—the little town of Malvina, not far from the Mississippi River—on July 9, 1940, the fifth of what would eventually be thirteen children (though two died in early childhood) born to Mary Ella and Barney Sawyer.

There was a crisis with the naming of this fifth child and fourth girl. Barney was away when the new arrival made her entrance. Mary Ella thoughtfully named her new daughter after her own mother, Abbie, so the child's recorded name became Abbie Sauer—a garbled misspelling of "Sawyer" entered by a White clerk. When Barney returned home, he seems not to have noticed the last-name mix-up. Instead, he took Mary Ella to task for the slight of providing a first name to "his" child. He renamed her Ethel because "it sounded biblical," Ethel would later say, a religious connection that was important to him. Indeed, the Hebraic meaning of Ethel is "noble one"—a fitting description of the woman that this fifth child would become.[4]

Before her second birthday, Ethel moved with her family to Memphis. Typical of the Great Migration participants, a family member had preceded them there, so Mary Ella and Barney decided to leave Mississippi to seek a better life for themselves and their children. They lived with Barney's mother, Odena, in a segregated neighborhood called "New Chicago" in North Memphis that bordered a White community. Ethel can remember her mother talking over the back fence quite regularly with a White woman, "Miss Powell," who would call Mrs. Sawyer by her first name. One day Ethel fussed at her mother: "Momma, stop calling her Miss Powell! She doesn't call you Miss Sawyer!" Mary Ella just smiled and said, "Oh, girl," as she motioned to Ethel to lower her voice so the White woman wouldn't hear her. Ethel was advocating for social equality even then, wanting her momma to be on equal footing with the White neighbor lady.

Ethel and her siblings would laugh and play with their friends in the neighborhood, which was situated so that some Whites, living on the upper end of their street, would have to walk through the lower Black section to get to the corner stores. Ethel's sharp memory recalls that on a few occasions, she and her younger brothers would hide in some bushes and throw little pebbles at the White kids as they walked down the street. "We'd hide behind the hedges and say to each other, 'That's OK. If there's a war, we'll win because there are more of us than there are of them!'"

Kid stuff. Kid's play. That's what segregation seemed to be. Ethel had a happy, well-adjusted upbringing. She remembers a night of childhood reverie—twirling in the street with a friend and looking up at the stars and exclaiming, "I never want to grow up! I *never* want to leave Memphis!"

Life wasn't all fun and games, though. When Ethel was about five, Mary Ella uprooted her by-then-seven children and took up residence in the small town of Rosedale, Mississippi, not far from where Ethel was born. Things may not have been going well with her marriage to Barney, or perhaps Mary Ella was just tired of living under her mother-in-law's roof. Whatever the reason, Ethel remembers a time of mixed joy and sorrow during this new Mississippi sojourn. She and her brothers had fun playing in the yard of the three-room shotgun house, sometimes venturing across the little road to pull tiny crawfish from the pond. Her slightly older sister would take care of them and their new baby sister, Geraldine, while Mary Ella and two of her older daughters worked in the cotton fields nearby to earn a little money. Tragically, the sickly infant would die not long after the family had arrived in Mississippi. Ethel would be haunted throughout her life by the memory of the night when she, Mary Ella, and the baby were sleeping in the same bed and a wheezing, laboring Geraldine "took her last breath." Shortly after that, her parents reconciled, and the family reunited in Memphis.

Interestingly, at about this time, just prior to the family's return to Memphis, the wider world broke through into Ethel's young consciousness. German prisoners of war were being housed and forced to work on the roads and cotton plantations of Mississippi, some near where the family was staying in Rosedale.

"The guards, the American guards were on horseback and were overlooking [the prisoners]. They would bring them to our little house, I guess for their break," Ethel recalled. "So, they would gather around the house and get water and stuff. And one of them would hold one of my little brothers."

"He would sit on the porch every day they came and hold this child in his arms," she continued. "So, I thought, 'It must remind him of his own child.'"

What an odd yet humanizing memory of an enemy combatant, who fought for racial purity in Europe, holding a Black child in Mississippi, of all places, to help remind him of the life that awaited him back home. It was a subtle suggestion to Ethel that racial barriers were porous and could be breached.

When the Sawyer family returned to Memphis, it was obvious why the city was such a draw: better jobs, decent schools, nicer neighborhoods, and a somewhat relaxed grip of Jim Crow racism. Barney Sawyer earned a living wage, first as an assembly-line worker for the Firestone Tire & Rubber Manufacturing Company and then, when a White woman took too strong an interest in him, as a freight handler for the Union Pacific railroad. Mary Ella took in ironing on occasion to make extra money for the family. And even Barney's mother, Odena, worked as a cleaning woman at a local factory.

It so happened that Odena's workplace was along the route traveled by the Sawyer children to and from school. Ethel recalled that on many afternoons, as she and her siblings walked home from school, their grandmother would be waiting for them outside the factory, waving and greeting them with a smile. No wonder Ethel loved Memphis so much. She had a sense of security, a sense of belonging, a sense of multigenerational love.

Ethel recalls that during these years, Barney was quite religious and used that focus to help with the children's education. "He would call us in from play," she reflected, "and he would have each one of us read a passage from the Bible . . . and you'd have to explain what it meant." This was an early way that Ethel learned to read and critique texts—good training for her future profession as an educator.

Neither of Ethel's parents had much more than a rudimentary education. Mary Ella completed the fourth grade, while Barney came close to making it out of the eighth. But both had been schooled in life's lessons, many of which they tried to convey to their children. One of those was the value of hard work. Every fall, Mary Ella would take her children with her into the cotton fields of nearby Arkansas on Saturdays to let them learn what it was like to put in a full day's work. "It was kind of a community thing," Ethel recalled. "Folks from our neighborhood would all get on a bus and be brought to the fields where we'd spend the day socializing, laughing, and picking cotton. It was actually kind of fun!" Ethel proudly recalled how once—and only once—she managed to pick one hundred pounds of cotton in one day.

Mary Ella had high expectations for her offspring, but she also kept them in check by not allowing them to brag about their accomplishments. One day, Ethel came running home from school with exciting news. "Momma! Momma! LOOK! I made all A's!!" she exclaimed as she rushed through the door.

"Oh, girl," Mary Ella responded. "You're *supposed* to make all A's. God gave you the brains to do so, didn't He?" That stopped young Ethel in her tracks. "I think my little heart sank a bit," she would later recall. But as she advanced through school, Ethel came to accept her achievements as natural. "I didn't have the attitude like 'I'm smart!' You know? I was just like, 'OK.' It wasn't a big deal to me."

Although Ethel *loved* her life in Memphis, it wasn't paradise, and Barney Sawyer knew it. Black people generally were only allowed certain jobs—rarely rising above the menial positions offered them—and always were expected to bow and scrape to the White man. "My father was not a fan of White people," Ethel noted. He would often be found grumbling about them— "Dirty bastards!"—referring to some slight either to his own prospects or to others like him. "He didn't like them, and I'm sure he feared them," she would later reflect.

Ethel also remembered vividly the touchstones of the burgeoning civil rights movement during her adolescence. She was shocked by the murder of Emmett Till in 1955. "That hurt me," she said, upon seeing the photo of Till's horribly disfigured face, which first appeared in *Jet* magazine. But equally of note were the gains Blacks were making in the courts and in the streets: the *Brown v. Board of Education* decision in 1954; the forced integration of Little Rock High School in Arkansas in 1957. "I thought it was great!" Ethel recalled. "I didn't think much about breaking into the White world," she continued. "I just thought that Black people ought to have certain rights and [be able] to do certain things."

This idea of equality, of standing up for equal treatment, came naturally to Ethel. And it was reinforced when she would travel to Chicago during the summers as a teenager to visit her older sisters, one of whom had married a White man and the other, a Puerto Rican.

Ethel made steady progress in the schools of Memphis. She was smart, and she surrounded herself with other kids who were smart. She was with the crowd that was going places. She attended the Manassas Elementary School from first through third grades. And although most of her classmates remained at Manassas through twelfth grade, Ethel was reassigned to the newer Klondike School for fourth through eighth grades. (Due to the tremendous influx of Black people migrating from the Deep South after World War II, the older schools in Memphis were becoming overcrowded, and newer ones were being built.) She returned to Manassas High School—a rival to Joe Jackson's Booker T. Washington High—for all four of her high school years.

One notable example of Ethel's smarts was the fact that her father would encourage her to "work the puzzle" that appeared each week in the *Memphis Press-Scimitar*, the local afternoon paper. When Ethel was twelve or thirteen, she completed the word puzzle and dutifully mailed it in, as always. This time, she was rewarded for her efforts with a complete set of the *Funk & Wagnalls New World Encyclopedia*! The books were delivered to her home with a note informing her that she had won that week's challenge—something Barney would brag about for years to come.

Ethel's intelligence was also recognized at school. A select set of Juniors at all of the city's Black high schools would compete on the radio show *Quiz 'Em on the Air*. Ethel was excited when she was chosen as one of the group to represent Manassas High. She worked hard in the weeks prior to the event to memorize various facts from the daily news, which made up the bulk of the questions students were asked during the quiz. She was crestfallen, however, when one of the first questions she got was about sports. "I read the newspaper. I read everything . . . *except* the sports page!" she would later quibble. "I wasn't all that interested in sports." The question she was asked had to do with how much money a certain popular ball player made during the previous year. "I gave some ridiculously low number . . . and everybody groaned," Ethel recalled. "I think I embarrassed everybody, including my grandmother." Ethel shrugged off the flub. "I just said, 'I guess next time I'll read the sports page!'"

Ethel was also industrious. During the summers with her sisters in Chicago, Ethel would babysit or, later, work in restaurants and even in an office environment for the Spiegel Catalog and Montgomery Ward mail-order franchises to earn money for the coming school year. One summer, following her sophomore year of high school, Ethel applied to work for the Illinois Bell Telephone Company, fudging her age to suggest that she had already graduated from high school. She never got a call back, but the following fall, back in Memphis, she was summoned to the principal's office. The phone company had been pestering the school for how to get in touch with Ethel. She had scored a near-perfect grade on the screening test they had given her, but somehow, they had failed to obtain her contact information in Chicago. After learning that the highly intelligent Ethel was still in high school, the telephone-company executive exclaimed, "Tell her when she graduates, we want her!"

But Bell Telephone wasn't the only entity to discover Ethel's smarts. Her Manassas High guidance counselor also took note. Ethel hadn't planned to go to college. She knew her family couldn't afford to send her. She had settled on the idea of either becoming a secretary—she had majored in secretarial training in high school—or joining some branch of military service as a way of making a living. But she had scored in the ninety-fifth percentile on her nationally ranked college entrance exams. "You're not going into *any* service," her counselor told her. "You're going to *college!*" Ethel went through the motions of applying to a few historically Black colleges—Wiley in Texas, Tougaloo in Mississippi, and a few others—without any idea how her family would pay for it. What Ethel didn't know was that her counselor had contacts at these colleges and in time would find scholarships and work-study arrangements so that with some extra effort Ethel could comfortably move forward with her education.

As Ethel was considering her college options, Jesse Turner Sr., president of the Memphis branch of the NAACP, tried to recruit her into being part of the first cohort of Black students to integrate Memphis State University (now the University of Memphis) right in her hometown. Turner had a keen eye for talent, had scoured the records of all four Black high schools in the city, and had come up with the names of students with the highest college entrance-exam scores. Ethel's name was on the list. One summer's evening in 1958, Turner called to inquire if Ethel might be interested. Ethel turned him down. "I told him that I wanted to live a normal college life," she said. "Maybe I didn't want any repercussions for my family," she also reflected, "but the thing that really stood out for me was, 'I don't want to spend my college years doing that.'"

It would be another year before Turner engineered the integration feat in Memphis. By that time, Ethel would have already finished her first year at Tougaloo and would be starting on her second. By year three, she would be ready for a different racial reckoning—and on her own terms.

JAMES "SAMMY" BRADFORD

In a strange twist of Memphis small-world connectedness, James "Sammy" Bradford would be inspired to go to Tougaloo by one of the students who *did* integrate Memphis State. Ralph Prater, who was a few grades ahead of Bradford at Memphis's Frederick Douglass High School, had first attended Tougaloo for a few years before being lured back to his hometown by the NAACP's Turner to become part of the group now known as the "Memphis Eight." Bradford's journey to Tougaloo, thanks to Prater's example, would be rather straightforward; his journey to graduation would be anything but that.

Sammy Bradford—he wouldn't reveal exactly how he came by that nickname, but nearly everyone called him "Sam" or "Sammy"—descended from Tennessee sharecroppers, was born in Shelby County in a rural area not far from the Memphis city limits. He can remember hearing stories as a child about the various places the family had farmed: the Floyd farm; the Bateman farm, the Harold farm. By age five, his family had moved into the Belmont community of north Memphis to a modest home where he, his mother, and three sisters lived with his maternal grandparents, Steve and Lizzy McNeal—affectionately known as Papa and Big Mama. Papa was illiterate ("He wouldn't recognize his name if it were in boxcar letters!" Sam declared) but more than made up for this deficiency by his sharp mind and clear, strong memory. As a sharecropper, Papa would always demand that a certain portion of the land that he tilled—five to ten acres—be designated specifically for his family's gardens. The crops grown on this land would not be "shared" with the landowner and would be used for feeding the McNeal family of ten children. Sam noted that Papa's demands often would be met with disbelief from the White landowners. "The arrogance of this nigger telling us what he wants and what he requires," Sam imagined the landowner thinking. But if such an arrangement wasn't acceptable, Papa would just move the family to another farm. Sammy would pick up on that determination—what might have been viewed by some as insolence—and carry it forward.

Big Mama was distinctive in her circle because she *could* read—something other family members would marvel at given her humble circumstances. And she read the Bible daily—a trait she passed on to her daughter, Sam's mother, Mamie Sue. Big Mama was also strict. Sam described her as "a tough little pigeon-toed lady." What she couldn't convey through commands, she put over with the switch. And Sammy got his share of lickings to keep him straight. "It wasn't child abuse," he was quick to point out. "It was training."

Big Mama took charge because the men couldn't or wouldn't. The family's move to Memphis was necessitated by Papa's stroke, from which he never fully recovered. Sam recalled the family having to feed his invalid grandfather daily—often some of Big Mama's homemade chicken soup. "For the longest time, as I got older, I couldn't stand chicken soup because I associated it with Papa." Sam's own father had separated from the family not long after Sam was born. He saw his father rarely during his childhood.

If Big Mama was strict, Sam's mother, Mamie, was a bit more accommodating—too accommodating some said—and she doted on her brood. As the only son, Sam was given something of a wider berth than his sisters. But Mamie was always concerned about Sam's outspokenness and his willingness to challenge authority—whether it was Big Mama or the White man. "She was afraid of that for me," Sam recalled. Still, he was allowed to go further from home than his sisters. For example, as early as age twelve, Sam would accompany his great aunt Sue, Big Mama's sister, on the bus back to her home in Jackson, Tennessee—seventy-five miles due east—and ride back home to Memphis all by himself. "She would encourage me to do that—to be manly."

Sam would also do errands for Mamie like going downtown to pay certain household bills. One time in his early teens, Sam got on the bus and "just sat down." Then he realized he had plopped himself in the White section. "Man, I automatically popped up as if I had been stuck by a needle or something, and I hurriedly made it to the back of the bus." Like Joe Jackson, Sam had been socialized to "know my place." For Sam, "segregation was a way of life" and even though he never accepted it, it didn't seem to cause him many problems. "It wasn't a daily fight," he said. "Life goes on, and you have to go on as well."

As for discipline, Mamie once said, "The only thing I know to do with them is to keep 'em in church!" Much like Joe Jackson, Sam was raised in the church—in his case, Summerfield Missionary Baptist. Mamie sang in the choir, and Sammy, with his bright tenor voice, was a showstopper. At Sunday services, Sam would be embarrassed when "little notes would be passed up to the pastor" asking Sam to sing a solo. Big Mama's favorite hymn, "How Great Thou Art," was a standard for him, as was Mamie's Christmas pick, "O Holy Night." It would be Sammy's voice that would eventually open up doors for his future.

At Summerfield Baptist, Sam met a mentor he would come to call his "adopted grandfather"—Jackson Gales—a highly successful insurance agent and a "real go-getter" Sam recalled. Gales provided Sammy with "a way up and a way out"—offering him a job as a driver to accompany Gales on his daily insurance route throughout Memphis. More importantly, Gales served as a male role model to Sam, teaching the impressionable youth important lessons on how hard work can often lead to respect and opportunities, even within the existing system of racial segregation.

Sammy attended Frederick Douglass Elementary, shifted to his neighborhood Hyde Park Middle School, and then back to Frederick Douglass High School—housed in the same complex as the elementary school in the nearby Douglass community. Though he was a good student, college never crossed his mind. No one in his family had ever stepped onto a college campus, let alone attended one. But Sam's vocal talent got him noticed by the school's choral director, Omar Robinson, and Sam was picked to participate in the annual Citywide High School Concerts during his junior and senior years. This is how he came to the attention of Tougaloo's Pops Lovelace.

Pops was asked to serve as guest conductor one year for the concert. Sammy was thunderstruck. "Pops was *great*!" he recalled. "I was so impressed with his arrangements of these songs we had been doing—these little mundane pieces. But he just wiped us out with his arrangements!" Robinson made plans for Sam to audition for Pops after the concert, and things went well. "I sang two or three songs for Pops, and he bowed his head in approval." In a week, Sam received a letter offering him a partial scholarship if he would come to Tougaloo and sing with Pops. The year was 1960. Sam accepted the offer, and his life would never be the same.

Chapter 5

CHILDREN OF THE DELTA AND RIVERSIDE

NOT SURPRISINGLY, THREE OF THE NINE TOUGALOO STUDENT DEMON-strators came from in and around the Delta region of Mississippi—that loamy, rich, cotton-growing fluvial plain offshoot of the Mississippi River in the northwestern section of the state. It was the Delta where the Black under-class was needed to chop and pick the cotton and where Black people, as a rule, outnumbered Whites. Interestingly, all three students from the Delta region came from small towns or cities, not from "out in the rural." Their experiences were less harsh than the stories one often hears of rural Delta justice—where Whites in the minority exercised nearly dictatorial power over their more populous Black neighbors and where Jim Crow segrega-tion was enforced with brutal efficiency. In the towns, there was a bit more breathing room as well as better prospects for employment outside of the stifling sharecropping system. One of the Nine hailed from a north-Delta enclave, while another was reared right on the river at the Delta's endpoint. The third, while technically not from the Delta, grew up just south of the region in a plantation town that benefitted mightily from its closeness to the rich cotton capital of the South.

JANICE JACKSON

Clarksdale was "a sleepy little Delta town" when Janice Jackson was born there on January 10, 1940. About seventy-five miles southwest of Memphis, Clarksdale is smack in the middle of Mississippi's cotton country and has come to be known as the Home of the Blues. Janice found her hometown to be a wonderful place to grow up. She lived only a few blocks from the Clarksdale drugstore, owned and operated by the now-legendary NAACP activist Aaron Henry. She held fond memories of visiting Henry's store as a teen, "one of the few forms of entertainment and recreation that teenagers had . . . going to the drugstore, getting a sundae, just sitting and talking to people." Better yet, Janice's home life was idyllic. "I could not have asked for a better situation," she would reflect years later.

Her father, Eugene Jackson, was an independent builder and contractor, a rarity for a Black man in the Mississippi Delta at that time. Eugene had worked his way up, initially learning his trade from White builders who hired him in subordinate positions. Eventually, Eugene staked his own claim on the future by starting his own construction business.

Janice's mom, Bertha, was a homemaker who longed to be an educator. She worked within the home out of deference to Eugene's wishes, though eventually she attended Delta State College and became a Head Start teacher.

Education was primary for the Jackson family, so much so that the public schools of Coahoma County were deemed substandard by Eugene and Bertha, so Janice and nearly all of her eight siblings were sent to the Catholic elementary school, Immaculate Conception, within walking distance of their Fourth Street home. The parish elementary school was just getting started when Janice entered school. It added on grades as the children advanced. Janice went all the way from second grade through twelfth, serving as the school's first valedictorian in the spring of 1958.

Janice responded to her parents' enthusiasm for learning. "Education was very, very important to me," she said. "And doing well was important to me. I wanted my family to be proud of me! So, it was just a built-in thing to excel academically."

It is hard to understand the marvel of security and well-being that got passed along to African American children who grew up within such a deeply segregated society. Janice is one of several of the Tougaloo Nine who report having been insulated from the most demeaning aspects of the Jim Crow racial caste system. She exudes an air of confidence—even superiority—and calmly describes her achievements as if they were preordained. She credited her accomplishments, in school and in life in general, to a stable childhood family life as well as to her own innate intelligence, ambition, and drive. And the security she felt from her father's somewhat elevated status in the White world seemed to offer a form of protection to the family. "I didn't feel any effects of racism [or] prejudice," she said. "I was sheltered from it, more or less."

"I kind of understood what was going on," she continued. "There were incidents and things that happened around us, which my dad could kind of explain to us, but I never felt threatened by anything because he was just so protective and could handle anything."

Janice explained that Eugene's status was such that he was invited to build a movie theater in Clarksdale's commercial district. This was a time, she said, when "Blacks and Whites didn't go to the movies together." At the grand opening, however, "they had a special section reserved for my dad and his family upstairs in the balcony, and we went to the opening," she related. "[This] was just not done!" she said. "Never done!"

"Because he was known and respected by the Whites in the area, we just got different treatment as a family," she said.

This may have been why the 1955 Emmett Till murder came as such a shock to Janice. She was "just horrified by the images and the pictures—and the cause. I felt it *so* deeply," she recalled. "I would see those pictures [in my mind] for years!" Her horror was all the more acute since she lived less than an hour's drive from where Till was killed.

Even so, Janice never felt that any such harm would come to her or to her family. "I didn't feel scared or troubled by any of the things that were happening in the world around us," she said. "We heard about lynchings and all kinds of crazy things happening to people, but I just felt insulated from it all."

One reason for this outsized confidence may have been that Janice's mother provided a stable home environment, which managed to keep the segregated world at bay. "We ate our meals at home. We had dinner at our dining-room table every evening, [a meal] that my mother had cooked for eleven people." Janice doesn't remember eating out at restaurants in Clarksdale. That's why her first memory of the personal slap of segregation seemed so harsh. She and her extended family took a trip through St. Louis when Janice was about sixteen years old. Her uncle, who was in the military, wanted to grab a bite to eat, so they stopped at some nondescript place along the way, and he went in to order a meal. He was refused service but was told he could go around back, and they would serve him a sandwich to go. Janice thought, "This is weird. Here's a place that serves food, but you can't get any food?!" It's not as though she hadn't heard about segregation, but even growing up in the heart of the Mississippi Delta, the effects of segregation were not obvious to her. "This was the first time I had experienced it first-hand," she said. Janice had to be taken outside of her insulated home environment to comprehend the bubble she was living in.

Even her economic situation seemed pleasant and "normal." "I didn't know that we were poor!" she exclaimed years later. "Because we had a life that was, I think, pretty good!" Indeed, living in town offered benefits that were unavailable to the rural families a little further out in the Delta. Janice remembered one summer when she and her sister Dorothy decided to go with their teenaged friends to chop cotton. "I thought it [would be] fun! Something fun to do!" She had noticed that most of the kids from the neighborhood would be gone all day, so she asked her mom if she and her sister could go do what the other kids were doing. "This was big time! Three dollars a day! Whoo-whee!!" The girls went out on the early morning truck with the rest of the kids to find out what this was all about. Janice found out quickly that there was no fun involved. "Is this what we're going to do all day?" she wondered. "Just chopping? This is *not* a picnic!!" After three days, she was done. Babysitting seemed a much more appealing way to earn some spending money.

But babysitting proved to be another landmine in the racial war zone of the 1950s Deep South—though in this case, a somewhat comical one. Janice was invited by a White family to accompany them to Mobile, Alabama, for their week-long beach vacation so that she could watch their young daughter while the parents took some time for themselves. "I was *so* excited to be going to Mobile on a vacation!" she recalled. Janice treated it as if this were *her* vacation, too. "I ironed all of my little shorts and my little halters and all my cute little outfits." When she accompanied the family onto the beach, other White vacationers noticed. "I got lots of stares," Janice remembered. After a few days, the wife talked to Janice about covering up a bit more on the beach. "From now on, when we go out, wear a dress," she was told. "But I didn't bring anything else!" she protested. Eventually, it all worked out, but Janice learned quickly that this was no vacation for her and that there was an invisible "line of demarcation" between the Black and the White worlds.

Nevertheless, Janice remembered her teenage life in Clarksdale fondly. Her world revolved around the church, the school, and the drugstore. Father O'Leary, the White priest at Immaculate Conception, created a safe and fun place for the Black Catholic youth, and, of course, there was Aaron Henry's drugstore. Henry was a pharmacist and a business owner when that was a rarity for a Black man in the Delta. His store was "*the* gathering place [during] all of my growing up," Janice recalled. Even though Bertha didn't want her children spending too much time at this local teen hang out, somehow, every Sunday after Catholic Mass, Janice and her siblings would end up there since it was on a direct walking path back home from the church.

In 1953, Aaron Henry organized a branch of the NAACP in Clarksdale.[1] Even as a child, Janice knew that Henry was an influential presence in the town. "He was a man of means and was well respected within the community," she recalled. "He had a lot of influence on the community and the people and what they thought." Janice also remembered her mother being particularly taken with Henry. "My mother thought he was just great," she said. "She just really thought Aaron Henry had it going on."

Eventually Henry became statewide president of the NAACP—just before Janice and her Tougaloo friends made their library stand—and he would prove to be a useful ally in her first freedom fight.

Janice had two best friends, Betty Jo Woods and Mildred Jean Hubbard—both a year ahead of her at school—who ended up deciding to go to Tougaloo College in 1957 to continue their education. When Janice inevitably began thinking about her next step as she approached high school graduation, she naturally thought of Tougaloo. Thanks to Father O'Leary's influence, Janice's older brother Ronald had gone away to attend high school at a Catholic seminary in Bay St. Louis—a rare training ground for Black priests in the South—so Janice was used to the idea of going away to school. And her father was, somewhat counterintuitively for that time, more interested in his girls getting a college degree rather than his boys. "He wanted us to have a sense of independence," Janice said, "so that we would never be dependent on a man."

"You need to be educated and take care of yourself," Eugene told her.

Even though Eugene had his own business, supporting nine children didn't leave much savings for sending kids to college. He struck a deal with his girls. He would do his best to send the first one (Janice) to college, and after graduation, she would get a job and work to send the next one, and so on down the line. In the late summer of 1958, Janice took that deal, and with her modest savings, with Eugene's promised family funds, and with a part-time academic scholarship and the guarantee of a work-study job on campus, Janice boarded a Greyhound bus headed for Jackson and Tougaloo College.

ALBERT LASSITER

The first thing one might have noticed about Albert Lassiter in 1961 would have been his height: at six feet, five inches, his lean frame towered above his classmates. Then, when he opened his mouth, out would come this deep bass voice. In the familiar photo of the Tougaloo Nine, taken after their ordeal, he stands head and shoulders above his other eight coconspirators. Albert hailed from arguably the most renowned Southern Civil War city, Vicksburg, "the Gibraltar of the Confederacy," whose high cliffs and placement right on the Mississippi River made it a strategic essential for both sides: Whoever controlled Vicksburg controlled the Mississippi and all transport up and down the river. The Lassiter family's modest homestead was just blocks away from Confederate Avenue, a main thoroughfare that leads directly to the Vicksburg National Military Park—the twenty-five-hundred-acre memorial grounds that commemorate some of the horrors of that most deadly war in American history.

Albert Lassiter came into this world on Christmas Day 1941, along with his twin brother, Alfred, to Ethel (Franklin) and Wright Lassiter—the third and fourth of what would eventually grow to a family of nine children. Although technically a city boy, some of Albert's earliest memories were of helping Ethel's father on their family farm outside of Vicksburg in Warren County. Ethel had grown up there and learned early the value of agriculture. Even in

Vicksburg, she kept an impressive garden, which the boys helped cultivate. "As youngsters, we would learn how to work the garden and hoe," Al recalled. "And during the summers, we worked with Papa (Franklin) on his small farm."

To help the family financially, the twins accompanied their grandmother into the fields to chop cotton. "We would get on the cotton-chopping truck at about four o'clock in the morning and ride with other adults and a few other youngsters, too," out into the vast cotton fields of Mississippi. "With a large family, everybody did something to earn a little bit of money to help," Al said. "We started at about age ten . . . chopped cotton to earn two or three dollars a day."

Wright Lassiter was a cement finisher, plasterer, and bricklayer. His boys would often work with him, particularly as they became teens. "That was big," Al recalled, "because I could make a dollar an hour then. We were digging footings for driveways, tearing down old barns and stuff." Albert and brother Alfred also helped build the new high school, Rosa A. Temple High, that the twins would later attend for their final year before both headed off to college.

It was Ethel Lassiter who emphasized the need for her children to get an education. She had finished high school—something of an anomaly for young Black girls in her day—but ended up working as domestic help in a White home anyway. She believed that higher education—college—would propel her offspring to better opportunities. "I want y'all to go to college," she would often say. Al remembered that it was not only Ethel, but also other family members urging the children to "put somethin' in your head!" "They exhorted us, they pushed us," he recalled. "Consequently, the Lassiters did well academically." Coming home with anything less than an A was generally unacceptable. "Albert, you'd better pull this one up," Ethel told her son when he came home once with an uncharacteristic C. "After that, I went back and got all As," he said. "You'd have to explain if you did anything less than an A or an A-minus."

Despite all their efforts to better themselves, however, the Lassiter children saw the great disparity between Black and White achievement. "We saw, even as children, just how things were," Lassiter recalled. "Most Blacks were obviously in meager homes; most had menial jobs, had modest automobiles, didn't have credit." Ethel and Wright saw education as a way out. Consequently, six of the nine Lassiter children would go on to earn PhDs in their chosen fields.

Even Al's father returned to school while working full time to support his family. Beginning in 1952, Wright attended evening and weekend classes at Union Theological Seminary in Monroe, Louisiana, about ninety minutes away. Wright continued his studies at Mississippi Baptist Seminary in Jackson and eventually earned not only his bachelor's degree but also a master's in theological studies. In 1956, he became pastor of the Vicksburg church where he had been serving as a deacon—Mt. Carmel Missionary Baptist—and would remain there, eventually becoming pastor and ministering until his death in 2001.

If education was the driver to a better life, though, Albert Lassiter would say that as a young person, it was hard to see how that life betterment might actually be achieved. "There was nothing in the South . . . nothing to say that there is some hope . . . hope that things will turn around." He remembered walking past the nicer White school on his way to Cherry Street Elementary. He recalled with some frustration the "hand-me-down" books he and his classmates would receive—the discards from the White schools. He recounted his trips downtown on the Drummond Street bus, how he would immediately scoot to the back of the bus after paying his fare, not wanting to disturb the peace of the Whites up front. "Don't do anything to cause any trouble." That's what his parents taught him. "They were teaching us how to survive," Lassiter reflected years later.

He remembered one incident in particular—how he and his brother at age eight were socialized to ensure their safe return. Ethel had her hands full at home with the younger kids, so one day she asked the twins to go to the store and buy her some stockings. She talked through every part of the transaction with her boys so they would come back in one piece: "Find the stockings; go to the counter; hand the lady your money; if a White person comes to the counter, you step back; let them pay for what they're getting, then you come back up; when they give you change, don't you count it; just put it in your pocket." The instructions were designed to ensure that there was no friction in the interaction, no chance for misunderstanding or disrespect. All this just to buy some stockings!

As Albert Lassiter became older, he found ways of challenging the system of segregation—though never really successfully. He once boarded the bus and sat in the Whites-only section—not to be a rebel, he claimed, "I just wanted to see how it would feel." He was chased to the back by the bus driver's command. Later, as a laborer, he learned the art of resistance from an older coworker nicknamed "Tea Cake." They were digging some footings, and they had dug down deep enough to meet the foreman's specifications. The foreman drove by and yelled, "OK, you monkeys can stop now. That's enough!" Tea Cake whispered to Al to keep digging as if they hadn't heard the command. "We just kept swinging, and then he got out of the truck and said, 'OK, y'all can stop now.'" The point was elegantly made without uttering a word: "We're not going to answer to that insult," he recalled. It was a rare moment of insurgency. Generally, Al found that "they talked to you the way they wanted to talk to you, and you had to take it. That was the way of survival."

But the 1950s were a time when some of Mississippi's Black citizens were beginning to take matters into their own hands and quietly agitating for societal change. Chief among them was Medgar Evers of the NAACP. One of Evers's primary responsibilities was to help reinvigorate local branches of the organization in communities that were ready to work for change. In the mid-1950s, Vicksburg was just such a community, and Wright Lassiter was one of the local leaders that Evers turned to for guidance and support.

"At that time, our dad was one of the leadership within the community—as a bricklayer, a preacher, a pastor. I remember Medgar coming to our house—I believe it was 1957—to gather some folks in the community and to set up a chapter of the NAACP," Lassiter recalled. "Medgar was quite an articulate and professional fellow."

"During those times, youngsters weren't part of the conversation," he continued. "I remember it really had to be hush-hush. But we had an idea of what was going on."

Lassiter recounts a story of when he and his twin Alfred were working with Wright on a construction project at a White man's home. Word was starting to get around that Evers had come to town. "I remember the man asked my dad, 'Hey, you're not going to join the NAACP, are you?' My dad, of course, had probably already joined, but he skirted around the answer."

"I don't know. I'm not sure," is what Wright said in response, not wanting to jeopardize his livelihood or the safety of his family. "He was pretty bold," Al said with pride of his dad. "He was not reckless, but he was courageous." Wright Lassiter Sr. became a charter member of the Vicksburg branch.

Another, less direct but no less effective resistance strategy was to get an education. By the time Albert and Alfred were ready to graduate from high school, their two older brothers had already finished college: one at Alcorn State College, about an hour south of Vicksburg, the other, at Arkansas AM&N—the same school Joe Jackson first attended in Pine Bluff. There was no question the twins would follow in their brothers' footsteps, but to which colleges? Al had been a natural leader throughout his high school years. He had been class president during his freshman, sophomore, and junior years; head of the Science Club; and student head of the area Hi-Y Club—a YMCA-sponsored club for high school boys and girls. He also played trumpet in the band, was center on the basketball team, and sang in the newly formed school choir.

Older brother Louis Lassiter by then had joined the air force, and he encouraged Al to seek an appointment to the Air Force Academy in Colorado Springs. Louis told Al that he was a perfect candidate because the academy focused on young men of academic achievement with leadership skills. Al dutifully went through the arduous process of seeking letters of recommendation from the school's Black principal, as well as from the White superintendent of schools, and even the affable White mayor of Vicksburg— John Holland (who incidentally would soon be tapped to lead the Mississippi Civil War Centennial Commission). But every appointment to a military academy required a letter of nomination from one member of the state's US congressional delegation—either a senator or congressman—all of whom were White. Al recalls receiving a rejection letter from Mississippi's then junior Senator, John C. Stennis—an avowed segregationist. Although complimentary of the young man's qualifications—"I understand that Mr. Lassiter is highly qualified for the Air Force Academy," Stennis's rejection letter stated, "however, I cannot nominate him at this time."

Albert was crestfallen but not defeated. He certainly understood that such a nomination was a long shot, particularly for Mississippi. In fact, in 1960, there were only a handful of Black students attending the Air Force Academy, all from states outside of the segregated South. Word soon got out around school that Lassiter's bid had failed. Mrs. Howard, his biology teacher, quickly came up with an alternative. A Tougaloo alum, Mrs. Howard put in a good word for Al with her Tougaloo connections. It didn't hurt that he played basketball and that he had experience using his rich, deep bass voice singing choral music. As with Sam Bradford and Joe Jackson, Pops Lovelace found a way of providing Al with a small stipend if he would agree to sing in the Tougaloo choir. So, with that scholarship, a work-study assignment, and a one-hundred-dollar award from the American Legion's oratorical contest, along with the funds he had saved from his construction job, Albert Lassiter cobbled together the funds necessary to attend Tougaloo College starting in the fall of 1960.

GERALDINE EDWARDS

Geraldine "Geri" Edwards has the Mississippi River itself to thank for her presence on this earth. Her parents met on the bridge that traverses the river between Natchez, Mississippi, and Vidalia, Louisiana. The story goes that Simuel Edwards and a friend were walking across the expansive bridge in one direction when they spied two young ladies walking across the bridge in the other direction. Simuel bet his friend that he could talk to the girl he had his eye on. Game on! That young woman was Thelma White. The year was 1940. Thelma and Simuel would quickly court and soon marry. Geri was born the following year on July 20, 1941.

Both the Edwards and the White families were hard-working sharecroppers from the plantations in and around Vidalia. Simuel wanted a better, less hard-scrabble life, so he joined the army and was part of the Black contingent who maintained the supply lines in the European theater during World War II—something he had in common with Medgar Evers. Upon his return, Simuel heard there was work in the booming Texas oil fields, so he uprooted his small family—which now included two children, Geri and Pete—and moved to Orange, Texas, near the oil hub of Port Arthur. After a few years, the family returned to Vidalia and moved in with Thelma's parents—or perhaps it would be more accurate to say with Geri's mother's father and Geri's father's mother. In an unusual twist, Thelma's mother, Alice, had died while Simuel was away in the war, and her dying wish was that her husband, Alfred, would marry Simuel's mother, Texanna, who had come to nurse her through her illness. Grandad Alfred complied, so the families became doubly joined.[2]

Mama Tex, as Grandma Texanna was called, had a deep and long-lasting influence on her grandchild Geraldine. Despite the fact that four families lived under one small roof, Geri remembered her return days at Vidalia as "the happiest years of my life." Mama Tex took a special interest in Geri and taught her how to cook, how to "forage for wild greens and berries, how to can and preserve foods for the winter months, how to make elderberry jam and wine." At Grandma Tex's instruction, Geri would go into the fields, armed with only a butter knife, and come home with armfuls of dandelion greens. Grandma Tex instilled in Geri a love of the outdoors, a love of cooking and creating healthy meals, a love of health and wellness in general—loves that would become passions throughout Geri's long life.

But that little house in Vidalia got a bit crowded. Geri, her parents, and their growing horde (there would eventually be five boys) lived with her grandparents, an aunt and her two children, and two of Texanna's grandchildren whom she was raising. Five adults and many children were living in a six-room house that Geri described as "not much more than a shack."

During this extended stay in Vidalia, Geri began to notice the differences in the quality of life between the small city's Black and White residents. The Black area she lived in on the north side had no sidewalks, no paved streets. "The residential area for Blacks had ditches in the front of their properties and gravel in the streets," she later remarked. "It was so dusty! When it rained, it was muddy. When it didn't rain, it was a cushion of loose dirt, just like talcum powder." An active child (some might have called her hyperactive), Geri would either bicycle or skate all over town. But skating on gravel just didn't work. She had to make her way to the White section of town and into the downtown area, where sidewalks and pavements were plentiful. She recalled skating all around the courthouse square to her heart's delight and wondering why the sidewalks didn't stretch out into her part of town.

"I remember letting my parents know that we should have sidewalks," she said with a laugh. Even at the age of seven, Geri knew something was different—something wasn't right—about how the two races lived.

Geri started first grade while the family was still in Texas, joined the second-grade class in Vidalia, and was in fifth grade when it came time to move to Natchez. Simuel had found a job with the International Paper organization and moved his growing family across the river to be closer to his work. Natchez, though a bit larger and more established than Vidalia, had the same living standards for Blacks—no sidewalks. And it was too far for Geri to walk into town, so her skating days were over. At first, the family stayed with Thelma's brother and his wife while Simuel purchased some land and built his own house a few blocks away.

It was that process of building that captured young Geri's attention: all of the planning that went into the construction of a simple home. Simuel built a miniature model and talked with the family about each step of the building project. Geri was fascinated as the plans became real. She marveled at how, through careful planning and step-by-step execution, a new reality could take shape. "We watched in amazement and anticipation as he showed us where he was in his progress at every step of the project," she recalled years later.

Natchez today represents the quintessentially Southern plantation town. Antebellum mansions gracefully line the eastern bank of the Mississippi River, recalling the days of King Cotton, when the city was a major trade and shipping crossroads. Natchez was largely untouched by the ravages of the Civil War and even served as temporary headquarters for General Grant and his army just after the Union victory at Vicksburg. For a time, Grant took over the grand plantation home Rosalie, situated along the Mississippi River. It still stands today as a prime example of Greek revival antebellum architecture and of the grandeur that was built on the backs of the enslaved and the slave-intensive cotton economy.

In the 1950s and '60s, when Geri called Natchez home, her memories of life in this historic port city seem tinged with regret that borders on bitterness. "We never were allowed to go to any of the antebellum homes or estates when I was in Natchez," she noted. Even so, the move to Mississippi opened up other vistas for the young Geraldine Edwards. Though she had lived near the great Mississippi River for most of her early life in Vidalia, when Geri's family moved to Natchez, she landed right on a Mississippi bayou. The change was transformative. She now lived on "an ecological paradise," as she put it, and her backyard became a place of adventure and discovery. "I loved to go into the bayou and swing on the vines and forage for fruit and berries," she said. "All of those goodies grew in abundance in the tropical landscape in the middle of [my] adopted playground."

She also noticed a difference in the recreational facilities at her new Mississippi school. It was there that Geri's natural athletic abilities began to blossom and get noticed. The larger Natchez schools had better playgrounds and more jungle-gym equipment, and Geri took to it like a pro—swinging on the bars and doing all sorts of tumbling exercises on the long, wide, paved, fenced-in playground. She couldn't remember where she learned her athletic skills: "It just came natural to me." She soon formed gymnastics groups with other girls who wanted to try her "stunts."

Interestingly, given that her later claim to fame would come as a result of "invading" a library, reading became her passion and her escape—"my own secret world." Through reading, "I could escape the reality of segregation and expand my thinking and my mind," she observed. But even here, she noticed that Black people were treated with less respect. She would go to the "Negro" library and saw that "the choices were limited, to say the least." Even so, she would read anything and everything that was available to her. *Jet* magazine—delivered to her home—became a favorite way of keeping up with Black celebrities and their globe-trotting lifestyles—something Geri imagined for herself. She noticed the difference between the White-focused local paper, the *Natchez Democrat*, and the Black-oriented *Chicago Defender*. She began to realize "why so many Blacks left Mississippi to migrate to the North." Through reading, Geri began to realize that the world was much larger than the confined milieu of the Miss-Lou region and this changed her perception of who she was and the possibilities for her life. "I read myself into an elevated self-appreciation for who I was," she said.

When the family moved into their newly completed home, Geri finally, as the only girl, was able to have a room to herself, and like the author Virginia Woolf a generation or two earlier, it transformed her life. "It was my little princess space," she recalled. "Now I could read in peace because I was in my own space."

"It was my freedom!" she declared.

But a reader requires books, and Geraldine, perhaps more than many of her contemporaries, observed the meager selection of books at the "colored" Natchez library—what was called the "auxiliary" library downtown. "The place must have been all of twelve feet by twelve feet in size. It was also limited in titles." She was aware of the larger, "Whites-only" library but noted with no small amount of sarcasm: "We couldn't go into [that] library. They made a *separate but equal* place for the colored citizens." Even so, Geri was thrilled when she learned that she could check out for free even the meager selections from the auxiliary space and take them home to read. If the public library held little charm for her, when Geri started attending Sadie V. Thompson High School, not far from where she lived, she discovered what a *real* library could be. "They followed the Dewey decimal system," she noted with an air of discovery and remembered that she now could "follow the titles of certain writers and read all of their works." It wasn't lost on her that she might have been doing this all along had the auxiliary "Black" library been better funded, or if she had had full access to the "White" library's collection.

During her teenage years, Geri also felt the sting of segregation when she wanted, but could not get, a summer job. "There is nothing to do all summer long," she would recall. "You go downtown, and you see [White] teenagers working in the five-and-dime store, [but] you can't get a job. You're capable, and you have the desire [to work], and you can't get a job! So, what do you do?"

Geri escaped into reading. "I was highly motivated to wanting to better myself." It was reading that kindled in Geri the desire to go further with her education. "My appetite for reading was insatiable," she recalled. "[And] my reading was a direct inspiration for the desire to attend college." Additionally, a favorite teacher, Miss Haynes, took summer classes at a teacher's college and would return and share with Geri her "excitement for learning on the college level." Always up for a challenge, Geri worked hard to get college ready. She ended up graduating fifth in her class—she flunked Algebra as a freshman, more because the male teacher was propositioning her regularly rather than any aptitude problem for numbers—and was on her way. She and her friend Betty, who finished a few places higher in the school rankings, visited Tougaloo and fell in love with the campus. They decided to attend the college together. Simuel and Thelma packed both of them up in the family station wagon in August of 1959, drove the ninety miles to Jackson, and dropped them off at campus for orientation. Geri Edwards had read her way to her own new reality.

Chapter 6

CENTRAL AND SOUTH MISSISSIPPI OFFSPRING

ALTHOUGH THE MAJORITY OF THE TOUGALOO NINE DEMONSTRATORS came from the Delta and from Memphis, a few represented other constituencies—specifically the areas in and around Jackson, the very seat of state power, and Laurel, a hotbed of Klan activity within the state. Both locales had their own unique charms and challenges for mid-twentieth-century Black youth. Alfred Cook and Meredith Anding Jr. grew up close to that power, perhaps frustrating them more than if they had never seen its two faces. Evelyn Pierce became a youth leader in her local YMCA and Laurel NAACP Youth Chapter. She learned to push for things that most people thought were beyond her reach.

ALFRED LEE COOK

Alfred Cook—one of the oldest of the Tougaloo Nine when they marched into that downtown Jackson library—was not one for interviews. He was guarded when discussing his own story, demurring by saying he was planning on writing his own book about his consequential life. It certainly would have been a tale worth telling. Sadly, Cook died before completing his memoir. As a result, there are only the barest of facts based on a few news articles that he agreed to participate in years earlier and some public comments he made at various alumni gatherings where the Tougaloo Nine were fêted over the years. The little that Al Cook revealed during those sessions, however, touches upon areas of Black life and education in Mississippi that bear exploration.[1]

Alfred Lee Cook was born in Vicksburg during the first days of 1938 to Queen Ella and Elijah Cook. The Cooks had another son, Elijah Jr., who arrived a year later. Calamity struck the family early when Alfred was only eighteen months old. His mother died, and Elijah Sr. removed himself from the family not to be seen again until the children were grown. Alfred and Elijah Jr. were raised by their maternal grandparents, the Reverend Jim Bell and his wife, also named Queen Ella. Though strict, the Bells, were "the most loving people around," Cook fondly recalled. Jim and Queen Ella owned some land near Edwards, Mississippi, a small enclave about halfway between Vicksburg and Jackson. Owning land was a far cry from the sharecropping life to which most rural Blacks were condemned. The children spent their early years in a picturesque, though racist, rural setting, where the family grew crops and raised farm animals.

It was in the Edwards community that Al Cook learned an enduring lesson about racism and how to resist it. "I had always been taught to say, 'Yes, Sir,' and 'No, Ma'am' to Whites," Cook reflected. "I *never* yielded to that request."

"I recall that as a ten-year-old boy," he continued, "a White man was talking to me, and I would only nod my head up and down." Seeing this, Cook's grandfather demanded that he say, "Yes, Sir," to the man. "I refused to speak," Cook remembered. Then Jim Bell put his shoed foot on little Alfred's bare toes to force him to say the honorific "for fear of my life." Still, the youthful Cook refused. The White man let it drop, though perhaps not without giving Bell a good talking to about how he was raising his grandson.

During these formative years, Alfred and Elijah Jr. were schooled by their grandmother, a high school graduate. The year Cook turned twelve, he and his brother were sent to school in Jackson so that they both could obtain a formal education.

Cook attended the high school that was connected with and run by Campbell College—an all-purpose elementary, secondary, and junior-college-level institution founded and run by the African Methodist Episcopal Churches of Mississippi. A somewhat precocious youth, Al Cook liked to flout the school's rules. After two years at Campbell, he was expelled when he was found in the girl's dormitory, a serious infraction of the religious school's strict code of conduct.[2] Cook was unceremoniously returned home to his grandparents in Edwards, where he found that his grandmother, Queen Ella, his rock, was seriously ill. She would die within the year, as would his grandfather, two months later.

"I was left so poor, hair wouldn't grow on my face," Al Cook later joked. The boys' circumstances were no joking matter, however, and Al, "being a thinking young person," devised to trick his way into the air force by lying about his age. He succeeded in this ruse, claiming to be eighteen, when, in fact, he was two years shy of this minimum age requirement. He signed up for a four-year tour of duty sometime in the mid-1950s. While serving in the military, realizing that education would be a key to his long-term success, Cook obtained his GED high school equivalency certificate.

But Al Cook found the military a miserable existence for a young Black man. Discrimination was rampant; Black recruits were forced to do the most demeaning jobs. "I was treated like a subclass citizen," he recounted. "I was never given the due I felt I was entitled to. Never! So, I began to rebel." Cook was released from the Air Force Military Police six months prior to the end of his tour of duty. "They asked me to leave because I was a troublemaker," he would later admit. "They didn't need people like me." Cook was offered an honorary discharge and moved on. He had dreams of becoming a doctor and realized he needed to get a good college education. Perhaps because it was known to him, he applied and was accepted back into the Campbell College community and its higher-education program.

Campbell College and the AME Church

The very first organized religious institution for African Americans in the United States was the African Methodist Episcopal Church. Organized in 1794 in Philadelphia by the ardent Christian devotee Richard Allen, the AME Church format quickly spread to other cities on the Eastern seaboard. The church itself was an outgrowth of the Free African Society, established in 1787, in which Allen also had a hand, along with Absalom Jones—both freedmen who objected to the harassment they experienced while trying to worship in mainstream churches. Each felt the need to band together with like-minded Black believers "to provide mutual aid in times of misfortune and to exercise a kind of moral oversight . . . by visitation and prayer." By 1816, the first conference of AME churches was called by Allen, who would become their bishop, and thus, the first Black Christian denomination in America was created.[3]

It is said that the formation of the AME Church through the direct lineage of the Free African Society created the template for all future Black churches in the United States: "A pattern of religious commitment that has a double focus—the free and autonomous worship of God in the way Black people want to worship him, and the unity and social welfare of the Black community."[4] This dual commitment would show itself in Mississippi through the creation of a school that would attempt to serve the needs of the Black community while focusing on moral development and biblical training.

Campbell College was established in 1890 under the leadership of the Mississippi and Northern Mississippi Conferences of the AME Church. Although initially located on a bluff overlooking the Mississippi River, just a mile below center-city Vicksburg, the college soon was shifted to just outside the city limits of Jackson—now West Jackson—to take advantage of capital city's centrality within the state as well as its expanding infrastructure of rail, telegraph, and telephone lines. This coeducational school was designed as "a college for all, regardless of creed or denomination, who would like to avail themselves of the opportunity to get a good education."[5]

From its earliest days, Campbell College operated as both a high school and a junior (two-year) college. As a "church" school, the college was deeply steeped in the Bible. Theological and biblical training were paramount and received top billing in the school's repertoire of majors for students. But the school also offered substantive technical training for those wishing to become teachers, nurses, carpenters, artists, and musicians. Even sewing—"domestic economy"—and agricultural courses were taught. To support its teacher-training curriculum, the school ran a full-service elementary school, mostly populated with students from Jackson and its surrounding counties.

The ethos of the school was expansive: "The advantages of Campbell College are offered to all persons of both sexes, without regard to sectarian affiliation, and in the broadest possible sense, race or nationality." But as a religious-based school, the behavioral expectations were strict: "Students who have no fixed purpose and who do not regard the improvement of their minds for larger usefulness and who have no desire to fit themselves for the emergencies of life, are not received as applicants, and the presence of such students will not be tolerated." Whatever infraction Al Cook ran afoul of during his first stint at Campbell was most likely minor: serious enough to get him expelled from the discipline-focused high school, yet insignificant enough that he was allowed to return for college.

During its entire operational tenure, from 1890 to 1964, Campbell College would be one of less than a handful of African American–funded and run colleges within the state of Mississippi. (Tougaloo and Rust Colleges were funded and run by White religious organizations and staffed on an integrated basis.) Campbell's reliance solely on Black-based philanthropy would be its undoing, as the school seemed always to be underfunded and financially struggling.

Despite its financial woes, the college's independence provided its administrators and students with an opportunity to act more aggressively with regard to civil rights agitation, a situation that would come into full flower in the early 1960s. Additionally, its location about a mile from downtown Jackson (as opposed to Tougaloo's campus about ten miles away) would offer a perfect location for leaders like Medgar Evers to use the college as an assembly area for press conferences or as a launching pad for some of the early civil rights protests within the city. It was during his freshman year at Campbell that Alfred Cook encountered Evers.

In April 1960, the NAACP's Mississippi field secretary and others announced an Easter boycott of stores in downtown Jackson because of the way their clerks disrespected Black customers. This was the first of several boycotts that Evers would lead in the wake of the galvanizing student-led lunch-counter sit-in staged two months earlier in Greensboro, North

Carolina. That sit-in inspired a wave of similar demonstrations throughout the South, although Mississippi remained strangely isolated and quiet. Evers hoped that a boycott would at the very least signal to Mississippi's power brokers that its Black populace was not satisfied with the status quo and was beginning to seek substantive changes to the racial dynamic. (Any sort of sit-in or in-your-face, direct-action campaign was deemed too dangerous at the time.)

The administrators and trustees of Campbell College were divided in their thinking about the burgeoning civil rights movement and the college's role in sparking change. Some, like chaplain and dean of religion Reverend Charles Jones went all in, offering the campus as a staging ground for demonstrations and, in the case of Jones, even participating in his own one-man protest by attempting to integrate the downtown Jackson Trailways bus depot. Jones had the support of college president Robert Stevens, but various trustees and faculty, including Stevens' outspoken wife, believed the college should "focus on academic and not political" activities.

Cook sensed these divisions as he became more interested in speaking out. "We students wanted to do something like others across the country were doing," he would later say. In fact, Al Cook became one of the student leaders of that first Easter boycott and of the group that it spawned, the Sacrifice for Human Dignity. At the same time, Cook soured on Campbell College's mixed messages on student activism and decided that his spring semester at Campbell would be his last.[6] Still needing to advance his education, however, Cook looked to Tougaloo College as a more welcoming campus and observed, correctly, that Tougaloo had a higher academic rigor and standing. Tougaloo was one of only two HBCUs accredited within Mississippi at the time and would be better positioned to provide him with the education he needed to launch a career in medicine. In the fall of 1960, Alfred Lee Cook transferred to Tougaloo as a sophomore science major and continued his quest for both higher education and stronger activism.[7]

MEREDITH ANDING JR.

Meredith Anding Jr. was born on August 31, 1941, in the deep woods of Mississippi in a little enclave known as Myles Station (Myles) in Copiah County—the adjoining jurisdiction to Hinds County, which houses the state's capital city. But Anding's birthplace of Myles was a far cry from the grandeur of Jackson. Meredith's maternal grandfather was a blacksmith who ran a small business out of "a little hut" where he created ironworks. It was the kind of place draped with newspapers that were pasted to the walls to keep the wind and rain out. Meredith remembered his early life as one of fishing and hunting and being part of the great outdoors. His father's people came from a region only slightly more populated than Myles—Monticello, Mississippi—the seat of Lawrence County, just a stone's throw from Jefferson Davis County, named, of course, for the president of the Confederacy.

The eldest of twelve children, Meredith Anding Jr.—they called him "Junior Man"—was the son of Meredith Sr. and Nellie (Marshall) Anding. For this narrative in particular, Anding thought it worth mentioning that his grandfather was the result of the rape of his great-grandmother by a White man named *Alred*, according to family lore. She later married Steven Anding, and, thus, the family surname, but Junior Man's light complexion can be traced back to the unacknowledged Alred bloodline.

When Meredith was about five years old, his family moved to Jackson into a little shotgun rental house not far from Campbell College. Meredith Sr. attended the school briefly while learning to become a self-employed air conditioning and appliance repairman. He was good with his hands and set about building a larger home just one block over on Hattiesburg Street, where young Meredith and the rest of his siblings would grow up. Meredith Jr. started his formal education at Adams Economy, "a little church school," he recalled. He later attended the public schools in his neighborhood—Sally Reynolds Elementary, Isable Middle School, Jim Hill High School—all of them, of course, segregated.

Even so, Meredith's Black neighborhood in West Jackson bordered a neighborhood where Whites lived at that time. M. B. Pierce, then a still-young, newish member of the Jackson police force, resided only a few blocks away. As he grew, the young Anding would occasionally see the future police chief around the neighborhood. Later, of course, he famously would come face-to-face with Pierce as a college student who dared to break societal strictures at the downtown library.

Meredith's home life was filled with family and friends. Once the Andings moved to Jackson, they got closer to his mother's siblings and their families, in particular, the Logans. One of Nellie's older sisters, A. M. E. (Marshall) Logan, was a dynamic force, not only within the family but also in the community. Named by her father to honor his deep affection for the African Methodist Episcopal Church that he served faithfully, A. M. E. and her husband, S. L. Logan had moved from Myles to Jackson only a year or so before the Andings did. In fact, Meredith and his family lived just down the street from the Logans on Biloxi Street for nearly a year while Meredith Sr. was building the Anding family place a few blocks away.[8]

A. M. E. would come to be known as the "Mother of the Jackson Civil Rights Movement" in Jackson, but even in the forties, while raising her four children, she was a force in the community. At first, A. M. E. worked as a self-employed seamstress and hairdresser, ingratiating herself with other members of her new community. Then she became assistant manager of the local grocery store. She was active from the start in the Pearl Street AME Church (of course) and even sold Avon products door-to-door. All these interpersonal connections that Logan made in her business and personal life would become ever more important as she immersed herself in the workings of the Jackson branch of the NAACP. Reinvigorated just after the *Brown v. Board of Education* decision, the Jackson branch provided the local support network for Medgar Evers and his plans for a city-wide movement. A. M. E. became a force within the group, eventually serving on nearly every committee.

Realizing how important a strong membership base was to the functioning of the branch, Logan set about calling on her connections, door-to-door, to sign them up as new members and to preach the values of sticking together. As often as not, she would have the door slammed in her face—membership in the NAACP in 1950s Mississippi was considered an act of a lunacy—but steadily, with all the conviction of a convert, A. M. E. helped build up the membership base of the Jackson branch.[9]

None of this was lost on Meredith Sr., who insisted that his children get involved in the branch's newly organized West Jackson Youth Council. "He signed me up without me even knowing!" Anding recalled. Meredith's cousin Willis Logan—A. M. E.'s son—was president of the group at the time. It was through these family connections that the Andings fell into the orbit of Medgar Evers and his persuasive arguments that local Blacks needed to begin finding ways to register their protest against the Whites-only power structure that dominated every aspect of Mississippi life.

As noted, the NAACP field representative became convinced that for Black citizens to rise up, it would be necessary to train the youth and develop an array of nonviolent tactics that might work in such a violent and repressive regime of White rule. And he found ways to encourage the most promising among them with opportunities to travel outside of the state to meet other youth engaged in similar plans and projects.

Meredith participated in two out-of-state annual conclaves of NAACP Southern Regional Youth Councils—the first in Georgia, the next in South Carolina—where Evers and other NAACP luminaries, including Evers's boss, Ruby Hurley, would facilitate dialog among the various Southern Black youth in order to inspire them to push against their second-class citizenship within the Southern social structure. Meredith recalled hearing at one of those gatherings, during the summer of 1960, that kids from every other Southern state had already taken action to express their collective objection to the status quo within their communities. It was only Mississippi that had not yet found the courage to protest. Meredith and the Mississippi contingent got together and said, "Let's go back and think of something to do!" he recalled. "That's how the [zoo protest] idea was born." The kids preempted the library sit-in by a few months, but because of their relative youth, nothing much came of their protest. They were sent home after a good talking to by the police.

Their brazen action occurred on a Sunday later that summer. Meredith, his cousin Willis Logan, youth leader Amos Brown, and a few others from the West Jackson Youth Council made their way over to the Jackson Zoo, about a three-mile bike ride from the NAACP offices at the Masonic Temple. Their idea was simple. The park benches throughout the zoo's campus were reserved for Whites only. Even though the zoo was open to Black visitors on certain days of the week, they were not allowed to sit on the benches while visiting the park. There was a bench across from the concessions stand. The adventurous teens decided to purchase some ice cream, sit on the bench, and see what would happen.

"In about five or ten minutes, the police came and took us out," Meredith recalled. He believed that this was the first such protest in Jackson. But the police, perhaps under instructions from headquarters, handled the situation with a light touch. "We're not going to arrest you," they told the youths, addressing them as if they were little children. "Just go home and be good boys and girls and don't cause any more trouble." This initial foray into civil disobedience never made it into the papers, but it certainly stayed in the minds of Anding, Brown, Logan, and the other participants. "That [protest] didn't work out," Meredith stated matter of factly, "but we got our feet wet." And despite adept handling of the situation by the police, it should have been an early warning signal that the Black youth of Jackson were beginning to catch the resistance fever that was inflaming the rest of the South.[10]

As for school achievement, Meredith wouldn't call himself a good student. "I didn't study," he claimed. Even so, he won the history and civics awards in high school. He also entered a statewide model-car-building contest sponsored by the Fisher Price toy company and won first place/junior division—an accomplishment that garnered some local accolades. (He would enter the contest two more times, coming in second and then third in the state, even as the building project became more and more challenging.) He was on the trade-school track, studying carpentry and masonry and with no interest or expectation of going to college. But since Jackson State College was right there—just a few blocks from his home, part of his daily newspaper route, in fact—he applied in the spring of 1958 along with many of his high school classmates, and he got in.

At Jackson State, Meredith found he was able to keep up with the academic work but realized that the college didn't have the major he was hoping to focus on—engineering. He was good at math and had a knack for solving complex technical problems, as the Fisher Price competition had demonstrated. During that first year at Jackson State, Meredith discovered that Tougaloo College, although not offering an engineering major, had a program with a heavy math and physics emphasis that would put a dedicated student onto the engineering track. The summer after his freshman year, Meredith found a job working construction. His White boss, Mr. Kane, saw the young man's potential and was impressed with his placement in the Fisher Price challenge. Kane urged Anding to take the engineering path. So, with that little push, in the summer of 1959, Meredith Anding transferred from Jackson State to Tougaloo College and started his sophomore year there that fall. His academic and activist inclinations were about to pique.

EVELYN PIERCE

In a cruel twist, not all of the Tougaloo Nine survived until their story became widely understood as an essential link in the Mississippi civil rights struggle. Evelyn Pierce—who would later become known as Ameenah Omar when she married the older brother of Malcolm X—died only a few years before this project got underway; few clues remain to piece together her activist journey. It is thanks to her older sister, Armendia (Pierce) Dixon and her younger sister Demathraus Pierce Perry, that we can draw a portrait of the Pierce family and the environment in which Evelyn Pierce came of age.[11]

By now, that story will sound quite familiar. It seems almost a composite of all the other stories presented thus far: Large family, newly moved from rural to urban setting; devoted parents; a charismatic father who works full time and also serves as a pastor or preacher; a mother who instills a love of learning; family emphasis on education as a way up and a way out; dedicated and industrious teachers who "make a way out of no way" to ensure that the youth in their care have access to a better life than they have known; a cocoon of protection that surrounds these children and attempts to keep from them, for as long as possible, from the scourge of racism and segregation under which they live; a success story of deep human striving and struggle for a better life, not only for oneself but also for one's community; and importantly, the role of the NAACP in raising awareness about how best to resist the oppressive White regime.

Evelyn, the sixth of eleven children, was born on April 3, 1941, to the Reverend Lou Edward Pierce and Denothraus (Pickens) Pierce in the southeastern Mississippi town of Laurel. Both parents came from nearby smaller locales—Denothraus from Bay Springs, a modest town in the southeastern, piney-woods section of Mississippi where lumber mills abound; and Lou Edward from Stringer, a smaller, unincorporated community—what we might now call a "truck-stop town"—halfway between Bay Springs and Laurel. Coming from Bay Springs, Denothraus hailed from the more affluent family. "Mother's parents owned property," Armendia recalled. "Her father was a music teacher. She probably had a very good life." Lou Edward, on the other hand, "grew up poor." As the family stories tell it, Lou Edward's mother, Nancy, had two names because "she and her family were sold twice into slavery." Granma Nancy would become an important figure in the lives of the Pierce children, but as Armendia noted, when Denothraus "married my father, that sort of put her in the poor category."

The Pierce family's early years were ones of struggle and survival—and tragedy. Both parents were well-educated, and both taught at the local "norm" school, as Armendia related—what were known as teacher-training, "normal schools." When their first child, Warren G., was born, Denothraus allowed Nancy to care for the child so that she could continue teaching to help make ends meet. But Warren developed spinal meningitis and died, causing Denothraus to swear, "I won't leave another child." Thus, Lou Edward became the sole breadwinner for the family. He made a living teaching returning World War II veterans who attended night school thanks to financial assistance from the GI Bill. In addition, he took on all sorts of additional jobs—selling cars, delivering milk—to make ends meet. "Whatever he could do to keep the family going, he did it," Armendia recalled. As many of his generation who were seeking a leadership role in the Black community, Lou Edward felt the call to preach. He eventually built and pastored his own church, St. Luke Missionary Baptist, and became an important Black leader in Laurel.

The family moved to Laurel in 1937, just prior to Armendia's birth and a few years before Evelyn's. At first, they settled in the poorest section, the K.C. Bottom, because that was all they could afford. They rented a little shotgun house with an outhouse just off Tallahalla Creek, a tributary of the Leaf River, which would flood seasonally and leave "water streets" which the Pierce children would float down in inner tubes, along with the snakes and the debris. "It wasn't the most sanitary place to live," Armendia wryly observed. Just after World War II, the family was one of the first to be invited to live in the new Triangle Housing Project—a subsidized community on higher ground, by the railroad tracks on Maple Street. Here the family would thrive in their new three-bedroom townhome: "One bedroom for Daddy and Mother, and the rest of us (ten children) crowded into two bedrooms!" The Traingle Projects were something of a self-contained community, with 124 housing units built in a triangular formation, with an inner common area and lots of running room for kids.

Armendia marveled at the thriving community that her family and others like them built during the depths of Jim Crow segregation. "We created our own middle class," she noted. She also pointed out that the world-renowned opera singer Leontyne Price came from their neighborhood and went to school with her older siblings. In addition, "[Leontyne's] mother was a midwife and delivered most of us into this world," Armendia recalled. "And my brothers would get their hair cut by Lenotyne Price's father," a part-time barber and lumber-mill worker. One of Price's earliest benefactors, Mrs. Elizabeth Wisner Chisholm—heiress of a local lumber baron's fortune—also provided funds for the youngest Pierce girls, Ruby and Elizabeth, to go to college.

But Evelyn's sister also remembered Laurel for its less-savory elements; it was known as a hotbed of Klan activity within the state. "We knew it was heavily infested with the KKKs," Armendia observed. In fact, "the Grand Wizard of the KKK lived at the end of the street!" Indeed, Sam Bowers, who would become the imperial wizard of the White Knights of the KKK, settled in Laurel in the late 1940s and ran a pinball-machine operation, Sambo Amusement Company, out of an industrial building near the Triangle Projects.[12]

Armendia remembered that groups of Klansmen would attempt to terrorize various sections of Laurel. "They would ride through and blow their horns and put on their lights and wear their KKK outfits," she recalled. But she also noted that the Klansmen would "*never*" ride through the Triangle Housing Project. "They were afraid to come through the project area," she said.

The counterbalance to the Klan activity, of course, was Laurel's strong chapter of the NAACP, to which all of the Pierce family belonged—parents and children. "If ever the NAACP had a positive [impact]," Armendia stated emphatically, "it had it on the African American community of Laurel, Mississippi." She described how the adults would gather regularly to discuss racial issues within the community and develop strategies to resist the blatant discrimination they experienced daily. The kids, too, became members of the Laurel NAACP Youth Council at an early age to steel themselves against the demeaning effects of living in a segregated society. "We got into the NAACP when we were eleven or twelve," Armendia recalled. "It was sort of like you had to be ready for responsibility. You learned early. The Youth Council of the NAACP greatly influenced our lives." The youth would gather, talk over their own struggles with racism, and find constructive things to do to build community.

Armendia described her younger sister Evelyn as "funny," "provocative," "very smart," and "a leader." She is certain that Evelyn led the youth chapter of the NAACP several times during her teenage years. "She was very outgoing," Armendia said. "I was older, but shy."

Evelyn's younger sister Demathraus concured. "My sister Evelyn was really a leader," Demathraus said. "We kind of did what she told us to do. We looked up to her."

In fact, Demathraus wanted to *be* Evelyn for a time. "I tried to emulate her dressing," she recalled. Even though the Pierce children mostly wore hand-me-down clothes, she noted that if Evelyn "wore a yellow sweater on Wednesday, the next Wednesday, I wanted to wear that yellow sweater," she said. "I would pick a date where I would be like Evelyn."

Demathraus also acknowledged the benefit of the family belonging to the local YMCA and YWCA. "That was really a main outlet for activities outside of the home," she observed. "And we did things like community involvement by helping older people, mowing their lawns or cleaning their houses, things like that."

Demathraus enjoyed telling a childhood story about how the Pierce kids would play cards and dance while their father, a strict Baptist, was away on weekends. By this time, Lou Edward Pierce had become a minister and served a series of churches far from home. He would leave Saturday evening, stay at a parishioner's home overnight, and return Sunday evening after the late service. So, Saturday nights and Sunday afternoons became the time the kids would try to fit in all of the taboo activities—with Mother Pierce's OK—while Daddy Pierce was away. One Sunday, Reverend Pierce returned home earlier than expected. "We were scrambling to get the card table out of the living room, and we dropped some cards in the hallway just as my father came in the door.

"Was somebody playing cards?!" Reverend Pierce exclaimed. Mother Piece allowed that, "Yes, they were playing cards."

"So, they went up to their bedroom and had a further discussion," Demathraus recalled. The upshot was that they would only play cards on Saturday nights when they *knew* Daddy wouldn't be anywhere nearby.

One activity that Evelyn and others in the family participated in was school choir. "[Evelyn] excelled at that," Armendia recalled. "She was a good singer." The skills Evelyn learned there would serve her well at Tougaloo, where she would join Pops Lovelace and the Tougaloo choir.

All of the Pierce children attended the same segregated Laurel public schools: Nora Davis Elementary, Southside Junior High, and Oak Park High School. From there, they went on to either college or into the military. Indeed, all of the Pierce siblings would go on to important lives of community service. This incredibly accomplished family would play major roles in the areas of education, military service, and social work in the communities in which they would eventually settle. Again and again, Armendia would come back to the formative role that the NAACP played.

But she also acknowledged the limits of the NAACP's accommodationist approach during those crucial years leading up to the outbreak of demonstrations. "All of us didn't buy into turning the other cheek," she said. Clearly her sister Evelyn was among these. Even her choice of college was intended as an affront to the status quo.

"Tougaloo was off limits," Armendia said. "Tougaloo was a school that we knew, without a doubt, that if we went there, we would be blackballed. We would not be able to get a job in the South."

Since Tougaloo had a reputation for providing many of Mississippi's Black schools with highly qualified teachers at the time, this claim seems a bit overwrought. But when pressed, Armendia persisted. "No, it was a given that you didn't go to Tougaloo," she insisted. "It was where White folks didn't want us to go."

"So," Armendia laughed, "that's probably why [Evelyn] went there!"

And this is what is known about Evelyn's choice: a budding NAACP activist with a desire for a good education chooses an in-state private school with a reputation for excellence and a history of pushing against the grain of established social norms. Hoping to learn more ways of changing Mississippi's status quo, Evelyn took the plunge and arrived at Tougaloo College in the fall of 1960, just as things were about to get very interesting. In short order, she and her eight schoolmates would get their chance to move Mississippi forward.

Part III

CULTURE CLASH

Chapter 7

TOUGALOO'S CULTURE OF RESISTANCE

IMAGINE IT'S THE MIDTWENTIETH CENTURY, AND YOU'VE JUST GRADU-ated from a segregated Black high school in Mississippi. Or maybe you're from an out-of-state state school looking for a new adventure. You some-how have found out about Tougaloo College—funny name, right?—maybe from a relative, more likely from a school counselor. You've heard that it's a cut above the kinds of schools that Negroes in Mississippi might aspire to. You've worked hard, and you think you might qualify. So, you apply. And after an interminable wait—isn't it that way for any college?—you find that you've been accepted. You got in! You start dreaming of what college will be like—the freedom, the fun, the opportunities. But you really have little preparation for the liberality you are about to experience. No matter, you start making plans and packing your bags.

Now, imagine you're on campus. Your first approach to Tougaloo College by car from County Line Road—the one that puts the college on the other side of the tracks (literally) from Hinds County and the city of Jackson. Who cares? Black folks are always doled out the scraps. We'll just see what's behind those arched gates that announce where you are: Tougaloo † College. The cross symbolizes that this is a Christian College, one started by White missionaries and abolitionists just after the Civil War. It is one of about one hundred Christian colleges started in the South between 1864 and 1875 for the formerly enslaved. And it is a *blessed* place.

You drive (or most likely are driven) under the gate and onto what seems a palatial preserve of peace. Indeed, the place once was a plantation, a forced-labor camp where people of color toiled for hours in the blazing Southern sun to enrich the plantation owner while they themselves lived like animals in slave quarters—the remnants of which are still visible beyond the dorms where you will be living. For the past ninety years, however, this place has been transformed into a reservoir of peace, a place of deep learning. Of education. Of uplift. You immediately feel at home.

How could this be? How could a place with such deep roots and a beautiful campus, with hundred-year-old live oak trees hung with long-flowing Spanish moss—how could this have all been prepared for you? Who knew this was even here? Who could have imagined a spot like this was possible . . . in Mississippi? You walk around the campus—on sidewalks! Sidewalks that you yearned for in your own little town where mud and dust were, instead, the norm. Sidewalks crisscrossing the main square—from your dorm to the classrooms to the gym . . . to the chapel.

And what a chapel! The finest building on campus. You tiptoe in and find a stunning polished wood-frame structure with sturdy wooden pews and a show-stopping pipe organ. Light fills the vast open space above like an angel announcing that you have entered a holy place, a sacred space, a place far removed from the indignities that you have suffered just outside those gates. This is a place of repose, of thought, of prayer and reflection. Take in this feeling. It is yours for only a brief time: this landscape; this oasis. Soon you will be sent back out into that world renewed and equipped to take on the demons that await.

You go to your assigned dorm. You settle in. You begin taking classes, meeting roommates and other lucky ones who got in and who will accompany you on your college journey. They are all "colored" but of varying hues and shades, from light mocha to deep chocolate. And what's this? Your teachers are not all Black like they were back home! You've got White teachers and foreign teachers, as well. You wonder if you'll be able to make the grade with what you know will be higher standards than what your local high school or previous college prepared you for. Better buckle down and get to work.

Now, imagine that after about a month of soaking up this exhilarating new environment, you're invited to an all-student meeting in that lovely chapel. It's early evening, after classes have concluded. The bell rings in the steeple high above the chapel, calling all students and much of the faculty to that most-holy shrine. You go expectantly, wondering just what is beckoning. Could it be your future calling?

You enter and immediately sense the crackle of electricity that permeates the humid air. Word is going around. Medgar Evers is in the house! The same Medgar Evers who has been attempting to rouse Black folks throughout the state to take on the mighty forces of oppression and to object to the Jim Crow racism you've experienced your entire life. Medgar Evers, the state leader of the NAACP, that vilified acronym you've heard so much about—the National Association for the Advancement of Colored People. The name that even Negro public school teachers throughout the South can't mention at school for fear of losing their jobs. And Medgar Evers! How on earth did he get in here? And who is giving him this platform? In this sacred space!? You hold your breath as he is introduced and begins to speak.

What could he say that would address the indignities that you and your family have already suffered? What might he suggest that you haven't already thought of privately, in the deep silence of your own reflections? And yet, have you ever heard these things discussed openly? Has any preacher at home ever talked directly to the crisis of the Negro in the South rather than to the spiritual needs and perils of your eternal soul? Has any leader in your locale openly addressed the discrimination, the lack of job opportunities, the limited options, the poor infrastructure in Black communities? These and other unspeakable topics are about to be addressed, and Mr. Evers will have a plan of action for making radical change to his native Mississippi.

As he speaks, you sit back and wonder how he could have the gall, the calm presence of mind, the audacity, the courage(!) to stand there in a public space and discuss alternatives to the reality that you now live. You think of your mother being beaten to the ground by a bus driver when she asked him a simple question. You remember the town of your youth where you couldn't roller skate in your neighborhood because there were no sidewalks on the Black side of town. You've had flashes of insight—and rebellious thoughts that you've held close—that perhaps if you all stand together, you might mount some strong opposition to the way things are and seemingly have always been. You become delirious with hope after hearing this youthful, thoughtful, serious renegade talk tangible strategy about what has been done and what might be done in the future to resist the culture of White superiority and Black oppression. You think maybe, just maybe, things could change. And you begin to dream a world of equality, opportunity, and accomplishment.

When Mr. Evers makes his final plea for support—"We need you . . ."— you rush to sign up for the on-campus College NAACP Youth Council and determine that you will make a difference in your time and place. If not now, when? If not me, who? If not here, where? The match has been lit, and you are ready to do your part to push for change.

– – –

This imaginative exercise—an amalgam of the reflections of several of the Tougaloo Nine—actually happened in the state of Mississippi in the fall of 1960. And the fact that Tougaloo College—so close to the political center of White power in the state—could operate independently and hold such a radical stance on racial equality at this particular time in Mississippi's history is testament to a long line of the school's teachers, preachers, and administrators. To allow Medgar Evers on campus for a presentation at that time was a radical act. But Tougaloo took it all in stride thanks to its culture of resistance, which had been fostered by Dr. Ernst Borinski, Reverend John Mangram, and Dr. Adam Beittel, all of whom were active at the college at the time of the library sit-in. Along with former chaplain Reverend William Bender and just-retired President Sam Kincheloe, these men served as an advance guard, countering the prevailing attitudes about Black inferiority in Mississippi's separate and unequal society with a firm belief in Black equality, in Black capability, and in Black advancement.

THE STARS ALIGN

There seems to be an ineffable synchronicity about key historical events that causes one to ask, "If this didn't happen, would that have occurred? If he/she hadn't arrived on the scene, would the decision to move have been taken? At this time? By these people?" The syzygy of the NAACP's Evers and Tougaloo's Beittel, Mangram, and Borinski, in perfect alignment, made everything that would follow possible. How and why these individual forces came together, managed to be in the precise location where they were most needed—Tougaloo College, Jackson, Mississippi—is the subject of this chapter. The outline of the Evers story was covered earlier. This chapter focuses on the trio of Tougaloo leaders whose teachings and example inspired their students to take action. Their presence on the scene and their support of what was to be put in motion in the Magnolia State—an all-out assault on Jim Crow segregation in the heart of Mississippi's power center—can be chalked up to a "meaningful coincidence" or, perhaps better, to the answering of a call of conscience and the desire to be at the heart of America's race problem. All four men—each in his own way—put their shoulders to the wheel and pushed, *pushed hard*, against the seemingly intractable, White-supremacist Southern culture. And it began to move.

DR. ERNST BORINSKI

To encounter Ernst Borinski in the 1950s or '60s on the Tougaloo campus was like touching a live wire. He was someone deeply energized and transformative, someone whose life experiences uniquely qualified him to catalyze the stagnant racial climate in Mississippi and inject new ideas and build bridges that could (and would) usher in a new day. Borinski's life story reads like an Indiana Jones adventure, encompassing nearly every major tragedy and conflict of early twentieth-century Western culture. Space allows for only the broadest sketches of his life before arriving at Tougaloo, but Borinski left a treasure trove of interviews with the Mississippi Department of Archives and History for those who wish to delve deeper.[1]

Born into a secular Jewish family in 1901 in far-eastern Germany—an area he would refer to as the "great empire corner," where the empires of Germany, Austria-Hungary, and Russia came together and battled for dominance— young Ernst Borinski was twelve years old when Archduke Ferdinand was assassinated in 1914 and the falling Jenga pieces of alliances brought on the First World War. Although fighting occurred all around his home on the Eastern front, he remembered that within his native city of Kattowitz (now Katowice) daily life went on "business like usual," as Borinski would later recount in his fractured English. He and his friends grew used to the daily gunfire and cannonade they would hear in the not-so-distant countryside. "You heard the shooting of guns all the time," he recalled. "It was like the tick-ing of a clock." This extended exposure to the instability of war gave Borinski a lifelong sense that things could change at a moment's notice. "Enjoy what you have," he would say. "It may not last."

This mantra proved true enough for Borinski after the war, when native Poles staged uprisings demanding their independence. These events pushed those hammering out the Treaty of Versailles—including President Woodrow Wilson, whose Fourteen Points included support for new democracies in disputed areas—to establish the Republic of Poland. Since Kattowitz was on the extreme eastern border of what had been Germany, just fifty miles from Krakow, a plebiscite was held to determine whether the area should stay in German hands or be annexed into the reconstituted Polish republic. A complicated set of decisions were made based on the plebiscite that resulted in Kattowitz and its surrounding area becoming part of Poland. Thus, over-night, Borinski became a Polish resident, and an enduring confusion over his country of origin ensued. Since he wanted to go to university in Germany, however, Borinski was able to hold onto his German citizenship.

The following decade was one of relative calm for the young scholar, who attended a variety of universities in Halle, Berlin, and Munich (including the famed University of Halle-Wittenberg—now Martin Luther University), and earning a BA, MA, and PhD along the way, focusing primarily on the history of the law as well as on the liberal arts.[2] Intent on law as his profession, Ernst next attended the Hague Academy of International Law in the Netherlands, earning his JD in 1930. Borinski triumphantly returned to Germany and set up his own law practice and even served as a local judge for a time. When the Nazis rose to power, however, Borinski clearly understood the ramifica-tions. "I was one of the few people who read Hitler's *Mein Kampf* and took it seriously," he drolly stated years later.

The at-risk Jewish lawyer held on as long as he could, but in 1938, shortly after the Nazis took over Austria, Borinski fled in a dramatic escape by overnight train to Holland ("with just a suitcase and a few thousand marks"), later to England, and finally to the United States.[3] He left everyone he loved and nearly everything he owned behind. When asked years later about his family and friends who decided to stay put, he would only say, "There are things in my past that I will not speak to at all. It was tragic. I liquidated this area completely for my own mental good health."

Borinski tried to start over in America, but World War II intervened. He was drafted into the US Army in December 1942 and was sent to various training camps, including Fort Bragg, North Carolina, where he first witnessed Jim Crow segregation up close. After basic training, Borinski shipped off to North Africa where his facility with European languages (he spoke German, Russian, French, and Polish fluently) provided him with privileges not typically enjoyed by a lowly military private. He often was called in by his superiors to translate during high level meetings and negotiations. His army service also earned him US citizenship.

After the war, Borinski knew he wanted to teach—he had done some teaching at the University of Jena before the war and loved it—but believed he would need American credentials to be fully accepted into the US academic community. He also wanted to "find an American perspective." So, with no time to waste—he was now in his midforties—Borinski tested into the master's degree program at the University of Chicago, where he studied, among other things, political science, sociology, and law. Meanwhile, he began looking for a place to land. He talked to friends at the International House, some of whom were Black, to help sort out his options. One of those housemates asked if he would "consider going into Black education." "Certainly!" he answered, not knowing exactly what this meant. He was clear, though, about one thing: "I didn't want to have a job in any established institution. I wanted a job somewhere nobody else would go."

That is how the newly Americanized Borinski found himself writing to the American Missionary Association to see if they would be interested in his services. In what he says was a "candid" ten-page letter to AMA secretary Fred Brownlee, Borinski poured out the twists and turns of his eventful life and asked Brownlee to consider putting him to work. "We would be interested," was Brownlee's reply. After a brief interview at the AMA's offices in New York City and admonishment that the work would be difficult and possibly dangerous, Borinski was on his way to another battleground, this time, Mississippi, USA.[4]

Borinski at Tougaloo

Borinski was the first of the aforementioned change agents to arrive on the scene at Tougaloo. In the midsummer of 1947, the naturalized citizen stepped foot for the first time onto Mississippi soil. It was hot. He arrived in the late afternoon on the famed *City of New Orleans* train from Chicago and immediately confusion over the color question reared its ugly head. Tougaloo's academic dean, the Hampton Institute and Harvard University trained Lionel B. Fraser, had agreed to be on hand to welcome Borinski and to drive him to the college. But when Borinski exited through the "Whites-only" door of the railway station, there was no one in sight. He attempted to walk the entire length of Jackson's famed Capitol Street—the eight-block business district bordered by the train station and trestles on the far western side and by the Old State Capitol Building at the farthest eastern outpost, from which the street derived its lofty name. The one-hundred-plus-degree heat and the high humidity got to the northern-bred German, however, and he soon returned to the station to try to find his ride. Only when Borinski sauntered over to the "Colored Only" section of the receiving area did he find Dean Fraser, who drove the new recruit up the half-mile stretch of Capitol Street, taking a left onto State Street directly in front of that old seat of power, past the site where the Jackson Municipal Library would be built a few years later, and due north nine miles out to County Line Road and on to the Tougaloo College campus.[5]

Borinski was initially housed in the men's dormitory, not yet occupied by students, who would show up a few weeks later. There was no air conditioning, and the air hung thick with humidity and sweltering heat. His first experiences must have caused Borinski to question his decision to come to this isolated, seemingly God-forsaken place. The next day, however, he was able to take stock of the campus, admire its calm beauty, and assess its somewhat run-down, ramshackle assemblage of old buildings, some of them condemned for use. What a come down from the grandeur of Halle, Berlin, and Munich, not to mention Chicago. Was this really where he was planning to spend the rest of his life? "I will see what happens here," he said to himself.

On his self-guided tour, Borinski came upon a large two-story building with a basement, Beard Hall, that was boarded up and marked "Condemned." He found an open door and slipped down into the basement, where he found a spacious, if gone-to-seed, academic setting. In a flash of insight, he realized, "This is a good place for developing something like a social science lab"—the kind of stimulating learning environment he encountered at the University of Chicago. When he met Tougaloo's newly installed president, Harold Warren (1947–1955), later that day, he mentioned his idea. "The whole building is condemned!" Warren exclaimed incredulously. "I've looked the place over, and I think if you condemn that building, you can condemn every one of them!" Borinski shot back. He encouraged the college president to reevaluate the building and its potential functionality. Days later, the building was reopened.

It was obvious, however, that Warren didn't think much of Borinski's scheme. He gave him only five dollars to clean up and refurbish the lower level for its new purpose. Borinski, well aware of how things can get done outside the chain of command, gathered a group of students who were beginning to make their way back to campus for the new semester and called them into service. Many of them were army veterans, so he used an army analogy. "Do you know what requisition means?" he asked his strapping team. They did. "In the next three hours, I need you to furnish this whole place with tables, chairs, typewriters . . . everything! I give you permission to break into any office that you see on campus and requisition what you need for this mission." By the end of the day, Borinski's Social Science Lab was up and running. President Warren called "Herr Professor" back to his office and gave him twenty dollars to ensure that no further such "requisitions" occurred.

In this and so many other key moments of his time in Mississippi, Borinski would play dumb and use his outsider status to advance his own agenda— the cause of racial equity. During his very first sociology class, Borinski announced to his students in his heavily German-accented English: "I am not from here. I am not even from America. But when I see the kinds of laws you have here, I assure you it cannot last very long. We will challenge all the laws. I don't want you to accept any one of them!" (Borinski's pitch could have been lifted directly from Myrdal's *American Dilemma*.) The students could hardly believe their ears. Who was this unusual, hard-to-understand foreigner, and how was he going to break down the seemingly intractable infrastructure of White-supremacist laws and practices? "Herr Professor" seemed more like an oddity, a wild-eyed radical—maybe even a Communist! Someone to watch out for rather than to follow.

Borinski, perhaps trying to build his credibility with his new students but also testing the boundaries of Mississippi culture, showed them how it could be done. During that first week of classes, he would later recount, he took a handful of his students to downtown Jackson and brought them into one of the five-and-dime variety stores found then in just about every urban setting across America. He had them sit down at the lunch counter, and he ordered ice cream for the entire group.

"I can't serve *them*!" the White attendant exclaimed.
Again, the German accent: "Vy don't you serf dem?"
"Why?" she nearly screamed. "You know why!!"
"I don't know anyzing," Borinski feigned.

Afraid that this suspicious foreign-sounding professor might cause trouble, the young counter clerk agreed to serve the integrated group but insisted that they must "get out of here right away!" or she would get in trouble. They complied, and perhaps the very first (undocumented) sit-in within the city of Jackson occurred—in 1947! This would be a ploy Borinski would pull often during his early years in Mississippi. "My advantage was that I was an outsider," he would confess years later. "I played this game very carefully by pretending 'I just don't know.'"

Borinski wagered his claims about the inevitability of desegregation based on his clear understanding of the American Constitution. "It seems to happen quite frequently with naturalized citizens," he observed. "They are really taken in by the American Constitution." This well-read fanboy of America had been a constitutional lawyer back home in Germany and understood the difference between the Nazi Nuremberg Laws, which stripped Jews and others of their German citizenship, and the protections provided by the American Constitution, particularly the Fourteenth Amendment, which provided citizen status to all native-born people, including its Black populace. Even in those early days at Tougaloo, Borinski would preach a sort of social gospel of radical resistance. "You have the right," he would say, "but every right in the Constitution is not a self-fulfilling prophecy. You have to fight for it!"

So obsessed was he by the American jurisprudence system that in 1952, when Borinski took a sabbatical to earn a PhD in sociology from the University of Pittsburgh, he ended up writing his doctoral dissertation on the laws—specifically on the court-made laws—related to the advancement of equal rights in America. "The Sociology of Judge-Made Law in Civil Rights Cases" became the émigré's touchstone for all of his future work with students and his long-time advocacy for cultural change within his new home. Besides being a unique contribution to literature in the field of civil-rights lawmaking, Borinksi's dissertation, like Myrdal's *American Dilemma*, foresaw the inevitability of the landmark US Supreme Court *Brown v. Board of Education* decision, which would occur the following year.

When Borinski returned to Tougaloo in the fall of 1953, doctoral laurels mounted on his balding head (thus, becoming "Herr Doktor"), any doubts he may have had about making a career there were swept away. "I came back to Tougaloo College and decided firmly to make Tougaloo my base of operations," he would later recall. "I would deal with the situation of race from the legal viewpoint right here in Mississippi." It would be a rocky, tortuous path—one with sweeping highs and tragic lows—but one that Borinski would find deeply satisfying during the next thirty years.

BORINSKI AND BENDER—EARLY RESISTERS

It must be said that Borinski was not the first—nor would he be the last—inspirational figure to tread the stony path of insistence on Black rights in Mississippi. Tougaloo has many examples of individual acts of courage displayed by its leaders, dating back nearly to its founding. One repeatedly referenced by Borinski himself is that of Reverend William D. Bender, who served as Tougaloo's chaplain and assistant to the president from 1934 to 1950 and then as the college's public relations director until his retirement in 1956, just two years before the first two Tougaloo Nine students arrived.

Bender was himself a late-blooming product of Tougaloo's then-complete educational system. He started out in its primary school at age fifteen, finished its high school, and graduated from its college, completing the entire trifecta in 1914 at the age of twenty-eight. He then enrolled in Chicago's prestigious Moody Bible Institute to prepare for the ministry. Bender would serve at pastor at various Southern Black churches in Mississippi, Louisiana, and Texas before circling back to Tougaloo as chaplain. He used that perch to begin his own assault on Jim Crow segregation by challenging the White political elite. His resistance to White rule culminated in his signing a complaint and later testifying in 1946—along with nearly three hundred other Black Mississippians—before a special US Senate committee investigating improprieties related to the reelection of the inflammatory White supremacist and self-proclaimed Klansman Theodore Bilbo.[6] Importantly, Bender's testimony helped convince the Senate to delay the seating of Bilbo for a third term. Bender further inflamed Whites by encouraging the creation of NAACP chapters throughout the state of Mississippi, by taking leadership of the Jackson branch in 1943, and by serving as president of the NAACP's Mississippi State Conference of Branches—from 1946 through 1953. For this last role, he was dubbed "our main man in Mississippi" by none other than Thurgood Marshall, who was then working as an attorney for the racial justice organization at its headquarters in New York City. Marshall said that Bender was "the one contact we can rely upon in Mississippi."[7]

Borinski would always make reference to Bender when discussing Tougaloo's unique role in leading the resistance in Mississippi: "We challenged the existing order," he noted with a degree of pride. "We all systematically made a contribution by making a confrontation; and of that confrontation, slowly the change occurred."

Herr Doktor's contribution would ratchet up markedly after the *Brown* decision, as Mississippi society retrenched into a disturbingly and aggressively reactionary stance in response to the Supreme Court's unambiguous ruling against the *separate but equal* doctrine. Though Borinski claimed that he always tried to build bridges with the White community, something that his AMA sponsors insisted upon—"They must have repeated it ten times!" he recalled about his initial interview—the sociology professor also became something of a pesky nudge, the pricking conscience of an otherwise recumbent and compliant White populace. After *Brown*, and with the shockingly swift formation of the Citizens' Councils—the powerful and well-organized political-action groups devoted to resistance to integration at all costs—Borinski's tone became shriller. He regularly wrote letters to the editors of Jackson's White-rule, status-quo newspapers—the *Jackson Daily News* and *The Clarion-Ledger*—both owned and overseen by the rich and ultraconservative Hederman family. But Borinski knew just who he was goading, and he did it repeatedly. The surprising thing is that they published his letters—at least some of them—and responded in kind. Excerpts from a particularly pointed exchange in *The Clarion-Ledger* provide some context:

December 2, 1955

Dear Editor:

At their meeting on Thursday, the Citizens Councils of our state again emphasized that they are dedicated to maintaining segregation by legal means and will disclaim any responsibility for the acts of violence which have recently been committed against Negro citizens. The honorable citizens of the Citizens Councils overlook, however, that specifically in light of the very recent decisions of the Federal Courts and many State Courts, segregation just cannot be maintained any more by legal means. They should, therefore, face squarely the fact that if they continue to [insist upon] segregation, they have to do it by illegal means, by straightforward violation of the law of the land and specifically of the Constitution of the United States. . . . [8]

Sincerely yours,

Dr. Ernst Borinski,
Tougaloo

A swift and relentless response was mounted in the same newspaper a few days later by *The Clarion-Leger*'s reliably racist columnist Tom Ethridge. In a 22.5-column-inch rant, Ethridge's regular Mississippi Notebook opinion piece, replete with a Confederate Stars and Bars graphic, reprimands Borinski—whose "professional function, we understand, is to lecture Negroes rather than members of the patriotic Citizens' Council"—to stay in his lane and "exercise his considerable letter-writing talents in behalf of better law observance among our colored race." Ethridge goes on to cite national crime statistics and defame not only Borinksi and Tougaloo, but the NAACP, the Supreme Court, and any other individual or organization that would dare challenge the Southern orthodoxy on race. "Although paid to educate blacks, he elects to instruct whites," Ethridge complains. "Mississippians will require some sounder legal authority than Dr. Borinski to convince us we are 'lawless' in seeking to preserve our racial integrity."[9]

Indeed, Borinski *had* ramped up his speeches to Black audiences, as well. Almost from the time of his arrival at Tougaloo, he had been invited to speak as a special guest—even to preach!—at Black churches throughout the area. Rather than chastise Blacks for, as Ethridge put it, their "disgraceful record" of crime, Borinski chose to hold forth on the inspirational topic of social uplift and the rights of all citizens accorded in the US Constitution. Though he knew very little about the Christian "literature" he was expected to preach on, Borinski later would slyly recall, "I was a great improviser." "They expected me to go to every Black church," he faux complained, "and I went!"

But it wasn't just the churches that wanted his reflections. In February 1955, just as Medgar Evers was taking the reins of the Mississippi State NAACP apparatus, the now-celebrated Black attorney Carsie Hall—one of less than a handful of Black lawyers allowed to practice in the state—invited Borinski to address the NAACP-sponsored "Negro Week" gathering at the renowned Farish Street Baptist Church in Jackson. Hall was then the president of the local Jackson branch of the NAACP. Although no record survives of Borinski's remarks, it is instructive to note that the very next day, one of Borinski's letters appeared in the morning's *Clarion-Ledger* going into great detail about why the *Brown* decision was legally sound, citing various case law to support the decision—*Jacobson v. Massachusetts (1905)*; *Pierce v. Society of Sisters (1925)*; *Mugler v. Kansas (1887)*—and urging Mississippi's White citizenry to comply. Likely some version of this topic, which had become Borinski's specialty since obtaining his doctorate on the subject, was discussed at the NAACP gathering. It is also quite likely that this occasion was the first time Borinkski met Evers in the flesh, though he certainly would have heard about Evers from Bender and others in the Black progressive community.

Outreach to Black churches and organizations, and didactic, preachy letters to the editor weren't Borinski's only avenues of community engagement. He found strong White allies at the White, Methodist-run Millsaps College just a mile from downtown Jackson. Despite its stated segregationist stance— a necessity for any White institution to flourish within the Magnolia State at that time—Millsaps College, its administrators, teachers, and students offered a welcoming hand to the German refugee and found ways, sometimes unwittingly, to help him advance his agenda of racial equality. In later years, Borinski would reminisce, "Whatever I did, I could do so well because I had always some backing from Millsaps College . . . the silent backing of Millsaps College."

Borinski's facility with languages and his growing renown as a sociologist made him a welcome presence on the Millsaps campus. For a time, he taught German to a mixed group of Millsaps and Tougaloo students. And Millsaps students would often be the only Whites, outside those from the Tougaloo College community, who would dare to show up at Borinski's Social Science Forums—informal integrated meetings held twice monthly in the basement of Beard Hall while school was in session. Borinski's Forums would become a thing of legend. At the time, though, they were low-key events where Black students and Tougaloo teachers and administrators would intermingle with Whites from the community to hear lectures on issues of local, national, or even international interest.

Coffee, lemonade, and donuts would be served, thus breaking Mississippi's restrictions against Blacks and Whites eating together. But the topics and speakers were often of such renown that it was hard not to attend. In time, with the help of Field Foundation funding, Borinski would attract people like UN special ambassador Ralph Bunche; journalist Pauline Frederick, an early female pioneer in broadcast journalism; and doctor Everett Hughes, the then-renowned sociologist under whom Borinski had studied at the University of Chicago. "We can't afford *not* to go!" many from Millsaps and other surrounding colleges would aver. Besides taking on global issues of war and peace, Borinski wouldn't overlook the prickly local issues. He once even invited Mississippi's secretary of education to discuss the prospects for Mississippi integrating its school system following the Supreme Court decision.[10]

The Forum fostered a healthy back-and-forth interaction with the audience. After brief introductory remarks, speakers would participate in an extended question-and-answer period, where students and community members would as often voice their opinions about the subject at hand as ask the guest speaker for further clarification. In this way, Borinski believed he was helping to forge new pathways to the integrated society he saw as inevitable.

George Owens, who would become Tougaloo's first Black president, began his tenure at Tougaloo as business manager in 1955. He had a chance to observe Borinski's methods for many years and had only the highest praise for the Forum and its impact. "Borinski had an outstanding array of presenters, lecturers in the Social Science Forums which involved people, Blacks and Whites, from all around the state," Owens observed. "We were exposed to international concerns and how they impacted on the domestic scene."

"It was a place where Blacks and Whites of goodwill got together to talk and plan strategies," Owens continued. "It was really a place where a good Movement in Mississippi got mobilized and started. It was a real force."[11]

One of the Millsaps students who came under Borinski's sway during this period was Edwin King—a bright, civic-minded scholar from Vicksburg whose own racial justice awakening happened during the Vicksburg flood of 1953 when, while assisting with recovery efforts, came in direct contact with the appalling living conditions of his city's Black residents. He began to wonder how he could help change those conditions and the circumstances that caused them. He entered Millsaps in 1954 with every intention of becoming a Methodist minister so that he could preach the social gospel and help change peoples' minds about race in his native state. Borinski's methods and programs were a balm and encouragement to King during his four years at Millsaps. "Borinski was like a second father," King would later say.[12]

King attended a number of Borinski's Social Science Forums while at Millsaps and recognized the professor's outlaw nature. "Borinski made sure that he violated *all* of the rules," King recounted. "He made sure that the Black teachers and some of his Black students didn't all huddle in one corner. And you knew [as a White person] you were liable to sit next to a Black person."

"He always served cider and doughnuts or cheese and crackers," King continued, "so you broke bread together. Just violating all the taboos!"

One important incident from this period that both Borinski and King had a hand in became a flashpoint in Mississippi's slow crawl toward integration. The trouble began when Borinski was invited to speak on the sensitive subject of Christianity and race relations at a Millsaps function in early March 1958. "They didn't want to have a Black person speak, so I was the closest to a Black they could get," Borinski wryly observed. During his presentation, Borinski called out everyone in the audience—everyone in White Mississippi, for that matter—by saying, "As I see the situation, segregation violates basic Christian principles." With that, according to Borinski, the crowd "got wild!"

Certainly, the press and the politicians had at him. The state legislature, which met only every other year, happened to be in session at the time and had already developed a bill to investigate the activities of the Mississippi NAACP as a possible Communist or subversive organization. After hearing about Borinski's criticisms, they added his name to the bill as another worthy subject of investigation. This brought significant negative public attention not only to Borinski and Tougaloo College—Borinski noted that a cross was burned on the college grounds after the public outcry—but his speech also caused Millsaps to be brought under the microscope for colluding with such a scoundrel. As a result, Millsaps was forced to cancel a highly anticipated lecture by a prominent antisegregationist Methodist minister due to the unwelcome attention. In addition, the chairman of the college board felt it necessary to reiterate the college's stated policy of segregation. "We didn't' realize how much the Citizens' Council was cracking down on everything," King would later say. "We had become their target."[13]

The entire situation demonstrates what a tightrope Borinski and others were walking as they tried to shift the consciousness of a recalcitrant people. King asserted that by the end of the 1958 spring semester, Millsaps students and teachers were forbidden from visiting Tougaloo and Borinki's Social Science Forum, and even White professors from Tougaloo were barred from visiting Millsaps if students were present. Borinski, always the trickster, ameliorated this situation by inviting leading local lights such as Eudora Welty, who existed outside of the academic community, to appear at his Forums for the cultural enhancement of his students, thus assuring an integrated audience.[14] Even so, this hyperskittishness about the sharing of ideas and crossing racial boundaries was exactly the situation that would confront the Tougaloo Nine cohort who would begin attending Tougaloo College that fall.

REVEREND JOHN DEE MANGRAM

After Borinski, the next person to arrive on campus who would have a significant influence on the Tougaloo Nine would be its beloved chaplain. Certainly, the chaplain at any AMA school played an outsized role in the life of the campus. This was always true at Tougaloo. Indeed, some of the school's earliest leaders served as both president *and* chaplain. The religious underpinning, the twice-weekly religious gatherings, and the prominence of Woodworth Chapel on campus made the Chaplain's role central to Tougaloo's beating heart. In 1951, the Reverend John Dee Mangram was an incredible find for Tougaloo.[15] Born in 1925 just outside of the small town of Pittsburg, Texas—not far from where Louisiana, Arkansas, Oklahoma, and Texas converge—Mangram distinguished himself as a scholar almost from birth. He served as the valedictorian at his eighth-grade elementary school graduation and repeated the feat at his graduation in 1941 from Frederick Douglass High School in Pittsburg. He steadily rose through the academic world, first earning a bachelor of arts degree, with a focus on religion and philosophy, from the nearby Jarvis Christian College in Hawkins, Texas, which he was able to attend, in part, due to a football scholarship; then heading to Howard University in Washington, DC, for a second Bachelor's degree, this time in divinity studies with an emphasis on Christian social ethics, graduating in 1948.

Mangram was obviously on a divine mission, though his first postgraduate job seems a bit random—likely due to the necessity to make some money. He spent his first year after graduating from Howard as a social studies teacher at a high school in suburban Philadelphia. He then shifted in 1949 to a more suitable post at the renowned HBCU Lincoln University, just an hour to the west at Oxford, Pennsylvania. It was here that Horace Mann Bond, the father of future civil rights icon Julian Bond, held sway as the university's first African American President. Mangram briefly served as the school's "university minister" (i.e., chaplain) and also taught religion. (It is tempting to think that Mangram and the younger Bond may have crossed paths during this time.)

Mangram was anxious to return to the South, however, and when the post of chaplain at Tougaloo came open the following year, Mangram jumped at the chance. Perhaps he just wanted to be closer to home, but as events would play out, it is also possible that he wanted to be where significant civil rights battles were brewing to help shape the outcome. In later years, while working on his doctorate in California, Mangram would step into the shoes once worn by the irreplaceable moral philosopher and theologian of nonviolence Howard Thurman at the Church for the Fellowship of All Peoples in San Francisco. But Mangram's most headline-grabbing moments would come during the decade or so that he spent in Mississippi.[16]

From the start of his Tougaloo chaplaincy, Mangram threw himself into community life both on campus and in the greater community of Jackson and beyond. He had married the former Bobbye Durham just before moving to Mississippi, and the two made a striking pair on campus, with Bobbye working in the college Treasurer's Office while Mangram held sway over the venerable Woodworth Chapel.

Of course, Mangram was cognizant of the fact that he was replacing a living legend as chaplain in the person of William Bender, who had stepped down from the post for health reasons but who continued to teach and remained active in his various social-justice commitments, including participation in the local chapter of the NAACP. Mangram literally followed in Bender's footsteps, joining the Jackson branch of the NAACP and eventually becoming the group's chaplain and chairman of its Executive Committee.[17]

It was Mangram, in fact, who helped raise funds from local donors to send Meredith Anding and his cousin Willis Logan to attend the NAACP Youth Retreat in Georgia during the summer of 1960—the event that sparked Anding's activism.[18]

Ed King, who himself would become a Methodist minister and serve as Tougaloo's chaplain beginning in 1963, met Mangram on several occasions while a student at Millsaps in the mid-1950s. As noted, the idealistic young student became enthralled with the leadership and mildly subversive approach of Ernst Borinski, who would become King's long-time mentor and eventual friend. But his association with Borinski brought King into

Mangram's orbit. The observant, aspiring change agent saw how the two colleagues were mutually supportive.

"Mangram might bring in visiting speakers, and Borinski would attend," King remembered. "And anything Borinski did or sponsored, Mangram would attend and urge students to attend." King described Mangram as "thoughtful and quiet, very much like Medgar" and "very pro-civil rights." King, looking ahead to when a movement might take off in Mississippi, recognized that "whenever the sit-ins started, I assumed Mangram would be one of the leaders."[19]

Indeed, by June 1960, Mangram was singled out by the Mississippi Sovereignty Commission as one of the key leaders of the emerging Mississippi civil rights movement, along with Medgar Evers, of course, as well as Reverend Charles Jones of Campbell College and Aaron Henry of Clarksdale, among others.[20]

But Mangram's gaze was not solely focused on Tougaloo. He kept up a substantive correspondence with both religious and secular leaders beyond the gates of the college. In the limited record of Mangram's letters still extant in the Tougaloo archives, we find a man deeply engaged in the broader community of philanthropy as well as religion. In the winter of 1960, the record shows him planning a meeting of the Alabama-Mississippi Conference of Congregational Christian Churches, to be held at Tougaloo from March 24 through 27, exactly one year prior to the library sit-in. It is instructive that he invited Medgar Evers to this meeting with a dozen or so Disciples of Christ ministers from the deepest of the Deep South to discuss the NAACP's perspective on race relations and plans that were in the works to address the dire need for change. (In a follow-up letter to Evers, Mangram is profuse in his praise of the civil rights leader's presentation. "Your address and the forum were the highlights of our meeting," he told the NAACP leader. "The delegates were deeply grateful that you had been asked to share the program and deemed your contribution as invaluable.")

That same month, Mangram is imploring a colleague from Howard University's School of Religion for talented students to consider taking up pastorates in the heart of Dixie, using enticing language to bait the hook: "The deep South is, perhaps, the greatest challenge to a dynamic ministry—one willing to pioneer, to be in the forefront in the immediate revolution which is underway in this country—that I know."

Mangram is also in regular correspondence with Kenneth I. "Kib" Brown, the executive director of the Danforth Foundation of St. Louis, Missouri. In one letter, he crows about having another Tougaloo student—the third in four years—winning a prestigious Woodrow Wilson Fellowship. In another, Mangram expresses appreciation for having been asked to serve as deputy director of a Danforth Foundation conference, where he came into contact with some of Black America's leading lights, including the Reverend Benjamin Mays, the long-serving and influential president of Moorhouse College, and Jeanne Noble, the noted scholar on Black women's education and then head of the Black sorority Delta Sigma Theta.

Perhaps most interestingly, Mangram carries on a spirited interaction with one of Martin Luther King Jr.'s early mentors, the Reverend Dr. J. Pius Barbour, an American Baptist pastor of Calvary Baptist Church in Chester, Pennsylvania. He parries with Barbour over the pastor's optimism, apparently over recent global developments, perhaps including the newly emerging student civil rights movement. Mangram takes a more skeptical view.

"I am not quite so optimistic," he writes to Barbour.

> What I see rising on the horizon is not new. It is as ancient as the "will to power" and the desire for relief from tyranny. This fact is revealed in (1) the rottenness and well-defined decadence of the West fraught with its racial antagonisms, the diabolical doctrine of racial supremacy, the ignominious whoring mother of racial antagonisms; (2) the desire to deify all of the tragic stupidities of the past which have historically destroyed whole nations and civilizations; (3) a weak as water, equally as stupid Church, which has capitulated to every destructive and death-welcoming device of blind, irreverent, greedy capitalism whose strength is weakness itself—all of these contribute to a kind of dirge with a 'rock and roll' beat for the death of the West.[21]

By all accounts, Mangram was an inspirational preacher. According to Joseph Jackson, who was already an ordained minister when he arrived at Tougaloo in 1960, Mangram was "the type of minister that I idolized." Jackson had a unique opportunity to hear and analyze Mangram's preaching style and thought processes every Sunday as a member of the Tougaloo choir. Mangram was "very intellectual," according to Jackson. "There was a presence about him. His sermons were coherent and always had a strong social action message." Geraldine Edwards agreed, noting that Mangram "was a serious person when he taught the philosophy classes." In fact, she observed, "He was serious about life in general."

Meredith Anding, however, had a quite different impression of Mangram. Unlike Jackson or Edwards, Anding had taken a religion class from the chaplain in the late 1950s during his first year at Tougaloo. He could recount Mangram's physical features—"a tall fellow with a receding hairline, slimly but well-built. I oftentimes thought that he had played football or something like that." His descriptions were accurate on every point.

Anding also distinctly remembered another aspect of Mangram's demeanor. "This is the cursing-est religion teacher!" he thought to himself during one spirited discussion. "This guy used profanity a lot! That's the most outstanding thing I remember about him."

Whether sacred or profane, Mangram is described by most of the students who took part in the library demonstration as a quiet, behind-the-scenes influencer. He was, in fact, the adult advisor to Tougaloo's NAACP College Chapter, which formed on campus during the 1959/1960 school year. As such, he would have attended most if not all of the chapter's monthly meetings and would also likely have fed information back to Medgar Evers and the Jackson adult branch regarding the students' interests, activities, and, crucially, their readiness for undertaking any serious direct-action initiatives. Geraldine noted that Mangram "was devoted and kept the operation [of the NAACP] on campus moving forward."[22]

It must also be stated that despite Mangram's seemingly subtle ways, having a Black authority figure—the campus chaplain, no less—serving as the adult coordinator for the most radical civil rights organization operating within the state at the time and having him gently boosting creative thinking about addressing society's wrongs with regard to race and discrimination must have been enormously inspiring to the youthful undergrads. Nearly all of the soon-to-be student demonstrators were from deeply religious upbringings. Nearly half were preacher's kids who had grown up in the shadow of the church and had great respect for ministers of the gospel. Mangram's presence and quiet encouragement would certainly have confirmed for them that they were on the right path in challenging the strictures of a segregated society.

From extant Mangram correspondence sent in the month after the library sit-in, it becomes obvious that he was the primary advocate on campus for the philosophy and practice of nonviolent resistance. Mangram wrote,

We had hoped that all of the going to jail would be unnecessary in solving some of the ugly problems we face in Mississippi, but this seems inevitable since there is not enough Christian concern or sensitivity of conscience on the part of white Mississippians to change.

They simply m[u]st be forced to do so. We cannot win by the force of violence, so we have elected the force of nonviolent direct action. The method is terribly slow, but much better for all concerned.

We pray that the college does not suffer unduly and that no one will suffer too much because of our actions. We are convinced that what we do is God's will for us and so we act. . . .

These are times that bring out the worst in people, but they also elicit the finest and best too. We pray that we shall be able to live creatively in these tensions and that Mississippi and the South will be better because we lived in this period of history.[23]

Unexpectedly, Mangram himself would emerge from the background and become a leading spokesperson for social change in the wake of the library sit-in. Although his contribution has largely been overlooked, John Dee Mangram's role was crucial in moving the students from discussion to action.

DR. A. D. BEITTEL

The Reverend Doctor Adam Dan "A. D." Beittel was the last to appear on the Mississippi scene prior to the Tougaloo students' life-changing decision to push openly against the boundaries of the closed society. Beittel seemed to be on a long, safe glide path toward retirement in the summer of 1960 after a full career in academia and the ministry. Among an array of other assignments, he had served as the president of Talladega College in Alabama from 1945 through 1952 and then was offered the opportunity for a respite from racial tension as chaplain and professor of religion at Beloit College in Wisconsin (1953–1960). Beittel and his wife, Ruth, were looking forward to a sabbatical year abroad studying the very real religious conflicts in the Middle East when they were visited by two trustees of Tougaloo College begging them to once again go South. The college unexpectedly was about to lose its then president Dr. Samuel Kincheloe, who had grown weary of college administration and wanted to get back to teaching, research, and writing. The need was desperate. Would they consider it? The decision to uproot yet again was a tough one for the couple, who had spent their entire adult lives working for racial justice in the vineyards of the Lord.[24]

What little we know of Dan Beittel's early life seems to have been wrapped in Christian progressivism. Born in Lancaster, Pennsylvania, on December 19, 1898, Beittel was reared in the Quaker-like atmosphere of that Pennsylvania Dutch and German community, where he absorbed the missionary spirit of a small evangelical sect native to the area, the Churches of God in North America (now the Churches of God, General Council). Young Beittel attended the private Christian Findlay College in Ohio, graduating with a bachelor's degree in 1922. He then went to Oberlin College "for theological seminary work" to earn a master's degree. Both of these choices point to a deep Christian spirituality and a desire to spread the Christian social gospel. Findlay was an interesting collaboration between the church and state, having been founded by the city of Findlay and the Churches of God. From its founding in 1882 through Beittel's graduation, all of Findlay's presidents had also served as pastors/chaplains of the college chapel. Thus, Beittel saw firsthand how academic scholarship, leadership, and intense Christian devotion could be combined to help shape young minds.

At Oberlin, this was taken a step further. Established in 1833, Oberlin was the first college in the US to admit women and one of the first to admit African Americans. Its missionary zeal to eradicate slavery—"America's most horrendous sin"—and "to educate a missionary army of Christian soldiers to save the world" inspired Beittel during his nearly three years there. Indeed, he came to believe that his work in academia could also play a role in what he saw as God's plan to end segregation and usher in a world of social equality for all Americans.[25]

In 1925, with a master's degree from Oberlin in hand, Beittel spent the next year at the University of Chicago earning yet another bachelor's degree, this time in divinity studies—so that he might eventually pastor a church. Upon reaching this milestone, Beittel married Ruth, whom he had met at Findlay (she was the dean's daughter) and had courted ever since. (Beittel would joke that he had to date the dean's daughter to graduate from Findlay, though in the same breath crowing about his achieving "all As and graduating in three and a half years.") Once hitched, the two embarked upon an immediate adventure, traveling to Montana so the new divinity graduate could serve as pastor of a Congregational church there. The assignment didn't last long. After two years, Beittel, perhaps realizing that running a church wasn't all it was cracked up to be, returned to the University of Chicago to begin doctoral studies in philosophy, concentrating on the New Testament and early Christian literature. Maybe teaching would be his thing. He graduated in the spring of 1929, just as the Great Depression loomed. By September, he had accepted his first academic job at Earlham College in Indiana, a Quaker school with deep roots in peace and social-justice work.

After three years in Indiana, Beittel took up the pastorship of a small Congregational start-up group that met near Nashville's Vanderbilt University. The pairing did not go well, likely because Beittel, something of a rebel himself, wanted to push on civil rights issues more than the congregation was willing to allow. Retreating again to academia, where Beittel and his wife, Ruth, would stay for the remainder of their careers, the two took up residence in the fall of 1936 at North Carolina's Guilford College—another Quaker school—where Beittel served as dean and taught courses in sociology for the next nine years.

In 1945, Beittel was scanning the Congregational newsletter and noted that the long-serving president of the historically Black Talladega College in Alabama had announced his retirement. Without much thought of success, Beittel dashed off a letter to the AMA inquiring about their plans for replacing him. To his surprise, Beittel received a very cordial invitation by Fred Brownlee, the head of the AMA, to travel to New York to discuss the matter. On the strength of that one meeting, which turned out to be an interview with Brownlee and several of the Talladega board members, Beittel was offered the job.

Thanks to a detailed history of the college, a more complete portrait of Beittel and his push for social change emerges.[26] Although the picture is clouded by the politics of race and the complicated dance between the AMA and the boards of its affiliated institutions, *Talladega College*, a book by Maxine Jones and Joe Richardson—two Talladega alums—fills out what is known of Beittel's assertive, some might say aggressive, stance on racial equality while also pointing to some of his strengths and weaknesses as an administrator and college president.

The search for a new president of Talladega took two years, mostly because the board of trustees realized the delicate nature of selecting someone who understood Southern mores while at the same time having the political acumen to push forward, however gently, with a progressive integrationist agenda. Beittel seemed to check all of these boxes and had another attribute that led to both his selection and his undoing: he was White. Although sentiment on campus was for the AMA and the Talladega Board of Trustees to choose a Black man for the job of president, neither group seemed quite ready to move in that direction. Despite the fact that Talladega had an extraordinarily capable Black academic dean, James T. Cater, who was recognized throughout the small world of Black education as being "the foremost dean" of all Southern Black colleges, the school's Board of Trustees made it clear that they would not be selecting him for the job of president. This set up an immediate rift between the new president and Cater once Beittel arrived on campus. The division would never completely be resolved, partly because of temperament and partly because prior to Beittel's arrival, Cater had, in essence, been running the school, not only during the two intervening years, but during the two prior administrations, as those previous presidents spent most of their time fundraising for the school. Beittel, however, was a hands-on administrator who had his own ideas about how best to run Talladega, and these ideas often clashed with Cater's, causing constant power struggles between the two men and eventually leading to the faculty and students taking sides.

Despite this ongoing difficulty, Beittel initially seemed like a perfect choice for the historically Black college. Just as he later would be for Tougaloo, Beittel was adept at fundraising, and he was a tireless booster for the school, reviving the interest of alumni nationwide and garnering headlines for his social-justice activism. In addition, Beittel set about raising the salaries of the faculty, which were woefully inadequate, to attract the best teachers. He also increased enrollment by 30 percent during his second year. (Returning Black soldiers, with financing through the GI Bill, certainly helped this jump in admissions, which had been flat for the prior ten years.)

But the truest measure of Beittel's character came in his relentless push for tiny, rural Talladega, Alabama, to open up to the idea of racial equality. In this way, Beittel seems to have come across as a glassy-eyed idealist, imagining a world that he wanted to see and then moving forward in the real world as if his imagined world already existed. As incredible as it may now seem, Beittel consistently urged his fellow White community members to make room for leadership positions for Black residents who showed promise. Jones and Richardson describe Betittel as "pestering the city commission about discrimination," urging them to provide services to Blacks that were then only enjoyed exclusively by Whites, pushing them to hire Black police officers, complaining about segregated hospitals, and lobbying for an interracial committee that might begin discussing how the community might one day do away with its racial inequities. This was Talladega, Alabama, in the late 1940s! The nearest large city was Birmingham, about fifty miles away. Think of the "tired old town" of Macomb, Alabama—the fictional setting of Harper Lee's *To Kill a Mockingbird*—but with a historically Black college set down just on the outskirts. Beittel's constant hectoring convinced the White power structure of Talladega that he was an "agitator," a "radical," and a "dangerous man"—exactly what the AMA had warned its employees who worked in the South *not* to be.

But Beittel didn't reserve his comments on racial practices only to the city fathers of Talladega. He managed to irritate the governor of Alabama, Progressive "Big Jim" Folsom, by publicly pushing for the equalization of pay among Black and White public-school teachers. Nearly twenty years before the name of Bull Connor would raise a national outcry, Beittel was chastising the Birmingham commissioner of public safety for not allowing Black people to attend public entertainment events with Whites and complaining to the governor about the police—under Connor's jurisdiction—and their heavy-handed tactics against Blacks. In other words, Beittel was way ahead of his time, what most Whites at the time would call a "troublemaker"—needling the community to make change faster than it was ready or willing to go. This aspect of his personality, that radical zeal to see the Kingdom of God fulfilled here on earth, explains much about how he would eventually handle the situation of nine student demonstrators from his campus at Tougaloo. He was at Talladega—and would be still at Tougaloo fifteen years later—one of the most radical college presidents in America, at least when it came to the issues of race and social justice.

Beittel developed programs to bring White students to Talladega for intercollegiate conferences under the guise of "free exchange of ideas." He also encouraged, without much success, White students from throughout the state to spend their college years at Talladega. Indeed, Beittel's youngest child, William, enrolled in Talladega in 1946 and graduated from there in 1950, though he spent at least one year "abroad." The record shows that only one native White Alabamian accepted Beittel's invitation to matriculate at Talladega. Beittel was more successful in creating student exchange programs so that his students might get a broader view of the world by attending colleges outside of Alabama for a semester and so that outside students might get a glimpse of the Deep South by coming to Talladega for a semester. One Talladega student called his semester away "one of the most broadening experiences imaginable."

Just as he would do at Tougaloo, Beittel kept in perpetual motion as a member, and often officer, of many religious and social-justice groups. He was instrumental in the formation of the Alabama branch of the Southern Regional Council—a racial-justice organization established in 1944 to promote racial equality in the South—and became the state organization's first president. He also ensured that Talladega joined the United Negro College Fund, which had just formed, also in 1944, thus ensuring that, despite the previous administration's reservations about the group, Talladega began to enjoy the benefit of UNCF's fundraising prowess. Beittel became the group's secretary beginning in 1950.

Despite these and other advances, Beittel's often tone-deaf and dismissive attitude toward students and faculty alike—one faculty detractor called him "curt" and implied that he had dictatorial tendencies—eventually wore down whatever goodwill he had built up through his progressive racial-justice boosterism and academically expansive programming. Beittel could be bullheaded on some issues, like refusing to allow intercollegiate football to be reinstated on campus, while otherwise promoting student fitness and various student travel initiatives. (Beittel may have been ahead of his time on this point, arguing that football took too many of the college's resources for the benefit of the few; instead, he wanted to build a better gym and give opportunity to travel to all students, not just the football team.) These missteps—combined with the poor judgment on the part of the trustees for not choosing a Black president in the first place—and the ever-present antagonism with Cater and his faction, eventually led to Beittel's dismissal in 1952. (In what seems like "just deserts," Cater was also forced to resign at the same time so that the school could make a fresh start.) Beittel took the year's-pay severance package that the board offered and, together with Ruth, traveled throughout Europe during the 1952 through 1953 school year.

They then took up residence at Beloit College in Wisconsin, snugly in the North, where Dan served as dean of the chapel and professor of religion. They planned to remain there, nestled in a beautiful home overlooking the Rock River, until Beittel's expected retirement at age sixty-five. Then the unexpected happened.

"A couple of people from the board of Tougaloo came up and said they were in a bad way—that Tougaloo needed a president," Beittel would later recall. "We sort of thought we had served our term in the South" was their initial reaction. "We had a very good time at Beloit and would have stayed on there until retirement," he continued. "We debated at some length." Indeed, one can almost hear the back and forth between the former dean's daughter and the quixotic Christian minister. Was it out of a need for redemption—an attempt to revive his flagging reputation after the Talladega dismissal—or simply another response to what may have been perceived as a divine calling? Perhaps a little bit of both.

After wrangling with the AMA board and leadership and wresting from them the promise that he could stay on as president until he reached the age of seventy—he was then sixty-one, and the standard retirement age was sixty-five—Beittel convinced Ruth that it was worth one more try. The two made an exploratory trip to the Tougaloo campus that summer to discuss the idea with President Kincheloe. Anxious to be gone and to leave Tougaloo in good hands, Kincheloe played up the strengths of the college, its closeness to Jackson, and the fact that the board had undertaken to build a new President's residence, which would be finished in a year's time.

The Beittels were smitten. Whatever inner calculus the couple contrived to convince themselves to leave Beloit and accept the job at Tougaloo may never be known. All Dan Beittel ever said for the record, in his typically understated way, was that the idea of going to Tougaloo offered "something of a challenge, so we went down to Mississippi about the first of August 1960 and [were] there for four very boisterous years." It would, indeed, be the capstone of his career and the making of his reputation.

Chapter 8

COLLEGE BOUND

STUDENTS WHO ATTENDED TOUGALOO COLLEGE DURING THE 1950S AND '60s generally make a point of describing their first encounter with this haven of racial amity in an otherwise hostile world. Geraldine Edwards certainly was taken by the place when she first set foot on the campus in the summer of 1959. "If I had any doubts or apprehensions about Tougaloo Christian College," she would later write, "they were all resolved when I first stepped on the campus. There were lots of majestic oak and fragrant magnolia trees all over campus. There were dormitories and a grand mansion that served at the time as the president's residence. There was even a library that was open in the evenings." Beyond that, Tougaloo featured the one thing that she had observed in childhood that every Negro neighborhood she lived in lacked: sidewalks! "The sidewalks that crisscrossed the campus were like a maze. On campus, you just had to head in the right direction traveling on one sidewalk or another. The sidewalk mazes were an opportunity to see the beauty of the serene campus and to carry you to the places to learn. The mazes of sidewalks were beautiful."[1]

Besides the obvious new access to what one might now consider basic accoutrements of neighborhood living, Geri noticed much more. The place was a wonderland. "You see," she said, "they have these kinds of trees in Natchez"—the live oak with Spanish moss hanging deeply down—"but we were never allowed to go to any of the antebellum homes in the area." Tougaloo College also had those old-growth trees and the beauty of a manicured garden paradise. "So, when I came to campus," Geri continued, "it was the most beautiful place I had ever seen."

Joseph Jackson, who would, to his surprise, be elected to lead the campus NAACP chapter within about a month of his arrival, had a considerably different impression of Tougaloo when he arrived in the fall of 1960. At age twenty-three, Jackson had had a broader life experience and had previously attended a better-funded state school. "Well," said Jackson, "you can imagine my experience coming from a college like Arkansas AM&N in Pine Bluff . . . modern buildings and everything. And so, when I went through the arch of Tougaloo, it was as if I had entered into the days of the antebellum South!"

"I'm a modern guy!" he laughed. "And here I am in Mississippi! And knowing the history of Mississippi when it came to the lynching of Blacks and castrating Blacks, etcetera, etcetera. . . . I didn't even know where Tougaloo was! It was *really* rural. And crossing that railroad and going on in. . . . I had entered a whole different era that I was not familiar with, and I was not prepared for."

Another member of the Memphis contingent, Sam Bradford, who at eighteen at the time, would become the youngest member of the Tougaloo Nine, recalled a much different welcome to the school. "The students were so cordial and friendly," he said. "I fell in love with Tougaloo. . . . 'The Tougaloo *thing*,' we called it. You know, the Tougaloo experience. . . . It'll grab you!"

Sam's roommate and fellow Tougaloo Nine member Albert Lassiter said his most lasting impression of Tougaloo was the commitment of the staff and the college's religious roots. "God bless the faculty," Lassiter commented. "I know they weren't paid very much, but they shared the vision that, you know, 'These young folks . . . we've got to get them an education. That's how we're going to improve the community.'"

Ethel Sawyer was more subdued about her initial reaction to Tougaloo. "I don't remember having a big [first] impression," she said. "It just looked like someplace I was going to like."

ETHEL AND JANICE—1958

First impressions aside, each cohort of Tougaloo Nine members to attend the college had their own unique experiences up until their consequential protest. Ethel Sawyer and Janice Jackson, who arrived for the fall semester of 1958 and would become lifelong friends, had a hard time even getting to campus.

The two had seen each other, improbably, while traveling for their first time to Tougaloo College in August 1958. "That was a fateful meeting," Janice would later recall. "Ethel was coming from Memphis on the Greyhound bus that comes through Clarksdale. I got on the bus in Clarksdale, and both of us were going to Tougaloo!" The two would become fast friends, eventually becoming roommates and even gravitating to the same place after college where they would settle and embark on long-term careers.[2]

Their first adventure together, however, was simply getting to campus. They hadn't spoken while on the bus together, but when Greyhound deposited them safely into the middle of downtown Jackson, they realized they were going to the same place. But how to get there?

"We were both standing there dumb," Ethel recalled. "Neither of us knew how to get to the campus. We hadn't made any plans to get to Tougaloo!" The two would tease each other mercilessly for the rest of their lives about how this first challenge was met, with Ethel being undecided about how exactly they reached their destination, although she was sure that paying for a taxi for the nine-mile trip had been out of the question.

Janice—often the hero of her own stories—said she took charge, calling the school and having a car sent to fetch them. "I had to help my little sister out!" she ribbed her less world-savvy friend.

Once at Tougaloo, however, they each blossomed, both academically and personally. On their way to the campus, the young women talked about maybe rooming together, but when they arrived, they found that Janice's buddies from Clarksdale had arranged for her to room with them. But Ethel was just a floor away in the same dorm, and Janice ended up spending much of her time with Ethel and her other freshmen classmates.

The school was a haven. And Ethel's connection with Dean Branch through her high school counselor paid dividends for both girls. Almost immediately, Ethel became the dean's work-study secretary, and Janice, at Ethel's suggestion, started her work-study job with the dean's wife, Rose Branch, who taught psychology. The two students would retain these assignments throughout their four years at Tougaloo. And the two adults became something of stand-in parents for the young women. "They were gentle people," recalled Ethel. "They were nice to us . . . and supportive to the students in general."

Ethel and Janice explored the campus together, as well as its nearby environs, and would make the most of what they found. On campus, below Judson Cross Hall, the girls' dormitory, Ethel discovered the Co-op, a place for students to hang out that served food and sported a juke box and a small dance floor. The two would spend hours of leisure time down at the Co-op playing bid whist or dancing the nights away. "Ethel and I would go down, and we would just dance and dance and dance!" Janice recalled. "And I *loved* me some bid whist!"

Just off campus, the girls frequented Moman's Grill, a "greasy-spoon" café within spitting distance of the campus. For a time, Janice dated Robert Moman, the son of the Grill's owners, who also attended Tougaloo at the time. "Good times," Janice said wistfully. "Those were good times."

The two friends eventually joined Delta Sigma Theta, the activist Black sorority founded in 1913 at Howard University by twenty-two Black collegiate women. Both would rise to important leadership offices in the Tougaloo chapter, Ethel becoming president during her senior year, and Janice serving as vice president of the pledgees during a particularly strong growth period. "Tougaloo helped me to grow," Janice noted. "It influenced how I came to think of myself, how I carried myself. I felt empowered."

Despite their many social activities, both women excelled academically. "I managed to keep my grades up," Ethel emphasized. Whereas Janice focused on the sciences, Ethel tended toward the humanities. Ethel invited Janice into the orbit of Ernst Borinski and his Social Science Forums. "Old Dr. Borinski down at the sociology lab doing all of those seminars and things," Janice recalled, "that was the first inkling of integration and activism I can remember. Ethel was a sociology major, so she would pull me into all of that."

Janice particularly recalled how White students from nearby Millsaps College would attend Borinski's Forums—her first real opportunity to participate with Whites on an equal footing. "It was an introduction to other cultures, other people, other ideas. It was a very mind-opening experience."

Even though Ethel ushered Janice into Borinski's milieu, she admitted that she herself was an "infrequent visitor" to the Social Science Lab at Beard Hall. She could, however, do a wicked impression of Borinski. "Ah, Zo, Meez Zawyah," Ethel wryly mimicked. "Why eez you not come to zee lab?"

One thing both women agreed on was the trouble they had with funding their education. During a joint interview, they recounted their nervousness about going to the Registrar's Office to sign up for the next semester.

"We had edgy stuff going on at Tougaloo," Janice said, eyes opening wide. "Every time it was time to register for classes . . ."

". . . we didn't have the money!" Ethel jumped in, finishing the sentence.

"We wouldn't know if our money was there!" Janice confirmed. "We'd be standing there, and I'd say, 'Girl, I don't know!' And we'd get up there and say, 'I sure hope Momma remembered to send the money!'"

Their concern was not unique. Nearly every student interviewed for this project had deep and sometimes overwhelming fears that, despite their best efforts and their obvious academic promise, their families just could not find the extra funds to send one of their children—often the very first in their extended families—to college, not even to a minimum-cost institution like Tougaloo. Some would have to curtail their college career for years until they could scrape up enough cash to return, either to Tougaloo or to another academic setting. Others would successfully cobble together funds from summer jobs and on-campus work-study programs to scrape by and finish. Every one of the Tougaloo Nine would eventually earn their bachelor's degree; most would go on to earn advanced degrees, as well.

GERALDINE AND MEREDITH—1959

Two additional Tougaloo Nine participants found their ways to the college at the beginning of the 1959 school year: Geraldine Edwards and Meredith

Anding. Geraldine's arrival at Tougaloo was memorable, almost like walking into a secret garden. "Coming to Tougaloo was a bonanza for me," she said. "It was an eye-opener."

She then described her first panoramic view of the campus as it existed then. "When I came here . . . there was Judson Cross. Then there was Beard Hall. And the Mansion. And it went around in a semicircle to the library, to Galloway Hall, the chapel, and the gym. So, it was a horseshoe, almost a semicircle around. It was the most beautiful campus. . . . I was just so grateful to be [t]here."

When Geri set foot on campus, she was a young woman on a mission. The first in her family to go to college, she was determined to finish in three years so that she could start working and help pay for her younger brother's tuition to the college of his choice—something she called "The Family Plan." "My parents had really sacrificed because I didn't get a full scholarship, so they had to put out about one hundred dollars a month and at that time that was a lot of money. And so, I wanted to repay them. And I wanted to help my brother go to college, too." Geri took as many classes as were allowed each semester during her entire time at Tougaloo, even attending summer sessions in order to ensure that her three-years-and-done plan would work out.

For some at Tougaloo, this was too much. Geri recounted how Mr. Dockins, the registrar, summoned her to his office for a private audience. "I never wanted to get in trouble, so I remember him calling me to the office, and I was sure I was in trouble," Geri said. "So, when I went to the office, and I sat down, and I waited. He had me to wait. And I'm sitting there almost mesmerized: 'What did I do wrong? I work on campus. I do what I'm supposed to do. I attend my classes. I don't cut. So, what did I do?' You know? 'How is this going to affect my plan?'"

Turns out that Dockins wondered why she was trying to hurry through Tougaloo. When he finally ushered Edwards into his office, here's how that conversation went:

"Geraldine Edwards!"

"Yes, sir, Mr. Dockins."

"Why don't you like Tougaloo?!"

"But I *do* like Tougaloo!"

"Well then why are you trying so hard to get out of here?"

"What do you mean?"

"You're down here carrying twenty-one units. That's too many classes!"

"Well, I'm passing them!"

Dockins and others, it seems, thought that Geraldine was trying to speed through her college experience without enjoying any of the extraordinary things Tougaloo had to offer. But Geri begged to differ. "He didn't know it, but I was having a great time at Tougaloo," she exclaimed. "I *was*! It was just my personality. It's me. I do all kinds of things. That's just the type of person I am."[3] Geri didn't back away from her plan, and by her third year—after two years at Judson Cross, she had accumulated enough credits to move into the girls' senior dorm.

It is also true that Geri enjoyed her down time at college. She recalled that "Tougaloo provided me with everything that you would find in a town or a city. We had the sock hops and things for dances. We had the movie times in the gym. We had drama over at the library. We had reading things that we could do. The campus was all-inclusive."

Geri considered joining the exclusive Alpha Kappa Alpha sorority but found their activities hard to fit into her exacting schedule. "I was recruited to be an AKA, but I didn't follow through because I didn't have the time *or* the money. I just had a different plan. But I always liked their group. And it seemed to me that they were just *so* sophisticated."

As for academics, the naturally talented athlete found her home in the Physical Education Department, led by Dorothy Redmond, who became a mentor to Geraldine. "She was so gracious in helping me get through my classes," Geri recalled, "even giving me extra things to do to help me to be the best physical educator I could be."

Geri also took advantage of the campus's cultural offerings, particularly Dr. Borinski's Social Science Forums every other Wednesday night. "I got to hear a lot of those people who were social-change agents," she remembered. "Dr. Borinski was very instrumental and helpful to me. He was never my professor except for the required sociology course that everybody had to take. But I attended the Forums pretty much the whole time that I was at the school."

Geraldine credited the Forums with sparking her activism. "They used to invite our thinking [such that] it was no longer acceptable to exist within the status quo," she recounted. "They also broadened my horizons and gave me the idea that I could do some of these things." Geri used to enjoy the social hour afterward "with day-old donuts, coffee or tea" where students could interact with internationally known thought leaders. "It was the Forums that really gave me the initiative to make changes and to seek challenges in my life. They were definitely a turning point for me." It was this spark that would lead Geri to join the NAACP College Chapter at Tougaloo and would draw her into her first experience of standing up to racial oppression in one of her favorite places, the public library.

Meredith Anding didn't spend much time declaiming the benefits of going to Tougaloo. Perhaps it was because he came from Jackson rather than some of the smaller enclaves throughout the state, so having access to activities hadn't really been an issue for him. Or maybe it was because he never lived on campus but was instead a commuter student, living at home in West Jackson and taking the Tougaloo commuter bus to campus each day for classes. After having spent his first year of college on the Jackson State campus, just steps away from his home, arriving on the Tougaloo campus must have seemed like an exotic getaway—the broad expanse of land miles from home, the ancient tall live oaks, the deeply draping Spanish moss, the historic buildings, the glorious chapel. Once in a while, he would spend the night in a friend's room so he wouldn't have to make the commute the next day, particularly if he had an early-morning class.

One element of Tougaloo society that Anding found noteworthy was the integrated nature of the faculty. He recalled his early life in Myles—and even as an older child in Jackson—and how as a child he could play with White children and have significant relationships with older White adults—all of which shifted when he became a young teen. Then it became, "You know, 'you go your way, I go mine' . . . or 'you stay over here, and I stay over there.'" This was true everywhere "except for places like Tougaloo." Meredith would remain a Tougaloo day student throughout his enrollment there until his participation in the library sit-in upended, at least temporarily, his dream of completing his college education.

POPS LOVELACE AND THE CLASS OF 1960

The other five members of the Tougaloo Nine all arrived on campus in the fall of 1960, meaning that most of the participants in the library sit-in were new to the college, if not necessarily new to college life. Alfred Cook and Joseph Jackson had already been to other colleges—Al to Campbell College and Joe to Arkansas AM&N. But both would find their footing and a deepening of educational rigor and focus at this private liberal arts school. Evelyn Pierce, too, would find a stimulating environment and an active social life. Sam Bradford and Albert Lassiter would discover an enduring connection to their alma mater through academic excellence, spiritual uplift, and service to community.

Notably, all five of these new Tougalooans—a majority of the Tougaloo Nine—sang in the choir; some owed their very presence at Tougaloo to the scholarship funds offered by choral director and music chair Ariel "Pops" Lovelace. It is possible, in other words, that the library sit-in may never have happened without the financial support these five students received from Tougaloo's music department. A brief detour, therefore, to examine Tougaloo's music program and get a glimpse at the life of one of Tougaloo's most beloved personalities from this period seems in order.

Almost from the founding of the college, music has been an integral aspect of the school's beating heart. Few records survive of Tougaloo's first years, but surely as a Christian school developed and run by missionaries, hymns and religious anthems must have permeated the early worship services held on campus. As early as the 1872/1873 school year—the year of the first extant catalog of classes—references can be found to rudimentary music instruction and to the formation of a chorus and a quartet. This same catalog references Tougaloo's emphasis on the training of music teachers for the various Negro schools that were forming throughout the state. Indeed, as the college developed from a mere high school to an actual institution of higher learning, classes in music, particularly vocal music, became a required part of the curriculum.[4]

As early as 1893, the Tougaloo choir performed concerts for the public, gaining honor and renown for their accomplished programming and polished performances. In fact, it is recorded that in the spring of 1893, a "special train brought 125 people to Tougaloo" to attend a concert of the college choir. In the days before radio, when live performance was one of the few diversions from everyday life, the Tougaloo choir enchanted its visitors, nearly 40 percent of whom were White, with classical selections by Weber, Grieg, and Mendelssohn as well as lighter, more popular tunes. These events were also interspersed with piano recitals of various classical pieces.

At about this same time, a "Male Quartette" was formed that specialized in singing the "old songs"—Negro spirituals—which would eventually become one of the choir's specialties. In 1894, this group traveled to Massachusetts to perform at the American Missionary Association's annual meeting and elsewhere in the region, thus initiating a tradition of the student choir taking extensive road trips to sing throughout the country to heighten awareness of Tougaloo College and to raise needed funds for various educational and building initiatives—a practice that would continue well beyond the Tougaloo Nine years.

By 1896, Tougaloo had its own music department, headed by Lydia Harris Hamlin, the wife of then-president of the college Reverend Cyrus Hamlin. Mrs. Harris Hamlin had the good fortune of being the sister of Murray Harris, a prominent organ builder, who in 1903 gave the college its own pipe organ and installed it in the campus's new Woodworth Chapel—an incredibly generous gesture that significantly enhanced Tougaloo's ability not only in music instruction and performance, but also in the efficacy of its worship services.[5]

An additional aspect of the music program at Tougaloo was inviting prominent and, in some cases, renowned musicians to perform on campus while instructing students during their stay. Male and female glee clubs would spring up at various times, as well. When the Jazz Age arrived, student bands and combos also formed. The music faculty, who were generally accomplished musicians and singers themselves, would give impromptu recitals and concerts throughout the year, making the remote campus seem far more cosmopolitan than its rural setting would have suggested.

In 1959, Tougaloo had the great wisdom to hire a bona fide musical prodigy to head its Music Department and lead its distinguished choir. Ariel "Pops" Lovelace hailed from Gary, Ohio. Born in 1908—coincidentally just as the Tougaloo music department was taking off—Lovelace found his niche in music and stuck with it throughout his academic and professional careers.

Lovelace's father was a musical minister, one who both preached *and* led the choir at his church in Gary. Ariel watched his talented father and decided he, too, wanted to become a musician and choir director. After completing his primary and secondary education at local Gary schools, Lovelace attended the American Academy of Music in Chicago, earning a bachelor of music degree. He then shifted to the Sherwood Music School, also based in Chicago, to gain both a second bachelor's of music and a master's of music education.[6]

The budding musician and music theorist did further study at both the Chicago Music School and at Northwestern University with plans to achieve a doctor of music degree, but it seems that life got in the way, and he found a job teaching music in the Dayton (OH) public schools.

No one, not even Lovelace himself, knew how he got the nickname "Pops." When asked about it in 1973, he simply said, "I've been teaching forty-one years, and for forty of those years, students have been calling me that." Lovelace posited that the name may have come about because from his earliest days as a teacher, he had helped students get scholarships and student aid packages to help with college expenses. Just as likely, it was his dignified manner combined with his preternaturally receding hairline.[7]

Wherever it came from, the moniker stuck. (All of his students from the sixties, certainly all of the Tougaloo Nine who were lucky enough to study and sing with him, used that endearment.) At some point along the way, Pops shifted from teaching secondary school to the college level, moving to Mississippi's capital city to teach music and direct the choral activities at Jackson State College.

In one of his early acts of genius, in 1940, Pops instituted a statewide choral singing convocation called "Songfest," which was still going strong more than eighty years later. "Much of the improvement in the quality of choral singing in the schools of the state may be attributed directly to the work of Lovelace with Songfest," a scholar of the period has noted.[8]

After a few years, in 1947, and by now with a wife and three children, Lovelace shifted his professional base to southeastern Arkansas to become the head of the music department at Arkansas Agricultural, Mechanical, and Normal College (now the University of Arkansas at Pine Bluff) but hoped to eventually return as chair of the music department at either Jackson State or at Tougaloo. His wish was fulfilled in 1959 when he was hired to head up Tougaloo's music program as well as to teach various music courses. With that assignment, Lovelace became the first male to lead the department.

Pops quickly set about putting his stamp on Tougaloo's music program, just as he "Popsified" every musical arrangement he ever touched, as Tougaloo Nine member Sammy Bradford, one of Pops's stand-out singers, would note. Pops threw his enormous energies into making the Tougaloo choir the best it could be while keeping the standard number of concerts on site as well as the bus tours to places far and wide during fall and spring breaks.

One such tour, documented in the Tougaloo Archives, gives a glimpse of the rigors of the road. In what might be called the choir's Midwestern Tour, the Tougaloo choir would leave on a bus along with a few faculty or parental chaperones and head to St. Louis, Missouri; Louisville, Kentucky; Oak Park, Illinois; Grand Rapids, Michigan; Waukasha, Wisconsin; Beloit College, Wisconsin; and Goshen College, Indiana. Every location would have some connection to the either Congregational or Disciples of Christ churches. Students would stay in the homes of church members—often White families—or on college campuses throughout the tour. An Eastern Tour, generally in the fall, would bring the choir to places as far away as Providence, Rhode Island; Hartford, Connecticut; and Plymouth, Massachusetts, with a stop in New York City thrown in for good measure, where the choir would serenade the Board of Trustees of the American Missionary Association to ensure the college stayed in good standing with its founders and major financial supporters. There is conflicting information about whether the tours made any money for the college, but the proceeds would at least pay for the buses and various expenses along the way.[9] Al Lassiter recalled going on just such a tour the very week after he had been in jail for the library sit-in. Indeed, for those five Tougaloo Nine participants, their first impressions of the college are intertwined with their memories of Pops and his choirs.

Two of Pops's star recruits were Sam Bradford and Albert Lassiter. Al had this booming, luxurious bass voice that could have rivaled that of Melvin Franklin, who was just beginning his rise to fame as a founding member of the Temptations, the Motown singing sensation. Bradford had a strong, sweet tenor that pierced many a heart. The two young men ended up as roommates during their memorable second semester—the one where they would etch their names in Tougaloo lore by participating in the library sit-in. And each would feel a debt of gratitude to Tougaloo and Pops Lovelace that neither believed he could ever repay.

In a joint interview with Bradford, Lassiter didn't talk much about his time at Tougaloo. His reticence comes from a certain shyness, perhaps, mingled with a deeply thoughtful mindset. The tall and lanky Lassiter's six-foot, five-inch frame dominates every photo of the Tougaloo Nine he appears in, and he must have been quite a player on the basketball court. But he is more conversant about Tougaloo's religious underpinnings. "As you know, Tougaloo was founded by the American Missionary Association, and the Disciples of Christ contributed to it. So, you had this moral underpinning there, which kept us straight." And, of course, both he and Sam had chorus scholarships, so they were required to sing at church services twice a week. "We went to chapel each Wednesday and Sunday," Lassiter noted.

For his part, Sam's career at Tougaloo was something of a patchwork. He described himself as a "persistent" student. "I was never known as a studious one," he said. "I didn't have the best grades, but I didn't have the worst grades either." But academics were only one part of Tougaloo life, and Sam wanted to take it all in, particularly the social side. "I enjoyed everything," he enthused. "I didn't get *involved* in everything, but I enjoyed the *prospect* of everything. I just liked being on the scene."

Another Pops protégé credits the modest showman with nearly everything good that ever happened in his long life. "He was 'The *man*,'" Joseph Jackson declared. "He alone—thanks to his getting me to Arkansas AM&N and then later to Tougaloo—he set me on the path of higher education. I owe him *everything*." As noted, Joe Jackson had a very different first impression of Tougaloo, given his wider experience and unusual status as a married man and ordained minister as well as a college student. His most lasting impression of the place, though, is about its power to broaden one's understanding of the world.

Jackson immediately recognized the interracial nature of the place. "Here you've got Dr. Beittel, and you've got his wife. And first and foremost, they were *White*! Arkansas State was all *Black*! So, to see that they've got integrated teachers. And they've got Dr. Schnell, a German teacher—from Germany! And you've got my idol, Dr. Ernst Borinski, sociology professor, who introduced us to a lot of international political figures at his Wednesday night forums."

"So, when I went to Tougaloo," Jackson concluded, "that's when my education really began."

As for Alfred Cook and Evelyn Pierce, little information exists to piece together their first impressions of Tougaloo or of Pops Lovelace. Both loved to sing, however. This is clear from their public comments and from interviews with various family members. So, one can expect that both thrilled at the full-throated experience of singing with a great choir and expressing themselves joyfully in song. In addition, both participated in the forty-fifth anniversary commemoration of the library sit-in, and Cook was also available for the fiftieth anniversary fete. At those moments, one can get a sense of their debt to Tougaloo.

Cook, of course, arrived at Tougaloo already a veteran and student leader of the burgeoning Jackson movement, but was most interested in the college's academic rigor. It was an accredited college and had a top-notch science department. Hoping to eventually go to medical school, Cook welcomed the more demanding scholarship of the place. "Tougaloo set a pattern in my life academically," he would later say. Cook also acknowledged that he joined Tougaloo's choir when he first arrived on campus and continued to sing for the rest of his life. "Tougaloo did so many things for me," he gratefully acknowledged.[10]

As for Evelyn Pierce, one can sense her feelings about Tougaloo by the reverence with which she speaks about the place. Evelyn was a good student and a good singer. Her sister Demathraus confirmed: "She *loved* to sing." But more than that, Evelyn thrilled at the *existence* of Tougaloo—the fact that such a place could thrive within the confines of the state of Mississippi. "Tougaloo is a *very* special place," Evelyn told students forty-five years after her courageous sit-in participation. "It fosters a mindset of dignity; a mindset of effort; a mindset of 'You can do what you want to do;' a mindset that lies are made to be challenged."

"We had something special at Tougaloo," she concluded.[11]

Chapter 9

COMMEMORATING A WOE-BEGOTTEN WAR

IN 1957, WHILE MOST OF THE TOUGALOO NINE WERE MAKING THEIR WAY through high school, a movement was afoot on the national stage to find an appropriate way to commemorate the centennial of America's most deadly fratricidal conflict, best known by most of its countrymen simply as "the Civil War." The idea had been brewing for several years in groups called Civil War Roundtables, which had emerged in the early 1940s and had become civic clubs, of sorts, where history buffs and Civil War enthusiasts gathered monthly, usually over lunch or dinner, to hear talks by knowledgeable experts on the war's battles, strategies, and personalities and to discuss—sometimes endlessly—their takes on the whys and the wherefores of the war's beginnings and its many twists and turns. In the mid-1950s, as the one-hundredth anniversary of the war approached, members of these groups began lobbying their elected officials—some of whom were members themselves—to pressure Congress and the president to create a national Civil War Centennial Commission well in advance of the actual centennial years of 1961 to 1965 to ensure the proper planning and coordination of a national commemoration. (As it turned out, these years nearly perfectly overlapped the zenith years of America's civil rights movement.)

Not everyone thought this was a good idea. In the wake of the 1954 *Brown* decision, when tensions were already running high and some Southern states were threatening "massive resistance" to the integration mandate, did it really make sense to further inflame sectional differences by digging up old grudges? Congressman Fred Schwengel (R-IA), who would eventually play an outsized role in the commission's oversight, urged caution. "I see the possibility of some ugly things creeping up as a result of this," he stated, accurately foretelling the "angry passions . . . reckless utterance . . . erroneous assumption . . . and pride in partisanship" that would eventually occur.[1] Even former South Carolina governor James Byrnes would later call the entire enterprise "a mistake" and observe: "After *two* centuries [the war's] battles might be commemorated. But one century is a short period in the history of a country and I fear it is quite impossible to re-live the four years of the Civil War without recalling experiences that will be unpleasant to the people of the North and South."[2]

Despite whatever limited opposition there was at the time, roundtable leaders pushed forward with their plan and developed draft legislation that was introduced into the US House of Representatives by one of their members, Congressman William Tuck of Virginia, whose grandfather had fought under Robert E. Lee. A willing Northerner introduced the same bill into the Senate, and the game was on. By September 1957, President Eisenhower signed Public Law 85-305 authorizing the creation of the national Civil War Centennial Commission (CWCC) and providing broad guidelines for its activities: "It shall be the duty of the Commission to prepare an overall program to include specific plans for commemorating the one hundredth anniversary of the Civil War. In preparing its plans and programs, the Commission shall give due consideration to any similar and related plans advanced by State, civic, patriotic, hereditary, and historical bodies, and may designate special committees with representation from the above-mentioned bodies to plan and conduct specific ceremonies."[3]

Congress decided that this national commission would have a limited budget under which to operate, so the planning and execution of the many commemorative events throughout the country would be delegated to the states to oversee. The national commission would mostly serve as a clearinghouse: encouraging states to form their own local commissions, developing a newsletter to promote centennial activities, calling annual assemblies to whip up enthusiasm for the effort throughout the anniversary years, and providing annual reports to Congress about these collaborative ventures.

Interestingly, most of the Southern states were skeptical of this national approach to commemorating the war. Local sentiment was so strong on the Confederate side that they feared a national approach would interfere with their own regional efforts to honor their dead and foster their *Gone with the Wind* Lost Cause traditions.[4] It didn't help matters that General Ulysses S. Grant III, the grandson of the man who more than anyone else was responsible for handing the North the victory (and a general in his own right), was selected as chairman of the commission. And a quick review of the twenty-five-member commission turned up only a few certifiable Southerners, suggesting that the heavy hand of the North would dictate the terms of the commemoration just as it had dictated the terms of surrender a century earlier.[5]

But the views of nearly every commissioner appointed to the CWCC were what today would be called "reconciliationist"—a consensus paradigm that attempted to create a narrative about the war and its causes that could knit the country's fractured core back into a single, unified whole. Developed exclusively by White journalists and historians, the consensus view espoused certain key principles:

- that the Civil War was a tragic battle between brothers;
- that it was a necessary squabble in order to ensure that the United States emerged stronger and more resilient than before—a force for good, standing up for democratic principles on the international stage;
- that the conflict was actually about tariffs and states' rights issues and had very little to do with the institution of slavery;
- that the practice of slavery had been a financial burden on the Southern ruling class, though a relatively benign practice in their hands, which helped elevate and civilize the enslaved; and
- that the period of Reconstruction was an abysmal failure—an ill-advised attempt by the North to impose its sectional values on the South rather than allowing the Southern ruling class to work out its own future in accordance with the Thirteenth, Fourteenth, and Fifteenth constitutional amendments passed in the wake of the Civil War.[6]

This reconciliationist view of the war that permeated the commission's thinking might have given Southerners confidence that their point of view about the conflict would be honored. Indeed, once he got to know Grant III, Tuck wrote to a colleague on the commission staff, "If I did not already know that General Grant is a Northerner and the Grandson of the victorious Union General, from everything he has said and done since I have known him, I would associate him with the South."[7]

The other obvious point about the commission that should have given the South comfort was that despite the fact that the Civil War had fought over the issue of slavery, and that the emancipation of the enslaved and the outlawing of the practice of slavery was the single-most significant outcome of the war, not a single representative on this important commemorative body was a person of color. There were many prominent Black figures of note—historians, sociologists, politicians—who might have fit the bill. But the only "diversity" provided within this group of (mostly) elderly White men was the appointment of Consuelo Bailey,[8] a White Republican female politician, who had just finished serving as lieutenant governor of Vermont—the first woman ever to have achieved this distinction in the country. Most of the men who served on the commission had been born prior to the turn of the century and had decidedly conservative views on racial matters. This glaring blind spot would seriously hamper the commission's ability to reach out to all Americans and would put it in significant jeopardy once commemorative events began in earnest in 1961.[9]

When the commission leadership began encouraging each state to form its own statewide commission and develop its own commemorative events, the South began to come around. This public-relations effort was furthered when Virginia governor J. Lindsay Almond addressed his colleagues at the May 1958 National Governor's Association and urged them all to get involved. In addition, the national commission selected as its executive director public relations wiz Karl Betts, a native of the border state of Kansas and a Civil War Roundtable enthusiast who happened to be a childhood friend of President Eisenhower. Almond's and Betts's entreaties to Southern states turned the tide, and by 1959, all the South had jumped on board, recognizing the opportunity for state boosterism and a chance for the South to tell its own story.[10]

Mississippi was an early adopter. At least one prominent Mississippian, Charlotte Capers, served as a reconnaissance scout at the commission's first National Assembly held in Washington DC in January 1958. She returned with a positive report about the group's objectives and its determination to let each state drive its own programming. Capers would become an important figure in helping to shape the Mississippi commemoration, particularly the day-long festival in Jackson. She came from a well-known family: her father, W. B. Capers, had served as rector of St. Andrew's Episcopal Church, directly across from the Governor's Mansion on Capitol Street, for twenty-five years. Her brother Walter had founded the Jackson School of Law. Capers herself, an able administrator and a wonderful storyteller—she was a close friend of Mississippi author Eudora Welty—had been selected in 1955 to head the Mississippi Department of Archives and History (MDAH). From that post, she advised governors and the state legislature about all things historical for the next nearly thirty years.[11] Capers's boundless energy infused the early planning for the Mississippi centennial with a positive can-do spirit. "Do something big or forget it!" she told the original state centennial organizing group of elected officials and interested citizens at one of their early meetings.[12]

Capers had convinced then-governor J. P. Coleman—a segregationist, but a moderate by Mississippi standards when it came to race relations—that full participation in the centennial could be an important archival and historical activity. Coleman and his team of bureaucratic professionals envisioned a "a relatively conservative commemoration—a respectful remembrance." Because he had only one year left in his term as governor, and he would be gone when the actual commemoration was to commence, Coleman appointed a temporary commission in the fall of 1958 to put in place plans for the centennial which, by necessity, would be carried out by the succeeding gubernatorial administration starting in early 1960. Coleman populated his commission with an impressive statewide team of Mississippi leaders, including Capers; prominent Vicksburg attorney and Civil War history buff Frank Everett; state tax collector and future governor William Winter, and various businessmen and Civil War heritage representatives, including J. Paul Faulkner, president of the Jackson Civil War Roundtable, and Ed Bearss (pronounced "bars"), an enthusiastic young National Park Service historian then serving at the Vicksburg National Military Park.[13]

At the group's organizing meeting in October 1958, Capers provided a summary of the first Assembly of the National Civil War Centennial Commission and solicited ideas for Mississippi's commemoration. Initial thoughts included celebrating the life and legacy of controversial Civil War personality Nathan Bedford Forrest; honoring the memory of Confederate president Jefferson Davis and his historic Beauvoir Plantation located on the Mississippi Gulf Coast; and commemorating the numerous battles and skirmishes fought on Mississippi soil, including, most importantly, the decisive battle of Vicksburg.[14]

The ever-efficient Capers wrote to Karl Betts about the formation of the Mississippi commission on the day of its first meeting. When Betts responded by inviting her to Washington to discuss the commission's longer-term plans for observances, Capers demurred, noting that "our Commission is 'un-' financed at present," so a trip to DC would have to be "worked out through other channels."[15]

The issue of financing for the Mississippi commission was problematic. Despite his strong picks to serve on the new commemorative body, Governor Coleman seemed in no hurry to obtain legislative approval nor funding authority for the new entity. In a letter to an interested Delta judge, he stated, "I believe we should go ahead with our plans and that we would have plenty of time to get the necessary appropriation in 1960, since the war did not begin until April 1861."[16] Indeed, the legislature had already appropriated funds for a two-volume set of essays documenting Mississippi's role in the Civil War, to be developed by two University of Mississippi history professors: Drs. John Bettersworth and James Silver.[17]

Coleman's temporary commission made significant progress in the fifteen months of its operation. The group had alerted various travel bureaus operating within the state of the centennial's approach and its potential for additional tourism; had connected with Betts, Grant III, and other members of the national commission staff; and had begun itemizing and planning for specific commemoration events, including the Secession Convention in Jackson to be held on January 9, 1961, exactly one hundred years to the day when Mississippi declared its independence from the Union. (For various reasons the date would shift to late March and collide with the Tougaloo Nine library sit-in.)

Also, under the leadership of William Winter, a subcommittee of the commission developed a twelve-point set of recommendations on how the commission should proceed with its work. These included encouraging local groups to organize observances; cooperating closely with the National Park Service to help preserve various battlefield sites; and, importantly, promoting "better understanding between the peoples of various states and sections of the country." Nearly all of the Winter subcommittee recommendations would be implemented in the coming years.

But Coleman's commission was hampered not only by its lack of funds, but also by its unclear mandate. Repeated attempts by Frank Everett, who had assumed the chairmanship of the group, to clarify with the governor the commission's remit proved inconclusive. By its September 1959 meeting, the group was foundering, and members knew their time was limited by the coming gubernatorial election. Since Coleman was constitutionally limited to four years, it was likely that the new governor would want to move in a different direction. It was also obvious that any longer-term commission would need funding and approval by the state legislature. This was made clear by Florence Sillers Ogden, a Delta aristocratic holdover from an earlier age whose brother, Walter Sillers Jr., was the powerful speaker of the Mississippi House of Representatives and whose own claim to fame as a socialite and woman of influence came through her leadership role in the state conference of the Daughters of the American Revolution, her membership in the United Daughters of the Confederacy, and her weekly column, Dis an' Dat, which was carried in both the *Delta Democrat-Times* and *The Clarion-Ledger*.[18]

Recognizing her well-connected status, the National Centennial Commission selected Sillers Ogden—at the recommendation of Mississippi's US Senator John Stennis—to become one of its first Advisory Committee members from Mississippi. Never one to hide her light under a basket, Sillers Ogden wrote on her Ogden Plantation stationery a fawning letter directly to General Grant III that oozed with Confederate charm and girlish coquettishness, though by then she was in her late sixties. "I am deeply interested in the Centennial and feel sure it will be a great success under your chairmanship," she wrote to Grant III. "That is, if you are anything like as good at Centennials as your grandfather was [at] running a war."

Sillers Ogden went on at some length about their shared histories:

Since your grandfather shelled my grandmother's plantation as he steamed down the Mississippi on his way to Vicksburg, I know a lot about your family. You may be interested to know that I still operate that plantation, raise cotton on it. It is located one hundred miles south of Memphis. My father, a ten-year-old boy, was on leave on his pony when your grandfather's fleet rounded a bend in the river and he saw and heard Confederate snipers fire on the gunboats and the boats then let loose their works.

I did not think I would ever receive an appointment from General U. S. Grant, but time and the river have run a long span since that August day in 1862 and the bitterness of those days is long spent. I consider it an honor to serve on your Commission.[19]

The letter was so full of sectional warmth, South for the North, that Betts made sure it ran in the national commission's newsletter *100 Years After*; Sillers Ogden also saw to it that it was carried in *The Clarion-Ledger*. She then began accepting every invitation offered to travel to national commission meetings, including to the second National Assembly, held in Richmond in the Spring of 1959.

"The Rebels outnumbered the Yankees!" she would exclaim in disbelief about the gathering since, like many Southerners, she expected the national commission to be overrun with Northerners. "And there was no animosity or hard feelings in evidence."[20]

At the Richmond assembly, Sillers Ogden encountered members of the Virginia Civil War Commission and brought back news of how Mississippi's commission could thread its way to statewide success by following the "Virginia Plan."

The grand dame was invited by Charlotte Capers to attend the faltering Mississippi commission's September 1959 meeting, where she made a fine showing just after Chairman Everett complained about not having a state congressional mandate. Waving the Virginia bill in front of the full commission, Sillers Ogden exclaimed that "the Virginia legislature had passed legislation establishing a permanent Civil War Centennial Commission and appropriating funds for the commission's use!" She then promptly walked the paperwork up to Everett, who passed it around to his fellow commissioners.

Next it was up to Sidney Roebuck, the man who would eventually become the Mississippi commission's executive director, to push the point. Roebuck was a well-regarded attorney and public servant from the small town of Newton whom Governor Coleman had appointed because of his connections to the travel industry. Roebuck had once been chairman of the Mississippi Highway Commission and in 1959 served a stint as president of the Mississippi Motel Association. More to the point, he was currently holding down the fort as president of both the Mississippi Travel Council and the Mississippi Automobile Club, the state affiliate of the American Automobile Association (AAA).[21]

Knowing that Barnett was Coleman's likely successor—by then he was the only one on the ballot—Roebuck suggested that the temporary commission make recommendations to the incoming governor and state legislature based on its months-long exploration of the centennial landscape thus far. He also recommended that all members of the commission tender their resignations to the new governor, thus allowing Barnett to choose his own team to further the commission's work. Roebuck also proposed a budget of half a million dollars—an incredible sum for Mississippi at the time—to fund the Centennial Commission's work for the coming four years. Roebuck's recommendations were adopted by the temporary commission, thus establishing him as a take-charge leader of the group, a point that would not be lost on the incoming governor.[22]

ROLLING WITH ROSS

As expected, when Ross Barnett assumed power on January 19, 1960, he set about remaking the Mississippi Civil War Centennial Commission in his own image and likeness. He saw the commission as one state initiative he could use to merge his twin campaign promises of economic development and Southern cultural purity.[23] Barnett intuitively understood the symbolic power of the centennial to communicate his White-supremacist and segregationist message. He also realized what a boon the four-year commemoration, which closely tracked his four-year term as governor, could be for tourism and Mississippi boosterism. The new governor quickly assumed control of the commission, thanked the temporary commission for its service, and promptly replaced all but three of its members with his own set of loyalists. Chief among the holdovers was Sidney Roebuck, whom Barnett appointed executive director of the newly named Mississippi Commission on the War Between the States. Roebuck became the equivalent of Karl Betts at the state level, with all of the public relations showmanship that the post required. And, like Betts, Roebuck would steer the commission toward the path of theatrical pageants and memorial events that would set Mississippi apart from most of its other state centennial commemorations.

The new name for the commission was adopted by the Mississippi legislature, which, at Barnett's urging, formally established the group early in its 1960 legislative session. It also appropriated $200,000 for the commission's operations during the coming two years, with an equally generous allotment expected to follow during the next two-year budget cycle—essentially in line with Roebuck's original proposal. It would be the largest amount allocated to any of the other Southern commissions save Virginia.[24] Although Governor

Barnett didn't announce his new commission line-up until late May, Roebuck had already been given the nod and had taken it upon himself to travel to Washington in April to meet with Betts and his team and get a better idea of what was going on from a national perspective.[25]

After his formal induction as executive director on July 1, Roebuck sent a letter of introduction to the leaders of every other state commission in the country soliciting their support and advice. He also seemed to apologize for the new commission's moniker. "The Commission was legally constituted as the Commission on the War Between the States, although everyone will know it as the [Mississippi] Civil War Centennial Commission."[26]

The new name was not a random creation, however. It was a pointed counternarrative to the "Civil War" terminology adopted by the North years earlier to suggest that the South's secession was an act of rebellion. Many Southerners had come to prefer calling the incivilities "the War Between the States"—thus highlighting the independent nature of each state in the conflict and insisting that each state had the right to withdraw from the Union at will. In addition, as many a Southerner has observed: "There was nothing 'civil' about it!"

In fact, the United Daughters of the Confederacy (UDC), a heritage group honoring all things Confederate, had lobbied the US Congress as early as 1911 to have "War Between the States" adopted as the official terminology to use when referring to the conflict. It may have been UDC influence that pushed the Mississippi legislature to adopt the commission's new name. (Until then, any documentation from Governor Coleman's temporary commission was titled "Mississippi Civil War Centennial Commission.")[27]

For Mississippi, the branding was important for another reason. It was a way for Barnett to send the signal that the reconstituted commission would take a different approach to the commemoration. Certainly, commissioning books and historical exhibits was fine, as far as it went, but this new commission would ensure that the entire nation would know that Mississippi was open for centennial business. To make the point, Barnett sidelined Charlotte Capers's role, allowing her to serve only in an "ex officio" capacity. He brought in the mayors of two of the most tourist-heavy cities within the state: Biloxi and Vicksburg. He invited in Florence Sillers Ogden (most likely at her insistence) and also elevated her brother Walter—the speaker of the Mississippi House of Representatives—to an ex officio position, as well. The formidable and well-connected Gladys Slayden, who had been part of Coleman's original commission, survived Barnett's purge, likely because of her newly elected status as a member of the state's House of Representatives and her role as president of the Garden Clubs of Mississippi, which oversaw annual "pilgrimage tours" to the Mississippi Delta's plantation town of

Natchez and other nostalgia-driven Southern cultural excursions. Vicksburg mayor John Holland ended up being chosen as chairman of the reconstituted commission; Mrs. Slayden was selected as vice chair.

Barnett also was savvy enough a politician to ensure that at least one "heritage organization"—read "Confederate heritage"—was represented on his commission. Though he dispensed with one Sons of Confederate Veterans representative and one United Daughters of the Confederacy member, he substituted another UDC representative with more clout. Kathleen O'Fallon, who, like Slayden, had just been elected to her first term in the House of Representatives as state delegate from Wilkinson County, could also boast of her connection as past chair of the state UDC organization. She joined and would also serve an important role on the new commission.

As for Capers, she seemed unconcerned about her shift out of the leadership of the commission. She had bigger fish to fry. Her Department of Archives and History was responsible for the complete renovation of the Old State Capitol Building, which was undergoing a million-dollar makeover, to be unveiled at the start of the 1961 centennial observances. The refurbished historic Capitol would serve as the backdrop for Mississippi's centennial kick-off event—the reenactment of the state legislature's secession vote to be held in the very same chamber one hundred years to the day after the initial disastrous decision was taken on January 9, 1861. She had her hands full and was fine with playing a back-bench role.

Of course, just as with the national commission, no one had considered—in Mississippi it would have been unthinkable at the time—including a Black person (or two) on the state commission. This was to be all White affair with Black citizens playing no substantive roles other than servile ones.

At its first meeting on May 27, 1960, the new commission met in the Office of the Governor at the State Capitol. Barnett welcomed them, and after the organizational formalities were dispensed with, he immediately launched into his joint message of economic development and positive PR for the state. The governor identified the "opportunities that the commission would have for bringing in tourist[s], promoting goodwill, and giving publicity to Mississippi during the next four years." The tourists, of course, would bring their cash, and the positive publicity would help blunt the negative impression most outsiders had of the state because of its insistence on segregation. Barnett also felt the need to present Sidney Roebuck as his pick to oversee the day-to-day work of the commission and to get their buy-in. Not to worry, the governor's hand-picked team unanimously supported his decision.[28]

At its next meeting, the following month, the commission was already discussing uniforms for the "Mississippi Greys"—the faux fighting phalanx that would represent their communities in the big Secession Day Parade that the governor had announced and in the various memorials and reenactments that would pepper the calendar during the next four years. Pageants were also on the agenda, and the commissioners wasted no time expressing their hope that Roebuck would hire "experienced personnel in the pageant field for consultation in this area." Branding was also on their minds. A motion was made to adopt a seal, an emblem, and a flag for the commission's public work. Roebuck was also directed to develop a manual and a handbook for instructing communities as to how to go about forming their own Mississippi Grey units and registering them with the commission. The Mississippi program was up and running.[29]

Though not mentioned in the official minutes, the new commission also adopted a three-page "Statement of Policy" that would become the group's operational guideline for the next four years. The document references the commission's legislative mandate and cites eleven key objectives—some pulled directly from the list developed by Coleman's temporary commission. The directives urged the commission

- to take responsibility for the proper commemoration of the Secession Activities of the Mississippi Convention on January 9, 1961;
- [to] encourage every city, town, community, and county in Mississippi to organize one or more units of the Mississippi Greys;
- to encourage the citizens of various communities in Mississippi to stage pageants commemorating the special events that transpired in their areas during the years 1861–65; and
- to publish a manual for the guidance of local groups who desire to participate in any way in the Centennial observance.

It was an ambitious list, one that would eventually garner national recognition.

From this point forward, Barnett largely stayed out of the commission's business, dropping by their bimonthly meetings occasionally to offer a word of encouragement or to comment on something notable they had accomplished. Roebuck proved a capable and energetic administrator. Realizing that his job was essentially state boosterism through Lost Cause mythological theatrics, he called in the most renowned public relations practitioner in the state and attached him to the commission as a consultant, with Barnett's blessing.

George Godwin was a whirlwind of ideas and had the strategic assets to get things done. He was a fixture in Democratic political circles and, as he would tell it, an "unofficial advisor to six administrations, major private corporations, and public area development corporations." In the 1940s, Godwin was instrumental in creating the state's Agricultural and Industrial Board—the powerful group of elected leaders whom Barnett would employ to push his probusiness agenda. Godwin also helped Barnett create his "Bill of Rights for Business and Industry" the same year he began working with the commission. The man knew how to craft ideas and sell them to wary politicians. He was a natural fit for helping to push the commission's agenda.[30]

On the darker side, Godwin was an incorporating member of the Jackson branch of the Citizens' Council—"the Klan without sheets,"[31] as civil rights activist Charles Evers would later refer to it—and served on the local group's board until his death in 1968. This strange link between White supremacy and ongoing efforts to attract outside businesses and tourism to the state suggests that Godwin—and by extension, most of Mississippi's power structure—operated in a weird information bubble that dismissed the risks associated with the state's intransigent stance on segregation. This anomaly was represented by the sentiment that many members of the commission, Barnett himself, and other elected officials like Jackson Mayor Allen Thompson, often repeated: "If only they [non-Southern White people] could come down and see how we operate, they'd have a better appreciation for our way of life." This bubble would be burst, first by the national press coverage in the aftermath of the Tougaloo Nine Library Sit-In and, eighteen months later to catastrophic effect, by the James Meredith University of Mississippi integration crisis. But that was all yet to come.

PLANNING FOR A BLOWOUT COMMEMORATION

Meanwhile, the commission was on a roll. They had engaged an in-state clothing manufacturer to mass produce, at an affordable price, a commission-designed uniform for the Mississippi Grey units that were slowly forming throughout the state. "The uniforms are to be made of a cotton wash and wear material from Mississippi cotton," crowed Charles Fulghum of the Mississippi Manufacturers Association.[32] Also, letters had been sent to mayors in forty-seven communities throughout the state urging them to name Centennial Committees for their communities. These committees could serve as recruitment centers for those interested in joining the Mississippi Greys. They could also be expected to develop plans to hold commemorative ceremonies in their own towns and hamlets. Uniforms had to be ordered no later than October 1 to meet a January 1 delivery schedule. There was no time to lose. The Secession Day commemoration was scheduled for January 9, 1961, and it was hoped that upwards of ten thousand Mississippi Greys would march in the massive parade that was scheduled to honor the Confederate dead and celebrate the South's Lost Cause Confederate culture.

In addition, Roebuck benefited from the work that Governor Coleman's temporary commission had started, much of which came to fruition soon after Roebuck took over. Charlotte Capers's capable hands can be seen all over two important initiating documents that Roebuck released in mid-1960. The first and most essential was *Mississippi's Greatest Hour*, a forty-eight-page how-to manual on the many ways the current citizenry could effectively organize their communities to honor and commemorate their fallen heroes of the Confederacy. The tone is pure Capers—direct, instructive, and encouraging, like your favorite teacher guiding you through a complex school project. There are checklists and reporting forms and a host of suggestions, from developing and sponsoring historical dramas and pageants, to creating museum-quality exhibits and display cases for local enjoyment, to finding and editing old first-person accounts of the war. Even doing a "general clean-up" of your town square is included so that tourists who may be ambling by will want to stay for a while: "Take inventory of your town's appearance. . . . Consider also the comfort of your visitors."

There is never a full-throated discussion of the reasons for the war in the manual—how could there be?—but Capers at least offered the even-handed observation that "the causes of the War were those which bring about all wars—greed, fear, ignorance, apathy, and emotionalism; and some Americans in every section of the country were guilty of harboring those qualities." Capers further noted, "No generation is entirely free of such evils, our own included."

Mississippi's Greatest Hour was adopted by Barnett's newly appointed commission at its second meeting in June 1960 and was finalized, printed, and released to the public—sent mostly to mayors of Mississippi towns, other elected officials, and civic groups—in late July. Even this, however, was a little late to rally the troops, particularly for those interested in forming units of the Mississippi Greys, which Capers described as "Mississippi's Centennial Military Force in Memoriam." Nonetheless, the publication was an important achievement and launched the commission's overall efforts with a bit of fanfare.[33]

The other major publication that Capers oversaw, released toward the end of 1960, just before the centennial began in earnest, was *Mississippi in the War Between the States*, a thirty-six-page historical summary of the war and Mississippi's role in it.[34] The booklet is a dizzying hodgepodge of facts, dates, and listings of the smallest of skirmishes that reportedly took place on Mississippi soil. Three bylines adorn various entries in this compendium: Capers's, of course, but also those of Frank Wallace, the commission's newest hire as information director, and Ed Bearss, the National Park Service staffer, then employed as resident historian at the Vicksburg National Military

Park, who, incidentally, had served as secretary on the Coleman temporary commission.

Wallace had just joined the staff of the commission in August, so most of the work must have been done by Capers and Bearss prior to Wallace's joining the team. Nevertheless, both Capers and Wallace share the byline for the opening essay about the war—the only place where the issue of slavery is addressed in any fashion. The full paragraph is instructive: "The causes of the war, of course, were many, and the seeds of sectional dissension were sown long before Fort Sumter, when the first Yankee traders brought the first black slaves from Africa to the new world. The immediate causes, however, were the fight over the extension of slavery into newly acquired territories of the United States, and states' rights, or the right of a state to secede from the Union."

Of course, the Yankees come in for criticism and blame for bringing the Africans here in the first place, but the mention of slavery as one of the causes of the war in a Southern publication at this time—when Lost Cause orthodoxy insisted that the war was fought solely because of tariffs, economics, and states' rights—is remarkable and a bit bold. The booklet also includes a detailed chronology of the life of the president of the Confederacy and long-time Mississippi resident Jefferson Davis, a discussion of various areas of Mississippi that saw significant fighting, a Civil War reading list, a compendium of Civil War historical markers throughout the state, and a final essay, "100 Years After—Mississippi Today and Tomorrow" that provides a substantive assessment of Mississippi's progress since the disastrous events of a century earlier.

Capers also managed to slip in an update on her own pet project—the Old Capitol restoration—primarily because of its importance to the centennial programs in Jackson. Indeed, when it reopened in early 1961, this historic structure had been reimagined as the Mississippi State Historical Museum. Two of its massive rooms would be devoted to Confederate relics: one would house various Jefferson Davis memorabilia ("Davisiana"); another would hold artifacts of the secession, Civil War weaponry, and a diorama of Vicksburg during the war.

Mississippi's Greatest Hour is also noteworthy because it presents the fledgling work of budding Civil War historian Ed Bearss, who had provided a two-page summary of the Battle of Vicksburg—one of his specialties—along with a ten-page list of every battle, every skirmish, every conceivable engagement between North and South that occurred within Mississippi's borders.

Bearss was an interesting outside addition to the mostly homegrown Mississippi commission team. Born in 1923 near Billings, Montana, on his family's homestead, which was literally on the edge of the large Crow Indian Reservation that included the Little Big Horn Battlefield, Bearss became enamored of all things historical—particularly anything connected to the history of the Civil War.[35] (As a boy, he named the cows on his father's ranch after Civil War battles and named the many family cats after Civil War generals.)

America joined World War II a few months after Bearss graduated from high school; he signed up for the marines. Severely wounded in early 1944 in a battle in the South Pacific, Bearss spent the rest of the war in various hospitals reading everything he could get his hands on that pertained to the Civil War. After VJ Day, Bearss determined to continue his education and become a historian. He received a bachelor's degree from Georgetown University in 1949, and a master's degree in history from Indiana University in 1955. The idea of working for the Park Service first came to him while researching his master's thesis. Bearss visited the Shiloh Battlefield to get a better sense of the situation Confederate General Patrick Cleburne faced while fighting there. As he walked the fields, deep in conversation with the park historian, Bearss found his calling. "That was the most important walk I ever took," he would later say. While walking the battlefield, Bearss would see why various key decisions had been made. Many of his observations were in direct conflict with then-current orthodoxy about the battle. His keen insight, to "walk the battlefield" would seal his reputation as an up-and-coming scholar of all things related to the Civil War.

Bearss joined the National Park Service in September 1955 and began working at the Vicksburg National Battlefield. "I'd have preferred Gettysburg," Bearss groused, "but it wasn't available." Not to worry. During the next eleven years, Bearss would make his mark at Vicksburg and eventually go on to become the chief historian for the National Park Service in Washington, DC.

By the time of Bearss's appointment to Governor Coleman's temporary Centennial Commission in October 1958, he was already a local celebrity. Partly to escape an uncomfortable internecine battle between his two bosses at the Vicksburg Park, Bearss undertook a search for the long-lost USS *Cairo*, a Union ironclad that had been sunk in 1862 somewhere in the Yazoo River when it ran into two Confederate underwater mines as it was slowly making its way to Vicksburg. Nearly one hundred years later, Bearss and two colleagues embarked on their day off—Armistice Day 1956—in a small boat to find the sunken remnants of the *Cairo*, and with the help of an old magnetic military compass and Bearss's deep research into the ironclad's possible locations, they managed to identify the likely location of the underwater ruins. It was an incredible find—the most important Civil War relic uncovered during the Centennial period. Eventually, more than ten thousand artifacts would be recovered from the waterlogged vessel.[36] As might be expected, upon the *Cairo*'s discovery, Bearss received an overwhelming amount of media attention and became a National Park Service star.

None of this kept him from his day-to-day duties, however. If anything, his success bred more work. Having already served as the Vicksburg battlefield's historian for four years, it made sense for Bearss to write the essay on the centrality of Vicksburg to the Civil War for *Mississippi in the War Between the States.* He had already agreed to author a definitive work on how what he considered the overlooked Battle of Champion's Hill near the town of Bolton, Mississippi, led to the inevitable Union victory at Vicksburg. (Frank Everett, chairman of Governor Coleman's temporary commission, had asked Bearss if he would undertake the project, and the young, as yet unpublished historian agreed to do so without pay as long as he was assured the work would find its way into print.) Bearss, described by some as a polymath for his extraordinary command of minutiae about the war, was well into the development of the manuscript for *Decision in Mississippi*—a book that would seal his reputation as one of the nation's most knowledgeable public historians of the Civil War—when he dashed off his two-page summary of the Battle of Vicksburg and his ten-page list of Mississippi skirmishes for *Mississippi in the War Between the States.*

Both *Mississippi's Greatest Hour* and *Mississippi in the War Between the States* were met with high praise by the Mississippi press and helped burnish not only the reputations of Capers and Bearss but also that of Roebuck, despite his limited involvement in either project. Aside from the exceptional content of both pieces, one of the things that people remarked upon was their high-quality production value. George Godwin knew a thing or two about presentation and saturated the covers of both booklets with a bright red and deep blue full-bleed covers, with the centerpiece being the centennial emblem: a representation of the Confederate Stars and Bars on a shield with the word *Mississippi* and an attractive magnolia blossom above. His effective printing technique—and yes, Godwin's company got the exclusive contract for all of the commission's printing needs for the entire four years—helped make both manuals sought-after mementos of the commemoration.[37]

Such exquisitely produced memorabilia made a mark in regional circles, as well. When Sidney Roebuck and Gladys Slayden unveiled the colorful materials at the first meeting of the Confederate States Centennial Conference in Atlanta that summer, eyes popped. "What you have already accomplished is astounding comparing it to what the rest of us have done," gushed the staff assistant to the Georgia commission in a follow-up letter to Roebuck.[38]

The materials were a big hit with those in the travel industry as well. The manager of the Sinclair Oil Auto Tour Service added her praises: "Congratulations to Mississippi on publishing the finest state folder on the Centennial that has come across my desk." She also asked for five hundred copies to supplement the company's own centennial advertising campaign.[39]

Godwin's execution of commission projects was garnering strong positive feedback for the group. And according to the commission's official meeting minutes, Godwin was also responsible for one of the most creative ideas for fostering sectional reconciliation of any that arose nationwide during the entire four years of commemoration. At the Mississippi commission's September 1960 meeting, Godwin floated the idea of inviting states with monuments at the Vicksburg National Military Park to visit the site and honor their war dead. Perhaps, he pondered, each state could have its own week of commemoration, and maybe "they could end the week by having the Governor from that particular state meet with Governor Barnett at that State's monument for remarks and a wreath-laying ceremony."⁴⁰

In the aftermath of the war, many states went into a monument frenzy to pay homage to their lost sons—attempting to carve into stone the extreme grief of a nation bereft. Vicksburg and Gettysburg—arguably the two most important battles of the war and both decided essentially on the same day—excelled at this memorialization. By 1960, the eighteen-hundred-acre Vicksburg battlefield site included fourteen monuments from Northern and Midwestern states as well as seven memorials from Southern states.⁴¹ Godwin's state commemoration idea likely emerged from his strategizing over how best to boost tourism during the centennial years. But it struck a chord that resonated with the entire commission. Perhaps it was just Southern hospitality, perhaps a genuine desire to bury the past and move forward together, or perhaps just crass commercialism—maybe a little of each. Whatever the motivation for the idea of inviting outsiders in, the concept caught fire, and within weeks, invitations were going out to all of the Northern and Midwestern states that had fought on the side of the Union to come during the spring and summer of 1961 to honor their war dead during a week of activities specifically tailored to each states' involvement in the war.

Indeed, Roebuck, commission chair John Holland, and information director Frank Wallace made it their mission to visit the office of nearly every Northern governor whose state had sent troops to Vicksburg and whose citizens had erected a monument in their memory to visit the National Military Park during the week designated for their special commemoration. Most governors received the delegation cordially but often demurred from attending the Vicksburg ceremony, sending a representative instead. Nevertheless, the effort seemed like a sincere offer of reconciliation and often garnered good press in whatever state capital the Mississippians were visiting.

A COMMEMORATION, *NOT* A CELEBRATION

While others were engaging in state-to-state diplomacy, George Godwin continued to cook up schemes for broader recognition of the Mississippi commission's work. Godwin's advertising prowess extended into media relations, as well. He seemed to be something of an unofficial member of Ross Barnett's staff. So close was he to the new governor that during the summer of 1960, Godwin accompanied Barnett to New Orleans where the Mississippi Governor would make one of his first major media appearances on the Sunday morning news and politics show *Face the Nation*. While there, Godwin chatted up Mike Marlow, one of the producers of the show, and gave him the lowdown about the spectacle Mississippi was planning for its centennial celebration, inviting CBS to cover the event for its viewers. Unwittingly, this invitation would ensure the presence of national media during the events surrounding the Tougaloo Nine library sit-in.

Godwin followed up with a letter to Marlow a few weeks later, suggesting that the Jackson gala would be "the first dramatic event of the Centennial in the Nation," coming as it would on January 9, the day after the planned kick off of the national centennial program. The advertising impresario gave the full run-down of events in his two-page detailed letter: the re-enactment of "Mississippi's Act of Secession . . . preceded by a colorful parade of 'Mississippi Greys'"; the opening of the Old Capitol, "which has recently been completely restored to its original 1833 form at a cost of more than $1 million"; and "a series of four or more Confederate balls," with "grand marches and everything."[42]

Godwin wasn't the only one going overboard to promote the upcoming centennial events. Despite the commission's best intentions, once information about the Secession Day Parade and other commemorative events began to be touted in the local press—ginned up, of course, by a seemingly inexhaustible series of commission press releases—a festal atmosphere began to develop around the Magnolia State's day-long community gathering. The first rebuke to the commission on this score came, surprisingly, from one of the heritage groups, the Sons of Confederate Veterans. Jim Collier, an elected officer of the Mississippi division of the organization, took Roebuck to task. "When the newspapers refer to this period in front page articles as being a period of celebration, I cannot refrain from registering a strong protest," he wrote. "I am sure that all who are working toward making this a success must realize that we of the South certainly have nothing to celebrate, and I certainly trust that in the future this period will be referred to as a Commemoration and not a celebration."

Roebuck responded somewhat defensively, noting that the commission's manual states emphatically that "the observance of the centennial is a commemoration, NOT a celebration" and lamenting that he had no control over how reporters refer to the upcoming events. But he also commiserated with Collier, saying, "I am sure my two grandfathers who fought in the Confederate Army would not think we had cause for a celebration if they could come back and speak their thoughts."

He also addressed the need to bring outsiders to Mississippi, obliquely defending the rah-rah atmosphere that was developing around the centennial. "If people are going to come South, we would like them to see Mississippi and its people and learn more about us," he wrote. "We think that if they come here, they will go back home with a kindlier feeling toward us than perhaps they have now."[43]

By late November 1960, shop owners on Capitol Street and throughout the downtown area were clamoring for more details about the parade and other festivities. Kenneth Primos—son of Greek immigrant Angelo Primos, whose four downtown restaurants (for Whites only, of course) were staples of the shopping district—wrote Roebuck saying, "We are interested in doing all we can to help promote the Centennial," and revealing his plans to "decorate our restaurant in the Old South Theme."[44]

Two other notable highlights from the commission's November meeting: It was announced that Mrs. Slayden had been elected as permanent chair of the Confederate States Centennial Conference during their meeting in Richmond in October, thus adding to her clout within the Southern centennial community; and Director Roebuck noted that Jackson's mayor Allen Thompson had recently invited eighty-eight business leaders to City Hall to encourage them to have their employees form units of the Mississippi Greys.[45] Although it goes unsaid in the minutes, this move on Thompson's part signals a looming problem for the Mississippi commission. The secession festivities were planned for January 9, just two months away, and Roebuck is still desperately trying to round up volunteers to participate in the Mississippi Greys marching army. The slow response by Mississippi's citizenry to this faux fighting force pomp and circumstance would end up delaying Mississippi's Secession Parade by almost two months and, as a result, will forever connect the start of Mississippi's nascent civil rights movement with the celebration of its Confederate past.

Part IV

GETTIN' READY

Chapter 10

FREEDOM'S EARLY STIRRINGS

IT IS INSTRUCTIVE TO READ THE HEADLINES OF MISSISSIPPI'S NEWSPAPERS during the early days of the student movement protests that began on February 1, 1960, when four Black students of North Carolina A&T State College walked into the Greensboro, North Carolina, Woolworth store and sat down at what until then had been a segregated lunch counter. Mississippians, at first, had no response; it seemed like an entirely local phenomenon. Even as similar demonstrations began cropping up in other border states such as Virginia and, especially, Tennessee, the news outlets' reporting is extremely limited, offering just summary newswire stories about these seemingly unconnected protests. It's like watching a tsunami happen in slow motion. Only gradually do the opinion and government leaders realize the calamity that is overtaking them. And by then, it's too late.

The Mississippi headlines seem much more concerned about the civil rights bill that is making its way through the US Congress—what would become the Civil Rights Act of 1960. The machinations of Senators Eastland and Stennis of Mississippi, as well as those of Russell of Georgia and Johnson of Texas take up much more ink about the watered-down legislation that would become largely a footnote to history compared to the swelling student movement, which would become a defining development in the push for civil rights.

In the jointly published *Clarion-Ledger/Jackson Daily News* Sunday edition on February 21, *JDN* editor Jimmy Ward finally begins to take the demonstrations seriously in his Covering the Crossroads column. Even then, he uses a story published in the ultraconservative *News & Courier* of Charleston, South Carolina, as his source in questioning just how and why these seemingly locally based outbreaks keep happening. He posits "the existence of some kind of underground apparatus of undetermined proportions."[1]

By early March, as the demonstrations start to creep closer to Mississippi's borders, particularly in Deep South Alabama, and headlines about "Negro Protests" begin appearing almost daily, sometimes in the top-right corner of the front page over three columns of type. Still, no one seems to believe that any of these disturbances will occur within the Magnolia State. As late as March 4, *The Clarion-Ledger* is crowing that "Jackson is one of the capital cities in the South that has not felt the sting of organized protests on the racial issue." And Mayor Allen Thompson declares that this is "not just luck."

"You can't say Jackson is just lucky," he states. "It's more than luck. It's the result of a lot of people working together, planning and praying together."[2]

This may be why on March 20, the *Clarion-Ledger/Jackson Daily News* Sunday story hit with such force. "Tougaloo Students Get Request for Sit-Down" the headline screamed from just below the masthead's front page. Editor Jimmy Ward's sources at the Sovereignty Commission had discovered that Tougaloo's student body president Eddie Irions had received an overture from "a band of professional egoists, hate mongers and racial agitators"— Ward's inimitable prose—"to organize lunch counter sitdown demonstrations." Irions was conveniently out of town when reporters called the college, but then-Tougaloo president Sam Kincheloe confirmed Irions had received the request, though he provided no additional details.

When asked about the explosive claim, the NAACP's Medgar Evers denied any involvement, noting that "it would not be the [Mississippi NAACP's] policy to stage sit-down strikes." He did, however, provide clarity on what his group *was* planning. "From now on Negroes will be urged to simply not trade at those establishments discriminating against them," Evers told a reporter. "We have had economic pressure applied to us. It is time we began using the same tactics."[3]

Nonetheless, Mississippi's political class was taking no chances regarding the possibility of direct-action protests. As reports about the impact of demonstrations elsewhere slowly sank in, Mississippi's attorney general, Joe Paterson, crafted language for three bills "designed to head off sit-down invasions . . . which have plagued other states lately." The bills called for a fine of $500 and the possibility of up to six months jail time for persons "going into or remaining in places of business after being forbidden to do so by the owner or manager"; for persons who "willfully obstruct the free, convenient or normal use of sidewalks, streets, alleys or other public passageways"; and for persons who engage in "soliciting or urging or procuring any other person to enter or remain in any place of business against the will of the owner or manager." The Mississippi House of Representatives introduced the bills one day and then brought them to the floor for a vote the next—an unheard-of scheduling feat. They passed with near-unanimous votes. The bills were sent to the state senate, where they were expected to have a longer slog through the typically deliberative legislative process.

Just after this alarming bulletin about Tougaloo hit the papers, however, the Mississippi Senate quickly brought these bills regulating public behavior, which had been languishing in committee for several weeks, onto the floor, thus bypassing entirely its calendar scheduling process. The bills passed unanimously in the senate without any debate and were then rushed to Governor Barnett's office for signature. After a gradual awakening to the gathering storm, Mississippi's lawmakers were preparing for the inevitable.[4]

EVERS'S FAITH IN THE YOUTH

Meanwhile, the forces pushing for freedom were not sitting still either. Indeed, Medgar Evers had been encouraging youth participation in the Mississippi freedom fight even before he signed on as a full-time staffer for the NAACP in late 1954. That summer, as a volunteer member of his local branch, Evers traveled to the NAACP's national conference in Dallas, Texas, with several promising young acolytes in tow, including the sibling of future Jackson NAACP youth leader Amos Brown. After hearing of his sister Gloria's extraordinary experiences meeting the leading lights of Black America's resistance movement, Amos Brown made sure he was part of Evers's retinue when the annual event was held in San Francisco in 1956. By then, young Brown had already helped establish Jackson's first viable NAACP Youth Council in December 1955—in the wake of the Emmett Till murder—and was serving as its president. Years later, Brown would recall traveling for hours on end with Evers and others—including Luella Bender, daughter of Tougaloo's Reverend William Bender—in "the Blue Goose," Evers's recently purchased company car, a blue 1955 Oldsmobile. At the convention, Brown met Martin Luther King Jr., who was in the midst of leading the Montgomery bus boycott, as well as Rosa Parks and NAACP leaders Roy Wilkins and Thurgood Marshall.[5]

The experience would change the trajectory of Brown's life and set him more firmly on the path of resistance to the established order in the South. Back home, Brown was inspired by the examples of everyday folk who volunteered their time and energy to ensure that the NAACP would thrive locally in Jackson and throughout the state of Mississippi: people such as John W. Dixon and Mary Cox, who will appear later in this narrative, as well as Essie Collins, treasurer of the Jackson branch; attorney Carsie Hall; and Sam Bailey, adult advisor to the Youth Council who would eventually become president of the NAACP's Jackson branch. It was people like this who would sustain the Jackson movement through its various iterations during the next several years as Amos Brown finished high school in 1959 and headed off to Morehouse College in Atlanta in the footsteps of Dr. King. But he left behind a strong and active Youth Council, one of whose members, Meredith Anding, would become part of Mississippi history as a member of the Tougaloo Nine.

INTERNAL STRUGGLES

When the nationwide sit-in movement began in February of 1960, powered by college students and enlivened by those even younger—many of them NAACP Youth Council members from various states across the South—Medgar Evers knew the time had come for him and his young protégés to make a move.

The only problem was that the organization he served, particularly its adult volunteer infrastructure in Mississippi, wasn't ready to make the move with him. Charles R. Darden had become an indispensable part of the NAACP operation in Mississippi. Not only was he president of one of the most important branches within the state—the branch in Meridian, located at Mississippi's far eastern end, bordering Alabama—but Darden also served as president of the NAACP's statewide apparatus, the Mississippi State Conference of Branches. On top of that, Darden had been elected to the national NAACP board of directors as Mississippi's representative. In other words, he was a big deal. Even though he was a volunteer, Darden's word meant something among the rank and file of the approximately two thousand Mississippi NAACP members scattered throughout the state. He also had the ear of Roy Wilkins and others at the national level of the organization. And he neither suffered fools nor took prisoners.[6]

Somehow, Evers had gotten on Darden's bad side. Most likely, it had to do with Evers's solicitation of new members from the ranks of World War II vets that he had served with, many of whom were ready to fight more aggressively for their freedom at home. The Mississippi field secretary courted them and ensured that they ended up in positions of authority within their own branches, thus diminishing Darden's omnipotent rule. In March 1960, Darden complained to Evers's second-tier boss, Gloster Current, that "he took his American Legion of Jackson, MS, took over the Jackson branch of the NAACP, and there has been nothing but confusion since that election of American Legion to NAACP branch officers." Ouch.

Medgar's wife, Myrlie, also suggested that Darden was after her husband's job. How uncomfortable must it have been, then, when Evers saw the opportunity to begin making substantive change in Mississippi through boycotts and protests that Darden blocked him at every turn? "I regret having to bring this matter to your attention again but I have had enough," Darden wrote to Current in that same March tirade. "Medgar Evers is too much of an antagonist in the board meetings to be tolerated." The issue this time was exactly the crux of the matter: How fast should the local branches be able to go in pushing for change knowing Mississippi's harsh and intolerant stance toward civil liberties for Black people? At a meeting earlier that week, Darden upbraided Evers in the presence of the entire statewide board for "going over his head and the authority of the board" by discussing strategies for change at an NAACP staff gathering earlier in the year in Memphis. Alarmingly, Darden interpreted Evers's conversations with other paid NAACP colleagues about "the ways and means of permitting Mississippi youth to participate in nationwide protests against racial segregation and discrimination" as insubordination. In essence, he was criticizing Evers for simply doing his job.[7]

The interchange sounds much more like a power play than an issue of policy, but Darden also was significantly more conservative in his outlook than was Evers; he opposed any sort of open challenge to Mississippi's existing power structure, fearing the negative impact such a challenge would have on the NAACP's viability within the state. This was not an unreasonable position, especially with the benefit of hindsight. But for Darden to openly castigate the NAACP's lead staffer in Mississippi for participating in a sanctioned staff meeting with other NAACP staff members while they discussed strategy seems heavy handed, to say the least. And this must not have been Darden's first breach of bureaucratic protocol. Evers calmly and objectively put in writing to Current what had happened at the meeting and let the chips fall where they may.

Apparently, Darden was too much for Current and Wilkins, as well. Evers kept his job, and before the end of the year, Darden was voted out as president of the State Conference, replaced by none other than Janice Jackson's mentor from Clarksdale, Aaron Henry. The activist army veteran and pharmacist sided with Evers on issues of policy, and, like many of the field secretary's other veteran friends, was ready to move.

In a memo to Current just the week before the dustup with Darden, Evers mentioned that he was planning on visiting Tougaloo College on Friday, March 11, 1960, to "organize a chapter there." Obviously, the explosive pace of the student movement since it burst forth at the start of the previous month in Greensboro, North Carolina, was having an impact on Evers's thinking. (By the end of February, the concept had spread to more than thirty cities and by year's end sit-ins had happened in nearly every Southern state.)[8]

Evers hoped to be on the forefront of the action in Mississippi, but even he wasn't advocating in-your-face direct-action sit-ins. Not yet anyway. He felt, however, that some sort of organized campaign was needed to show the nation that Mississippi would not be left out of the resistance movement. Perhaps a boycott of the downtown business district would be in order. White businesses, especially those in Jackson's central business district on its main merchandising avenue, Capitol Street, loved getting Black business, but they treated Black customers as second-class citizens when it came to service, courtesy, and respect. The message seemed to be that Black shoppers didn't belong on Capitol Street at all. This had to change.

SACRIFICE FOR HUMAN DIGNITY

Despite ongoing friction with Darden, Medgar Evers kept his meeting with Tougaloo students in mid-March and also visited the Reverend Charles Jones, dean of the Lampton School of Religion at Campbell College—where future Tougaloo Nine member Alfred Cook was enrolled—to attempt to get something started. Jones was an important ally of Evers as the NAACP field secretary attempted to get adult support for student engagement in the nascent Mississippi student movement. Jones had recently moved to Jackson from Washington, DC, and must have been surprised by the lack of any real push for change going on in the Magnolia State. He joined Evers and the NAACP as soon as he got settled at Campbell College in the fall of 1959, and by early 1960, he felt sufficiently secure in his position to begin speaking out.[9]

According to Evers, the trigger point for acting was provided by former Mississippi governor J. P. Coleman when, in response to sit-ins taking place in other parts of the South, he suggested that "our Negroes are satisfied." Evers thought that such a misleading comment could not be allowed to stand. After a long discussion, Evers and Jones fixed on the idea of "a sacrificial boycott during the Easter season." They shared their idea with various "civic leaders, students, businessmen, clergy and others" and formulated a plan to move forward.[10]

By early April, a plan was in place for a boycott of any White chain stores known to have disrespected Black customers in Jackson, as well as of any and all stores up and down Capitol Street. The initiative was called "Sacrifice for Human Dignity." It would take place from April 10 through 17, during the height of the Easter shopping season. The "sacrifice," of course, would mean that Black families who had not yet done their traditional clothes shopping for display at Easter church services would have to go without. The idea could be a hard sell to many Black families that often spent substantially on Easter finery. No problem. Jones and Evers had a plan. They galvanized some 350 students from Tougaloo, Campbell, and Jackson State to turn out one rainy Sunday in early April to knock on doors and deliver handbills urging the Negroes of Jackson to stay away from Capitol Street during the week before Easter Sunday. "These young people were overwhelmed with enthusiasm to have been able to contribute in the struggle for first-class citizenship," Evers gushed to his direct supervisor, Ruby Hurley. Despite pronouncements from the president of Jackson State College (a state-supported school that relied on White funding to operate) that students were forbidden "to participate in any demonstrations against segregation," another two hundred students from all three colleges showed up the following Thursday evening to again carpool and fan out through Jackson, distributing leaflets in the

Black sections of town. Evers estimated that students handed out more than ten thousand fliers.

The next day, Friday, April 8, Jones, Evers, and future Tougaloo Nine member Alfred Cook—who by then was serving as Campbell College student body president and was an important instigator of this initial foray into mass protest—held a press conference to announce the initiative publicly and to garner whatever press coverage might be offered to amplify the message. Jones announced the boycott and emphasized that there would be no demonstrations or picketing "of any sort" to accompany the boycott. "Demonstrations tend to antagonize rather than harmonize," Jones noted. He also predicted that the boycott would be 70 percent effective and said students from Campbell, Tougaloo, and Jackson State Colleges were participating in getting the word out about the boycott, as were local high school students.

Al Cook then stepped to the podium, becoming one of the first student organizers within the state to publicly criticize Mississippi's wrongheaded approach to race relations.[11] Reading from a prepared statement, Cook noted that the boycott had been "organized to stop all patronage of all White businesses in the City of Jackson." He also announced the group's name—*Sacrifice for Human Dignity*—and clearly stated that the effort is "designed to show the people of Mississippi that the Negro is not satisfied with his condition."

Evers then spoke and coyly insisted that the boycott was not an NAACP-sponsored event, stating that it was a "community-driven project," but said his group "would cooperate." This seems like an unusual step for the NAACP's man in Mississippi to take, particularly since he was the one who called the press conference. Clearly, Evers was still smarting from his recent run-in with Darden and thus was stepping lightly into his activist role. Years later, Al Cook would confirm what an Associated Press story reported at the time, that Evers joined the protest only in an "advisory capacity" and not as a representative of the NAACP.[12]

That afternoon, the *Jackson Daily News* trumpeted the message: "Jackson Negro Boycott Vowed" the headline announced. The following morning, Jackson's *Clarion-Ledger* carried a front-page story: "No Easter Buying: Negroes Pledge Jackson Boycott." No doubt, both stories must have been something of a shock to those who thought that all their Negroes were "satisfied."[13] Like a charm trying to ward off a bad omen, *The Clarion-Ledger* pluckily posted a short "Congratulations, Jackson!" editorial squarely in the center of its front page, applauding the citizens of Jackson, White and Black, for the calm and quiet that they had maintained thus far in the wake of "an NAACP appeal for a business boycott in our city." The opinion piece continued, "Sane leadership exists in our respective communities, and the Jacksonians who stay with this leadership, despite violence elsewhere, merit commendation."

In a related news brief, *The Clarion-Ledger* reported that a bottle was thrown through Charles Darden's front window shortly after the NAACP news conference ended. Although police chalked the incident up to "juveniles," Darden—and Evers—must have known that the vandalism was related to the launch of the boycott. This certainly must have caused heightened friction between the two men.[14]

On Sunday, April 10, students again fanned out to nearly all of the Black churches in the city, Evers reported to his superiors, "to appeal to the various congregations to cooperate in the movement." The use of the term *movement* must have thrilled Evers. Finally, Jackson—and therefore, Mississippi—had a viable movement![15]

EVERS AND MANGRAM

One additional outcome of the Easter boycott and the Evers visit to Tougaloo College to gather recruits for the distribution of leaflets is that the NAACP leader got to work more closely with Tougaloo's chaplain, John Mangram. There must have been strong synergy between the two men because the reverend ended up addressing the Mississippi NAACP's spring membership campaign meeting in early April while the boycott campaign was ramping up.

In his efforts to stir the crowd and bring in new members, Mangram pulled no punches: "At a time when our country needs to be unified, when we need to be teaching our youth the very best that we know—not only to keep in the race of democracy against totalitarianism, but to win friends and influence people who can and would come into our camp—our State, through its representatives, both in the State Government and the National Government, seem to go out of their way to prevent democracy." The Tougaloo chaplain was just warming up:

> They pass laws which are insulting to human beings and blasphemous and idolatrous before God. At a time in the life of our part of the country, when every experience seems to point out the utter stupidity of segregation, they preach it and write about it as though this were the highest and most wholesome way of life known. It is an attitude of defiance, of hatred, of flouting laws that are for the justice of all so that the privileged few might continue to bask in the sunlight of an ignominious idolatry which dubs Mississippi as the hinterland of the Nation.
>
> There can be no justice in a segregated community! Negroes have known this for a long time, and white people have known it, too. If you agree when the enemies of democracy tell you that the NAACP is a

Communist front organization, you are asleep! If you want to awaken from your long sleep and join and become active in an organization dedicated to making all America free and decent, then join the NAACP.

Those who have eyes to see and ears to hear know that it is the one organization that has done more to help make America the land of the free and the home of the brave than any other![16]

The audience surely had not heard such a direct assault on the White power structure and on segregation. Evers thought enough of the Yale-educated theologian's remarks to include extensive excerpts in his April monthly report—something unprecedented during the five-plus years he had been sending these off to the national office. Perhaps he was trying to alert his own organization to the changes that were developing within his territory. Or perhaps he was simply bringing to his supervisors' attention the presence of an ally in the fight for racial justice. Whatever his intention, Evers also reported that Mangram's address had its intended impact. More than fifty new members of the NAACP were signed up that day. Clearly, Evers and Mangram were forging a partnership that both men hoped would reap even more far-reaching results in the future.

THE SPIES OF MISSISSIPPI

These early efforts at developing a movement were not lost on those determined to keep any form of change to the status quo at bay. In an incredibly detailed eighteen-page memorandum, Zack Van Landingham, a former career FBI special agent then working for the Mississippi Sovereignty Commission, provided a blow-by-blow summary of the entire Easter boycott campaign, including copies of the "Blue Dodgers"—the mimeographed sheets, replete with blue ink typical of this printing process—that announced the Capitol Street boycott. He also supplied his supervisors with a list of the license plate numbers and car models of all those attending NAACP public meetings and rallies, mostly at local Black churches, where the boycott may have been discussed.[17]

Besides this typical Dick Tracy showmanship, Van Landingham's memo provides an interesting outsider's view of how the movement was put together and who its leaders were. The detective's version of events begins on April 6 when a Black maid tells her White employer about "college students going around to the various negro high schools and elementary schools soliciting their support for the easter boycott."[18] The White woman, of course, called the police, who then alerted the state spy agency. Although the rumor of the school visits seems to have been false, the idea that something awry was afoot caused alarms to go off within the halls of the White establishment.

What is revealing even from this early date is that there are paid informants already operating at Tougaloo College who are watching for any signs of "trouble" on campus. A "confidential informant" listed as "T-1" told his Sovereignty Commission handlers that Evers had been on campus on April 6 to promote student participation in the boycott effort. This informant also provided the commission with a copy of the mimeographed boycott flier. It conveys a simple, hand-lettered message urging readers: "LET'S CELEBRATE EASTER IN OLD CLOTHES!!—It is a Human Sacrifice for the Cause of Human Dignity."

Van Landingham also points out in his memo that only wire service and TV reporters—and not anyone from the local Jackson newspapers—were invited to the April 8 early-morning press conference announcing the boycott, suggesting that Evers was seeking broad coverage for this first major foray into public social activism within the state. Van Landingham reports that he "immediately tipped off" both Jimmy Ward at the *Jackson Daily News* and Bob Webb at the *State Times* about the press briefing, thus pointing out the close association between the spy commission and the local press (though he says nothing about *The Clarion-Ledger*).[19]

The Sovereignty Commission spy also suggests that Reverend Mangram ("Rev. Mangum") had been suspended from teaching or preaching by the Tougaloo board of trustees for "advocating the boycott" and for having "spoken at the NAACP meeting on April 3"—the speech Medgar quoted from so extensively. This is a dubious claim, since Mangram had spoken many times at NAACP meetings and, as noted, had served as chairman and chaplain of the Executive Committee of the Jackson branch for years. The Tougaloo Board may certainly have heard about Mangram's involvement, but even under President Kincheloe—Dan Beittel wouldn't arrive until September—such precipitous action against an admired campus figure is unlikely.[20]

Importantly, given Alfred Cook's later role in the library sit-in, Van Landingham's extensive memo cites Cook as a significant leader in the boycott movement and notes correctly that he was then serving as president of the Campbell College student body. The spy had done enough digging to report that Cook "had originally come from Jackson" but that "his family presently live in the State of Michigan," which was a bit garbled but essentially correct. (Cook had been born in Vicksburg but did have extended family members living in Flint.)

The Sovereignty Commission memo goes on to quote several Black leaders' opposition to the boycott, including, predictably, the reactionary Percy Greene, editor of the Black weekly newspaper *The Jackson Advocate*. Van

Landingham had included in his memo a copy of an editorial Greene had written opposing the boycott: "Right off in answer to Mr. Evers we would say the reason why there has been no sit down demonstrations in Mississippi is because of the good sense of the masses of Negroes." Greene also took a personal swipe at Evers, calling him a "zealot and a paid advocate of the NAACP," estimating Medgar's and Myrlie's combined salaryies from the NAACP ("something like $10,000 per year") and noting that they were insulated from any economic repercussions from the White community. "Knowing that the NAACP can do nothing to get jobs for Negroes here we would regard as a fool any Negro who takes such advice" as to participate in the boycott. He ends the piece by comparing Evers and the NAACP to the Communist Party, suggesting that the storied civil rights organization was "trying to destroy everybody and everything which refuses blind following of its leadership."

Greene was not wrong in pointing out the dangers of Black resistance to White rule in Mississippi. He was stating the obvious. And even though Greene's early career as a journalist in the 1940s championed Black causes, by the 1960s his editorial judgement was compromised. He had begun taking money from and serving as a paid hack for the Sovereignty Commission, opposing just about any activity that smacked of civil rights agitation. Since he was the most notable Black journalist in the state, Greene and his accommodationist stance on Black rights issues infuriated many Mississippi progressives including Evers, who had been a target of Greene's bile ever since taking the top NAACP job in the state. As Myrlie Evers would observe, Greene's editorial position on issues of race progress "left no doubt as to his allegiance."[21]

Van Landingham ends his lengthy surveillance memo by reporting on specifics of the Easter boycott, suggesting it was a total flop. Citing prominent Black Jacksonians as well as news reports from various locally based reporters, the former G-man concludes that the effort had limited impact. "Generally speaking, boycott was ineffectual in downtown area," he reports. "However, in outlying area close to negro districts and some credit stores accustomed to large negro trade, reported boycott was felt by them. Boycott was considered an overall failure."

Even the national press agreed that the boycott was less than successful. "In Jackson, Miss., police officials and merchants said a boycott of downtown stores, if there was one, fizzled," the Associated Press concluded in a larger story about ongoing protests throughout the South. "Several merchants claimed there were more Negroes shopping downtown than usual."[22]

It may be anticlimactic to consider the effectiveness of that 1960 Easter boycott. How, exactly, can it be measured? In his initial predictions for the boycott, Evers thought it might be 50 percent effective, whereas Reverend

Jones, who was charged with day-to-day implementation of the boycott, forecasted 70 percent. In the end, Evers believed it had been closer to Jones's number, using primarily visual data for his conclusion. Foot soldiers had been watching activities on Capitol Street and at the various chain stores throughout the week. Few Black customers were shopping at the White stores; those who did, Evers alleged, were from rural areas who came to Jackson on weekends to shop and who may not have heard about the boycott. He also cited reports of Black-owned shops "over-run . . . particularly in the field of foods and millineries." And some of the White merchants on Capitol Street "admitted that they were hard hit." In his monthly report, after summarizing the campaign's highs and lows, the NAACP field secretary simply noted, "The 'Sacrifice for Human Dignity' was a success."[23]

Perhaps it doesn't really matter how effective the boycott was. The *fact* that Evers and his allies were able to so quickly mobilize that many students—his final estimate was that seven hundred had participated in the canvassing—hold a press conference, get publicity, and mount a significant challenge to the existing order was an impressive accomplishment, an announcement that a new day had arrived in Mississippi's capital city. The Negroes were not at all satisfied; nor were they complacent or compliant. In fact, they were just getting started.

Colia Liddell, one of the founders of the Tougaloo College NAACP chapter, agreed. She was there at the start, when stirrings of the need to stand up to Mississippi's racist practices began. And she participated in the Easter boycott, the leafleting, and much that would follow, including preparations for the Tougaloo Nine protest. Liddell estimated the effectiveness of the Easter boycott at a more likely 35 percent. More importantly, she understood the boycott's broader significance: "At least for us," Liddell noted years later, "it was the beginning."[24]

WADE IN THE WATER

Before the Easter boycott was technically over—Easter Sunday was April 17 that year—members of Mississippi's Gulf Coast NAACP initiated their own campaign for human dignity. Perhaps inspired by the speed with which Evers was able to gather his forces for the boycott, two professional Black NAACP members from the Mississippi coast sparked what many now consider the first "direct-action" mass protest in the state. To say it was a planned, well thought out affair might be a stretch. But on the very Easter Sunday that marked the end of one NAACP campaign in Mississippi, another one began. On that day, Dr. Gilbert Mason, long-time NAACP member and vice president of the NAACP's Mississippi State Conference of Branches, walked onto what was considered, at least by custom, the "Whites-only" beach in Biloxi. In broad daylight, the Howard University–trained doctor and former swimming star strode to the water's edge, jumped in, and went for a swim. Biloxi police arrested the good doctor and carted him off to jail.[25]

On that same day, Doctor Felix Dunn, president of the Gulfport NAACP, in sympathy and coordination with Mason's protest, took an Easter stroll on the nearby Gulfport beach with his wife and family. He was respectfully invited to leave the beach by Gulfport's mayor; the Dunns complied, and no arrests were made.

The mayor of Biloxi, however, had already proved he was not the kind of man to show such restraint. Laz Quave, who in just a few months would be appointed by Ross Barnett to serve on the states' Civil War Centennial Commission—in part because of his showdown with Mason—was a man of little tact and few social graces when it came to interacting with the Black residents of Biloxi, particularly ones he might consider "uppity." In fact, the year before, when Mason first attempted civil disobedience by swimming at the beach, Mayor Quave reprimanded him and not-so-subtly threatened him, saying, "If you go back down there on the beach, *we're going to leave you down there!*"—an obvious suggestion that some unspoken harm would come to the Black doctor if he were once again to go wading in the "Whites-only" water.

When Dr. Mason returned to the Biloxi beach for his 1960 Easter "wade-in," Mayor Quave let his law enforcement officers handle matters. Mason was charged with "disorderly conduct" (a charge usually reserved for domestic disputes or drunken brawls) and "disturbing the peace." This time it was Biloxi's police chief, Herbert McDonnell, who berated and threatened Mason, suggesting that he'd find someone to beat the NAACP official if he ever put his "ass on that goddam beach again." Mason's response to what seemed like a hollow threat by McDonnell was to call for a second "wade-in" for the following Sunday, April 24.

Although Mississippi's coastal towns and cities had a somewhat more relaxed approach to segregation than its inland rural areas—and certainly had the reputation of being laxer than the capital city of Jackson—this breach of segregation etiquette was noteworthy and, therefore, needed to be dealt with. When groups of Black residents entered the beaches in three separate locations on that following Sunday, the White brigade was ready. After allowing the bathers to get comfortable in the water and on the beach, White men with "bricks, baseball bats, pipes, sticks and chains" descended on the unsuspecting rule breakers and chased them violently away, The police chief was true to his word. His police officers, out in force, did not intervene. Instead, as would happen with later civil rights confrontations, "the law enforcement officers were just standing around," Mason reported. Black citizens could go onto the beaches and into the water, but they were on their own when it came to defending themselves against White rampaging attacks.

One immediate result of the Biloxi "wade-in" was the further awakening of Mississippi's political class to the fact that the public behavior laws they had enacted just six weeks earlier did not take into consideration all of the possible ways protest to the status quo could emerge. Within days, the Mississippi Senate toughened an already-passed house bill that sought to redefine "breach of peace" to include various emerging protest tactics such as defying a police order to disperse and refusing to leave another's premises. Both houses immediately passed the amended bill and sent it to the governor for signature. This breach-of-peace law would be the one used against the Tougaloo Nine less than a year later.[26]

The one positive outcome of the Biloxi wade-in was that it caught the attention of the national NAACP's legal team. Medgar Evers had already been alerted to the plans for the April 24 return demonstration. But "the shit hit the fan" as Mason would later describe, when he and Dunn took full advantage of the NAACP's considerable skill in making the incident into, literally, a federal case. The national NAACP's lead attorney, Robert Carter, was called in, as was their chief lobbyist, Clarence Mitchell. The two men immediately contacted the Justice Department and attempted to bring the full force of the federal government into play. Evers took affidavits from those who had been brutalized. In the end, the Justice Department filed suit against the Harrison County officials, charging them with breach of federal contracts since the beach had been created by federal funds and with the expertise of the federal Corps of Engineers.[27] Even though it would take more than twelve years for the suit to be settled definitively in the plaintiff's favor, the message had been sent. The Negroes of Mississippi would no longer docilely take whatever was served to them. The national NAACP was flexing its power in the most recalcitrant state in the nation. And Medgar Evers began to see how, with proper planning and execution, direct-action tactics could work, even in Mississippi.

JUST ANOTHER DAY'S WORK

To read the regular reports that Evers sent along to his superiors and to sift through the in-depth accounts of the incredible breadth of his work throughout the state is to conceive of a man who never stopped. He was someone who seemed to be everywhere all at once. He also knew everything that was going on. He was a one-man nerve center for those afflicted by, abused by, and tossed aside by the state. "Please help me" was, as his wife Myrlie would later write, "a cry that Medgar heard in his sleep, a cry that haunted him, that drove him to frenzies of activity, that took him into danger and brought him back weak with rage and powerlessness."

"It was," she continued, "the call that ran through the stumbling words of every affidavit, the look in the frightened eyes of a man in a jail cell, the hope in the face of a Negro child too young to know what 'Negro' meant in Mississippi."[28] And yet, despite all of this exposure to trauma, Evers somehow had an eye for educating the next generation of leaders. He never lost sight of the need to work with the youth, to bring them along, to show them how to stand up.

Take the case of Johnny Frazier and Meredith Anding. Frazier's name appears often in Evers's reports, his press releases, his notes. Frazier was a standout youth leader from the Mississippi Delta town of Greenville, located right on the banks of the great river. Greenville was the home of Hodding Carter Jr. and his *Delta Democrat* newspaper; it was known as a progressive town with what, for Mississippi, passed for liberal attitudes toward race. Frazier grew up somehow learning that the existing segregated world needed to be challenged, to be fought against, to be defeated. In his early teens, Frazier joined the Youth Council of his local Greenville NAACP branch. He eventually rose in the ranks to become the group's president, then eventually advanced to become the NAACP youth leader for the entire state. Evers rewarded his leadership by sending him, along with other promising youth, to the organization's Southeast Regional Youth Retreat held each year, generally in some remote location in the South. In 1960, that place was Keysville, Georgia, a rural outpost on the outskirts of Augusta. Evers attended the ten-day conference and drove Frazier there along with another youth leader, the future Tougaloo Nine participant Meredith Anding.

When the conference ended, Evers transported Anding and Frazier most of the way home. At some point, however, he dropped them off at a bus station in Mississippi—perhaps urgent business took him elsewhere—gave them bus fare, and cautioned his youthful protégés: "Don't be heroes going home. Sit where you're supposed to sit!" Anding followed his mentor's sound advice and made it safely back home to Jackson. Frazier, however, had a different idea. After more than a week of getting revved up over how to fight segregation, Frazier decided this was the time to make his mark, just as Evers himself had done while traveling by bus a few years earlier.[29] When the bus Frazier was riding made a brief stop in the town of Winona, Mississippi—a town that would later become infamous for its savage treatment of civil rights icon Fannie Lou Hamer—Frazier decided he needed to integrate the "Whites-only" waiting room. He never made it back onto the bus.

Frazier was beaten senseless by the sheriff and deputy sheriff of Montgomery County and thrown into jail. When he came to, he asked for his one phone call, called Medgar at his home, and asked him to come bail him out. It was Saturday night, and with cash bail set at $2,000, there wasn't much Evers could do until Monday morning. He contacted Anding to make sure he had made it home safely, then invited him to travel with him to Winona to get Frazier out.

Anding vividly recalled the scene. "I met [Medgar] at about 5:00 a.m. that [Monday] morning. We went up to the county seat to pick up Johnny. We walked in, and the sheriff said, 'What can I do for you niggers?'"

As a city boy from Jackson, Anding wasn't used to such crude talk. His eyes widened, and his face reddened. He was about to say something when Evers pulled him by the arm and firmly shifted Meredith behind him. "I just kind of reacted, but Medgar, he expected it," recalled Anding.

Evers calmly said, "We're here for the young man, Johnny Frazier."

"Yeah, we've got the nigger," the sheriff spat back, pushing Anding further toward rebellion. Evers realized that the quick-tempered youth might prove less of an asset than he thought, so after discovering that springing Frazier from jail might take longer than he had hoped, Evers ushered Anding out, and they went to get some breakfast at a nearby Black-run café. There they met one of Evers's World War II veteran comrades, Amzie Moore, a leader of the Cleveland NAACP who had driven over from his nearby Delta town about an hour away to provide moral support. According to Evers's lengthy report on the matter—fifty years later, Anding's memories were a bit fuzzy—the three then headed over to the courthouse, where a hearing was scheduled on Frazier's case.

On the short walk over, they were confronted by "a sullen crowd of white men, mostly farmers in overalls, who stared menacingly at the three of us as we talked among ourselves." Of course, the courthouse, like every other aspect of Mississippi life, was segregated. The Whites were ushered into the ground-level courtroom, while Evers, Anding, and Moore were sent upstairs into the balcony. When Johnny Frazier was trotted out in handcuffs and with no attorney to represent him, he was asked if he wanted to talk to anyone. "Yes," he said.

"Who?" he was asked.

"Mr. Evers."

The NAACP leader descended to the main level to confer with Frazier amidst a cackle of taunts. He could see with his own eyes that Frazier's injuries were worse than the youth could have explained in a phone call from the sheriff's office. Evers suggested that Frazier plead not guilty so as to preserve his right to appeal. Frazier then represented himself before the judge—a justice of the peace—and was given the opportunity to cross-examine the arresting sheriff and deputy who had brutalized him. Frazier described his treatment by the cops and then asked the deputy "Are you a Christian?" The law officer fumbled for an answer until the judge came to his defense, ruling the question out of line and unrelated to the case. To the sheriff, Frazier pointedly asked, "Did you not call me a 'nigger'?"

"Yes, I called you a 'nigger,'" came the sheriff's swift reply. "That's what you are! A 'nigger'!"

The crowd of White spectators came to life with jeers, as if they were witnessing a comedy routine. In the end, Frazier was convicted for disorderly conduct and resisting arrest, fined twenty-five dollars for each charge and a twenty-three-dollar court fee. Evers urged Frazier to notify the judge immediately that he intended to appeal the charges. This was granted, but to get Frazier released, the cash-strapped Evers had to come up with the additional court fees. Frazier waited in a holding cell for most of the rest of the day while the NAACP field secretary dropped Anding back at the café and then scrambled back to Jackson to grub up the funds. Returning to Winona after the courthouse had closed, Evers had a difficult time getting the sheriff to release Frazier. Most likely, the soft-spoken Evers appealed to the sheriff's sense of decency, noting Frazier's youth and, with a deft touch, referring to his need for medical attention due to the treatment the teen had received at the hands of Winona's finest. The sheriff finally relented and told Frazier, still in his bloody T-shirt, to "get out of town!"

The two then walked over to the café to retrieve Anding, who had spent the afternoon thinking over his poor showing with the sheriff earlier in the day. "Even though at the regional meeting they train you, you know? They tell you what *not* to do and how *not* to react, *not* to fight back. But when I reacted to the sheriff, it was just instantaneous! The training just didn't pop in!" Once all three were in the car, Evers did his best to get them to safety. "Before we could get out of town," he later wrote, "three cars made it their business to check our every move, and as we proceeded to the city limits, we were followed quite some distance by these cars."

For Anding, the experience was disconcerting. "Johnny's T-shirt had blood and all of that kind of stuff . . . and a car fell in behind us. I was scared! Probably as scared as I've ever been. Medgar had a .45 pistol, and he pulled it out from under the seat. And so now I'm thinking, 'OK, you're in over your head. We're getting ready for violence!' They followed us for five or six miles and just turned off."

Without further harassment, the three weary freedom fighters made it safely to Greenville, where a shaken but triumphant Frazier walked into the arms of his worried parents. Rather than risk the 120-mile nighttime drive back to Jackson, Evers decided that he and Anding would stay overnight at the home of an NAACP supporter that Evers bunked with when visiting the river town. "Had a great breakfast" the next morning, Anding recalled, and the two refreshed agitators made their way back to Jackson.[30]

Meredith Anding might have found the experience of springing his friend from jail harrowing, but what Evers had introduced his young follower to was the harsh reality of working for civil rights in Mississippi. It *was* harrowing and shocking and deeply troubling; yet Evers faced these horrible odds day after day after day. One wonders how he coped. What inner strength allowed him to calmly face down Mississippi's psychotic racial climate. That really is the only word for it: "psychotic." Myrlie Evers said it best: "For Mississippi is the state with the split personality, and it bequeaths this psychosis to many of its sons and daughters."[31]

For Evers, however, this was just another day's work. And he got up the next day to sally forth again into this troubling, maddening Mississippi mire. Unbelievable. Incredible. And all too true. Anding would remember this experience when it was his turn to face the police and later appear in a Mississippi courtroom after the library sit-in. Thanks to his mentor, Anding would be ready for his own ordeal with Mississippi justice.

Chapter 11

A CHANGE IS GONNA COME

MEDGAR EVERS SEEMS NEVER TO HAVE RESTED DURING THIS PERIOD OF intense movement development. In June and again in September 1960, he testified before the federally created Mississippi Advisory Committee to the US Commission on Civil Rights about the state's impossible racial situation. In July, he spearheaded a public relations campaign skewering the state Sovereignty Commission for funneling $20,000 of state funds to the Citizens' Councils to continue their campaign of ensuring staunch adherence to Mississippi's segregationist laws and practices. He kept up with a myriad of investigations of abuse by Whites seeking to terrorize their Black fellow citizens. One of these included the emasculation and murder of a Black laborer in Amite County in the southwestern part of the state. Another was the second "harassment" arrest of Otis Smith, head of the Tougaloo College Chapter of the NAACP, who had been one of the student leaders of the Easter boycott campaign. It must have been a relief when Evers received an invitation in September from the chairman of the Tougaloo College's Student Political Action Committee to provide his thoughts on Mississippi's racial and political climate and what Tougaloo students could do during the coming school year to help advance his agenda for change.[1]

The committee met on Thursday, October 6, in the peaceful setting of Tougaloo's Woodworth Chapel, and all students were invited to attend. About two hundred showed up to hear the man who had orchestrated the Easter boycott the prior spring. It was a reunion, of sorts, and many were eager to hear what Evers might be planning for the coming school year. Of course, he talked about the results of the Easter boycott and his desire to boycott the upcoming segregated Mississippi State Fair, held every year in Jackson in October. He also mentioned the recent public-school desegregation lawsuit that the NAACP had entered into on behalf of his own family and several other Jackson parents of school-aged children. He discussed the upcoming presidential election and his desire to turn out a record number of Black voters. And undoubtedly, he talked up membership in the Tougaloo College Chapter of the NAACP as the most direct way for those present to get involved in the movement for racial equality within the state.[2]

For one new student, Joseph Jackson, what Evers had to say was mesmerizing. "Just the idea that someone of his stature was coming before us," Jackson recalled. "It didn't take long for him to inspire us." While listening to Evers lay out his program for change, Jackson realized "you never heard anyone else speaking like that!" Finally, someone was speaking his language—a well-thought-out plan to make things better for Black people, not only in Mississippi but throughout America. Joe Jackson was instantly sold. "After listening to Medgar explain the challenges he was faced with and the plans he had for (the city of) Jackson," the young student preacher recounted, "I wanted to become a part of it."

Jackson's wish didn't take long to fulfill. Sometime during the following week, a meeting was held for all those who had signed up or recommitted to the Tougaloo College chapter. Jackson was eager to attend to find out how to begin making the change he so deeply wanted to see. At that meeting, it was discussed that because Otis Smith was facing serious criminal charges for what were likely false claims that he had been stealing cars along "the Natchez Trace Lover's Lane," it might be wise, at least reputationally, to have a new president of the chapter until the charges were resolved. An election was proposed and held during that very meeting—Joseph Jackson's first-ever NAACP involvement. And who was nominated for the position? The studious, well-spoken Joseph Jackson himself!

The young preacher could hardly believe that he was hearing his name put into nomination. "I had no idea that the members of the NAACP Youth Chapter were going to elect me president!" Jackson would exclaim years later. "I'm thinking that they're going to elect, you know, a Mississippian—maybe a junior, maybe a senior. I was a sophomore. And low and behold, they elect me!"

Although the move shocked the newly initiated freedom fighter, the choice was no surprise to one particularly observant member of the chapter, Geraldine Edwards. "I was impressed by Joe Jackson," she would later recall. "He was an older student, he was going toward the ministry, he was studious, and he was a very handsome young man." Years later, Jackson would remember something Geraldine had said during a reunion event of the Tougaloo Nine. "There was a focus about you," she told him. "Not only your focus, but it was your presence. You had a presence about you." For whatever reason, the members of the Tougaloo College Chapter decided that this newcomer could guide them during this new era of social change, even in the seemingly intractable setting of Jackson, Mississippi.

One person who seemed desperate for that change to come to the state's capital city was Medgar Evers. Not long after Joe Jackson's installation as president of the Tougaloo College Chapter, Evers wrote to Dr. Gilbert Mason, the leader of the Biloxi movement. Mason was proposing to file a desegregation suit against the city of Biloxi school system, and Evers was trying to get the assistance of the national NAACP for this new initiative. Evers was impressed with what Mason was doing on the coast and wanted to somehow get that same level of commitment and activism started in his base of operation. In what may be one of Evers's most unguarded and heartfelt moments, he shared with Mason that "I am anxious to get something going here in Jackson to the point that *I am willing to risk even life itself.*"[3] Evers knew he was playing with fire. Nevertheless, in time, he would help coax Joe Jackson and the students from Tougaloo into the lion's den and shift the movement in Mississippi's capital city into a higher gear.

ALFRED COOK AND THE STATE FAIR BOYCOTT

At about the same time as Joseph Jackson's installment as president of the NAACP's Tougaloo College Chapter, a dozen or so miles away in West Jackson, another plan was hatching to stir the local Black populace to push for equality. Alfred Cook—still at Campbell College—and his like-minded friends had been encouraged by the impact of their Sacrifice for Human Dignity Easter boycott. As Student Council president—and in consultation with Evers and Campbell College dean Charles Jones—Cook and his school mates organized the Student Committee for Human Dignity to help continue the push for equal treatment in all aspects of Jackson civic life. The committee's first target? The segregated Mississippi State Fair. Held annually at the State Fairgrounds, located directly behind the historic Old State Capitol Building—the same structure that would play an outsized role in the state's Civil War Centennial observance a few months later—the Mississippi State Fair was a ten-day extravaganza. It was a carnival open to all of the state's citizens—though on a segregated basis—and thousands flocked to it from Mississippi's rural areas as well as from its urban centers. Like any state fair, particularly one with a majority agricultural economic base, there were livestock and 4-H demonstrations and prizes for the best-bred cows, goats, sheep, and chickens. Families came from miles around to enjoy a day at the fairgrounds, have some cotton candy, get taken for suckers in some shooting game or hoop toss, ride the Ferris wheel, maybe win a stuffed animal, and return home tired but happy. It was a time to relax a little from the daily cares and woes of life. It was a cheap way to escape into a fantasy land of bright lights and hot, buttered popcorn. It was pure joy.

In earlier years, the fair had been held at the fairgrounds for White people and then relocated to the Negro section of town for the state's Black citizens.

Cost cutting forced a shift in logistics, and it was decided that the event would stay at the fairgrounds, with the first week opened exclusively to Whites and the final three days opened to Blacks. The shift felt like a diminishment for the Black attendees. They were an afterthought. They were invited in after Whites had enjoyed the fair, dirtied up the grounds, taken all the good prizes, and then left the dregs for their darker-skinned neighbors. It was an insult.

Al Cook and his crew, most of whom had participated actively in handing out leaflets to promote the Easter boycott, saw the fair as the perfect next target for their ire. They called for a boycott of the Negro State Fair—the three days tacked on at the end. Again, leaflets were distributed, and Jackson's Black residents were urged to stay away from the fair. "We believe that no Negro person who believes in human dignity and democracy will participate in or attend the Mississippi State Fair for Negroes this year."[4]

The Mississippi NAACP issued a statement backing the students' project: "All people who believe in human dignity will support these students in this fight against discrimination and bigotry."

"It's not fair that Negroes have to have a separate Fair here when that's not done anywhere else, not even in county fairs around the state," said Tougaloo junior Eugene Carter during a press conference called by the NAACP to announce the boycott.

"There is ample space for people of all races during the Fair," Evers chimed in, "and relegating Negroes to a special period works undue hardship on us. It is purely a result of prejudice and discrimination."

But Evers hedged his bets on this first fair boycott, saying "I don't expect we'll get one hundred percent cooperation, but you can be sure the support among students and many adults will be considerable. This is just the beginning."

Press reports about the fair boycott suggest that it was less than a rousing success. "Despite rumors circulated Sunday afternoon of an intended 'student boycott' of Fair gates," *The Clarion-Ledger* noted, "attendance was actually heavier than generally anticipated on the first day." Percy Greene's *Jackson Advocate* was even more direct: "According to observers we talked to . . . and what we saw . . . the crowd was the biggest ever before seen at the fair."[5]

Not to worry. Evers knew he and the students were just getting their feet wet. Just as with the Sacrifice for Human Dignity, there had been no picketing or outward display of protest at the fairground gates to dissuade Black customers from entering. Just a simple announcement followed up with a press release. The Jackson freedom brigade would have to up their game if they were to begin getting the hoped-for results.

In the aftermath of the first attempted boycott of the Negro State Fair— there were to be at least two more, each more successful than the previous— Evers began searching for his next target. He was beginning to realize that pressure needed to be consistently applied for any change to occur in the hidebound political center of the state. But what would stir things up while at the same time keeping participants relatively safe from Mississippi's brutal racial reprisal system? He wasn't exactly sure. But he knew for certain that the kids at Tougaloo would have some ideas and most likely would become part of the solution.

HOW ABOUT A LIBRARY SIT-IN?

Gunnar Myrdal doesn't spill much ink talking about libraries in his magnum opus *An American Dilemma*. What he does report is damning enough, though. In chapter 15, titled "The Negro in the Public Economy," he wrote, "There is an amazing discrimination against Negroes in the segregated school system of the South. Virtually the whole range of other publicly administered facilities—such as hospitals, libraries, parks, and similar recreational facilities—are much poorer for Negroes than they are for whites." And, "Damaging from both cultural and recreational viewpoints are the restrictions of public library facilities for Negroes. In 1939 it was found that of 774 public libraries in 13 Southern states only 99, or less than one-seventh, served Negroes. Of the 99 libraries, 59 were concentrated in four states." These states, he tucked in a footnote, were Virginia, Kentucky, Texas, and North Carolina. This meant, of course, that there were only forty libraries that Black residents could access in the remaining nine states of the South, including Mississippi. Myrdal also noted, "It was estimated that only 21 per cent of the Negroes in these 13 [Southern] states had access to public library services."[6]

Later, in a chapter titled "Social Segregation and Discrimination," Myrdal compared the types of social segregation practiced in the North versus the South, and observed, "Most other public facilities—such as libraries, parks, playgrounds—are available to Negroes with about the same amount of discrimination and segregation, in the various regions of the country, as in schools. Negroes are not permitted to use these in the South unless they are acting in a servant capacity. Many Southern cities have separate parks, playgrounds and libraries for Negroes, but in all cases they are poor substitutes for those available to whites."[7] Is it any wonder, then, that the libraries and parks would become key targets for racial protest?

The concept of a sit-in at a library wasn't exactly a novel idea in 1961. Ever since libraries became public, tax-supported institutions, Black people had been wanting to find points of entry. Perhaps the earliest nonviolent demonstration to gain admittance to a Southern "Whites Only" bastion of books was the 1939 Alexandria, Virginia, library sit-in.

The protest was orchestrated by Black attorney Samuel Tucker, a twenty-six-year-old native of the city located just across the Potomac River from Washington, DC. Because of segregation laws, Tucker, in his youth, had been forced to attend high school in DC rather than at the one reserved for Whites just four blocks from his home. Tucker later graduated from Howard University and studied for the bar at the Library of Congress and the DC Public Library, both of which by then were open to Blacks. In 1937, the city of Alexandria opened a new, well-equipped public library less than two blocks from Tucker's family residence, but he was barred from entering it because of his race. While at Howard, Tucker had learned of the nonviolent tactics used by Mohandas Gandhi and his followers to gain political rights in India. He was also aware of the US labor movement's use of sit-down strikes to improve working conditions. Fed up with the strictures of segregation in his hometown, Tucker decided to try to stage a nonviolent protest at the library. In March 1939, Tucker convinced a friend—a retired army sergeant—to go with him to the new library and request a library card.[8]

When the two men entered the "Whites-only" facility on Queen Street and asked for library cards, they were denied. Expecting the brush off, they simply left, but Tucker then filed suit to force the library's hand. While awaiting the outcome of his legal challenge, Tucker convinced several younger Black residents of Alexandria, including his younger brother, to stage a sit-in at the library. In a scene similar to the one later staged more than twenty years later in Jackson, five well-dressed young Black men successively approached the librarian, asked to apply for a library card, and when refused, walked over to the aisles of books, picked one off the shelves, and sat down to read.

Alarmed, the librarian rushed to the library director's office shouting, "Oh mercy! . . . There's colored people all over the library!" Police were called, and the youth were ordered to leave. None budged, whereupon they were arrested and taken to jail. A long court battle ensued; results were not immediate. Alexandria's libraries were finally opened to all citizens on an equal basis in 1962.[9]

This was just the first of many large and small efforts by Black citizens to gain access to their local libraries. In his autobiography, *Walking with the Wind*, civil rights icon John Lewis, who loved to read, described his ardent desire to gain a library card from the small-town library of Troy, Alabama. "There was the public library, where I longed to go, but through whose doors I was not allowed to set foot. That killed me, the idea that this was a *public* library, paid for with government money, and I was supposedly a US citizen, but I wasn't allowed in. Even an eight-year-old could see there was something terribly wrong about that."

At age sixteen, Lewis decided it was time to address this inequity. "I didn't hate the librarian at the Pike County Public Library who turned me away—very politely—when I walked up to her desk in the spring of [1956] and said I would like to apply for a library card so I could check out a book. I knew I would be refused. But that was the first step of the first formal protest action of my life." Being refused that card was the affront that radicalized the future chairman of the Student Nonviolent Coordinating Committee.[10]

Along those same lines, the future executive director of Martin Luther King Jr.'s organization, the Southern Christian Leadership Conference (SCLC), Wyatt Tee Walker, also had a library story. Though born and reared in the North, Walker went South to Richmond to attend college at segregated HBCU Virginia Union University. After college, Walker became pastor of Gillfield Baptist Church—one of the oldest Black churches in the country—twenty-five miles south of Richmond in Petersburg. From that pulpit, Walker began agitating for change. He joined and later became president of the local chapter of the NAACP. In 1957 he helped form Dr. King's Southern Christian Leadership Conference, eventually serving on its national board.

By 1959, Walker had built up enough of a following that he was able to rally Petersburg's citizens to take action; his first target—the public library. That summer, Walker marched through the Petersburg Public Library's front door and strategically requested Lost Cause historian Douglas Southall Freeman's hagiographic and Pulitzer Prize–winning biography of Robert E. Lee. He was, of course, refused service at the front desk. Instead, he was politely instructed to go to the basement, where Negroes were served. Walker left, but rather than visit the poorly lit, dingy basement reading room, Walker instead instructed the NAACP to file suit against the city council in what would turn out to be a protracted legal battle. When the student sit-ins began the following year, one of the first targets for student protesters against segregation in Petersburg was the library. On February 27, 1960, more than 140 high school and college students descended upon the Petersburg library, found ample reading material, and eagerly started to read. Rather than integrate, the city manager closed the library. The standoff that ensued made national headlines. In November 1960, after months of protests, arrests, and lawsuits, the Petersburg City Council agreed to reopen the library on an integrated basis.[11]

It is doubtful that any of these examples were known by the students at Tougaloo College in early 1961. Nevertheless, for such a volatile racial environment as Jackson, Mississippi, staging a demonstration at a library rather than at a lunch counter or a park made perfect sense. First of all, libraries were places of quiet and repose. No one entered the library to make a ruckus. They were viewed as safe spaces—aloof from the hustle and bustle of daily life. Second, it was unlikely that a large, hostile crowd would develop within the walls of a library, at least not like those that typically congregated at the many lunch-counter sit-ins that had been staged throughout the South—some of which had turned shockingly violent. Third, as Medgar Evers often remarked, public libraries, as well as public parks and public swimming pools, were funded by tax dollars paid by *all* citizens, not just Whites. Therefore, it could reasonably be argued that Black residents had a right to use the library in exactly the same way as Whites did because their tax dollars helped to fund the facilities.

The best that can be surmised about the genesis of the Tougaloo Nine demonstration is that after Joseph Jackson assumed leadership of the NAACP Tougaloo College Chapter, ideas began to get batted around about how to challenge Mississippi's strict racial codes. Years later, there were various opinions about how the idea of a library sit-in rose to the top. Some, like Ethel Sawyer and Geraldine Edwards, remember standing around on the sidewalks outside their dorms talking about the fact that no substantive student demonstration had yet happened in Mississippi. "Shouldn't we be doing something?" they asked.

Some suggest the idea came from a student bull session—or perhaps during one of the regular NAACP College Chapter meetings on campus. Meredith Anding suggested that the idea was one floated initially by West Jackson Youth Council members after their nonstarter sit-in at the Jackson Zoo. Anding conjectured that he might have even mentioned the idea at one of the few Tougaloo NAACP meetings he attended.

Sam Bradford and Al Lassiter believed the idea was derived from a composite of suggestions from Evers combined with input from the College Chapter students and their on-campus mentors. "We were advised by Dr. Borinski, John Mangram, and ultimately Medgar Evers," Bradford recalled. "We kicked around what we might do—Medgar *and* us. We concluded that since the public library was supported by tax dollars, we could make the case for going there."

"Right!" chimed in Lassiter. "It would be commensurate with college students. Nobody could argue with that."

"And besides," Sam concluded, "a library would be quite different from other places people were protesting about."

Joe Jackson, on the other hand, had no doubt about where the idea for the library sit-in came from: Medgar Wiley Evers. "This was *his* brainchild," Jackson firmly stated. Nearly sixty years later, Jackson could still remember Evers standing at the lectern in Woodworth Chapel as he calmly laid out his plan. "Now, we are going to be involved in a sit-in demonstration in the city library of Jackson." And, Joe Jackson said, the Mississippi field secretary began describing exactly how he saw the demonstration unfolding.

But Alfred Cook vehemently insisted that it was *he* who brought the idea of a library sit-in to Evers and to his fellow Tougaloo students once he transferred from Campbell College that fall. The idea, he said, came from his frustration over having to use the inadequate College Park branch library, designated specifically for Black patrons and located on the first floor of the College Park Auditorium on Lynch Street, just steps away from his Campbell College dorm. Cook knew of the better-equipped libraries throughout the city, the ones reserved only for Whites. And though he realized books could be ordered from any branch and delivered for pickup by him at the College Park location, Cook bristled at the inconvenience and even more at the unfairness of it all. "My [grand]parents paid taxes for seventy years in Mississippi before they died. And those monies went to support those libraries, yet we could not go! I just couldn't accept that. And I thought that would be a good target for us."[12] Cook, of course, already knew Evers from their work together on the Sacrifice for Human Dignity. He said he brought the idea to the NAACP leader's attention soon after he transferred to Tougaloo.

For her part, Geraldine Edwards admitted that even though the idea for the sit-in may have come from the students, "we needed some strong advisors and leaders to pull the planned caper off. Thankfully," she observed, "we had both Medgar Evers and John Mangram who were dedicated to the cause."[13]

PREPARING FOR THE BIG DAY

Perhaps it doesn't really matter how the idea came into being. As historian John Dittmer jokingly told a group gathered to celebrate the fiftieth anniversary of the Jackson library sit-in, "There are lots of creation stories about the Tougaloo Nine—and they're all true!"

What is certain is that beginning in November, the group that would come to be known as the Tougaloo Nine, and their supporters began meeting regularly with Medgar Evers and Reverend John Mangram in the chapel to plan strategy, practice what-if scenarios, and get "brainwashed" as Joe Jackson put it, in the practices of nonviolent resistance.

Evers asked each of the initial two-dozen or so volunteers if they could handle the expected harassment without reacting. "Can you not fight back if you are hit or kicked?" Al Lassiter remembered Evers quizzing each of the volunteers. "'Can you just ball up on the floor or block a punch?' He interrogated and prepped us." There were some who figured they might not be able to stay nonviolent, and they were weeded out. Better to have them stay in the background as support rather than risk breaking discipline. Besides, Lassiter pointed out, "If you fought back, you might get killed!"

Nearly every single participant in the library sit-in had this same observation. Because this type of open resistance to established norms had never been attempted in Mississippi's capital city, the price for their brazen behavior might be steep. Years later, when asked to articulate the potential cost of such open resistance to Mississippi's strict racial codes, a flummoxed Sam Bradford loudly blurted out a single word: "*Death!!!*"

It was just a small group that met regularly with Evers and Mangram once the training got underway. No more than twenty-two participated, said Colia Liddell, who was excited to see an idea finally coming to fruition that might really grab attention and challenge the entrenched Jim Crow system. "It was happening!" exclaimed Liddell. "It was on!"

The meetings were generally held in the Chapel under Reverend Mangram's supervision and always on the down low. "You couldn't shout out loud what you were doing," Lassiter pointed out. "But word would get around."

The group wasn't exactly sworn to secrecy, but they knew what they were about to undertake was unprecedented, and they realized that stealth would be an important element of the plan's success. So, the group generally only talked about their plans amongst themselves and tried to keep a lid on outside speculation—particularly with faculty—in order not to spoil their plans.

The date for the sit-in seems to have been kept secret, as well. According to Liddell, a date in January was scuttled when somehow word of the planned demonstration leaked, and police got wind of it. After that, Evers and Mangram decided to keep the proposed date to themselves until just before the day approached. They simply told the students to be ready.[14]

By mid-February, however, the sit-in seems to have taken a back seat to other college activities. Two of the Nine, Albert Lassiter and Evelyn Pierce, were part of a delegation of eight Tougaloo students who traveled to Austin, Texas, along with Reverend Mangram, as representatives to a YMCA and YWCA convention being held on the campus of the University of Texas. (The "Y" organizations were important sources for recreation and leadership development for both the Lassiter family in Vicksburg and the Pierce family in Laurel.)[15]

In the run up to the sit-in, Meredith Anding recalled attending a meeting of the NAACP Tougaloo College Chapter in the chapel one evening just a week or so before the demonstration took place. After the meeting, Meredith walked out into the night air to find a campus-wide "serenade" in progress. "There were maybe three or four hundred students out that night," he recalled. It was "a really good rally," Anding recounted, where "some of the more prominent and popular students would speak." Although none of the specifics of time or place for the sit-in had been shared with the wider student body, it was well known that some sort of demonstration was in the works. One speaker after another declaimed the necessity of standing up and being counted in the coming fight for freedom. "It was very 'rah-rah.'" Meredith recalled. "You would have thought that there would have been ten thousand people going to the library!"

Evers had been attending the earlier NAACP chapter meeting and exited the chapel with Anding. It was there that he suggested to Anding that he would be a good candidate to participate in the planned sit-in, although at that point, no specific date had been announced, nor had Anding committed to participating. In fact, Anding believed several dates had been floated—the 29th of March, April 4th—in order to throw the opposition off should they get wind of the plan. He explained, "Whenever there was any kind of activity planned, any show of resistance, somebody within the Black community would always tell. So [the opposition] always knew, and they were always prepared." He understood that Evers's fuzziness about the date would ensure that when the big moment came, the students' action would be a bolt out of the blue. "We caught them off guard," Anding said with a smile years later.

Despite the delay, preparations for the library sit-in continued, either at Reverend Mangram's home or at the Woodworth Chapel, even though there was no fixed date for the showdown. "Reverend Mangram was devoted and kept the operation on campus moving forward," Geraldine recalled.

For Joe Jackson, the repeated run through of what might happen when they entered the library—what could happen when the police arrived, what was likely to happen should a crowd of hostile White citizens surrounded them—only fed into his trauma over what had happened to his mother and the White bus driver when Joe was a child and powerless to protect her. "It really brought out that inner rage within me that I had suppressed for a long time going back to when I was eleven years old," Jackson recalled. "When those (NAACP) members acted out the behavior of those Whites, they spit on us. They called us 'niggers.' They pushed us. They got in our faces." The intensity of these mock demonstrations had their intended effect. They steeled the nerves of the would-be demonstrators, pushed them to work through their anger and resentment at Whites, and strengthened their resolve to see this thing through. "We were so mentally prepared, we were like Zombies," Joe Jackson said. "At least I was."

Medgar Evers was never one to get ahead of himself, and he even managed to keep from his superiors the date and time for the planned demonstration. But seeing the need to prepare for what he saw as the legal battle ahead—assuming the students would be arrested—Evers contacted the NAACP's general counsel, Robert Carter, to seek the organization's assistance.[16] In mid-March, Evers wrote his colleague that "at long last we are about to commence direct protests against racial segregation in Mississippi, Jackson in particular."

Just those words must have given the civil rights leader much satisfaction, particularly given his recently settled battle with nemesis Charles Darden. But even here Evers was vague about the timing and the exact form these protests might take. "Our moves will be directed against public conveyances, terminals (including air terminal café), public library and parks."

Although he provided no specific date, Evers acknowledged that he was currently working "to secure bondsmen" and said he had already contacted local lawyers Jess Brown and Jack Young, "who have agreed to work with us in these cases." He went on to say that Brown and Young believed that they would need legal advice from the national office, particularly should the potential court cases need to be appealed. Of course, Evers also requested that the national office help with legal fees. He then carefully noted that "the youth are planning to make their move before Easter" and asked Carter to contact Brown and Young "immediately." Direct-action protest in Jackson was imminent.[17]

Chapter 12

MISSISSIPPI PREPARES FOR A RAUCOUS CELEBRATION

AS 1961 DAWNED, THE NATIONAL CIVIL WAR CENTENNIAL COMMISSION took center stage in a series of events meant to draw attention to the commemoration and the four-year-long saga it had been formed to honor. The national commission's first public memorial occurred on Sunday, January 8, 1961, at the tombs of the war's most celebrated generals, Grant and Lee. The dual ceremony was intended to demonstrate national unity by honoring the martial heroes of both North and South. Two of the commission's highest-caliber members—Chairman U. S. Grant III for the North and commission vice chairman and US congressman William M. Tuck for the South—played prominent roles in the ceremonies, simultaneously held in New York City (at the extraordinarily elaborate Grant Tomb on the Upper West Side just off the Hudson River) and in a small town in the Shenandoah Valley where Lee's remains are buried beneath a modest chapel that bears his name on the campus of Washington and Lee College (now University) in Lexington, Virginia.

Both ceremonies dripped with Lost Cause romanticism and reunionist rhetoric, but in an attempt at regional reconciliation, each gave credit and honor to both prominent generals. In New York, the weather was bitter and cold. "A chill wind blew in off the Hudson," *The New York Times* reported, and "flurries of snow swept through the ranks." More than fifteen hundred federal troops in full dress uniform were assembled to honor the Northern conqueror whose military genius preserved the Union. "We humbly repent the bitterness that turned brother against brother," the Reverend William R. Robbins—chaplain to the Military Order of the Loyal Legion, a fraternity of Union officers and their heirs—proclaimed during his opening benediction. Grant III, suffering from a cold—no small thing for a man of seventy-nine—abbreviated his prepared remarks in the frigid thirty-degree weather to simply indicate that the importance of the Civil War commemoration was to remember that the "country was able to reunite after four years of strife." He then placed a wreath at his grandfather's tomb, under the embossed emblem that came to characterize President Grant's postwar perspective, "Let

Us Have Peace." Afterward, the West Point Military Academy Band played "America the Beautiful."

In a gesture of sectional amity, Grant sent a prearranged telegram to Tuck honoring Lee's memory. Tuck read it at the opening of his remarks in Lexington: "WE PAUSE HERE TO PAY TRIBUTE TO A VERY GREAT GENTLEMAN WHO ADVANCED THE AMERICAN IDEAL OF LIVING IN HONOR, IN DIGNITY, IN UNION, AND IN FREEDOM," the telegram read. "I DIRECT THESE REMARKS TO THE TRADITION THAT IS ACCEPTED AND TREASURED AS AN AMERICAN IDEAL . . . COMPLETE DEVOTION TO THE MEMORY AND THE LEGEND OF ROBERT E. LEE."

Tuck sent a corresponding conciliatory telegram to Grant III, which apparently was not read due to the chilly conditions: "MY THOUGHTS ARE WITH YOU ON THIS OCCASION WHEN TRIBUTE IS BEING PAID TO THE MEMORY OF YOUR ILLUSTRIOUS GRANDFATHER. WE PRAISE HIM HERE IN THE SOUTH AS A MAGNANIMOUS LEADER. HE WAS DEDICATED TO THE PRINCIPLE OF AMERICAN UNITY TO WHICH WE ALL SO HEARTILY SUBSCRIBE TODAY."

In his remarks at Lee's chapel, Tuck honored Grant III for "extolling the virtues of our great leaders, North and South" and noted, "This is a great day for America." In true reconciliationist style, Tuck declared that the centennial would provide the country with an opportunity to "look back into our history and to evaluate anew the great test of a century ago that threatened to tear us apart, but, in the end, brought us closer together."[1]

The day was filled with the tolling of church bells throughout the nation, including the bells of the famed Riverside Church, just across the street from Grant's tomb, as well as those at the little chapel in Lexington.[2]

MISSISSIPPI DELAYS

Mississippi had planned to be the first state commemoration out of the gate on the day following the official opening of the Civil War Centennial. January 9, after all, was the actual day—one hundred years earlier—on which the Magnolia State's specially elected Secession Convention delegates decided to break ties with the Union. But Governor Barnett's relatively late formation of the Mississippi Commission on the War Between the States just six months earlier put planners at a significant disadvantage and caused them to reassess the timing of their festivities.

First off, there were not enough men signing up to march as stand-ins for their Confederate forebears in the Secession Day parade. The trouble began long before Mayor Allen Thompson convened Jackson's top business leaders in early November to try to beat the bushes for more Mississippi Greys. Even by September 1960, it was becoming obvious that orders for Mississippi Grey uniforms and requests for the commissioning of Mississippi Grey units were lagging far behind. By November 23, with the deadline for ordering uniforms long passed, only 723 had been paid for and delivered. Even with the additional 800 or so uniforms ordered but not yet paid for, the total number of marching men fell far short of the 10,000 hoped for. Charles Fulghum of the Mississippi Manufacturers Association had given multiple deadline extensions, but it was clear that a "fighting force" would not be raised in time for the planned Secession Day Parade in early January.[3]

Not only that, but the renovation of the Old Capitol Building had fallen behind schedule, as such major projects are wont to do. Charlotte Capers could not assure the commission that the Old House of Representatives chamber, where the three-day debate over Mississippi's decision to secede from the Union took place, would be ready in time for the reenactment. In addition, the weather was a concern. Who had decided that early January would be the best time for an outdoor parade? As the problems mounted, Roebuck and the Mississippi commission realized they would have to push back the date for the parade and the secession reenactment, no matter that it might not be historically precise.

From the earliest discussions of the commemoration, January 9 had been chosen for its historical significance. Had the event gone off as planned, it would have given Mississippi pride of place in having the first major state-sponsored commemoration after the January 8 national centennial kick off. Roebuck must have eaten a good deal of humble pie when reporting in late November to Barnett that the event would have to be postponed. It certainly was not for lack of trying. Since he assumed his role as executive director of the commission on July 1, 1960, Roebuck and his small staff had sent out letters to mayors of every city, town, village and hamlet in Mississippi trying to gin up interest in the centennial and playing upon their civic pride to initiate a local Mississippi Grey unit of at least forty men to march in the Secession Day Parade as well as to participate in any local commemorative events. Additional pleas were made to various civic and commemorative organizations, including the Sons of Confederate Veterans, the American Legion, VFW units, and members of the Elks clubs and Masonic lodges.[4]

The pamphlet *Join the Mississippi Greys* laid it all out. For $21.50, a prospective candidate could purchase a Confederate uniform, made with "attractive, all-cotton, gray fabric" by a Mississippi manufacturer, complete with tunic and insignia, trousers, and Confederate forage hat, all of it braided with gold and topped off with the Mississippi Centennial insignia. Special color designations were assigned for artillery, cavalry, and lowly infantry.[5]

Despite Roebuck's determination and George Godwin's public-relations prowess, the pitch fell flat. Throughout the summer, only a trickle of applications had been received for the establishment of Mississippi Grey units. But as summer turned to fall, interest began to build, and the constant beating of the Confederate drums began to arouse the locals to their "patriotic" duties. By January, applications for eighty-seven units of the Mississippi Greys had been approved and activated with about thirty-two hundred men willing to parade not only in the Secession Day events but also in any local events that may be sponsored during the centennial period. Although this was significantly fewer than the ten thousand troops hoped for, it was good enough for a decent showing.[6]

The Mississippi commission, always with an eye toward history, finally decided that the next feasible date for a commemoration would be March 28, the day one hundred years earlier that Mississippi had petitioned to become part of the Confederacy. The extra two-and-a-half months gave the "troops" extra time to prepare—some actually did train to march the two-mile parade route—and for the final touches to be put on the Old Capitol Building's renovation. Given the uncertainty surrounding the building's readiness for visitors, however, the reenactment of the secession convention was shifted to an outdoor setting on a special stage erected in front of the historic edifice's expansive entrance area. It was taken as a matter of faith that the weather would cooperate.[7]

But Mississippi couldn't allow the date of the actual centennial of its secession to pass without some sort of recognition of its historic importance, so a small indoor ceremony was held on January 9. By then, the renovation of the Old Capitol was far enough along that a small gathering was allowed inside the actual House of Representatives chamber where the original vote to secede had taken place. Members of the commission and a smattering of city, county, and state legislators, along with members of the press, entered the grand entrance to the Greek Revival Old Capitol Building and made their way to the second floor. Permanent seating had not yet been installed, so the honored guests milled around in the expansive hall gawking at its fresh, new look. Simple folding chairs had been arranged in front of a lectern; the guests would just have to make do to mark the solemn occasion.[8]

Charlotte Capers had arranged for the original, signed Ordinance of Secession, then housed and on display at the Department of Archives and History, to be on hand for the ceremony. At 10:00 a.m., the gathered group of about 150 guests took their seats as Vicksburg mayor and commission chairman John Holland rose to open the proceedings. Holland welcomed those gathered and called upon prominent Presbyterian minister Dr. Albert Sidney Johnston, nephew and namesake of the famous Confederate general, to offer a prayer. Then Holland read from the actual journal of the convention a summary of the steps that led to Mississippi's decision to break with the Union.

Governor Barnett spoke next. He had prepared a brief but pointed oration to honor the occasion, drawing a direct connection between the decisions faced in 1861 and those the state faced currently. Without mentioning racial tensions that were brimming over throughout the country—at that very time the all-White University of Georgia was being forced by a federal court order to integrate—Barnett made clear that Mississippi would likely take a hardline approach. Referring to his counterparts a century earlier, Barnett said, "Consciences were searched and divine wisdom was sought. It is a credit to our Mississippi forefathers that they chose the way of hardship because it is the way of honor." No doubt, Barnett was not so obliquely signaling that Mississippians should take the same approach on looming civil rights issues.[9]

"The period of commemoration celebrates neither the victories nor the losses of the War," he went on. "Nor does it attempt to recognize and recount the dividing forces which prompted the War. Instead, it is a period in which Mississippians of the present will honor devotion to principle, adherence to faith, and courage in adversity—qualities which served our forbearers well and can serve our generation equally as well."[10]

The local press picked up on Barnett's coded language immediately. "Drawing a parallel without going into details of today and a century ago" is how the *Jackson Daily News* described the oration. Barnett was gearing up for a battle that he knew would eventually come to his state and seemed to be seeking guidance from those who had had to make hard choices a century earlier. Little did he know that plans had already been hatched to begin the push for the integration of schools and libraries throughout the state. Within the month, James Meredith would petition to integrate the University of Mississippi; by the end of March, the Jackson Municipal Library would be breached. His decisions, particularly with regard to the Meredith affair, would be nearly as disastrous for his state as the ones taken a century before.

ALABAMA SLIPS IN

After Mississippi's ceremonial launch of the Civil War centennial, Roebuck and his staff continued furiously working to organize the bigger event now planned for the end of March.[11] Roebuck continued to urge local groups to form Mississippi Grey units so as to have a good showing for the Secession

Day Parade. And he did his best to drum up national support by corresponding with executives at all three major television networks, regaling them with specifics of the planned extravaganza and urging them to cover the proceedings.[12]

But the ten-week delay allowed Alabama to slip its centenary commemoration ahead of its rival neighboring state. And perhaps this was as it should have been. The first state to secede from the Union, South Carolina (in December 1860), would be holding its commemorative fire until mid-April, the anniversary of when its forces fired on Fort Sumter one hundred years earlier, and the actual war began. Plans were in place to light up Fort Sumter like a powder keg, this time with fireworks rather than cannon fire. In February, therefore, Alabama planned to showcase its primacy as the state that hosted the original capital of the Confederacy by reenacting the inauguration of Jefferson Davis as president of the renegade nation in Montgomery exactly one hundred years to the day, on February 18.

Indeed, the Bamas had planned an entire week of festivities leading up to the swearing-in ceremony. These included a Religious Rededication Day, a Junior Citizens' Day, and a Confederate Ladies Day. Governor Barnett was invited to attend the entire week's festivities, but he decided to fly in just for the day of the ceremonial swearing in where he could get the most media bang for his limited presence. And what a day it was. Barnett joined Governor Lindsay Almond of Virginia (author of the massive resistance campaign against integration of public schools) and Governor James Patterson of Alabama, another "Never" proponent, on the portico of the Alabama State Capitol to watch the proceedings. All three were dressed in "vari-colored" antebellum costumes and served as stand-ins for their counterparts who actually had been in attendance one hundred years earlier.[13]

A local attorney, dressed in long, black coat and high hat made a dashing appearance as the tall, lanky Davis and was sworn in by a state judge. The three governors as well as the Davis stand-in were transported in a horse-drawn surrey up Dexter Avenue—the same Dexter Avenue that houses the Dexter Avenue Baptist Church, MLK's church during the Montgomery bus boycott five years earlier—on their way to the inaugural reenactment. Of course, "Dixie" was played by minstrel bands, and a "lengthy" parade followed the ceremony, with stand in troops from various Southern states, including Mississippi and Georgia, as well as from the host state.

Alabama crowds were out in force despite a driving rain that parted briefly for the ceremonies then resumed with a vengeance during the parade that followed. A requisite Confederate Ball was held that evening, but Barnett and company by then were safely back home in Mississippi after suffering a travel scare due to the stormy weather.[14]

The troublesome weather was a bit of a preview for what would threaten to transpire in Jackson the following month. No matter. Barnett got his photo op, compared notes with other Southern governors also intent on celebrating the centennial as Confederates, and experienced a taste of what to expect when Mississippi's turn came around.

The next day, the combined *Clarion-Ledger/Jackson Daily News* Sunday edition ran a front-page photo of the three governors, Barnett in the center with a forced smile, along with a descriptive article about the events in Alabama from the day before. As if to compensate for the national attention provided to their neighboring state, the paper's editors also ran a prominent story on the editorial page touting Mississippi's upcoming ceremonies. "No State Has More to Offer for Civil War Centennial Observance" the two-column headline somewhat defensively opined, signaling to readers that the Magnolia State would not be outshone.

"No other state has more to offer in the way of history, tradition, charm and hospitality," the opinion piece concluded. "Mississippi's communities and citizens must take fullest advantage of the opportunities afforded by the Civil War Centennial which will bring thousands of welcome visitors to our midst."[15]

MISSISSIPPI UP NEXT

Work continued apace on Mississippi's soon-to-be-splashy entrance into the Centennial programming sweepstakes. It is noteworthy that the Mississippi commission chose to hold its February meeting—just one week after the Alabama Jeff Davis blowout—at Beauvior, the final home of the Confederate president, located in Commissioner Laz Quave's bailiwick of Biloxi. Perhaps they felt starved of Davisiana since only Holland accompanied Barnett to the swearing in reenactment at Montgomery. More likely, the commission was beginning to hold meetings outside of Jackson to break the monotony and to reward themselves for work accomplished thus far. (Travel expenses were typically paid for out of the commission's budget.)

Beauvoir was an interesting choice of venue. The former 608-acre cotton plantation had dwindled by 1961 to just 52 acres and was called "The Jefferson Davis Shrine." It included Davis's gravesite as well as a Confederate museum, An old soldiers home, "beautiful landscaped grounds," and a Confederate cemetery housing the remains of more than five hundred fallen Confederate military men. One could not have chosen a more symbolic Lost Cause relic of past glory and defeat. It was here that Davis spent the final years of his life, writing his two-volume *Rise and Fall of the Confederate Government* and reflecting on what might have been as he peered out over the shores of the Gulf of Mexico, which touch the property's southern border.[16]

The place also served as a lightning rod for racial tensions. During the midst of the Gulf Coast "wade-ins" the year before, a harmless, mentally challenged Black man named Bud Strong was brutally murdered—nearly decapitated—and his body was dropped in front of the Davis Shrine as a retributive White protest against the Black uprising. "Of all the places in our community to kill a black man," wade-in leader Dr. Mason later wrote, "none could have sent a more sinister or a more powerful symbolic message than Beauvoir."[17]

Nonetheless, Laz Quave, who had stoked the racial tension during the wade-ins, played the gracious host to his all-White guest list at Beauvoir. Even Governor Barnett decided to take a day and soak up the Confederate memorabilia, as did Charlotte Capers, happy to escape for a while the stresses of ensuring the Old Capitol Museum's timely restoration. With just a little more than a month before Mississippi launched its foray into Confederate boosterism, one might have thought that the meeting would be consumed with details of the parade, the pageant, and the balls. But it seems as if the Jackson Centennial Committee took on the main responsibility for these events. The only reference to the upcoming Secession Day program was a request that tours be offered of the Old Capitol during the day-long celebration. Capers, feeling confident that most of the work would be completed by late March, allowed that the tours could, indeed, be arranged.

Mayor Holland offered one other piece of news that titillated those present. On the night before the Secession Day festivities, WJTV Channel 12 would air a ninety-minute program primarily focused on the Civil War, with thirty minutes of the time devoted to a telethon to solicit funds for the raising of the Union warship, the USS *Cairo*, which Ed Bearss of the National Park Service and Ken Parks (who worked at the TV station) had discovered in the shallows of the Yazoo River back in 1956.[18] A gasp of excitement shot through the room. In addition, towns and cities that were sponsoring upcoming centennial events would be afforded time on the TV program to tell the viewing public about their plans.[19]

Other than that, the commission turned its focus to other matters, primarily the Vicksburg weekly visitations by Northern and Midwestern state delegations. Because of the rescheduling of the Secession Day program from early January to late March, there was now a conflict with the visit by the New Hampshire delegation to Vicksburg National Military Park. This schedule had been announced back in October, and invitations had already been extended. In fact, commission information director Frank Wallace had recently traveled to the Granite State to personally deliver an invitation to the governor during a New England tour that brought him to the state capitals of Rhode Island, Massachusetts, and New York for a similar Southern-charm offensive. Governor Barnett had even issued an official proclamation with all of the states and dates listed in chronological order, as if setting them in stone. Shifting the date for this first of fifteen consecutive weeks of hospitality was not an option.[20]

As it would turn out, not only would New Hampshire Week coincide with Mississippi's over-the-top Confederate salute, but also, Granite State representatives would be on hand to witness one of the state's first brushes with serious opposition to its segregationist culture. Though no one knew it yet, March 26 through April 1 was gearing up to be one of the most eventful weeks for Mississippi since it joined the Confederacy one hundred years earlier.

By early March, Sidney Roebuck had put out a press release providing the full schedule for the March 28 Secession Day celebration, including the 10:00 a.m. parade, the 1:00 p.m. Secession Reenactment, the 3:00 p.m. tea at the Governor's Mansion, and the requisite four Confederate Balls commencing at 8:00 p.m. The fuss over the rescheduling of events seemed to be entirely forgotten. The local press had offered Roebuck a lifeline early on in the crisis, applauding the decision to delay. By February, he also was getting glowing comments from Karl Betts of the national commission in Washington, DC. "Believe me," Betts cooed, "Everybody around here is talking about the magnificent planning of the Mississippi Centennial Commission." By early March, Betts was in ecstatic expectation. "Your program in Mississippi leaves me absolutely breathless," he exclaimed in a letter to Roebuck.[21] The game was on, and it was almost showtime.

THE NAACP WEIGHS IN

Roy Wilkins and his colleagues in New York read with disgust stories about the Alabama festivities and those being planned by Mississippi and other Southern states. By mid-March, he could no longer contain his frustration. He let loose with a press release condemning the direction that the Civil War Centennial was trending. "The NAACP has warned its units in 45 states that the outpouring of 'pro-South' propaganda during Civil War Centennial celebrations now underway could 'strike a hard blow at our present-day movement toward equality.'" In his communiqué to NAACP branches, Wilkins was even more direct: "The Southern states . . . have appropriated large sums of money and are going all out to present the Confederate side as effectively as possible. They see this as a great opportunity for pro-South and pro-segregation propaganda. As in the past, they hope for a great deal of success in selling to the rest of the country a distorted version based on alleged inferiority of the Negro, upholding the Confederacy and repudiating the great moral issue which lay at the bottom of the Civil War."

Wilkins instructed NAACP members to contact the head of their own state Civil War Centennial Commission and to draft press statements to register their "resentment at efforts to commemorate the Civil War with meaningless pageants and spectacles which overlook the real meaning of the War." He also called upon his members to "Make it clear that the Civil War was fought to preserve a union 'conceived in liberty and dedication to the proposition that all men are created equal. . . . ' Any celebration which does not make this plain is a dishonor to the men who laid down their lives in this country's costliest conflict."[22]

Although there is no evidence that Medgar Evers or anyone at the state NAACP operation registered a complaint with Roebuck and the Mississippi Commission, it is conceivable that Evers and Mangram saw Wilkins's statement as an endorsement of their planned library sit-in. This call to action may even have had something to do with the scheduling of the sit-in the day before the Mississippi Secession Day blowout as a preemptive strike against Southern propaganda. After all, Wilkins's statement called for "countermeasures" to thwart the South's Confederate messaging. Coming as it did just ten days before the sit-in, Wilkins's statement surely would have provided Evers with some cover should Darden or any of the other members of the state board question his move toward direct-action tactics. For Evers and Mangram, the message must have been interpreted as "full speed ahead."

Chapter 13

"WE'RE NOT SITTING STILL"

ONE WEEK BEFORE THE LIBRARY SIT-IN OCCURRED, *THE CLARION-LEDGER* ran a front-page story by enterprising reporter Jerry DeLaughter that was something of a warning of the imminent race storm. Titled "Jackson Negro Speaks: 'Second Class' Citizenship Galling to Educated Group," DeLaughter described in depth a surreptitious conversation between two non-Southern Whites and an anonymous, educated native Mississippi Black man. "While most of Mississippi's white leadership would like to believe their own statements about how satisfied Negroes in the state are with 'separate but equal' facilities," the piece begins, "the point of view in this article would seem to invalidate some of such hopes."[1]

DeLaughter then quotes the anonymous Black man's views at length.

[Mississippi's Negro leadership] intends to do everything we can in our own time and our own way to integrate the state at every level. . . . Negroes will no longer be satisfied with second class citizenship.

We're not in a big hurry about things, but we're not sitting still.

Don't you understand? As long as the law says we *cannot* do something that white people do, just because we're Negroes, then we believe that law is bad and should be changed.

Southern white people seem to think all we want to do is eat in their homes or marry their children. This is completely absurd!

The only thing—how strongly can I stress this?—the *only* thing we want to do is remove those barriers which keep us second class. Or, like white people say, "in their place."

Yes, we're going to integrate Jackson and Mississippi. We won't do it tomorrow, and we hope of course it won't be a sensational or bloodletting thing, but we're going to do it.

I believe every single informed Negro leader in the state believes that sincerely. It's not that he's angry or wants a fight. It's just that he believes that full-fledged respectability and citizenship cannot not exist—under God and the US Constitution—in the present situation in Mississippi.

The speaker ominously predicted exactly how things would unfold: "I think [White] political leaders think they've got a good thing in this hobby-horse and are going to ride it until some of us get killed. That scares us, but it doesn't stop us."

This unnamed savant even expressed empathy with the segregationists: "We can understand the background to some of the white man's prejudice. It's deep-rooted, far back [to] the Civil War. But don't you think a hundred years is long enough to wait for a prejudice to mellow into tolerance?"

The forthright statements were shocking, appearing as they did in the state's paper of record. DeLaughter and *The Clarion-Ledger* editors justified running the story by suggesting that Jackson would eventually have to face "thorny Mississippi versions of Little Rock and New Orleans" where school integration crises had caused massive confrontations and negative media attention. Importantly, DeLaughter also noted that the statements represented "an attitude not previously publicized by Negroes" and thus were worthy of front-page coverage. History does not record who exactly this native Mississippi Black leader was—he only agreed to be quoted if his name was not used—but clearly a message had been sent: "Be ready; we're coming for our rights."

The anonymous commentator's remarks dovetail with the tone of Medgar Evers's speeches, which had begun to take on a more assertive tone at the beginning of 1961. Perhaps this was due to the new NAACP state leadership under Aaron Henry, which allowed him a wider berth to speak his mind. But surely, he was also well aware of what new tactics he had up his sleeve and was also trying, in his own quiet way, to send a signal.

In mid-February, Evers spoke to the NAACP Jackson branch at a public meeting at the New Mount Zion Missionary Baptist Church, just blocks away from the Mississippi Memorial Stadium where Governor Ross Barnett would stage one of his most renowned stands for segregation eighteen months later.[2]

The reason for Evers's oration was the commemoration of Abraham Lincoln's birthday—a day that well into the twentieth century was celebrated by African Americans nationwide. It also coincided with the date of the founding of the national NAACP in 1909. Evers told the assembled crowd:

> The occasion for which we are assembled here today is a glorious one. It symbolizes a long struggle for human rights in this great country and it commemorates the beginning of an organization that has uncompromisingly led the fight for total democracy.
>
> Our job is not complete, and because we have made great strides in the field of human rights, we cannot let up now!

Today we live in an age in which man has accomplished scientifically the unbelievable. Leontyne Price sang at the Metropolitan Opera in New Your City while at the same time she was seen in her hometown of Laurel, Mississippi on television. Spaceships read about in Buck Rogers comic strips 20 years ago are realities today.

Even with this amazing advance in science and technology, man has not until this day done what God would have us do and that is: Love our neighbor as ourselves, especially if your neighbor happens to be black and the other neighbor white.[3]

Evers acknowledged that "we have a great challenge before us here in the city of Jackson" and then itemized areas where the local branch should place its focus:

- more and varied jobs for Negroes (including in factories, city employment (police and firemen), and federal employment (postal clerks, typists, office personnel);
- more registered voters;
- implementation of the US Supreme Court decision regarding schools;
- unrestricted use of public facilities such as parks and libraries; and
- removal of segregation signs at bus and train stations, as well as unrestricted seating arrangements for all passengers on city bus lines.

This is the first detailed plan of attack that Evers had laid out for the Jackson movement, and it is significant that libraries are on the list. It must also be noted that this is the first of several speeches Evers would give where he mentioned Mississippi native Leontyne Price.[4]

Price's rapid ascent in the opera world had recently landed her with her first leading role in the pinnacle of the American opera: the Metropolitan Opera in New York City. There on January 27, 1961, she debuted as Leonora in Verdi's *Il Trovatore*, for which she received a thirty-five-minute ovation—one of the longest in Met history. She took the Met by storm that season, singing in five operas, including one that would become her signature role, *Aida*.

So phenomenal was Price's assault on the cultural barriers to Black success during that period, *Time* magazine featured a multipage profile of her along with a cover illustration of the diva in all her imperious glory just weeks before the Tougaloo students made their assault on the downtown library in Jackson. Evers clearly saw Price's triumph as a sign that the time had come for Black people in Mississippi to make their move. Surely Evelyn Pierce, a Laurel native herself and someone who knew Price and her family personally, would have felt pride in her compatriot's rise and perhaps might have taken some courage from these recent developments.[5]

TWO MORE MISSISSIPPI FREEDOM FIGHTERS

The lead up to the library sit-in would not be complete without briefly profiling two additional young women from south Mississippi whose lives would be forever changed by the events surrounding the Tougaloo Nine demonstration. Their story demonstrates once again how Medgar Evers worked to develop young talent and how that preparation paid off once the Tougaloo Nine stepped into history.

These two key movers in what would play out as Jackson State College's response to its sister school's lead-off of the student demonstration era in Mississippi were sisters themselves. Dorie and Joyce Ladner hailed from the all-Black enclave of Palmers Crossing just outside of the South Mississippi city of Hattiesburg. Both would later make their marks on the Mississippi movement as important members of the Student Nonviolent Coordinating Committee (SNCC). Their actions in the wake of the Tougaloo Nine sit-in would hasten their radicalization and propel them first to transfer to Tougaloo College and then to rise up against the Mississippi political power structure that had kept them, their family, and their community in a state of perpetual poverty and submission.

Dorie Ann Ladner was born on June 28, 1942, at the home of her grandparents on what was then Royal Street (now MLK Street) in Hattiesburg.[6] It was her grandmother who named her, having been impressed, as were many Americans at the time, by the story of Dorie Miller, an African American US Navy cook who on the morning of December 7, 1941, had jumped into the seat of a wounded White antiaircraft machine gunner and, without any preparation or training, managed to shoot down at least one Japanese kamikaze plane as it attacked the ship *West Virginia* in Pearl Harbor, Hawai'i. Just one month before Ladner's birth, Dorie Miller was awarded the Navy Cross for his extraordinary bravery and clear-headedness under fire. "This marks the first time in the present conflict that such a high tribute has been made in the Pacific fleet to a member of his race," said Admiral Chester Nimitz, who pinned the medal to Miller's chest, "and I am sure that the future will see others similarly honored for brave acts."[7]

For years, no one quite understood that her name was *Dorie*. All the way through high school, her friends knew her as *Doris*. So, it wasn't until college that this young Black freedom lover would grow into her name, along with its symbol of courage under fire.

Dorie's sister, Joyce, came along a little more than fifteen months after Dorie on October 12, 1943 (coincidentally on the birthday of Dorie Miller!). Though the two were not quite what might then have been called Irish twins—two births within the same twelve-month period—their attachment was nonetheless intense. As Joyce would later recount, early on, the girls' mother "twinned" the two girls—dressing them in similar outfits and treating them as if they were both the same age. Almost as soon as Joyce could walk, she followed her older sister around wherever she went. When Dorie left for her first day of school, Joyce cried and cried, so much so that her mother, Annie Ruth, after several weeks of watching Joyce sulk around the house during Dorie's absence, finally took Joyce to school and asked the principal if the younger girl could join her sister in class. "I was three and a half years old, with one little braid on the top of my head," Joyce said with a laugh years later, "and this is the first memory of anything in my life!"

"Can't she at least come and play for a while with her sister?" Annie Ruth begged the school administrators.

The principal, a Mr. Travillion, said, "If you can have this little girl bring me a cigar tomorrow," patting little Joyce on the top of her head, "I'll see what I can do." Not taking any chances, Annie Ruth dressed both Joyce and Dorie in their finest matching Sunday dresses "with ruffles and patent leather shoes," and as Dorie went off to her first-grade class, Joyce was brought up to the principal. "Here's your cigar that you wanted, Mr. Travillion," little Joyce said, extending the thick, cellophane-wrapped stogie. Sure enough, he told the preschool teacher to accept the not-yet four-year-old into the class.

But even this wasn't enough for the young, determined Joyce. Within two weeks, the preternaturally brilliant girl had insisted repeatedly to her preschool teacher that she needed to be *with* her older sister. Eventually, the exasperated instructor marched Joyce up to Dorie's first grade classroom and deposited her there; the two would remain classmates for the next twelve years. They would prove to be the smartest of their generation of Palmers Crossing youth, with Joyce serving as valedictorian and Dorie as salutatorian at their high school graduation. The sisters then decamped to Jackson State College as both classmates and dormmates in the fall of 1960.[8]

Dorie and Joyce also learned about the Black freedom struggle together as youth when as teens they joined the NAACP Youth Chapter in Hattiesburg. Indeed, one could say that their lineage as freedom fighters extends through some of Mississippi's most ardent champions—Vernon Dahmer, Clyde Kennard, Victoria Grey, and of course, Medgar Evers. "These were the brave souls who were shepherding us along," Dorie said years later.

It was Clyde Kennard who served initially as the Hattiesburg Youth Chapter's advisor when Dorie and Joyce helped organize it in 1958. Kennard had been born in Hattiesburg but was sent to Chicago as a teen to live with his older sister to obtain a quality education. After a career in the US Army, first in Germany helping to clean up after World War II and then as a paratrooper in the Korean War, Kennard returned to Chicago and was accepted into the prestigious University of Chicago, where he came close to earning a bachelor's degree. At the end of his junior year, however, Kennard's mother begged him to come home to Mississippi to help run the family farm; her husband had died, and she needed help.

Ever the dutiful son, Kennard left school and returned home. Seeking to complete his undergraduate education at a nearby accredited college, Kennard attempted to enroll at the "Whites-only" Mississippi Southern College (now South Mississippi University). For this egregious flouting of Mississippi's rigid segregationist codes, Kennard was framed, twice, on minor law violations and eventually sent to Parchman Farm, Mississippi's hard-time penitentiary, for seven years.[9]

Between his return to Mississippi in mid-1955 and his removal to Parchman in late 1960, Kennard reengaged with the Hattiesburg Black community, teaching Sunday school at a nearby Baptist Church, and became involved with the resurgent local NAACP branch, thus entering the orbit of Medgar Evers and the Ladner girls.[10]

It was Vernon Dahmer and his sister Eileen (Dahmer) Beard, who drove Joyce and Dorie to Jackson in the late 1950s for them to attend their first statewide NAACP meeting. Dahmer was a businessman, a cotton farmer, and an active NAACP member. (He would later be killed when his home was firebombed in 1966 by the Klan for the transgression of helping Black citizens register to vote.) Eileen (Dahmer) Beard happened to be Annie Ruth's best friend. "My mother entrusted us with Ms. Dahmer and her brother to go to Jackson to go to statewide NAACP meetings," Joyce remembered. "We were just kids." Thus, the young Ladner sisters were transported from the small world of Palmers Crossing to the burgeoning flow of civil rights activism in Jackson and across the state.

It must have been at that first statewide meeting that Dorie and Joyce heard Medgar Evers speak. With his "ready smile" and his natural ability to articulate the grievances of Mississippi's Black populace, he would have spoken clearly and directly to the gathered statewide group about what they should be advocating for and why.

"All of you are paying taxes for roads and lights," Dorie recalled him saying. "There's no reason why you should have to walk in the middle of the gravel road. You should have sidewalks. You should have lights. You should have sewer lines, not outdoor toilets." All of these claims resonated with the Ladners, as did "Mr. Evers's" easy way of connecting with the youth. "He had the ability to make you feel comfortable," Dorie remembered. "And so, somehow we were able to meet him one on one and to form this kind of communication with him."

JACKSON STATE COLLEGE

The Ladners' occasional visits to Jackson also brought them into the orbit of Jackson State College, literally across the street from Evers's NAACP office on Lynch Street in the Black Masonic Temple where all of the statewide NAACP meetings were held. When it came time for the girls to pick a college, therefore, Jackson State seemed like the logical choice. "Halleluia!" shouted Dorie when she heard she had been accepted. She would be leaving little Palmers Crossing behind and bringing her lifelong companion, younger sister Joyce, along with her.

Jackson State, like Tougaloo, had its start as a religious school—in this case, formed in 1877 by the American Baptist Home Mission Society as Natchez Seminary "for the moral, religious, and intellectual improvement of Christian leaders of the colored people of Mississippi and neighboring states." Originally located in Natchez, just across the river from Louisiana, the school shifted its home base to a more centralized location in Jackson in 1882, where it eventually became Jackson College. When the American Baptists faltered in their financial support of the growing educational mecca, the state of Mississippi stepped in, and in 1940 it became part of the state's higher education system, first as a school for training teachers and later, in 1956 after years of building its faculty, as a four-year liberal arts college and modest graduate school. It was thus renamed Jackson State College.[11]

From the start of its public oversight, the college has been managed by Black officials appointed by the state. The first of these was Jacob L. Reddix, an able though overly strict college president who had an incredible "up from (near) slavery" ascension story. Born in 1897 and reared in a small south Mississippi lumber town to formerly enslaved parents, Reddix pursued higher education as his way out of poverty. After graduating from the Miller's Ferry Normal and Industrial School, a "Tuskeegee-like" elementary and high school just over the border in Alabama, Redix enlisted in the US Army during World War I. After the war, he taught in the segregated public schools of Birmingham, Alabama, for two years before migrating to Chicago and earning, at age thirty, a bachelor's degree in engineering from the reputable Lewis Institute (now the Illinois Institute of Technology). For the next decade, Reddix taught math at the newly formed, innovative, all-Black Roosevelt High School in Gary, Indiana—at what today might be called a "community school," where both the educational and recreational needs of the child and the neighborhood were accommodated on one campus. Reddix later studied economics at the University of Chicago on a Rosenwald Fund scholarship where he became something of an expert in the emerging field of community-based cooperative economics.[12]

His success in finding alternative ways for wealth accumulation for the hard-pressed Black community made him a favorite speaker about cooperative development at various colleges, church groups, and public-interest clubs. This, in turn, brought him to the attention of FDR's Farm Security Administration—part of the US Department of Agriculture (USDA)—and he was invited to join the agency to help coordinate its activities with the emerging agricultural cooperative movement. Reddix's time with the New Deal agency was short-lived, however. His boss at USDA also served as the vice president of the Rosenwald Fund, a philanthropic organization focused primarily on the education of African Americans in the South. This felicitous connection caused Reddix's boss to identify him to the Jackson State recruiters as the man whose background perfectly prepared him "to change over a small, church-related college into a key institution that may become one of the outstanding institutions in the state of Mississippi." Reddix jumped at the chance and never looked back. His life mission, thus, became the transformation of a failing church-run school into a thriving HBCU. He would stay at that pinnacle of Black achievement for the next twenty-seven years, gaining the support and trust of the White Mississippi political establishment and wresting ever-larger sums from them as well as from private institutions to plow into the college's physical infrastructure and academic reputation.[13]

During Reddix's tenure, the school's annual appropriation from the state legislature grew from $10,000 in 1940 to $1.6 million in 1967. Reddix was a rainmaker. But that ability to shower the college with needed funds came at a cost—ensuring that his White overlords were not disturbed by anything on campus that would smack of racial agitation. Under duress, Reddix's loyalties eventually would be revealed, and his shocking behavior would fan the flames of unrest on the Jackson State campus in the wake of the Tougaloo Nine demonstration.[14]

THE LADNER SISTERS SAY A LITTLE PRAYER

At Jackson State, the Ladner sisters were assigned to board at Ayer Hall, the freshman women's dorm at the center of campus. They both would complain in later years about how restrictive the campus rules were, particularly for females. "I thought mother was strict," Joyce would later remark, "but Jackson State was much worse! We had to be in our dorm at dusk. We had to sign out anytime . . . wherever we were going. If you were going to the [campus] library, you had to sign out. It was like a prison!"

Both sisters found release regularly when they would sneak off campus during their "free period" to visit Medgar Evers and catch up on what was going on in the world of "Negro rights." "On many a Wednesday afternoon, Dorie and I signed out to go shopping, whereas in actuality, our destination was Evers's two-room, no-frills office," Joyce recalled. "We never stayed long—just long enough for Medgar to update us on NAACP activities in Jackson and civil rights events at large around the state."

During one of these visits with Evers, he let them know on the down low that some of the Tougaloo students were about to do something big, but they must keep it absolutely secret. "There haven't been any sit-ins in Mississippi yet," he told the girls. "But there's going to be one very soon."

"He then proceeded to tell us," Joyce recalled, "that a group of students from the Tougaloo College NAACP chapter were going to stage a sit-in. We were shocked, but also ecstatic! Like, 'Finally! At last!!'"

The excited Ladner sisters asked if they could join in. At first, the eager leader agreed, but later he thought better of it. It was one thing for students from Tougaloo to protest—a school with strong abolitionist roots and deep financial ties with organizations outside of the state. It was something else again for students to rise up from Jackson State—a college completely controlled and funded by the state itself. "Medgar didn't want to assume responsibility for us getting kicked out of school," Joyce opined, "because he would have to answer to our parents."

Instead of greenlighting the sisters' involvement in the sit-in, Evers suggested that they attend a meeting coming up that weekend at Tougaloo with some of the collaborators to see if there might be a supporting role they could play. The young women jumped at the chance to be part of this unheard-of challenge to the state enforced system of segregation. "We had a tremendous interest in what we called back then 'Negro Rights,'" Joyce said. "All we knew is that we wanted to be a part of change in Mississippi."

That is how the Ladner sisters found themselves the following weekend—just a day or so before the sit-in took place—being driven for the first time to Tougaloo College by Aurelia Young, a Jackson State music teacher and the wife of Jack Young, one of the few Black attorneys authorized to practice law in Mississippi.[15] At that clandestine meeting, Joyce and Dorie met some of the students who were planning to sit in, as well as some adult advisors who were helping with logistics.

Dorie recounted the meeting in detail: "We were upstairs in the Mansion in the president's quarters. And we stayed there quite a while. It was on a Sunday afternoon. I remember Dr. Beittel was there; an art professor from Mississippi State, a Dr. Ryder, was there; Mrs. Young; some more students from Jackson State; and some Tougaloo students—I didn't know them at the time."

While most of the Tougaloo Nine had no recollection of such a meeting on campus with outsiders, one—the silent one throughout this exploration—recounted a specific memory of the gathering. On a phone call during a Tougaloo Nine anniversary conclave in 2006, Evelyn Pierce clearly recalled the gathering. "I was invited to the president's home before we demonstrated," she said, "and met with them—Dr. and Mrs. Beittel, who was so refined. And over tea, we talked about their concern for our safety."

"Now, I don't remember that they knew the exact plan," Pierce continued, "but I very, very vividly recall sitting in their parlor, and their expressing their concerns for our safety."

That such a meeting would take place during a time of heightened concerns for security and the need for absolute secrecy caused many of the Tougaloo Nine to discount the story. The fact that one of their number recalled it so clearly, however—as did one of the Ladner sisters—suggests it likely *did* take place but perhaps without the full participation of the entire group.[16]

It was at this meeting, Dorie insisted, that she and others were casting about trying to find some way of supporting the Tougaloo students while not jeopardizing their positions at Jackson State. Dorie recalled that after a long discussion, including concerns similar to the ones Evers had raised about Jackson State students getting involved in the demonstration, Dr. Ryder suggested, "Why don't you have a prayer meeting" in support of the students once they've been arrested?

Dorie answered him sheepishly, "OK." She also noted that the president of the Jackson State Student Government, Walter Williams, a senior, was in attendance as was Emmett Burns, a popular junior at the state-run school. Both would be crucial, as would the Ladner sisters, to the planning and execution of the Jackson State uprising that would ensue in the wake of the Tougaloo students' library action.

When they returned to their dorm room at Jackson State, Dorie and Joyce wondered how they would develop interest in the upcoming sit-in when they couldn't really talk about it openly. They hatched a simple plan that would at least introduce the idea without giving anything away. Dorie was the president of the Ayer Hall Dormitory Council, a group that met weekly to discuss issues with other freshman women living on campus. Perhaps at the upcoming meeting, Dorie could turn the meeting over to Joyce for a brief prayer. Joyce recalled that she was "so fundamentally religious" in those days, as was the culture, that "every public or private event started with a prayer." Dorie questioned Joyce about what she might say in her prayer that would alert the students without giving anything away. Joyce was circumspect. "I don't know," she told Dorie. "You've got to trust me!"

Thus, when all were gathered for their weekly dorm meeting, Dorie called on Joyce to lead the group in prayer. Joyce reached deeply into her heart, first "thanking God for all of us being alive and being there in our dormitory that night," she would later recount. "I went on to talk about the 'dark days ahead.' I said, 'God, please give us protection and guidance as we approach these dark days that are upon us.'" That was it. A cryptic message that something was about to happen, though no reference to specifics. Signal sent.[17]

PREPARING FOR THE WORST

Back at Tougaloo, all was not tranquil. Despite all of the advance planning and nonviolence drills, nothing could completely wipe out the fear that some of the soon-to-be demonstrators felt while preparing to face Mississippi's finest. Joe Jackson was particularly rattled the night before they were to head downtown. It almost sounds like if he had had the chance, he would have bolted. By that point, however, Jackson knew that he had "come too far."

"It makes a difference when you have leadership responsibility," Jackson said. "I knew that my colleagues were not going to turn around. But I knew by me being president, whether I really wanted to follow through or not, I had no choice but to go."

All night, Jackson tossed and turned, preparing himself as best he could for whatever might come. "I'm thinking about the state of Mississippi and its history," said Jackson. "And here I've got a wife and two young children. And I don't know what's going to happen to me. It was the uncertainty of the moment. And that's when I realized what leadership means."

This was the exact purpose for Mississippi's cruel and violent racial terrorism—to keep Black people in such fear that they would never dream of stepping out of line, knowing the severe consequences that might await them. Somehow Jackson and the others managed to face that monster and walk into the very heart of danger to see what might happen if they poked the beast.

Other students were more blasé about the whole thing. It was not until Sunday evening, March 26, after chapel services that Reverend Mangram called the group of volunteers together and told them the plan was to be put in action the next day. The severity hit some hard. But Ethel didn't even bother to go to the meeting, figuring it was just another walk through and delay. Her roommate tried to get her to go. "Lucille told me, 'They're going to be deciding what to do tonight.' And I said, 'Well, y'all just tell me what's decided. We're going out!' Ethel and her boyfriend Roger were headed to Moman's Grill "to eat hamburgers, play the juke box, and dance. So that's where I was!"

When Ethel returned from her night out, Lucille was visibly upset. "Tears were visible in her eyes," Ethel recalled. "And she *never* cried!" Mangram had advised the students to call their parents to clue them in on what was about to happen. Lucille, who had gone through all of the extensive training for months, was told that under no circumstances was she to participate the next day. "I called my parents, and they said, '*No!*'" Lucille wailed. Ethel looked at her squarely with resolve and said, "I can do this. Don't cry. I can do this."

Some of the others who ended up participating called home but were not quite as direct as Lucille must have been. Geraldine Edwards got in touch with her parents but was vague about the specifics. "We were instructed to call our parents and tell them not to be surprised at anything they might hear," Geri recalled. "But we were not to tell them exactly what we were going to do."

Sam Bradford clearly remembered calling his mother the night before because he didn't want her getting a surprise call the next day telling her that her son was dead. "Momma, I'm going to jail," he blurted out once she came to the phone.

"For what!?" she asked incredulously.

"Well," Sam said, recovering himself, "we're going to demonstrate, and we just don't know how this thing will turn out."

"Lord, Take care of my boy!" Momma cried. In that instant, she even prayed for the entire group, Sam recounted. Then she gave him her signature line—"Just don't say anything"—as if this well-practiced incantation was a guarantee to keep him safe.

Others decided not to follow Mangram's advice at all. Albert Lassiter made no move to call home. He hadn't really thought ahead to consider what impact his actions might have on his family or on his father's employment. That would come later. At the time, he just figured, "If I'm going to do something, I'm going to do it. We were already committed."

Janice Jackson, too, felt no compunction about stepping into history without parental approval. "I didn't know how my dad would take it," she said and worried that he might do something rash should the police or a White mob attack the protesters. But more than that, she felt that the decision was hers to make. "It was my obligation to do this," she said. "I've got to do something. I *want* to do something."

And so, each in their own way, the group soon to be known as the Tougaloo Nine prepared as best they could for whatever might come.

Part V

THREE DAYS
OF CONFLICT

Chapter 14

DAY 1:
THE STUDENTS TAKE CHARGE

THE OUTLINES OF THE STUDENT DEMONSTRATION ARE PRETTY SIMPLE from the vantage point of more than sixty years later. A group of nine Black students from Tougaloo College entered the Jackson Municipal Library's "Whites-only" main branch on North State Street; they looked for reading material, sat down at various tables throughout the facility, and began to read. In short order, the police were called, and the nine were duly arrested, marched out of the library, put in police cars or paddy wagons, and carted off to the city jail a few blocks away. The Nine—five men and four women— were kept overnight and throughout the next day, during which time they were interrogated individually but otherwise treated civilly and released once their bail was secured.

From this broad perspective, it seems a cut-and-dried story without much fanfare, little drama, and cause for only modest notice, if any, in the local and national press. But context is everything; and for such a defiance of local race laws to be abridged in the city of Jackson, the heart of the Deep South, this breach of protocol was more than just a slap in the face. It was nothing short of the start of a massive cultural shift and a shock to those who thought segregation would endure in perpetuity. Here are the specifics of what happened that day.

HEADING TO THE LIBRARY

Monday, March 27, 1961, dawned chilly and damp. Rain was expected later in the day. Most of the soon-to-be demonstrators busied themselves with getting dressed and grabbing a bite to eat before heading downtown. Everyone seemed to be concerned about dressing properly for the occasion. Janice Jackson had troubled one of the girls in the dorm to style her hair the night before. The guys pulled together their best clothes as if they were going to church. Albert Lassiter remembered specifically deciding to wear a trench coat to keep off the chill and the rain, yes, but also "to provide an extra layer of protection" against whatever beatings might come. Sam Bradford thought that was a good idea, so after he pulled on his best clothes, including a sporty sweater—despite later insisting that "it wasn't like we were *GQs*"—he went next door to borrow a trench coat from a friend who was about Sam's size and build. Joe Jackson was similarly attired with a crisp white shirt, thin dark tie and warm knit sweater with a collar. Alfred Cook may have won the male style contest that day. He wore a trendy striped blazer, along with requisite tie and dress shirt, looking much like the entrepreneur that he would ultimately become. Meredith Anding, similarly blazered up, completed his ensemble with striped tie, dress shirt, comfortable pants, and sporty tennis shoes.

The women were even more focused on their attire. Geraldine had the same idea as Al Lassiter. "I was very concerned that I dress *well* and that I dressed *warm*," she recalled. "That I was comfortable. That I was well protected." She selected "a suit that I designed and sewed: a two-piece, double breasted outfit, which had a comfortable feel. It was warm and had three-quarter-length sleeves." In addition, Geri wore her green raincoat, which was lined and waterproof and had deep pockets "to put things for safe keeping." The raincoat came with "a matching cap"—an accessory that would follow her the rest of her life thanks to the photos taken that day. "I was dressed for the weather and any circumstances that may have occurred."

Janice remembered choosing her wardrobe carefully, as well: "a plaid skirt and a matching tan sweater. Heels. Stockings. We wanted to look very, very good," she said.

Ethel kept it simple, with a thick white turtleneck sweater and calf-length skirt, while Evelyn looked all business with a dark blouse buttoned to the neck and a trendy vest-skirt combo.

The plan was to meet at Judson Cross dorm—the closest to the exit gate—at 9:30 a.m. sharp. Just as she was coming down to the gathering spot, Geraldine spied Colia Liddell getting off the Tougaloo commuter bus and running toward the Science Building. "Come on, Colia! We've got to go *now*!" Geri yelled. But Colia had a different idea. "I just *know* I've got to get to that Science Hall because my professor—an Indian brother (Professor Shamim Siddiqui)—wasn't going to forgive me for skipping that biology class. And my grades were terrible because I was spending too much time working on movement stuff rather than working on academic stuff."

Colia wasn't the only one to back out at the last minute. Joseph Jackson, the leader of the group, got concerned when only a few of those who had been participating in their training sessions showed up. He remembered Medgar suggesting that Meredith Anding would be an asset to the group because he was a local and had some experience with the Mississippi police. Although

Anding had attended a few of the practice sessions, he felt more affinity to the West Jackson Youth Council and had remained mostly aloof from the Tougaloo College Chapter. Jackson hurried to find Anding and called him out of chemistry class. "We're going down to the library," Jackson excitedly told him. "Medar thought you might be interested." Thus, what might have been the Tougaloo Eight became the Tougaloo Nine.

Reverend Mangram met those willing to participate in the parking lot and gave them one more pep talk, with instructions to remain nonviolent no matter what. Dean and Mrs. Branch, Registrar Dockins, and Dr. Borinski, were all there to see them off. Then two cars—Mangram driving the girls in his sedan and soon-to-be graduating senior Jerry Keahey, a budding photographer, driving the guys in the school's yellow station wagon—pulled away from the farewell committee and headed to whatever fate awaited them downtown.

If the others were in a state of excitement as they rode out of the Tougaloo gate, Joseph Jackson was in a trance, fearful of all of the things that might happen. He remained so as the vehicles approached the Carver Library on Mill Street—the main library for African Americans in Jackson. The students disembarked to visit Carver to ensure that none of the books they had chosen in advance were available. A few of the nine approached the information desk and requested their preselected research book. The Black librarian assured them that their books were not in the library's limited collection. But she said she could send over to the main branch, the larger "Whites-only" library on State Street, to inquire as to the books' availability. She was told not to bother. "We'll just go there and get it ourselves," one of the students said.[1]

The group left in a flash. "We were in and out of there so fast!" Ethel recalled. As he made his exit, Meredith Anding, who knew the librarian on duty from her work at the other Black library in the city—the College Park branch near his home—gave the now-curious woman a wink and a grin. She responded with a shy, knowing smile. Then they were off.

Nearly everyone's nerves were taut as the two cars approached the State Street library, an imposing, four-story modernist concrete and glass structure. Geraldine recalled being "apprehensive," but unlike Joe Jackson, "I had no fear for my life," she said.

Driver Jerry Keahey remembered that both cars pulled into the Sears Department Store parking lot directly across the street from the library. As the students piled out of the cars, newsmen emerged out of nowhere. "As we crossed the street, the media came out of the bushes with cameras rolling," recalled an excited Sam Bradford. "And that was part of the strategy." Medgar Evers, indeed, had called various media outlets to alert them to the "invasion."[2]

The entrance to the library was situated at the corner of North State Street—a busy north-south thoroughfare through the city—and the smaller

Yazoo Street, with the front doors facing State. Two small concrete steps led to the wide glass doors that served as the entry point to this temple of knowledge where only Whites were allowed to tread.

STEPPING INTO THE SURREAL

The anxieties of many of the students began to get the better of them as they stepped into the bright, airy, open space of the Jackson Municipal Library on State Street—such a contrast to the smaller Carver space they had just visited. Both Janice and Geraldine remember being dazed, almost as if they had entered another dimension of consciousness. "It was a feeling of numbness," Geri says, "like I was anaesthetized."

"To me, it was surreal," remembered Janice. "It was like I was there doing what I was supposed to do, but I felt like I was lifted out of my body or something." The reality of what they were attempting—challenging the deeply entrenched and violently enforced Jim Crow system of segregation in the state of Mississippi, of all places—was finally hitting them. This shift in consciousness, however, did not deter them from their goal. "I was determined," said Geraldine fiercely. "I was *not* going to let *nobody* turn me around!"

Janice, too, struck a rebellious pose. "I felt defiant," she later recalled. "They can't tell me this is not right! *We* ought to be able to use the library, too!"

For all of Joe Jackson's earlier jitters—which had become severe as the caravan made its way over to the library's main branch—when he entered that White bastion of knowledge, everything changed. "When I entered the library, all fear left from me," Jackson would recount more than fifty years later. "I became emboldened."

At the information desk, Joe Jackson spoke first. "I said, 'Ma'am, I've been to the Black library, but they didn't have this book that I need for this project I've got to complete.'" In a studied, steady voice, he continued, "I'm here because I believe you have the book.'" He then took a deep breath.

"You went to the Black library on Mill Street?" she asked.

"Naturally, I went to the Black library, Ma'am, but they didn't have this book, and I need it."

Although the librarian looked at him "in disgust and anger" Joe would later assert, she eventually went to retrieve the book and handed it to him. Then, he walked a few steps to the study area, sat down at one of the expansive tables, opened the book, and began to read.

Geraldine also picked up on the librarian's reaction. She could hear "that rustling, that discontent. And at the same time, there was a kind of disbelief: 'Oh, no they didn't! They didn't enter *this* place!'"

Janice, too, focused in on the librarian's state of mind. "I remember the librarian coming up to us and asking what we were doing there, what we wanted. A little, thin lady, about forty-ish, all nervous or whatever. Looked like she was more nervous than I remember being!"

Not everyone needed the librarian's assistance. Ethel went straight to the card catalog, thumbed through its offerings, and discovered that her preselected book wasn't listed. So, she simply perched herself at one of the large reading tables nearby and opened the college textbook she had brought with her and acted like she was reading.[3]

Geraldine went directly to the stacks to find the book she had selected, bypassing the card catalog altogether. A voracious reader since childhood, "I was very proficient in the library," she noted. "I knew the Dewey Decimal System and went right around to the shelves to look for the book." As it turned out, the library didn't stock the book she was looking for either, but Geri just pulled one on the same subject—human anatomy—which she was studying for her phys ed major.

Sam remembered exactly which book he had chosen: *Introduction to Parasitology*! "I had gone to one of our professors and asked for his suggestion for a book that I might not find at the Carver Library, and he said, 'Try to check out *Introduction to Parasitology*.' I had never heard of it in my life!"

Alfred Cook chose a similarly obscure text: *Bergey's Manual of Systematic Bacteriology*—a text that would become central to his later profession but now was a convenient foil. "I knew nobody in the state had it!" he would later claim.

Al Lassiter wasn't all that concerned about which book he should get. Since he was the tallest of the nine, he was more interested in finding somewhere that would shield him from a policeman's billy club should one be raised against him. "I positioned myself near the card catalog," he recalled, "so that the police would not be able to get a good swing at me because we expected to be physically attacked."

Joe Jackson described how the whole scene unfolded in eerie quiet. "Oooh, you know, you could hear a pin fall! Seeing nine Black faces in an all-White library!"

While everyone was getting settled, the librarian went into her office and called the police. Though Joe Jackson didn't hear exactly what transpired, he is certain she must have said something like, "We've got nine niggers down here in our White library!"

Thanks to the fact that the NAACP would file a discrimination lawsuit on behalf of the students, we have access to the name of this White librarian and her recollections of what happened that day. Frances French was a ten-year employee and the acting librarian on duty when the nine entered that Monday morning. In her testimony, French stated that she had been forewarned about the imminent visit of the Negro students by two reporters—Bill Minor of *The New Orleans Times-Picayune* and Cliff Sessions of United Press International—who had arrived shortly before the students did and told her they had been contacted about the impending demonstration.[4]

As Minor would later tell it, "I had been tipped off by Medgar Evers." Minor gave a heads up to his friend and colleague Ken Toler of *The Memphis Commercial Appeal*, and the word must have spread to others in the office, including to Sessions. "We went straight to the library," Minor recalled. They got there just before the students arrived.[5]

"After talking to [the reporters], I did call the police," French continued. "I didn't know whether it was a rumor or not. I just called because I didn't know what was going to happen." The police told her to call back if, in fact, anything actually *did* happen.

French informed the students that it was "custom" for Negroes to use one of the two Negro branches, Carver or College Park. She also advised them to return to Carver and formally request that the Jackson Municipal Library forward the books there for them to review, which was the standard practice. She testified that she then, once again, "called and notified the police that the students had arrived." Having been alerted earlier, the police surely had begun preparations to head to the library, which explains how they arrived there so quickly. "They were there lickety split!" recalled Janice.

Even though most of the Nine suggested that the cops arrived within ten or fifteen minutes—Jerry Keahey claims it was only four or five—as far as Ethel was concerned, they couldn't get there soon enough. When she took her seat to read, she decided to situate herself to see out of the large picture windows facing State Street, where a group of rowdies had begun to gather across the street. Somehow, they had been alerted to the demonstration almost as soon as the students entered the building.

"The way I was facing, I could see them," Ethel said of the crowd. "And they were shaking their fists, and I was thinking, 'Hurry up and come on, police!' Because I was feeling kind of threatened by the crowd and wondering if they were going to come on in."

Janice noticed her best friend's agitation and, perhaps to help quell her own nerves, kept checking on Ethel. When asked more than fifty years later about what she did in the library, Janice demurred. "It's not vivid enough for me to just remember precisely what I was doing. I just know I milled around and looked through the card catalog and did the stuff I was supposed to do." Only one memory stood out for her: "I remember kind of looking out of the corner of my eye to see if Ethel was OK," Jancie said. "I looked to see if everything was cool."

Soon enough, Ethel got her wish. The police arrived, but not with guns blazing or even drawn. "They were very respectful," Geraldine noted. "There were no guns pulled, no billy clubs pulled out. Nobody put their hands on us."

"WHO IS THE LEADER?"

The police "were a little cautious," Joe Jackson confirmed, not surprising perhaps since this represented the city's first encounter with the kind of non-violent protest tactics that had already swept through the rest of the South.

Outside, Jerry Keahey was mulling over exactly what he should do when he saw the police pull up to the library. After dropping his group of students off across the street from the library, Keahey drove around the corner on Yazoo Street, parked the car, and jumped into a phone booth to call back to Tougaloo to let Dr. Borinski and Dean Branch know that all nine students had made it into the library. He could actually see the demonstrators thanks to the large picture windows that went all around the building. Then he waited to see what would happen next.

"It took a few minutes until a police car came up. And then another police car. And then *another* police car!" he recalled. He quickly placed another call back to campus to provide an update. At that point, "Dr. Borinski told me to get out of there!"

Borinski, alarmed that Keahey was still on the premises, barked into the receiver, "Get back to zee campus! I don't vant zem to arrest you! And I don't vant zem to take zee station vagon!!" Keahey sped off but wisely took an alternate route back to Tougaloo. He later heard that police were driving up and down State Street looking for him. "I went the back way, he later recalled, "and once I got inside the gate, I was safe."

Back at the library, Al Lassiter clearly remembered his first interaction with the Jackson police. Since he was still standing by the card catalog when the police entered the building, his tall frame commanding attention, an officer immediately approached him.

"Boy, what you doin' at this library?!" the man in blue demanded.

"I'm here looking for a book, Sir," the lanky, slow-talking, deep-bass Lassiter responded.

"Your library is down on Mill Street!" the officer replied impatiently.

"Yes, Sir. But they don't have the books I'm looking for."

(This was beginning to sound like an Abbott and Costello comedy sketch.)

"Well, you still gotta go down there anyway!" the policeman said with finality.

"Yes, Sir!" Lassiter replied.

And then the two just stood there facing off.

Geraldine, too, remembered her first interface with the officers of the law. "One came up to the table and asked me my name," she recalled. "He wanted to know what I was doing in the library. And I'm sure I said something like, 'I'm here to read a book!'"

It all sounds quite perfunctory, even though such a direct assault on segregation had never been tried before in Mississippi's capital city. Obviously, the police had anticipated this eventuality and had previously talked through how best to handle it. So much for the myth that "all-of-our-niggras-are-happy" routine Mayor Thompson and others kept pushing. Much of official Jackson must have known this day would come.

Thanks to the presence of the press, what happened next is clear. First, Chief of Detectives M. B. Pierce—the same Pierce who lived not far from Meredith Anding's family in West Jackson—spoke up.

"Who is the leader, please?" Pierce asked a "smartly dressed girl"—most likely Geraldine.[6]

"Suh?" she answered inquisitively. "Leader of what, Suh?"

"You will have to leave," he commanded. "You all know you're not supposed to be here."

No response.

"If you leave now and go down to the Carver Library," Pierce said calmly, "you'll be served there, and you won't be arrested."

Silence.

"If you don't leave within the next two minutes, you'll be arrested."

No movement.

"Alright, you're under arrest. Now, move out!"

At that, just as the students had been instructed, they all rose and began to make their way to the front door, each escorted by a man in blue. The students clearly understood that arrest was the goal so that the NAACP legal team could use the event as a test case to challenge Mississippi's entire segregationist infrastructure. They followed Medgar Evers's instructions perfectly and made sure not only that the NAACP got its test case but also that they were not arrested for anything other than "breach of peace." (Had they continued to sit, for example, they might have been charged with resisting arrest.)

A moment of unexpected levity occurred to break the tension, at least for one of the demonstrators. As she was rising out of her chair, Ethel later recalled that "I looked down to pick up the book I had been 'reading' all this time, and it was upside down!" Instead of being amused, however, Ethel was afraid that one of the policemen had seen it and would draw the conclusion that she and the rest of her Tougaloo colleagues were stupid. "I thought, 'Oh, I'm so glad nobody saw this!' I could just hear them say, 'One Negro had a book upside down!'" It was only later that she and her Tougaloo pack would howl with laughter at her discovery.

LOOKS OF DEFIANCE AND MOMENTS OF GRACE

There is one photograph that stands out among the several that were snapped as the students exited the library on their way to the police cars. It is notable for many reasons, not least of which is that, besides the police, only three of the young women being arrested are pictured. They are not handcuffed. They are perfectly coiffed and dressed. They are making a statement—not with their words but with their body language. Their faces are defiant. There are no smiles typically found when cameras are around. There is a determination and grit in their expressions announcing that this is a new day for Mississippi. A policeman walking next to the women seems to be lecturing them, which is simply adding fuel to their fire.

The women are marching forcefully to a destination unknown, without a care for the outcome. Rage would not be too strong a word for their attitude. "Don't you dare try to put a hand on us!" they must be thinking. "We are moving with our own agency and in our own time to a place that you cannot even imagine. We are coming for what is rightfully ours. You will not be able to stop us. Just watch!" It is an image unlike any other in the Mississippi civil rights portfolio. And it comes at the very beginning of the long public struggle for Black freedom in the Magnolia State.

The photograph captures Ethel Sawyer, Janice Jackson, and Evelyn Pierce, surrounded by police, in what can only be described as "a perfect moment." They have been led out of the library with their comrades but somehow have been separated by just a few feet as they are about to turn the corner toward the waiting police cars. Across the street, out of the frame, more than one hundred screaming Whites are hysterically deriding them with jeers and curses. "They were yelling all kinds of stuff," recalled Ethel. "That was one menacing crowd! And that's when I threw my head in the air and said to myself, 'The hell with you!'" Indeed, Ethel's nose is high, her neck outstretched, and her gaze steely. She is impudent.

Janice remembered this moment, as well. "Everything was unfolding as it was supposed to. And I felt defiant. It was just, 'Hey, look at us! We're doing something to make a difference! Take us on to jail. So what!?'" Thanks to her sheltered upbringing, and perhaps a healthy dose of youthful naivete, Janice somehow felt protected. She recalled the shouting crowds across the street as well as her extraordinary composure. "I didn't look directly at anyone. I just kept . . . I contained myself. The way I managed to get through this was that I kept everything contained. There was like a shield around me," she said. "It was like, 'Hey, I'm doing this. Nothing is going to happen. And bring whatever it is you want to bring on!'"

Evelyn, too—all five-feet, two-inches of her—looks self-possessed and undisturbed, carrying some books and a large handbag as if she were walking to her next class at Tougaloo.

The police managed to get the entire group into the waiting squad cars. Then they sped the five blocks past the Governor's Mansion and City Hall to the city jail.

It wasn't until he was on his way to the pokey that the full force of what he just had done hit Joe Jackson. "It was almost like a dream," he would later say. "That's really when fear . . . I felt fearful then. Because we were in the custody of the police."

Once they arrived, the students were booked and fingerprinted. Then one by one, they had their mug shots taken, with a front and a side view, and an individualized tracking number as well as the date of arrest posted on a board that was hung around each one's neck. A lovely souvenir portrait for posterity.[7]

In these snapshots of history, no one's face gives anything away. Certainly, fear does not seem to be present. Nor are there any smiles. Three of the nine—Joseph, Geraldine, and Albert—are wearing glasses, which reflect light and thus partially obscure their eyes. Evelyn is the only one who looks openly hostile, though Meredith and Janice come in a close second and third, scornful, perhaps, of the whole procedure.

For his part, Meredith recalled feeling almost drugged when his "portrait" was being taken. "It was kind of like I was going in for surgery," he said. "I was calm, but it wasn't me. I'm spiritual, so I knew somebody was holding me up [in prayer]. Otherwise, my knees would have buckled!"

Alfred Cook seems above it all, looking quite dapper in his thin tie and natty sport coat. All of the portraits are remarkable for the calm they exude. Perhaps the students were just grateful to have made it that far without incident, without assault.

Taken together, these portraits form a composite of African American life in the twentieth century. Each of these determined faces will disprove the bankrupt stereotypes of Black deficiency. They will be the part of the first generation to fully throw off the shackles of White suppression, to rise like none of their ancestors had risen through the White world—the soon-to-be integrated world—and to achieve remarkable things. Thanks to their education as well as to their own gifts and grit, they will find professional-level jobs in military service, in academia, in medical technology, in government, in education, in social work, and in politics. This will be their only arrest and this for the audacity of breaking barriers, which they will continue to do throughout their mostly long lives. Theirs will be a testament to the possible, to what can happen when individuals are afforded the opportunity to explore their full potential. All of this is presaged in their youthful, forthright faces. And all of it will come to pass. It is their destiny.

JAIL TIME

After the police formalities, the groups were separated—the guys were brought into one area of the facility, the women to another. The two groups would not see each other again until they were released the following evening. After being booked and fingerprinted, both groups were taken to their respective holding cells—what is commonly known as "the drunk tank"—to await further processing or until they could obtain bail and be released. Whatever their preconceived notions of jail may have been, the students were not disappointed.

"We all got put in the tank," Al Lassiter recalled of the five male demonstrators. "It's a holding cell with all the other inmates. Very crowded. Dirty. Smelly," he said. "And there was a hole in the floor where you did your business, you know? And what did they say? Uh, 'Flush the mule!' You know, the hole."

The women were equally grossed out. Geraldine in particular was horrified. "I remember specifically being in that nasty, stinky jail holding cell. It was so terrible!"

Medgar Evers had told the students that they wouldn't have to wait long to get bailed out, so their expectations were that they'd be back on campus by late afternoon, certainly by suppertime. But the bailiff, Hinds County sheriff J. R. Gilfoy, "conveniently made himself absent" either out of personal pique or institutional revenge, so the bond money that Evers had managed to scrape up from three of his local NAACP stalwarts—the R. L. T. Smiths, both Senior and Junior, and John Dixon, a postal worker—sat idle until the sheriff returned the next day.[8]

Somehow this message wasn't conveyed to the jail-bound students, so as afternoon turned into evening, some became incredibly troubled. Joseph Jackson in particular was a basket case. When the group didn't get released immediately, Jackson's imagination went wild. "That's when I knew they were going to pull some tactics on us," Joe said. "They're going to take us out one by one, and they're going to do us in."

The group was served what passed for lunch while still in the drunk tank. Just about everyone complained about the food. "They served some old salt pork or something," recalled Janice. "And some beans. Some sort of biscuit. It didn't look good. I had never seen food like that. I thought, 'This is how they treat people in jail?' It was awful."

Janice also worried about how long it was taking to get bailed out. "This isn't the way this was planned," she thought. "This is *not fun* up in here! This is *not* gonna be just some little thing, and we're out!"

To help calm their nerves and create a better atmosphere, all of Pops Lovelace's male students banded together—Joe, Sam, and the two Als—and began to sing. Meredith Anding, not musically inclined, listened in wonder. "These guys were members of the choir, and so they start singing. They sang several songs, but the one I remember was 'Bless the Lord, O My Soul.' It was one I had heard them sing before. A lot of harmony there. And the girls picked it up, and they were singing back and forth to each other." It was a moment of grace, briefly transforming those dank, depressing holding cells into anointed sanctuaries.

For her part, Geraldine found solace by turning the women's cell into a dance studio. Almost from the time they were closed up with the imprisoned Black women of the city, Geri began first pacing, then stretching, then full-on dancing in whatever available space she could find. "I was active," she said. "I was a physical education major. I was used to dancing. And I just couldn't be still in that place."

If she remembered nothing else, Janice recalled Geri's unlikely choice for a studio. "Oh, I remember Geraldine dancing!" she exclaimed. "I'm thinking, 'Girl, sit down! Sit down!' But she was doing her twirls and pirouettes and whatever."

Ethel confirmed: "Geraldine entertained us by dancing. I think she was doing ballet!"

"I would move around and do things," Geraldine gleefully stated. "I guess I got people laughing. So, it got a little lighter mood in there."

When the noonday news announced the arrest of the Tougaloo students, Dean Branch decided it was time to get President Beittel involved, or so the story goes. Beittel had traveled to Atlanta that morning to attend a United Negro College Fund board meeting. There are conflicting views over how much Beittel knew about the planned demonstration. Obviously, if he had hosted a tea in his residence a day or two earlier, he was aware that something big was about to happen, though he may have been kept in the dark about where and when. Nonetheless, Tougaloo's new president took a laissez faire approach to student activism. He would publicly say that what the students did on their own time was their own business; privately, he would later admit, "I stood with the students." Even if he knew about his youthful charges' plans, it is unlikely that Beittel would have intervened to stop them.

His being out of town when the library sit-in occurred offered him a level of plausible deniability that he would not have been able to claim had he had been on campus when the students left in a school-owned vehicle to head downtown. Upon receiving the news of the sit-in from Dean Branch by phone, Beittel calmly said he would conclude his business in Atlanta and be back on campus the next day.[9]

THE SHOW MUST GO ON

While the Tougaloo Nine were holed up in the Jackson City Jail, White Jackson proceeded with plans to celebrate its Confederate heritage as if nothing out of the ordinary had happened. For his part, Sidney Roebuck spent the day nailing down last-minute details for the parade. One of those details was ensuring that Governor Barnett and Mayor Holland would travel up Capitol Street in style. He confirmed arrangements with Robert Stockett, operator of Stockett Stables down by the fairgrounds, to supply two carriages and four horses, as well as drivers to ensure a smooth and historically accurate ride for the grand occasion.[10]

The most pressing concern, however, was the weather. "Thousands of anxious Mississippians who have spent time and money on the Civil War Centennial parade and pageant scheduled for tomorrow are holding their breaths at the weatherman's forecast of 'scattered thundershowers' for the day," wrote *Jackson Daily News* reporter Pat Flynn. When asked, "What would be done with the giant parade in case of rain?" chairman of the Jackson Centennial Committee Robert Nichols said, "We'll just get wet." *Daily News* editor Jimmy Ward was not so resigned. In his Crossroads" column, Ward begged for a reprieve from the storms. "It just can't rain tomorrow," he whined. "Here Mississippi has waited 100 years to have a Centennial parade and the skies look heavy today. It simply can't rain on Tuesday!" The commission's information director, Frank Wallace, told it straight: "The parade has to go on. The people are here, and it will go on."[11]

"Frantic" last minute preparations were being made for the big day. Twenty-four hours earlier, "hoop-skirted belles and frock-coated men" rehearsed their parts for the pageant reenactment of the 1861 Mississippi legislature's deliberations on secession at the Old State Capitol. The pageant, called "The Outset," dramatically recounted the debate on secession and the vote to join the Confederacy. As an added bonus for attendees, a recitation of Jefferson Davis's final speech to the Mississippi legislature just before his retirement from public life was also planned. It promised to be an emotional, heart-tugging theatrical event for the Lost Cause crowd.

White Mississippians loved nothing if not their history and traditions. Secession Day had been planned, commission press releases repeatedly said, not as a "celebration," but as a solemn "commemoration" of all that had transpired one hundred years previously. Indeed, all of the more than three thousand troops that would be marching were being touted as "The Mississippi Greys—Mississippi's Centennial Military Force in Memoriam" to honor all those who had fallen in defense of the Confederacy.[12]

Somehow between the announcement and the implementation, the solemnity of the day was all but forgotten. The parade about to commence the next day would be a raucous celebration of all things Southern, most especially all things Confederate. The Outset, planned for later in the day, would provide a more solemn backdrop to the commemoration, offering a moment of reflection about all that had been lost as a result of the decision to secede.

"HOW COULD YOU DO THIS TO ME?"

It is hard to know exactly what the response of White Jackson was to the Tougaloo Nine's direct and public assault on segregation, particularly since it preceded a day of festive celebration. There are clues, however, in the actions of the police throughout the city as well as in the alarmed expressions from the mayor. According to Colia Liddell, despite her reluctance to accompany her classmates downtown that morning for fear of missing yet another required class, once news got back to campus in early afternoon that the library sit-in had gone off as planned, she and about twenty other Tougaloo students, having finished classes for the day, piled into cars and headed downtown.

As they rode, the students thought up ways in which they might support their now locked-up confreres. Someone suggested another sit-in to amplify that the library demonstration was not a one-off event. They drove to Capitol Street and scouted out all of the likely places—Walgreens, Woolworth's—but they were too late. "We went downtown to all of the places with lunch counters," Liddell reported. "That was our project. [But] every place we went, the police had already arrived! And they told us that if we were going to pull off a demonstration, we'd really have to do some scheming because they were already there waiting for us. So, the bus station and everything had policemen to make sure anything that was for Whites was protected."

Despite their preemptive presence, Jackson's finest made a strong impression on the plucky undergrad. "Each place had four of the loveliest state troopers you ever wanted to see," Liddell remembered with a smile. "I never knew men grew so tall and big!"

The attractive collegian claimed she tried flirting with the youthful police officers stationed at each site. "And those poor boys would turn red!" Colia mischievously recalled. Nevertheless, at each location, access was blocked.

Liddell admitted that these stops all over town were really an attempt to intimidate the authorities and keep them guessing about what might be coming next. "It was a threat that we might come down there any day, any hour, and sit in," she recalled with glee. "The Jackson police were nervous. The Tougaloo demonstration hit them *so* hard and *so* cold and *so* fast!"

As another sign of brazen contempt for the established order, the students decided to make their way to City Hall and seek an unlikely audience with the mayor. "We could not have done this under normal circumstances," Liddell admited. "Blacks couldn't just go in the mayor's office." What they found there on that day shocked even them.

Perhaps in an attempt to discover what might have caused their fellow students to take such assertive action within his city, Mayor Thompson decided to allow this impromptu discussion with the Tougaloo delegation. According to Liddell, the group entered the mayor's office to find a man shattered and distraught. "He just broke down and started crying!" Liddell later described. "He's actually crying! He felt that we had just destroyed his city."

"I don't believe you all did this to me!" he kept repeating. "How could you do this to me after all I did for Tougaloo?"

"He's popping his heart pills," Liddell observed. "He was *so* upset, I thought he was going to have a heart attack!"

Liddell credited Thompson with a fair amount of foresight. "He lived in this city and realized it was up for grabs. He knew that after that demonstration, there would be more and more and more and more. And that Jackson would have to change. That's the kind of moment this was for him. He literally had tears running down his red cheeks because he was angry."

After leaving this seemingly broken, beaten man—a victim of his own rosy narrative of the positive aspects of segregation—the students returned to Tougaloo to find many of the students also in an uproar. "Some were just frightened to death," Liddell remembered, because state troopers had driven up to the gates of the college threatening to enter.

Other students were packing their bags. They had heard from their parents, who were unnerved by the action of the Tougaloo Nine and were on their way to remove their young adult children from what they must have seen as a dangerous situation. "I actually saw one kid being taken away," Liddell recounted. "How many students Tougaloo lost in that moment, I don't know. But I know ten or fifteen left."[13]

"YOU GUYS ARE ON TV!"

Back at the jail, the students were still in the holding tank. All afternoon, they had been confident that they would be sprung quickly, but as the hours stretched into evening, some began to lose hope. Something must have gone terribly wrong. Suddenly, they heard someone whispering, "You guys are on TV! You guys are on TV!!" It was the Black kitchen worker delivering their second inedible meal. Their confidence soared as they realized the outside world, indeed, was aware of their plight. Talk sprang up among the students and the vagrants about what had transpired earlier in the day. "Keep up the good fight!" the inmates called out to their young cellmates.

At some point, the police realized the students would be spending the night, so they decided to move them into longer-term quarters upstairs. Once escorted there, the guys were made to wait outside of their cells for an extended period. With no place to sit except on the hard, cold concrete, Sam spied pillows and blankets inside their soon-to-be cell and did his best to fish them out by sliding Lassiter's long trench coat through the bars and then using it as a fishing net, of sorts, eventually coaxing the soft, warming cotton bedding toward him, where he could shimmy it out into the hallway. When the police returned with keys to let them inside, the enterprising young men had already made themselves comfortable on the floor. "One of the guards came by, and he had this 'What the hell?' look on his face," Lassiter recalled. "We were trying to be creative and resourceful to try and make this thing a little more palatable," he continued. "Later they let us go inside the cell."

Meredith Anding recounted a rather harrowing detail once the students had all settled comfortably onto their cots. "We were up there for about thirty minutes, and then they brought the dogs in. Placed the dogs inside the cell with us." The dogs were two German shepherds that the Jackson Police Department had borrowed from the city of Vicksburg, which had recently purchased them from a Kansas City trainer. Prepped to be attack dogs, the hefty animals failed their first test. "They brought them in, and we had to scramble to get up on the upper bunks or climb the bars. They were somewhat vicious at first," Anding recalled. "They were definitely not to be played with." But "after about five or ten minutes, the dogs calmed down and actually became tame!" Anding observed. "The dogs were kind of like, 'Hey, we're all in this together!'" When they realized the dogs were no longer a source or terror, the cops retrieved them and left the young men alone for the rest of the night.

That did not end the monkey business, however. Perhaps as an attempt to harass the police who had sicced the dogs on them, perhaps as a release from the various tensions of the day, or perhaps, as he suggests, as a way to cheer up his terrorized cell mates, Alfred Cook decided to stage his own animal protest. As he would tell it years later, Cook said, "I just thought of a chimpanzee I had seen when I was in the air force and all the things that he would do when he became upset." Cook then decided to act out the chimp's behavior in front of his aghast classmates. "I climbed up on the bars of our cell, mimicking a chimpanzee. And I jumped down." He then walked around the cell on all fours like the primate would do. "And then I jumped off the wall and went across the cell."

Albert Lassiter, who dealt with the day's tension by taking long naps, confirmed Cook's antics. "I remember waking up to squealing and carrying on," Lassiter said. "It was Al Cook acting like a monkey and climbing on the bars!" And that is how this wild day ended for those holed up in the Jackson City Jail. Outside it was another story.[14]

ANOTHER PROTEST BREAKS OUT

With nine Black students jailed downtown, with thousands of White citizens making their way to Jackson to participate in the Confederate Parade festivities the next day, and with Black Jackson riled up about the failure of the police to release the Tougaloo students on bail, Jackson State's students stepped into the breach. As noted, the Ladner sisters had been forewarned by Medgar Evers that something big was about to happen, and soon. Joyce Ladner's Sunday evening prayer had been overheard by dorm matron Miss Rose, and she became alarmed. The next morning, as the Tougaloo Nine were getting ready to head downtown, Miss Rose reported what Joyce had said—something about "dark days ahead"—to the school's dean of students, Dean Oscar Rogers, a Tougaloo alum and a Harvard-educated minister. Rogers called both Ladner girls into his office, along with Miss Rose. This was highly unusual and caught the young women off guard. "It couldn't be the prayer," Joyce remembered telling Dorie as they marched to the dean's office. "I mean, I can't imagine!"

"No, it's not your prayer," Dorie retorted. "Nobody knew what you were talking about."

Crestfallen that her effort may not have had the intended impact, Joyce entered the dean's office with Dorie just a step behind. Miss Rose was already there. Dean Rogers was uncharacteristically stern. "Sit down, ladies," he said coldly. Looking at Joyce, he said, "Miss Rose here said you gave a prayer last night and talked about the 'dark road ahead.' What were you talking about?!"

Joyce hesitated, wondering how best to respond.

"Is there something I need to know about some trouble about to take place?" Rogers persisted.

Remembering that Rogers was a Baptist preacher, she blurted out, "What right do you have to ask me about my prayer?!" All of seventeen years old and looking smaller and more child-like than her age, Joyce would remark years later: "To this day, I have no idea how I got those words out of my mouth!" She also noted, "All of my life I had drawn strength from my older sister. She always made me feel larger and tougher. And on this day, I came out swinging!"

Dorie, too, was both alarmed and incensed. Figuring the best defense was a good offense, she said, "Anybody who's scared of a prayer, I don't want to be around him!"

"Miss Ladner," Rogers said coolly to Dorie, "I'm going to hip you before I ship you," meaning he was going to set her straight before he expelled her.

Joyce jumped in: "Anything I say in prayer is between *me and my Lord!*" — with great emphasis on the last four words. At this, Rogers seemed disarmed. "Befuddled . . . really taken aback," Joyce recalled. "And Miss Rose looked like a deer caught in the headlights."

"You wouldn't want anyone interfering with your worship of the Lord, would you?" Dorie, more calmly queried.

Rogers, still sensing trouble but realizing the interview was going nowhere, softened. "Yes, yes. Prayers are a very private matter. I apologize for this intrusion into your religious beliefs," he said. "You're both excused."

The sisters had a hard time keeping a straight face as they exited the office, realizing they had outsmarted a Harvard grad. "Dorie and I were quite pleased with ourselves," Joyce allowed.

But as they made their way back to Ayer Hall, Dorie in particular grew more incensed at the matron's role in the matter. Both girls strode into Miss Rose's office, and Dorie, shaking her fist, said, "We don't appreciate you spying on us and snitching to Dean Rodgers! What my sister says in prayer is none of your business!"

Miss Rose seemed on the verge of apologizing but refrained. "She was a mean, tough bird," Joyce would later remark.

Instead, Miss Rose defended herself. "I told Dean Rodgers what I overheard because I was scared that some agitation might be about to happen. I thought he should know because it might affect the safety of the students. I was just doing my job!"

"As far as I'm concerned," Dorie hissed, "you better keep my name out of your mouth! And my sister's too!!" And the two coconspirators left the office, aghast at what they had just done yet exhilarated that nothing had been revealed that might have foiled the Tougaloo students' efforts. All they could do now was wait.

The sisters retreated to Dorie's room, cutting their classes to see if any developments with the library sit-in had yet taken place. "We were on edge, in a hush by the radio in anticipation of a news bulletin," Joyce recalled. "Before long, it came. The Tougaloo sit-in had gone off as planned. Talk about jubilation!"

Soon, the entire Jackson State campus was buzzing with the news. At this point, a plan was hatched to get the broader Jackson State community involved. Joyce recounted that at 5:00 p.m. that evening, a group of committed students, including all of those who had attended the meeting at the Beittels' residence the day before as well as others who had already demonstrated their commitment to activism (including James Meredith, soon to be internationally known, who at the time was attending Jackson State) gathered to hatch a plan for a sympathy prayer vigil later that evening. Everyone was told to spread the word: "I heard there's going to be a sympathy prayer for the Tougaloo students tonight in front of the campus library." The message was discretely prepared so that no one could pin its origin on anyone else.

By Joyce's estimation, a small crowd began to gather at around 6:45 p.m., causing others to stop and ask what was up. By 7:00 p.m., "several hundred students had gathered," she recalled, "more than any of us expected." It had been decided that Emmett Burns—a junior and "a very popular fellow"— would lead the prayer on behalf of the jailed Tougaloo students. No sooner had Burns begun than a loud racket could be heard coming from the direction of the president's residence, which was adjacent to the library. "Emmett wasn't even half-way through his prayer," Joyce recalled, "when we heard a familiar voice shouting, 'Stop this! What's going on here? Break this up right now!'"

It was Jackson State president Jacob Reddix, who had somehow heard about the gathering and was determined to end it before any damage was done to the college's state funding or to his reputation as president. "His power, because it was conferred power," Joyce explained years later, "would only last as long he kept happy the White power structure: the Governor, the state legislature, the board of education and, very importantly, the State Sovereignty Commission and the White Citizens' Council."

The Ladner sisters had a front-row view of all that happened next.

"Reddix, in a frenzy, huffing and puffing," Joyce recalled.

"Here comes the president, screaming and yelling and thrashing his arms," Dorie noted, "carrying on and cursing."

"He was wailing his arms just really like a chicken with its head cut off," Joyce allowed.

In his alarm, panic, and rage, Reddix grabbed a freshman girl—Joyce's roommate Eunice, in fact, who was standing right next to Joyce—pulled her to him, and then pushed her away so hard that Eunice fell down. In the confusion of the moment, a rumor began to circulate that Reddix had slapped a student to the ground. Only someone close to the action, like Joyce was, could have seen what actually happened. "He didn't slap her," Joyce would later say, "he knocked her to the ground."

Nevertheless, Reddix's actions shocked and enraged the gathered youth. "We students turned on President Reddix at that moment," Joyce vividly recalled, "pointing accusing fingers, shouting invectives, and pleading with him to understand that we were only holding a peaceful prayer vigil." Nevertheless, "wild man that he was," Joyce continued, "President Reddix heard nothing as he spun away from us and raved on."

Joyce and her other roommate, Margaret, helped Eunice up, dusted her off, and tried as best they could to stop her from crying. "We had no idea what to do next," Joyce later said. "Things were happening so fast!"

"We started scattering, running to the dorm, running everywhere," Dorie remembered. "But within minutes, the police were on campus!"

"We saw a unit of the all-White Jackson City Police, armed with guns and billy clubs," Joyce concurred. "We knew what their next move would be."

Soon, the police were roughly moving through the crowd, ordering everyone to disperse. "[They were] shoving students right and left, demanding that we break it up right away," Joyce recalled. "Fearing serious violence, we immediately retreated to the library and to the dorms with our angered and our hurt feelings over President Reddix turning the police loose on us. He had violatcd us!"

That night, word spread throughout campus that students should boycott classes the next day, wear black arm bands, and meet at the Field House after breakfast for further instructions.

A more immediate drama played out in Joyce's room that evening. Reddix's rumored "slap heard round the city" had spread to reporters, and they were calling Ayer Hall asking to speak to Eunice. "Housemother Rose refused to allow Eunice to talk to the reporters or to anyone else who called," Joyce noted.

Late into the night, one of the deans arrived to tell Eunice she needed to clear out of the dorm by morning. When Eunice shrieked, "Why?!" she was told, "You have been expelled." Joyce, Margaret, and Eunice pleaded with the dean for clarification, but all they were told was that President Reddix had ordered the expulsion. A stunned Eunice began packing.

With fifty years of hindsight, Joyce Ladner would come to realize that the events of that night "had transformed many of us from sympathizers [with the Tougaloo Nine] to protesters." The next day, they would get their chance to show just what they were made of. Reddix's ill-conceived tirade inflamed the students more than any quiet vigil might have done, bringing them dangerously close to a collision with a city full of neo-Confederates the next day.[15]

A DARK AND STORMY NIGHT

Meanwhile, Colia Liddell, who lived in Jackson, remembered that night as being a particularly stormy one. An early spring squall passed right over the city. "It stormed all that night, and Black folks kept their lights on around the city. Anywhere we drove through town that night, lights were on," Liddell clearly recalled. "People were having prayer sessions, and folks were concerned about the lives of those [Tougaloo] students."[16]

Liddell also captured the mood of the Black community at this critical juncture. "The city really began to develop an atmosphere of struggle around this first incident," she said. "And Black folk just felt the Lord was on their side."

The community's outpouring of sympathy for the nine jailed students was demonstrated most tangibly in the cookies, cakes, hot food, and snacks that individual families, mostly Black women, brought to the jail to help support this newly forming resistance movement. Rather than give the provisions to the by-then-famished young freedom fighters, however, the police let it all pile up near the entrance to the police station.

Meanwhile, hungry, tired, and overwrought Joseph Jackson spent a sleepless night on his jail bunk. Tossing and turning, his brain could not turn off. "We weren't released that Monday. That's what I think did us all in. At least that's what did *me* in," Jackson said. "I was in no kind of mental state to eat that food. I starved myself because my fear had taken over," Jackson recounted. After a while, in the middle of that hellish, stormy night, Joe Jackson's spirit broke. "Your mind was going a mile a minute," he recalled, describing his mental state. "I've read about Emmett Till. I've read about the history of Mississippi. And I just said, 'OK, I've got a script.' If any of those cats come in and pull us out one by one, my script will be: '*Please*, Mister White Man! *Please* don't do anything to me. *Please* don't take my life. I've got a wife and two little children in Memphis. If you let me go, I *promise* you, I will never *ever* come down here and break your Jim Crow laws again, Sir.'" But a small, persistent voice in his head kept pestering him—just as a friend would put it to him years later—"Nigger, you should have thought about that before you broke those laws."

Jackson would later admit that he was delirious with fear. "It was real! I couldn't eat. I couldn't sleep. I really never have had a feeling like that in terms of being that close to death."

Chapter 15

DAY 2: SECESSION DAY

WHEN SECESSION DAY DAWNED, JIMMY WARD GOT HIS WISH, SORT OF. THE storms that had raged during the night ended just before the parade began. But the harsh winds, flood-inducing rains, and tornado-like conditions that had so disturbed Colia Liddell overnight would continue to harass the city for the duration of the Tougaloo Nine saga. However, daytime temperatures in the low seventies on Secession Day turned out to be perfect for marching.[1]

SECESSION DAY FEVER

The excitement over the impending celebration was palpable throughout most of White Jackson. The morning newspaper headlines screamed the latest update about the upcoming events: the midmorning blow-out Confederate Parade; the early afternoon outdoor dramatic pageant reenacting the Secession Convention; the dainty midafternoon tea at the Governor's Mansion hosted by Governor and Mrs. Barnett for all parade participants; and the evening Confederate Balls, four in all, in three separate locations in downtown Jackson. The day was not declared an actual holiday, but school schedules were relaxed, and kids were excused should they choose to skip to attend the parade. And the many stores on Capitol Street would open just after the parade and stay open late into the evening.

Sidney Roebuck's press apparatus at the Mississippi Commission on the War Between the States ginned up a seemingly endless series of press releases and human-interest stories to attempt to get as much publicity as possible for the commission's signature event, put on in collaboration with the Jackson Civil War Centennial Committee. Outlandish predictions that 150,000 eager parade watchers would line the streets of Jackson were taken as gospel by the willing hacks at the Hederman papers for what was billed repeatedly as likely to be the largest single parade in the history of the state.

Not all the Whites in Jackson were thrilled with what was about to be an outrageous display of Confederate values as the state grappled with the reality of rising inequality and dissent among its Black population. Little Martha Bergmark, who would go on to found the Center for Mississippi Justice, was a sixth grader at Pearl Spann Elementary in northeast Jackson during the opening of the centennial ceremonies. Her teacher that year was Carl Barnett, a cousin of the Governor, who, weeks in advance of the celebration, began to come to school dressed in the faux Confederate uniform that he planned to march in during the Secession Day Parade.

Bergmark's father, Robert Bergmark, the distinguished—now legendary—professor of philosophy and religion at the liberal-leaning Millsaps College, took a dim view of Carl Barnett's Confederate boosterism and the upcoming orgiastic revelry that would soon envelop the city. "I remember my father being horrified," Martha said. "This is *treasonous!*" she recalled him saying. Both her father and mother were "appalled by the whole centennial of the Civil War." They realized that it was a way for Mississippians to thumb their noses at the US Supreme Court's ruling on school desegregation and the burgeoning movement for civil rights. "It was clearly a way of saying 'We're against what's happening right now,'" she said.

Martha was not one of the youth who made their way down to Capitol Street on the day of the parade. "Oh, heavens!" she remarked. "I would have gotten in trouble for *that!*"[2]

But the Bergmarks were in the minority of Jackson families. Hundreds of kids showed up for the mammoth parade along with their parents, who took the day off from work to join in the festivities. By the parade's ten o'clock start time, both sides of Capitol Street were packed six-to-eight deep with people trying to catch glimpses of the floats, the marching bands, the high-stepping drum majorettes and the trudging modern-day Confederate soldiers from every part of the state that were about to make their way up Jackson's widest and grandest thoroughfare.

INTERROGATING THE TOUGALOO NINE

While thousands of flag-waving Confederates were assembling along Capitol Street, the Tougaloo Nine were still holed up in the Municipal Jail just two blocks over on Pascagoula. The students had awakened—those who were able to sleep—to another lousy meal. "Molasses, a biscuit, grits, some dry salt meat—a strange combination," Meredith Anding recalled. Then another type of harassment ensued. One by one, the students were removed from their cells and slow walked to an interrogation room where two of the Jackson PD's finest tried to break them down and get information about how they planned the sit-in and, more importantly, who had put them up to it. Fifty years later, Janice still held a clear memory of the incident. "The detectives or police or whoever they were [took] us into the room by ourselves," she recalled. "[One of them] had the coldest, grayest, steel-coal eyes I had ever seen in my entire life. You know? He was just looking through me!" The questions were mostly about "Who put you up to this? Who made you do this? You couldn't have come up with this yourself." Rather than feel intimidated, Janice was incensed. "Why would you say that? What makes you think I'm not smart enough?!" Her heart "might have been pounding, pounding, pounding," but Janice stood her ground. The detective pushed further. "What must your parents think? They must be so ashamed of you!" Janice straightened her spine and snapped right back: "You don't know my parents! How can you say they'd be ashamed of me? My parents would *NEVER* be ashamed of me!" That same defiance she felt while exiting the library showed itself again.

"I had never faced a White man in that manner before," she would later say. "And he looked so menacing! And he just kept on pounding with the same questions, the same insistence that 'You couldn't have done this. Who? Come! Tell me! You didn't. . . . Who? Who?! *Who is behind this*?!'"

Each student faced the same test, the same badgering, the same questions. None of them broke ranks. The police were trying to get them to admit that Medgar Evers had put them up to it. That HE was to blame. That they were just innocent victims. Everyone stuck to what apparently was their "standard, pat answers," as Janice put it. "*We* did this. *We* came up with the plan. It was *our* idea!"

Ethel confirmed that the police were looking for a bigger fish. She recalled being brought into "a little closet-like room. They sat me in a chair. And I just remember these two very tall men asking me a number of questions. The major thing they wanted me to say was that Medgar had put us up to do this." "We don't want you!" they screamed at her. "We know you all are not smart enough to do this. We *know* that Medgar Evers put you up to this!" Ethel became indignant at the suggestion that they didn't think college students could come up with a plan to integrate the local library. "I was pissed off, so I said, 'I'm tired of your penny psychology! I want my lawyer!'" With those magic words, the interview was concluded, and she was escorted back to her cell.

"The most degrading part was going into those rooms and the detectives trying to bend our minds," recalled Geraldine. "It was like 'divide and conquer.'" Her memory of the interrogation is consistent with the others'. "I know you didn't have enough sense to set this up," they told her. "I know you must have been persuaded by someone else to do this!" But Geraldine responded in her patient, quiet demeanor: "Nobody persuaded us to do this." And "I made this choice on my own." Geri remembered her inquisitors "being frustrated and telling me that I was lying."

It seems likely that the interviews were conducted concurrently so that the prisoners wouldn't be able to coach each other how to respond. Perhaps they took the ladies in one shift and the young men in another, since they were in different cell blocks. Meredith Anding believed that "they must have been doing some of us simultaneously. In other words, they didn't string it out, one after another." Perhaps because he was local and the police had a sense of his local ties, he got some questions the others seem to have avoided. "They basically tried to put words in your mouth," he remembered. They asked him, "Who's been working with you? Where did you come up with this crazy idea?"

"I don't know if they used the word 'nigger' or not," Anding reflected, "but they forcefully emphasized, 'You're in the *N-A-A-C-P!*' I was somewhat concerned that they could hit me, but they never did."

Years later, Joe Jackson took pride in the fact that everyone stayed on script, and no one betrayed their adult advisors. Besides being asked the obvious questions—"Who put you up to this? Who is your leader?"—Jackson also remembered more subtle attempts to get him to break. "We have a suspicion of who your leader is, but we want to hear it from you," they said to him. "*We* did this," he insisted again and again. "We *chose* to do this!"

"They knew," he would observe years later. "But they could not really have any evidence that it *was* Medgar if we did not implicate Medgar. None of us did. We knew not to give up Medgar."

Joe Jackson noted, as did others, that this was a practiced response. "Medgar had said, 'They're going to want to find out who orchestrated this. And all of you will have to just say, 'Nobody planned this. We have a research project in college, and we needed these books to complete our research.'"

"But actually," Joe Jackson continued, "they wanted to pressure us to the point where we gave Medgar up. Nobody did."

This now seems like such a remarkable feat. With all of the pressure the Mississippi power structure could have put on these students and their families—nearly all with Mississippi ties—none of the students gave into those pressure tactics, not even the skittish Joe Jackson. In the coming months and years, hundreds of young people would find inspiration in the example of these nine fearless first-time offenders for freedom.

Once returned to their cells, Janice and Ethel spent hours going over what the police had said to them, outraged over their dismissiveness of the abilities of college students. "We were really fussing and mad!" Janice recalled.

MARCHING FOR THE CONFEDERACY

Out on the streets, even as the night's torrential rain slowed to a drizzle, thousands of spectators began lining up along the parade route in hopes of getting a prized front-row spot. Thousands more were gathering out of sight down the four-mile stretch of adjoining Mill Street to participate in the grand march up Capitol Street. There were thirty-eight marching bands from high schools and colleges from all over the state. Even junior high bands were counted in that number. Twelve- and thirteen-year-olds marched with the Hardy, Peeples, and Bailey Junior High School Bands from Jackson. Older students from nearby Brandon marched with their high school band. Members of the Pearl, Meadville, Decatur, Union, Hazelhurst, Purvis, Florence, and Leland High Schools were all lining up along the four-mile staging area. Bands from all three of Jackson's White high schools—Murrah, Central, and Provine—were represented.

Interspersed among the bands were the adult marching units, decked out in their Confederate look-alike uniforms, purchased for twenty-one dollars either by individuals or by the companies they worked for—all in the spirit of civic pride which gripped the populace like nothing had since the days of Forrest and Beauregard. One hundred and twenty-five marching units, comprised of about twenty-five marchers each, took their places amidst the floats, the dignitary cars, and scantily clad majorettes as everyone put on their best faces to show the world their abiding pride in their White, Confederate heritage.

There were no "Negro" faces among the more than five thousand who marched that day, despite the fact that more than 40 percent of Mississippi's population at the time was Black.[3] The only hint of diversity among the nearly thirty-five thousand who showed up to watch were a very few Black children in the crowd and the several Uncle Tom-like characters who were hired to pick up the dung droppings from the horses who pranced up Capitol Street. News coverage carried photos of the bucket brigade—Black men clad in servile white coats and black pants—who, with brooms and dung buckets, stayed between the horses and the dainty majorettes or marching bands behind them. Even Jimmy Ward himself found the graciousness to mention the crew in his column the next day, if only to point out their submissiveness: "That was excellent foresightedness to provide the clean-up details to go behind the cavalry, sweeping up the 'little touches of authenticity' the horses added to the parade, Ward noted."[4]

Black people, of course, were beside the point, as evidenced by the names of some of the marching units: Yankee Hunters of Itawamba, Jackson Blue Flame Rebels, Forrest County Raiders, Meridian Invincibles, Brice's Crossroad

Critters. It was all in good fun, as long as the ruse could be maintained. Even a sensible reporter like Bill Minor joined in the party atmosphere, grabbing a fake Confederate rifle, smiling broadly and posing for a picture with a somewhat skeptical Ross Barnett, himself dressed in full Confederate General regalia, along with commission head Sidney Roebuck, also rebel-clad and definitely in on the joke.[5]

Later Minor would decry the event, saying, "I was so exasperated by the whole thing. Just think, *celebrating* seceding from the Union! You'd think that would be something they'd want to forget about." But on the day itself, Minor seemed to be playing along. What else could he do? Anything less would have seemed uncomfortably out of place.[6]

JACKSON STATE STUDENTS BOYCOTT

Not all of Jackson's citizens were planning to march in lock step with the city fathers and the heritage brigade, however. The surprise library demonstration the day before had stirred something deep within the heart of Black Jackson and it would not be easily quelled. On the campus of Jackson State College, the students who had been chased away from a simple prayer meeting by their college president and the Jackson City police the evening before were now ready to take more decisive action.

When daylight arrived after a long, unsettled night, students' passions moved from disbelief to anger, and they too were ready to march. Dorie Ladner noticed something strange as soon as she woke up and looked out her dorm window. "I saw police officers walking around with these dogs—German shepherd dogs. And I said, 'Oh, my God! What are they doing with the dogs?' I had never seen a police dog before!"

Nevertheless, Dorie and others she had rounded up, including her sister, began gathering just outside Ayer Hall, refusing to go to class in order to protest President Reddix's outrageous behavior the night before. The students made their way to the Field House after breakfast. Joyce recalled that the venue was "wall-to-wall people." A delegation of student protesters was sent to visit the classrooms throughout campus to encourage other students to join the boycott. When all who could be persuaded were assembled, Student Body President Walter Williams addressed the gathered throng and spelled out the students' grievances. At the top of the list was the reinstatement of Joyce's roommate Eunice.

Before long, however, the police, along with their attack dogs, put a halt to the rally. Fifty years later, Joyce Ladner would observe: "The terror that the sight of those dogs aroused within me is with me still. It was like slavery!

It appeared that Reddix was no longer calling the shots and that the Mayor and the Governor had seized control of the campus."

CONFEDERATE PARADE BEGINS

At that very moment, Mayor Allen Thompson and the Governor Ross Barnett were being feted as they waved to adoring crowds as the Secession Day Parade finally got underway. Governor Ross Barnett, along with Vicksburg Mayor and Centennial Commission head John Holland, led the parade, pulled in Robert Stockett's horse-drawn carriage up the long, half mile, eight-block expanse of Capitol Street, waving and smiling all the way. For the sixty-three-year-old Barnett, whose father had fought in the Civil War, it must have been a highlight of his life.

Once Barnett's carriage had made its way up Capitol Street to cheering throngs, he joined his wife in the reviewing stand in front of the Governor's Mansion that graced the north side of the street, just two blocks away from the newly restored Old Capitol. There they would stand and wave for the next two hours as floats and horses and bands and majorettes and troops—lots and lots of Confederate troops—made their way uphill from low-lying Mill Steet. Barnett's horse-drawn carriage was followed by a second one packed with city officials. Mayor Allen Thompson along with his fellow city commissioners Tom Marshall and Dock Luckey—all of whom were up for re-election and all dressed in faux Confederate uniforms—rode in a horse-drawn "fringed vehicle of the era." Thompson, ever the affable politician, got out of the cart halfway up the street as the crowds got thick with potential voters. He greeted his constituents with handshakes and hugs, hoofing it the rest of the way before detaching himself from the festivities and making his way back to City Hall.

When the other dignitaries were properly placed in their observation area, the parade began in earnest. A cohort of Jackson City Police on motorcycles led the way, followed by the now-standard parade participants known simply as "the Shriners." This philanthropic group of men in their fez hats and robes seemed to mock the police escort as they, on their mini-motorcycles, zig-zagged their way up Capitol Street to announce the zaniness of what was about to follow. Then, a most extraordinary Confederate artifact showed itself rounding the corner of Mill and Capitol Streets. When unfurled fully, the largest Stars and Bars Confederate flag ever produced stretched the entire width of the six-lane Capitol Street and extended nearly half a block in length. The crowd roared with excitement as their symbol of defiance made its way up the wide avenue, carried by twenty ROTC cadets from nearby Central

High School. This relic belonged to the University of Mississippi, so of course, the Ole Miss Rebel Band and the University of Mississippi Greys received pride of place, marching and booming Southern melodies directly behind their treasured symbol.

Then, the vast array of horses, floats, marching bands, hi-steppers, cannon, and other artillery began their glorious trip toward gauzy, mythical Confederate nirvana. A dozen Daughters of the Confederacy, mostly middle-aged women and beyond, stood on the steps of the Governor's Mansion bedecked in period costume—hooped skirts, parasols, shawls, and bonnets—cheering on their favorite baton-wielding marchers, forceful drummers, and attractively groomed horses. The equine specimens spent the prior night at the state fairgrounds just behind the Old Capitol where they were fed and bedded down in the same stalls that just two years later would house massive numbers of young Black Jacksonians who would march and protest on this very same street that now celebrated the glories of the Old South. But any suggestion of such societal transformation was out of sight on *this* day.

It can be speculated that the decision to keep the Tougaloo Nine in jail overnight and throughout the entire day was to ensure that not a hint of racial strife could raise its head and spoil what otherwise was a complete return to the world when White supremacy fully reigned. During the day, however, Medgar Evers, John Mangram, and other members of the Jackson NAACP's Executive Committee began planning a mass meeting for later that evening to protest the extended jailing of the Tougaloo Nine and to provide a counter-narrative to all of the Confederate hoopla.

Such cheekiness could not even be contemplated by those drifting deeper into their mint-julep dreams of a century gone by. Most of the men were ogling the pretty young things passing by in their short skirts and bare legs. Of special interest were the lovely Delta Belles, clad in brand new outfits of thigh-high, flouncy, canary yellow gingham with matching parasols that they twirled endlessly, to the crowd's delight. The Belles preceded the Delta State College Band, which according to one report, was the first brass ensemble to play "Dixie" on this day where one might have thought such a selection would have been required of each musician walking up the grand boulevard. Coming as the song did half-way through the parade, it caused one spectator to remark, "*It's about time*!!" Another just stared at the high-stepping co-eds and sighed "Y-E-A-A-H!"[7]

One observer's thoughts were of a less carnal nature, perhaps one of the few taking seriously Roebuck's entreaty to commemorate rather than celebrate the occasion. "This Centennial should serve well as a reminder of the horror of war on our own soil," Delle Dale of Jackson wrote to the *Jackson Daily News* following the parade. "Above the din of rebel cries, brass bands, marching feet of grey-clad soldiers, the songs of Dixie, echo the screams of the dead and dying and the crackle of flames that made a 'Chimneyville' of Mississippi's capitol city and spread ruin and destruction across the Southland."[8]

Such was the spirit of the day that Department of Archives and History head Charlotte Capers tried to convey the tragedy of the hour with her elaborate war-widow's outfit, but her broad smile and waving arms, despite their black-gloved hands, sent a mixed message. Seymour Gordon, "Women's editor" of the *Jackson Daily News*, recorded that Capers "was attired in a maise yellow taffeta antebellum frock" with "matching yellow straw hat swathed in black veiling and lace" and "black sheer shawl." Capers traveled in style up Capitol Street, sitting high in the passenger seat of a bright white convertible Chevy, the official car of the Mississippi Commission on the War Between the States. She apparently was one of the few commissioners willing to participate in such a public way in the festivities.[9]

Most of the others gathered in the Governor's reviewing stand, happy to observe the first fruits of their labors. Florence Sillers Ogden and Representatives Gladys Slayden and Kathleen O'Fallon were there in Ross's orbit that day, along with commission director Sidney Roebuck. So was Biloxi Mayor Laz Quave, who just a year before opposed with force the integration of his city's beaches.

Some actual artifacts of the war were in evidence in the parade. Chief among these was a cannon recovered from the federal ironclad USS *Cairo*, which was still submerged in sandy silt along the banks of the Yazoo River just north of Vicksburg. A foundation had been established to raise the vessel—a multi-million-dollar effort that would see success a few years later. No matter. A cannonade from the sunken Union vessel would do just fine. It made its way up Capitol Street on a float designed to give the "Operation Cairo" maximum publicity on a day when the capture of any Yankee booty could raise a cheer. Additional artillery—some authentic, other recreated— was pushed up the heavy-laden street. At times the cannons were fired with fake ammunition which nonetheless made a piercingly loud noise and emitted large puffs of smoke. It's a wonder the glass storefronts remained intact.

Not far behind the USS *Cairo* float followed a Dixieland Band atop a flatbed truck. Accompanying the jazz combo's melodies was a large sign: "The South Shall Rise Again!"

Rufus Dorsett—who at eighty-three was the eldest marcher trooping up Capitol Street—stood out in his bright Stars and Bars vest among his fellow marching 'soldiers' of the Biloxi Mississippi Grey Infantry Company.

At times Ross Barnett would make his way down from his perch and deign to sign autographs for the many school children, some in raincoats, who gathered nearby. One such photo gained a good deal of attention. A young Black boy who dared to show his face on Mississippi's Whitest Way was rewarded by an autograph from the Governor. "See how we treat our Darkies?" the photo seemed to shout.

Another float whose theme was in tune with the spirit of commemoration recounted the day that Confederate recruits marched off to war. The Deer Creek Raiders of Hollandale had built a large model plantation home at the back end of a long, flatbed trailer which was pulled by a truck. A white picket fence surrounded the rest of the mobile structure to represent the front lawn where middle-aged Confederate-uniformed men bid farewell to their wives by hoisting mint juleps in the air, *Gone with the Wind* style.

Cars were interspersed with the marchers. These chauffeured representatives were members of various Confederate heritage groups, including the Sons and Daughters of the Confederacy. Interestingly, there was a car carrying members of the youthful "Children of the Confederacy"—a project of the United Daughters of the Confederacy that educated children of Confederate ancestry as young as babies to "honor and perpetuate the memory and deeds of high principles of the men and women of the Confederacy."[10] Incredibly, there were also a dozen cars transporting the "Real Daughters of the Confederacy," living relics whose fathers had actually fought in the Civil War.

Another curiosity was a miniature hot air balloon provided by the Mississippi State University's "Aerial Observation Corps." The colorful, patchwork-quilt-patterned inflatable remained tethered to two earthbound corpsmen who, when it could be done safely, raised the balloon high above the adoring gawkers, thus making quite a statement as it moved slowly along the parade route. The display provided a teachable moment, reminding viewers young and old that the Civil War pioneered the military strategy of spying on the enemy from above.

Perhaps the most innovative float was presented by the Washington County Swamp Rangers, who had built a replica of a "ten-gunner" ironsides gunboat on wheels, complete with narrow rectangular slats where guns on each side emerged and shot plumes of smoke into the air. A tall smokestack and a large Confederate flag hoisted above the contraption gave it a whiff of authenticity.

Other rural districts also went big. The Wirt Adams Cavalry brigade brought nearly "100 prancing mounts" and their accompanying uniformed riders. Another rural region represented by the Washington County Sheriff's Posse transported nearly eighty horses and their mounted "Confederate" soldiers to Jackson to be part of the parade. Others were more modest. The Union Cavalry of the Confederate Army—you read that correctly—brought thirty "high-stepping mounts" to the show.

Beards were the stylistic innovation for men participating in the parade. Many had sworn off shaving for months to be able to authentically play their part in the march up Capitol Street. One observer of the parade, keeping a running list about each passing float or regiment, noted the "L. Q. C. Lamar Artillery Unit, most all members heavily bearded." Even the *Jackson Daily News* got into the act by printing photos of many state and local legislators and artistically illustrating what they might have looked like one hundred years earlier—all with penciled-in full beards.

If Southern heritage was on full display on this day, so was American capitalism. In the run-up to the centennial parade, businesses up and down Capitol Street concocted ways to lure customers into their stores during the few days that thousands of out-of-towners were visiting. Many had developed unique Confederate displays to grace their storefronts. McRea's Department Store came in for special commendation from Jimmy Ward for its "impressive collection of Civil War guns on display." Others took out ads in the local papers offering discounts on various centennial-themed products. Some went so far as to print fake Confederate money that could be cut out and used to purchase trinkets inside the store—anything to get shoppers, and their children, to march right into their business establishments and buy, Buy, BUY!

Although the hoped-for number of attendees was 150,000—a figure repeated by Jackson boosters in the weeks preceding the parade, a more realistic estimate of the actual crowd was offered by several news outlets as being closer to 30,000, with another 5,000 marching—respectable numbers given that Jackson's entire population at the time just topped the 150,000 mark, but nowhere near the hoped-for throng.[11]

For two hours this ostentatious display of a foregone era played itself out on the streets of Jackson as thousands took it all in with excitement. The city had never seen, nor would ever see again, such an ardent and potent symbol of its former glory. It was as if Sherman had never marched through and torched everything in his path, as if the derogatory nickname Chimneyville— only the brick chimneys were left standing—had never been uttered. This was a resurrection, of sorts. A wiping clean the slate of defeat and by sheer will and imagination, raising from the dead—for one day only—a lost civilization. It was a culture set in amber, pretty to look at but going nowhere. And most of Mississippi's White citizens were caught in this time warp with no way out.

The bubble would soon burst. The nine Black students in the city jail that day were the canaries in the coal mine. No one wanted to think about them or hear what they were chirping about, but by their outrageous display of cheek in the run-up to this day they had sent a signal. Their real, direct protest stood in stark contrast to this fairy tale. The "Whites-only" myth would have to make room for the other half of Mississippi's populace. And it could be done easily, like the nine students had shown by example—"Just let us in"—or it could be done the hard way. Change was on the way, and Mississippi would have to deal with it one way or another. We all know how this story plays out, and it is not a happy tale. But at this moment, Mississippi still had a choice. The tragedy is that it chose then, and in many ways still chooses now, to resist those winds of diversifying change.

THE SPARK OF STUDENT ACTIVISM

After police broke up the impromptu gathering of Jackson State students at the Field House that morning, it took some time for the youths to recover their composure and figure out their next move. By early afternoon, a group of more than 50 had gathered near the Pearl Street side of campus and began marching eastward in the direction of the downtown area, hoping to make it to the city jail about a mile away. The improvised march was designed both as a rebuke to the campus administration (and the police), as well as a sign of support for the Tougaloo students still stuck in jail. Joyce and Dorie Ladner were among this group, ready to march.[12]

Somehow the police had gotten word of the defiant protest and lined up not only reinforcements but also tear gas and, of course, the dogs at a strategic location along its expected route. After marching several blocks, the students were stopped by a phalanx of police in riot gear urging them to turn around and go back to campus. The students refused to turn back. All of a sudden, one of the cops yelled, "Kill the niggers!" and all hell broke loose.

"There were cracking sounds in the air," Joyce recalled, "and someone screamed, 'They're shooting us!'" Suddenly the police charged the students with their dogs and their billy clubs, "knocking students everywhere."

The cracking sounds were not bullets but tear gas cannisters being shot into the air to disperse the crowd. One of them hit Dorie Ladner in the back of her head, leaving scars that would last a lifetime. "It was bedlam," she recalled years later. "Turn those dogs loose on those God-damned niggers," she heard police yelling. The students began running in whatever direction would get them away from the police and the dreaded dogs.

The Ladner sisters got separated, Joyce running one way and Dorie another. All along Lynch Street was a Black residential area, with many low-slung shotgun houses stretching several blocks. "We started running to the houses and people let us in," Dorie explained. She had run to the back door of one of the homes. "C'mon in!" cried the matron. "Here! Wash your face!" she told Dorie. "Tear gas was burning my eyes and back," Dorie recalled. Once her eyes stopped burning, the lady suggested that Dorie sit on the front porch as if she lived there so police would not think the lady was harboring one of the protesters. Dorie complied, looking cool and collected. "I'm sitting there like I live there and police were running up and down the street with these dogs in the alley."

Dorie stayed on the porch until the police were no longer scouring the streets. Then she made her way back to campus to look for Joyce and see what might have happened to the other students involved in the melee.

Joyce had experienced her own miraculous retreat from terror that afternoon. She and another student ran down a different side street and heard a radio playing inside another small shotgun house. Joyce, panic stricken, knocked loudly on the front door, screaming, "Let me in! Let me in! The police are trying to kill us!!" When no one came to her rescue, Joyce let herself in by reaching through a hole in the screen door and unlatching the hook.

Eventually, "a middle-aged woman was rushing to the front of the house," Joyce recalled. "After we told her what had happened, she assured us that she would let us stay and wouldn't let the police in if they conducted a house-to-house search." The lady went back to her housework. Joyce noticed that gospel music was playing on the radio and a pot of greens was cooking on the stove. "It was so comforting," she recalled.

Several other girls showed up at the back porch and the woman let them in, as well. "Stay as long as you like," she told them. She went back to her ironing and Joyce heard her mutter in something of a stage whisper, "God is going to wreak his vengeance on these low-down, dirty White people one of these days." And later, "It's a sin and a shame to chase people down the street with dogs and hit them over the head like cattle."

"We four, scared, angry students stayed with this woman in her three-room shotgun house for about an hour, which seemed like an eternity. I will always remember the generosity of this woman—who asked nothing of us in return—for braving potential danger on our behalf."

When Joyce got back to campus, she was heartened to see Dorie waiting for her by the cafeteria. After grabbing something to eat, the two newly minted freedom fighters returned to Ayer Hall to recap the day. "That night we sat and talked for a long time," Joyce recalled. "We were unable to conceal our excitement over the fact that finally there was an organized civil rights protest, and that we had been a part of it."

Dorie was thankful to hear that there had been no arrests. "We all scattered and got away." But she also reflected on the impact of the past few days on her consciousness. "It made people like me more determined," she remembered feeling. "A spark had been ignited."[13]

SECESSION DAY CONTINUES

While police were battling the Jackson State students in West Jackson, Secession Day activities continued downtown as if nothing were awry. The Secession Parade ended at about noon, then Governor Barnett, his wife and their big family of children and grandchildren, along with commission members and other local dignitaries, withdrew into the Governor's Mansion for a quick lunch. They reappeared less than an hour later for the short walk up Capitol Street to the large terrace of the Old State Capitol, where a stage had been erected and reserved seating for government dignitaries and special guests had been arranged.

The expanse of State Street that fronted the Old Capitol building had also been blocked off for spectators. It was time for the day's next event, a performance of "The Outset" a one-act play encapsulating the legislative debate and discussion that led to Mississippi's two-step process of its secession from the Union and its entry into the Confederacy.

The Mississippi Commission on the War Between the States had hired Louis Dollarhide, local arts critic and literature professor at Mississippi College, to develop the "pageant" based on the actual transcripts of the Secession Convention, as it came to be known, which lasted, on and off, from January 7 to 26, 1861.

When one o'clock rolled around, and with most of the spectators having sufficiently refreshed themselves with lunch or snacks at the many diners and lunch counters that peppered Capitol Street, the throng was ready for the next event. "More than 7,000 jammed the front of the Old Capitol for the spectacle," wrote *The Clarion-Ledger*'s Jerry DeLaughter. An enormous temporary platform had been erected in front of the historic building that had been the site of the original debate one hundred years before.[14]

The mood shifted from party celebration to poignant reflection as the sun came out and shone down upon the cast of one hundred—mostly students from local colleges and volunteers from the State Highway Department—representing the actual state legislators from the various Mississippi counties of a century earlier. The group had practiced for months for the fifty-minute presentation under the direction of Millsaps theater director Lance Goss. The drama injected a sense of reality into what had up until then been a mythic bacchanal. The audience was exposed to the actual debate that took place in 1861 by then-leading political lights, including L. Q. C. Lamar and James Alcorn. They heard the arguments made by those in favor of remaining in the Union as well as by those for setting off on a separate, unknown course.

The mood was solemn as Governor Barnett took to the stage and made some brief remarks honoring "the noble deeds and sacrifices of men and women who a century ago staked lives and fortune in defense of a Cause. . . . In November 1860, Abraham Lincoln was elected President of the United States. With that election the time had come for Governor Pettus to fulfill a promise he made in his campaign . . ."

Dollarhide's script skillfully called for an actor impersonating Civil War Governor John J. Pettus to pick up the narrative as the current governor finished and took his seat: " . . . a promise made to the people of Mississippi that if the party of Lincoln triumphed in the November elections, I would call a special session of the Legislature to consider the course of action our state must take to insure not merely its survival, but its survival with honor."

The audience then got various tableau of the events of January 7, 8, and 9 as the decision to secede was discussed and taken. Of course, the man with the lofty name, Lucius Quintus Cincinnatus Lamar—former US House member from Mississippi and future US Supreme Court judge long after the war was lost—was featured for his role in helping to write and maneuver the Ordinance of Secession through the specially called convention of one hundred delegates to determine the Magnolia State's course of action. Also highlighted was the role of Mississippi legislator James L. Alcorn, a Unionist (or Co-operationist) who urged the delegates not to secede but to try and work out their differences within the structure of the US Constitution.

The fever to secede was not as acute in Mississippi as it had been, say, in South Carolina and other Southern states. Indeed, one delegate urged his fellow delegates to closely consider the purpose of their likely action, noting that many of them owned no slaves and most had only a few house servants. He called out three delegates who each stood to lose a million dollars or more should slavery be outlawed but noted that most would easily recover from the economic impact of emancipation, short of war.

"I should like to call a few facts to your attention," he said. "The basis of our anger against the North, against Mr. Lincoln, consists in his purpose to free our slaves. Is this not right? And yet how many of us stand to lose much if we lose our slaves?"

Alcorn also urged delegates to consider the consequences of their precipitous action. "What we propose is the division of a people who are organically one; and such a division, I maintain, can have calamitous results for both North and South. . . . With a gesture we can wreck a great and growing nation. I maintain that we must stand within the Union. . . . If we do not, I foresee disastrous results for us all and for all we hold dear."

The reenactment, so faithfully presented, must have caused some in the 1961 audience to think, "What if?" But the pageant kept moving toward its inevitable conclusion.

Lamar eventually called the question to consider the Ordinance of Secession "to dissolve the Union between the State of Mississippi and the other States."

Three amendments were put forward to blunt or slow down the impact of the final decision to secede. All of them failed with at least seventy delegates consistently favoring secession. When the question was finally called for passage of the Ordinance, the vote was "84 yays" (for secession) and "15 nays." In the end, even Alcorn voted for the measure and then, ominously paraphrasing Julius Caesar, stated "The die is cast, the Rubicon is crossed, and I enlist myself with the army that marches on Rome."[15]

As a denouement to the historical pageant, since all in the audience knew what disastrous results the decision had reaped on the state, Dollarhide decided to append to the secession re-enactment a dramatic oration of the farewell remarks that Confederate States' President Jefferson Davis made to the Mississippi legislature in 1884. In its entirety, Davis's speech is a biting rebuke to the forces that won the war—and an exhortation to keep on fighting. ("I deliberately say, if it were to do over again, I would again do just as I did in 1861" and "I cannot believe that the cause for which our sacrifices were made can ever be lost.") But with Dollarhide's revisionist editing, the revised speech suggests a leader who had accepted his fate and that of those he once led. All offensive passages had been excised to avoid any Sectional discomfort. *"Friends and brethren of Mississippi,"* the Davis stand-in began:

> We are now in a transition state, which is always a bad one, both in society and in nature. What is to be the result of the changes which may be anticipated is not possible to forecast, but our people have shown such fortitude and have risen so grandly from the deep depression inflicted upon them that it is fair to entertain bright hopes for the future.
>
> No one is the arbiter of his own fate. The people of the Confederate States did more in proportion to their numbers and means than was ever achieved by any in the world's history. Fate decreed that they should be unsuccessful in the effort to maintain their claim to resume the grants made to the Federal Government. Our people have accepted the decree. . . . Let them leave to their children and children's children the grand example of never swerving from the path of duty, and preferring to return good for evil rather than to cherish the unmanly feeling of revenge.[16]

Davis was played by a twenty-one-year-old drama student from Millsaps College named Richard Pierce. By all accounts his portrayal of the aging former president of the Confederacy—Davis would die five years after delivering his Mississippi farewell—was the highlight of the pageant. Pierce/Davis delivered the remarks from a balcony on the museum's second floor, high above the audience, adding a sense of historic weight to the proceedings.

As Pierce exited from the portico above the stage, a choir sang "America, the Beautiful,"—*not* "Dixie"—as a way of signaling that the country had been handily knit back together. Though Pierce's portrayal had an impact, and his recitation of Davis's cleaned-up remarks seemed to genuinely move the crowd, all efforts at North-South amity were for naught. Just blocks away, nine students were still sitting in jail for having peacefully entered a library and thus declaring their social equality nearly one hundred years after the war began, and no one seemed all that concerned about it. The pageant observers were still caught in the grip of a long-held myth—the "Lost Cause" myth that Davis's original text alluded to—and they could not shake it loose.

OLD CAPITOL RESTORED

Once the pageant ended, the doors of the newly renovated Old Capitol Building swung open wide to welcome its first visitors. "The hallowed halls of the old building had likely not witnessed such a spectacle since secession itself," *The Clarion-Ledger* opined. Charlotte Capers and the chief curator of the new museum, archaeologist Robert Neizel, were on hand to greet the many visitors as they entered. While the crowds flowed in, including many parents with small children, a receptionist jokingly commented to the architect in charge of the renovation, "We may have to ask for another appropriation to restore the building again after today!" Her concerns were unfounded, however, as *The Clarion-Ledger* reported, "The dignified shrine was treated as just that."[17]

At $1.6 million, the renovation was so successful that some might have wondered why the space had ever been abandoned. Original construction of the building had begun in 1839; with the restoration, the 122-year-old structure regained its glory as one of the best examples of Greek Revival architecture in America. Ross Barnett couldn't take full credit for the glorious re-imagining of the once-crucial seat of government. The renovation had begun under his predecessor, J. P. Coleman, but Barnett relished the opportunity to show it off.

Just before opening time, as Charlotte Capers later recorded, the Governor toured the restored facility on his own and got stuck on the new, impossibly difficult-to-open elevator. "At one point, Governor Barnett was seen to enter the elevator on the ground floor," she wrote, tongue-in-cheek, "and we rushed to greet him on the second. The elevator ground by, went up to the third, came back down on the second, and we flew down to remove His Excellency on the first. No such luck. He went up again, and after quite a trip, he did manage to stop the machine at his destination. This was a relief, as he was to open 'the exercises,' as we say, in his Confederate uniform."[18]

By all accounts—hilarious Barnett mishap aside—the overhaul was a triumph for Capers, who oversaw every aspect of the renovation. Architecturally, the restoration once again brought out the building's "majestic symmetry and simplicity" after years of disuse and neglect. All of the historic spaces were preserved, including the House and senate chambers, the Governor's office, and the "High Court of Errors and Appeals" as the state supreme court was once called.

Capers and Neizel brilliantly reimagined the remaining space as a museum of the state's history. The newly renovated rooms displayed specially constructed dioramas, including those of Desoto 'discovering' the Mississippi in 1541; the Indian Treaty of 1820, which opened up new lands for White settlers; and Union ships attempting to run the Confederate batteries along the Mississippi River at Vicksburg in 1863.

Of course, there were rooms filled with Confederate memorabilia. But there were also areas set aside to explore archeological finds, Native cultures, and the complex history of Mississippi's provenance prior to its being admitted into the United States in 1817. The building would serve as a museum for more than fifty years until 2017, when a new state-of-the-art nouveau-classical building was completed, interestingly paired with Mississippi's latest tourism magnet, its modernist Civil Rights Museum. For now, though, that history was in the process of being created.

If the new museum grew tiresome to visitors, the local papers offered suggestions to out-of-towners for other locations throughout the city they might want to check out. Chief among them were two Civil War–related sites. A new community center was being dedicated at Battlefield Park, where actual breastworks and other entrenchments used during the bloody fighting in Jackson in 1863 had been preserved. And tours were available for the antebellum home of Charles Manship, successful businessman turned politician who served as mayor of the city during the period of "unpleasantness." It had been Manship's difficult task of surrendering the city to General Sherman after the Battle of Jackson in May 1863. His had been one of the few residences left standing by Union troops in their warmup to the sack of Atlanta and their march to the sea.

But mostly everyone just wanted to go to tea at the Governor's Mansion. Unfortunately, due to limited space, the afternoon gathering had to be limited to the Mississippi Greys who had marched in the parade along with their families. (Surely this perk was offered in order to help wives encourage their reluctant spouses to sign up and march.) Ross and Mrs. Barnett, along with the wives of various state officials and members of the Centennial

Commission, graciously greeted their gallant visitors. Many of the host wives dressed in hoop skirts and crinolines to honor the spirit of the day.

Those who couldn't get into the invitation-only soiree could cool their heels on the Mansion's expansive lawn and be serenaded by three marching bands still on duty: those from Mississippi Southern, Mississippi State, and, of course, Ole Miss. Surely by now, however, some spirits—at least those of the small children—must have been flagging. For those locals who had ventured downtown for the festivities, this was a good opportunity to head home, make dinner, call the babysitter, and get ready for the final phase of the day's commemoration—the Confederate Balls.

The Jackson police also saw the opportunity provided by this opening in the Secession Day schedule to remove the thorn in their side and release the nine Tougaloo demonstrators from jail.

TOUGALOO NINE SPRUNG FREE

It seems that nearly every one of the Tougaloo Nine lost his or her sense of time while in the custody of the police. Although Joe Jackson remembers a small window high above their men's cell where they could manage to see whether it was dark or light outside, Geraldine recalls no such window in the women's quarters. The hours seemed to stretch on for an eternity. When later told she was only in jail for about a day and a half, Janice Jackson was astonished. "What!?" she asked in disbelief. "It was only thirty-six hours or something? I said, 'Please!' Looked to me like it was at least three or four days!!"

Al Lassiter concurred. "Oh, yeah. I thought it was like two-and-half or three days." Geraldine also lost all sense of time.

"I tell people it *had* to be three days," she said. "But we couldn't tell! We couldn't tell day from night! We were just sort of lingering in time. And when you're not doing anything, time seems longer."

Jackson Daily News editor Jimmy Ward had a suggestion for the students. In his front-page Crossroads column, adjacent to a cartoonish stars and bars illustration celebrating the day's events, he penned this: "One Tougaloo co-ed to another: 'Is you did yo' Greek yit?'" His audience certainly got the joke, even though he didn't mention the read-in. But just in case they needed a reminder, he followed this imaginative racist quip with a longer made-up story about "publicity-seeking Negroes" who "invaded" a library in Atlanta.

When Ethel saw these front-page affronts later in the day, she was hopping mad, but when she showed them to Janice, the two burst out laughing. "We didn't know whether to be pissed or entertained," Ethel would later say. It was that kind of day.[19]

At some point prior to their release, Dr. Beittel stopped by the jail to check on his students. It was the first sign in more than twenty-four hours that someone from the outside world was, in fact, concerned about their well-being. Beittel says he returned from his UNCF meeting in Atlanta and "as soon as I got back, I went to the jail. And the jailer was very decent to me. He brought the group to another room, away from their cells. And I had a chance to talk with them."[20]

In his comments to the press after visiting the students, however, Beittel said he had simply visited his charges "to discuss mid-term exams, which are underway at Tougaloo" and to make arrangements for them to take the exams at a later date. He observed that "all were in good spirits" and noted that attorneys Jack Young and Jess Brown were arranging for their bail, which he expected to be posted later in the day. Then, in response to a reporter's question, he let it be known that "no disciplinary action is contemplated" by the college for the students' actions. "They were acting completely on their own and their demonstration was in no way related to school policies," he said. Beittel's hands-off stance dramatically contrasted with the harsh, "hands-on" approach of Jacob Reddix at Jackson State from the night before and would set the tone for his remaining three years at Tougaloo.[21]

As the college president predicted, the bond money was finally accepted by the sheriff early that evening. When the students were led down to the booking station while awaiting their final release papers to be signed, they saw all of the food and snacks that had been delivered to the jail the evening before and had been trickling in throughout their second day of incarceration. As they waited, a few of the guys began to pretend to reach out and grab some of the food from the makeshift shelves that had been created. The girls chided them, not knowing that the food had actually been brought there for them. "Don't do that!" they whispered. "That's just what they expect us to do! Don't steal those cookies!!" It was only later, when the snacks were stuffed into the police cars that were to transport the students back to campus, did they realize that the cache of goodies was for them.

After an interminable period of alternating between heightened awareness and extreme boredom, the students were released from jail just after 7:00 p.m. on Tuesday evening, March 28, and driven by the police back to the Tougaloo campus. They, in fact, had been in jail for nearly thirty-two hours. Much had transpired in their absence.

What most students remember about their trip back to campus was the way the cop cars went careening through Jackson to get them there. "We were speeding *so* fast down the highway," Ethel recalled. "This is the way they gonna get rid of us!" she thought ominously. "Get those niggers out of here!"

a less serious Al Lassiter imagined the police thinking. "We were going one hundred miles an hour!" Sam remembered. "They were flying!!"

When the shaken students arrived safely back at Tougaloo and were driven through the wrought-iron gates, a crowd of hundreds awaited them. The patrol cars rumbled down the gravel path, past the president's new residence—still under construction—and up to the left toward Judson Cross Hall. The police drivers were uncertain what to make of the throng of celebratory students, particularly as they began to make their way boisterously toward the police cars. Those gathered, of course, were there to greet and welcome back their schoolmates, relieved that they were safe and deliriously happy that they had done their part to throw off the Jim Crow shackles that had held them all in check for their entire lives.

"The students just stormed the police cars," Sam remembered. "They were coming to greet *us*! But the cops became a little bit concerned because the students were headed toward *them*."

Instead, when the demonstrators exited the patrol cars, some were hoisted on shoulders and paraded around campus. "Coach Coleman picked me up," Sam proudly recalled. "He certainly did! We were treated as heroes."

"Proud," Al Lassiter interjected. "They were proud."

Ethel remembered the jubilation but also recalled keeping one eye on the food that the police began pulling out of the car. "So here come a lot of guys to welcome us back," she noted. "But some guys from Galloway Hall said, 'Oh, let *us* carry that for you.' And we never saw that food again. I bet they had a ball down on Galloway Hall!"

"Now that I think about it," Ethel reflected, "I think we were hurt and mad and tickled all at the same time."

After this unprecedented celebration of this cohort of nine students who had done Tougaloo proud, everyone retired to their dorms to prepare for whatever repercussions the next day might bring.

Not everyone returned to campus right away, however. Alfred Cook and Meredith Anding stayed downtown and headed over to College Hill Missionary Baptist Church near Jackson State to participate in the extraordinary turn out at the NAACP's mass meeting called in response jailing of the students and the Secession Day events. Local news reporters were on hand to capture at least part of the celebratory mood, recording that between four to five hundred participants "jumped to their feet and yelled, 'Glory,' when the Tougaloo students made their entrance." Both Anding and Cook recalled the pumped-up gathering. "Once the crowd saw Alfred and I, they started to yell and to applaud," Meredith remembered.

But Reverend Mangram, who was in the middle of his presentation as the featured speaker at the rally that night, unexpectedly ordered the two young men to move to the back of the stage, away from their enthusiastic admirers. "He shooed us back in the background," Anding recalled. Al Cook believed this was done for the youths' safety, although it is also possible that their unanticipated arrival interrupted his flow.

Mangram was just warming up the audience to his theme. "This is just the beginning," he said of the library sit-in. "These nine students are bearing the sins of segregation because they are Blacks and they are getting out of their place!" Mangram shouted. Then, clearly understanding the historic juxtaposition between Jackson's first civil rights sit-in and the over-the-top celebration of all things Confederate, Mangram threw down the gauntlet. "I'm so glad the damn Yankees won the war, I don't know what to do!" he exclaimed to thunderous applause. He went on in this vein for forty-five minutes.[22]

Prior to the students' arrival, Medgar Evers had updated the crowd on their recent release from jail and also about the Jackson State student uprising from earlier in the day. He denounced the "police state tactics" used to intimidate the JSC students (many of whom were in the crowd) from their "use of peaceful protest against segregation and discrimination in Jackson." Evers also took note of the historic nature of the library protest, saying that it "is the beginning of the fight to make us first class citizens in Mississippi!"

"In the past few days," he continued, "there has been history made in Jackson and in Mississippi. And we will move ahead from this day on."

Meredith Anding remembered being congratulated by one of his neighbors, R. L. T. Smith. "I'm proud of you! I'm proud of you!" Smith kept repeating as he pumped Anding's hand. As one who put up the bond for the students' release, Smith had also addressed the gathering earlier in the evening, declaring that "I am a Negro who won't go along with the way things are now, and I plan to change it!" Smith was one of those challenging in US District Court the monthly payments being made by the state government to the Citizens' Council to promote segregation.

Also, on the dais that evening was Alfred Cook's former mentor from Campbell College, Reverend Charles Jones. One can imagine a similar joyous reunion between Cook and Jones as they celebrated the latest milestone in the Mississippi movement's long slog toward freedom. "It took nine brave students to stage Monday's sit-in," Jones observed. "White people say we want to be with them," he continued. "We do not want to be with them. We want to have what they have! And we are here tonight to start to get some of it!!"

After Mangram's oration, a Jackson State student who was taken into police custody and held for two hours for questioning after the aborted march to the city jail earlier in the day offered a warning, of sorts, to the assembled crowd. Randy Parker, who had carried a small American flag in the march, along with an armful of schoolbooks, described what he had been through—the tear gas, the police batons, the dogs. Then he simply said, "My experience was one that many of us will have to endure" in the quest for freedom. Within twenty-four hours, Parker's statement would seem like a prophecy.

As an indication of the show of force to come, more than twenty of Jackson's finest had arrived at the scene of the rally and were staking out the church from across the street. But as the two-hour meeting ended and the crowd quickly began to disperse, it was clear that the police presence was unnecessary. The *State Times* reported that "following the meeting, the Negroes began quietly filing home and the police did not need to interfere." Meanwhile, one of the premier social events of the spring season had begun for White Jackson.

REBEL YELLS AND DANCING INTO THE NIGHT

Ah, the Confederate Balls. How to put it? Just about everyone who was anyone—and even some of those who weren't—turned themselves out as if Scarlet O'Hara and Rhett Butler themselves would be in attendance. It was full-on *Gone with the Wind* at least at three of the four balls on tap for the evening.

All four had been meticulously planned to ensure everyone interested in attending could do so, and so that those who had played important roles in the day's events would feel appreciated. Two high-end hotels in the city   the King Edward, the Heidelberg—and the large municipal auditorium, also downtown, were conscripted into service to handle the thousands of revelers. The Heidelberg did double duty, holding events in both its Victory and Olympic Ballrooms.

The City Auditorium hosted the more than three thousand Mississippi Grey marching troops and their wives—the only place large enough to handle such a crowd—and it was the first ball visited by the governor and other political elites. The ball kicked off at 8:00 p.m. sharp with "the Grand March"—the entrance of the poohbahs—before the dancing commenced. The order of the march was staged for maximum impact, saving the best for last. "Colonel" (Mayor) Allen Thompson and his wife led the march, followed by "Adjutant-in-Chief" (Commission Chairman) John Holland and his bride. When "Major General" (Governor) Barnett and his missus arrived, the crowd went wild.[23]

All three couples were turned out nicely, with the men wearing the same faux Confederate uniforms they had donned for the parade and the women displaying their exquisite ball gowns, all fashioned in the Southern style. For the record—and Seymour Gordon made sure her readers had every breathless detail—Mrs. Thompson "was lovely in an aqua silk taffeta. Its softly shirred ruffled skirt blossomed with handmade roses."

We are told that Mrs. Holland, wife of the mayor of Vicksburg, wore an antebellum gown "of black silk taffeta with wide tiers of black French lace. The bouffant skirt, worn over hoops, was accented with cream-colored roses." And Mrs. Barnett, "our gracious First Lady, was attired in a turquoise blue pure silk organza. The authentic costume was detailed with gracefully draped overskirt caught up at intervals with large pale pink cabbage roses." She also displayed "turquoise plumes in her hair and long white kid gloves."

As the power couples made their entrance, the band struck up "The Bonnie Blue Flag"—the first anthem of the new Confederacy, which had been written by an Irish immigrant entertainer who premiered it in Jackson in the spring of 1861, likely when the state legislature voted to join the Confederacy, exactly one hundred years earlier.

> We are a band of brothers, and native to the soil,
> Fighting for our Liberty, with treasure, blood and toil;
> And when our rights were threaten'd, the cry rose near and far,
> Hurrah for the Bonnie Blue Flag, that bears a Single Star!
>
> Hurrah! Hurrah! For Southern Rights, hurrah!
> Hurrah! For the Bonnie Blue Flag, that bears a Single Star!
>
> As long as the Union was faithful to her trust,
> Like friends and like brethren kind were we and just;
> But now when Northern treachery attempts our rights to mar,
> We hoist on high the Bonnie Blue Flag that bears a Single Star! . . .
>
> First, gallant South Carolina nobly made the stand;
> Then came Alabama, who took her by the hand;
> Next, quickly Mississippi, Georgia and Florida,
> All rais'd on high the Bonnie Blue Flag that bears a Single Star!

The crowd could hardly contain itself at the sound of this fighting/drinking song—the second-most-popular Southern ditty to come out of the war. As the Grand March ended, there was an immediate move to the dance floor, where there was "mass confusion of grey coats and swirling silk skirts."

Each ball was hosted by various units of the newly formed Mississippi Greys. Leaders of such groups as "the Sons of the South Artillery Unit," the "VFW Barksdale's Raiders," and the "Gulf South Defenders" greeted guests as they arrived. It is an indication of how deeply entwined were the politics of the day with the commemoration of the past by noting that the "Citizens' Council Unit" helped with hosting duties at the City Auditorium, the largest of the evening's four celebratory balls. The arch-segregationist civic organization likely saw it as a recruiting opportunity.

The City Auditorium event was a classic affair. Period costumes and music were the order of the evening. The Jules Barlow orchestra provide the sounds while the actors from the long-running Vicksburg pageant "Gunboats 'Round the Bend" demonstrated "Old South dances." The drift into the deep past was complete.

Barnett and company repeated their Grand March routine down at the Heidelberg Hotel events later in the evening as the sextet of ladies and their prominent gentlemen put in an appearance at three of the balls. The only exception was the one held at the King Edward Hotel, located at the foot of Capitol Street, just across the street from the railroad station. Here, all of the young college and high school students who had marched and jammed that morning on the streets of Jackson kicked off their marching shoes and danced the night away to the contemporary songs of Elvis, Chubby Checker, the Everly Brothers, and the like, provided by the band "The Red Counts." "The merrymaking could be heard for three blocks" away, wrote one surprised observer. "Virginia reels and waltzes were forgotten as the joint really rocked!" The future was quickly overtaking the past.

The big moment at the Heidelberg came late in the evening as Jerry Lane's orchestra, holding down the Olympic Ballroom, launched into a loud rendition of "Dixie." Partygoers in the Victory Ballroom informed the Ole Miss dance band that they were being outdone. Soon, "Dixie" was blaring from both rooms. "The crowd was wild!" a reporter noted. "The bands played louder, the screams of the crowd grew wilder, and those who couldn't manage the difficult Rebel Yell gave a reasonable facsimile, which left no doubt how they felt about the 'Confederate National Anthem.'"

The parties continued late into the night, and no one seemed to want to let go of the great, gripping Lost Cause dream. Eventually, overcome by exhaustion, "the tired colonels and their wives decided to close this first and grandest chapter of Mississippi's Civil War Centennial."

INTRODUCING THE TOUGALOO NINE: THE MEMPHIS CONTINGENT

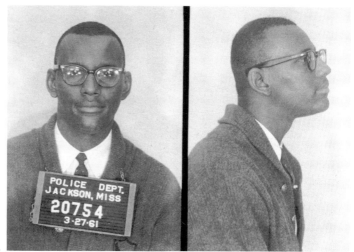

JOSEPH JACKSON JR.

ETHEL SAWYER

JAMES "SAMMY" BRADFORD

CHILDREN OF THE DELTA AND RIVERSIDE

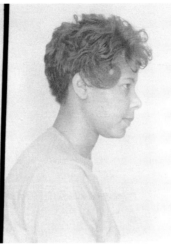

JANICE JACKSON

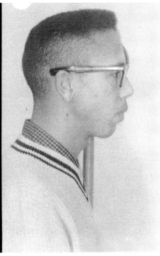

ALBERT LASSITER

GERALDINE EDWARDS

ALFRED COOK

MEREDITH ANDING JR.

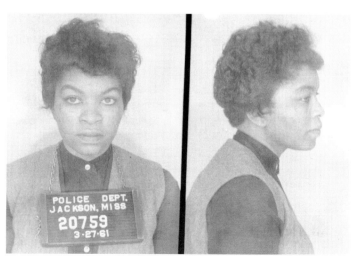

EVELYN PIERCE

TOUGALOO COLLEGE—THE OASIS

The Hallowed Entrance Gate of Tougaloo College as it appeared in 1961. (Tougaloo College *Eaglet*, 1961)

Exterior, Tougaloo's Woodworth Chapel, where most of the Tougaloo Nine first met Medgar Evers. (M. J. O'Brien)

Interior, Woodworth Chapel, where chaplain John Mangram preached every Sunday throughout the 1950s and early 1960s. (M. J. O'Brien)

The Mansion, which in the early spring of 1961 still served as the president's residence. (M. J. O'Brien)

President Adam D. Beittel
(Tougaloo College *Eaglet*, 1963)

Chaplain John Dee Mangram
(Tougaloo College *Eaglet*, 1957)

Professor Ernst Borinski
(Tougaloo College *Eaglet*, 1961)

Dean A. A. Branch
(Tougaloo College *Eaglet*, 1961)

Business manager George Owens
(Tougaloo College *Eaglet*, 1961)

Music teacher/choral director Ariel Lovelace
(Tougaloo News, September 1980)

SCENES FROM CAMPUS LIFE

Dr. Borinski's Social Science Lab. (Borinski, right; Ethel Sawyer, third from right.) (Tougaloo College *Eaglet*, 1960)

Dr. Borinski's famed Social Science Forum, where Black and White alike could sit together and hear leading scholars discuss issues of national and international importance. (Borinski seated front, center; Geraldine Edwards, front-right, looking back at camera.) (Keahey Collection, A&RSD, MDAH)

The Tougaloo College Choir appearing on a local TV program. (Joseph Jackson Jr., back row, third from left; James "Sammy" Bradford, fourth from left.) (Keahey Collection, A&RSD, MDAH)

Tougaloo students and staff heading to Texas to attend the annual conference of the YMCA/YWCA organizations, just six weeks before the library sit-in. (Evelyn Pierce, front row, second from right; Albert Lassiter, back row, far right.) (Keahey Collection, A&RSD, MDAH)

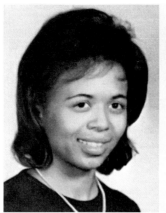

Colia Liddell organized the Tougaloo College Chapter of the NAACP and served as special assistant to Medgar Evers. (Tougaloo College *Eaglet*, 1961)

The Ladner sisters—Dorie, left, and Joyce, right—were students at nearby Jackson State College when the Tougaloo Nine took their historic action. They participated in JSC's student uprising to protest the arrest of the Tougaloo Nine and would go on to become important Mississippi members of the Student Nonviolent Coordinating Committee. (Tougaloo College *Eaglet*, 1964)

Medgar Evers worked to organize the youth of Mississippi from the time he took on the role of Mississippi's field secretary for the NAACP in late 1954. He advised the Tougaloo Nine prior to their historic action and helped organize their legal defense in its aftermath. (Albert Lassiter's brother Lewis was teaching art at Tougaloo College during the summer of 1963 when Evers was assassinated. Upon hearing of the tragedy, he quickly sketched this pen-and-ink portrait of Evers and presented it to his brother, knowing Albert's deep association with and affection for his mentor. This marks the first publication of this work.) (Used with permission of Albert Lassiter Sr.)

Roy Wilkins served as executive secretary of the NAACP from 1955 through 1977. Wilkins was a harsh critic of the Civil War centennial celebrations conducted by the Southern states. (NAACP Photo Collection, LOC)

AT THE LIBRARY

James "Sammy" Bradford studies as police confer about how to proceed. (NAACP Photo Collection, LOC)

A screen capture of newsreel footage reveals the scene as police have announced that the students are under arrest. Geraldine Edwards (seated) prepares to gather her belongings as Meredith Anding (right) and Albert Lassiter move toward the exit. Ethel Sawyer (in white sweater) can be viewed just behind Lassiter's shoulder. (Screenshot from WLBT-TV footage. [MDAH])

The Tougaloo Nine exit the Jackson Public Library under police escort. From left: Meredith Anding, Evelyn Pierce, Janice Jackson, Alfred Cook, Geraldine Edwards, Joseph Jackson, Ethel Sawyer, Albert Lassiter, and James "Sammy" Bradford. (Screenshot from WLBT-TV footage. [MDAH])

The start of Mississippi's Civil War centennial commemorations began on January 9, 1961, with a declaration by Governor Ross Barnett in the newly refurbished Old Capitol, where the original Articles of Secession were drawn up, debated, and approved. Top row, from left: Dr. Albert Sidney Johnston, nephew and namesake of the prominent Confederate general, provided the invocation for the event; Barnett; and John Holland, mayor of Vicksburg and chairman of the commission. Bottom row, from left: Byrd Mauldin, Thurman Bryant, Laz Quave, Kathleen O'Fallon, Charlotte Capers, Florence Sillers Ogden, and Gladys Slayden. All but Johnston were members of the commission. (A&RSD, MDAH)

Reporter Bill Minor (left) clowning with high-ranking members of the Mississippi Civil War Centennial Commission prior to the Secession Day festivities. Pictured with Minor (from left) are Honorary Colonel William Gupton, Governor Ross Barnett, and Sidney Roebuck. (Bill Minor Private Collection)

Thousands of men dressed in faux Confederate uniforms marched up Capitol Street, along with baton-twirling majorettes, school marching bands, and riders on horseback to honor their defeated forebears and celebrate Confederate culture. (A&RSD, MDAH)

Variously themed floats accompanied the marchers. This one, representing the Deer Creek Raiders of Hollandale, went full-out *Gone with the Wind*, with a plantation house and a sign that reads, in part, "Farewell Mint Julep Party—OFF TO WAR!" (A&RSD, MDAH)

An honorary Confederate colonel and his family are greeted by (from left) Governor Ross Barnett, Centennial Commission director Sidney Roebuck, and Commissioner Byrd Mauldin at the Governor's Mansion tea for parade participants. (A&RSD, MDAH).

A reenactment of the Secession Convention of 1861 on the portico of the Old Capitol during Mississippi's Civil War centennial celebration, March 28, 1961. (A&RSD, MDAH)

Across the street from the courthouse, police sicced dogs on Black bystanders awaiting the outcome of the trial of the Tougaloo Nine. (NYWT&S, LOC)

Photographer and Farish Street Newsstand owner Thomas Armstrong being chased from the courthouse by police and a threatening dog. "Before Violence Struck" read the accompanying headline. Armstrong would be brutally beaten by bystander Red Hydrick before finding shelter in the nearby *Clarion-Ledger* building. (NYWT&S, LOC)

Medgar Evers points to the broken arm of eighty-one-year-old W. R. Wrenn, the result of police brutality against peaceful Black citizens congregating outside the courthouse during the trial of the Tougaloo Nine. (NAACP Photo Collection, LOC)

STOP THIS DOG!

THIS IS A VICTIM'S VIEW OF A POLICE DOG

A pastor was snagged by teeth like these when Mississippi police used dogs on Negroes demonstrating their support for the sit-in students on trial at the Jackson courthouse on March 29.

Do You Want To Fight The Dogs?

You can lick the police dog spirit, wherever it may be. Join the NAACP, the organization with the year-in, year-out driving power. Send your check or money order (see below) and *you will be enrolled in the Army to Fight the Dogs.*

Nationwide Spring membership campaigns in most localities from April 15 through June 30. Annual memberships: $2.00, $3.50, $5.00, $10.00 and up. Life memberships (payable in installments) $500.00. Contributions in any amount. Join your local branch or send to:

NAACP fundraising flier calling attention to the dogs used to disperse the crowd at the trial of the Tougaloo Nine. (NAACP Papers, LOC)

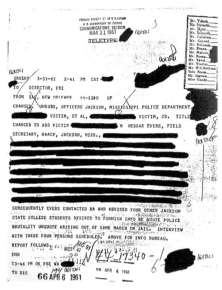

Medgar Evers was one of many of those brutalized by the police to be interviewed by the FBI in the wake of the police riot during the trial of the Tougaloo Nine. Most of the testimony remains heavily redacted more than sixty years after the incident. (Printout, FBI Vault)

TOUGALOO NINE TRIUMPHANT

In the days following the Tougaloo Nine protest, student photographer Jerry Keahey gathered the relieved and jubilant group on campus for a historic portrait. From left: Joseph Jackson Jr., Geraldine Edwards, James "Sammy" Bradford, Evelyn Pierce, Albert Lassiter, Ethel Sawyer, Meredith Anding Jr., Janice Jackson, and Alfred Cook. (Keahey Collection, A&RSD, MDAH)

Keahey also included several behind-the-scenes collaborators while attempting to recreate the library scene of students seated at tables, reading books. Besides the Tougaloo Nine, additional key players include Joan Collins (seated, second from left); Mary Allen (standing, second from left), and Reverend John Dee Mangram (standing, second from right). (Keahey Collection, A&RSD, MDAH)

During the 1961 NAACP National Convention in Philadelphia, the Tougaloo Nine rubbed elbows with the likes of drummers Max Roach and Babatunde Olatunji in the lobby of the Sheraton Hotel. Here, Roach's wife, Abbey Lincoln (left), performs Roach's recently released avant-garde "Freedom Now Suite" at the convention with Olantunji (center) and his dancers, as well as Roach's band (right). (NAACP Photo Collection, LOC)

Although several of the Tougaloo Nine rode the Freedom Train from Philadelphia to Washington, DC, with many of their NAACP counterparts in July 1961, they were not included in the meeting with President Kennedy—something Meredith Anding Jr. would grumble about for years to come. Here, Bishop Stephen Gill Spottswood, recently elected chairman of the NAACP national board, reads a statement urging the president to take action on his civil rights agenda. Kennedy, seated in his famous rocking chair, reads along. Medgar Evers, standing just behind Kennedy (far left), was present, as were many other regional NAACP leaders. (JFK Library)

Arrest portraits of the Tougaloo Nine appear in many major civil rights museums across the country and emblazon T-shirts, mugs, and other memorabilia. It may be useful to remember, however, that at the time of their historic protest, the Tougaloo Nine were ordinary citizens and college students. (Photo of T-shirt by M. J. O'Brien. College photos taken from Tougaloo College *Eaglet*, 1960 and 1961.)

Police photo collage and college student photo collage are arranged in the same order as follows: Top row (from left), Joseph Jackson Jr., Albert Lassiter, Alfred Cook; Middle row (from left) Ethel Sawyer, Geraldine Edwards, Evelyn Pierce; Bottom row (from left) Janice Jackson, James "Sammy" Bradford, Meredith Anding Jr.

HONORS AND COMMEMORATIONS

In 2006, members of the Tougaloo Nine were awarded keys to the city of Jackson when they returned for the forty-fifth anniversary of their heroic action. (Key from the archive of Meredith Anding Jr. Photo by M. J. O'Brien)

In August 2017, a historical marker was dedicated just outside the library that the Tougaloo Nine attempted to integrate. Many of the Nine were on hand to honor the moment. From left: James "Sammy" Bradford, Janice Jackson Vails, Ethel Sawyer Adolphe, Geraldine Edwards Hollis. From right: Alfred Cook and Meredith Anding Jr. (AP)

Images of the Tougaloo Nine are prominently displayed at the Mississippi Civil Rights Museum, which opened in December 2017 in Jackson. (M. J. O'Brien)

Members of the Tougaloo Nine family returned to Jackson in 2021 to receive honorary doctorate degrees from Tougaloo College. From left: Albert Lassiter Sr., Armaan Anding (son of Meredith), Alfred Cook, and Geraldine Edwards Hollis. (M. J. O'Brien)

Prominently displayed in the Washington, DC, congressional office of Representative Bennie Thompson of Mississippi is a portrait of the Tougaloo Nine (above mirror). (M. J. O'Brien)

Chapter 16

DAY 3: THE TRIAL, THE DOGS, THE BEAT DOWN

WHEN DAYLIGHT CAME, *JACKSON DAILY NEWS* EDITOR JIMMY WARD got to work crafting a laudatory editorial that ran in the afternoon paper. He wrote,

> Yesterday's colorful parade, the dramatic rebirth of the Secession at the Old Capitol, the multitudes touring the Historical Museum and the gala festivities last evening all combined to make a memorable occasion for Mississippi.
>
> Few, if any, parades in the state's history could match the color, enthusiasm and reception given the nearly two-hour performance that moved with clocklike precision up Capitol Street on Secession Day. A rewarding scene for those who participated was the excitement it gave the many, many youngsters who waved Confederate flags and saluted the forces of the Mississippi Greys.

Ward went on to praise that master of public relations George Godwin for coming up with the idea in the first place. "What started as an idea nearly two years ago became a remarkable reality," Ward purred. "The idea of mobilizing the memorial units of the Confederacy sprang from George W. Godwin, Sr., of Godwin Advertising agency." Ward himself took a bow for spreading the idea on the front page of his newspaper in April 1959. (An uncharacteristic photo of Ward, along with Godwin—both dressed in their faux Confederate colonel jackets and Johnny Reb forage caps—accompanied the piece.)

He also noted that at the time, the idea seemed a bit far-fetched for some other Southern opinion leaders. "*The Richmond Times-Dispatch* didn't quite like the idea," Ward observed. "That journal called the Godwin idea a nightmare, proclaiming the suggestion would cost millions, or billions, of dollars." Ward noted that despite "token opposition, Mississippians in all walks of life pitched in with a delightful sense of cooperation and the show moved off on schedule Tuesday."

Ward went on to heap praise on the Centennial Commission and the legis-lature, among others, before congratulating himself once more. "In exploring the Centennial idea for the first time nearly two years ago, this newspaper said: 'We can envision no single activity of the Centennial that could possibly have the dramatic significance that would come from the reactivation of all the military forces of the Confederacy.'" He went on to say, "We have seen that vision put into action. It deserves to grow into greater things."[1]

Not everyone was so sure that the idea of recreating the genteel South and having Confederate military units, unarmed and untrained though they may have been, was the best way of commemorating the Civil War. Such an outrageous display of Southern "culture"—honoring the very values of rebellion that brought about a breach to the Union and contributed to the loss of more than six hundred thousand lives, not to mention the near com-plete destruction of the South's infrastructure—was viewed as an enormous breach of etiquette. It played poorly in the Northern press and even in some progressive areas of the South.

In his front-page daily column in the *Atlanta Constitution*, Ralph McGill condemned Mississippi's and Alabama's commemorations thus far, saying, "What we have now are increasing numbers of persons wandering about the South wearing sleazy imitations of Confederate uniforms, growing beards, stirring up old hatreds, making ancient wounds bleed again, reviving Ku Klux Klans, working themselves into immature fits of emotionalism, recreating old battles, and otherwise doing a great disservice to the memory of those who fought and died in the war of 1861–65. . . . We do not need to refurbish old myths."

"By all means," he concluded, "let us memorialize the war and those who served it honestly and well. But let us have done with all else."[2]

The bad publicity that the Mississippi Confederate extravaganza engen-dered, coupled with similar concerns expressed when Alabama kicked off its commemoration the month before, rolled off the backs of quacks like Jimmy Ward. But a more immediate and distinctly local dose of reality was awaiting the capital city at precisely the same time as the day's *Jackson Daily News*—including Ward's self-congratulatory homage—was rolling off the presses.

ANOTHER DAY OF FIRSTS

After their glorious reception back on campus, the Tougaloo Nine retired to their dorms to get showers and settle down for a good night's sleep. The next day dawned still cloudy and with a chance of scattered showers. The newly minted activists' schedule was already set for the day: attend classes as per usual in the morning, have lunch, maybe get one more afternoon class in before getting ready to head downtown for their trial, which had been hurriedly scheduled at the end of the court day at 4:00 p.m. If the students were restless about appearing in court, they didn't show it. It was going to be just another day of firsts for them.

If the star attractions seemed unfazed, most of Jackson was anything but. The fact that the nine demonstrators were to make an appearance, however perfunctory, in the downtown area in the late afternoon had much of Jackson in a tizzy. Black and White citizens alike wondered how things would play out. Would the students be found guilty and sent back to jail? Would the judge be lenient and let them back on the streets to cause more "trouble"? Were more protests planned in a coordinated attempt to disrupt the rhythms of the capital city's daily routine? Coming as the trial did the day after the Confederate Parade and its accompanying grand balls that went far into the night, the reminder of the brash protest must have seemed like a splash of cold water on the faces of White Mississippians. Indeed, a few days later, the staunchly old guard columnist Charles Hills at *The Clarion-Ledger*—with a gruesome wit to rival that of Jimmy Ward at the *Jackson Daily News*—asked the question that seemed to be on everyone's minds: "If the Negroes want so much to be whites, why don't they just skin themselves?"[3] Yes, this is what passed as levity in Mississippi's paper of record. Shocked astonishment with a wish to flay those who would dare disrupt the established order.

In the run up to the trial, Jackson's power structure seemed to expect the worst, if their show of force was any indication. An hour before the trial of the students was scheduled to begin, police ringed the Municipal Court Building. It looked as if Jackson's entire police force—all White, of course—was called out to ensure tranquility among the populace. Photographs of the scene show at least a dozen armed officers of the law standing on the second tier of a three-tiered set of steps leading up to the imposing courthouse entrance. On the second tier—the one with the longest terrace—Jackson's finest stand, dressed in pressed white shirts and ties, guarding the sacred white-block limestone temple of justice. Two men in blue stand with seated guard dogs—the same dogs that had been used to quell the Jackson State uprising the day before. They are stationed, one cop and one dog, on either side of the extra-wide stairs, as if they were some ancient Egyptian guardians of the galaxy. Additional police surround the entire building, press reports note. They seemed ready for anything.[4]

Citizens interested in the proceedings, both Black and White, began arriving almost as soon as the police got into formation. By 3:40, the entire limited-seating courtroom was packed—with one side of the courtroom filled with Whites, the other with Blacks—120 in all—observing the segregated custom and almost making the point for the prosecution that what the students had done, well, it just isn't done around here.

Police had spread the word that once the gallery in the courtroom was filled, no one would be allowed in or around the building. Spectators continued to arrive, and police turned them away. The disappointed ended up forming two separate groups just across Pascagoula Street—a wide throughway that left plenty of space for cars to come and go.

Once again, the now-infamous nine Tougaloo students were driven downtown, and this time dropped off in front of the courthouse. By then, hundreds of bystanders, Black and White, had gathered outside in anticipation of their arrival—some to heckle, some to cheer. It was now standing room only, inside and outside of the courthouse. And the presence of the dogs had already heightened the tension on the street.

As the defendants emerged from their vehicles just before 4:00 p.m., their supporters in the crowd erupted in cheers and well wishes, thrilled to see all of their new heroes and heroines—so young, so fresh—for the very first time. The attention was welcome recognition for the nine, although for some, it was a bit overwhelming. "Going back and not knowing the outcome of what we were about to do made me a little bit apprehensive," recalled Janice. "I remember lots of people outside, and that was more intimidating than going into the library!"

The students headed up the grand limestone steps, but the police and their dogs were blocking the way. Once they saw the dogs, the students became hesitant, not exactly sure what to do. For their part, the police were confused about who these young people were, despite the fact that they had just left their custody less than twenty-four hours earlier. Unhappy about the cheering from the crowd, the police began to move toward the Nine.

"They had those police dogs on leashes, and they let them come up real close to us," remembered Albert Lassiter.

"One came towards me," Ethel recalled. "Then somebody said, 'Those are the defendants!'" Embarrassed and frustrated, the police let them pass and turned toward the crowd of Black enthusiasts, who were still cheering. The police crossed directly in front of the students to get at their admirers.

"When they started to applaud, the police ran across with the dogs," Meredith Anding observed. "I was kind of glad they did because I didn't want to have to walk through those dogs."

As if the Red Sea had just parted for them, the students quickly ascended the remaining stairs and entered the courthouse. Thus, most didn't witness what happened next—the second time in as many days that the police sicced dogs on defenseless Black citizens. It was only tall, lanky Al Lassiter, the last defendant to enter the building, who turned his head toward the crowd and caught a quick glimpse of the developing storm.

At least a dozen police officers, including those with the dogs, rushed across the street to quell the loud cheers and applause for the students. It was all too much for the officer in charge, Captain Beavers Armstrong, who loudly called out, "That's it! Move 'em out! Get 'em!!" Without warning, that "*Wagon Train* fashion" order, as one observant pundit would later put it, turned the police and their dogs onto an unsuspecting group of Black bystanders and turned those bystanders into a stampeding crowd attempting to flee.[5]

Various news reports detail what happened next. "Police moved quickly into the Negro group, swinging their sticks and shoving. The German shepherd dogs lunged at the people." The crowd, made up mostly of students and faculty from Jackson State, Tougaloo, and Campbell Colleges, scattered. Many of the young people quickly made their way to an adjoining parking lot and out of danger. The older residents had a harder time of it. Reverend S. L. Whitney—a distinguished scholar, prominent pastor of Farish Street Baptist Church, and vice president of the nearby Mississippi Baptist Seminary for Negroes—was attacked and bitten by one of the dogs.[6]

Others, including Medgar Evers, were beaten with billy clubs and chased away from the courthouse. Alarm and chaos broke out as the crowd realized they were under attack. Some reports cite the beating of an eighty-one-year-old woman who wasn't even part of what the police began calling a "demonstration" even though it was simply a crowd of people attempting to witness a bit of history.

News reports don't really do the mayhem justice: "The younger Negroes quickly scattered through a parking lot to safety, but some of the slower ones were clubbed on the head and back. The dogs bit and ripped the clothing of several persons."[7]

Still-extant video of the scene, now housed at the Mississippi Department of Archives and History, tells a more harrowing tale. Screaming, scrambling hordes run in every direction as police—clubs raised in fierce battle-ready poses—and snarling dogs, loosely leashed, give chase. What the crowd and the media witnessed that day—as did the Jackson State students the day before—was the first attacks by police dogs on nonviolent crowds during the civil rights era, two years before the more sensational attacks in Birmingham grabbed national headlines.

Much would be made later, particularly by the Black press, of the fact that the White bystanders faced no such outraged attack by the police. They were simply ordered to move along, which they did, happy to escape the wrath of the now out-of-control police force.

As both groups were making their exit—one hasty, the other more orderly—a well-known Black freelance news photographer, Thomas Armstrong, tried heading up the stairs, assuming he'd be allowed into the courtroom. When he approached the phalanx of police guarding the building, one of the cops said, "It's full up, Uncle. Let's move along." Armstrong, upset that he would miss the opportunity for some additional work and noting that White journalists were still being admitted, was a bit slow heading back down the steps. Police, already worked up by the earlier excitement, began to nudge Armstrong with their night sticks. Then one of the officers with a dog began following him. That was too much for Armstrong; he mumbled some derogatory comment under his breath—or so he thought. The cop with the dog overheard him and the chase was on.

Armstrong took off across the street, through the still-dispersing crowd, and into an adjacent parking lot. Just then, Red Hydrick, an ardent racist familiar to police, pulled out a gun and began pistol-whipping Armstrong on his head and shoulders. Armstrong, somewhat delirious from all that was happening to him and to those around him, ran through the parking lot to get away from both dog and assailant and escaped into the back of *The Clarion-Ledger* newspaper offices, where he was well-known. He was bleeding from two head wounds and was eventually taken to a doctor, who sewed him up and sent him on his way.

Hydrick, a fifty-five-year-old bootlegger and club owner from nearby "wet" Rankin County, was allowed to simply move along with the exiting White crowd. To reporter Bill Minor, this was a moment of awakening. He was familiar with Armstrong's work as a photojournalist and was on the scene getting ready to enter the building himself when the photographer was first chased and then attacked. He also knew Hydrick—"He was notorious," said Minor—and watched as Armstrong was assaulted while the police failed to intervene. "I saw him slug the poor guy with a pistol butt," Minor recalled, "and the police did nothing about it." For Minor, the event was fraught with foreboding. He observed that the library sit-in was "the very first [protest] that ever happened, and it gave you an idea of how any challenges against segregation were going to be treated."[8]

Later that evening, when cooler heads prevailed (and likely after the FBI had been contacted and urged to investigate the incident at the courthouse), police went searching for Hydrick and arrested him. He was charged with assault and battery and for carrying a concealed weapon. Hydrick paid the $125 bond and was released immediately, though his gun was confiscated.[9]

In contrast to the outside mayhem, inside the courtroom, the tone was quiet and solemn. Sam Bradford was positioned as the first in the line-up of students to face the judge. Both of Jackson's Black attorneys, R. Jess Brown and Jack Young, were present in the courtroom at the behest of the NAACP. Again, the students had dressed in their Sunday best to appear in court and were poised and collected despite their uncertainty about what might happen to them.

Their attorneys had briefed them on what the worst outcome could be. The new breach-of-peace law allowed for punishment of up to a two-hundred-dollar fine and, more importantly, up to four months in jail.[10] Somehow, the reality of what that would mean for their everyday lives—no more school, no more dances, no more summer jobs—hadn't quite sunk in for most of them.

"My mind was fixated: 'This is just a process. This is something I'm going through. It's going to come out well,'" Janice Jackson thought. "I always had this in the back of my mind: 'Everything's going to turn out well.' Even though I didn't fully understand what the process was!"

One of the Nine felt grateful to be in the middle of the pack and not the first one to face the judge. Ethel felt completely unprepared for the courtroom proceedings. When the judge declared that the defendants were charged with "breach of peace" and then asked, "How do you plead?" The question caught Ethel completely off guard. "Shit!" she thought. "What do I say?!" She couldn't remember being briefed about this. And there was an interminable pause with all of them facing the judge, and perhaps no one knowing who should go first or how they should plead.[11]

Ethel began to ponder the charge and her role in the library sit-in. "You know, if my presence in this White library disturbed your peace, then I guess I'm guilty!" After what seemed like an eternity, Sam's mellifluous tenor voice finally stated loudly and clearly, "Not guilty, Your Honor." And then, right down the line, "boom, boom, boom," recounted Ethel, "'not guilty,' 'not guilty,' 'not guilty'" until all nine had entered their pleas.

"It's a good thing I didn't go first," Ethel would later joke. "I would have blown the whole thing! And this was going to be a test case right from the beginning."

A brief trial ensued. The prosecution called only two witnesses, both of them police officers who had been on the scene at the time of the arrest. The first, Captain John L. Ray, would soon become a household name for his strict adherence to the letter of the law in the many civil rights demonstrations that would follow. He testified that the presence of the students in the library constituted a breach-of-peace situation. Their presence "would have caused trouble" had they been allowed to remain in the library, Ray asserted. In fact, there were several White patrons in the library when the students arrived, none of whom seemed particularly disturbed according to press reports. Ray also described coming upon them "pretending to read" and suggested that none of them "had obtained a book from the library." Ray's assertion might have been technically true, since none of them was able to check out a book from the library, but most of the students had grabbed books from the shelves and were, in fact, reading them.

When Ray was cross-examined by the defense team of Brown and Young and asked what exactly was the breach in the peace at the library, the police veteran simply said that this "was the first time that the group—or any other out-of-town group—had gathered there." Ray did admit that the students "were orderly and created no disturbance when told they were under arrest." No mention was made of the racial makeup of the group, in keeping with the tenets of the breach-of-peace law, which purported to be colorblind.

Ray's brief testimony was followed by Lieutenant C. R. Wilson, who repeated Ray's claim: "There could have been serious trouble from the presence of this group in the library." The lieutenant also made a near slip that could have completely shifted the course of the case. When asked to describe his role in the arrest, Wilson explained, "I was called to the library, and upon arriving, found a group of Nee—uh, people there." Had the word Negro slipped from his lips, the defense team could have jumped on it and made the case about race. As it was, Brown and Young had to attempt to prove that the visit to the library was *not* a breach of peace, an argument that the judge would rule they had not conclusively made.

Not that they didn't try. Attorney Jack Young argued that there was no evidence of intent on the part of the students to trigger a breach of peace and insisted that the students "had not broken any law." Young tried to reason with the judge: "We have not yet come to the place where this is a police state, have we, your Honor?" (Young clearly was unaware of the police-state tactics going on just outside the courthouse.)

Jess Brown firmly declared that the arrest was illegal "whether in Mississippi or Soviet Russia." He went on to say that under the terms of the arrest, he himself would be fearful of entering any public building, "including this one."

"Just to be present would be sufficient to be arrested," Brown concluded. One of the prosecuting attorneys helpfully stated that Brown was "always welcome" in the courthouse, which also doubled as the police station—a smug reference no matter how one might interpret it.

It is not clear why, but the students were not called upon to defend themselves or to explain their actions. Their obvious testimony would have been that they were working on school projects and needed access to books they could find nowhere else. But given the speed of the scheduling of the trial, the attorneys may have been hesitant to put witnesses on the stand that they had not properly vetted and prepped.

It is unlikely that their testimony would have done anything to change the outcome. Municipal judge James Spencer, while praising the students' impeccable behavior in the library—"there was no proof of disorderly conduct whatsoever"—suggested that the defense had not adequately addressed the threat of their being there. "You have overlooked pertinent parts of the statute," he admonished Young and Brown. "The actual conduct of the defendants is not the test under the statute." He said the students were guilty because their conduct, although orderly, would have touched off a breach of peace. "Such violations have resulted in clashes and breaches of the peace elsewhere. This community has avoided such troubles and by the grace of God will continue to do so."

The judge ruled all nine defendants "guilty as charged." As for their punishment, because this was, for all of them, their first offense—in fact the first time most of them had ever stepped inside a courtroom—the judge went easy on them. Each of them received a sentence of a one-hundred-dollar fine and thirty days in jail, with the jail time suspended contingent upon their refraining from any further protest activities within the state. Judge Spencer noted for the record, however, that he would likely be tougher the next time should protests continue.

Brown and Young immediately announced that they would seek an appeal of the verdict in the Hinds County Court. (Indeed, the case of the Tougaloo Nine would be combined with other NAACP test cases in Jackson and would make its way for consideration all the way to the US Supreme Court.)

All of the Nine seemed to breathe a sigh of relief, especially Joe Jackson, who had been haunted by his involvement from the beginning. The entire proceeding took no more than half an hour. Then the students were ushered out of the courtroom, through an unfamiliar corridor, down the back stairs, and out to where cars were waiting to whisk them back to campus. They did not witness, therefore, the continuing assault by the police on their peaceful, cheering fan club. Instead, they were brought back to the safety of the Tougaloo campus, where their lives returned to normal.

This time, there was no fanfare, no cheering fellow students to welcome them back, no more snacks from the community to bolster their spirits. The students were simply dropped off on campus, walked back to their dorms, and life continued as it had before their historic protest. For some, this seemed anticlimactic. Geraldine would later observe with regret, "We were not a cohesive group that worked [to accomplish] other things." But surely their suspended sentences kept the group from participating in additional protests if they wanted to stay out of jail. Others were just happy to get back to the normalcy of their college lives. "After the sit-in, Janice and I just went on," Ethel recalled. "We had our work-study jobs, our classes, our social life. We were busy!" They took it all in stride and moved on to the next phase of their very full college lives.

THE NATIONAL NAACP GETS INVOLVED

It wasn't until early Wednesday afternoon, just before the trial, that Medgar Evers finally had a chance to sit and process all that had happened during the past forty-eight hours. He had, of course, been on the phone constantly, keeping the NAACP's national office apprised of events starting with Monday's sit-in. But it occurred to him to put in writing the basic outline of events and to develop some suggestions for the future in a short letter to Roy Wilkins.[12]

Dear Mr. Wilkins:

The first "Sit-In" type demonstration in Mississippi, as I am sure you already know, took place Monday, March 27, 1961 at the Jackson Municipal Library, by nine young NAACP Members from our Tougaloo College Chapter.

These young people exhibited the greatest amount of courage in the face of mounting tension and were reported in our local newspapers as being "orderly, intelligent, and cooperative."

Their stay in jail was for approximately thirty-two (32) hours, primarily because the sheriff, (J. R. Gilfoy) in Hinds County, conveniently made himself absent, rather than approve the property bonds which had been secured. Finally, however, at 7:10 p.m. on Tuesday evening March 28, 1961, the young people were released.

The act of bravery and concern on the part of these nine young people has seemed to electrify Negroes' desire for Freedom here in Mississippi, which will doubtlessly be shown in increase in memberships and funds for 1961.

Mr. Wilkins, my main reason for writing this letter is that, it would be an inspirational gesture for these nine young people if we could arrange to have them attend our National Convention in Philadelphia, July 10–16. While we realize this would be an expensive item which is not necessarily included in the budget, it would give further inspiration and leadership to our cause, here in Mississippi.

Please consider having these young people attend our National Convention. I would appreciate an early reply.

Respectfully yours,

Medgar W. Evers
Field Secretary

Evers was already looking ahead, no matter how the trial turned out, as to how these youth would be viewed in the light of history. He was also considering his own legacy within the organization, asking to show off his prized activists in front of his colleagues from other states who had doubtless had their own student leaders paraded before the membership in years past. Most telling is Evers's use of the terms Wilkins could understand—money—letting him know that there was a heightened expectation for more funds to flow in the form of new memberships and other contributions. But this letter, dashed off before Evers headed downtown to witness the students entering the courthouse, perhaps most of all demonstrates his pride in the fact that he had helped usher in a new day for Mississippi. "Now the battle has begun in earnest," he seems to be announcing.

The letter to Wilkins was not Evers's first attempt to contact Wilkins about the goings on in Jackson. His first recorded communique with the national office about the library sit-in occurred on March 28, while the students were still in jail. Apparently, Gloster Current and Roy Wilkins were unavailable when he called the New York office, so Evers dictated a message over the phone with the basic facts, precisely recounted: "Nine students of Tougaloo . . . also members of our college chapter went to Jackson municipal library, arriving at 11:12 a.m., Central Standard Time. . . . police arrived at 11:35 . . . escorted them out under arrest. They were placed under $1,000 bond each. They are still in jail."

He reviewed the Jackson State "uproar" from the evening before, as well, including rumors that "some of the students will be expelled" and the whispers among students that "if one is expelled, all should be expelled." He credits a recent investigation of police conduct by the US Civil Rights Commission as the reason that "the police have been overly courteous to the arrested students and there has been no brutality."

In the formal way of communicating that his superiors seemed to expect, Evers stated the obvious in a wrap-up paragraph: "Our long-range goal is to make it possible for Negroes to go to the city library without difficulty. This is part of our campaign to eliminate segregation in Jackson and throughout the State of Mississippi."[13]

Still unable to get his bosses on the line the next day, Evers sent messages through Herbert Wright, the association's national youth secretary. Again, Wright's formal memorandum to Wilkins and Current dated the day after the students' arrest is striking given the historic nature of the incidents described. Evers had explained to Wright the entire story about what happened with the bail money. Evers "had previously arranged to secure bail bonds through a local bonding firm. The bondsman was notified of the arrests and he came to the City jail immediately. . . . After the bonds had been completed, it was discovered that the sheriff was out of town. . . . The students were forced to remain in jail over-night and are still in jail awaiting the return of the sheriff to the city. We have been advised that the sheriff is expected in town before noon today."[14]

No matter how Wilkins heard of the new developments in Jackson, there can be no doubt as to his excitement over the events that were beginning to unfold. His actions in the following weeks would demonstrate that. But Wilkins didn't jump into high gear until Evers called him and spoke to him directly about what might today be called a "police riot" against Jackson's Black citizens as they cheerfully welcomed the arrival of the Tougaloo Nine to the courthouse for their trail.

Upon hearing of the breakdown of any artifice of cordiality on the streets of Jackson, Wilkins first fired off a terse telegram to "Honorable Ross Barnett" letting him know of the NAACP's immediate protest against the use of "DOGS ON PEACEFUL CITIZENS WHO COULD NOT FIND SPACE IN COURTROOM AND WERE STANDING OPPOSITE COURTHOUSE AT POLICE DIRECTION." Calling the police "ATTACKERS RATHER THAN PROTECTORS," Wilkins noted that he was aware that a minister had been bitten by one of the dogs, that other men and women were "CURSED AND CLUBBED" by police, one of those being the NAACP's very own Medgar Evers. "WE DEMAND THAT YOU PROVIDE PROTECTION FOR CITIZENS AND PARTICULARLY SECRETARY EVERS." Then Wilkins threw out his sharpest, high-brow blow. "CALL OFF THE DOGS, LEGREE," he demanded, the disgust dripping off the telegram's still-wet teletype with the reference to the arch villain of *Uncle Tom's Cabin*. "SLAVERY IS OVER."[15]

There seems to be no documentation as to Barnett's response to Wilkins, if any. Indeed, his only comment to the press when asked about the melee at the courthouse was to tell reporters: "I don't know a thing about the facts. I have so many things that are more important to attend to!"[16] This must have been something of a Humpty Dumpty moment for someone who just the day before seemed on top of the world, parading about in his fake Civil War regalia and being feted at the Confederate Balls late into the night. Wilkins sensed an opening that could serve the NAACP's purposes and went full bore to exploit it.

Part VI

AFTERSHOCKS

Chapter 17

REACTIONS PRO AND CON

THURSDAY MORNING ARRIVED WITH A RENEWED THREAT OF SEVERE thunderstorms and perhaps even a tornado later in the day. The entire week had been a bit of a washout as far as the weather was concerned. "Two or three more days of showers, thundershowers, and squall lines over the state is the best that the Weather Bureau can offer," announced *The Clarion-Ledger* that morning. The weather had become the subject of front-page news throughout the week, rivaling the history-making events of the library sit-in and its aftermath along with the centennial celebrations. The threat of flooding in low-lying areas throughout the state became an ever-increasing concern as the week progressed, and the hard rain continued, filling rivers large and small, from the mighty Mississippi to the Delta's Yazoo to Jackson's Pearl. Rain was expected through Saturday, with a glimmer of hope for a bit of sun and respite by Easter Sunday.[1]

The day's news also brought an interesting profile of the dogs used by police during the events of the past three days. An enterprising reporter for the *State Times* was able to ascertain the names of the dogs—*Happy* and *Rebel*—and how they had come to be available to the Jackson police. The German shepherds were "charter members of the Vicksburg Police Department's canine corps," the reporter unveiled and had been loaned to the city of Jackson once news of the library sit-in had set off alarm bells in police stations statewide.

This front-page story also revealed that the one-hundred-pound dogs had been trained in Springfield, Missouri, at an academy run by a "former Nazi storm trooper"—one Harry Nawroth—who had once trained "killer Dobermans to guard Hitler's airports." Happy and Rebel had been brought to Vicksburg the previous December after a sixteen-week "rigorous" training program with their handlers from the Vicksburg PD. Since then, the dogs had been tracking prowlers and burglars in the Vicksburg area. This was their first deployment in "crowd control." Additionally, the *State Times* lamely joked that "Happy and Rebel are making the Jackson Police Department's orders to racial demonstrators more meaningful."[2]

FREEDOM COMIN', AND IT WON'T BE LONG

On Thursday evening, March 30, little more than twenty-four hours after police had raged against an excited crowd of Black bystanders at the courthouse, another mass meeting of the Black community was held, this time at the Masonic Temple's auditorium in the very building where Medgar Evers's NAACP offices were housed. More than eight hundred mostly Negro citizens turned out to hear a line-up of speakers that in normal times Evers would have found difficult to summon even for his annual Mississippi Freedom Fund benefit banquet. The NAACP's top lobbyist and head of its Washington Bureau Clarence Mitchell—the man who would come to be known as the 101st senator because of his influence on civil rights legislation within the halls of power—served as the headliner. Mitchell flew to Mississippi's state capital from the nation's capital that day to reassure Jackson's Black citizens that the NAACP was with them in their fight. He said that the national NAACP was pushing for stronger legislation in the US Congress—another civil rights bill, to strengthen the rights and protections of America's disenfranchised. He told the crowd that he had already contacted the Judiciary Committees of both the House and the Senate "about the shocking, disgraceful action in Jackson" and urged "the passage of strong civil rights legislation to give Americans the same kind of protection in Mississippi that we seek to give our fellow humans in remote corners of the world."

Mitchell brought the discussion back to the student sit-in at the public library and titillated the crowd with his mastery of language. "I don't know how dictionaries in Mississippi define 'public,' but those we use in Washington—and they're the ones that count—say public includes everybody, white and colored." Citing the recent upswing in enthusiasm for demonstrations in Jackson and contrasting these with the police crackdown, the lobbyist continued, "There is not enough power in the state of Mississippi to match those determined to have their civil rights!" And taking on the powerful Sovereignty Commission, which in recent days had come under considerable criticism by detractors even within the state, Mitchell jousted about the commission's speakers' bureau, which was sending home-grown enthusiasts of segregation into Northern cities to explain its benefits. "I would like to know how they're going to explain the events of recent days in Mississippi," Mitchell taunted.[3]

The Tougaloo student sit-in and the subsequent Jackson State support demonstrations had unleased a feeling of joy and unity within the Black populace previously unseen in Mississippi's capital city. Before Mitchell took the stage, the jubilant crowd acted more like they were attending a religious revival rather than a political rally. They danced; they sang; they even marched around the auditorium. Their enthusiasm could not be contained. Freedom was coming! One of the songs circulating on the protest circuit was "The Freedom Song"—Freedom lyrics set to the popular Harry Belafonte tune, "Day-O! (The Banana Boat Song)":

> Free-ee-ee-dom! Free-ee-ee-dom!
> Freedom comin', and it won't be long.

It was the song the students had been singing on the Jackson State campus the morning after their prayer meeting had been shut down. Now it was being sung jubilantly in the Masonic Temple by eight hundred souls ready to march into a new day.

Aaron Henry, president of the Mississippi State NAACP, informed those gathered that he had immediately wired President Kennedy and the Justice Department, urging them "to halt this savage attack on Negro people in Mississippi." (Mitchell had also telegrammed Attorney General Robert Kennedy almost the moment he heard about the police misconduct: "URGE THAT YOU DO EVERYTING POSSIBLE UNDER EXISTING LAWS TO PROTECT THE CIVIL RIGHTS OF OUR CITIZENS IN JACKSON, MISSISSIPPI, AT THIS TIME.") Indeed, Henry noted that FBI agents had already arrived in Jackson—some were in the crowd—to begin their investigation into Wednesday's police attack. Even so, Henry told the crowd that up until now, Mississippi's Black citizens had been handed a "do-it-yourself kit" in the struggle for human dignity."[4]

Tougaloo chaplain John Dee Mangram served as emcee of the gathering. The spiritual advisor to the Tougaloo Nine urged all present to keep this growing movement nonviolent: "Even though we be struck dead, we will not strike back," he told the crowd. "We must not become embittered at our white friends, who do not have the maturity we thought they had." But Mangram also tapped into the energy in the crowd, enthusiastically noting that "all the things our white friends may do to us cannot stop the forces which have been unleashed in this city and state!"

"We must face what we have experienced," the Tougaloo chaplain declared, "and, in a measure, accept it." He prayed "for the Holy Spirit to visit Jackson and touch the leadership—in the Governor's Mansion and in City Hall." Again, the White press felt compelled to report that the large gathering broke up "without incident."[5]

AN ATTEMPT TO MUZZLE THE PRESS

At about this time, some concerned prominent Jacksonians tried to shut down any negative reports about the goings on in Mississippi's capital city. The effort wasn't reported until a week later by Hazel Brannon Smith in her *Northside Reporter*. The day after the "dog bites man" incident, as she called it, "a meeting was held in which some of the most prominent men in Jackson attempted to tell newspaper, television and radio people how to handle news emanating out of Jackson." The city's elite were trying to muzzle reporters and their cameras, attempting to limit the damage that the city's image was suffering as a result of the police overreaction to an enthusiastic crowd. "Fortunately for the people of Mississippi," Brannon Smith noted, "most of the men, representing a majority of the mass communication media in Jackson, refused to go along with this attempted blackout of the news." Smith acknowledged, however, that some of the photos of the "dog bites man" variety had been locked up and might never see the light of day.[6]

Official Jackson was trying to make like nothing really happened, but it was far too late for that ruse. The wire-service reporters and photographers had already exported their stories and photos, which appeared in many major newspapers across the country, including in *The New York Times*, which covered the sit-in, the Jackson State uprising, and the courthouse melee with substantive text and graphic photos in back-to-back stories over two days.[7]

If Jackson's power elite were trying to silence the press, Mayor Allen Thompson was trying to get its attention. He announced Thursday afternoon that he was asking for airtime the following evening to plead with the people of Jackson for racial calm and peace. This was the first racial crisis Thompson had had to face publicly in his nearly twelve years in office. And it couldn't have come at a worse time. He was up for reelection and was being challenged by an upstart candidate who seemed to be running as a "realistic" segregationist and suggesting that Thompson's bromides about the race issue weren't working.[8]

Thompson was anxious to get in front of the mostly White voters and share his thoughts. Two networks offered him ten minutes on Friday evening, and he grabbed it. Thompson then attempted to craft a message that would appeal to the full spectrum of his constituents: the upset and beleaguered Negroes seeking respect and some semblance of equality; the fierce and now-defensive White supremacists who vowed to give no ground on the race issue; and those in between, who most likely weren't quite sure what to make of recent developments.

By Friday, it was beginning to sink in that the ground had shifted a bit in Mississippi's tug of war on race. The students' library sit-in and the subsequent Jackson State uprising and police riot at the courthouse; the presence of federal officials in the form of FBI agents on the ground in Jackson; a mass meeting of Negroes to openly and vociferously demand their civil rights—all during a week when Mississippi had just recommitted itself to Confederate values—it was too much for the local media. In his regular Affairs of State column, Charles Hills circled the wagons, stood up for Jackson chief of police W. D. Rayfield, and misconstrued the facts to his own liking. Rayfield "and his fine department, have been quick to break up demonstrations and trouble-making," Hills opined. "They have discouraged disturbances, treating one and all alike."

Hills tried mightily to make the case that there was nothing to get excited about and that all citizens in Jackson are treated equally. "If there are continued attempts to flaunt the laws of this state, the law-breakers may as well expect discouragement." As to the new sense of pride among Negroes, Hills suggested such a sentiment was misguided: "Fines and suspended sentences were given several persons for the recent library 'study-in,'" he noted. "This is nothing to inspire pride, any more than application of the term jailbird, generally applied to those who have been incarcerated for law violation."[9]

WILKINS GETS RILED UP

If in Jackson there was a certain amount of handwringing and retrenchment, at the NAACP's New York offices, there was nothing short of jubilation that comes with a long-sought breakthrough. By midday Friday, Roy Wilkins had ordered the sending of a two-page telegram to its largest and most well-heeled NAACP branches across the country—an expensive enterprise—announcing the national organization's way forward in Mississippi: "NAACP WILL DEFEND NINE TOUGALOO COLLEGE STUDENTS ARRESTED AND FINED FOR ATTEMPTING TO USE WHITE LIBRARY IN JACKSON, MISS. SHOCK AND ANGER AT USE OF POLICE DOGS AND CLUBS ON PEACEFUL PERSONS ASSEMBLED TO WITNESS TRIAL OF STUDENTS MARCH 29 HAS SWEPT NATION. NAACP IS MOBILIZING EVERY POSSIBLE STRENGTH TO PROTECT PEOPLE FROM PERSECUTION BY POLICE AND OTHER AUTHORITIES."[10]

The dispatch goes on to discuss the association's plans to launch an "EDUCATIONAL CAMPAIGN TO TELL THE TRUTH ABOUT MISSISSIPPI IN DETAIL TO COUNTRY AT LARGE." Wilkins urges the selective group of branch presidents throughout the country to issue statements denouncing the violence in Mississippi and also asks each to flood the office of Robert Kennedy, thanking the attorney general for triggering a prompt investigation of the events of March 29. Of course, Wilkins being Wilkins, he begs all branches to send contributions to help with the new Magnolia State initiative, which he calculates could cost as much as $40,000. "MISSISSIPPI, THE SNARLING DOG STATE, MUST BE THE TARGET HENCEFORTH OF ALL DECENT AMERICANS IN AN EFFORT TO ERASE THE DISGRACE THIS STATE HAS BROUGHT UPON OUR COUNTRY IN THE EYES OF ALL HUMANITY," he concluded.[11]

Wilkins also thoughtfully arranged for brief telegrams of sympathy to be sent to photographer Thomas Armstrong, Reverend S. L. Whitney, and Bishop David McPherson, head of Jackson's Christ Temple Church—one of the most prominent Black ministers in Jackson, who apparently had also been attacked during the police riot.

The Magnolia State initiative, formally called "Operation Mississippi," would eventually turn into a five-point program aimed at bringing attention to the plight of Mississippi. It included efforts to:

- ramp up voter registration and voting by the state's more than nine hundred thousand African Americans, noting that fewer than 4 percent of eligible Black residents were registered to vote in Mississippi, "the lowest figure in the nation";
- focus on law enforcement, "including not only justice in the courts themselves, but proper police action outside the courts" and noting that "this includes police brutality and the improper use of police force (including dogs) to harass peaceful assemblies of colored citizens";
- opportunity for employment without discrimination, particularly in "plants having government contracts";
- access to public accommodations, such as "parks, beaches, playgrounds and other recreation areas"; and
- desegregation of public education within the state. "The University of Mississippi and other tax-supported colleges ought to have Negro students."[12]

One note that adds poignancy to Wilkins's long-in-coming decision to finally throw resources at what previously must have seemed to him and his team as a lost cause is the then-little-known fact that Wilkins himself had deep family roots in Mississippi. Both his mother and his father had escaped the place just a year before his birth. "I was not born in Mississippi," Wilkins allows in the opening sentence of his posthumously published 1982 autobiography, "but my story begins there all the same, deep in the rolling hill country of Northern Mississippi." Late in life, after his retirement from the NAACP, Wilkins tracked down his ancestors and, remarkably, the location of their gravesites behind "a little country church called Beverly Chapel." Both of his father's parents had been enslaved, born just a decade or so "before Abraham Lincoln set them free."[13]

Thus, Wilkins took great interest in what happened in Mississippi during his professional career, but ever the realist, he was doubtful of ever changing the savage racial mores of his ancestral region. When the Tougaloo Nine took their decisive action, however, Wilkins saw an opening, and he jumped at it. For the next two years, the NAACP would flood the state with legal and financial support. As a result, there would be some huge wins but also some tragic losses.

THE NATIONAL MEDIA WEIGHS IN

Reaction to the Tougaloo Nine sit-in, and particularly to the police overreaction on the day of the trial, hit many of the major US newspapers and even merited mention in the weekly news magazines. *Time* magazine, for instance, kicked off a piece titled "The Education of the South," with a paragraph about both the library sit-in and the police beatdown. It even ran the photograph of the three women exiting the library, referring to them as the "wholly New Negro." In fact, the uncredited reporter noted that "the fact that Negroes even raised their heads in last-ditch Mississippi bespoke a new attitude."

The popular weekly large-format photojournalism of *LIFE* magazine included a large Associated Press picture of Happy or Rebel striking at Reverend Whitney with the caption "A Police Dog's Supremacy in Mississippi." *US News & World Report*'s coverage included a similar photo on its "Front Page of the Week" section with an accompanying article titled "When Dogs Were Used to Break Up a Crowd."

Newsweek provided the most fulsome coverage, highlighting the library sit-in, the Jackson State sympathy protests, *and* the police overreaction on the day of the trial. Titled "The Read-In," the brief article made note that "while the crowd was fleeing the dogs and nightsticks, the nine students were convicted for refusing to move along when directed by a police officer. . . ." The magazine also rightly predicted that the students' "appeals—when they are heard—will raise the first legal challenge to Mississippi's state segregation laws, which date back to 1890."[14]

The reach of this coverage cannot be underestimated. A detailed, scientific readership study sponsored by *Newsweek* in early 1962 concludes that these four magazines had a national readership of more than fifty million individuals per week. Word was spreading far and wide that Mississippi's Black populace was finally rising up.[15]

MAYOR ALLEN THOMPSON SPEAKS

Back in Jackson, the city seemed ready to hear what the mayor had to say. The afternoon *Jackson Daily News* not only announced Thompson's double appearance that evening—6:15 on WJTV and 7:30 on WLBT—it also had obtained a copy of his speech and printed it in its entirety to ensure the widest distribution. (The mayor had also used his Municipal Association contacts to wrangle an appearance on NBC's *Today* show that morning, "condemning racial unrest.")

The speech begins more like a campaign presentation, with the mayor enumerating all of the great things he had done for the city during the past dozen years: road projects, water and sewer improvements, a new airport, a new auditorium, and coliseum. He detailed the number of schools—both "white and colored"—that his administration was either building or improving and noted that more than $21 million had been spent on city schools since 1950. It was all quite impressive but hardly addressed the crisis at hand. (His competitor in the mayor's race requested and received equal TV time the following week due to the campaign-style aspect of Thompson's speech.)

Halfway through, however, Thompson shifted and tried his best to focus on the events of the past week, although obliquely. He never mentioned the library sit-in or the subsequent demonstrations by the Jackson State students. Nor did he refer directly to the police action against peaceful Negroes awaiting the outcome of the students' trial. But he did refer to Jackson's library system, saying, "We take particular pride in the Carver Municipal Library for our Negro citizens on North Mill Street and in the library for our White citizens on North State Street"—clarifying, one supposes, should there be any question, that the branches were still segregated. He also praised "our excellent police department" and the city's "remarkably low crime rate."[16]

Thompson then warmed to his announced topic: "Up to this point, I have not mentioned our most valuable asset," the mayor declaimed. "This is the friendly spirit of cooperation and harmony which has consistently existed among our people of every race, creed, and color." He even tied in the Civil War history lesson from earlier in the week, noting, "Almost a hundred years ago, among the few structures which remained standing in Jackson after Mr. Sherman's visit were your City Hall, your Governor's Mansion, and the State Capitol. Our city became known as Chimneyville." He noted that it took collective action by all residents—"white and colored, Gentile and Jew, Protestant and Catholic"—to rebuild and thrive. "This fine spirit of harmony has existed without incident until the past few days." Thompson then falsely asserted that the week's turmoil had been "planned and promoted" by people outside of the city and state. "Let's not permit organized incidents created by outsiders who have no real interest in our welfare, destroy our mutual good will which we have built up over a period of one hundred years."

Next, he offered a warning: "Our laws will be strictly enforced. Any infraction of the law by either a white person or a colored person will be vigorously prosecuted. The rights and safety of every citizen will be protected."

Wrapping up, Thompson turned conciliatory, mawkishly so, and circled back to his boosterism of the city: "Let's join hands in a spirit of genuine friendship and keep Jackson one of the finest cities on earth in which to live and raise our families."[17]

Thompson's TV appearances were largely lauded the next day. "Mayor Right Not to Ignore Crisis," one headline opined. His competitor in the upcoming election, however, carped that it was "80 percent politics and 20 percent about the racial situation." Percy Greene aptly summed up the Black response to the mayor's speech in his weekly *Jackson Advocate*. Greene observed that the mayor had made no mention of the use of police dogs at the courthouse earlier in the week. Also, "the speech made no mention of the conditions that lead to the sit-in demonstrations at the municipal library. No mention was made of the real or alleged grievance of the Negro citizens of the city, and no promise in regard to a program for the future." Even the conservative Greene, who was in the pocket of the Sovereignty Commission, was showing some sass.[18]

The big news that emerged after the mayor's speech, however, was not what Thompson said, but what he had done before he took to the airwaves. In something of an unprecedented move, Mayor Thompson called three Black ministers, leaders of the (Black) Interdenominational Ministerial Alliance, to his office to have a frank discussion of the week's events. Also present were his city commissioners and police chiefs Rayfield and Pierce.

The meeting apparently had been requested by the ministers even before the week's events unfolded, but the fact that the mayor granted it was evidence that the sit-in was already having an important desired effect. Ostensibly, the ministers—Reverend E. A. Mays, pastor of Central Methodist Church; Reverend T. B. Brown, pastor of Mount Helm Baptist Church; and Bishop David McPherson, who had been attacked by the police dogs—originally wanted to discuss police brutality against Black prisoners in the Jackson City Jail and the fact that only the Black convicts were forced to wear traditional black-and-white-striped prison garb. But the events of the week pushed other matters onto the agenda.

When the ministers accused the police of brutality against its Negro citizens, police chief Rayfield objected, saying, "The Jackson Police Department has certain policies."

"And that policy is never to use force unless it becomes a matter of necessity," chief of detectives Pierce added helpfully.

Commissioner Tom Marshall, whose portfolio of city oversight included the Police Department, noted that the police had, in fact, fired two of its own during the past two years for "excessive roughness."

Pierce once again chimed in, "We have received more complaints of police brutality from White people than Negroes."

It is unclear how someone who was attacked by police dogs on Wednesday was able to sit through such a session without lashing out at those responsible for the chaos at the courthouse. But it was reported that McPherson and the other ministers seemed "satisfied" with the lame assurances given by city officials. (An indication at how cowed the ministers were is that one of them, Reverend Brown, was scheduled to speak at the mass meeting the night before but bowed out at the last minute, most likely so that he would not jeopardize his chance to meet with the mayor directly the next day.)

All was not sunshine and rainbows, however. The three Black spiritual leaders urged the mayor to invite a committee of Negro leaders to meet "at least every three months" to discuss race relations. "If we intend to continue to live together in peace and harmony," Mays told Thompson, "then we must clear up certain grievances."

The mayor responded, "The doors of City Hall are always open to the Negroes of this city."[19]

THE FBI STEPS IN, THEN STEPS OUT

The need to regularly check in with the mayor would be important since the feds seemed to be losing interest. When first told by Medgar Evers of Wednesday's alarming police overreach in Jackson, newly appointed US Assistant Attorney General for Civil Rights Burke Marshall said, "I have Mr. Evers's story. I'm trying to find out if it's true. If it is, it's a disgrace." It was Marshall's very first day on the job. The former corporate lawyer, thirty-eight, had been confirmed by the Senate to serve in the Kennedy administration just the day before. The inexperienced civil servant who formerly represented corporate clients such as Standard Oil followed up on his expression of outrage with this comment: "I may say, though, that I've been told by local authorities that the instructions to the police were not to use force."[20]

After just twenty-four hours in Mississippi, FBI agents seemed to be all too willing to accept the party line as well. An FBI spokesman noted that "the only violence so far uncovered was between a white man and a Negro [the altercation between Hydrick and Armstrong] and did not involve police." The spokesperson also allowed that he had received "assurances from responsible leaders in Jackson that no unnecessary force will be used." He added, "We are continuing to investigate and have asked for further facts on the situation."[21] He said nothing, however, about the dogs or the clubbing of innocent bystanders, despite evidentiary photos in the local and national press. The federal government's ineptitude at not seeing through the false claims of city officials was on display from the start.

It is thanks to the FBI's presence in Mississippi, however, that a sworn affidavit from Medgar Evers provides an eye-witness account of the police riot. Provided on March 31, just two days after the disturbance, Evers's statement is a vivid and chilling description of what he experienced in the midst of the mayhem.

The NAACP field secretary said that he and two companions—the names are redacted but most likely are those of his boss, Ruby Hurley, who was in town "on business" (probably to check out the status of the Tougaloo Nine case and to be on hand for the trial), and perhaps Evers's nemesis, C. R. Darden, who was also on the scene—arrived at approximately 3:25 p.m. Evers dropped off his two visitors in front of the courthouse and went to park the car in a lot nearby. As he walked toward the front of the courthouse, he passed the Jackson police station, which was housed in the same building as the court. He saw three policemen "looking out the window at me." "There he is," one remarked casually. "We ought to kill him." Evers looked at them, registered the remark, smiled, and kept on moving.

It should be noted that this form of harassment would become commonplace in Evers's life, and in the life of his family, for the next twenty-seven months, until he was finally gunned down in June 1963. It is a measure of the man that he seemed to take it all in stride, never letting his detractors see his concern over such callously violent statements. His rising profile in the wake of the Tougaloo Nine demonstration and the vast civil unrest that would occur in the months ahead put a target on his back that would become irresistible the more he became identified as the leader of the Jackson movement.

Like so many others who arrived too late to get into the courtroom, Medgar Evers and his guests were told to stand across the street "in the parking lot in the rear of the Mississippi Publishing Company building." They were there at about 3:45 p.m., when the Tougaloo students arrived and "the Negroes applauded in spontaneous recognition." It was then that all hell broke loose. As Evers reported, "an officer yelled, 'Disperse them!'" and the chase was on. Darden, it seems, made haste to get away, and Evers didn't see him for the rest of the day. Ruby Hurley also got lost in the shuffle as the two of them scrambled to safety. Evers stated that he was headed north toward Pearl Street when "I was struck once on the left rear part of my head with an object I assume was a revolver by a white man in plain clothes." This, of course, was Red Hydrick, who had also chased and similarly assaulted Tom Armstrong. Hydrick was likely making his own getaway when he saw Evers and decided he, too, needed some vigilante justice.

"I believe the object that struck me was a revolver because immediately after being struck, I saw a snub-nosed revolver, blue steel, approximately .38 caliber, in his hand," Evers explained. The former army man and avid hunter knew his guns. "This blow did not knock me down and must have been a glancing blow," he said. The two men did not exchange epithets, nor pleasantries, for that matter. Evers "kept on going as uniformed officers were hurrying Negroes along away from the parking lot." As he turned onto Pearl Street, Evers saw police "chasing and striking Negroes indiscriminately with 'billy' clubs." Evers even thought he recognized one of those being beaten as a Tougaloo student.

The police then spotted Evers and moved toward him. "As they approached me," the harried NAACP field secretary recalled, "one of them who was ahead of the others said, 'Get going, Boy!'" "I am going!" Evers replied. At that, "he struck me across the back just above the waist with his 'billy' club."

"The other officer," he reported, "also struck me with his 'billy' club in the same general part of the back."

Incredibly, in this melee, the thirty-five-year-old Evers came upon the seventy-nine-year-old Reverend Whitney, "who had been bitten by a police dog and whose coat, I observed, was torn on the forearm and the sleeve." He, thus, was an eyewitness to the results of what was likely the first police dog attack in modern civil rights history.

After that, Evers said he was rescued by some friends, who picked him up and drove him to his office on Lynch Street. Not long after arriving there, however, he was called to Dr. A. B. Britton's office to witness the injuries of photographer Thomas Armstrong, "who was being treated . . . for lacerations of the head and bruises of the right shoulder and right arm." Armstrong explained that he had both been beaten by police (on arm and shoulder) and also "struck on the head by a white man not in uniform." It was almost the same exact beating that Medgar had received, though somewhat more serious.

Since he was at the doctor's office, Evers "asked him to examine me, which he did." The Doc said he wasn't seriously hurt, Evers recounted to the FBI special agents from New Orleans, "but the places where I was struck give me pain now." The agents observed him rubbing the back of his head repeatedly throughout the interview but "observed no visible marks or swelling."

When asked if there was anyone who could verify the account of his beating, Evers mentioned the name (redacted) of a newsman who "was alongside him momentarily while he was leaving the scene and was taking moving pictures of the action."

Finally, Evers made sure to make the point at the end of the interview that while "all Negroes present in the area of the trial were dispersed by many police officers using 'billy' clubs and two dogs, whites in the same area were not molested."[22]

Nothing much came of Evers's sworn testimony nor that of others who risked life and livelihood to make a statement to the feds about what happened to them that day. Most of these reports contained in the Evers FBI file are redacted. Importantly (and inexplicably), one statement is entirely readable. This is the statement of eighty-one-year-old Willis Randall (W. R.) Wrenn, who, while following police orders to vacate the area across the street from the courthouse, "felt a blow across my left wrist and back. The blow knocked me down on my back," Wrenn said, "and I looked up and saw a uniformed police officer standing over me. He had a billy club in his hand." After seeing a doctor and getting an X-ray days later, Wrenn discovered that his arm had been broken. A photo of the forlorn, elderly Wrenn, standing with Evers and displaying his left arm—completely covered in a cast and supported by a sling—would be featured later that spring in the NAACP's first long-form, professionally designed four-page fund-raising brochure itemizing the Operation Mississippi program and why it was needed.[23]

Red Hydrick, the man who had assaulted both Thomas Armstrong and Medgar Evers, was brought to trial two days later—Good Friday on the Christian calendar—in the same courtroom where the Tougaloo Nine had been tried. Tom Armstrong, however, likely fearing for his life, did not show up to testify against Hydrick. Thus, the bootlegger with the handy pistol and the hair-trigger temper was only convicted of carrying a concealed weapon, a misdemeanor. Hydrick was fined $125 and released.[24]

A CRACK IN THE MONOLITH

One immediate implication of what was becoming known as the Tougaloo "read-in" was the development of a surprising fault line in what had seemed an unshakeable ability of Mississippi officials to hold the line on segregation at all costs. In the immediate aftermath of the library sit-in, state representative Phillip Bryant, a twenty-two-year-old elected representative from Oxford—home of the University of Mississippi—laid the blame for the sit-in squarely at the feet of the Sovereignty Commission. Two weeks earlier, Bryant had condemned the spy agency as a "private gestapo" that was engaged in "witch-hunting" and "private character assassination." Bryant's tirade—a result of the Sovereignty Commission's whisper campaign against a liberal-leaning Ole Miss student who was in the running to become editor of the school paper—had become national news.

Now, the young legislator—he was the same age as some of the Black students who sat in at the library—pushed his attack further, suggesting that the sending of Mississippi boosters North to defend segregation with canned speeches by the Sovereignty Commission's publicity director, Erle Johnston, was the bait needed by racial-equity groups to launch direct-action protests against the practice.

"We send these speakers North, and they tell their audiences glowing tales of racial harmony," Bryant said. "What do we expect? We're building a glass house in Mississippi for the NAACP to cast stones at! They have to come into Mississippi now and try something just to save face." Declaring that the state had "created a monster," Bryant urged the legislature to reign in the Sovereignty Commission's reach.[25]

Such open criticism of the established order was anathema to what had seemed to the world outside of Mississippi a monolithic bastion of segregationist unanimity. And Bryant's attack was not singular. Newsman Hodding Carter noted how, in many instances, the "large number of young legislators" elected two years earlier were beginning to assert new thinking within the legislature. "Finally, the young men in the legislature have begun to attack the most sacred cow of all—the State Sovereignty Commission. They are vigorously questioning the commission's actions, its worth in the state, and the necessity for its existence. In doing so, these young men are also breaking from the traditional pattern of blind acceptance of any action which was taken in the name of segregation."[26]

Of course, there was pushback from the established order, but the cracks were becoming more visible and the internal dissent more vocal. As Carter further observed, the dissent of this new wave of younger legislators "will be speaking for large numbers of Mississippians who are tired of taking what the clique of Big Brothers have been handing out for so long."

Progressive news outlets also began trying to make the failure of the Sovereignty Commission a wedge issue, particularly because the spy agency apparently was caught completely flat footed by the Tougaloo Nine action. Sovereignty Commission director Albert Jones, "whose job," the *Jackson Daily News* reminded its readers, "is to preserve segregation," told reporters that "he was informed of the 'read-in' shortly after it took place and had no advance warning." Such a complete and immediate admission could not have inspired confidence in those who had put their faith in Barnett and his state apparatus to maintain the racial status quo.[27]

RAMIFICATION OF STUDENTS' PROTEST

Easter Weekend passed quietly in Jackson, with most residents absorbing the events of the week and preparing their hearts for the celebration of the Lord's Resurrection. In an unusual show of racial amity, on Good Friday, the *Jackson Daily News* showed a front-page photograph of a three-year old African American child with her live white Easter bunny that she had rescued as her family was evacuated to a Red Cross shelter from their flooded home in Hattiesburg. Though powerful storms had dumped extraordinary amounts of rain throughout the state, even causing tornadoes in some areas, by Easter Sunday, the storms seemed to have subsided, and all was calm.

Most of the Tougaloo Nine students went home for Spring Break that weekend and began to better understand the repercussions of their actions. Aside from the brief appearance of Alfred Cook and Meredith Anding at the College Hill Missionary Baptist Church the night of their release from jail, and, of course, showing up for their trial the next day, the students had stayed out of the public eye. Their court conviction and its requirement that they participate in no further demonstrations curtailed their activities in a city where even attending a mass meeting could be considered an infraction of their probation agreement.

When he returned home to Vicksburg briefly during the Easter break before heading out on a Tougaloo choir tour, Albert Lassiter had a heart-to-heart talk with his father, who explained to him in no uncertain terms the seriousness of what he had done and the impact it could have on the Lassiter family. "Albert, we didn't know y'all were going to do that," Wright Lassiter Sr. told his son. Albert's heart skipped a beat. "Then it hit me," he said. "Dad could have lost all of his work because he was a self-employed bricklayer. That's the only time I guess some fear came over me." The elder Lassiter went on to say that despite the threats to the family, they supported what their son had done. "He survived that and did alright," Albert recalled. "I was so relieved but also very proud of Dad."

Geraldine also had misinterpreted her family's tenuous "independence." While she later expressed relief that neither she nor her family members were "beaten, hung, or harmed" after the read-in, she also acknowledged that "we really were much more liable than I knew at the time." Her father was a pastor, which shielded him somewhat, and he also worked as a sawmill worker for the International Paper Company, a corporation with its senior management outside of the state—another buttress against retaliation. But Reverend Edwards also owned and operated a gas station and small recreation area for Black people on the outskirts of Natchez. Geraldine reported that her father was "physically and emotionally attacked" in the wake of her participation in the sit-in. Also, during the summer of 1961, "the KKK, in their white pillowcases with holes cut for eyes, rode horses *inside* of our small family business!"—a threatening gesture meant to intimidate the Edwards family.[28]

Meredith Anding also had a rude awakening. Although his family was supportive of his budding activism, those who were funding his education were not. Anding had been receiving a monthly stipend from the Disciples of Christ's First Christian Church of Jackson, a White congregation that was also a significant local supporter of Tougaloo College. He lost that funding as a result of his participation in the sit-in and had to drop out of Tougaloo at the end of the spring semester until he could make other financial arrangements.

Perhaps the most dramatic immediate impact fell upon Evelyn Pierce. Her family in Laurel began getting death threats, and her father heard from sources in the community that he needed to get his daughter out of state to ensure her safety and that of the entire Pierce family. There was serious concern that the newly built family home would be firebombed. A cross was burned in their front yard. "That was a *very* stressful time," her sister Armendia reported. Demathraus Pierce, Evelyn's younger sister, who was living at home at the time, recalled her father staying up all night to guard the home with her grandmother's shotgun. "He put it in the window so everybody could see it," she stated. "And I remember being shocked that there was even a shotgun in the house!!"

"My father got my sister off Tougaloo campus and sent her away," Armendia said. Reverend Lou Edward Pierce drove to Tougaloo, picked Evelyn up for Spring Break, and shuffled her off to Buffalo, where there were extended family members ready to take her in. But the stress was too much for Reverend Pierce, however. After multiple nights of standing watch over his home and repeated threats by phone, he had the first of several strokes that sidelined him for a time. Despite it all, Demathraus said, "I remember us all being very, very proud of my older sister."[29]

BEITTEL QUESTIONED

If the students and their families were facing various ramifications from the protest, so were Dr. Beittel and Tougaloo College. On April 5, exactly one week after the courthouse smackdown in Jackson, Beittel received a call from S. C. Meisburg, an official with the First Christian Church of Jackson—Meredith Anding's former benefactor and a significant local funding source for Tougaloo College. Meisburg, who also served as a member of Tougaloo's board of trustees, asked for a meeting with the college president and a number of other church representatives to discuss Tougaloo's role in the protest events of the prior week. Due to scheduling difficulties, the group didn't meet until the afternoon of April 17 in the office of one of the church members, attorney Charles Clark, in the Lamar Life Building, an imposing eleven-story, white, gothic revival building—considered one of Jackson's first skyscrapers when it was built during Jackson's boom years of the 1920s—located on Capitol Street, just across from the Governor's Mansion.

Although Meisburg stated that the meeting was not intended to be "an inquisition," the group questioned Beittel relentlessly for two-and-a-half hours about the propriety of Tougaloo's involvement in the library sit-in and the students' appeal of their conviction. Handwritten notes from the meeting show that Beittel was put through his paces:

- What do you think of the library sit-in?
- What disciplinary measures have been taken or are planned against the students?
- Did you know the library sit-in was to take place?
- What is the official position of the college on demonstrations of this kind?
- Don't you have responsibility to the college as well as to the students—to see that the college continues to function after the present generation of students has gone?
- Did any members of the faculty confer with the students on the sit-in?
- Did the NAACP pay the students to sit in?
- Do the students know how much harm they have done to the First Christian Church—one of the supporting denominations?
- Are more demonstrations of this kind apt to happen?

The ambush must have been difficult for Beittel to handle, seeing as he alone was facing several attorneys, an insurance executive, and a local business proprietor—all of whom had some influence over the amount of support that the church provided to Tougaloo.[30] But from what can be discerned from Beittel's notes and his follow-up letters to the group, he did not waver in his support for the students nor from his belief that they were free to function in society without the school's oversight or discipline.

It appears that the group offered to pay for the students' fines if they would only return to court and plead guilty or at least plead *nolo contendere* (no contest) rather than allowing them to work with the NAACP to appeal the charges. They wanted Beittel to broker such a deal with the students and report back. Beittel wasn't willing to approach the students with such an offer but suggested that one or more of the group come to campus and make the offer themselves. There were no takers.

Then Beittel raised the crucial question of how, exactly, does a compromise by the students change the situation they were protesting? Beittel chided the men that such a deal "only closes the case and involves no compromise on the issues" of segregation.

"What compromise are you suggesting?" they asked, not considering the broader question.

"Opening the library," Beittel shot back.

"That's impossible!" they replied.

"Only concessions of this kind will stave off further demonstrations, I believe," the clear-eyed Beittel responded.

The meeting ended inconclusively, with Beittel agreeing to reconsider the group's request to discuss a deal with his students and, at the very least, talk it over with his staff back at Tougaloo.

Two days later, Beittel wrote cordial yet decisive replies to each of the meeting attendees, indicating that he had talked the matter over with Dean Branch, business manager George Owens, chaplain Mangram, and PR director Henry Briggs and "the consensus of the group is that the students have already made up their minds to carry through the appeal of the case and that it would not be desirable to urge them to reconsider a decision which they have already made."

"Furthermore," Beittel continued, "it was felt on the part of my colleagues that to suggest that someone might be willing to pay the fine for them might be misinterpreted by them in an unfavorable light." In other words, the gesture might be looked upon as a bribe.

Beittel then pressed his larger point: "If Jackson were willing to do what Memphis did under similar circumstances, that is, to open the library to all citizens of Jackson without discrimination, it is probable that the students would reconsider the matter and be willing to have the suit closed."

"If no adjustment of this kind can be made," Beittel continued, "it appears that the appeal will stand and the case will go to the County Court."[31]

This was likely the final word on the subject. The appeal of the students' convictions went forward, though at a snail's pace; no request ever seems to have been made for them to back off; and within a month of Beittel's reply, the First Christian Church of Jackson withdrew its support of Tougaloo College.[32]

"THE SPIRIT HAS CAUGHT FIRE"

While Beittel was on the hot seat, another key figure in the sit-in planning was receiving accolades for his role in helping to orchestrate the demonstration. Reverend Mangram, who in the immediate aftermath of the sit-in seemed to be one of the most prominent public faces of the incident, received congratulations from around the country from the notable as well as the everyday citizen.

Leaders at the national office of the United Church of Christ's Council for Christian Social Action expressed their gratitude "for Christian leaders like you, who are not blinded by the customs of the past nor the mores of region or community, but are willing to work effectively to achieve equal treatment for all God's children." Bob James, a leading Quaker from the Tanguy Homesteads near Chester, Pennsylvania, and a recent visitor to Tougaloo, penned a note on Easter Sunday asking Mangram to convey his appreciation in the wake of the demonstration to the Beittels ("who even under great pressure will stand stalwart and firm"), to the faculty ("so many of whom I came to know and appreciate"), to Mangram ("steady, imaginative, courageous, an inspiration"), and to the students ("especially the Nine, each struggling with the next steps he or she ought to take").

Another handwritten fan letter for Mangram came from the prominent African American religious leader William Lloyd Imes, another recent visitor to Tougaloo's campus, who commented about the library sit-in that "it is such faith in action that gives us all cause for hope in a day of almost unparalleled difficulty and distress in our nation and the world." He also offered sympathy for Reverend Whitney, whom Imes had met during his visit: "who suffered injury from the barbarity and ruthlessness of those who were supposed to uphold the law."

To Imes, Mangram wrote a hasty reply, saying, "We are all very proud of the stride toward freedom made by the one dozen students who participated in the March 27th 'read-in' at the Public Library in Jackson. They represent a new day and a new kind of person among Negroes in Mississippi and the South."

"Keep praying for us and keep encouraging us," Mangram concluded. "We need both."[33]

Perhaps most importantly, Mangram received a letter from Anne Braden of the Southern Conference Educational Fund (SCEF), the left-leaning racial justice organization devoted to "dismantling racial segregation in the South."[34] Mangram had presciently sent Braden various news clippings of the library sit-in events and suggested she publish a summary for the readers of SCEF's monthly newsletter *The Southern Patriot*. Braden published the most thoughtful piece in the aftermath of the landmark demonstration, criticizing the White silence in the wake of the courthouse attack. "White Jackson reacted with silence and fantasy," Braden wrote. "No voice was raised in protest over the use of vicious dogs to attack human beings. "Rather," she continued, "police officials said that reports of the incident were 'lies' by the NAACP."

The *Patriot* also carried the most pointed and poignant comment captured from any of the demonstrators themselves—a statement covered nowhere else. "Our goal is to establish an equal place for the Negro alongside the white man," Janice Jackson is quoted as saying, "with all justice and all opportunities for *all*.

"We do not hate those who oppose us," she continued, "we blame it on ignorance. We grew up in Mississippi, and we know these people. We are sorry for them."

Braeden also sent Mangram a copy of her book *The Wall Between*, thinking he might be encouraged to "read the story of one white southerner who saw the light." She was speaking of herself, of course. "There are many others and I believe there will soon be many more because of the brave actions of you and the Tougaloo students and students all over the South are taking."

"Truly what you are doing is not for the Negroes alone," Braden concluded, echoing Myrdal. "You are offering to the white South an opportunity to save its soul."[35]

At some point in April, Reverend Mangram spoke at an NAACP gathering, giving his assessment of the impact of the Tougaloo Nine demonstration. Titled "Spirit Has Caught Fire," the oration in part describes Mangram's understanding of the students' frame of mind and suggests the kind of training he had attempted to instill in them. "There is not a single one of the students who sat in who would not do it again, and many more would join them. They are prepared for whatever happens; they are not playing. They have counted the cost carefully and prayerfully. They stand for their own rights but with a spirit of forgiveness and understanding of their opponent which transcends the issue of Negro rights. . . . *The spirit that motivates them has caught fire in the hearts of others who heretofore have been afraid.*"[36]

Chapter 18

RISE UP

THE JACKSON STATE CRISIS SEEMED TO HAVE TAMPED DOWN AFTER THE Easter break. President Reddix had called an early, extended Spring Break on the Wednesday before Easter after the police riot in downtown Jackson during the Tougaloo Nine trial—an event that many Jackson State students had witnessed. Reddix's hope was that by disbursing the students a few days early, their zeal for overturning the established order would cool. When they returned, perhaps the Tougaloo Nine demonstration would be in the rearview mirror, and there would be less cause to protest. The gambit worked.

"As he expected," Joyce Ladner later recalled, "when students returned from Spring Break, the campus was calm. The militant mood had vanished."

But that was not the end of the saga for the Ladner sisters. When they came back to campus after the break, they were once again trotted into Dean Rodgers's office and told in no uncertain terms that they would not be returning to Jackson State after the end of the term. He considered them to be two of the "ringleaders of the demonstrations," Joyce recounted. He also let them know that he had caught on to their sneaking off campus to visit Medgar Evers on Wednesday afternoons. "I found out about you girls!" he told them triumphantly.

The young women were unfazed. Dorie, fighting fire with fire, immediately stood up and announced, "We don't want to stay here anyway! We hate this school! We're transferring to Tougaloo!" This was news to Joyce, but she inwardly smiled at Dorie's resilience. "Dorie and I were not ashamed of our actions," she would later state, "and we were *not* going to be humiliated."

Joyce came to believe that Dean Rogers was secretly relieved that the two would be escorted out without a fuss. One less issue to deal with. Walter Williams, president of the Student Council, had been immediately expelled before the Easter break and just weeks before his graduation because of his role in the campus uprising; students were upset enough about that. "I believe Dean Rodgers heaved a sigh of relief," Joyce later opined. "We were going without a fight." Upon leaving the dean's office, the sisters broke into peals of laughter. "It was a 'victory laughter,'" Joyce explained. "We were as defiant as ever. Even at the very end when he was kicking us out, we refused to give in."

One person who didn't get away so easily was Joyce's roommate Eunice. President Reddix made her pay for having been in the wrong place at the wrong time. During Spring Break, she was called back to campus and made to sign an affidavit that she was "not struck or otherwise harmed" by Reddix. The *Jackson Advocate* reported that in her statement Eunice said that she had scattered to get away when she saw Reddix coming toward her and "slipped and fell to the sidewalk." Further, she said that "Reddix and a companion stooped down to pick her up."[1]

Surely, this must have been a tale concocted by Reddix to restore a bit of his tattered reputation and allow him to keep his job. He likely extracted the statement from Eunice and her reportedly livid parents in exchange for a recommendation to get her into another Black college elsewhere in the state. In any event, there were no obvious signs that further disturbances were in the offing when students at both Jackson State and Tougaloo returned to classes on April 10. That, however, would soon change.

AN ALL-OUT CONTINUOUS DRIVE

For its part, the NAACP was forging ahead with a plan to keep Mississippi in the spotlight. The week after Easter, Roy Wilkins summoned to the NAACP's New York headquarters Medgar Evers, state president Aaron Henry, and Evers's nemesis and national NAACP director, Charles Darden, along with attorneys Jack Young and Jess Brown, to brief the staff about the goings on in Mississippi. He also arranged for a press conference on Friday of that week to get additional national media attention for the plight of Black Mississippians.

A reporter for the *Pittsburgh Courier*, a Black news outlet, provided striking details of the deliberations. "The never, never stand of Mississippi against any form of integration or civil rights for Negroes will be met head on, Roy Wilkins, NAACP secretary, announced, by an 'all-out and continuous' drive to eliminate discrimination." Wilkins laid out the five-point plan, developed jointly by the Mississippi/New York team, to combat what he called "Mississippi-ism." The plan included the following:

- voting and voter-registration drives;
- a focus on law enforcement, including police brutality tactics;
- access to jobs, particularly in facilities with federal government contracts; and
- access to public accommodations such as parks, playgrounds, swimming pools, and beaches.

The stars of the press event, of course, were the "grim-faced" Mississippians themselves. Aaron Henry cautioned that the project would be tough going because "many Negroes, as citizens, have to think twice about registering in Mississippi because of the prompt reprisals from whites in firing them from jobs, because of beating, and even murder."

Darden recounted what he saw at the courthouse and revealed that he, too, had been beaten by police and interviewed by the FBI. "Although they were Southern agents," he said, "they seemed sincere in the investigation." He also detailed the beating of the eighty-one-year-old woman who was just passing by on the day of the courthouse incident.

Evers spoke of the unequal justice system in the state, citing the case of Clyde Kennard, whose appeal to the Mississippi Supreme Court had been denied during the week of protest and backlash, adding insult to injury. The ruling meant that Kennard would have to serve a seven-year term in Parchman penitentiary for allegedly agreeing to buy twenty-five-dollars-worth of stolen chicken feed. Evers explained how he had publicly criticized the ruling a "mockery of justice" and for this was sentenced to thirty days in jail and a one-hundred-dollar fine—a case that was itself now being appealed.

The reporter characterized the attitude of the delegation as "completely disgusted" with the intractable denial of civil rights to Negroes. When asked how Mississippi's NAACP contingent would respond should it encounter violent pushback by Whites to its initiatives, Wilkins coldly replied, "The NAACP is *not* a turn-the-other-cheek organization."[2]

When Medgar Evers returned from New York, he found a letter from his second-tier boss, Gloster Current, honoring the beleaguered freedom fighter for his leadership and bravery. "Just a note to tell you how much I personally appreciate what you are doing and how proud of you I am," Current wrote. Having just listened to a news program, Current was effusive in his praise:

> Listening to the CBS broadcast Sunday night, the commentator did a round-up story on Mississippi and your name was prominently mentioned along that of the citizens council. It seems as if we are, at long last, getting results. Certainly, the tone of the radio editorial was commendatory of the Association's work and of yours in particular.
>
> Courage undaunted will get its reward and certainly as long as we have you in Mississippi the Negro still has hope.[3]

No doubt Current was sincere in his appreciation for Evers's efforts to crack open Mississippi's closed society as well as for the positive press that the NAACP was receiving. It was one of the few unequivocal expressions of support for Evers's singular contribution that he would receive from his sponsoring organization. It must have confirmed his belief that, after years of internecine battles with Darden, he and his statewide association were finally on the right path.

That Sunday, April 9, just as students were returning to campus after Spring Break, Evers held a "mass protest rally" at Farish Street Baptist Church to update Black citizens on the NAACP's national plan for Mississippi. *The Jackson Advocate* reported that the place was crawling with undercover cops and reporters anxious to hear the next steps for the burgeoning movement that had been inspired by the library sit-in. What they heard, instead, was "speaker after speaker denounce the use of police dogs against spectators." Evers did end up giving some details of Operation Mississippi, and several West Jackson Youth Council members spoke of their determination to keep up the fight.[4] All in all, however, it was a missed opportunity to keep the pressure on. No further demonstrations were announced.

Whatever was to come, though, it was clear that the Tougaloo sit-in and subsequent events had grabbed the attention of Roy Wilkins and the national NAACP staff. This in itself was a major accomplishment. The NAACP would pour thousands of dollars into Mississippi in the coming years in an attempt to uproot entrenched attitudes about segregation. The outcome of those efforts, for good and ill, could not be clearly foreseen. For now, it was enough for Medgar Evers, John Mangram, and the students who had started it all to bask in the glow of their initial success of calling attention, finally, to Mississippi's separate and unequal society.

ROSS BARNETT RETURNS TO FORM

On April 15, Ross Barnett made one of his first major public appearances since the outbreak of racial demonstrations in the Magnolia State's capital city. The governor traveled to the University of Mississippi to address the annual convention of the local district of the Phi Alpha Delta legal fraternity. Though he never mentioned the racial tensions that had erupted in Jackson in the wake of the Tougaloo Nine demonstration, Barnett made it abundantly clear where he stood on the race question.

The Governor first launched into his now perfunctory defense of states' rights, suggesting that like-minded states should enter into a "compact" to fight the "usurpations" of the federal government. "Democracy is not a thing of Washington," he exhorted. "Democracy is a thing of the crossroads." He continued, "We in the South know that the laws dealing with the separation of the races are necessary to maintain the public peace and order where the races live side by side in large numbers. We know that they are essential to the protection of the racial integrity and purity of the white and Negro races alike."[5]

"The good people of the North," Barnett asserted, "have been sold a bill of goods by expert propagandists in the highly emotional field of race relations." He then posited the unlikely, fearmongering theory that, based on the then-current birth rate, "the colored population of the US will increase from 18.8 million to 150.4 million in a century. And a great majority of these will be in the North."[6]

As he wrapped up his increasingly paranoid assessment of race relations, Barnett said, "If the State of New York wants to integrate and promote intermarriage and a mongrel race, it is not Mississippi's or Alabama's business. However, if Mississippi and Alabama want to maintain purity and integrity of both races, that is Mississippi's and Alabama's business."

Barnett finally made a plea for action by the audience. "It's time to separate the men from the boys," he said. "Take cowards out of the front line—identify the traitors—hang on."[7]

MEDGAR EVERS USHERS IN A NEW DAY

By this point, Jackson seemed to be returning to its pre-"read-in" comity, with elected officials hoping that the seemingly out-of-character demonstration and its harsh aftermath was a one-and-done affair. But the capital city's first sit-in had stirred ripples, especially in the hearts and minds of Jackson's Black youth, and those stirrings of imagination—the rethinking of what was possible in terms of resistance to the status quo—would soon bring further unrest to this once-tranquil Southern town. When Jackson State's students returned from their Easter break, a small group began to ponder new ways to challenge Mississippi's race rules. Soon, they were ready with a plan.

On April 19, four collegians—three from Jackson State and one from the ever-ready Campbell College, all members of the newly formed NAACP Intercollegiate Chapter for the city of Jackson, boarded a city bus on Capitol Street and refused to move to the back area relegated to their race. The four were quickly arrested and this time, just as quickly bailed out by long-time staunch NAACP supporters. Two days later, their trial was held in the same courtroom where the Tougaloo Nine had been found guilty. The foursome received the same sentence—a one-hundred-dollar fine and thirty-days, suspended—from the same judge who had adjudicated the Tougaloo Nine case. Upon hearing of this new arrest, Jackson State students once again held a prayer meeting on campus and this time were undisturbed either by President Reddix or by the Jackson police.[8]

The night before the trial of these newly initiated freedom seekers, Medgar Evers headlined a mass meeting at Jackson's Black Masonic Temple. His comments, preserved in the NAACP archives at the Library of Congress, are worth quoting at length because they show the new militancy that he and the state NAACP had adopted in the wake of the library sit-in and, now, the bus demonstration.

> The occasion for which we are assembled here tonight is a righteous one. It symbolizes a mere beachhead of a dedicated struggle to make possible the fulfillment of the American dream that is of justice and equality for all without regard to race, creed, or color. It is significant that we are here tonight, for it indicates that at long last we here in Mississippi are determined to protest injustices through the courts and through such demonstrations as we are having here tonight. Let it be known to those who say that Negroes in Mississippi are satisfied, that tonight we are here to indicate to the world that so long as there is segregation and discrimination anywhere in the state of Mississippi—or the United States of America for that matter—we are not and shall not be satisfied.
>
> We are making gains in our struggle for first class citizenship, but it cannot be overemphasized that we have only begun this fight, and that there must be many sacrifices. It was well said by an early American patriot that "These are the times that try men's souls. The summer soldier and the sunshine patriot in the time of trouble will shrink from the services of his country. But those who stand by it now deserve the love and admiration of man and woman alike."
>
> Those words were spoken in part by Tom Paine during the crises of the early history of this country. Today, these same words describe these young people who have taken a giant step for freedom in the face of tremendous odds and impending crises. Americans and Mississippians of good will everywhere applaud the courage and foresight of these young people and are willing to stand behind them to the end that justice be done.

Evers then declared that the national NAACP "stands 100 percent behind" the Tougaloo Nine students as well as the youth who staged the bus sit-in. And he goes on to exhort the crowd assembled to action. "We cannot let up now," he extolls. "Let it not be said of us when history records these momentous times that we slept while our rights were being taken by those who would keep us in slavery and by those who say that we are doing 'all right.'"

The leader of this new movement then itemizes areas where pressure needs to be brought, including:

- more and varied jobs for Negroes in the local factories of General Electric and the Vickers manufacturing company;
- city and federal employment of Negroes as policemen and women, firemen, and postal workers;
- expanded voter registration efforts;
- unrestricted use of public facilities such as parks and libraries; and
- the removal of segregation signs at bus and train stations and all remnants of segregated seating on busses and trains.

The energized Evers ended his oration on a high note. "These and many other opportunities are available through persistent effort for their attainment. We must be ever-vigilant lest we lose sight of our objectives. In closing, may I say, let men of good will and understanding change the old order, for this is a new day!"[9]

A new day, indeed. The Tougaloo Nine demonstration and those that inevitably would follow were ushering in a new level of resistance to the established order. One can sense Evers's growing excitement over the developments during the past month. He later reported to his supervisors that the crowd at the mass meeting, which he estimated at seven hundred souls, was cheering him on. He also believed that the police missteps in the arrest of the Nine (i.e., holding them overnight) and their outrageous behavior outside the courthouse during their trial "brought on greater unity in the Negro community and projected the NAACP in a position of being the accepted spokesman for the Negro people."[10]

This was a new position for Evers to find himself in—a respected leader on civil rights issues. The novel feeling must have been gratifying after years of struggle to gain a foothold with a large section of Jackson's Black populace. He redoubled his efforts to instigate lasting change. "Negroes were finally on the move," Myrlie Evers would later recall of this period, "and Medgar, after all the years of frustration, had time for nothing else."[11]

As always, however, with progress in Mississippi, there was a countervailing pushback to put this "New Negro" in his place. An NAACP press release reported that the Jackson City Police Department had purchased its own police dog, no longer willing to rely on a borrowed canine corps to deal with the city's race problems. (The dog had been purchased as the "personal property" of Sheriff Gilfoy—the same official whose absence kept the Tougaloo Nine in jail overnight—until administrative approval could be obtained to shift the dog to the Police Department.)[12]

More ominously, on Friday, April 21, the same day as the trial of the bus demonstrators, Evers was called into the office of the Jackson Police Department's chief of detectives, M. B. Pierce, for a chat. According to Evers, for at least twenty minutes, Pierce tried to "explain" how police actions at the courthouse during the trial of the Nine, with the Jackson State students that same week, and with the new wave of bus demonstrators, were designed to try to "protect" Black demonstrators as well as White citizens. Evers was having none of it. He responded by asking, if Pierce's statement were true, why was it necessary for police to take down license plate numbers of people attending NAACP meetings since such intel led to harassment, not protection, of the attendees.

Although the rank-and-file police officers that day were courteous enough to the NAACP leader to his face, their intentions seemed anything but gracious. Evers overheard them whispering behind his back: "It's that Medgar Evers! Let's get a good look at him so we can shoot straight." If the stage whisper was supposed to strike fear in the heart of this newly militant Black leader, the thirty-five-year-old Evers didn't show it. He just kept on pushing forward.[13]

ROY WILKINS TAKES AIM

At about this time, the national NAACP released a massive fundraising effort on behalf of its Operation Mississippi initiative. From the sentiments expressed in this three-page cri de coeur signed by Wilkins himself—an early example of what would become a staple of all advocacy appeals in the late twentieth century—it appears that the NAACP was finally ready to commit to a full-on assault of Mississippi's racist ways. After describing the circumstances of the March 29 police riot outside the Jackson Municipal Courthouse, with special attention given to police dogs biting unsuspecting bystanders and the police themselves "swinging clubs, blackjacks and pistol butts," the letter gets to the point.

> This happened because Mississippi is, in a way, a snarling dog state, a state dedicated to upholding white supremacy by any means at hand, even those of animalism, terror, and murder.
>
> If this sounds like Hitlerism, it *is* Hitlerism—right here in the U.S.A. in 1961.
>
> This kind of thing cannot be "dealt with." It must be stamped out. Help stamp out Mississippism, the snarling dog philosophy. Help Negro citizens fight this savagery. Help protect Negro youth which wants a fresh deal, with every American making his way, under freedom's rules, according to his abilities, not according to his color.

Wilkins offers a robust endorsement of Operation Mississippi, committing to "the removal of degrading racial proscription from all areas of Mississippi life, using old and new techniques, and employing every available resource in the process. We are determined to bring the United States Constitution to the State of Mississippi."

"It will be a continuous campaign," Wilkins promises, "for as long as it takes, to combat injustice and barbarism in Mississippi. The plan is to proceed in depth and without cessation." Of course, there is the standard request for funds. "Fifty thousand dollars is sought as a kick-off sum," Wilkins allows, "with increased amounts needed as soon as the program gets under way."

Wilkins concludes with a damning connection between what had happened at the Tougaloo Nine trial and the Confederate celebration staged the day before. "Your contribution will translate your indignation into practical action. You cannot go to Jackson . . . but you can send your word to Mississippi Governor Ross Barnett. He has declared [March 28, 1961, at the re-enactment of Mississippi's 1861 secession from the Union] that the Confederacy is 'an undying cause.' You can make a human, person-to-person move in sending your check; you can help rescue both white and black Mississippians from the hateful hand of the dead past."[14]

By early May, the checks were rolling in. So were representations of the conflicting currents of American life with regard to race. Some were highly congratulatory and encouraging. "I certainly appreciate the wonderful work you and our NAACP are doing," wrote a member from of St. Louis. "This is the only kind of answer to Barnett and his fellow swine in Mississippi," wrote a supporter from Farmingdale, New York, in a brief note accompanying her contribution. A doctor from Cleveland, Ohio, helped out with a small check and some addresses of others who might be able to provide more if asked. "There is no question that this matter—as well as the entire matter of racial inequality in this country—must be vigorously fought," he wrote.

Others were less appreciative of the effort. One detractor cheekily sent along a Confederate twenty-dollar bill as a form of protest against the fundraising appeal. Another wrote, "Thanks for the reminder. Sent my contribution to Mississippi at once to buy bigger and fiercer dogs." It was signed "One of the White Majority." The most outraged of the bunch simply sent back the last page of the appeal with a note scribbled at the bottom: "Sir" [with an arrow pointing to Wilkins's signature] "For you to address me is an indignity to which I never expected to be subjected." It was signed by a retired US Navy admiral.

America may, indeed, have been deeply conflicted on matters of race. Wilkins and the NAACP, however, seemed resolved as never before that the time to crack open the Closed Society was now: now that protests had broken out, now that the lie of racial amity within the state could be disproven, now that the students—chief among them, the Tougaloo Nine—had taken a stand against the status quo. One can sense the vast arsenal of NAACP resources shifting from other priorities to focus on Mississippi. That shift would come into full focus the following year, when NAACP lawyers would accompany James Meredith onto the campus of the University of Mississippi, backed by the forces of the federal government and setting up a clash that continues to rankle some to this day.

For now, however, an issue garnering national attention was threatening to swamp the NAACP's Mississippi initiative. It was called "the Freedom Ride."

THE FREEDOM RIDERS "INVADE" MISSISSIPPI

The Freedom Ride was a Congress of Racial Equality (CORE) initiative meant to test a recent US Supreme Court ruling on integrated interstate travel. In 1948, buses, trains, planes, and other conveyances that traveled between states were deemed by the Court to fall under federal law and thus needed to allow for integrated seating. In 1960, the Court extended this ruling to apply to bus terminals, airports, and train stations that supported interstate travel. No longer could there be segregated eating facilities or restrooms in such places anywhere in the nation. All interstate travel facilities must also be integrated.

Just as CORE had tested the 1948 ruling by sending an integrated group on a bus across the upper South, so James Farmer—one of those who had participated in the 1948 rides and who in 1961 headed CORE—decided a similar set of rides could force the integration issue again, this time throughout the Deep South. The Freedom Ride began on May 4 with two busses setting out from Washington, DC, on their way through Virginia, the Carolinas, Georgia, Alabama, and Mississippi to their hoped-for final destination of New Orleans, Louisiana. The riders encountered modest resistance until they arrived in Alabama on May 14, where one bus was sabotaged and, after being forced to stop, was firebombed. The second bus made it safely to Montgomery, where the riders were brutally attacked as they exited the bus to enter the bus station—the police conveniently nowhere to be found—while a mob of angry Whites beat the riders with pipes and sticks. All of this made national news, of course, and after nearly a week of delays and the near collapse of the rides due to rider defections for fear of their lives, a group of deeply devoted students from Nashville, members of the Student Nonviolent Coordinating Committee (SNCC), joined the Ride. On May 24 the buses rolled into Mississippi.[15]

The only stop that the buses made in the Magnolia State was in downtown Jackson, where the riders were arrested immediately upon integrating the bus stations—thus violating local laws—and taken to the city jail for booking and processing. CORE had decided, and SNCC agreed, that any arrests should be handled as "Jail, No Bail." That is, upon arrest, the riders would accept whatever jail term was given them and would not ask to be released from jail on bail to await their appeal. It was hoped that this Gandhian technique would put pressure on the authorities—particularly if more riders followed—by filling the jails to overflowing. And follow they did. More than four hundred riders would be arrested that summer, overcrowding not only the Jackson City Jail, the nearby Hinds County Jail, but also the State Penitentiary at Parchman up in the Delta where most of the Freedom Riders were eventually sent.

As might have been expected, such an influx of "outside agitators" caused alarm, confusion, and anger among many Jackson residents, though they took pride in the fact that no violence had broken out in their state thanks to the quick action on the part of the police. In his daily Crossroads column, *Jackson Daily News* editor Jimmy Ward did not disappoint in his critique of the "foreign invasion." On the first day the riders arrived, Ward wrote, "This should be made clear to all Mississippians. If these so-called 'freedom riders' choose to visit Mississippi, the state and local authorities are fully equipped to handle the situation. These people are crackpots. Any unauthorized citizen who shows up around them will be reducing himself to arguing with a crackpot. If anyone insists on even taking a look at them, kindly wait until officers have promptly locked them in cells at the Jackson Zoo and then go out and observe these human freaks for free."

The zoo remark went over so well with his readers that Ward returned to it the next day: "Some good can come out of the invading screwballs. Since this crew is trying to conduct themselves as animals, why not evacuate our well-behaved monkeys from the Jackson Zoo. Confine these freaks to their cells and let the US Government feed them hot, buttered surplus peanuts."[16]

The riders kept coming day after day. The national media had a field day. All of a sudden, Jackson had become ground zero for the nation's civil rights struggle. As a result, Governor Ross Barnett and Mayor Allen Thompson were invited onto national television shows to provide insight into their state's plight while also being grilled by liberal-leaning reporters and talk-show hosts. Barnett went on *Face the Nation*, and Thompson appeared on the *Today* show.

It was Thompson's comments that caused the local Jackson movement to retaliate. "A great majority of our Negro citizens . . . why, they accept segregation as the white people accept it," Thompson told the show's popular host,

Dave Garroway.[17] He also said that both Blacks and Whites were able to use the Jackson Zoo "without being discriminated against." That was enough for half a dozen of Jackson's Black youth, led by Amos Brown, who was home on summer break from Morehouse College in Atlanta, to go pay a visit to the much-discussed animal park. When the six sat down on the park benches, they were promptly arrested. But Mayor Thompson, fresh from his national TV debut, told the police that the segregation rules at the zoo had changed and not to charge the youth.[18]

Several days later, Brown returned with another NAACP youth member James Hopkins. This time, when the two sat on the benches, they were arrested, charged, and held overnight in jail. Two weeks later, the same thing happened to a group of seven NAACP youth members, including Meredith Anding's cousin Willis Logan. The local movement was continuing to ramp up even as the Freedom Riders had sucked up all of the national media attention. These local transgressions were only reported locally.[19]

In early July, a Jackson State student attempted to enter the swimming pool out at Livingston Park, adjacent to the zoo. She and three others were arrested for sitting on the zoo benches after being stopped by police from entering the pool area. Mayor Thompson completely reversed himself and threatened to close all of the city's parks and pools unless the demonstrations stopped.[20] It was clear that the example of the Tougaloo Nine and the extraordinary day-after-day news coverage of the Freedom Rider "invasion" were having an impact on the local youth. In fact, a number of Freedom Riders, particularly a determined group of SNCC members from Nashville, decided to relocate to Jackson and make it one of their long-term bases of operation. Together with Medgar Evers, this group would work closely with the local youth to encourage continued resistance against segregation in all of its forms. Both the city of Jackson and the Jackson movement began preparing for a long siege.[21]

Chapter 19

HISTORY MARCHES ON

FOR SIDNEY ROEBUCK AND HIS COHORT AT THE MISSISSIPPI COMMISSION on the War Between the States, the Freedom Rides and the growing local movement against segregation could not have come at a worse time. After spending nearly $100,000 in Civil War centennial tourism advertising in magazines like *The Saturday Evening Post, Holiday, Redbook*, and *National Geographic* during March and April, the commission was poised to see a significant uptick in visitors during the spring and summer months.[1] But once civil rights demonstrations broke out locally and then the Freedom Rides began, Roebuck feared that it had all been for naught. Indeed, his charm offensive to the state of Minnesota that spring was blunted because of the bad press the South was getting from the harsh way Freedom Riders were being treated in Alabama and elsewhere.

Roebuck happened to visit Minnesota at the very time the first Freedom Riders were entering Mississippi and getting arrested. Minnesota Week at the Vicksburg National Military Park was scheduled for May 21 through 27. Minnesota's governor had already declared May 27 as "Mississippi Day." And a federal judge named after one of the Minnesota colonels who served in the Battle of Vicksburg was sent as the governor's special representative at the Vicksburg ceremonies. But any positive press for Mississippi's outreach to its Northern neighbors was drowned out by the state's chilly reception of the Freedom Riders. Tom Deale, a representative of the Minnesota Historical Society, admitted as much in a letter to Roebuck. "We got very poor coverage" in the local press about the Vicksburg event Deale reported. "Two possible reasons for this: (1) the Governor's grossly inefficient press secretary; and (2) the bad press Mississippi has been getting up here with the 'Freedom Rides.'"[2]

FETED IN PHILADELPHIA

While Roebuck and his team struggled with how to overcome unwelcome bad publicity due to civil rights agitation, the Tougaloo Nine were taking a victory lap. The summer of 1961 will be remembered by many of them primarily as the time they were celebrated by the national NAACP at the organization's annual convention in Philadelphia. Medgar Evers's entreaties to Roy Wilkins just days after the historic library sit-in to have the Nine attend the upcoming conference had not fallen on deaf ears. In fact, Wilkins saw an opportunity to crow a bit about how the NAACP was making in-roads with the youth movement in, of all places, the great sovereign state of Mississippi.

The NAACP invited any of the Tougaloo Nine who could make it to an all-expenses-paid week-long trip to the City of Brotherly Love and welcomed them to participate in all of the events surrounding the convention, to be held at the Philadelphia Sheraton from July 10 through 16. The thought was thrilling to a number of the newly initiated freedom fighters. Albert Lassiter remembered riding up on the Trailways bus with Sam Bradford and others from the Mississippi delegation. "It was a *very* big deal," said the future air force colonel. "We stayed at the Ben Franklin Hotel . . . it was like the Waldorf or something . . . and ordered room service!" Lassiter, Bradford, and Meredith Anding roomed together, as did Geraldine Edwards, Ethel Sawyer, and Janice Jackson. "Medgar set it up for us," Lassiter recalled.

Sam remembered being short of cash just before boarding the bus, so he asked his mentor who was there seeing them off for a loan. Evers reached into his wallet and pulled out what little cash he had—eight dollars—and handed it to his young protégé. It was a debt Sam would talk about for the rest of his life.

Ethel remembered the long bus ride—"all the way to Philadelphia and back!" Geraldine also had strong memories of the trip. "I have sketches in my mind of the various mountain ranges and the cities that we traveled through," she would write after fifty years had passed. "The mere fact that this convention happened in Philadelphia, and we were given the opportunity to attend was a treat as well as an honor."

"I shook hands with Martin Luther King," Geri marveled and "was in the presence of Andrew Young and many others."

Al and Sam stuck together for most of their time in Philadelphia, each recalling more and more exciting moments:

"Meeting Martin Luther King and Roy Wilkins!" recalled Al.

"Seeing Brock Peters perform 'Freedom Now!'" piped in Sam.

"The Max Roach combo playing!" shouted Al.

"And Babatunde!!" (the Nigerian drummer), inserted Sam.

"He played! He *played*!!" declared Al.

"I got Max Roach's autograph," Sam crowed, sounding still a bit star struck more than half a century later.

"We were just meager Mississippi boys," Al remarked.

(Bradford's and Lassiter's memories are accurate. The drummer Max Roach and his future wife, Abbey Lincoln, had released their avant-garde

Afro-jazz album *Freedom Now Suite* in late 1960 in part as a response to the student sit-in movement sweeping the country. They were invited to perform the piece at the NAACP convention in Philadelphia. Brock Peters served as narrator, and Babatunde Olatunji provided both African drumming support and six African dancers.)[3]

"What I remember, too, was the Freedom Train to Washington, DC," Sam reported. "We had a *big* crowd there. One *heck* of a crowd!"

During the 1961 convention in Philadelphia, the NAACP chartered a twenty-two-car "Freedom Train" from the Pennsylvania Railroad Company for more than twelve hundred of its members to travel to the nation's capital to lobby Congress about civil rights issues. It was the NAACP's answer to CORE's Freedom Ride. The train left out of Philadelphia's ornate Thirtieth Street Station at 8:30 a.m. on Wednesday morning, July 12, and arrived in DC's majestic Union Station a little before 11:00 a.m. From there, the convention delegates fanned out and visited the offices of congressmen and senators with whom they had prearranged appointments.[4]

Meredith Anding had vivid memories of traveling on the Freedom Train to Washington, DC, and especially of being wowed by the city's grandeur. "I remember going into the Capitol and being impressed with the magnitude of the Rotunda," he marveled.

But regarding a visit with his Mississippi legislators, Anding said, "I don't think our congressmen were willing to meet with us," though he wasn't completely sure of this assertion. It is unlikely that most of the all-White elected members of the Mississippi legislative delegation (with the possible exception of liberal-leaning Frank Smith from the Delta) would have even countenanced a meeting with an all-Black group of citizens from the Magnolia State, especially since antilynching and anti–poll tax legislation, home rule for the majority Black city of Washington, DC, and making the US Civil Rights Commission a permanent agency were the issues the group was lobbying for.

The NAACP was prepared for such an eventuality, however, and had advised its Southern members to seek meetings with leaders of various government agencies, such as the Department of Commerce (to urge "immediate action to strike down segregation on interstate travel"—a key demand of the Freedom Riders) and the head of the National Guard (to lobby for inclusion of Black recruits in its ranks, particularly those from Southern states).

Anding was particularly put out when he was told that he and his fellow Tougaloo Nine members would not be able to accompany Medgar Evers and other NAACP top leaders when they went to the White House to meet with President Kennedy that afternoon. "Medgar got there," Meredith noted dejectedly, "but none of us [did]."[5]

It is notable, nonetheless, that Kennedy met with a small delegation of NAACP visitors that day. Indeed, to his credit, when the president learned of the Freedom Train idea, he invited Roy Wilkins and his chief lieutenants and board members to visit him at the White House. A photograph of the group was taken, and both the president and the civil rights leader used it to their advantage—Kennedy to show he was open to hearing directly from Black leadership and Wilkins to demonstrate that the NAACP had access to the highest halls of power. The meeting itself, however, was far from a success.

In his autobiography, Wilkins describes how he and newly elected NAACP board chairman Bishop Stephen Gill Spottswood were invited for a brief private conference with the president in his upstairs living quarters as the others gathered in the Oval Office below. "Jackie Kennedy came rushing up from the basement," Wilkins recalled, just as the three men were headed back down to the larger gathering. "Oh, Jack!" she exclaimed breathlessly. "I've found the Lincoln china!" The president quickly introduced her to his guests, and some minor pleasantries were exchanged. "Then, turning radiantly to Kennedy, she repeated, 'Jack! The Lincoln china!!'"

Later, when the president and the NAACP leaders had joined the larger group downstairs, Spottswood read to him a prepared statement expressing the NAACP's dismay at the administration's lean list of accomplishments thus far in the realm of civil rights. "The absence of a clear call from you for enactment of civil rights legislation has become a source of dismay," Spottswood declared. "In view of the specific pronouncements of the platform on which you were elected . . . there is grave concern over the prospects that without support from the White House, there might be no congressional action of the various urgently needed bills."

After hearing the NAACP chairman out, the president delivered the difficult news: "We remain convinced that legislation is not the way; at least it is not advisable at this time."

Wilkins recounts that he was "extremely disappointed" with the president's quick dismissal of the NAACP's overture. Evers, too, must have been crestfallen. "It was a measure of Kennedy's political smoothness that just about everyone left the White House that day feeling charmed by the man," Wilkins recounted. "But when we reported back to the full delegation of the Freedom Train, the pain was obvious: we had heard plenty about the Lincoln china, nothing about . . . a meaningful legislative program."[6]

Despite Meredith Anding's frustration at being excluded from the White House visit, and the entire delegation's dismay over the president's firm—though gracious—rebuff of immediate legislative action, on their return train back to Philadelphia, everyone had stories to swap about their day of lobbying the top legislators of the land. For many this was their first time ever even considering such bold, direct political action. (Wilkins surely must have been thinking of the positive aspects of the Freedom Train event when he gave his organization's assent to participate in the larger March on Washington two years later.)

For the Tougaloo Nine, the Freedom Train was just a warmup for their moment in the spotlight. The next evening, the students were the NAACP's special guests at the annual Freedom Fund banquet, where Jackie Robinson presided, and Thurgood Marshall gave the after-dinner address. It was here that they were brought on stage to wild applause as the conventioneers got their first good look at the Mississippi vanguard that they had heard so much about. At the opening of the convention earlier in the week, Bishop Spottswood gave a shout-out to various youth councils throughout the country, including "our student chapters at Tougaloo College and Jackson State College in Mississippi" for "being jailed for challenging a lily-white 'public' library and segregated bus lines." Now a majority of the Tougaloo Nine were taking a much-appreciated bow on the national stage. "I remember a big auditorium . . . and they applauded us!" Ethel enthused, still a bit surprised by the attention they received.

On the final day of the convention, Roy Wilkins made his traditional "State of the Association" speech. It was one of his finest. After the requisite pleasantries of platform etiquette and after acknowledging the more than 1,750 delegates from 38 states who had attended the convention—the largest number ever save for the group's fiftieth anniversary two years earlier—Wilkins acknowledged the substantial number of young people attending the conference. Chief among these, he called out "members of our youth chapter in Tougaloo College in Mississippi." These were "the young people who walked into the library," he explained, "and tried to get a book and read. And they were tapped on the shoulder by a policeman and taken to jail." He said, "This is probably the only country in the world where a boy or girl who tries to go to school or tries to get a book out of the library is sent to jail."

Wilkins extoled the presence of so many young people—as well as those forty- and fifty-year-olds "who never admit they're getting old." He said the youth "came at a time of crisis, when talk of freedom [was] in the air." He noted President Kennedy's recent call for freedom and neutrality in Laos, in Angola, in Kenya and in Rhodesia. "Well, my friends, to put it simply, our delegates came to Philadelphia because we *unfree* Americans want to be free in our own country."

"We are interested in Angola, and we want Angola to be free; we are interested in Kenya, and we want Kenya to be free . . . but we want to be free in Mississippi and Alabama and Georgia and South Carolina," he exclaimed. Going even further, Wilkins made a more striking point: "We want to be free in San Francisco and Boston and, if you please, [in] Philadelphia."

The NAACP head acknowledged the contributions of "other groups" in the civil rights space making "excellent, effective and spectacular work"—a notable tip of the hat to SNCC, CORE, and even Dr. King's SCLC, but he claimed that "the backbone of the organized movement was the NAACP." He then ticked off the various local NAACP branches doing valiant work "in Virginia, in North Carolina, in South Carolina, in most of Florida and Arkansas and Tennessee . . . in Georgia . . . in Texas, in Oklahoma, and even in Mississippi."

He then summed up the mood of the 1961 convention about to conclude: "It is one of impatience with the slow pace of integration in American life," he noted, "and of impatience with the time-worn and transparently invalid excuses for that slow pace."

"Let it be said here and now," Wilkins continued, "that wherever segregation and inequality persist, whether naked or camouflaged, we in the NAACP intend to see that there is no peace!" He then ticked off a list of injustices that might still be referenced more than sixty years later: inequality in housing, in employment, in training, in policing, in voter registration and in schooling.

Wilkins went on to list various NAACP-led boycotts and defended the ongoing protests. "Agitation is American and democratic and always has been," he declared. "And no American can be an outsider in his own homeland." He called for "a crusade for freedom" in "every village and every city" in America as "the best guarantee that our beloved country will have the strength and the integrity necessary to maintain its freedom in a threatening world."[7]

It was a powerful and inspiring ending to what, for the Tougaloo students, was an eye-opening experience. As a souvenir of her first trip north, Geraldine Edwards chose a miniature Liberty Bell, so omnipresent at Philadelphia tourist spots, because "I got the feeling of freedom as I sat in those restaurants and ate without any hassle," she said. "I make sure that I always have a Liberty Bell in my possession as a reminder of why I walked into that library in Jackson, Mississippi. It is my symbol of freedom."

Later that summer, Geri was asked by Medgar Evers to represent the Tougaloo Nine at an event in Washington, DC. She was one of the few members of the group to be in town as she was finishing up her second year of summer classes so that she could finish her degree in three years. "Medgar facilitated the entire trip and my being able to represent Mississippi," she recalled. The trip had a shaky start. Geraldine had never flown before, and her tight schedule necessitated a quick up-and-back with an overnight hotel stay.

Already nervous because of first-time flying jitters, Geri's experience was marred when a White Mississippi woman refused to sit next to the young Black college student when she arrived at her assigned seat. "A compassionate White man took her seat and helped me endure my first time flying," Geri reported. The trip and her talk—sharing her experience as one of the Tougaloo Nine—all went well, and the next day she winged her way back to Jackson. Evers was there to greet her and get her back to Tougaloo's campus in time for her next class.[8]

BEITTEL IN THE HOT SEAT

The grilling of Tougaloo's president, Dan Beittel, did not end with the interrogation he endured from five officials from the First Christian Church of Jackson weeks after the library sit-in. Questions remained about his handling of the situation, particularly about his unwillingness to discipline the students for their defiance of local laws and customs. In early September, just as students were returning to campus for the fall semester, Beittel was invited to appear on a public-affairs television program to discuss his views on student protest with a panel of prominent journalists. These included Ken Toler, Jackson-based reporter for the Memphis *Commercial Appeal*; United Press International (UPI) Southern bureau chief John Herbers; Jackson *State Times* managing editor Paul Tiblier; and Dick Sanders, news director of Jackson television station WLBT, who also served as host. The conversation was civil but pointed.[9]

Beittel was asked if he were a member of the NAACP. "Not technically, but I subscribe to their literature," he answered. Was Tougaloo's library inadequate for the students' needs? "I don't think the students came to the Jackson city library primarily for books," he parried. Would he expel the students if they lost their judicial appeal? "There's a difference between going to jail for stealing something and going to jail for a conviction," Beittel noted. "I should respect [the students] for being willing to pay the price for what they believe to be right."

Do you think it's right to go against community customs and rules? "All customs and rules should be abided by when they are consistent with our highest ideals," he pointed out. "But when people pay taxes to support an institution, [they should be able to] participate in the benefits." Beittel added that he thought the students "could have integrated the library without trouble if they had been ignored. There would have been no trouble had they sat there and read for three hours."

Will you discourage off-campus activities in the future? "No, I don't think so," the college president curtly replied. Beittel's only concession was to suggest that he might remind students that their primary purpose for going to college was to learn and that they would not be excused from their classes or homework just because they were off demonstrating.

The conversation must have been eye opening to Jacksonians deprived of alternative local viewpoints. For Beittel, the experience seems to have been exhilarating. In a letter to a colleague about the incident he wrote, "Last week I was invited to participate in a 'meet the press' panel on one of the local TV stations. Some of my friends were afraid that the affair was a setup simply to give the college unfavorable publicity and perhaps to get my scalp. . . . I received many telephone calls and letters of commendation from both the Negro and white communities." Nonetheless, Beittel's TV appearance further heightened local officials' concern over the existence of such an openly divergent voice in their midst and invited further scrutiny of Tougaloo and its administrators by the Mississippi Sovereignty Commission.

THE LEGAL APPEAL OF THE TOUGALOO NINE CASE

One unresolved issue for the members of the Tougaloo Nine upon their return from Philadelphia was the status of the appeal of their conviction for breach of peace. It seems that the leaders and lawyers of the national NAACP believed that the Tougaloo Nine case could be used to help challenge racial segregation in all of its forms in Mississippi—and throughout the South—and possibly even destroy the entire legal underpinning of the practice in public spaces, just as the *Brown v. Board of Education* case had done for public schooling. As noted, the conviction of the Tougaloo Nine on March 29, 1961, was immediately appealed, and the NAACP was prepared to provide legal backing for the students all the way to the US Supreme Court, should it be necessary.

But Mississippi had a different plan. Rather than allow the appeal to proceed up the chain of various courts, the Hinds County Court simply found a way to delay hearing the case. It was first set to be heard in April. Delayed. Then in May. Delayed. Next in June . . . Mississippi's legal minds knew that should the case proceed to courts outside of Mississippi that the entire structure of the law it was built upon might collapse. Breach of peace? There was no indication that anyone was upset within the library other than the police themselves. And although the cops took great care not to use any racial terms in the arrest or during the trial, it was clear the whole set-up was denial of citizen rights and privileges due to racial animus—a blatant violation of the Fourteenth Amendment's equal-protection clause. This would obviously come up as the case progressed. Better to delay rather than have the entire edifice of segregation come tumbling down.[10]

This same strategy happened with other local public-facilities demonstration cases as they came before the court. The bus-seating incident, the zoo sit-in, and the swimming pool attempted-entry cases faced similar fates: guilty in the municipal court. Appeal. Delay. More delay. To deal with this frustration of justice, it appears that the NAACP's legal team decided to go around the local courts entirely and file the cases in the federal court system, where they'd have a better chance of being heard. In January 1962, in an unprecedented move, the NAACP filed a class-action suit against the city of Jackson, using the various examples of arrest for breach of peace as evidence that the Black citizens of Jackson were being discriminated against due to race. Cliff Sessions of UPI called it "the first legal attempt to integrate public facilities in Jackson."[11]

The NAACP attorneys asked representatives of each infraction to provide testimony of such discrimination but chose not to name them as defendants. Instead, in a novel twist, the NAACP chose as defendants three long-term local members of its Jackson branch—all adults and economically independent of the local White control—to serve as samples of the entire class of citizens who were being discriminated against throughout the city. These three—Reverend L. A. Clark, Mary Cox, and W. R. Wrenn—testified, as did Ethel and Janice for the library sit-in, James Hopkins for the zoo demonstration, and Eddie Jean Thomas for the swimming pool infraction. This was typical NAACP legal protocol—not to escalate but to litigate.

Most of the trial was rather matter-of-fact. Ultimately, the case turned on a technicality. After losing at each level through the lower courts, the case made it all the way to the US Supreme Court. But the high court rejected the NAACP's class-action strategy, reading the cases narrowly and ruling that none of the three defendants named—Clark, Cox, and Wrenn—had been legally harmed in any of the various demonstrations or arrests and thus could not represent the "class" of citizens in the court. In other words, they had no standing. The case was remanded back to the lower court, which let its guilty verdict stand.[12]

Meanwhile, the original appeal of the Tougaloo Nine case languished in Hinds County Court and in fact never was heard. This point is confirmed by an NAACP Legal Team summary of cases pending before the Mississippi court system in July 1964. It lists all of the names of the Tougaloo Nine and simply says that the case had been "continued." And again, in a 1965 oral history, Dr. Beittel observed that the case still had not been heard despite the fact that the 1964 Civil Rights Act had been passed, and all public conveyances and facilities were required to desegregate.[13]

While still at Tougaloo, therefore, the students found that they could not participate in any further demonstrations for fear of violating the terms of their parole and having their thirty-day suspended sentence remanded—another reason, surely, for not allowing their appeal to be heard. Nevertheless, sometime in the early 1980s, some of the Tougaloo Nine reported that they received a letter from the city of Jackson absolving them of the breach-of-peace violation (though some complained that the misdemeanor continued to show up on their formal criminal record for years to come).

CONTINUED TURMOIL IN JACKSON

In the run up to the March 1961 Secession Day, Sidney Roebuck and the Mississippi commission staff received a strange, anonymous postcard from Yonkers, New York. On the front, along with the commission's address, was an ominous note: "Chimneyville 1963?"—an obvious reference to the nickname for Jackson after Union troops, soon after the fall of Vicksburg, retook the city of Jackson in July 1863 and destroyed nearly every semblance of civilization in the process, leaving mostly burnt-out homes with only the chimneys still standing.[14]

On the reverse side, a brief note, hastily scribbled, read, "To your five Centennial tours—Red, Green, Orange, Yellow, Blue—add a *Black* tour!" (The reference is to a colorful centennial tourism brochure, distributed widely, that suggested various self-guided tours throughout the city to see Civil War sites.) "Unless you give the Blacks equal rights," the correspondent continued, "a voice from above was heard saying: 'July 1963 Jackson will be burned and destroyed by African missles [*sic*].'"[15]

The card may have been written by an unstable history buff, but the author's message was prescient. By the spring of 1963, two years after the Tougaloo Nine demonstration, Jackson was once again engulfed in seemingly intractable racial discord, with more than one thousand of its residents, mostly teenagers, having been arrested in antisegregation demonstrations that were ignited by another sit-in, again led by Tougaloo students, this time at the Woolworth's five-and-dime store on Capitol Street.

By this point, Medgar Evers was right out front, leading the charge along with John Salter, a radical Tougaloo political- and social-science professor. Even Roy Wilkins inserted himself into the mix when he decided to directly intervene in the proceedings by picketing with Evers in front of Woolworth's four days after a raucous and violent response to the student-led sit-in there. Both were arrested and charged with breach of the peace. Wilkins was treated respectfully by his jailers and was out on bail later that afternoon, but his bond had been set unreasonably high ($1,000), and he carped about that all the way home to New York the next day. Evers was left to figure a way out of the impasse, along with his bosses from the national office who had come down to assist with the effort, but whose unwillingness to use more mass demonstrations and marches to advance the movement's demands left the local Black populace—and Evers in particular—exposed and without sufficient momentum for success.

Two weeks after the Woolworth's sit-in, as White Mississippi became increasingly agitated, Evers was shot and killed, inflaming tensions even further and leading to a near-conflagration at his funeral on June 15. Only the quick thinking of Robert Kennedy's deputy assistant attorney general for civil rights, John Doar—who waded into the middle of a militia-mad, rifle-toting enormous police presence and a distraught, rock-throwing crowd of mourners—kept the incident from turning into a massacre.[16]

The day after the funeral, it was announced that Medgar's brother Charles would take over the lead of the NAACP's operation in Mississippi. Even so, the assassination of Medgar Evers took all of the wind out of the sails of the Jackson movement, and its shattered adult representatives let go of nearly all of the movement's demands to ensure that the killing would stop. Evers's meticulously crafted youth strategy was momentarily thwarted, though his belief in the power of young people to boldly seek change would be wholly vindicated in the years to come. Meanwhile, the Civil War commemorations continued unabated. There was another Confederate defeat to celebrate.

VICKSBURG CENTENNIAL

Nothing could come close to the over-the-top Secession Day festivities of 1961, so the Mississippi commission recommended small, tasteful, local events throughout the state during 1962, whether or not actual battles or skirmishes were fought there. These were called Rededication Days, and the commission crassly sold this idea as "an outstanding opportunity to get FREE ADVERTISING FOR YOUR TOWN ALL OVER AMERICA" by having their event listed in the commission's annual calendar of events. A *Special Rededication Day* flier was developed to provide guidance to local planning committees on how and when to develop their local events.

Given the blowback from national media regarding some of the South's earlier Confederate bashes, the recommendation was to tone it down. "In whatever manner you plan your Rededication Day, though, bear in mind that it should at all times be dignified. Raucousness, commercialism, or any displays of bad taste that might detract from the National flag, the Confederate flag, or the purpose of the Rededication ceremonies are to be carefully avoided."[17]

Commission director Sidney Roebuck made it a point to request that "each Mississippi community schedule a re-dedication ceremony some time in 1962" and suggested how to set up a program and even which organizations and individuals to contact—"Sons of Confederate Veterans, United Daughters of the Confederacy, mayors, school officials, history teachers and public spirited citizens—in order to have a meaningful community event."[18] Indeed, the commission's report for 1962 lists more than 150 such events—balls, pilgrimages, memorial services, pageants and, yes, even parades.[19]

Yet if things went small scale for 1962, the commission planned one final big blowout for 1963. This, of course, was the commemoration of one of the most significant turning points of the war—the Battle and Siege of Vicksburg. That General Grant and the Union army ultimately won the day seems not to have bothered the Southern planners of the battle's commemoration. Everyone knew it was a big deal, and Mississippi was going to celebrate its primacy of place (and gain the tourism benefits) despite having to admit defeat.

The one major problem with the Vicksburg commemoration was that a century earlier, Confederate general John C. Pemberton had the temerity, unbeknownst to him, to wave the white flag of surrender at Vicksburg on the very same day that General Robert E. Lee turned around and high tailed it out of Gettysburg, giving the North two major victories on the same day, July 4, 1863. Historians still dicker over which battle was more significant for the eventual overall Union triumph, but for the planners of the centennial, it seemed to become a battle over who could put on the better commemorative show.

As early as 1960, the Gettysburg planning committee reached out to the Mississippi commission hoping to coordinate their centennial events. Not much came of the effort, however, as both groups were determined to hold their festivities concurrently, combining them, of course, with the national Independence Day celebration. As it turned out, Gettysburg would have the better speaker lineup, owing to its victorious Northern location and independent planning organization—the unwieldy sounding "100th Anniversary of the Battle of Gettysburg and Lincoln's Gettysburg Address Commission."[20]

Mississippi would have to settle for a decidedly Southern affair with mostly local speakers. Any thought of some sort of regional reconciliation program seems not even to have been considered, even though the Mississippi commission had extended itself so graciously two years earlier with its weekly memorial ceremonies for all Northern states that had sent soldiers to fight in the battle.

Both locales offered a full week of commemorative events. In Mississippi, planners had "deliberately determined that the tone of the observance of the Siege Centennial should be serious commemoration rather than celebration—thoughtful non-partisan appraisal instead of commercialization or carnival revelry." Surely the presence of the commission's original chairman, Frank Everett—not a rah-rah Barnett Confederate—on the Vicksburg planning committee helped keep the party atmosphere in check.[21]

The sequence of planned events began on Sunday, June 30, with the call for a Day of Prayer and Devotion. All churches in the city held special services honoring the occasion, and a special memorial service was held at the Vicksburg National Military Park which, thanks to the intervention of Mississippi's junior US Senator John Stennis had been significantly spruced up with the help of more than $300,000 of federal, National Park Service funds.[22]

During the lead up to July 4, daily seminars were held on various aspects of the battle by nationally recognized scholars, including the ubiquitous Ed Bearss of the National Park Service, who had just completed a second volume of Mississippi Civil War history, the counterintuitive *Rebel Victory at Vicksburg*, at the request of the Mississippi commission.[23]

The Vicksburg National Military Park was open for tours, and it was reported that nearly fifty-six thousand visitors entered the park during the five-day commemorative period. (In fact, the Park Service reported that more people had toured the park on June 30, the opening day of the ceremonies, than had visited the park since its creation in 1899!)[24]

On July 4, a special luncheon was held, sponsored by various local civic clubs, to honor the opposing generals in the battle—Ulysses S. Grant and John C. Pemberton—another gracious nod to reconciliation. The namesake grandsons of each military leader were in attendance, bringing special poignancy to the gathering, which more than 350 enthusiasts attended.

Of course, a parade was held that morning with bands, floats, and even some units of the Mississippi Greys, but nothing as raucous as the Secession Day Parade of 1961.[25] And in the afternoon, a special memorial program was held outdoors featuring Governor Ross Barnett and Mississippi's senior US senator, the deeply conservative and racist James O. Eastland, as speakers. The speeches were interrupted briefly by a summer squall. But the program was rescued by "a thrilling air show" by the "talented and daring" Air National Guard that followed, to the delight of the estimated eight thousand spectators.

That evening, the largest fireworks display in the history of Vicksburg was illuminated, intended to recreate the dramatic bombardment of the city by the Union navy, as well as the return fire by the Confederate army from high on the Vicksburg bluffs one hundred years earlier. By all reports, the five-day commemoration was a triumph.

Coming as it did little more than three weeks after the assassination of Mississippi's own Medgar Evers, however, the commemoration was an almost entirely White affair. Any local Blacks who might have wanted to attend would not have been welcome anyway. In addition, the National Baptist Convention, the largest US Black Christian denomination, had called for a sixty-day mourning period for the civil rights martyr, with the public grieving to begin on the very day of the Vicksburg commemoration, July 4.

Undoubtedly, the date was chosen to highlight Evers's patriotism as a World War II veteran and also to point out that his death was an American tragedy.[26] But the juxtaposition of the two events—the assassination and the celebration—once again paired the Mississippi Civil War Centennial and the Black Freedom Struggle just as the Tougaloo Nine Library Sit-In had done with the Secession Day events two years earlier.

It was a harsh reminder of what Evers had often said: "Freedom has never been free." One hundred years after the last major campaign of the war on Mississippi soil had been won by the North, more than 40 percent of the state's citizens were still not enjoying the full rights of citizenship as promised under the Thirteenth, Fourteenth, and Fifteenth Amendments to the Constitution. It would take the signing of the Civil Rights Act of 1964 (on Evers's birthday, no less) and the Voting Rights Act of 1965 before any significant progress would be made on that front. By then, the Civil War Centennial in Mississippi would have ended, and the Mississippi civil rights movement would have shifted to another phase.

ROEBUCK CALLS IT QUITS

Mississippi Centennial Commission director Sidney Roebuck threw in the towel a year early, recognizing that there were precious few victories for his Magnolia State Confederates to commemorate after their defeat at Vicksburg. A great deal was made of the skirmish at Brice's Cross Roads, where Nathan Bedford Forrest and his wild horsemen gave the Union army one of its few defeats in early June 1864 as Sherman was making his determined march to Atlanta and onward to the sea. The event was the last gasp for the Mississippi Commission on the War Between the States, and this minor victory was exuberantly celebrated over a three-day weekend, from Friday, June 5 through Sunday, June 7, 1964, with a street dance Friday night, a Confederate Ball on Saturday, and a reenactment of the rout on Sunday morning, followed by a commemorative program in the afternoon.[27]

Although invited to speak at the ceremony, Mississippi's new governor, Paul Johnson Jr., politely declined, citing a scheduling conflict—something his predecessor would never have done. It seems celebrating past glories and honoring lost causes was becoming passé. Instead, Governor Johnson was trying his best to help his constituents realize that "we are Americans as well as Mississippians" and that they had to get on with the business of building the state's troubled economy and civil society in the twentieth century rather than glorying in its mythic nineteenth century past.[28] Nevertheless, twelve thousand people attended the Brice's Cross Roads reenactment on a very hot and muggy Mississippi morning to witness one of the few remaining Confederate "wins" in the state and to be on hand for one of the commission's final commemorative programs.[29]

Well before the Brice's Cross Roads event, Roebuck had realized there was no sense in prolonging the inevitable. In October 1963, he wrote to members of the Mississippi commission that he planned to close up shop on June 30, 1964, due to "lagging interest" in Civil War commemorative activities not only in Mississippi but "in every state and community." Roebuck well understood that there was little enthusiasm even within the state legislature for renewing funding for the commission and thus declined to ask for any during the upcoming legislative session. "There will be no money after June 30, 1964," he told the commissioners. Whatever unexpended funds might have been left in the commission's coffers were used to fund a diorama of the Battle of Brice's Cross Roads in the refurbished Old Capitol Museum. (Roebuck even pressed his colleagues at Brice's Cross Roads to get their final invoices in quickly. "We will be out of business as of July 1, 1964," he wrote. "We are going to have to work fast to be able to clear the bills by that time.")

Thus, the Mississippi commission limped to a close, allowing the historians to take over and finally freeing Mississippians to move on to more pressing matters.[30] These would include the coming "invasion" of the state by thousands of mostly Northern, mostly White college students to help with Black voter registration during Freedom Summer and, two weeks after the Brice's Cross Roads commemoration, the murder of three civil rights workers 150 miles south of the celebration site near Philadelphia, Mississippi. It was clearly time to leave the past behind.

Part VII

LEAVING THE NEST

Chapter 20

THE FIRST TO GRADUATE

IF THE SPIRITS OF THOSE CARRYING THE BANNERS OF THE PAST WERE flagging, those with their minds stayed on freedom and the future were enthusiastically marching on. All of the Tougaloo Nine would go on to lead extraordinary lives—at least from the vantage point of those who came before them. They were part of the generation of young African Americans whose possibilities broadened almost beyond belief by the tremendous strides pried open by the demands of the civil rights movement. Every one of them would use their education to find jobs that were meaningful, not menial. They each would gradually join the burgeoning Black middle class. Most would take part in one of the last big waves of the Great Migration—moving North or West, away from the South, to find their footing and experience a very different life (and lifestyle) than the one that awaited them had they stayed in Mississippi. Like their peers, however, nearly all of the Nine would fight discrimination and racism in its various forms as they rose in their chosen professions.

ETHEL SAWYER ADOLPHE AND JANICE JACKSON VAILS

The two best friends who had met while at the Jackson Greyhound bus station trying to find their way to Tougaloo were the first of the Nine to graduate in June 1962. Their last year at Tougaloo was filled with activity and accomplishment. Ethel served as president of the Tougaloo chapter of the Delta Sigma Theta sorority, while Janice held the position of secretary. Janice was elected "Miss Tougaloo" that final year, while Ethel was reselected "Sweetheart" for one of the campus fraternities, Omega Psi Phi.

Both women had been exceptional students, and both graduated with honors: Ethel, cum laude, and Janice, magna cum laude. A few days after their commencement exercises, Jimmy Ward of the *Jackson Daily News* had a gift for them—the gift of wry laughter that would stay with them throughout the rest of their lives. "A dreadful thing has happened out at Tougaloo College," Ward noted in his Covering the Crossroads column. "Some of that institution's most outstanding racial agitators graduated last week."

"Incidentally," Ward continued, "when degrees were passed out, several were cited as 'freedom riders cum lawd.'"

The derisive tone and comic spelling would stay with them, as would his "Is you did yo' Greek yit" silliness from the day after the library demonstration. "Janice and I would alternate between being real pissed off and falling out laughing," Ethel would record years later. More than six decades after their historic sit-in at the downtown Jackson library, Ethel and Janice would greet each other with Ward's intended put downs, laughing all the way because they knew they had bested him and the system he represented.[1]

Ethel Sawyer was the first Tougaloo grad to be admitted into the sociology master's degree program at Washington University in Saint Louis (WashU), thanks in large part to the unceasing efforts of Ernst Borinski to place his best students at high-profile institutions of higher learning. During the next five years, Ethel would earn her master of arts degree and complete all requirements for a PhD except the dissertation. Today she is recognized as a pioneer in the field of queer studies—a subject only discussed in hushed tones in academe in the mid-1960s. At that time, however, WashU was engaging in a comprehensive study of urban poverty in the Pruitt-Igoe housing projects, a series of thirty-three eleven-story apartment buildings located on the north side of St. Louis that served as the living quarters primarily for the city's African American poor and working class.

A group of WashU's grad students were being employed as research assistants to study various aspects of the housing project and its residents.[2] Ethel initially was part of the group studying the housing project and was visiting the area one day when a young woman invited her to meet some of her female friends. They turned out to be a group of lesbians who would gather regularly and swap stories. Although Ethel wasn't exactly sure what she had stumbled into—"Ignorance is bliss," she would later joke—she returned to the campus, taping and submitting (as required) the recording of her work experience for that day.

Shortly afterward, she was summoned to a meeting with two faculty advisors, who discussed with her the importance of her recent findings, the need for research in the area of female homosexuality, and their hopes that Ethel would consider researching this area. Ethel agreed to try and thus was released from the public-housing study in order to do more extensive research on the women she had met, their habits, their interactions, their lifestyles. "I spent the next several years doing research on female homosexuality," she remembered. It was one of the first in-depth studies of its kind in the United States.

During this time, Ethel put together some academic papers on the subject and completed her master's degree (with essay honors), but she kept delaying writing her dissertation.

By the end of her fifth year at WashU, she had completed all of her coursework but stalled when it came to writing up her deep research into her assigned topic. "I lollygagged, goofed around, wrote papers when I had to," she said. "And I did sort of have the intent to go ahead and finish." But Ethel apparently wasn't convinced that a sociology PhD focused on gay Black women would be a strong calling card in academe in the late 1960s. Nor did she believe it would be in her long-term best interest. So, a year or so after leaving graduate school, Ethel made the decision not to complete the dissertation.

In 1967, leaving grad school to join the workforce, Ethel took a job on another pioneering project that would take her back to Mississippi. It was then that Tufts University greenlighted an innovative community-health initiative inspired by Dr. Jack Geiger's experiences during Freedom Summer, when he visited Mississippi as part of the Medical Committee for Human Rights. The poverty and lack of any access to even the most basic medical care for most of the Mississippi Delta's poor Black sharecroppers pushed the young doctor to conceive of community health centers that would provide at least a modicum of medical support for the impoverished workers and their families. The program was in its start-up phase when Ethel and another WashU grad student joined the team, spending a year working on this groundbreaking initiative.

Though she downplays her role in the project—"I was out of my depth," she would later say—Ethel nevertheless recalled the many off hours she and her fellow WashU colleague spent hanging out with the handsome Meharry Medical College students from Nashville who rotated in and out of Mound Bayou as medical interns at Taborian Hospital.

After a year in Mound Bayou, Ethel moved to Pennsylvania to take up a teaching job at Haverford College just outside Philadelphia. It was there that her crisis over her dissertation reached a decision point. Her advisor at WashU was urging her to finish. "Just work on what you've got," he encouraged her. "We'll take it!" But Ethel decided it would not be helpful to her career, so she ended up ABD (all but dissertation), realizing the challenges that would follow in academia but resolved to put it all behind her. "I remember making that decision at Haverford. I kind of cried a little bit. But I said to myself, 'I don't think this is what I want, and I'm not going to do it.' So, pfft, there it was."

After a year at Haverford, Ethel shifted to teaching at Temple University for two years before moving back to St. Louis in the summer of 1971 to marry Edward Turner, whom she had met during her years in grad school. The marriage lasted only a year, but her return to St. Louis stuck. She would settle there for the next fifty-plus years and would carve out a career in the just-emerging branch of higher education that would come to be known as community college.

In the fall of 1971, Ethel began teaching at St. Louis Community College's Forest Park campus. She spent the next twenty-nine years with the organization in both teaching and administrative capacities. Ethel rose quickly through the ranks, becoming department chair in sociology followed within a few years as Social Sciences Division chair. An improbable consolidation in 1978 of her division with the Business School put Ethel in competition with several other college staffers (including the then Business Division chair) for the deanship of the new division, which she won. But the victory set up an ongoing, if undercover, battle with her Business School colleagues during the next three years. "Those people up in Business didn't want this little miniskirted, Afro-wearing, Black sociologist" to be their leader, Ethel allowed.

An incoming dean of instruction to whom Ethel reported decided to try to solve the ongoing power struggle after taking into consideration only input from the Business School faculty. He called Ethel in and told her she'd have to go back to the Sociology Department as a teacher for the upcoming academic year. She was livid. "I'm the only Black dean. I'm the only female dean, and I'm coming to the end of the third-year probationary period for all new associate deans, and he pulls *this*??!!" she exclaimed, still fuming about the dust-up more than thirty-five years later.

Her loyal following of social sciences teachers threatened to go on strike when they heard of the betrayal. The ever-loyal Ethel, however, urged them to get back to work, but "the faculty were in an uproar," she recounted. "And so were a lot of students!" After a brief meeting with the campus president, who alleged ignorance of the situation, Ethel received a letter from the college chancellor telling her that she was not being recommended for a permanent division deanship. "I went down immediately to the EEOC" and filed a complaint, she recalled. The Equal Employment Opportunity Commission found in her favor. (She would subsequently file a discrimination lawsuit against the college.) "Seems like I've been fighting for something all of my life," Ethel observed, harkening back to her Tougaloo Nine days.

After a drawn-out process, Ethel lost her discrimination lawsuit against the college, though her nemesis, the dean of instruction was soon let go while she remained as division dean, business and social sciences, for the next eleven-plus years. Eventually, after another series of mergers and cutbacks, Ethel was named dean of the combined Humanities and Social Sciences Departments, remaining in that post until her retirement from the college.

Some of Ethel's most valued educational contributions were those in the area of global education. Under her leadership (and often, her direct participation), extensive course, curriculum, and program development occurred at her campus, including the awarding of associate degrees and certificates in international business and international studies. In addition, she arranged for international faculty exchanges and faculty-led student-travel-abroad programs similar to those occurring at four-year institutions.

For these and other contributions, Ethel was awarded the Innovator of the Year and President's Star Award in 1998 and 1999, respectively, and her college campus received the 1999 Achievement Award from the American Council on International Intercultural Education in recognition of "its extensive contributions to Global education."

While officially retired from St. Louis Community College, starting in the year 2000, Ethel continued her work in global education, serving part time as global education specialist for the Missouri Community College Association, applying for grants and codirecting a three-year project entitled Enhancing International Studies and Foreign Language Teaching and Learning at Missouri Community Colleges. She was awarded the newly initiated Global Educator of the Year Award in 2003 for her contributions at the state level.

In a faculty Roast to the Conquering Tigress at Ethel's retirement party, one of her long-term colleagues honored her for her "'methodicalness,' her ability to get things done, her being a "Do-Right-Person", and her willingness to put it all on the line in the name of fairness and justice." That seems to sum it up nicely.

After retirement, Ethel continued to reside in and manage an apartment building she purchased in 1978 when she was thirty-eight years old. Over the years, she participated in the fight to prevent a proposed corporate takeover through eminent domain and the gentrification of her St. Louis neighborhood not far from the WashU campus, thus allowing more African American residents to remain in their apartments and their homes. She also made extensive renovations to her property, converting a six-unit building to five units (the larger one for her family's occupancy) and became skilled at property ownership, care, and management. In 2022, Ethel finally sold the property and moved into a senior living facility nearby.

On the personal side, Ethel married again, in 1974, this time to Max Gerard Adolphe, and together they had one child, Karim Gerard Adolphe, her much-loved son. At this writing, Ethel expresses gratitude for the long life she has lived and for her many loving and supportive family members and friends. She feels she has lived "a good life."

As for her time at Tougaloo and her membership in the Tougaloo Nine, she put it all in perspective. "I'm glad I did it," Ethel said of her demonstration at the library, "but I never felt the need to get accolades for it. It was just one piece of a long life of working and playing and fighting for change."

Through it all, Ethel maintained her devotion to Tougaloo for all it had given her. At the forty-fifth anniversary commemoration honoring the

Tougaloo Nine in 2006, Ethel concluded her remarks with this observation: "Tougaloo's respect for human dignity and its treatment of us during that time [of the library sit-in] simply added to what was already—and has remained through the years—my love affair with Tougaloo."

As for **Janice Jackson,** her years at Tougaloo were a time of achievement and expansion of possibilities, though there were times she would have to fight for her place in a man's world. Even fifty years later, it pained her to remember that she came in second in the grades race in her graduating class from Tougaloo. "Yeah, a guy beat me out at the very end," she said. And she believed even that defeat was a result of sex discrimination rather than anyone else's better intellect or stronger drive.

She majored in biology, a somewhat unorthodox field for women at the time, and she was still stung by the unfair treatment she received from one of her professors. "I remember one in particular who didn't believe that women should be in the sciences," she would later confide. "And he gave me a real hard time. My tests and my grades . . . would always be lower than the males." In one particularly problematic grade dispute, Janice even enlisted the aid of the dean of students, Dean Branch, to intervene. Nevertheless, she would graduate with a degree in biology with a minor in psychology and a full-ride scholarship to Columbia University. "I was going to get a PhD in biology," she later wistfully recalled. "I often wonder how my life would have changed had I done that."

But Janice had agreed to be part of the "family plan"—having her family sacrifice for her to go to college if she returned home, found a job, and helped fund the next child's higher education. Dutiful daughter that she was, Janice passed up that scholarship, returned home, and taught science and biology classes at Coahoma Community College for a year to help pay for her sister to go to Tougaloo.

Then a fateful call from Ethel changed Janice's trajectory. "Girl, you've got to come to St. Louis!" Ethel enthused. "Come for a visit this summer and see what it's like." That was the summer of 1963. Janice would remain in the Gateway City, with its iconic Arch, for much of the rest of her life.

Janice had every intention of returning home to Clarksdale once the summer ended, but Ethel wouldn't hear of it. "Girl, you're not going home!" Ethel said incredulously.

"Yes, I am!" exclaimed Janice. "You said just for the summer!" Somehow, the discussion caused Janice to rethink her priorities. By then, her sister had left Tougaloo, and Janice realized that her prospects for advancement were limited in Clarksdale. So, she finally got up the nerve to call her father and tell him she wasn't coming home. Despite his vociferous objections, Janice stayed and roomed with Ethel until 1967, when Ethel headed to the Tufts Health Care facility in Mound Bayou.

With her Tougaloo degree, Janice easily landed a job as a case worker with the Missouri Division of Family Services, where she worked until she could obtain the state teaching credential. In 1964, she started teaching biology and general science at St. Louis's Beaumont High School, just across the street from the State Fairgrounds north of the downtown area and not far from the Mississippi River. It was at Beaumont that Janice's civil rights experiences began to take root as she advocated for her students at this predominantly Black secondary school. "That's where my activism really kicked in," she would later recall. For the next five years, Janice worked with the students to form a Black Student Union and served as a liaison between the students and the school's older White principal, whose cultural awareness of the Black consciousness movement was, to put it kindly, more than a little deficient. When students wore dashikis to school to show their racial pride, he would complain they were dressing in costumes. "He just didn't understand," Janice explained. Eventually, he resigned, largely due to these cultural issues, and was replaced by a Black head of school.

Janice continued to advance in her career, shifting in 1969 to Lindenwood College as a counselor and director of the school's intercultural programs. The majority White school was attempting to diversify, and Janice oversaw about thirty Black students who had been attracted to the school primarily from the northeast. "The students kind of glommed onto me," Janice recalled. A key complaint was the lack of diversity within the teaching staff, which was overwhelmingly White. At one point, the students took over the school library because they didn't feel their concerns were being adequately addressed. "We stayed there for two weeks," reported the woman who knew a little something about library sit-ins.

Surprisingly, rather than take their ire at the disruption out on the students (and on Janice), the leadership of the college worked hard to find additional professors of color. Somehow, Janice was able not only to survive this challenge, but she came out in a stronger position. Her positive attitude and her ability to bridge racial divides kept her on the right side of Lindenwood's administrators, and she was given broader latitude to develop additional diversity programs. "They loved me there," Janice stated unequivocally.

"It seemed like everywhere I was going, this whole thing of activism and movements and sit-ins was following me!" she continued. "And I was always thinking that this is something that I *have to* do, you know? I *have to* step out here and do this."

In 1980, she shifted gears again and joined the staff of the University of Missouri/St. Louis, this time to help the college develop programs to retain students, particularly students of color, from entry point to graduation. During the next twenty years, she became a leader in the development of student-retention programs. Janice was so successful that she was invited to become a part-time presenter for the Noel-Levitz company (now Ruffalo Noel Levitz), a premier consultancy on student recruitment and retention.

After two decades at the University of Missouri/St. Louis, Janice stretched her wings and became an entrepreneur. "I took early retirement so that I could develop a nontraditional school for women who were transitioning from welfare to work." This was the era of "ending welfare as we know it," to quote President Clinton and one of his signature initiatives. Janice provided strong leadership in establishing her "City House Learning Centers" and obtaining government funds to train women, many of whom had never held a job, how to develop a resume, dress for success, and basic computer skills so they could transition to full-time employment. About five hundred St. Louis women went through the program before the funding ran out and was not renewed in 2005 during the George W. Bush administration.

But Janice's entrepreneurial spirit, once awakened, could not be extinguished. When she shuttered the schools, Janice shifted to selling real estate, buying, renting, and managing properties in and around the Ferguson, Missouri, area, where she eventually settled. By 2014, she owned and was managing about thirty units.

On the personal side, in 1969, Janice met and later married Jerry Herman, a fellow teacher, and the two of them vowed to travel the world during their summer breaks. And travel they did, to Russia, Western Europe, Haiti, Mexico, and various countries in Africa. "That was a really important phase of my life," Janice reflected. "I attribute a lot of my growth to that period—really educational and mind expanding."

By 1976, however, Janice found the relationship foundering. "He belonged to the world and didn't want to be tied down too much," Janice said. "I wanted to have some roots." By then, the two also had a daughter, Carla Gbassa Herman; Janice felt the need for a more stable environment for her little girl, as well. The split was amicable.

In 1978, Janice met and married a corporate attorney, Ronald Vails, and moved to University City, a small enclave just west of St. Louis, where the two bought a three-story home and settled down. "He was a wonderful guy," she says. "He was a wonderful stepdad."

This daughter of the Mississippi Delta views her married life in stages. "I had the Bohemian, traveling, world adventure man for my first husband," she observed. "My second one was a conservative lawyer, and we had the house, the yard, and people to take care of it all. We even owned an oil company in Texas! So that was an exciting, different period of my life."

Somehow that idealized life crumbled, as well, in 1993. After that, Janice vowed never to marry again. She did, however, meet someone in 1994 with whom she lived for the rest of her life. "He's my partner and friend," Janice said. "But I don't want to get married anymore."

Through all of the ups and downs of their lives, Janice and Ethel remained close. They would tease each other constantly but also shared each other's sorrows and family dramas. When Janice died unexpectedly in 2021 due to complications from surgery, Ethel eulogized her friend, celebrating her "Beauty of Heart," her "Loveliness of Physical Feature," and her "Bravery." In recalling how much time they spent together, both in college and afterwards, Ethel said, "Try to imagine people sharing a room in college and two different apartments and never having one single argument with each other!"

Ethel also confessed that she literally owed her life to her longtime friend. "Janice saved my life!" she recalled. While the two shared one of their early St. Louis apartments, Ethel said, "I was being electrocuted standing in a bathtub full of water [and] she pulled the switch to the electrical box (fortunately located inside the old apartment), releasing me to live to this day." How fortunate, indeed, for both of them that they met on their way to Tougaloo College and that they remained close to each other—"sisters" they would say—for the rest of their lives.

GERALDINE EDWARDS HOLLIS

Geraldine Edwards stayed on track to finish college in three years. She completed all of her coursework by the end of Tougaloo's 1962 summer semester. All that was left to do to graduate with a degree and a teaching certificate was to spend a semester student teaching. She was assigned to a school in Hollandale in the Mississippi Delta. Although the town was only about 140 miles due north on legendary Highway 61 from her home in Natchez, for Edwards, it was like entering an entirely new universe.

Schooling in the Delta was on what was called a "split session" so that kids could help with the planting and harvesting seasons. Geraldine's teaching session would start in July and go through September. That was her first surprise. More importantly, she was awakened to what she would come to call "agricultural feudalism" as practiced in the Delta—the system of sharecropping. "In my thinking, this was just another form of slavery," she would later write.[3] In essence, what she witnessed was Black people working and living on a White owner's land, planting, weeding (chopping), and harvesting crops for half of the value of the crops they brought in—their "share" of the "cropping." She came to understand what her uncles had often talked about, but she had never actually witnessed. The experience was eye opening, to say the least.

Nevertheless, Edwards stuck it out, daily teaching physical education to every grade level, from first through sixth. She thought the principal was autocratic, and she never got used to the idea of students being on separate schedules so that they could be released early or come late in order to work in the fields. She also found that small-town living was boring, with very little to do on weekends.

Because she had limited funds, Geraldine found ways of stretching her dollars by buying and preparing food for the other teachers-in-training she was living with and charging them for it. Despite this enterprising venture, she herself became undernourished that summer. She was worried about her mother, whose breast cancer had returned, and she was being pressured by a young man she had met the summer before when she attended the NAACP convention in Philadelphia and whom she had promised to marry. Too much change was happening all at once, and Geri was rethinking her priorities. She eventually called off the engagement and after her months in the Delta, returned home to Natchez to figure things out anew.

Although she wouldn't formally graduate from Tougaloo until the spring of 1963, Edwards received her teaching certificate in the mail in the fall of 1962 and started looking for a job. Despite having been offered a scholarship to the University of Michigan to pursue a master's in physical education and dance, like Janice, Geraldine was on the family plan. She took seriously the commitment to help repay the one-hundred-dollar-a-month sacrifice her family had made to send her to college and was determined to find a teaching job within the state to earn enough money to support herself and to help send her younger brother to college.

The job hunting didn't go well. Despite sending resumes and applications to nearly every school district in Mississippi, there seemed to be no takers. Some have suggested that after the Tougaloo Nine sit-in, there ensued a period when many Tougalooans had a difficult time getting a job as teachers in the Magnolia State. "Tougaloo grads were not welcomed in all parts of Mississippi," Geraldine would later write, "for fear of disrupting the system by bringing political views into the classroom." She also remembers being branded as "that [Tougaloo Nine] instigator" and being told, "You will cause trouble if you come to work here."

While waiting for a job offer, Geri didn't stand still. She became a substitute teacher in the Natchez school district and also volunteered her services at the nearby North Natchez Recreation Center, organizing a dance troupe and giving dance classes.

After months of hoping for at least one job lead, she finally received an invitation in early 1963 to visit Meridian—on the opposite side of the state—to interview for a job at Harris Junior College. Edwards traveled to Meridian during Spring Break and aced the interview. She was offered a job that summer teaching remedial math to student athletes, and if that went well, a full-time job in the fall.

Geraldine recounted how well Tougaloo had prepared her for the challenges ahead. "I was able to land that job. I was able to work that summer. And that put me on my feet. And I was ready to go because I had so many things that I could do. I could teach physical education. I could teach biology. I could teach math. I could teach dance. All of that worked out for me. I was so well rounded."

Of course, she was offered the full-time job at the end of the summer and signed a contract for the 1963/1964 school year. Her salary was $3,250. Not much in today's economy, perhaps, but at the time, it was more money than she could have imagined. She began sending home funds for her brother Peter, who entered Mississippi Valley State College that fall. And in this case, the family plan worked. Each sibling completed college and then helped pay for the next one. "Geradline set the example," they would later say.

It was just before Christmas during that first semester of her teaching career that Geraldine's mother, Thelma, succumbed to the devastation her body was absorbing as a result of breast cancer treatments. The loss was devastating—"My mom was my hero," Geri would often say. She forced herself to go on working, however, grateful for the job and the ability to contribute financially to the family during its time of need.

The following year, Geri vacationed with the family in Galveston, Texas, where once again, as at the NAACP convention in Philadelphia years earlier, she experienced what life could be like without the degradation of segregation. She could walk along the beach without fear of assault and eat wherever she pleased. It gave her a "feeling of freedom." On her way home, Geri stopped to visit family in Ferriday, Louisiana, and met the man who would become her life partner, Jack Hollis.

At the time of their meeting, Jack was at loose ends, moving between Galveston, Houston, and Oakland, California, trying to find his way. In the midst of this peripatetic life, he got drafted into the US Army. Through it all, his bond with Geri deepened. Perhaps it was that draft notice that caused him to realize what he really wanted in life. Jack sent an engagement ring in the mail and asked Geri to marry him—an unusual proposal—and she accepted. "For me," she said, "the commitment was an answer to my prayers."

The wedding was held in Natchez with Geri's father serving as officiant. In the inevitable confusion of wedding preparations, Jack forgot to bring the wedding ring, but somehow the marriage was consummated. The reception was held at the very Recreation Center where Geri had volunteered before landing her teaching job. After a week's honeymoon back on Galveston Island, the couple went their separate ways—Geri back to Meridian to teach and Jack to Fort Polk in Louisiana where he was then stationed.

Geri soon learned that she was pregnant with their first child and continued teaching up until the baby came two months earlier than expected—a little girl, whom they named Thelma after Geri's mom. Geri kept teaching while the baby, seriously underweight, was kept for two more months at the segregated hospital in Meridian.

When the school year ended, Geri found it necessary to resign her position and move back to Natchez so that she could have her family's help caring for baby Thelma while Geri continued to work. She found a job at the Natchez school district as a school counselor and also taught in the adult literacy program at night. She and the baby moved into their own apartment in Natchez and held tight while Jack commuted back and forth from his newly assigned post in Texas—a five-hundred-mile trip each way—whenever he could. It was not an ideal setup.

After a few years, Geri was pregnant again. This time, the premature boy she delivered didn't make it, and Geri ended up with a severe case of toxemia and lost her eyesight for a time. Meanwhile, after his two years in the army were up, Jack moved to Oakland to live with family and find work. Geri had to endure the loss of a baby essentially alone. Eventually, the family was reunited in Oakland, where they finally settled. Jack found work with the Mack Truck company, and Geri threw herself back into teaching and pursuing further degrees in her chosen field. In 1976, she earned a master of physical education degree at Hayward University (now the University of East Bay) and in 1982, a master of adapted physical education degree at the University of the Pacific at Stockton.

A fitness enthusiast before that term became embedded in the American lexicon, Geri produced several fitness handbooks specifically designed for the teaching of adapted PE, one of which was used by the school system of Oakland. She also became an active member of the California Association for Health, Physical Education, Recreation and Dance (CAHPERD), where she would occasionally offer papers on her teaching methodology and chair various committees for the furtherance of her profession. She retired from the Oakland school system in 1997; then she and Jack relocated seventy miles east to Stockton. But Geri never stopped. She took up volunteerism as a second career, getting involved in the local NAACP and in various community groups pushing for positive, inclusive change. She taught Black history classes during the city's Juneteenth celebration decades before the event was recognized as a national holiday. And she became deeply committed to her local Missionary Baptist Church and to her Christian faith.

In 2006, Geraldine was invited back to Tougaloo with all of her Tougaloo Nine colleagues to participate in a program seeking to honor their bold protest forty-five years earlier. It was one of the first official recognition events that Tougaloo held to pay tribute to its groundbreaking alumni. In Geri's mind, the recognition "was a long time coming." Indeed, she would often think that she and the others "had made a choice to put our lives on the line" but she felt that their efforts had not been appropriately appreciated. As the study of the Mississippi movement became part of the vanguard of historical investigation with the publishing of Dr. John Dittmer's landmark *Local People* in 1994, she saw that other civil rights activists who came after the Tougaloo Nine were being celebrated and held in honor, while "no one had really recognized our sacrifice."

At that forty-fifth anniversary event celebrating the Tougaloo Nine, Geri finally began to feel appreciated, acknowledging that "in some small way, I needed this approval." Thanks to Dr. Daphne Chamberlain and Dr. Leslie McLemore (both then affiliated with the Fannie Lou Hamer Institute at Jackson State University), as well as to Beverly Hogan, Tougaloo's then president, the Tougaloo Nine were finally being reclaimed by the institution that had given them the confidence to present a different narrative to the world about how African Americans felt about their treatment in the Magnolia State. Geri admits that she "welled up in tears" as Dr. McLemore—at that time a Jackson city councilman—acknowledged that the recognition was "long overdue." McLemore had also arranged for all of the Nine to receive a key to the city of Jackson and a proclamation from the city honoring their "monumental steps in the civil rights movement in Mississippi." Geraldine Edwards Hollis felt especially grateful that her father had lived to see this turnaround from "jailbird to honored guest." Indeed, at one of the events during that Founders Day weekend in October, Reverend Simuel Edwards stood up and said how proud he was of his daughter. This public accolade meant the world to Geri, particularly since Reverend Edwards passed away less than eight months later.

This 2006 gathering along with the blessing she received from her father was a turning point for Geraldine. She realized that she could carry forth the message of the Tougaloo Nine on her own, if necessary. She began writing a book about her life, centered on the Tougaloo Nine demonstration. *Back to Mississippi* was published in 2011, and Geri began giving lectures to schools and libraries all over America to tell the story of the Tougaloo Nine and her role in standing up to an unjust system. It was one such talk, presented at the Eudora Welty Public Library in Jackson while Geri was in town honoring the fiftieth anniversary of Freedom Summer in 2014, that led to the push to have a historical marker placed at the spot where the students had entered the original library just across North State Street. That happy day occurred on August 17, 2017, and Geri and most of her Tougaloo Nine cohort were on hand to witness another public recognition of their courage and commitment to social equality.

The anniversary commemorations of the library sit-in kept coming, as well. Geraldine had been on hand with nearly all of the Tougaloo Nine in 2011 as Tougaloo honored the fiftieth anniversary of the "read-in." And she would gather with them once again on the sixtieth anniversary in 2021 when Tougaloo awarded all nine with honorary doctorates of humane letters for their principled stand against an unjust system. For Geraldine, this was the crowning moment. "We put our lives on the line at early ages sixty years ago to make a difference in this city and this state," she said to a documentarian filming the event that day. She marveled that their example might be serving as inspiration for another generation of newly graduated Tougaloo students and how the story of the Tougaloo Nine had begun to gain traction. "I am encouraged," she said. "We stepped up to make a difference," she noted, "not for ourselves, but for all the people that live in this country." After sixty years, she finally felt fully seen and was ready to pass the torch.

Chapter 21

THE FOLLOW-ONS

ANOTHER COHORT OF THE TOUGALOO NINE GRADUATED FROM THAT storied college, though a bit later than the first three—either because they had started later or because it took them a bit longer to reach the finish line. But they eventually made it. Here are their rest-of-life stories.

ALBERT LASSITER SR. AND JAMES "SAMMY" BRADFORD

Sam Bradford and Al Lassiter were two of the youngest members of the Tougaloo Nine and, as such, had a number of additional years to spend at the college before moving on with the rest of their lives. Both men recall times at Tougaloo just after their heroic library sit-in when Freedom Riders began coming to Mississippi and trekking out to campus once they had served their jail time or upon returning for their court appeals. And big-name performers showed up intermittently to offer their encouragement. "So many folks came to campus after that timeframe," Al recalled. "Pete Seeger! Joan Baez! Dick Gregory! There were so many celebrities coming in to show their support."

But with the increased traffic came unwanted attention. "There were some folks who would easily throw firebrands across the campus," Al continued, referring to rowdy White locals who would drive by the campus, guns blazing, when some particularly noteworthy demonstration might have taken place downtown. Sam recalled that two maintenance men were drafted to provide a security detail for the college; "Will Shoot" and "Won't Shoot," they jokingly called them. All jokes aside, however, their services were welcomed during times of unusual stress.

Sam, like a number of those of his Tougaloo Nine contingent, had to leave before completing his degree, in his case because of lack of funds. Sam would struggle throughout the decade to get back and finish at Tougaloo. He would return—sometimes for just a semester, sometimes for a full academic year—only to then have to take a year or two off to earn enough money to return. But he kept coming back and kept being welcomed back as a struggling "eaglet."

Albert Lassiter had an easier time of it, graduating with his class in 1964. It was an auspicious time. Dr. Beittel had tendered his resignation under pressure because of his laissez-faire attitude—even open support for—civil rights activism on campus. In Lassiter's graduating class were three standouts from the 1963 Jackson Woolworth's sit-in—Anne Moody, Memphis Norman, and Joan Trumpauer—Jackson movement descendants of the Tougaloo Nine, if you will.

Lassiter steered clear of all that. Having kicked off student activism in Mississippi with the library sit-in, he left it to others to keep moving things forward. Besides, he and the Nine were still on probation. Had they tried anything that smacked of protest, they would have been hauled back in to serve out the thirty-day sentence for their library misdemeanor.

During his remaining three years at Tougaloo, Lassiter had gone from one success to the next. When he returned to campus in the fall of 1961, Albert was assigned as a chemistry lab assistant for his work-study program, an important leadership role "which was, for a sophomore, rather unusual," he observed. He continued to sing in the choir with his velvety bass voice, play sports, and study hard.[1] One summer, he was awarded a place in a National Science Foundation project as a chemistry lab instructor, teaching advanced high school students who were about to enter college. "That was truly special," he recalled, "because that stipend covered my Tougaloo room and board for the next year." Lassiter eventually pledged Alpha Phi Alpha and became president of the Black fraternity's chapter on campus. Notably, he also served for a time as president of the NAACP's Tougaloo College Chapter, following in Joseph Jackson's footsteps. Recognized in Who's Who among Students in American Colleges and Universities, Albert Lassiter graduated with a Bachelor of Science degree with an emphasis on chemistry.

The ever-humble Lassiter needed prodding from his college buddies to finally confess that his college nickname was "Prez" because in each class, club, or organization, he was regularly voted president or vice president. "I never campaigned," Lassiter protested. "I was just habitually nominated and humbly accepted."

After graduation, Lassiter entered the air force. He had, in fact, signed up even before graduation and been granted a student deferment from the draft with the understanding he would enlist immediately following graduation.

In short order, Lassiter was recognized as a talented leader and was given the opportunity to go to Officer Training School. When he successfully completed that hurdle, Albert Lassiter was commissioned as a second lieutenant in the US Air Force—a silent rebuke to Senator Stennis, who had declined to recommend him to the Air Force Academy years earlier.

Lassiter made a career of the air force, spending a total of thirty-two years in active and reserve military service, building an impressive résumé along the way. "I served in Aircraft Maintenance, Supply and Logistics, Radar Air Defense, Military Intelligence, and even as a chief of staff," he fondly remembered. "I stuck around for a while." By the time of his retirement in 1995, Lassiter held the rank of colonel—just one step removed from a brigadier general—and could look back with satisfaction on a stellar career of military service, with many of its awards and decorations.

Along the way, Lassiter picked up additional formal training and another degree. While stationed in California in the late 1960s, he found time to attend the University of Southern California and earned a master's degree in systems management, graduating in 1970. Later, while stationed near Philadelphia, he attended Temple University and took classes that nearly earned him an MBA. In addition, because of his consistent outstanding performance and leadership in the air force, Lassiter was selected to attend the prestigious Air War College in Residence during the 1989/1990 academic year. In all cases, he found that his Tougaloo College education served him well. "I didn't understand how well until I went to grad school," Lassiter observed. "When I first went to Southern Cal, in my class were Harvard grads, folks from MIT, military academy graduates. Stellar schools! I looked around and said, 'Am I going to be able to compete with these guys?' Turns out I was!"

Albert Lassiter graduated from the University of Southern California's master's program cum laude—another rebuke to Mississippi's unreconstructed columnist Jimmy Ward. When he shifted to Air Force Reserve status in 1975, Lassiter found interesting and impressive work in the private and public sectors, including a stint as production supervisor with medical manufacturer Merck; a few years as distribution manager with American Hardware Supply; and then as a regional vice president for distribution for a Jackson firm supporting various Pizza Hut franchises in seven states.

As his management and financial skills became more widely known, Lassiter came to the attention of the State of Mississippi's state auditor. From two years—from 1983 to 1985, he served as the head of Mississippi's Department of Public Accounts, managing a budget of $3.8 billion and auditing expenses for the state and all of its agencies, boards, and institutions. Surely there was some irony—as well as a commentary on the state's ability to adapt and change—that a Black college student arrested and convicted for breaching the peace in segregated Mississippi in 1961 could rise to such a high-ranking post within state government in a little more than two decades. It certainly was a testament to Al Lassiter's ability to build bridges while demonstrating excellence at every turn.

In 1985, the ever-adaptable Lassiter shifted gears again, becoming vice president for business and finance with Alabama A&M University, where he stayed until 1987, all the while maintaining one foot in the military through its active reserve service. Then, beginning in 1989, he was called back into full-time military service until 1995.

When he finally retired from the air force, Lassiter put his financial expertise and training to work, becoming a licensed financial planner. For the next twenty-five years, he worked for the Woodmen of the World Life Insurance Society, helping retirees like himself ensure their families' financial security through the purchase of annuities and insurance policies and earning many sales-and-management awards in the process.

On the personal side, in 1973, Al married Josephine Johnson, a speech pathologist, and together they raised two children, Albert Lassiter Jr. and Jansa Hope Lassiter. Remarkably, the entire Lassiter brood raised by Wright and Ethel Lassiter became people of accomplishment. The family could boast of a doctor, an artist, an architect, several professors and educators, a college dean, and even a college president. "My parents were good role models," Lassiter reflected, "and they exhorted us to go on." One of Albert Lassiter's younger brothers, Ralph Bunche Lassiter, was one of the first cohorts—after James Meredith led the way—to integrate the University of Mississippi. Al's sister Linda did the same at the University of Southern Mississippi. The Lassiter children forged paths of accomplishment hardly imaginable by their parents. They came along just at the time that opportunity was opening up for African Americans in this country. And they made the most of those chances to bring about change not only for themselves but for the entire society.

When he reflects on these enormous strides taken by himself, his family members, and his colleagues from Tougaloo, Albert Lassiter has a short phrase that sums it all up: "Times change, and people change, most often for the better."

James "Sammy" Bradford had a much harder time making it through to graduation at Tougaloo. Though he and Al Lassiter started in the same class in 1960, Sam finally crossed the finish line in 1969. The story of what happened in between he tells tearfully, but with deep appreciation for all those who helped him along the way. Bradford always seemed in need of funds while at Tougaloo. He barely scraped enough together with his choir scholarship and the many odd jobs he did around the school to pay his tuition and room and board. Occasionally, even those funds were not enough, so he'd get an extension of credit from the college. But Sam worked—and worked hard—for the college. At various times throughout his years at Tougaloo, Sam cleaned the library, he cleaned Pops Lovelace's music building, he cleaned Ernst Borinski's

Beard Hall. He cleaned the dining hall and drove the school bus to get kids living locally back and forth to Tougaloo. "I ended up with more work hours than I had academic hours," he later said. But with all of that hustling—he even hand washed and detailed students' cars for two dollars a pop—by the end of his second year at Tougaloo, spring 1962, Sam was broke, and there was no way he could return in the fall.

Bradford went home to Memphis and got a job, though he was always determined to return and finish his degree. He started working for a company that made Christmas wrapping paper, the Cleo Wrap Company. Later, he got a job driving a laundry truck for Hulbert Cleaners, a local Memphis establishment. His former high school music director helped Sam organize a music recital within the community to raise additional funds for his education. "My family and friends supported the recital, and I raised $400!" Sam recounted with pride.

With his full-time employment and the recital boost, Bradford was able to return to Tougaloo a year after he left. In May 1963, he stepped back onto Tougaloo's campus, not to go to summer school, but to work until classes began in the fall. Just weeks after returning, Sam heard that Medgar Evers had been assassinated. His unpaid debt to Evers from two years earlier when he traveled to Philadelphia with the Tougaloo Nine came rushing back. "Dang! I owed Medgar eight dollars!" he thought. He would later tearfully acknowledge: "I never gave Medgar his eight dollars because I didn't have it!" Later in life, once he was earning real money, he made it a point to donate to causes he knew that Evers would have supported—his way of making sure his debt to his benefactor was more than repaid.

Bradford was able to return to academics in the fall of 1963. It was then, too, that his life would take a considerable turn for the better. That first semester, Sam met the woman who would become his wife, Shirley Faulkens, then an entering freshman. But it would take a while for that relationship to blossom. Sam was a friendly guy and known by just about everyone on campus. "I liked to get my groove on," he recalled. Let's just say he wasn't the bookish type. He was very sociable and enjoyed a good party. About his studies, he would admit: "I didn't have the best of grades, but I didn't have the worst of grades either. I just was not known for my studiousness."

Sam changed his major at least once, which also delayed his eventual graduation date. He started out majoring in history, but like so many of those who attended Tougaloo in those days, he got interested in sociology thanks to the passionate interest in the subject instilled by Dr. Borinski. But even Borinski couldn't solve Sam's money problems.

Bradford stayed on to work on campus over that fateful Freedom Summer of 1964. He recounted how in late June, he and a friend lit out in a borrowed car "hell-bent to get over to Philadelphia (MS)" to try to find the three missing civil rights workers—though "not realizing the dangerousness of that venture." The two returned safely to campus, but events kept tripping Sam up. In August, he was called up for military service and was ordered to report to the draft board back home in Memphis. Sam went home and dutifully showed up for his appointment, not knowing what to expect. The draft board rejected him because of the inflexibility of the fingers in his right hand. The physical impairment was caused by not one, but two accidents earlier in Bradford's life. The first happened in high school, when the tips of three of his fingers were sliced off, shockingly, when the lathe he was resting his hand on in shop class was accidentally turned on. The second accident, which essentially sealed the deal, happened at the Cleo Wrap Company when Sam got his hand caught in the massive rollers that handle the cutting and packaging of the wrapping paper. Perhaps it was all for the best, considering the high rate of casualties in Vietnam.

By then, however, Bradford acknowledged that his money "was definitely funny"—meaning he was again coming up short to pay Tougaloo's tuition. In fact, he was even in arears to the college. He was forced to put his education on hold again. Realizing his limited options for work in Memphis, Sam headed to Chicago to stay with extended family and look for a better-paying job. He found one, working for the US Steel Company's Alloy Bar Mill, a short distance from the shores of Lake Michigan. But the plant was frigid in the wintertime—the kind of cold Sam couldn't get used to, so he switched to working for the Chicago Transit Authority and drove a city bus for the next two years.

"I didn't want to get stuck in Chicago," Bradford said, "so I lived like a hermit and managed to save a little money." During the summer of 1966, Sam wrote a letter to Grace Caldwell, Tougaloo's Admissions Office secretary, with whom he was friendly, asking her—no, pleading with her—to find a way for him to return. He let her know he had enough money to pay any outstanding debts and wanted to enroll for the fall semester. Caldwell wrote back, saying, "If you can get here, I believe we can get you in." That was all Sam needed; that September he was back at Tougaloo as a full-time student. It would take Bradford three more years, with summers spent in Chicago driving for the CTA, but in May of 1969, he would walk across Tougaloo's stage and joyfully and firmly grab hold of that elusive diploma.

"I was able to do it with the help of a lot of people," Bradford emotionally recounted. "Man, it was rough! But I was the first in my family to do it." The accomplishment did not go unnoticed by his kin. Sam's aunt chartered a bus from Memphis to take forty or so of his relatives and friends to Tougaloo to see their native son make good. "That bus was full!" he recalled in amazement.

That same summer, Tougaloo's administrators realized what a gem they had with James "Sammy" Bradford and hired him to be the college's first director of giving. Sam and Shirley got married and settled in the community of Tougaloo, just outside and down the road from the college gates. The couple would eventually have two sons, Ako and Pili.

After a three-year stint at Tougaloo, Sam spread his wings and took a job with Liberty Mutual insurance company, becoming their first Black claims adjuster, first working out of the Memphis office and later transferring to Jackson. Two years later, in 1975, he shifted again, becoming a lead trainer for Mississippi's Head Start Training Coordinating Council. Always adept at finding better opportunities, Bradford jumped again to the Zurich North America insurance company in 1976, again becoming the company's first Black claims representative.

Finally, in 1979, Sam went to work for the State of Mississippi's Division of Medicaid and found stability there for the next twenty-seven years, working his way up from field auditor to program administrator. "And that's the story of my life!" he said triumphantly. He retired in 2006.

Bradford's feelings about Tougaloo never wavered. "I fell in love with Tougaloo," he would often say. "That's what Tougaloo will do for you. It'll grab you. It's kind of the tie that binds." Sam's love for Tougaloo was so great that he picked out his burial plot on the campus and bought the headstone decades before his actual death. He was buried there in 2023 in the small cemetery that dates back nearly to the time of the school's founding. There he rests along with the remains of some of his heroes, including his beloved choir director Ariel "Pops" Lovelace and his much-admired sociology professor Dr. Ernst Borinski.

MEREDITH COLEMAN ANDING JR.

Meredith Anding also took a circuitous route to completing his Tougaloo degree. After he lost his funding and dropped out as a result of his involvement in the library sit-in, he hung around his family's home in Jackson and took a class or two at Jackson State that summer, hoping to continue his education. At loose ends, however, and recognizing his limited options in Mississippi, Anding contacted an uncle in Chicago and moved there to find work. He spent the next two years working at Presbyterian/St. Luke's Hospital as a lab technician. "Basically, the clean-up boy," he said. "I did stuff like sterilizing cultures and things like that." Later, he took a part-time job in the pathology department while attempting to restart his education at the Illinois Institute of Technology. "That didn't work out," he recalled. "It was too much for me."

While working one morning at Presbyterian/St. Luke's, Anding learned of the assassination of his mentor. Meredith saw Medgar Evers's photo on the cover of the *Chicago Tribune*, but it didn't register. "At first I just thought his picture was in the paper," he said. "I didn't put two and two together." Once he realized what had happened and after the initial shock wore off, his mind drifted back to when the two were riding in the Delta trying to get Johnny Frazier out of jail. He also remembered a time after the library sit-in when Evers had told him how proud he was of him. It was little consolation.

On the heels of Evers's death, Anding, still in Chicago, was robbed. He decided he had had enough of the big city; he enlisted in the air force. After some basic training in Texas, the new recruit ended up with a four-year tour of duty, mostly spent guarding American bases in Turkey under the auspices of USAFE—the US Air Force in Europe. "I was part of the Military Air Police," he noted. "I got to go to Ephesus, Athens, all over Greece." Late in his tour, he was transferred to California and assigned to the Tactical Air Command unit.

After his discharge, Anding returned to Tougaloo to finally complete his undergraduate degree. He had three more semesters to go. He enrolled in January 1968 and completed his bachelor of science degree with an emphasis in mathematics in the spring of 1969. Meredith completed his degree at the same time as fellow Tougaloo Niner Sam Bradford; they walked across the baccalaureate stage on the same day.

During his last few semesters at Tougaloo, educators noticed Meredith's acuity with numbers and suggested he go to graduate school. They helped open the doors for him to higher education by connecting him to the University of Buffalo (now State University of New York/Buffalo) where he not only found his vocation but also met and married the love of his life, Maurice Dianne Buggs. Maurice was enrolled in the same graduate program as Meredith, and they hit it off. They would end up spending the next fifty years together, raising their two sons—Gordon and Armaan—and becoming partners in education as well as in life.

Anding began teaching at the college while still a graduate student. After earning his master's degree, he took a job teaching advanced mathematics at nearby Niagara University. A few years later, he was recruited to return to State University of New York /Buffalo to teach at the university's Educational Opportunity Center, which focused on providing underserved urban communities with tuition-free academic assessment, skills building, and job-certification programs to help lead them to higher education or full employment.

Meredith and Maurice developed courses in mathematics, as well as assessment tools to give students and faculty a real-life measurement of each student's math-skills level. Meredith also supervised the graduate students who made up the core of the teaching staff at the center. Maurice branched off and taught high school locally, while Meredith stayed with the center for the next thirty years, retiring in 2007.

In their remaining years together, Meredith and Maurice bought a comfortable class A RV and traveled throughout the country, mostly dividing their time between their homes—summering in Western New York and wintering in Mississippi. When asked about his historic step into history with his Tougaloo Nine cohort, Anding responded, "We were the first to resist. We were the pace setters. We seized a moment in time that had arrived for the state of Mississippi to move forward." Meredith Anding died in January 2021 at the age of seventy-nine.

Chapter 22

THE ÉMIGRÉS

FOR VARIOUS REASONS, THE FINAL COHORT OF THE TOUGALOO NINE LEFT the college and sought their dreams and futures elsewhere. The whys and fascinating wherefores comprise the following chapter.

ALFRED LEE COOK SR.

Alfred Cook had various stories about what happened to him—and why—once his 1961 spring semester at Tougaloo concluded, and he disappeared. Cook had referenced Flint, Michigan, as his home to the booking officer after the library sit-in. Indeed, he did have some extended family living there. Just days after Tougaloo's spring 1961 semester ended in late May, "I was put on a bus by Reverend Mangram and Mr. Evers," Cook recalled. "There had been threats on my life." This was to be expected, one supposes, given that Cook had served as the student lead on the Sacrifice for Human Dignity campaign in 1960 and then as a member of the Tougaloo Nine a year later.

Cook spent the summer working at Flint's Hurley Hospital as a medical technologist, fully expecting to return to Tougaloo in the fall. Two things intervened. First, his family, having heard of the death threats, urged him to stay in Michigan. Second, he received a life-altering phone call informing him that his girlfriend, Barbara Gill—a rising senior at Tougaloo—was pregnant. "I got a call from a family member that my girlfriend and I needed to get married," is how he put it. "I did the honorable thing and married her that summer. Three months later, we had a child who at birth weighed two pounds, eleven ounces."

The baby was delivered and, for a while, boarded at the same hospital where Cook was working, so he was able to see her daily. In a sweet gesture, he insisted he take over the drawing of blood from his baby girl when he watched a nurse having trouble performing the task. "Ma'am, from here on, if it's twenty-four hours a day, I'm drawing my own baby's blood," he said. "I did that for the next six months before she was able to come home."[1]

Since Cook had a good job, he suggested that his wife complete her college degree while he worked full time at the hospital. During this time, the couple had another daughter. "I did most of the babysitting," Cook claimed. Barbara ended up getting both her bachelor's degree with a focus on education and a master's degree in counseling from the University of Michigan and would spend her forty-year career as a high school educator.

Once Barbara graduated, it was Alfred's turn to return to college, with the hope of fulfilling his dream of becoming a doctor. He entered the University of Michigan's competitive and all-consuming premed program, but for various reasons was unable to achieve the required 3.0 grade-point average to be accepted into medical school. Disappointed but undaunted, the resourceful Cook made a hard pivot. "I embarked on the clinical sciences," he said, becoming highly successful in the process.

After graduating from the University of Michigan with a bachelor's in biology, Cook enrolled at Wayne State University and earned a master's in biochemistry. His years at the hospital as a lab technician gave him an idea. He noticed that Black patients were reluctant to work with anyone other than Black lab technicians. He decided to open his own private lab service to cater primarily to a Black clientele. The idea took off. He became one of only three labs in the United States at the time that focused on Black patients.

"I opened a private testing lab in Flint, Michigan, and it grew to twenty-one locations around the Midwest," Cook recounted. "I had several hundred employees, and I did quite well." After twenty-eight years of managing his successful business, Clinical Laboratory Consultants, Cook sold it and retired, though he discovered that retirement wasn't all it was cracked up to be. "I got bored," he admitted. Restless by nature, he began looking for his next challenge.

He found it through the then-emerging field of financial planning. Cook became certified to sell insurance and became a part-time division leader for Primerica Financial Services. Given his impoverished early circumstances, perhaps it is no surprise that Al Cook reveled in his good fortune. "I *love* money," he enjoyed saying. "I have always *loved* money and dealing with finances." Wealthy himself after the sale of his prosperous lab business, Cook delighted in working with others to help ensure their financial success and security.

He also taught science and coached the golf teams at local high schools. "I said I was only going to do it for a couple of years," he claimed. Thirteen years later, he was still at it, finally retiring from everything in 2010.

Cook was a "joiner." He originally pledged Alpha Phi Alpha at Tougaloo, but because of his hasty departure, he never actually "crossed" to become a member of the historically Black fraternity. He eventually picked up again with the Alphas when he reenrolled in grad school at Wayne State, later serving as president of his local chapter. In addition, He became a lifetime member of the NAACP and various scientific associations. He also served on a number of nonprofit boards, including a stint on the Flint Area Chamber of Commerce.

Al Cook also loved to sing. At the fiftieth anniversary gathering of the Tougaloo Nine held on campus at the Woodworth Chapel, Cook exuberantly recounted how he had been part of the Tougaloo choir. And "fifty plus years since I left Tougaloo, I'm still singing in the choir! I love it! I'm an Episcopalian; I go to church every Sunday; and I sing!" Pops Lovelace must have been smiling from above that night.

About his short time at Tougaloo, Cook was quick to point out his love for his "college family." Although he knew it was a necessary decision to stay in Flint once his life had been threatened, Cook said it was a decision "that I have regretted since the day I decided not to return. Because Tougaloo was so dear to me and did so many things for me. Tougaloo set the pattern for my life," he told the packed audience of mostly students and alumni, "and I have not let you down."

JOSEPH JACKSON JR.

Were one to happen to call **Joseph Jackson Jr.** on the phone and get his answering machine anytime in the twenty-first century, he or she would have been welcomed to "The Temple of Peace" with John Coltrane's *A Love Supreme* playing in the background. The message was emblematic of how far the former Reverend Joe Jackson had traveled on his spiritual journey from his days as a young Christian minister and radical protest instigator. The trip had not been an easy one.

After the library sit-in, Jackson remained at Tougaloo for the remainder of the spring semester and then summered at home in Memphis, continuing to serve as minister of his small flock at Riverview Christian Church and working to earn money to support his growing family. As such, he was unable to accompany his Tougaloo Nine colleagues when they were feted in Philadelphia at the NAACP convention. Indeed, with the fog of time, he couldn't even recall getting an invitation. Too bad. Had he gone, he might have met his heroes in the struggle—MLK, Roy Wilkins, Andy Young—and that might have changed his entire trajectory.

As it was, the standout singer returned to Tougaloo in the fall of 1961 for what he thought would be another year of study and philosophical musings mixed with NAACP activism. Joe was a star in the choir and was even part of Pops Lovelace's Schola Cantorum, an elite group of singers who would travel the country and sing selections from opera, sacred music, and spirituals to raise the profile of Tougaloo, as well as to raise some needed funds for the choir and the school. Joe also pledged with the Omega Psi Phi fraternity at this time, an association that would endure throughout his long life.

By the end of that semester, however, Joe's wife, Clara, still back in Memphis, was finding it impossible to manage the household by herself, work full time, and care for two young children—particularly because young Joseph Jackson III was battling a life-threatening intestinal virus. Money was tight, and Clara was at the end of her rope. "I can't go on any longer," she told her husband during the Christmas break, so Joe was forced by circumstance to put his dream of a college education on hold. The crestfallen Jackson returned to Tougaloo in January 1962 for final exams and then dropped out. "I left that part of my history behind," he said. "I had to take care of my family."

His dream of a ministerial career was also slipping away. The church had promised to help keep Clara and the family afloat while Joe was away at school, but the funds never materialized. "That hurt," Jackson said. He was also beginning to lose faith in the confining strictures of the gospel, as uplifting as its proclamations were. He had taken a number of religion and philosophy courses during his year and a half at Tougaloo, one of which was taught by his "spiritual director," Dr. John Held.[2] The theology professor taught a course called "The Social Action Jesus," which prompted students to consider Jesus as something akin to "a social-justice action figure," said Jackson, "a human person as opposed to his status as Savior of the world."

"That was my radicalization," Jackson said. "All of us could become Social Action Jesuses with regard to social inequality and challenging the injustices of society. When I left Tougaloo, I never believed in the [Christian] dogma anymore."

Starting in February 1962, Joe Jackson began his quest to find his place in the world where he could fulfill his own social action mission. It was slow going. He first had to put food on the table. Improbably, Jackson literally sang for his supper—and that of his family—by taking a job as a busboy at one of the most exclusive, all-White supper clubs in Memphis. The Summit Club sat high atop one of the city's tallest and most celebrated buildings, the twenty-nine-story Sterick Building. Whenever a club member or guest had a birthday, Jackson would be trotted out to use his operatic tenor voice to powerful effect. His boss even invited him to sing for a reporter at the bar downstairs, and Joe found himself an overnight sensation. The attention caused three members of the club to pitch in and fund voice lessons for the struggling "ministerial student—now Lanza-like busboy—with great stage presence" to continue his singing career.[3]

In June of 1963, Joe heard that Medgar Evers had been assassinated. "I was saddened," he commented years later, "but I saw it as 'par for the course.' It was inevitable that such a thing would happen in Mississippi."

"It was a loss for me," he continued. "But I was involved in family matters and had to move on."

The family couldn't live on tips and a busboy's salary, however, so after about two years, Joe shifted to working for one of the club members at his lumber company. The money was better and more consistent, but the work environment was toxic. "My boss was a young, tobacco chewing White boy, and he was all over me!" Jackson recalled. In 1965, Joe shifted again, this time working at the local RCA Victor TV plant, producing television cabinets on the assembly line. "It was kind of like a breakthrough," he remembered. "Things were integrated then, and you worked right beside Whites on the line." After about a year, he was promoted to a cabinet-refinishing job, fixing and patching some of the imperfections of the cabinets as they rolled down the assembly line. In early 1968, Joe got into a dispute with his White supervisor and quit, refusing to be denigrated by "the master."

By then, Jackson had had enough of the South. He decided it was time to strike out and head west like so many of his contemporaries had done by then. Clara had a sister who lived in Santa Ana, California, with her husband. Joe set out in March to stay with his in-laws temporarily while looking for work. Clara and the children would follow a few months later. Joe immediately found a job at the Fisher Furniture Company—a competitor of RCA—in Fullerton and quickly went searching for housing. He was shocked to find that Jim Crow was alive and well in California, though in a more subtle form than what he had experienced in his home region.

Joe found a duplex just perfect for the family in a nice neighborhood just north of Seventeenth Street. What he didn't know was that Seventeenth Street divided the city racially and class-wise. Unwittingly, he had overstepped. When he asked to see the place, the owner claimed she had just rented it out. A few days later, he passed the home and saw "that damn 'For Rent' sign was still up!."[4] Welcome to Paradise.

What Jackson didn't realize was that Orange County had been established by a former Klan member from Tennessee, of all places, and that the enclave had a history of racial intolerance. "Someone told me, 'This is John Birch territory,' and I said, 'What? What?! You gotta be kidding!!'" In fact, just the year before, the US Supreme Court had handed down a ruling, *Reitman v. Mulkey*, outlawing housing discrimination. It was based on a case from Santa Ana. No matter. Jackson decided to stay and tough it out. It would be his way of pushing integration, whether the community liked it or not. He found suitable housing on the south side of Seventeenth Street.[5]

Joe Jackson was in a grocery store when he heard that Martin Luther King had been shot and killed in Joe's hometown of Memphis. "I almost went into shock," he recalled. "My wife and children were still there. For the first time in its history, the city of Memphis is placed under martial law." Both of his civil rights heroes—Medgar and Martin—were now dead; Joseph Jackson had to find a way to move forward and make his own mark on the world.

He saw that the US Post Office was hiring, so he took the test and passed. He was offered the opportunity to be a mail carrier or a custodian. Counter-intuitively, he chose the custodian's job. Although it paid less, the hours—3:30 p.m. to midnight—would afford him the opportunity to go back to school and complete his degree—another stake in his quest for economic independence and social equality. At the start of 1969, after the family was safely moved and settled, Jackson began attending California State University at Fullerton while working full time. By September 1971—and with his credits carried over from Tougaloo and Arkansas AM&N—Jackson had earned a bachelor's degree in sociology with a minor in psychology.

Neither of his parents lived to see him graduate. In 1962, just as Joe had returned to Memphis from Tougaloo, his mother died of a cerebral hemor-rhage—perhaps as a result of her husband's violent alcoholic rages. His father, whose alcoholism had only progressed since his parents separated in 1957, died in 1969 of complications from a simple hernia operation. Joe Jackson Sr. had not kept the wound clean as instructed and died of gangrene.

Nevertheless, Joe Jr. pressed on. He was ready for a professional job with a professional salary. He first found work as a personnel analyst with the city of Santa Ana; then, the following year, he started work as a probation officer for Los Angeles County, and something clicked. Finally, Joseph Jackson Jr. had found his life's mission, his personal ministry to the "Blacks and Browns" as he called the African American and Latino men who so frequently get caught up in the carceral state. "This really meshed," he noted. "This was my calling. I became a social action minister dealing with real life social events. My calling was to make significant changes for the betterment of humanity." For the next thirty years, he would serve as an interlocutor, of sorts, between the largely White world of power and the Black and Brown world of the everyday people caught up in a troubled system.

He would come to marvel at the position of trust, even respect, that he commanded within the juvenile justice system. For most of those years, he was the only Black serving in overwhelmingly White police stations and sheriff's departments—Lakewood, Norwalk, Pico Rivera, Whittier, Hun-tington Park—making decisions as to whether or not to arrest or detain any juveniles of color that were brought in. "If they wanted to detain a Black or Brown kid, they had to run the case by me," he recalled. "That didn't sit too well with some of these sheriffs, but that's what I did. I was rendering service to society by counseling youngsters. That was my calling." When a worried mother of one of the youth whom Joe had counseled told the inspirational probation officer that he was serving God through his work, her words were a welcome affirmation. "That really confirmed my feeling that this was my ministry," Jackson acknowledged.

Unfortunately, Joe's calling didn't coincide with his wife's sensibilities. Just as he was settling into his new position and professional life, the marriage unraveled. Joe and Clara divorced in 1975. In 1976, Joe married Jamie Mantell, a White marriage-and-family therapist, and together they had a son, Anthony. The couple remained married for twenty-one years and stayed on good terms despite divorcing in 1997.

It wasn't until after he retired that Joe Jackson had time to reflect on his activist career and to reconnect with his former Tougaloo Nine colleagues. In fact, most of them thought he was either dead or had just vanished. It wasn't until 2014 that Geraldine, who also had migrated to California, found him and brought him back into the fold. That same year, Joe decided to make a pilgrimage with his son back to Mississippi to rediscover his youthful activist locales.

The two Joseph Jacksons timed their visit to coincide with the annual Medgar Evers Homecoming Parade, held each year over the second weekend of June. It was Blues legend B.B. King who had mentioned to Medgar's brother Charles after playing at Medgar's ten-year anniversary memorial service in 1973 that "there ought to be some kind of yearly event to keep Medgar's dream alive." Charles took the suggestion and ran with it. By 2014, the parade had been held for thirty years straight, first in Fayette, Mississippi, where Charles had been mayor and then, starting in 1982, in Jackson in order to take full advantage of the capital city's amenities and venues.[6]

Joe Jackson introduced himself to Charles Evers, and Evers invited him to ride in the parade. So, Joe Jr. and Joe III felt like celebrities riding down Medgar Evers Boulevard and Martin Luther King Drive in the same parade that in earlier years had hosted the likes of sports icon Muhammad Ali and comedian Redd Foxx. The two also made a trip out to Tougaloo College, and Joe once again stood by the school's storied wrought-iron arches and walked the "pathways of greatness," recounting his glory days to his attentive son. "It was a bittersweet feeling when I left Jackson," Joe admitted.

As he aged, Joseph Jackson's sight began to give way to the ravages of undiagnosed glaucoma. Nearly blind, he rarely traveled anymore but remained active in telling the Tougaloo Nine story. He was honored by various civic groups in California, and his story got picked up by local community-interest reporters. In addition, Jackson provided a first-person account of his involvement in the Jackson Library "read-in" to the Library of Congress, part of its Voices of Civil Rights series. The young-in-spirit Jackson continued to sing and stay on top of local and national political news. He became a doting grandfather and great-grandfather, with six grands and eighteen great-grands (and counting).

He felt proud of his service to the greater community, both on the frontlines in Mississippi and in his career-long effort to soften the blows against the "Blacks and Browns" of society in California. "My life has not been in vain," he once said. "It has been all about service." Regarding his involvement in Mississippi's first important student-led demonstration, Joseph Jackson Jr. felt certain that the library sit-in and its aftermath "really elevated the history of Tougaloo." In addition, for Jackson personally, "Tougaloo College was the foundation for the shaping and understanding of my life as a minister and a leader."

EVELYN PIERCE—AMEENAH OMAR

When Evelyn Pierce was whisked away from Tougaloo by her parents and out of Mississippi in early April 1961, she first went to stay with relatives in Buffalo. Soon, however, her immediate family needed her elsewhere. So, Evelyn went to stay with her brother Lovely and his wife to help care for their sickly first child while both parents worked for the army at Fort Polk in the wilderness of Louisiana. With nothing else to do, Evelyn became interested in following the footsteps of her brother into military service. She became enthralled with military life and in 1962 joined the army and became a WAC, one of the Women's Army Corps.

That same year, Evelyn, along with Lovely, began agitating for change in her new hometown. It had been a long-standing custom that the US Post Office did not deliver mail to the homes of African Americans in the town of Leesville, just outside the army base. Instead, their mail had to be picked up at the local post office in town. Evelyn and Lovely led a demonstration to insist on equal treatment by this institution of the federal government. The local Klan threatened Evelyn and her brother for their effrontery to suggest that African Americans be treated as equals to Whites. In this case, however, Evelyn didn't have to flee. Instead, the members of the Military Police from Fort Polk created a security guard patrol to defend the Pierce home from attack. Later that year, the postmaster general ordered mail delivered to all citizens of Leesville.

As a WAC, Evelyn was trained in chemical, biological, and radiological warfare, eventually achieving the rank of staff sergeant. She became a member of the Pistol Team and reportedly was one of the first females to train male soldiers. During this time, Evelyn met and married her first husband, Alfred Johnson, also an army recruit. Once their military service ended, Evelyn and her husband went to live in Detroit, where Al had some family. Johnson was also a devout Muslim and a follower of the Reverend Elijah Mohammed, who had a large and militant following in Detroit. Evelyn converted and began attending religious services at the Detroit mosque. She and Johnson eventually divorced sometime in the mid-1970s.

In 1973, Evelyn went back to school and completed her bachelor's degree in English and social studies from the University of Detroit and later, in 1981, a master's degree in education with a specialty in curriculum development and personnel management. While still an undergrad, Evelyn pledged with the Alpha Kappa Alpha sorority with which she remained involved throughout the rest of her life. Eventually, Evelyn would travel to Africa on a mission of personal discovery and while there completed her PhD in education from the University of Ghana.

As for her career, Evelyn devoted herself to educating others as a teacher in the Detroit school system (1970–1977) and later in the small community of Highland Park (1977–1986) just north of Detroit where Evelyn moved. She eventually became a school administrator, including serving a ten-year stint as dean of students at Highland Park Community College (1986–1997).[7]

Evelyn's personal life took a fascinating turn when she met and later married in 1979 the older brother of Malcolm X, Abdul Aziz Omar. Abdul was still a devoted follower of the Reverend Elijah Mohammed, despite rumors that Mohammed's henchmen from the Nation of Islam (NOI) had murdered his brother. "Abdul was in it much more for the spiritual side and not the politics," Evelyn's older sister Armendia explained. In fact, Abdul was rewarded for his loyalty by being placed in charge of a number of NOI mosques throughout the Michigan area. Evelyn was immediately drawn to Abdul because of his peaceful demeanor. She joined him in helping to manage the NOI's Detroit temple, over which he had recently become leader. Evelyn Pierce also changed her name upon marriage and became Ameenah E. P. Omar. Eventually, she and Abdul would sour on the teachings of Elijah Mohammed and gradually managed to slip away from the grasp of the NOI, although Abdul remained a devout Muslim for the rest of his life. Ameenah and Abdul adopted two daughters, Neeyah and Lakisha, and remained married for nearly fifteen years until Abdul's death in 1994. Ameenah eventually returned to her Baptist roots and became an active member of the New Grace Missionary Baptist Church in Highland Park.[8]

In 1995, Ameenah embarked on a political career when she was elected to the Highland Park city council. She remained on the council for the rest of her life, serving as its president from 2003 to 2009. The public service initiative for which Ameenah was best known is the "WEED and SEED" program, which *weeded* out drugs and the criminal element from the community and *seeded* it through prevention, intervention, and treatment of drug-addicted community members. Ameenah found federal, state, and county funding for this work, as well as private foundation support.

But her tenure was colored by the economic forces that were becoming apparent in most of the industrial Midwest at that time as skilled jobs were being shipped overseas and industries, including the automotive industry, began shifting their factories to lower-tax and nonunion regions of the country. Highland Park, which was completely surrounded by Detroit—a city within a city—and which once was home to both Ford and Chrysler production facilities, became increasingly gutted as its tax base moved away. City services like water, sewer, garbage collection, and even policing were spotty at best. Crime became an increasing problem. The city found itself unable to perform its basic functions. Municipal lighting and water bills went unpaid. Bankruptcy loomed. At the end of 2000, Michigan officials decided they needed to put Highland Park, by then a city of just fifteen thousand residents, into conservatorship. Thus, the city's mayor and City Council ceased to have any substantive say in the budget or the day-to-day running of Highland Park.

Although the mayor strenuously objected to the takeover, suggesting that he had made improvements that were beginning to turn things around, Ameenah bowed to the inevitable. "I take no excitement that we are going to get a financial manager," the deflated city councilwoman said at the time. "But the way things are now, we can't do it (by ourselves)."[9]

Through it all, Omar managed to maintain a positive attitude and strong personal relationships not only with her constituents, but also with those at the state level responsible for the city's fate.[10] As a result, she was elected to chair the city council in 2003. "She was well-loved," her sister Armendia recalled. While serving in a leadership role, Omar dealt with many difficult issues, but none got her more attention than the one involving Eminem. The popular White rapper happened to be making his breakthrough film *8 Mile* in late 2001 when, for various plot development reasons, there was the need to blow up a house. The producers found an abandoned home in Highland Park and sought permission to use it as the prop. The state conservator thought it was a good idea. The production company would donate $2,000 to a local charity and agreed to visit some schools to discuss how movies are made. And the conservator would be rid of a city eyesore. That's not how Omar—then serving as President pro tem—and the rest of the city council saw it. "What Eminem stands for is the antithesis of what I stand for," she told a group of 50 residents protesting the decision. "I see no entertainment value in burning homes," said another city councilman." But the defanged city government had to bow to the decision of Highland Park's conservator, despite their 4–0 decision to deny Eminem his dramatic prop.[11]

As for the city's governance, it took nearly nine years, but Highland Park finally was returned to solvency and restored to local control. At that point,

Ameenah stepped down as chairwoman, though she continued to serve on the city council.

Omar's most cherished role was as queen mother of a small rural village of Akwakrom, Ghana. While serving as dean of students at the Highland Park Community College, Ameenah began sponsoring annual trips to Ghana so that both she and her students could connect more directly with their African heritage. Rather than the trip being a sightseeing tour, Omar wanted it to be more of a Peace Corps experience, where students worked to improve the lives of those they were visiting. So rather than stay in Accra or one of Ghana's other cities, Ameenah arranged to have the students stay and work in Akwakrom, a rural area southwest of the capital.

"They helped people so much," Armendia recalled, "and after about three years, the people in the village voted to make Ameenah 'queen' so that Americans could continue to help bring economic security to the village." Thus, Ameenah became an ambassador for African culture in America, dressing in African robes and visiting schools to educate children about Ghanaian customs and practices. She returned to Ghana, when possible, to stay connected to her "subjects" and to help implement a series of economic and female empowerment reforms that she believed were needed.[12]

By 2006, Ameenah was suffering from the emphysema and the COPD that would eventually take her life. She could not travel to Mississippi for the forty-fifth anniversary commemoration of the Tougaloo Nine sit-in that year. As noted, she did join the group by phone and recounted her days as a freshman there, recalling especially the contributions of Drs. Beittel and Borinski and commenting that as one of the Tougaloo Nine, "We accepted a challenge where there was no indication that we would be successful. But we were committed." She also noted, "We had something special at Tougaloo. And God has blessed the Spirit to remain with us." In her final recorded words of that call, Omar addressed the students present at the gathering to remind them how privileged they were. "I want you to remember how sacred, how special is the ground that you walk on," she told them. Ameenah Evelyn Pierce Omar died in 2010.

Part VIII

WHERE THIS STORY ENDS

Chapter 23

THE END OF AN ERA

MOST OF THE MENTORS, PEERS, AND EVEN ADVERSARIES OF THE TOUGALOO
Nine survived those early years of strife and struggle that we now call the
sixties. Their stories are collected here to help complete this narrative.

TOUGALOO COLLEGE

Once through the gates and onto the campus of Tougaloo College, a small,
half-acre cemetery, Tougaloo Garden Memorial Park, sits hidden among tall
pines just past the president's residence on the right. One can trace the history
of the college by simply reading the headstones. Among them are the names
of some of the most inspirational teachers, preachers, and administrators to
have blessed the place.

REVEREND WILLIAM BENDER

William Bender and his wife, Julia—one of Tougaloo's devoted librarians—are
buried there on the grounds of the college. Bender did not go quietly into his
good night. In his final years, he continued to preach while also participating
as an emeritus member of the state and local NAACP executive committees.
He also pulled together a scholarly article for *The Journal of Negro Education*
entitled "Desegregation in the Public Schools of Mississippi." In it, he offers
a biting rebuke to the White power structure of his state while delighting in
the fact that for all of their chicanery, the powerful White jurists, lawyers, and
politicians were unable to convince the one hundred or so "Negro leaders" they
corralled in 1955 to go along with their plans to ignore the US Supreme Court's
Brown v. Board of Education decision. The article also presciently quotes from
an Ernst Borinski piece that prophesied that Tougaloo would lead the way in
the battle for desegregation of Mississippi's schools and, by inference, of Mississippi public life. "Upon us rests the full responsibility for rejecting accommodation to the traditional pattern of segregation and humiliation," Borinski
wrote. "Tougaloo Southern Christian College has accepted the challenge."[1]

Bender would not live to see Tougaloo College play a leading role in publicly protesting Jim Crow segregation with the breakthrough library sit-in. But he plowed the ground and planted the seeds, which came to fruition less than four years after the day of his death, July 1, 1957.

Tougaloo students themselves, perhaps recognizing that Bender's time was short, dedicated their May 1957 yearbook, *The Eaglet*, to him: "With appreciation, profound admiration, and respect, we dedicate this annual to Reverend William A. Bender, alumnus, Christian minister, defender of civil liberties, former college administrator, friend and helper of Tougalooans, and an inspiration to lovers of humanity."[2]

The gesture must have thrilled the man who had dedicated the better part of his long life to those students on that campus. For them to have recognized him as a "defender of civil liberties" likely meant the world to him.

It was none other than the Reverend John Mangram who preached Bender's funeral. The two had grown close during their seven-year overlap at Tougaloo, and Mangram had nothing but praise for this early civil rights champion and man of the cloth who preceded him as Tougaloo chaplain.

"He loved life and dared to live as whole, as nobly, and as adventurously as he could," Mangram said of his elder. "Mr. Bender was one of the men who was always out in the front ranks in the fight for civil rights," he observed. "This meant that he was a marked man."

"His friends told him, his family reminded him, and even though he possessed the knowledge of the stark possibilities, he never ceased riding the buses, walking the highways at night as well as in the day, hitchhiking a ride with whomsoever would give him a ride. He walked in the very 'shadow of death' and feared no evil."

Mangram ended his ten-minute oration by imagining a letter Bender might have left his friends and family, saying that had he done so, Bender would have urged his brothers and sisters in the struggle to "Keep up the good fight! Don't give one inch of ground! Never quit until the victory is won!"[3]

ARIEL "POPS" LOVELACE

Pops Lovelace is another Tougaloo faculty member who gave his very best to the college and is buried on the campus grounds. After the historic 1960/1961 school year ended, Pops continued his stellar career at Tougaloo. He simply moved from glory to glory, spreading the joy of singing and appreciation for music wherever he went. He also encountered some extraordinarily talented musicians and singers along the way. Two of note were Robert Honeysucker (class of 1964) and Walter Turnbull (class of 1966). Both would go on from Tougaloo to have nationally renowned professional careers in classical music and choral conducting.

In 1967, Pops was called back to Arkansas AM&N to fulfill the necessary requirements to qualify for the Arkansas state pension plan, cutting short his first stint at Tougaloo. In 1970, however, Pops returned to his favorite college—"I'm in love with Tougaloo," he was known to say—and spent another decade capping his career teaching music and voice and again shaping the talent available to him into an extraordinary choral showcase.

It is important to note that Pops also did his part in helping to shift perceptions of Black people during the civil rights years. It is a little-known fact that for eighteen years, starting in the 1960s, he spent his summers back in his native Ohio working with the Farm Bureau Training School, teaching mostly White rural farm youth the basics of singing and group leadership. His extraordinary charisma with youth melted away any divisions the kids might have been racially programmed to feel as Pops brought to his charges not only his musical expertise but also real-world dispatches from the minefield of the South. "This was the first experience with a black man for many of these mostly rural children," recorded a Farm Bureau administrator. "They would ask him to describe his life in Mississippi and couldn't believe what they were hearing."[4]

Besides his "kids" from college choirs and summer programs, Pops also had a full and active family life. He and his wife, Edna, had three children, all of whom were born and raised in Jackson and Pine Bluff. One of them, Mary Lovelace O'Neal, seems to have inherited her father's artistic talent and passion. With Pops's loving support, Mary would grow into an accomplished professional artist—one of the relatively few African American women during the mid-to-late twentieth century to successfully incorporate the formal aspects of abstract expressionism, colorism, and minimalism into her work. O'Neal credits much of her success to her father's early encouragement: "He is the one who let me do what I was supposed to do," she told a *New York Times* reporter in 2021.[5]

The only entries in the Mississippi Sovereignty Commission files that include the name *Ariel Lovelace* relate to Pops's successful attempt in 1964 to integrate the Jackson Music Association, which sponsored several high-brow and family musical entertainments each year. Tougaloo students had staged successful boycotts of various musical events sponsored by the association earlier that year because their events were segregated; Blacks could not attend.

One such booking—canceled just minutes before showtime—was a concert by the popular jazz trumpeter Al Hirt. Instead of just calling off his engagement ahead of time, which is what many acts did once they were informed by Tougaloo student activists of the segregated nature of the event they were about to play, Hirt waited until Jackson's new Coliseum was full and then walked on stage armed not with his trumped, but with a statement about why he could not in good conscience play to a segregated audience. The rebuke stung the all-White audience and made national headlines, causing the Jackson Music Association (JMA) to fear that it would no longer be able to obtain bookings through its New York–based agency unless it could prove it did not discriminate.

In October of that year, Pops, along with a few others from Tougaloo, applied for membership in the association. The once staunchly segregated group decided it needed "a select few Negroes" to become members so that JMA could claim it was an integrated organization. In two memos, the Sovereignty Commission details two meetings where the applications of Pops, his wife Edna, and the other Black applicants were considered and ultimately approved. It was a subtle yet effective assault on the established order.[6]

Pops retired at the end of the 1980 school year. He was feted during Tougaloo's Founders' Day celebration that October with a plush dinner at the Jacksonian Inn and a convocation at Tougaloo's Woodworth Chapel.

The much-loved Lovelace proved just how much he loved Tougaloo when he decided that he and his wife should be interred on the college premises. He bought a small double plot just in time. Pops died unexpectedly six months after his big send-off from the college. Edna joined him in death twelve years later. Their tombstone is appropriately engraved with two treble clefs and says, "We Will Love You 'Till the End of an Endless End." The sentiment was crafted by his daughter Mary to memorialize her family's eternal affection for their devoted parents, but it could just as easily have been written by Pops himself to characterize his love of Tougaloo and its students.

ERNST BORINSKI

The beloved German émigré was not long in following Lovelace to the grave. Like the choral director, Borinski gave his all to Tougaloo. It appears that he decided to work until the very end. What else was there to do? George Owens, who by then had been president of Tougaloo for nearly twenty years, described Borinski's final days. "Borinski spent his summers at Vanderbilt or North Carolina [teaching] summer school," Owens recalled. "On this particular summer [1983], he loaded up his books and everything to go to Vanderbilt. He decided to go by his doctor's for one last check-up. The doctor slapped him in the hospital. Within a week, he was gone."[7]

Borinksi must have known he was in bad shape, thus his last-minute visit to the doctor. His death certificate lists congestive heart and renal failure as well as a heart attack as the causes of death.

Herr Doktor Borinski was eighty-two years old and had spent thirty-five of those years giving every ounce of his energy to Tougaloo. And his giving continued after his death.

President Owens, who served as the executor of Borinski's estate, made the professor's last will and testament part of Tougaloo's permanent archival collection. This public record shows that besides bequeathing his beloved Käthe Kollwitz self-portrait to the Mississippi Art Association, Borinski gave the entirety of his personal possessions—his books and furnishings—to Tougaloo College. He also bequeathed 20 percent of whatever additional revenues and income his estate might receive from insurance policies to the institution, with additional funds going to his long-term personal secretary, to Jackson's Temple Beth Israel "as a representative of the Jewish community," and to various godchildren he had collected along the way, including the elder daughter of "my friend Ed King."

Borinski asked that his "funeral arrangements be as simple as possible," with "no flowers" and "preferably a pine box" for a casket, "in keeping with the Jewish tradition, which I respect."

This extraordinary personage, who had lived through many of the worst events of the Twentieth Century and devoted his life to improving on that history, is also buried on Tougaloo's campus. His ground-level gravestone reads simply, "Ernst Borinski—Inspiring Teacher."[8]

There are others in this story, of course, who are not buried on or near the Tougaloo campus. Their endings are equally as important to the completion of this tale.

REVEREND JOHN DEE MANGRAM

Chaplain Mangram stayed at Tougaloo long enough to usher in the first flowering of the school's prophesied promise. Then just as quickly, he was gone. Some of the Tougaloo Nine would come to believe that at the end of the 1961 school year, Chaplain Mangram was run off of campus by those conservative forces on the Tougaloo Board who balked against having the school associated with the burgeoning Mississippi freedom movement. This was not the case, however.

Mangram's departure seems to have been a planned next step in his career development plan. As early as October 1960—months before the Tougaloo Nine protest—Mangram had written to his colleagues that he was contemplating a "year of study" away from Tougaloo. After a decade of serving as campus chaplain and associate professor of religion, Mangram was searching for a new challenge. By November, it appears that he communicated his full plan for the future with a highly placed confidant. Kenneth "Kib" Brown was then serving as executive director of the Danforth Foundation, a richly endowed philanthropic organization funded by the heirs of the Ralston-Purina dog food fortune. The foundation focused on improving educational opportunities for college students and teachers, primarily within the St. Louis, Missouri, area where the foundation and the company were based.

Tougaloo had developed an important relationship with the foundation, and both Borinski and Mangram maintained strong professional and personal ties to the organization's leader. (As noted, Borinski funneled some of his most promising students—Ethel Sawyer and Joyce Ladner chief among them—to Washington University in St. Louis, a prime recipient of the Danforth Foundation's largesse.)

Mangram's November letter to Brown makes a passing reference to a prior letter he had sent "indicating my plans for the future." In fact, as a result of that communique, Brown would secure for Mangram a one-year fellowship to study at the Pacific School of Religion in Berkeley, California, for the coming 1961/1962 academic year. Mangram's plan was to work toward a doctorate in theology, and he likely knew he wouldn't be returning to Mississippi anytime soon if he could make other arrangements during his year-long sabbatical. In an earlier letter, he had confirmed to Brown that he had been accepted into the school and that they had accepted "the work that I did at Yale, all of it. This brightens the day and sets a rainbow in the West for me."[9]

Indeed, Mangram stayed in California for the next six years. By the time the Danforth funding ran out, he was serving as pastor (or copastor—the record is unclear) of the Church for the Fellowship of all Peoples—the interracial and interfaith house of worship founded by the esteemed Reverend Howard Thurman in 1944 in collaboration with the nonviolence-advocating Fellowship of Reconciliation. Surely Mangram's credentials in Mississippi—both with the NAACP and as advisor to the Tougaloo Nine—helped secure him this plum post. His birthplace may have also played a role, since the church's original mission was to serve the many African Americans from Oklahoma, Texas, and Arkansas who had migrated west during World War II to secure jobs in the defense industry.

From 1964 to 1966, Mangram also worked as a graduate assistant at the Pacific School of Religion. He earned his doctorate in theology from the school in 1966. His doctoral dissertation was titled "H. Richard Niebuhr's Concept of Faith and Its Relevance for Campus Ministry"—a subject he knew well after his eleven years of providing spiritual direction to his Tougaloo students.[10]

Doctorate secured, Mangram moved in 1967 to Dallas, Texas, to become the chairman of the Division of Religion and Philosophy at Bishop College, where he would remain for the next twenty-one years. It was there that Mangram would become known as the preachers' teacher for the many ministerial students he would train. In 1988, Mangram returned triumphantly to his alma mater, Jarvis Christian College (JCC), to finish out his career. To honor one of its most notable graduates, JCC now hosts the annual Mangram Ministerial Institute Revival and Scholarship Conference to celebrate his legacy. The college also offers an annual John Dee Mangram Religion and Ministry Award to the most promising ministerial student in its graduating class.[11] The Reverend Doctor John Dee Mangram died in 2014 at the age of ninety, just as this study of the Tougaloo Nine was getting underway.

Reverend Gerald Britt eulogized his former teacher from Bishop College with these words: "I greatly admired John Mangram. He was a great preacher. He was a marvelous teacher. He was a wonderful man. I'm of the opinion that if those of us who sat at his feet were to become half the preacher and man he was, this world will be a much better place in which to live." Britt, a longtime Dallas activist and community leader, also noted, "At one point, all four presidents of the black churches conventions were headed by Bishop College preachers, and Dr. Mangram was an adviser to one and had taught the other three."[12] It was a well-earned tribute to a man who operated mostly out of the limelight, but who at a critical time was on the frontlines of the Mississippi Freedom struggle.

ADAM DANIEL BEITTEL

Dan Beittel continued to serve as the president of Tougaloo College for several years after the Tougaloo Nine demonstration opened the flood gates to student activism in Mississippi. Beittel never wavered from his belief that the college administration should not interfere with students' exercise of their citizenship rights outside of the classroom—a decidedly minority view in the early 1960s as student protests mounted across the country. As a result of this principled stance, Beittel was harassed by the Citizens' Council, spied upon by the Sovereignty Commission, and threatened with having Tougaloo's academic certification credentials withdrawn by the State of Mississippi. Still, he wouldn't budge.

He continued to raise funds for the institution, oversee an incredibly diverse and academically challenging environment for Tougaloo's near-capacity five hundred students, and managed a revved-up building and renovation plan for the college's aged infrastructure. In just four years, Beittel had increased the school's assets by more than $1 million, from $1.6 million to $2.7 million.[13] Nevertheless, by the spring of 1964, Tougaloo's board of trustees—and the board of the American Missionary Association (AMA), which held the purse strings for much of Tougaloo's funding—were looking for a new leader for their flagship HBCU in Mississippi. There are many explanations for this development depending on which sources you consult.

Historian John Dittmer tries to get to the bottom of all of them in his 1994 expansive history of the Mississippi movement, *Local People*. He points the finger at one Barnaby Keeney, then president of Brown University, who had offered to help Tougaloo raise funds for additional buildings and expansion of the campus if only the board of trustees would retire Beittel and "reduce Tougaloo's active involvement in the black struggle." Keeney, a well-liked college administrator, had a shadowy side that included stints with the intelligence operations of the US government dating back to his service as an intelligence officer for the US Army in World War II and continuing through his time at Brown, where he allegedly took a sabbatical in 1951 to work for the CIA. While president of Brown, Keeney apparently was also on the CIA's payroll, thus linking him directly to forces that may have wanted Beittel out of the top spot at Tougaloo in order to tamp down student protests.[14]

Another explanation for Beittel's early exit comes from none other than Erle Johnston, who by then had become head of the Mississippi Sovereignty Commission. Just days before Beittel's retirement was announced, Johnston visited the offices of the AMA and offered a deal to have the Mississippi legislature drop its threat to revoke Tougaloo's charter if the board would remove Beittel as president. Johnston alleged that Tougaloo had "become more of a school for agitation than a school for education." A week later, when news of Beittel's ouster was announced, Johnston implied that he had had a hand in toppling the troublemaker.[15]

A third line of reasoning from someone with an insider's view of the Beittel removal offers a less conspiratorial, more "official" justification. George Owens, who was chosen to replace Beittel, becoming the first Black president of the revered or reviled institution—depending on one's point of view—said that Beittel was told as early as October 1963 that the board would be expecting his resignation letter by the end of the school year since he had turned sixty-five, the required retirement age. Beittel believed he had a special deal with the AMA that would allow him to stay until seventy, so he rebuffed the board, even during a heated January 1964 exchange.

The reason for the board's insistence "had absolutely nothing to do with" student activism on campus, Owens alleged. "Dr. Beittel didn't invent civil rights activity [on campus]." Owens pointed to Reverend Bender's activism in the 1940s and '50s to bolster his point. "Reverend Bender was involved," he said, "and people tried to bring pressure . . . to fire Bender. But no, the board was totally supportive of that." And as for Keeney, Owens was adamant: "Keeney might have been placing himself where he could learn about our involvement in civil rights, but Tougaloo had nothing to hide, and Keeney wasn't going to decide what we did."

In two wide-ranging oral histories, Owens asserted that Beittel was pushed aside for the necessary purpose of executing on the board's new ten-year plan of operation and development, which included not only a building program but also an expansion of Tougaloo's academic offerings to prepare its Black students for a world where opportunities were opening up for them. "Things were changing," Owens recalled. There was "a new thrust to change the entire curriculum to prepare young people for a broad range of careers—a ten-year plan—and [the board] wanted a person to start with that who would have enough time to see it through rather than have a person start it and in the midst of it, leave."[16]

Beittel's dismissal could have been a combination of all three of these explanations. In any event, Beittel was forced out. He announced his resignation in April and was gone by August. George Owens was named acting president starting September 1, 1964, and was installed as full-time president in April 1966, with Barney Keeney serving as a keynote speaker at his inauguration.

But if Mississippians thought they were done with Dan Beittel, they were sorely mistaken. Beittel understood that he was at the heart of America's race problem and continued to work toward his vision of a more equitable society for the next five years until he was ready to retire on his own terms at the age of seventy. Upon his departure from Tougaloo, Beittel immediately accepted an offer to direct the Mississippi arm of the American Friends Service Committee and continued his many volunteer activities, including serving on the Mississippi Advisory Committee to the US Commission on Civil Rights. In 1965, he became a founding member of the Delta Ministry, a community- and economic-development organization initiated by the National Council of Churches. That same year, Beittel became the first board chairman of the Child Development Group of Mississippi—a pioneering statewide umbrella organization funded by the newly created US Office of Economic Opportunity (OEO) to establish Head Start programs for impoverished children to assure their readiness for elementary school learning. All of this suggests that he was not forced out due to a lack of energy or enthusiasm for the work at hand.

Dan and Ruth Beittel finally brought their sojourn to Mississippi to an end in 1969 and moved to California, where they continued to be engaged in various community projects. Dan Beittel died in 1988 at the age of eighty-nine, having contributed mightily to advance his vision of a more just and equitable society.

JACKSON STATE COLLEGE

JACOB L. REDDIX

Unlike Beittel, Jacob Reddix managed to keep his job during the heyday of student protest and retired from Jackson State on his own terms in March of 1967. During his twenty-seven-year tenure, Reddix oversaw extensive development of the college's physical infrastructure as well as its academic excellence. At the start of the 1940 academic year when Reddix took over as president, Jackson State enrolled a total of 108 students; when he retired, the enrollment was up to 5,000. Similarly, the college began with a state appropriation of $10,000 (supplemented by an annual $30,000 from the Rosenwald Fund for the first several years); when Reddix retired, Mississippi was funding the institution to the tune of $5.4 million annually. Equally as important, the school's academic achievements grew just as impressively as did its physical plant. Reddix managed to attract dedicated and skilled educators to the school's ranks. Pops Lovelace was Jackson State's first music instructor; Dr. Jane Ellen McAllister, the first Black woman to earn a doctorate from Columbia University's Teachers College, also joined the faculty at the start of Reddix's tenure and remained there for a decade.[17]

Perhaps Reddix's greatest hiring coup, however, was attracting the celebrated poet and novelist Margaret Walker (Alexander) to teach at the college. In 1942, Walker had won the most prestigious poetry accolade in the country, the Yale Younger Poets Award, for her poetry collection *For My People*, thus making her the first African American woman to win a national literary prize. In 1943, she married Firnist Alexander and started a family. With her husband and their three children, the poet moved to Jackson in 1949 to begin a thirty-year teaching career at the invitation of President Reddix.

The Alexander family would eventually take up residence in a newly developed Black neighborhood on Guynes Street (now Margaret W. Alexander Drive) in northwest Jackson, just a few houses down the way from where Medgar and Myrlie Evers had also settled. Margaret Walker Alexander stayed at Jackson State through all of its civil rights upheavals and managed to maintain a cordial relationship with Reddix despite his short fuse over student protest, which she, instead, praised in her poetry collection *Prophets for a New Day*.

Before all of that, however, in 1952 Walker Alexander wrote a series of sonnets honoring the first five presidents of what eventually came to be known as Jackson State University, including Reddix, on the seventy-fifth anniversary of the institution's establishment. She dubbed him "The Builder" and with obvious admiration wrote:

> O Reddix, builder for another Age,
> We follow you now with our hearts upheld
> We look to you and truly mark full well
> Your firm footstep across our desert space.
> You are our leader in this tortured sphere;
> We look to you and follow without fear.

In his 1974 memoir, Reddix returned the favor by using Walker Alexander's poem "A Litany from the Dark People" to close out the story of his life.[18]

President Reddix never recanted his harsh behavior against the students in his care on that early spring night of March 27, 1961. Nor did he seem to regret the three expulsions that followed. In his 232-page memoir, he provides exactly two sentences about student protest, neither of which directly addresses what happened on the Jackson State campus. He first references student upheaval while discussing, of all things, Jackson State's winning football seasons of 1961 and 1962. "I feel that as the great influx of college students in public institutions becomes a reality," Reddix wrote, "a good program of intercollegiate sports has the effect of counteracting group uprisings and other difficulties in large institutions."[19]

Indeed, Reddix put more emphasis on Jackson State's football team after the Jackson State student uprising, and in the fall of 1961, the college had an undefeated record, losing only to Florida A&M at the post-season HBCU championship Orange Bowl Classic. The following year, Jackson State won the championship in a rematch with Florida A&M.

Reddix's second reference to student protest occurs late in his lengthy reflections in a chapter titled "Race Relations One Hundred Years After Emancipation." "I remember the days when black citizens could not borrow books from the public libraries in certain states," Reddix, wrote, "Peaceful protest is a powerful and dramatic instrument for bringing about social change, especially for the poor and neglected citizens in a democracy. Of course, no change can be effected by peaceful protest that could not also be accomplished by means of the ballot. . . . The poor and the young want changes now, not tomorrow. This haste could be a dangerous trend in our democratic process."[20]

After his retirement, Reddix ran unsuccessfully for the Mississippi House of Representatives. His lasting impact, however, must be measured not only by the enormous growth and success of Jackson State, which became a full-fledged university in 1974, but also by his contributions to cooperative development within the state of Mississippi. In 1941, just after arriving to take up the leadership of Jackson State, Reddix helped organize what became the Hinds County Educational Federal Credit Union, which at the time of his retirement held $1.7 million in assets—then the second largest financial organization operated by Blacks within the state. And in 1955, he oversaw the creation of the State Mutual Federal Savings & Loan Association, which surpassed his credit union creation with $3.7 million in assets in 1967—"the largest amount of capital ever owned by Black people in the history of the state," he noted.

Jacob Reddix died in 1973 after having just completed his memoir *A Voice Crying in the Wilderness*, which was published the following year by the newly formed University Press of Mississippi.[21]

THE LADNER SISTERS AND WALTER WILLIAMS

Dorie and Joyce Ladner did, indeed, transfer to Tougaloo College in the fall of 1961, where they found a strong culture of scholarship combined with burgeoning student activism. Both joined the Student Nonviolent Coordinating Committee (SNCC) and became ever more involved in the flowering Jackson movement. Both also joined the Delta Sigma Theta sorority, known for its social activism and its "against-the-grain" ethos. In 1963, Joyce was asked by SNCC to become one of its two representatives to go to New York in the summer of 1963 to help Bayard Rustin plan and coordinate the March on Washington. Dorie joined her there for part of the summer and they both traveled to Washington, DC, to be part of that wonderous gathering in late August. A photograph taken just after the speeches concluded, as most of the quarter-million people had dispersed, shows a long line of SNCC members grasping hands and spreading out across the width of the Reflecting Pool, facing the Lincoln Memorial, where Dr. King had just delivered his "I Have a Dream" speech. The group—beaming with youthful optimism—includes Dorie and Joyce, with SNCC's chief Mississippi strategist, Bob Moses, in between, all singing "We Shall Overcome" at the end of a glorious day.

Joyce graduated from Tougaloo College in 1964 and, with the recommendation of her mentor Ernst Borinski, followed in Ethel Sawyer's footsteps to

Washington University in St. Louis for graduate school. There she earned her master's degree and PhD in sociology, doing her field work among the Pruitt-Igoe Housing Project residents, just as Ethel had done. In 1971, she turned her stereotype-shattering dissertation about the young women of Pruitt-Igoe and their coping strategies into a book, *Tomorrow's Tomorrow: The Black Woman*. She followed that up in 1973 by editing a series of essays by prominent Black sociologists and authors provocatively titled *The Death of White Sociology: Essays on Race and Culture*. Among submissions by E. Franklin Frazier and Ralph Ellison, Albert Murray and Kenneth B. Clark can be found one by Ethel Sawyer, "Methodological Problems in Studying So-Called 'Deviant' Communities.'"

The two volumes put Dr. Ladner onto a successful career path in academia, where she flourished, reaching the pinnacle of the profession in 1994 when she was named interim president of Howard University. The male-dominated board, however, denied her a chance to serve as the storied HBCU's first female president. No matter. In 1995, President Bill Clinton tapped her to serve on the District of Columbia Financial Control Board to help restructure the finances of the city's troubled schools. She also was named a senior fellow at the Brookings Institution, a DC think tank. Dr. Ladner retired in 2003 and after a brief relocation to Florida, returned to Washington DC, where she maintains an active social and postprofessional life, including a strong social-media presence. She is currently working on a memoir of her eventful life.[22]

Dorie Ladner took a different path than her younger sister. After two semesters at Tougaloo, Dorie dropped out to join the movement full time. She went to Atlanta to work at the SNCC office there and, significantly, went to Chicago, where her Hattiesburg mentor, Clyde Kennard, was dying of colon cancer after having been released on parole from Mississippi's Parchman penitentiary to get medical treatment. While in Chicago, Dorie saw TV footage of her former classmates being harassed and beaten at the Woolworth's lunch counter and decided to return to Jackson. After the assassination of Medgar Evers that June, Dorie spontaneously led the most memorable march of her civil rights career when, after the mile-long silent funeral march honoring Evers—from the Black Masonic Temple near the campus of Jackson State to the Collins Funeral Home downtown on Farish Street—she encouraged other SNCC volunteers to break into Freedom Songs and march past police barricades in an attempt to reach the downtown shopping district on Capitol Street, where the 1963 Jackson movement boycott had begun.

In 1964, Dorie was a key organizer for Freedom Summer and became SNCC's first female project director when she took over the leadership of the group's Natchez project, where she remained until 1966. In 1968, she participated in the Poor People's Campaign and later moved to St. Louis to become a community organizer for an antipoverty program there. Like Sammy Bradford, Dorie would return intermittently to Tougaloo when she could to pick up a semester of credits, but then she would leave again to work in the movement. "I just can't study while my people are suffering," she once told Joyce.[23] After a brief marriage and the birth of her only child, Dorie returned to Tougaloo College, finally earning her bachelor of arts degree in 1973. She then moved to Washington, DC, earned a master's in social work from Howard University, and worked as a social worker for the next thirty years in the city's only public hospital, DC General, in its emergency room and Psychiatry Department. She retired from this grueling work in 2006.

For a decade, 2013 to 2023, listeners of WPFW radio in Washington—"your station for jazz and justice"—were treated to Dorie's snippets of elder wisdom and stories of her time in the movement nearly every Saturday morning on the *DJ Lance Reynolds Show*. On any given appearance, she might go into detail about meeting Sidney Poitier after the March on Washington (with folk legend Bob Dylan in tow) or compare her own path as a young 1960s activist to that of those in the new century's Black Lives Matter movement. "I tried to do the best I could to make a change," she would often humbly confess. Dorie Ladner died on March 11, 2024.[24]

Walter Williams was the president of the Jackson State student government when the school's 1961 uprising took place; he led the student meeting at the Field House that authorized a march to the downtown city jail on March 28 while the Tougaloo Nine were still incarcerated there, and the city was filled with make believe Confederate soldiers and Lost Cause celebrants. As a result, Williams was expelled immediately from the college by President Reddix. The expulsion had serious consequences for the student leader. Unlike the Ladner sisters, who were just completing their first year of college when they were pushed out, Williams was in his final year at Jackson State. Expulsion meant that he would not graduate, would not receive a degree, could not move forward with his postgraduate plans.

It was a shocking blow for Williams and his family. But Williams turned what could have been considered a tragedy into a triumph. Having committed himself to nonviolent resistance, he stayed the course. When the Freedom Riders arrived in Jackson two months later, he took an even greater interest in the events that were grabbing the attention of the nation. When some of the Riders decided to stay in Jackson after their release and tried to foster a more vigorous local movement, Williams joined them. For the next two years, he became part of the vanguard of local Jacksonians joining with members of SNCC and CORE to try to bring about consensual change to the city. No matter what they tried, however, nothing worked. Mayor Allen Thompson and Governor Ross Barnett were not about to budge in their defense of segregation, nor were many White city residents ready to countenance a change.

Williams ended up at one of the most violent sit-ins of the era—the Jackson Woolworth's sit-in—on May 28, 1963, joining a number of Tougaloo students and some of their teachers to more directly—though still nonviolently—insist that the old ways had to go. They were met by a mob of more than one hundred White patrons, mostly teens as well as some adults (including the notorious Red Hydrick), cursing them, wildly haranguing them, dumping sugar, mustard, and ketchup on them, throwing store merchandise at them to try and get them to leave their posts at the lunch counter. Williams was struck in the head by a heavy glass ash tray and momentarily fell to the floor. Eventually, he got back on his stool and continued to suffer the verbal and physical blows of the crowd, all the while hoping his quiet witness would help change hearts and minds to enable Whites to recognize his humanity and that of his fellow Black citizens. After a three-hour siege, the police finally put an end to the ordeal, cleared the angry mob from the store, and let the demonstrators go, no longer feeling the need to arrest them for "breach of peace," though neither did they help "keep the peace" by putting a stop to the violence of the mob.[25]

Williams made his way to Chicago, where he applied for law school despite not having a college diploma. After explaining his situation, administrators at the John Marshall Law School waived the degree requirement, particularly after seeing his high LSAT score. In 1970, Williams graduated from Marshall with a law degree and began his career as a criminal-defense lawyer at Williams, Slaughter, and Williams law firm. In 1986, he was appointed to the Cook County Circuit Court as an associate judge, focusing primarily on juvenile cases. "It was gut-wrenching, but it was rewarding," Williams allowed. In 2008, the Illinois Supreme Court appointed Williams as a circuit judge, and for the next eight years, he became the supervisor of the traffic section, mentoring dozens of newly appointed judges along the way. Williams retired in 2013 but continued to serve in an advisory capacity on Cook County's New Judges' Education Advisory Committee. One of his colleagues said, "He was perfect . . . for this job because he was so good at mentoring people." All this could have been lost because of the rash act of an insecure college president in 1961.

Even that mistaken judgement was righted. In 2010, JSU president, Dr. Ronald Mason Jr., apologized to Williams and to the Ladner sisters on behalf of the institution for having expelled them in the wake of their Tougaloo Nine sympathy protest. In his statement, Mason observed: "The expulsion of the Ladner sisters and Walter Williams cannot be undone. Perhaps, however, the scales can be partially set right by publicly acknowledging that the acts for which Dorie, Joyce and Walter were separated from Jackson State were righteous, and the action of Jackson State, while within the law of the time, was nevertheless the wrong thing to do. Jackson State University therefore belatedly, but sincerely apologies."[26]

The following year, Jackson State finally awarded Walter Williams the diploma he had earned fifty years earlier. He was invited to participate in the 2011 baccalaureate ceremonies that year with all the other graduating seniors. "I was very proud the day I walked down the aisle," Williams noted. "They made quite a bit about it."[27] As well they should have. He had twice stood in the breach and helped usher in a new era for his home state.

OTHERS IN THE MIX

MEDGAR WILEY EVERS

The legacy of Medgar Evers did not die with the man upon his assassination on the long night of June 11/12, 1963. "Nothing can bring Medgar back, but the cause can live on," declared his wife, Myrlie, from the podium of Pearl Street AME Church the following evening. At its July National Convention that year, the NAACP posthumously awarded its fallen Mississippi freedom fighter its highest honor, the Spingarn Medal, thus carving his name into the highest echelon of the organization's activists and cultural heroes. In further recognition of Evers's dedication, the NAACP now annually recognizes three members of its staff—one each from its administrative, managerial, and executive ranks—with the Medgar Wiley Evers Award for Excellence.

But Evers's legacy lived on equally as large outside of the organization to which he had devoted his life. In 1964, the writer and cultural firebrand James Baldwin dedicated the first of his plays to be performed on Broadway, *Blues for Mr. Charlie*, "to the memory of Medgar Evers and his widow and children . . ." Baldwin had met the civil rights leader and his family when visiting Jackson during a speaking tour of the South sponsored by CORE at the start of 1963. (There is a photo of the two men standing in the driveway of the Evers home—the very same driveway where Evers would be assassinated less than six months later.) Baldwin had been considering writing a play using the Emmett Till murder as a jumping-off point, but he couldn't seem to convince himself that it would have any effect. It was Baldwin's direct interaction with Evers, and then the NAACP field secretary's subsequent assassination, that pushed Baldwin to put pen to paper, as he describes in his introductory note about the play's provenance:

I once took a short trip with Medgar Evers to the back-woods of Mississippi. He was investigating the murder of a Negro man by a white store-
keeper, which had taken place months before. Many people talked to
Medgar that night, in dark cabins, with their lights out, in whispers; and
we had been followed for many miles out of Jackson, Mississippi, not by
a lunatic with a gun, but by state troopers. I will never forget that night,
as I will never forget Medgar—who took me to the plane the next day.
We promised to see each other soon. When he died, something entered
into me which I cannot describe, but it was then that I resolved that
nothing under heaven would prevent me from getting this play done.[28]

Medgar's brother Charles, who took over as head of the NAACP in Mississippi after his brother's murder, also kept Evers's legacy alive, first in 1966
with the Medgar Evers Memorial Observance—an event that brought Roy
Wilkins back to Mississippi to honor the NAACP hero and to march with
other loyalists through the streets of Jackson along the same route as the Evers
funeral march three years earlier.[29] Charles later initiated the Medgar Evers
Homecoming Celebration, an annual parade held in Jackson in mid-June
to commemorate his brother's memory and to honor the distance the Black
community had come since Medgar's passing. (This is the parade Joe Jackson
rode in when he returned to the city of his Tougaloo Nine protest in 2014.)
    Myrlie Evers did her part to keep her husband's memory alive, first by
writing a dual memoir of their lives together—a best seller in 1967 entitled
For Us, The Living—and later by collaborating with scholar and renowned
author Manning Marable to compile Medgar's most relevant documents,
speeches, memos into a powerful compilation called *The Autobiography
of Medgar Evers: A Hero's Life and Legacy Revealed Through His Writings,
Letters and Speeches*. The book is a marvel, telling the history of the Jackson
Movement through Medgar's own words.
    The Evers family also established the Medgar & Myrlie Evers Institute in
1989 to honor this power couple of the Mississippi civil rights movement
and to advance the causes for which Medgar Evers had given his life. In 2013,
the institute held a fiftieth-anniversary commemoration of Medgar's death
to keep his flame alive, with a day-long series of events, culminating in an
evening gala where keynote speaker Vernon Jordan reminisced about his
days as a young Georgia NAACP field secretary who was mentored by the
older, more experienced Evers and where entertainer B.B. King provided an
appropriately bluesy ending to an extraordinary day.
    The pinnacle of all of these days of remembrance occurred in May 2024,
when the daughter of Medgar Evers, Reena Evers-Everette, accepted the
Presidential Medal of Freedom from President Joe Biden on behalf of her

ailing mother and grateful family. It was the culmination of decades of work, spearheaded by Mississippi congressman Bennie Thompson, to have Evers's civil rights career and military service appropriately appreciated by his country's highest officer. "This is such an extraordinary honor for our family," Evers-Everette told a reporter afterward. And when Myrlie Evers received the award from her daughter days later, she held it to her chest and tearfully exclaimed, "Medgar, you are finally recognized as a first-class citizen!"

"He was a warrior," Evers's daughter Reena said, "and he still lives on."[30]

AARON HENRY

The World War II veteran who helped Medgar Evers wrest the leadership of the Mississippi NAACP Conference away from less activist leaders such as C. R. Darden, became a force in Mississippi politics in the wake of the assassination of his friend and colleague. The Delta pharmacist, whose Fourth Street Drug Store provided a modicum of freedom to youth like Janice Jackson, had helped form and then lead—even prior to Evers's death—the Council of Federated Organizations (COFO), a consortium of civil rights groups working within the state of Mississippi to ensure a cohesive message and coordinated, effective activism. In 1963, COFO organized the Mississippi Freedom Democratic Party to pointedly show up the state's establishment, segregated Democratic Party and to advocate for an integrated, big-tent party structure open to all of Mississippi's citizens.

At the 1964 Democratic National Convention, Henry—along with freedom fighters Fannie Lou Hamer and the Reverend Ed King—testified before the party's Credentials Committee, urging the group to certify and seat the upstart, more representative Freedom Democrats and oust the segregated "regulars." The gambit failed, but in 1968, Henry (along with Hamer and King) was seated as a full-fledged member of the Mississippi delegation.

In 1979, Henry ran for a seat in the Mississippi House of Representatives and won, representing his home county of Coahoma and the city of Clarksdale. During all of this, he continued to serve as president of the Mississippi NAACP—a post he held for more than thirty years, finally stepping down in 1993 as his health began to decline. He lost his elected seat in the Mississippi legislature in 1995 and died in 1997, having helped usher in a completely new, multiracial political landscape in his native state.[31]

PERCY GREENE

Percy Greene, who started his career as an enterprising, even radical, Black journalist in the late 1920s, had become by the 1950s—and there is no other way to say it—an accommodationist Uncle Tom. *The Jackson Advocate*, the newspaper he started in 1939 to rave reviews and awards from the *Chicago Defender* and the *Pittsburgh Courier*, had become a joke to Jackson's Black community during the years of the civil rights movement. Greene consistently denigrated Medgar Evers, the NAACP, CORE, the Freedom Riders, COFO, and Martin Luther King Jr., among others, and urged compliance with all of Mississippi's laws and customs, no matter how discriminatory or obviously racist. In the late 1950s, Greene also began accepting payments from the Mississippi Sovereignty Commission to continue lambasting those who were trying to move Mississippi forward.

"Percy Greene? Everybody knows he's sold out," a Black Jackson businessman told a rival paper. "I regard his paper just as I regard the White Citizens' Council paper." Nevertheless, Greene managed to keep *The Jackson Advocate* going through the funds he received from his White "sponsors" and from primarily White advertising. His catering to White authority worked in his favor to a degree and once even saved his life. In 1976, he was invited to attend a political event with President Gerald Ford on a Mississippi riverboat cruise. Greene had a heart attack while on the boat and would have died but for the quick action of the president's physician, who was on board. He lived for another seven months and died in April 1977 at the age of eighty-two.

His newspaper was taken over by a more in-tune owner, who transformed it into a community asset that still operates today. Both Colia Liddell (in the 1970s) and future NAACP President and CEO Benjamin Jealous (in the 1990s) served as editors of *The Jackson Advocate*.[32]

COLIA LIDDELL LAFAYETTE CLARK

The young woman who helped establish the Tougaloo College Chapter of the NAACP—the group that sponsored the Tougaloo Nine sit-in—went on to become something of a fire starter all over the South during the civil rights years. In 1961, she initiated the North Jackson NAACP Youth Council to get her siblings and others not yet in college interested in the freedom movement. Crucially, she asked the new social science teacher at Tougaloo, John Salter, to serve as the adult advisor for the group. Together they would build a strong youth movement that in 1963 would challenge Jackson's status-quo segregationist policies through boycotts and sit-ins and lead to the city's largest civil rights uprising during the civil rights era. By then, however, Colia had moved on to an even harder gig.

In the summer of 1962, she joined SNCC and worked in various places throughout Mississippi running voter-education programs and promoting voter registration. In early 1963, she moved with her new husband, Freedom Rider Bernard Lafayette Jr., to Selma, Alabama, to help establish a voter-education and registration program there. Thus, Colia Lidell Lafayette helped to seed the ground for a movement that would blossom two years later and become one of the most consequential uprisings of the entire civil rights era, leading to the passage of the Voting Rights Act of 1965. But Colia only stayed in Selma for a few months. Her organizing skills and ability to connect with young people caused SNCC leader James Forman to send her to Birmingham during the height of its civil rights reckoning in 1963. She was there to face Bull Connor and his water cannons along with many of the youth she had encouraged to join that movement.

The Lafayettes left Alabama in 1964 to attend Fisk University in Nashville. She eventually returned to Jackson in 1973 and as noted, became a consequential editor of *The Jackson Advocate* at the time of its transition to a more clear-eyed media source for Black Jacksonians. She eventually earned her bachelor of arts degree from Jackson State University and later a master's degree from the State University of New York at Albany.

Liddell Lafayette Clark tirelessly organized wherever she found herself, whether in the Mississippi Delta, rural Alabama, or Albany, New York, where she eventually settled. Her advocacy became more expansive as she became more exposed to the cross-currents of international movements sweeping the world. "These struggles around issues of imperialism, colonization, capitalism, racism, environmental-ism, anti-woman, anti-youth, anti-age, anti-human struggles must be internationalized," she once told an interviewer later in life. "It is important that the struggle of the African in the USA be removed from domestic servitude to international leadership—human at last." In 2010 and again in 2012, Liddell Lafayette Clark ran unsuccessfully for an open US Senate seat for New York on the Green Party ticket. This lifelong freedom fighter died in November 2022 at the age of eighty-two, free at last.[33]

JOHNNY FRAZIER

The young man from Greenville whom Medgar Evers and Meredith Anding spent the better part of a day in August 1960 springing from the Winona jail would prove more than worth the effort. For his early protest, he was rewarded by his peers by being elected president of the Mississippi State

Conference of Youth Councils—a consortium of all of the youth councils throughout the state. (Later, as an adult, Frazier would take on the role of adult advisor to the group.) By 1964, he was representing Mississippi's youth at the NAACP National Convention, and thanks to his tireless activism, he was elected to the national board of the NAACP—an impressive feat for a twenty-something youth activist from the Magnolia State.

By then, Frazier, like the Ladner sisters' mentor Clyde Kennard before him, attempted several times to integrate Mississippi Southern College (now the University of Southern Mississippi) but was rebuffed. Frazier decided to attend Tougaloo College and, after graduating in 1968, traveled to Boston to prepare for the ministry at Crane Theological School at Tufts University. Frazier was ordained in the Unitarian Universalist Congregation in 1968 and was invited the following year to become pastor of "an experimental ghetto ministry" in Cleveland, Ohio. There he formed the Black Humanist Fellowship of Liberation and remained for half a decade ministering to a small congregation and involving himself in the Black Power movement. In 1974, Frazier left urban life behind and joined former CORE director Floyd McKissick to help build Soul City, North Carolina, a new city venture established in the rural, north-central part of the state. Intended to mimic the success of the planned community of Columbia, Maryland, Soul City never fully achieved the grandeur of its founder's imagination. Nevertheless, Frazier stayed and made community development his life's work, ministering mostly to the poor and the incarcerated "and a myriad of other activities."[34]

AMOS BROWN

The young man who started the West Jackson Youth Council back in 1955 with the encouragement of Medgar Evers and who participated in some of the earliest student protests of the Jackson movement would go on to become an esteemed pastor and leader of one of the largest and most politically potent branches of the NAACP in the country. "It wasn't by accident that I was involved in the movement," the elder Brown would explain. As noted, Brown attended Moorhouse College and was one of the only eight students to take a class from Martin Luther King Jr.—the only college course King ever taught. Brown had heard King preach years earlier, however, on Youth Night at that NAACP National Convention in San Francisco in 1956. During that same eventful trip, Brown had attended church services at the Third Baptist Church of San Francisco, the oldest predominately African American Baptist church in the West. Incredibly, after being schooled at Moorhouse—and later at Crozer Theological Seminary (PA) and Union Theological Seminary

(NY)—and after serving apprenticeships at churches in Pennsylvania and Minnesota, Amos Brown was invited to become pastor of San Francisco's famed Third Baptist Church in 1976. He would remain there for the entirety of his long career, ministering to church members while also building an activist movement, eventually becoming the president of the San Francisco NAACP and later, a member of the NAACP's national board of directors. As of this writing, he remains active in all three of these leadership positions.

In the summer of 2024, Brown became known for another reason: pastor to Kamala Harris, then vice president of the United States and the Democratic Party's nominee for president. Harris, whose home is in San Francisco, was by then a twenty-year veteran member of Third Baptist. "She came to this church because she knew our ways, she knew our history," Brown said. "This church has always had a balanced spirituality: social justice and personal fulfilment and salvation." In nearly every interview he has ever offered about his long life of service and activism, Brown recalled that 1956 trip with Medgar, "my mentor," to San Francisco in Evers's "Blue Goose" Oldsmobile—the one without air conditioning—in which they traversed the desert heat and dust (with bags of ice on the hood of the car "to keep the engine cool"). And he has always provided Evers primacy of place among his many mentors, teachers, and advisors.[35]

Chapter 24

THE OLD GUARD DIES BUT NEVER SURRENDERS

THE LIVES OF WHITE ESTABLISHMENT JACKSON ALSO REACHED THEIR natural endings in the years following the racial reckoning brought on by the Tougaloo Nine sit-in. Here are some of their "rest-of-life" stories.

GOVERNOR ROSS BARNETT

Ross Barnett's term of office nearly perfectly overlapped that of the Civil War centennial commemoration. Barnett made his four-year term memorable through his own full-throated resistance to federal rule. That "Never!" strategy culminated in the ultimately unsuccessful effort to keep Jackson State student James Meredith from enrolling in the University of Mississippi in the fall of 1962. Barnett's showdown with federal troops caused untold damage to the reputation of the state of Mississippi and left the university's campus in a shambles after a night of rioting as federal troops escorted Meredith onto campus and protected him throughout the melee, during which two people died and more than three hundred were injured.

Barnett, though defeated, was unbowed. He continued to lead the charge against integration—in schools and elsewhere in Southern public life—until he was eclipsed in 1963 by the ascendancy of George Wallace in Alabama, a younger and more articulate proponent of the "Never!" ethos. When his term ended in January 1964, Barnett returned to his law practice but made a habit of appearing in public whenever White supremacy could be supported. One such notable appearance was during the last day of Byron De La Beckwith's first trial for the murder of Medgar Evers. Despite calling the assassination "a dastardly act" upon hearing of it in June of 1963, Barnett strode into the courtroom just a month after he stepped down as governor and walked up to the beleaguered Beckwith, shook his hand, and chatted him up for five minutes while the jury looked on, leaving no doubt as to where Barnett's White-supremacist allegiances lay.

"Ole Ross" ran again for governor of Mississippi in 1967 (term limits prevented him from serving consecutive terms) but lost badly, coming in fourth in the Democratic primary, thus ending his political career. By then, Mississippi had moved past "Never!" to a somewhat more accommodationist stance. Barnett, however, never recanted his staunch defense of segregation. "I wouldn't do a thing in the world I didn't do," Barnett told historians John Jones and John Dittmer in 1981. "I did the best I could and what I thought was right all the way down the line." Ross Barnett died at the age of eighty-nine in November 1987.[1]

SIDNEY ROEBUCK

Mississippi Commission on the War Between the States Director Sidney Roebuck remained a loyal servant to Ross Barnett's vision of what the Civil War centennial could mean for Mississippi—expanding tourism, celebrating Confederate mythology, and attempting to improve the image of America's poorest state. But it was an impossible task, given that the effort came at exactly the time when Mississippi's reputation was being tarnished by Barnett's intransigent segregationist rhetoric and actions. Roebuck gave up the ghost about a year prior to the official end of the centennial when the second biennial funding ran out on June 30, 1964. A year before that, in May of 1963, Roebuck wrote Barnett to update him on the commission's progress but also to let him know that things were winding down. "The question that is worrying me is this:" Roebuck stated, "Just what can we do during the last year to justify the expenditure of public funds?"

"We know that the people of this state are losing interest in the Centennial," he continued. "After July 4th [the Vicksburg commemoration] this drop in interest may be more apparent. It is remarkable that we have kept interest as high as we have in view of the turmoil created by the Kennedy Administration, with the help of the agitators, the Cubans and the Russians."

Roebuck, of course, was referring to the James Meredith crisis of the prior year, as well as to the ongoing racial disturbances that were then roiling the city of Jackson. "This is your Administration," Roebuck went on. "I am proud to be a part of it, and want to do all that I can to keep its activities on a high plane."[2]

In February of 1964, Roebuck wrote to Mississippi's newly installed governor, Paul Johnson Jr., inviting him to participate in the ceremonies at Brice's Cross Roads in June, noting that "this will be the last major event of this Commission because our appropriation runs out on July 1."[3] That's about as close as Roebuck came to saying farewell. Like an old soldier, he just faded away.

It might be a stretch to say that Roebuck "returned" to his law practice in Newton. Indeed, he had never left it. The commission's work had been an add-on gig for him from the get-go. Nevertheless, Roebuck resumed his Newton affiliations, his full-time law practice, and his volunteer engagements, thankful to have escaped Barnett's service with his reputation intact. He continued his work with the Lions Club, with the Mississippi Automobile Association, and as a Sunday school teacher with the First Baptist Church of Newton. He died in November of 1982 and is buried at Lakewood Memorial Cemetery in Jackson.[4]

JAMES MYRON WARD

Jackson Daily News editor Jimmy Ward continued to spill his bile into the news stream of Jackson for the next twenty-three years, never retreating from his racist, arch-segregationist positions long after they had ceased to be talking points for the Citizens' Council crowd. In 1964, when a small number of Black children were scheduled to begin integrating Jackson's public schools, Ward railed against the powers that had forced this eventuality upon his beloved city. "Time has taken its toll and Jackson falls unwillingly as a bastion of segregation," Ward lamented. "As the event came to pass," he continued, "the city becomes a little bit pregnant with integration, but the condition came about not voluntarily but with Federalized rape."

Ward finally retired from his post as *JDN*'s editor-in-chief at the start of 1984. He had been struggling with cancer for the prior eight years. The new editors for the paper, which had somewhat adapted to the times by then, gave a nod to the former editor's failings but overall gave him a pass. "Jimmy Ward's place in Mississippi history we leave to Mississippi historians," a *JDN* editorial pronounced. "To them he will be another figure in Mississippi's turbulent past." To the *JDN* staff, however, he was "someone special, more human than the pages of any historian."

With nothing left to say and nowhere else to say it, Ward died two months into his retirement at age sixty-five.[5]

ALLEN CAVETT THOMPSON

If obituaries and commemorative articles are to be believed, Mayor Allen Thompson was the most affable resident of the city of Jackson. That is how he managed to stay above the political fray for more than twenty years as the capital city's chief elected officer. In 1948, when Thompson was running for his first term as mayor, one of his buddies quipped that "Allen is going to smile himself into office. That's all he's got, a smile." His friendliness and good manners may have proved helpful on the campaign trail, but once in office, Thompson also showed himself to be a more than capable executive, overseeing key building programs and road projects that would transform tragic "Chimneyville" into a robust and thriving city. He was a visionary with one gaping blind spot: native Jacksonian Allen Thompson could not envision a world where Black and White people lived together equally in the same neighborhoods, shopped at the same stores, or ate at the same restaurants. It was impossible for him to imagine how people of differing racial compositions could enjoy together the many features of modern living that he so mightily labored to develop—schools, parks, buses, libraries, swimming pools, even golf courses.

Instead, Thompson became the spokesperson for segregation. He traveled far and wide telling citizens from all over America about "our way of life down South." As president of the American Municipal Association (now the National League of Cities), he had a platform to promote the benefits of the separate-but-equal doctrine, and he used it. Perhaps his most widely seen performance was in May 1961 with Dave Garroway on the *Today* show. In the wake of the Tougaloo Nine incident and the onslaught of the Freedom Riders, Thompson artfully and gregariously declaimed that "segregation is a way of life best for us," and, like Sidney Roebuck, "If we could just get some more of you Yankees and northerners down here, even if we don't' convince you, we can show you our wonderful way of life." (The prior year, Thompson had been invited to debate Martin Luther King Jr. on TV but demurred, realizing that even his ready smile and disingenuous way with words had their limits.)[6]

In the wake of the Jackson movement uprising of 1963, Thompson finally caved to the inevitable—and then only after intense pressure from President Kennedy himself—offering to hire one or two Black policemen and a few Black female crossing guards to help Black children cross the street to attend Black schools. For this minor affront to segregation orthodoxy, he was harassed and threatened by his former White supporters. The following year, in preparation for Freedom Summer, Thompson slipped back into his "law-and-order" stance and purchased a used, retrofitted US Army tank for the Jackson police force to patrol the streets of Mississippi's capital city. This may be the first example of the militarization of American policing.[7]

Thompson continued to resist the inevitability of integration. He testified before the Senate Judiciary Committee against the Civil Rights Bill of 1964, calling it "the most destructive Bill that has ever been presented to [this] august body." Even so, when the bill was signed by Lyndon Johnson in July 1964 and became the law of the land, Thompson urged his city's residents to comply. "We'll go along with it, though we don't like it," he said at a press conference just after the bill was signed. His reasoning had more to do with protecting the city he had worked so hard to modernize. He wanted to avoid race riots as well as federal intervention. "We'll operate within the law and you'll be protected from violence, bloodshed, . . . harassment and discomfort," he assured his skittish citizens.[8]

In July 1969, Thompson completed his fifth term in office and happily retired as mayor—the only job he ever really wanted. He then showed his true colors by helping to form and then lead the group Freedom of Choice in the US (FOCUS), which advocated for families to be able to choose the type of school their children attended and have the government pay for it—a not-so-subtle denunciation of public-school integration and a precursor of what would eventually become the charter-school movement. In October 1980, at the age of seventy-four, Thompson died of a heart attack while vacationing in Florida.[9]

MEADY BRADFORD (M. B.) PIERCE

Meredith Anding's neighbor, chief of detectives M. B. Pierce, died in 1979 of a heart attack at the age of sixty-one at the Mississippi Baptist Medical Center just a mile or so from police headquarters in downtown Jackson. He had lived most of his adult life at 1044 Claiborne Avenue, just blocks away from Jackson State College and from the Anding family homestead on Hattiesburg Street. Pierce had joined the Jackson Police Department in 1939 when he turned twenty-one. He was at the pinnacle of his power as chief of detectives in the 1960s and had a role in dealing with every major civil rights demonstration in the city of Jackson during that turbulent decade.

Pierce retired from the force in 1972 with a worn-out heart and having been demoted a few years earlier to assistant chief of detectives. He and his wife, Maude, had no children, so policing had been his life. By the time of his retirement, Jackson had moved on from its rigid segregationist stance. Odds are that Pierce had a hard time adjusting to the changing times. On the very same day that a brief notice of his death appeared in *The Clarion-Ledger*, the paper also carried a story about complaints over police brutality. A Black legislator stated that "if anything, relations [between police and the community] have deteriorated" in the past several years. M. B. Pierce is also buried at Jackson's Lakewood Memorial Park.[10]

G. W. "RED" HYDRICK

The man who accosted Medgar Evers as police chased Black onlookers away during the trial of the Tougaloo Nine would continue to harass civil rights demonstrators throughout the movement's days in Mississippi. His most infamous appearance would come on May 28, 1963, when a photographer captured his presence at the Jackson Woolworth's sit-in, this time not physically abusing the demonstrators, but instead breaching the peace by encouraging younger Johnny Rebs to perform more outrageous acts of violence against the "agitators." The bootlegger from across the river, who for most of his adult life was in trouble with the law himself over illegal alcohol sales and the resulting violent lifestyle that this entailed, even found himself deputized by Hinds County law enforcement "to help keep the law and order during these marches and sit-ins." This is according to his daughter, Willie Mae (Hydrick) Bradshaw, who wrote an adoring and mostly accurate (though incomplete) biography of her colorful father's antics. No mention is made of his mad, brutal assaults on Black photographer Thomas Armstrong and on Medgar Evers outside the courthouse during the Tougaloo Nine trial. The closest she comes to acknowledging her father's racial animus is admitting that "Big Red was a staunch segregationist," and noting that "he could become an irate person as he defended his family's honor or protected what was rightfully his."[11]

Hydrick's temper continued to get him in trouble with the law, including a charge for assault and battery with intent to kill just six months after his courthouse scuffle during the Tougaloo Nine trial and another assault charge two years later when he attacked two Black men whom he claimed were driving drunk and whose car had rolled down an embankment. The tipsy men were swearing when they (miraculously) exited the car. Red slugged the driver because, as he testified, "he was cursing in front of white women"—that is, those who gathered to see what had happened.[12]

Red Hydrick retired from "liquor distribution" when the State of Mississippi took over the regulation and sale of alcohol to increase its own coffers in July 1966. By then, he had made and lost several fortunes, and his family had seen much tragedy as the result of his chosen profession. He died in 1974 of a heart attack and collapsed behind his home, falling down a twenty-foot embankment into the Pearl River. His body was discovered two days later.[13]

WILLIAM JAMES SIMMONS

Of all the "Old Guard" characters in this chapter, William Simmons—"the brains" of the Citizens' Council movement according to journalist Bill Minor—was the most dogged, and his body of work had the longest reach. Through his various council information outlets—primarily *The Citizen* magazine and the *Forum* TV and radio series—his insistent call for White-supremacist rule found an ample audience far beyond the boundaries of Mississippi and even the American South. As the implications of the *Brown v. Board of Education* ruling became clear to White Americans throughout the country, Simmons's audience grew to include disgruntled Whites across the nation. These stirrings only increased over time as the US Supreme Court continued to break down racial discrimination in other areas of American life, especially in housing.

It was Simmons, beginning in 1964, who worked tirelessly to create the alternative "council schools"—seg (segregation) academies, as they were known—as options for Mississippi parents who refused to send their children to integrated public schools. In 1968, he also founded the Mississippi Private School Association to help coordinate activities among the growing number of private academies of which there would be more than 110 by 1972, spread across four states (Mississippi, Tennessee, Arkansas, and Louisiana) and boasting an enrollment of more than thirty thousand students. The organization, now known as the Midsouth Association of Independent Schools, continues to exist with more than 120 school affiliates, though many are now integrated.[14]

Not content to contain his objections to integration only to the South, Simmons looked beyond the borders of the United States for examples of White rule. He made an exploratory trip to Rhodesia (now Zimbabwe) and South Africa in 1967 and recorded eleven segments of his syndicated *Forum* TV and radio program with various leaders in the region, including Ian Smith, Rhodesia's White prime minister. Simmons returned praising the apartheid systems he encountered. "Whites are so united on the race question," he marveled while addressing a Jackson Citizens' Council meeting, "even 'moderates' believe in and advocate social separation of the races."[15]

Simmons also began dabbling in national electoral politics when he volunteered for the 1968 presidential campaign of George Wallace. Historian Stephanie Rolph notes, "Support for a white counterrevolution aligned the Council's priorities with a political insurgency that extended well beyond the South." But Wallace's near assassination and withdrawal from presidential politics in 1972 left Simmons and the council once again out in the cold, though moving more and more closely to an alignment with the quickly shifting Republican party, which was intent on capitalizing on White disenchantment. With the election of Ronald Reagan in 1980, Simmons finally realized the acceptance of his once-radical beliefs in what he hoped would be a forceful expression of white majority rule. "Almost too good to be true" an editorial appearing in his *Citizen* magazine proclaimed. He was now becoming mainstream.[16]

In 1989, the Citizens' Councils of America finally closed up shop, realizing that its programs of White defiance were being absorbed into national politics. Bill Simmons then made a hard pivot, at the age of seventy-three, and opened a bed-and-breakfast establishment in his expansive 1908 colonial revival childhood home in Jackson, which he managed, along with his wife, until shortly after his ninetieth birthday. (The Fairview Inn operates today under new management.) During his long life, Simmons had been a member of the Sons of Confederate Veterans and the Jackson Civil War Roundtable as well as various other civic and professional associations. William James Simmons died at age ninety-one in 2007.[17]

Some of those supporting the Mississippi infrastructure technically should not be included as members of the "Old Guard." They were mostly working to try to move Mississippi forward. Their stories are also captured here.

CHARLOTTE CAPERS

Charlotte Capers's can-do spirit infused everything she involved herself in, particularly her oversight of the Mississippi Department of Archives and History. Rarely did she allow her own political feelings to show while working for the state, even during the darkest days of the Mississippi's civil rights conflicts. Once, however, her guard slipped. It was in February 1964 during an evening over drinks and dinner with her friend Eudora Welty and the noted poet and author Robert Penn Warren, who was working on what would become the book *Who Speaks for the Negro?* Apparently, the threesome had a fine time sending up such Mississippi public figures as recently retired Governor Ross Barnett and newly sworn in Governor Paul Johnson Jr. Warren later wondered if he might use some of the material discussed without divulging the names of the women interviewed. Capers immediately saw the danger in such a plan and nixed it. "I think they would be reasonable in firing me when considering the use of the words: Idiot, drooling, face like an old wash rag, ripped right open like a hog killing, and defective child, in connection with the chief executive and the chief executive-to-be," she wrote Warren. He dropped the idea, and Capers kept her job.[18]

Capers continued to apply her unrelenting energies to State of Mississippi projects. After her success with the restoration of the Old Capitol Building, she was tasked with similar duties for the Governor's Mansion on Capitol Street and the William Faulkner House at Oxford on the Ole Miss campus. She also served for a time as the editor-in-chief of the *Journal of Mississippi History* and, in her spare time, wrote nearly one hundred book reviews for *The New York Times*. A small collection of her occasional column Miss Quote that appeared in Jackson newspapers over the years was published by the University Press of Mississippi in 1982 as *The Capers Papers*. Charlotte Capers left an enduring legacy to the State of Mississippi when she secured an agreement from Eudora Welty to leave her papers to the Department of Archives and History—a gift that keeps on giving to Welty scholars and historians of the period. Charlotte Capers retired in 1983 and died unexpectedly in 1996 at the age of eighty-three.[19]

EDWIN COLE BEARSS

After his surprising find of the USS *Cairo* along the banks of the Yazoo River in November 1956, Ed Bearss's reputation seemed to expand with every succeeding year. After the success of his Mississippi Civil War centennial–sponsored book *Decision in Mississippi* in 1962, Bearss produced *Rebel Victory at Vicksburg* the following year—this time sponsored by the Vicksburg Centennial Commemoration Commission and published on July 4, 1963, during the week-long Vicksburg centennial celebration. As a result, it too received a wide distribution within the state and earned Bearss a loyal Mississippi following. But it wasn't just Bearss's writings or his important discoveries of Civil War artifacts that distinguished him. Bearss was an "impresario of public history," as his biographer noted. He gave spellbinding tours of the Vicksburg battlefield and was able to keep in his head names, dates, and stories of various heroes of the war on both sides—and spout them at will—to the delight of all. For a time, his local fame rivaled that of the affable Vicksburg mayor and Mississippi Centennial Commission chairman John Holland.

After the centennial, Bearss' star began to burn so brightly that in 1966, the National Park Service (NPS) brass enticed him away from the Magnolia State to install him as one of the NPS's new stable of program developers and historians centralized in Washington, DC. There he distinguished himself as the most knowledgeable historian of all nineteenth- and twentieth-century national parks in the country. By 1981, he was named the NPS's chief historian, a post he would hold until 1994. In that capacity, Bearss often served as the NPS's star witness at congressional hearings, particularly as the agency attempted to beef up Congressional funding for this or that national park initiative. After a forty-year career with the NPS, Bearss retired in 1995 and embarked on a twenty-plus-year career as a battlefield tour guide—one that gave him unending joy and won for him an ever-widening circle of fans.

"My classroom is thousands of acres," he once told a *Washington Times* reporter. "I have thousands of students of all ages and expertise. I can't see being confined to a single room."

On a sunny afternoon in the spring of 2019, in perhaps the last substantive interview of his long life, Bearss held forth on his Arlington porch overlooking the Potomac about any number of issues and people associated with the Mississippi centennial, his important USS *Cairo* find, and the various NPS officials who helped advance his career. Six months later, in his last appearance before the DC Civil War Roundtable, he recounted his long career while describing in depth how he and some of his buddies discovered the Union ironclad ship and the years it took them to raise the funds to eventually have it resurrected, cleaned, and put on permanent display at the Vicksburg National Military Park. About a year later, on September 15, 2020, Ed Bearss died back where his career had begun, in Mississippi, where he had moved to be with one of his children who had settled there. He was ninety-seven years old and had been the last living member of the Mississippi Civil War Centennial Commission.[20]

Chapter 25

COMING FULL CIRCLE

SURELY BECAUSE OF HIS PERSONAL CONNECTION TO THE STATE, ROY Wilkins must have been elated to finally begin to crack open Mississippi's intractable segregationist culture with the Tougaloo Nine library sit-in of 1961. He seemed particularly proud that it had been college students aligned with the NAACP who had made the first move. For more than a year, the Student Nonviolent Coordinating Committee (SNCC) and its sponsor, Martin Luther King's Southern Christian Leadership Conference, had been taking a victory lap over the new spirit of assertiveness shown by the student movement that had emerged, seemingly spontaneously, in February 1960. But Wilkins was quick to point out that many of the students at the forefront of the emergent movement had come up through the NAACP's youth divisions: young people such as Evelyn Pierce, Albert Lassiter, Meredith Anding, and the Ladner sisters. At his speech in Philadelphia in July 1961, though preaching to the choir of NAACP members, he pressed the point: "The registration of these young people, these youngsters in the youth section and the men in their young business careers who have chosen to function through this organization would seem to disprove any idea that we have hardening of the arteries. . . . These delegates came to Philadelphia to report a year of tremendous activity over the whole range of civil rights issues."[1]

Wilkins also batted down the idea that the NAACP was past its prime. "It has been said that the NAACP is not dramatic and that it goes in the courtroom only and that nobody hears it argue but the judges and the lawyers. This is not exactly true," he proclaimed and then gave examples of progress made thanks to the NAACP's efforts. But these types of catty comments he heard from detractors about the NAACP being washed up must have stung a man who had spent nearly his entire adult life in the trenches building an effective organization that could become large enough and strong enough to take on the entire entrenched racism of American life. It had delivered with the *Brown v. Board* decision, only to be pushed aside by new upstart groups seeking quicker ways to freedom.

In his memoir, Wilkins tends to downplay his rivalry with the new vanguard, suggesting that he only once publicly criticized Martin Luther King Jr.

It was over a remark that King reportedly made to the gathering of young student activists on the campus of Shaw University in Raleigh when they were in the process of forming SNCC in April 1960. King was said to have taken a swipe at the go-slow process of the NAACP when he praised the students for "moving away from tactics which are suitable merely for gradual and long-term change." Wilkins took the remark as "a very low blow" and "felt called upon to respond harshly to Dr. King."[2] The two men patched up their differences privately, but woven through his Philadelphia speech runs a strong defense of the NAACP's local branch activism, supported by an over-arching national organization with the financial resources and legal muscle to front a challenge to Jim Crow laws and practices—gradually, perhaps, but persistently—in both the South and the North.

While touting the NAACP's fifty-two years of forceful attacks against lynching, redlining, and job discrimination, Wilkins makes the point that "the NAACP is the most powerful organization of its kind in the country."

Indeed, in his memoir, Wilkins showered faint praise upon those engaged in direct-action campaigns against discrimination while maintaining the need for a longer-term strategy. "I knew it was essential to keep the sit-ins and the prospect of direct action within proportion," he wrote. "The students were young, committed, and valiant, but . . . they would have no staying power beyond a few short years' time. My own experience had taught me that the struggle would still be going on long after they were out of college and immersed in other concerns. Only a strong organization like the NAACP could survive the wear that went on year after year after year."[3]

And survive it did. Long after SNCC fell apart; long after CORE inexplicably transferred into the hands of a right-wing extremist; long after SCLC, weakened after Dr. King's assassination in 1968, became not much more than a regional power; the NAACP kept pushing forward, always with a national agenda as well as a local presence nationwide. Wilkins himself began to slow down in the 1970s, though he never lost his commitment to the US Constitution nor his belief in the power of the rule of law, equally applied, to create gradual, sustainable change.

Wilkins retired as head of the NAACP in the mid-1970s after more than twenty years at the helm of the nation's most potent agency for social change. His transition to private life was "quite a rugged passage," he wrote. Bishop Spottswood, who served as board chairman from the time of the Freedom Train in 1961 until he died in late 1974. That loss to Wilkins's leadership team was followed a few months later by the death of long-time NAACP board president Kivie Kaplan, who, incidentally, had been a trustee of Tougaloo College. Into that vacuum swept a new breed of racially assertive Black leaders who felt Wilkins had outlasted his usefulness.

In July 1977, nearly fifty years since he began working for the organization, Wilkins stepped down as its leader. He then began writing his autobiography with the help of *Newsweek* reporter Tom Matthews. The work, *Standing Fast*, is a fascinating look at the life and times of a man who was in nearly every room where things happened with regard to civil rights in tumultuous mid-twentieth century America. Wilkins died in September 1981, a year before the book was released. It would be listed by *The New York Times* as one of its 1982 "Notable Books of the Year," along with biographies of other luminaries of that age, including social reformer Dorothy Day, Supreme Court chief justice Earl Warren, and Martin Luther King Jr.[4]

As for the organization that Wilkins led, the NAACP itself was in for some hard sledding in the decades ahead. A series of sexual-harassment and financial scandals rocked the civil rights bastion in the 1990s, forcing out the organization's executive director and spotlighting the lavish expense account of its chairman of the board. The ship was righted in 1995 by none other than Myrlie Evers, who by then had relocated to Los Angeles and married Union leader Walter Williams. Mrs. Evers-Williams won the NAACP's board chair seat by one vote and set about putting the organization's house in order. She was aided in this effort by future firebrand radio personality Joe Madison, who served as her campaign manager, and former SNCC communications director and former Georgia House of Representatives member Julian Bond, who succeeded her as chairman of the NAACP board three years later and held the post until 2010.[5]

Improbably, at least for this narrative, in 2017, the NAACP board selected Derrick Johnson as its new president and CEO. Johnson, a native of Detroit, traveled to Mississippi to attend Tougaloo College in the early 1990s, majored in political science, and graduated in 1994. He then earned his law degree from South Texas College of Law in Houston. Johnson returned to Jackson and became Mississippi's top NAACP representative, following in Medgar Evers's footsteps. Later, Johnson was elected to the NAACP's national board and served as its vice president before being elevated to the organization's top leadership position in 2017. A Tougaloo alum, a direct heir to the Evers legacy, now heads the most storied and respected civil rights organization in the United States. It is an improbable, full-circle occurrence that Roy Wilkins, with his own Mississippi story, would surely have relished.

For this work, achieving a complete full circle means a return to Gunnar Myrdal and *An American Dilemma*. Myrdal made an astute observation within the first several paragraphs of his mammoth work. In chapter 1, titled

"American Ideals and America's Conscience," Myrdal asserted that in attempting to live up to its foundational promises, "America is continuously struggling for its soul."[6] Seventy-five years after this assessment was first recorded, then-candidate Joe Biden made "A Battle for the Soul of America" the central theme of his presidential campaign.[7] At the time, this concept seemed a bit of a throwback, somewhat old fashioned. Who talks about *souls* anymore in this age of data-driven analytics and economic imperatives? And yet, the winning Biden call to conscience is a reminder that members of each generation must find a way to hold America responsible for fulfilling its aspirational ideals. The Tougaloo Nine—and many others of that generation—did their part to remind the country of its unfulfilled promise and of its untapped potential. As a result, things changed, and we are a better people because of their activism. May their example lead us to take up that same banner and run with it.

Epilogue

THE LEGACY OF THE TOUGALOO NINE

IN 2014, JUST AS THIS PROJECT WAS GETTING UNDERWAY, I HAD THE opportunity to sit down with legendary Mississippi political reporter Bill Minor at his home in north Jackson. He was in his nineties by then and had been covering Mississippi for more than sixty years. He had seen it all, from Bilbo to Barnett, through the Citizens' Council and the Sovereignty Commission years when the state spied on its own people just to preserve racial purity and its much-revered segregated society. He had been on the scene at all of the major civil rights protests that happened in Jackson and thus had a unique perspective on the one that, for all intents and purposes, started it all—the one he tagged as "the *so-called* read-in."[1]

For Minor, the demonstration pulled off by nine Tougaloo students and their advisors seemed like "the most timid challenge" to segregation that he could imagine. "I mean, people didn't stand up waiting to get into the library back then," he observed, so what, he seemed to ask, was the point? Perhaps like many White progressives, the seasoned reporter was looking for bombast, for drama, for a big, bold march with hundreds if not thousands in the streets demanding change. That would come two years later as Mississippi's power structure dug in its heels and refused to compromise on even the most modest of demands for social equality from its African American citizens.

Minor's assessment seems to jibe with that of many White observers who felt that Mississippi's docile Black populace just wouldn't have the nerve to shake up the racial status quo. "Blacks had done nothing to challenge any segregation laws or customs," Minor complained. (Not exactly true since, as we have seen, Dr. Mason had challenged the "Whites-only" beaches along the Gulf Coast in 1959 and again in 1960.)

"Blacks in Mississippi were more docile," Minor continued. "They were not nearly as activist as they were in Virginia and North Carolina."

"I think it was the plantation mentality that had been handed down to them," the seasoned reporter opined. "They had lived a life that really didn't have any individual freedom."

For Minor, the question seems to have been: Would Mississippi Blacks ever have stood up for own their citizenship rights without the help of what came to be known as "outside agitators"? Had all of the Freedom-minded Black people already been chased from the state and moved elsewhere? Would Mississippi's seemingly invincible fortress of segregation ever be challenged from within, given the harsh and potentially violent consequences to anyone who dared to push for change?

Minor wasn't so sure. But it appears that if the Tougaloo Nine demonstration—as timid as it may have seemed—proved anything, it proved that challenging the system (albeit politely, positively, and nonviolently) was indeed possible. And such challenges would only get more forceful and more focused once this first student-led direct-action protest occurred.

As this volume chronicles, after the Tougaloo Nine demonstration, local youth began sitting in on the buses, sitting down at the zoo, and even attempting to enter the public swimming pools. A local movement *was* under development even before the Freedom Riders arrived to steal the headlines and shock the local citizens into believing they were under attack from an outside force.

Not only that, but the "read-in" caused Jackson State's mostly Mississippi-born and -bred students to become deeply engaged in the struggle. Their uprising—even at the risk of expulsion from this publicly funded institution—shocked not only Whites but the Blacks who were responsible for the school's management and development.

It must also be remembered that the harsh way the police reacted to the exuberant crowd at the trial of the Tougaloo Nine—with vicious police dogs attacking defenseless Black citizens—made national news and put the state on notice that such behavior was un-American. The FBI stepped in and started taking depositions the next day.

Perhaps more importantly, the Tougaloo action and its aftermath caused Roy Wilkins and the national NAACP finally to believe that putting the full force of its considerable legal and fundraising prowess behind a local movement in Mississippi would be worthwhile, particularly because it *was* homegrown and supported by the local Black populace. Although it is difficult to assess the overall impact of Operation Mississippi, what is clear is that for the first time, the civil rights organization put significant effort into telling the true Mississippi story, countering the false narrative being peddled by the Sovereignty Commission and the Citizens' Council propaganda.

In addition, it cannot be underestimated that the Tougaloo Nine demonstration occurred the day before Mississippi's blowout Secession Day festivities, poking a hole in that Lost Cause hot-air balloon before it even got off the ground—a deep embarrassment to Barnett, Thompson, Roebuck, and all those who saw the Civil War centennial as an opportunity to sell the state's "mint-juleps-and-magnolias" image to tourists nationwide. Concerns by American citizens that Mississippi was a scary place to visit would be completely confirmed the following year when the NAACP-funded challenge to the Magnolia State's strictly segregated educational system blew up with the Meredith crisis, leaving two dead, many more injured, and the campus of Ole Miss in ruins.

This "most timid challenge" to segregation at the library wrought huge changes to the consciousness of Mississippi's Black populace. It was a start. It showed that with proper planning and flawless execution, Blacks citizens could effectively and publicly resist segregation's strong grip, point a way forward to a more equitable society, and live to tell the tale. "It lit a light in the darkness," Minor finally conceded, a light that inspired others to do their part to challenge the prevailing White-supremacist orthodoxy and created a more just society.

THE INSPIRATION OF THE TOUGALOO NINE

In the Rayburn House Office Building, just steps from the US Capitol, on the wall of Congressman Bennie Thompson—the only Black member of Mississippi's US congressional delegation—hangs a colorful artistic rendering of the Tougaloo Nine. The painting, by artist and former Tougaloo College art chair Johnnie Mae Maberry, includes caricature portraits of the nine individuals who changed history, along with a collage of news reports announcing their breakthrough feat. Their countenances hover like angels over the room, welcoming each visiting group of constituents who enter Thompson's comfortably furnished and spacious office.

"I've had that picture on my wall ever since I moved here to Congress in 1993," Thompson told me. "The Tougaloo Nine were an inspiration to me to get more involved in activism and in trying to make a difference."

Thompson, you see, is also a Tougaloo grad, entering just after the heyday of the Tougaloo Nine and the heroes of the Woolworth's sit-in. He graduated from "The Loo" in 1968. And what specifically did they inspire him to do? "As a student, I did voter registration, in the Mississippi Dela, primarily"—the area for which he now has served as congressman for more than thirty years. "And I participated in the Meredith march from Memphis to Jackson," he recalled—that 1966 culturally transitional march that transformed the quest for equality into a demand for "Black Power."

"I was inspired by the fact that these brave Tougaloo students had the audacity to go to downtown Jackson to the library," Thompson said. "That was unheard of at the time."

We inevitably mused over what it was like to attend Tougaloo College during that ripe period of change. "Tougaloo, for people like me, helped take the blinders off in terms of what needed to be done to make a difference," Thompson told me. "But it also gave me courage that not only was it the right thing to do, but it was what we still call that 'Tougaloo Spirit.' Folks who went to Tougaloo," he chuckled, "were just a little different."

He reminisced about seeing such movement luminaries on campus as Stokely Carmichael, H. Rap Brown, Dick Gregory, and Harry Belafonte—even Martin Luther King Jr. "on numerous occasions" before his tragic assassination in April 1968. In fact, he recounted with grief, "one of the sadder moments: I'm one of two students selected from Tougaloo to attend the funeral of Dr. King."

As he spoke to me, despite discussing some dark topics of the past, Thompson seemed grateful to have an excuse to take a break from his high-profile duties. After paying his dues on the back bench of the Democratic Party's congressional caucus, Thompson, at the time we spoke in late September 2022, was serving as chairman of the House Committee on Homeland Security—a key post in defending the country's security from "enemies foreign and domestic." He was named by House Speaker Nancy Pelosi to head the House's Select Committee to Investigate the January 6 Attack—that day when hordes of mostly White American citizens brought implements of war (and even a large Confederate flag) to the US Capitol, engaged in hand-to-hand combat with Capitol police, and fought their way into America's sacred shrine of democracy in an attempt to stop the certification of the election of the president of the United States.

I caught up with Thompson just two days before the last of his nine flawless and impactful televised hearings on the attack was ready to kick off.[2] You would have thought he had nothing else on his mind. The memories of his time at Tougaloo—and the impact that college experience had on his life—was all he wanted to talk about. "The 'Good Ole Days' are the best," he remarked. Besides the inspiration of the Tougaloo Nine and their movement prodigy, Thompson readily talked about the Tougaloo culture. "It was a place that fostered diversity, fostered individualism, to 'Dare to Be Different.'"

As so many who took in the Tougaloo vibe, Thompson mentioned listening to the lectures of Dr. Ernst Borinski and attending his Social Science Lab. "You can only imagine . . . a student from Bolton, Mississippi, sitting in the Social Science Forums listening to Martin Luther King Jr. or Stokely Carmichael!" Bolton, Mississippi, then a rural town on the western edge of Hinds County, had a population in 1960 of about eight hundred souls. At Tougaloo, the world came into sharper focus for this small-town dreamer.

Thompson graduated from Tougaloo College in 1968 and almost immediately entered politics, winning a seat in 1969—at the age of twenty-one—as
alderman on Bolton's town council. Four years later, after earning a graduate
degree from Jackson State, he was elected Bolton's mayor. After more than
ten years serving in local elective offices, Thompson won a seat on the Hinds
County Board of Supervisors in 1980. He then shifted onto the national stage
by winning election to the US House of Representatives in 1993, where he
continues to serve the second district of Mississippi—a district that includes
parts of Jackson and nearly all of the Mississippi Delta.

Once he arrived in the halls of Congress, Thompson worked to show his
love for Tougaloo—the place that seems to have made him what he is today.
He helped raise funds for a complete restoration of the Woodworth Chapel
and created a lasting memorial to Borinski by finding funds to build a modern meeting space, complete with auditorium and brightly lit classrooms and
conference areas, on the grounds of what had once stood Beard Hall, the site
of Borinski's Social Science Lab. This modernist building is now called the
Bennie G. Thompson Center for Education and the Study of Civil Rights,
honoring one of Tougaloo's more recent guardian angels. Given pride of place
in the entrance to the building is a floor-to-ceiling photographic mural of
the Tougaloo Nine being escorted from the library by a cohort of Jackson's
finest, providing activist inspiration for generations to come.

Thompson draws a throughline from his time at Tougaloo to his time at
the top echelon of power in the US Congress. "If it's not right, then you need
to do everything you can to change it," he said. "I kind of have lived that my
entire life and continue to do that."

And how does the Tougaloo Nine demonstration fit into all of this? "Well,
first of all, it gave bragging rights to Tougaloo," Thompson says with pride
about the first student-led demonstration for civil rights in the state of Mississippi. "But they also set a high bar for everybody who matriculated [there],
that you had to be involved; that sure, it was about academics, but it was also
working to make this country a better place."[3]

There are other voices to consult about the impact of the Tougaloo Nine.
One of them is Myrlie Evers, wife of Medgar, who served as his secretary at
the NAACP offices on Lynch Street until their third child was born in 1960.
Myrlie tends to agree with Bill Minor's assessment of the initial impact of
the Tougaloo Nine. But she put it in a broader context and thus elevated it
to pride of place, just as Congressman Thompson did. "The change of tide in

Mississippi did not begin until 1961," she wrote in her memoir *For Us, the Living*. "Then, almost imperceptibly, Negroes took the offensive in the struggle for full citizenship. It began . . . when nine Negro students from Tougaloo Southern Christian College . . . entered Jackson's white public library, sat down, and began to read."[4]

A change of tide, the start of a wave, almost imperceptible, yet with mounting power, the civil rights movement—with leaders from without and from within—began to change the fabric of the closed society. By 1969, the Mississippi Sovereignty Commission closed its doors. The spying on private citizens for exercising their rights of assembly and speech had ended. It took another twenty years for the Citizens' Council to shutter, having lost most of its members and all of its unconstitutional state funding long before. "Organized racism" went out of business.[5] And it all happened because of the radical idea that everyone is equal: everyone, for example, should be allowed to go to the library, sit down, and read. It is an idea that continues to have currency today as school boards ban books and libraries become the last bastion of an open, civil society. Congressman Thompson's example demonstrates that this so called "most-timid challenge" of the Tougaloo Nine still has relevance and power today. A small ripple of hope, "a light in the darkness" as Bill Minor came to understand it, can, indeed, begin to change the world.

HONORS AND COMMEMORATIONS FOR THE TOUGALOO NINE

Sometimes it takes a while for history to catch up with itself and recognize the start of an important social movement. By 2006, it seems, all had been forgiven the Tougaloo Nine when the Jackson city council welcomed them back to town. No longer under threat of arrest, the seven of the nine who were able to attend received the red-carpet treatment, complete with a key to the city and special proclamations. By then, of course, Jackson had changed dramatically. Despite the fact that it continued to serve as the state capital, White flight from the city in the late 1960s and throughout the 1970s had hollowed out its tax base, thus eroding the ability for the city to provide essential services. Politically, Jackson became a majority Black city with a majority Black city council and a Black mayor. It was, in fact, city councilman Leslie McLemore, a contemporary of the Tougaloo Nine and then-Jackson State professor and founder of the Fannie Lou Hamer Institute on Citizenship and Democracy, who sponsored the proclamation honoring the "valiant efforts" of the Tougaloo Nine. In connection with the city's fete, Tougaloo College held an all-day seminar in commemoration of the Tougaloo Nine's contributions.

This was not the first time the Nine had been invited back to Tougaloo to be honored. In 1991, on the thirtieth anniversary of the historic library sit-in, Tougaloo College held a special program commemorating the school's singular role in kick starting the student movement in Mississippi. Then again, in 2011—the fiftieth anniversary year of the demonstration—the group was invited back for the college's Founder's Day week and honored at an evening event where historian John Dittmer emceed a program of recollection, calling upon the activists to reach deeply into their memories to recall specifics of their experiences at the forefront of Mississippi activism.

In 2017, thanks to the efforts of Jackson Municipal Library workers, the State of Mississippi erected an historic marker at the site where the Tougaloo Nine entered the library on North State Street. Once again, those available gathered to swap stories and commemorate their bold action. Then in May 2021, to honor the sixtieth anniversary of their breakthrough achievement, Tougaloo College awarded the Nine with honorary doctorates in humane letters. Three of the Nine were on hand to accept their scrolls. Later that year, all surviving members of the group participated in a Tougaloo video conference recounting their historic stand while encouraging students to get involved in the challenging events of the current day just as they themselves had done during their own college heyday. In addition, *USA Today* developed a long-form newspaper and podcast series titled *Seven Days of 1961* exploring "how sustained acts of resistance can bring about sweeping change." The Tougaloo Nine Library Sit-In was featured along with the Freedom Rides and the integration of the University of Georgia, among other events that helped move the push for equality forward.[6]

Appreciation for the Tougaloo Nine has only grown over time, with many civil rights veterans recognizing that before the Student Nonviolent Coordinating Committee came to Mississippi, before the Freedom Riders reached Jackson—in other words, before outside help arrived—the Tougaloo Nine made it their mission to call for a free and open society within the confines of a determinedly closed Mississippi. They were early participants in the long, hard, and still-current effort of direct, nonviolent resistance to the oppressive forces that seem to morph and reappear with each successive generation. As the song says, "Freedom Is a Constant Struggle." And that struggle continues . . .

ACKNOWLEDGMENTS

IT COULD REASONABLY BE SAID THAT THIS BOOK HAD ITS START AT A reception at Jackson State University in the spring of 2013. That's when the documentary film *An Ordinary Hero*—in which I provide on-camera commentary—had its Jackson premier on the fiftieth anniversary of the Jackson Woolworth's sit-in, the subject of my first book. While balancing a small plate of veggies and fruit in one hand and a plastic cup of chardonnay in the other, I spied Sam Bradford, one of the Tougaloo Nine, across the reception area adjacent to the screening room just before the film was about to begin.

I knew James "Sammy" Bradford from photos and by reputation. He was a short, well-built, distinguished man who had made it part of his life's mission to promote the importance of the Tougaloo Nine at any and every opportunity. For him, there were many of these, seeing as how he lived in the small enclave of homes adjacent to the campus of Tougaloo College and was therefore called upon regularly to represent the Nine whenever academics or administrators put together a panel lauding the heroism of its students and faculty during the civil rights era. What I didn't know is that he could be *very* convincing.

I slow walked my way over to meet Sam, wondering how I'd manage to hold both drink and plate while shaking his hand—a perennial problem at receptions. Luckily, he was standing by a table, so I put down my drink, reached out my hand to him, and introduced myself. After some small talk, mostly about my book and the sit-in anniversary we were there to celebrate, Sam baited the hook. He intently looked me in the eyes and earnestly said, "I know why this demonstration gets all the attention . . . it was so *dramatic*. But ours was the *first*!" His determined stare and his quavering voice both beckoned me to pay attention as he laid out the reasons why *somebody* ought to write a book about the Tougaloo Nine; *somebody* ought to make a movie.

Apparently, this was a practiced pitch Sam had perfected over the years. I wasn't getting any special treatment because I was the "author in the room." It was clear he had made the same plea hundreds of times. You could see it in his eyes, hear it in his weary voice. His direct approach took me aback at first. Here I am, a first-time author, having just completed a twenty-year saga to get my first book published, and he's suggesting I take on another impossible project? It was more than I could reasonably consider at that moment. I made some encouraging, noncommittal remark like, "You've got a good point there, Sam," picked up my drink, and made my way to the theater.

Not until months later, while casting about for my next project, did I realize Sam had hooked me. I couldn't get his desperate eyes and his convincing arguments out of my mind. No matter what other concept I considered, I always came back to the Tougaloo Nine. It was a no-brainer. I was already familiar with many of the Tougaloo and Jackson figures who would come into play. And I had done a good deal of research at the two most relevant archives where materials could be found: the Library of Congress in Washington, DC, near where I live, which contains the millions of pages of the NAACP archives, meticulously kept and catalogued; and the Mississippi Department of Archives and History in Jackson, which houses nearly all of the relevant newspapers and journals—and, as I would discover, even diaries and interviews—that could provide many of the first-hand accounts of the Tougaloo Nine incident.

Still, though, did I want to spend another ten years focusing on Jackson? It would certainly allow me to go deeper into the origin story of the Jackson movement and the early days of Medgar Evers's activist period, which I thought had received limited exposure in my first book. I decided to consult John Dittmer's *Local People*, the first major historical look at the civil rights movement in Jackson (as well as other places in Mississippi) during the 1950s and 1960s, before making my final decision. I remembered that Dittmer had touched on the library sit-in as one data point of a growing movement in Jackson. A closer look showed that his three-page summary of the event was loaded with important details, including the fact that the sit-in had touched off an uprising of sympathy at nearby Jackson State College; that the next day Mississippi celebrated the centennial of its secession from the Union; and that the trial of the Tougaloo Nine the day after the centennial caused the police to overreact to enthusiastic Black supporters of the demonstrators as they made their way to the courthouse. Dittmer's concise yet dramatic description sealed the deal. Sam Bradford had finally won his point and *someone*—me—was going to finally write a book about the Tougaloo Nine.

There are many people to thank for help along the way. Although writing is often a singular profession, it is rarely done without the help of many others. Chief among these were, of course, the Tougaloo Nine themselves, nearly all of whom gave their time and, importantly, their recollections to this examination of their lives and the historic sit-in that they planned and executed flawlessly. Those who participated fully with this quest were Meredith Anding Jr., James "Sammy" Bradford, Geraldine Edwards (Hollis), Janice Jackson (Vails), Joseph Jackson Jr., Albert Lassiter Sr., and Ethel Sawyer (Adolphe). Fortunately for me, despite the more than fifty years that had intervened from the time of the sit-in to the time I undertook its chronicling, only one of the Nine—Evelyn Pierce—had passed on. Her older sister Armendia Dixon and her younger sister Demathraus Pierce Perry provided crucial family background and personal stories about Evelyn, who later in life would be known as Ameenah E. P. Omar. Alfred Cook was the only holdout—there always seems to be one. Al was planning on writing his own book about his eventful "rags-to-riches" story but never lived long enough to complete the task. We met several times at public events celebrating the Tougaloo Nine and he was always encouraging about the overall project but was adamant about not sitting for an interview. Fortunately he left enough of a public record of his life and legacy through his various public speaking engagements, newspaper accounts, and even an authorized Tougaloo Alumni Facebook post so that much of his inspiring story can be presented amid these pages.

I might never have met the members of the Tougaloo Nine except for the generosity of Dr. Daphne Chamberlain, formerly of Tougaloo College. Dr. Chamberlain had planned both the forty-fifth and the fiftieth anniversary celebrations and was one of the few (if not the *only*) to have the contact information for most of those still living when I embarked upon this project. She graciously offered to provide an introduction and get authorization from the Nine for me to contact them directly. I am forever in her debt, not only for that intervention but also for her extraordinary dissertation about youth activism in Jackson from 1947 through 1970, which provided a map to follow in the early stages of my research. Not only that, but Dr. Chamberlain also served as one of the readers of the first draft of this manuscript, providing critical insight that helped shape its final form.

When I told him what I was up to, Dr. John Dittmer gave an important "thumbs up" to the project. Dr. Robert Luckett of Jackson State University's Margaret Walker Center provided important resource suggestions. He also directed me to the center's own cache of oral histories, collected mostly in the 1970s, which enriched my understanding of the events of March 27, 28, and 29, 1961, most importantly through an early interview with Dr. Colia Liddell Lafayette Clark—a significant and often overlooked figure in the early Jackson movement. I am also grateful to have had the opportunity to interview Dr. Clark myself as the project unfolded.

Not only libraries, but librarians were crucial to this work. I want to thank several by name: Patrick Kerwin at the Library of Congress's Manuscript Reading Room proved crucial in finding several needles in the large NAACP Papers haystack. In addition, Adrienne Cannon, manuscript specialist, provided me with a sneak peek at the library's newest catalogued NAACP archive, its "NAACP Records X" (named thus—I call them the X Files—because there are nine [IX] earlier sections to the NAACP Papers). This latest addition to the library's cache incorporates all of the documents that had once been housed in the NAACP's own Henry Lee Moon Library at its headquarters in Baltimore. That archive in its entirety was sent to the Library of Congress sometime in the early 2000s and has only recently (2023) been opened to the public. Many thanks to Ms. Cannon for listening to my pleas and those of other researchers to get these files catalogued and open to the public.

At the Mississippi Department of Archives and History (MDAH), I have been served by many excellent archivists. Two of note are Clint Bagley (now retired) and William Thompson. It was at MDAH that I found, among other treasures, the extensive records of the Mississippi Commission on the War Between the States, which provided an extraordinary look into the workings of this commemorative group. In addition, MDAH holds the Myrlie and Medgar Evers archive, part of the Tougaloo College Collection. That's where I found the ledger books with handwritten minutes of the meetings of the Jackson NAACP branch (many written by the hand of Myrlie Evers) from the years 1955 through 1959, among other gems.

One additional archivist who was inordinately helpful was Tony Bounds, Institutional Historian at Tougaloo College. At small independent colleges, individual staffers typically wear many hats. This is true of Tony Bounds, who not only oversees Tougaloo's special collections, but he also teaches, engages the student body on research projects, and serves as liaison with the Mississippi Department of Archives and History on their collaborative records sharing partnership. I am grateful for Tony's time and assistance on several occasions, allowing me to page through Tougaloo's yearbooks from years past, offering me the opportunity to look through the John Dee Mangram collection, and even facilitating the permissions for me to review the Tougaloo Board of Trustee minutes from the 1950s and early 1960s.

Finding photographs to help visually tell the story of the Tougaloo Nine proved particularly challenging. Many thanks to Andrew McNulty, Historic Research Specialist, and Celia Tisdale, Audiovisual Archivist, at MDAH for their sleuthing and assistance. Thanks as well to the archivists at the Library of Congress's Prints and Photographs Division.

Of course, I am indebted to Craig Gill and his team at the University Press of Mississippi (UPM), who have guided this manuscript from its earliest stages and who have produced, as always, a top-quality work of craftsmanship and editorial finesse that any author would be happy to be associated with. Thanks, too, to the additional UPM-commissioned civil rights scholars who read and commented on earlier drafts of this work. Their efforts brought clarity and focus to the work, and I am indebted to their thoroughness and candor. I also must thank the Author's Guild, of which I am a proud member, who helped review my contract with UPM and made important suggestions, including in the crucial new area of artificial intelligence protections.

I must thank family and friends who during the past dozen years listened to endless stories about whatever aspect of the Tougaloo Nine saga I was uncovering at any given time. In particular, thanks to Dick and Jane Vodra, Libby and Don Robinson, Dana Greene and Richard Roesel, Jack and Paula Bruggeman, and Jeff and Diana Burnam for their seemingly unquenchable appetite for the smallest detail and their willingness to keep asking "How's the book coming along, Mike?" Dick Vodra in particular had a unique part to play in the book's development. Once he heard me talking about the Civil War Centennial Commission, he quickly put me in touch with his brother Bill, a trustee of the American Battlefield Trust. Bill Vodra is the one who introduced me to his good friend Ed Bearss, who recounted in detail his time with the Vicksburg National Military Park and his role in the Mississippi centennial. Small world.

Professional acquaintances were also a great gift during this period. In particular, Leigh Ann Wheeler of Binghamton University/State University of New York, would often send me a clipping or a reference to the Tougaloo Nine as she worked away at her own project, a biography of activist and author Anne Moody, whom I had earlier written about in *We Shall Not Be Moved*. We have swapped notes repeatedly over the years, and I am grateful for her involvement and her friendship.

A big shout out also goes to Kathy Mosely, president of the Washington Area Tougaloo Alumni Chapter, for arranging the introduction to Congressman Bennie Thompson. Many thanks, also, to the congressman and his capable staff for their time and efforts on my behalf.

And then there's my family, most especially my wife, "Lady Allyson"— Tougaloo Nine member Joe Jackson gave her that moniker during our many calls with him over the years. Writing this book took me away from home more times than I can remember, but Allyson was always accepting, always cheering me on, always interested in how things were progressing during our nightly calls while I was either away researching or writing. Her interest and support are what kept me going, and that is why the book is dedicated to her along with the amazing Tougaloo Nine themselves. Thank you, Allyson, for your constant support and encouragement. Thank you Tougaloo Nine for sharing your memories of those troubled yet glorious times. And thank you, dear reader, for your interest in this vital part of our American story.

ABBREVIATIONS

A&RSD	Audiovisual and Research Services Division
CL	*The Clarion-Ledger* (Jackson, MS)
CWCC	Civil War Centennial Commission
DDT	*Delta Democrat-Times*
HBCU	Historically Black College and University
JA	*The Jackson Advocate*
JDN	*Jackson Daily News*
JSU	Jackson State University
MDAH	Mississippi Department of Archives and History
MCWBTS	Mississippi Commission on the War Between the States
MSCP	Mississippi Sovereignty Commission Papers
MWC	Margaret Walker Center
MCA	Millsaps College Archives
NA	National Archives
NPS	National Park Service
NYT	*The New York Times*
NYT Mag.	*New York Times Magazine*
NOTP	New Orleans *Times-Picaynne*
NR	*Northside Reporter*
NYWT&S	*New York World Telegram & Sun*
PC	*Pittsburgh Courier*
ST	(Jackson) *State Times*
SCSL-W&M	Special Collections, Swem Library, William & Mary College
TCC-MDAH	Tougaloo College Collection at MDAH
TCA-TC	Tougaloo College Archives at Tougaloo College
TSCC-BoTM	Tougaloo Southern Christian College-Board of Trustees Minutes
WP	*Washington Post*

NOTES

PROLOGUE

1. Gunnar Myrdal, *An American Dilemma: The Negro Problem and Modern Democracy* (New York: Haper & Brothers, 1944—single volume ed.), 3.

CHAPTER 1—AMERICA'S DILEMMA

1. See Keppel's foreword to Myrdal, *An American Dilemma*, v–vi. The Laura Spelman Rockefeller Fund was absorbed into the Rockefeller Foundation in 1929, just after Myrdal was awarded his fellowship.

2. For a list of possible study leads, see "Negro Study, Personnel Suggestions through July 15, 1937," Carnegie-Myrdal Study, Carnegie Corporation of New York Records, Columbia University, https://doi.org/10.7916/d8-af26-8q30, accessed January 31, 2024. Myrdal background derived from Egon Matzner, "Portrait: Gunnar Myrdal," *Challenge*, 20, no. 2 (1977): 67–68; and "Gunnar Myrdal: Biographical," The Nobel Prize, https://www.nobelprize.org/prizes/economic-sciences/1974/myrdal/biographical/, accessed January 13, 2024.

3. Initiation of study: Myrdal, *An American Dilemma*; Keppel's foreword, vi; Baker's background: *An American Dilemma*, vi; and David W. Southern, *Gunnar Myrdal and Black-White Relations: The Use and Abuse of An American Dilemma 1944–1969* (Baton Rouge: Louisiana State University Press, 1987), 1–4.

4. Myrdal, *An American Dilemma*, ix–xx.

5. "American Dilemma," *Time*, February 4, 1944, https://content.time.com/time/magazine/article/ 0.9171.791292.00.html. For a summary of various reviews and reactions to *An American Dilemma*, both in the academic and popular press, see Southern, *Gunnar Myrdal and Black-White Relations*, 71–99. Also see Walter A. Jackson, *Myrdal and America's Conscience: Social Engineering and Racial Liberalism, 1938–1987* (Chapel Hill: University of North Carolina Press, 1990), 231–71.

6. For Myrdal's in-depth discussion of the "American Creed," see Myrdal, *An American Dilemma*, 3–25.

7. Joseph Jackson Jr., the oldest member of the Tougaloo Nine, was born in 1937; the youngest member, James "Sammy" Bradford, was born in 1942.

8. Myrdal, *An American Dilemma*, li–lii. At the time, Black people comprised about 10 percent of the US population. See US Census data, 1940, https://www.archives.gov/research/census/1940.

9. Myrdal, *An American Dilemma*, 24.

10. Martin Luther King Jr., "I Have a Dream" (emphasis added), https://www.npr.org/2010/10/18/122701268/i-have-a-dream-speech-in-its-entirety, accessed January 11, 2024.

11. For Bunche contributions, see David W. Southern, "An American Dilemma after Fifty Years: Putting the Myrdal Study and Black-White Relations in Perspective," *The History Teacher* 28, no. 2 (1995): 239. Also see Jackson, *Gunnar Myrdal and America's Conscience*, "Myrdal and Bunche," 121–31. Bunche's four essays were titled as follows: "The Political Status of the Negro," "The Programs, Ideologies, Tactics, and Achievements of Negro Betterment and Interracial Organizations," "Conceptions and Ideologies of the Negro Problem," and "A Brief and Tentative Analysis of Negro Leadership." "The Political Status of the Negro" was eventually edited and published as *The Political Status of the Negro in the Age of F. D. R.* by the University of Chicago Press in 1973.

12. W. E. B. Du Bois, "Review: The American Dilemma," *Phylon* 5, no. 2 (1944): 118, 121–24. Myrdal consulted at least twice with Du Bois on the project and borrowed liberally from his scholarship. See Southern, *Gunnar Myrdal and Black-White Relations*, 21, 212. For characterization of Du Bois, see Roy Wilkins, *Standing Fast* (New York: Viking Press, 1982), 93, 149.

13. Niebuhr as quoted in Southern, *Gunnar Myrdal and Black-White Relations*, 97. Southern also records Howard Odum and other Southern intellectuals' reactions, 77–85.

14. Myrdal, *An American Dilemma*, 60–61.

15. Richard R. Aguirre, "Martin Luther King Jr.'s Visit to Goshen College in 1960 Inspired the Entire Campus," Goshen College, https://www.goshen.edu/ciie/intercultural/goshen-visit/, accessed October 8, 2022.

16. For an alternative critique of Myrdal's work and the Carnegie Corporation's involvement, see Maribel Morey's *White Philanthropy: Carnegie Corporation's 'An American Dilemma' and the Making of a White World Order* (Chapel Hill: University of North Carolina Press, 2021).

17. As quoted by David M. Kennedy, "The Making of a Classic," *The Atlantic*, May 1987, 86–89.

18. Charles E. Wilson (chair), "Assignment from the President," *To Secure These Rights: The Report of the President's Committee on Civil Rights* (New York: Simon and Schuster, 1947), vii.

19. For more on the impact of *An American Dilemma* on various American institutions, see Southern, *Gunnar Myrdal and Black-White Relations*, 101–54. The Symington story appears on p. 120. The footnote that Symington refers to appears in Myrdal, *An American Dilemma*, 101. Shaw's actual quote is "The haughty American Nation . . . makes the negro clean its boots and then proves the moral and physical inferiority of the negro by the fact that he is a shoeblack." In addition, see Jackson, *Gunnar Myrdal and America's Conscience*, 293–302. Myrdal is formally referenced just once in *To Secure These Rights*, 145.

20. Humphrey story and quote found in Southern, *Gunnar Myrdal and Black-White Relations*, 124.

21. Brown et al. v. Board of Education of Topeka et al., 347 US483 (1954), n. 11. The footnote specifically references several psychologists and social scientists, including Kenneth B. Clark and E. Franklin Frazier. It ends: "And see generally Myrdal, An American Dilemma (1944)." For more on how *An American Dilemma* and other social science texts entered US jurisprudence discussions, see Southern, *Gunnar Myrdal and Black-White Relations*, 127–50.

22. See Ernest W. Burgess, "Social Planning and Race Relations," in *Race Relations, Problems and Theory: Essays in Honor of Robert E. Park*, ed. Jitsuichi Masuoka and Preston Valien (Chapel Hill: University of North Carolina Press, 1961), 20–21.

23. *Saturday Review*, August 29, 1964, 74–76, as quoted in Southern, *Gunnar Myrdal and Black-White Relations*, xiv.

24. See Myrdal's preface in *An American Dilemma*, 20th anniversary ed., (New York: Harper & Row, 1962), xxv.

25. Southern, "An American Dilemma after Fifty Years," 239. A search on the scholastic site JSTOR turns up more than seventy-one hundred articles on the subject in various academic journals, books, and research reports. Search conducted December 11, 2023.

26. Ibram X. Kendi, *Stamped from the Beginning: The Definitive History of Racist Ideas in America* (New York: Nation Books, 2016), 506; Isabel Wilkerson, *Caste: The Origins of Our Discontents* (New York: Random House, 2020), 24. Myrdal repeatedly refers to America's system of segregation as a caste system.

27. Oscar Handlin, "A Book That Changed American Life," *New York Times Book Review*, April 21, 1963, 1, 26–27. Handlin was then director of Harvard University's Center for the Study of the History of Liberty in America.

CHAPTER 2—*MISSISSIPPI, USA*

1. To view *Mississippi, USA*, see YouTube, https://www.youtube.com/watch?v=qMa1-Jy5Er8, accessed September 27, 2019, transcribed by the author.

2. See "William J. Simmons" entry, mississippiencyclopedia.org. Also see "Racists' Strategist," in *NYT*, September 28, 1962, 22, as well as Hodding Carter III, "Citadel of the Citizens Council," *NYT Mag.*, November 12, 1961, 23. "Dixieland apartheid's number one organization man," see Neil R. McMillen, *The Citizens' Council: Organized Resistance to the Second Reconstruction 1954–1964*, 123.

3. For membership numbers, see McMillen, *The Citizens' Council*, 27 (Mississippi), and 152–54 (overall). These figures are disputed, however, and may be a bit conservative. The mississippiencyclopedia.org, for example, claims that the Citizens' Council movement "peaked at around one million" at its zenith. See "Robert 'Tut' Patterson" entry.

4. Carter III, Hodding, "Citadel of the Citizens Council," *NYT Mag.*, November 12, 1961. 23, 125.

5. For Barnett background, see *NYT* obituary, November 7, 1987, sec. 1, p. 35. Also see *WP* obituary, November 8, 1987, and "Ross Robert Barnett" entry, mississippiencyclopedia.org. Propeller incident referenced in Erle Johnston, *Mississippi's Defiant Years: 1953–1973* (Forest: Lake Harbor, 1990), 85. Also noted in Ed Williams, "Changing of the Era in Mississippi . . . A Southern Tragedy," *Southern Changes—The Journal of the Southern Regional Council* 10, no. 3 (1988): 10. RFK observation included in Arthur M. Schlesinger Jr., *Robert Kennedy and His Times* (New York: Ballantine Books, 1979), 342.

6. Curtis Wilkie, *DIXIE: A Personal Odyssey through Historic Events That Shaped the Modern South* (New York: Simon and Schuster, 2001), 91–92.

7. Erle Johnston, *I Rolled with Ross! A Political Portrait* (Baton Rouge: Moran, 1980), 2.

8. See John Jones and John Dittmer, "An Interview with Ross Barnett, February 11, 1981." MDAH Online Catalog, accessed December 7, 2020. Barnett's own biographical sketch from 1960 states, "He is a veteran of World War I." See MCWBTS, box 708, "Barnett, Ross R."

folder. Also see "Barnett, Ross Robert" entry in mississippiencyclopedia.org. In addition, see Gene Worth, "A New Resident in the Nation's Oldest Governor's Mansion," in MS Power and Light Company bulletin, Helping Build Mississippi, January–February 1960 edition, found in CWCC, box 117, "State Commission—MS 1958–1965" folder, NA.

9. "Vigorous Segregationist" quoted in "Ross Robert Barnett" entry in MississippiEncyclopedia.org.

10. Walter Lord, *The Past That Would Not Die* (London: Harper & Row, 1966), 243.

11. Frank E. Smith, *Congressman from Mississippi* (New York: Random House, 1964), 273.

12. McMillen, *The Citizens' Council*, 326.

13. See Yasuhiro Katagiri, *The Mississippi State Sovereignty Commission: Civil Rights and States Rights* (Jackson: University Press of Mississippi, 2001), 5–6.

14. Although this claim was demonstrably inaccurate, as this chronicle will show, already the local spark lit by the Tougaloo Nine was being minimized by the White media.

15. For a deeper exploration into the life of Medgar Evers, see Michael Vinson Williams, *Medgar Evers: Mississippi Martyr* (Fayetteville: University of Arkansas Press, 2011). To view original documents from Evers's NAACP work, see Myrlie Evers-Williams and Manning Marable, eds., *The Autobiography of Medgar Evers: A Hero's Life and Legacy Revealed through His Writings, Letters, and Speeches* (New York: Basic Civitas Books, 2005). For a dual biography of Medgar and Myrlie Evers, see Myrlie Evers (with William Peters), *For Us, The Living* (Garden City, New York: Doubleday, 1967). For a contemporary telling of the couple's activist story, see Joy-Ann Reid, *Medgar and Myrlie: Medgar Evers and the Love Story That Awakened America* (New York: Mariner Books, 2024). Also see "Chapter 1, Medgar's Mississippi" in M. J. O'Brien, *We Shall Not Be Moved: The Jackson Woolworth's Sit-In and the Movement It Inspired* (Jackson: University Press of Mississippi, 2013). For an overview of the entire Mississippi movement, see John Dittmer, *Local People: The Struggle for Civil Rights in Mississippi* (Urbana and Chicago: University of Illinois Press, 1995).

16. See Evers, *For Us, The Living*, p. 21. Mrs. Evers suggests the distance was more like twelve miles, although the distance from Decatur to the current Newton High School is ten miles.

17. W. E. B. Du Bois, "Returning Soldiers," *The Crisis* 18 (May 1919): 13.

18. For more on Evers's early life and eventual hiring by the NAACP, see Williams, *Medgar Evers: Mississippi Martyr*, 1–83; Evers, *For Us, the Living*, 7–33, 120–32. Also see Medgar Evers (as told to Francis H. Mitchell), "Why I Live in Mississippi," *Ebony*, November 1958, 65–70.

19. See "The Call," *National Negro Committee: A Call for a National Conference*, 1909. Manuscript/Mixed Material, https://www.loc.gov/Item/mss34140_01/, accessed March 11, 2024. Also see Mary White Ovington, "How the NAACP Began" reprinted in *NAACP 100: Celebrating a Century* (Salt Lake City: Gibbs Smith, 2009), 12–17.

20. For early NAACP presence in Mississippi, see Neil R. McMillen, *Dark Journey: Black Mississippians in the Age of Jim Crow* (Urbana: University of Illinois Press, 1989), 314–17; Dittmer, *Local People*, 29–40; and Patricia Sullivan, *Lift Every Voice: The NACP and the Making of the Civil Rights Movement* (New York: New Press, 2009), 86, 400–402.

21. Dittmer, *Local People*, 29.

22. McMillen, *Dark Journey*, 316.

23. Evers, *For Us, the Living*, 133.

CHAPTER 3—THE OASIS

1. Joan Traumpauer, "The Plantation and the Oasis," fall semester, 1961 (emphasis added), https://www.crmvet.org/lets/61-/traumpauer.pdf, accessed November 15, 2023. Joan's "movement" name is variously spelled Traumpauer, Trumpauer, or Trumpower. She was the first full-time White student to enroll at Tougaloo College. She arrived at the college as a Freedom Rider in 1961 and would later distinguish herself in the Jackson movement by participating in the Jackson Woolworth's Sit-In of 1963.

2. Summary of AMA history derived from Clifton H. Johnson and Christopher Harter, "Historical Note" in the "Collection Overview" section of the AMA archives housed at Tulane University's Amistad Research Center, https://amistad-finding-aids.tulane.edu/repositories/2/resources/37/, accessed November 30, 2023.

3. Clarice T. Campbell and Oscar Allan Rogers Jr., *Mississippi: The View from Tougaloo*, 2nd ed. (Jackson: University Press of Mississippi, 2002), 82.

4. Campbell and Rogers, *Mississippi*, 6.

5. Campbell and Rogers, *Mississippi*, 7, 8.

6. Besides from the AMA and the Freedmen's Bureau, Tougaloo would eventually receive funding from the United Church of Christ (Congregationalists) and the Disciple of Christ through its missionary branch, the United Christian Missionary Society (UCMS), as well as from the United Negro College Fund (UNCF).

7. McMillen, *Dark Journey*, 99.

8. Maria R. Lowe, "An 'Oasis of Freedom' in a 'Closed Society': The Development of Tougaloo College as a Free Space in Mississippi's Civil Rights Movement, 1960 to 1964," *Journal of Historical Sociology* (Oxford) 20, no. 4 (December 2007): 496–97.

9. Campbell and Rogers, *Mississippi*, 14–15, 19.

10. For list of presidents and their terms, see Campbell and Rogers, *Mississippi*, 331.

11. Miner would be the school's only White graduate for the ensuing eighty-five years. In 1964, Joan Harris Trumpauer (Mulholland) and Stephen Manson Rutledge would become Tougaloo's first White college-level graduates. See Campbell and Rogers, *Mississippi*, 197.

12. Campbell and Rogers, *Mississippi*, 103–8.

13. Campbell and Rogers, *Mississippi*, 167.

14. Campbell and Rogers, *Mississippi*, 215.

15. Campbell and Rogers, *Mississippi*, 135–36.

16. Due to the accreditation crisis, Tougaloo's enrollment dropped precipitously to only 197 students during the 1952/1953 school year. By 1959, however, it had climbed to more than 501 students, the maximum the school could accommodate at the time. See "Report of the Dean," October 27–28, 1959, 3, TSCC-BoTM, TCA-TC.

17. Lowe, "An 'Oasis of Freedom,'" 487.

18. See Campbell and Rogers, *Mississippi*, 182. Also see Tougaloo College website, "Our History" section: https://www.tougaloo.edu/about-tougaloo-college/our-history, accessed April 12, 2025.

19. Campbell and Rogers, *Mississippi*, 133, 226.

20. Samuel C. Kincheloe, "Basic Assumptions of a Christian College" delivered October 20, 1956, TSCC-BoTM, TCA-TC.

21. For more on Kincheloe's background, see "Tougaloo College Plans to Install President," *CL*, October 9, 1956. Also see "University of Chicago Settlement," https://socialwelfare.library.vcu.edu/settlement-houses/university-chicago-settlement/, accessed November 24, 2023.

22. See "President's Report to the Board of Trustees," April 16–17, 1957, 2, TSCC-BoTM, TCA-TC.

23. Student enrollment numbers: 305—"Report of the President, Board of Trustees," April 11–12, 1956; more than 520—"Report of Dean to President and Board of Trustees," April 1, 1960. TSCC-BoTM, TCA-TC.

24. See "President's Report to the Board of Trustees," April 16–17, 1957, 3–4, TSCC-BoTM, TCA-TC.

25. See Campbell and Rogers, *Mississippi*, 185. The prior president had authorized the establishment of Greek organizations but would not allow the formation of an NAACP college chapter.

CHAPTER 4—THE MEMPHIS CONTINGENT

1. Unless otherwise noted, all quotations in this work by members of the Tougaloo Nine are taken from author's interviews. See the selected bibliography for specifics of date and location of each interview.

2. WDIA went on the air in June 1947 initially with a country and western format. Gradually, the station's White owners shifted to R&B, gospel, and soul music. B.B. King and Elvis Presley, both from just over the border in Mississippi, credit the station as an early influence on their musical careers. For more on WDIA's rich history, see Louis Cantor, *Wheelin' on Beale: How WDIA-Memphis Became the Nation's First All Black Radio Station and Created the Sound That Changed America* (New York: Pharos Books, 1992). Stax stars Isaac Hayes and Carla Thomas began their careers as Teen Town Singers.

3. Beatrice was from Belzoni proper; Joseph Jackson Sr. hailed from Swiftown, a tiny enclave about ten miles northeast of Belzoni along Highway 7.

4. Unfortunately, no one ever bothered to have Ethel's name properly recorded. Since Abbie Sauer and Ethel Sawyer don't exactly match up, this would become an ongoing problem for Ethel in a post-9/11 world of heightened security.

CHAPTER 5—CHILDREN OF THE DELTA AND RIVERSIDE

1. For more on the establishment of an NAACP branch in Clarksdale, see Françoise N. Hamlin, *Crossroads at Clarksdale: The Black Freedom Struggle in the Mississippi Delta after World War II* (Chapel Hill: University of North Carolina Press, 2012), 24–29.

2. Besides from the author's interview, information about Geraldine's family connections and early life is derived from Geraldine (Edwards) Hollis, *Back to Mississippi* (Bloomington, IN: Xlibris, 2011), and her *March Memories: A True Reflection of Time, Then and Now!* (Bloomington, IN: AuthorHouse, 2014).

CHAPTER 6—CENTRAL AND SOUTH MISSISSIPPI OFFSPRING

1. Alfred Cook's profile has been pieced together from several sources: Doris Durr Ross's profile of Cook (with his review and approval) posted on March 25, 2015, on the Tougaloo Alumni Facebook Page, (entry in the author's possession); and two public gatherings of the Tougaloo Nine commemorating the library sit-in's forty-fifth and fiftieth anniversaries (recordings and transcripts in author's possession). In addition, Cook made public comments in August 2017 during ceremonies dedicating a historic marker at the site of the library sit-in (recording and transcript in author's possession) and gave various brief interviews when receiving an honorary doctorate from Tougaloo College in May 2021. He also provided comments to reporters at *The Jackson Advocate* during the sit-in's fiftieth-anniversary commemoration (*Jackson Advocate*, October 13, 2011). In addition, see Alfred Cook Sr. obituary, Lawrence E. Moon Funeral Home, Flint, MI, https://www.legacy.com/us/obituaries/name/alfred-cook-obituary?id=51945870, accessed July 2, 2023.

2. Cook revealed this detail during a 2021 ZOOM gathering of the surviving Tougaloo Nine convened by the author to commemorate the sixtieth anniversary of the library sit-in. (From author's notes of discussion, March 29, 2021.)

3. Brief profile of the African Methodist Episcopal (AME) Church is derived from C. Eric Lincoln, *Race, Religion, and the Continuing American Dilemma* (New York: Hill and Wang, 1984), 64–67. See also Henry Louis Gates Jr., *The Black Church: This Is Our Story, This Is Our Song* (New York: Penguin, 2021), 47–48.

4. Lincoln, *Race, Religion, and the Continuing American Dilemma*, 66. Here author C. Eric Lincoln is quoting from Gayraud S. Wilmore's *Black Religion and Black Radicalism: An Interpretation of the Religious History of Afro-American People* (Maryknoll, NY: Orbis, 1983), 113–14.

5. Profile of Campbell College is taken from two sources, both accessed February 12, 2019: The 1908 Campbell College Catalog, found online through the Hathi Trust Digital Library, https://babel.hathitrust.org/cgi/ls?field1=ocr;q1=Campbell%20College;a =srchls;lmt=ft and "Lost Colleges," at www.lostcolleges.com. For additional information about Campbell College's 1960s activism, see Joy Ann Williamson, "Quacks, Quirks, Agitators, and Communists: Private Black Colleges and the Limits of Institutional Autonomy," in *History of Higher Education Annual: 2003–2004*, vol. 23, ed. Roger L. Geiger (New York: Routledge/Taylor & Francis, 2005), 49–81.

6. During the Tougaloo Nine sixtieth anniversary ZOOM gathering on March 29, 2021, Cook acknowledged that he had been hounded out of Campbell College by President Stevens' wife because of his activism. Notes in author's possession.

7. Jackson State College was the other accredited college. For more information about Southern college accreditation, see the Southern Association of Colleges and Schools Commission on Colleges (SACSCOC), www.sacscoc.org. Rust College became accredited in 1970.

8. Biloxi Street was renamed A. M. E. Logan Street in 2011 to honor Anding's community-minded aunt.

9. A. M. E. Logan profile derived from *JA* "Reflections on the life of Mrs. A. M. E. Logan," by Stephanie Parker-Weaver, February 2011. Also see Tiyi M. Morris, *Womanpower Unlimited and the Black Freedom Struggle in Mississippi* (Athens: University of Georgia

Press, 2015) 31–34. Both families were also active in the Hair's Tabernacle AME Church just across the street from the Logan home on Biloxi Street.

10. The Jackson Zoo, located in the northwest section of the city, continues to operate and looks very much like it did in the 1960s. With its vast shady expanses and the adjacent Livingston Park (complete with a large fishing lake), it is clear why protests against segregation and limitations on Black admittance would have been staged there. It offered a place of rest and repose from the hustle and heat of the city along with educational and experiential enrichment for adults and youth alike. Though most wooden benches have been replaced by modern metal ones, some—like the ones used for protest by Anding, Logan, and Brown—can still be found within the zoo's gates (visited by author, May 2023).

11. The outlines of Evelyn Pierce's early life were drawn from an extensive interview with Armendia (Dixon) Pierce, October 26, 2014, Meadville, Pennsylvania, as well as a shorter telephone interview with Demathraus Pierce Perry, May 19, 2021.

12. For more on Bowers and his Klan activities in and around Laurel, as well as his headquarters near the Triangle Projects, see Charles Marsh, *God's Long Summer: Stories of Faith and Civil Rights* (Princeton: Princeton University Press, 1997) 49–81.

CHAPTER 7—TOUGALOO'S CULTURE OF RESISTANCE

1. This profile of Borinski is drawn primarily from two extraordinary oral histories Dr. Borinski gave while at Tougaloo. The first provides background information from 1914 through 1920: *An Oral History with Ernst Borinski*, with Eric Garnes, n.d. but likely 1960. T-005, box 1, folder 10, TCC-MDAH. The second is a five-part tour de force: *An Interview with Dr. Ernst Borinski*, with John Jones, part 1 (November 18, 1979); part 2 (December 9, 1979); part 3 (January 13, 1980); part 4 (January 27, 1980); and part 5 (March 9, 1980). T-005, box 1, folders 8 and 9, TCC-MDAH. Parts 4 and 5 deal with Borinski's time at Tougaloo. Also see *Personal Vitae of Dr. Ernst Borinski*, T-005, box 1, folder 24, TCC-MDAH, and *Ernst Borinski—Application for Job with U.S. Office of Education*, T-005, box 1, folder 4, TCC-MDAH.

2. It was in Berlin that Borinski met the German artist, sculptor, and social critic Käthe Kollwitz (1867–1945) and became a lifelong admirer and promoter of her work. Kollwitz—associated with both the realist and expressionist schools of German art—reportedly created at least fifty self-portraits during her lifetime, one of which—from 1922—Borinski purchased from the artist to celebrate the successful completion of his law examinations. It was one of his prized possessions that he managed to smuggle out of Germany as he fled Nazi oppression. The lithograph hung in Borinski's home at Tougaloo until his death. His last will and testament gave the drawing to the Mississippi Art Association "to be added to its permanent collection." It is now owned by the Mississippi Museum of Art. See "Last Will and Testament of Ernst Borinski," T/005, box 1, folder 28, TCC-MDAH.

3. Borinski had friends who had worked for the Zeiss Optical Company in Jena, Germany, one of whom had been transferred to the company's plant in Rochester where Borinski settled before his service in the US military. In addition, while in Germany, Borinski had struck up a friendship with the popular American journalist Hans von (H.V.) Kaltenborn, who had spent time in Germany as a newspaper reporter and who at the time was reporting for CBS Radio. (Broadcaster Edward R. Murrow called Kaltenborn "the dean"

of radio commentators.) Kaltenborn encouraged Borinski to flee Germany and come to the United States.

4. Borinski notes that having accepted the job at Tougaloo, he told one of his White graduate-school friends, Edna Davis, who was on sabbatical from Mississippi State College working on her doctorate in statistics. After a long pause, Davis responded, "Anybody else who would have told me this, I'd have said he was out of his mind. But I think you are the kind of character that can make it down there. Go!" See Jones, *Interview with Borinski Part III*, 6. Also see Maria Lowe, "'Sowing the Seeds of Discontent': Tougaloo College's Social Science Forums as a Prefigurative Movement Free Space, 1952–1964," *Journal of Black Studies* 39, no. 6 (2009) 865–87.

5. Jackson's Municipal Library, scene of the Tougaloo Nine sit-in, was built in 1954. "Historic Resources Inventory—Fact Sheet, (Old) Jackson Municipal Library," https://www .apps.mdah.ms.gov/Public/prop.aspx?id+11889&view+facts&y+1176, accessed December 17, 2023.

6. Bilbo's claim to Klan membership came just after winning his third Senate election. *The New York Times* questioned his motives for such a claim since, according to the *Times* reporting, there had been no official Klan established in Mississippi since its abolishment in 1924. See "Senator Bilbo States He Is a Klan Member," *NYT*, August 10, 1946, 15. However, at least five crosses were burned in various locations during the campaign, suggesting a Klan resurgence. See *Hearings before the Special Committee to Investigate Senatorial Campaign Expenditures, 1946, United States Senate, 79th Congress, Second Session* (Washington, DC: Government Printing Office, 1947). The hearings were held in Jackson from December 2 through 5, 1946. Bender's testimony appears on pp. 88–94.

7. For more information on William A. Bender and his important contributions to racial justice, see Dittmer, *Local People*, 2–3, 9, 30–32. There is also an entry, "Bender, William Albert," in mississippiencylopedia.org. In addition, Reverend Bender's one box of personal and professional papers can be found at TCA-TC.

8. The date is significant. The letter appeared just a few months after the murder of Emmett Till.

9. See Mississippi Notebook column, *CL*, December 12, 1955.

10. Description of the Social Science Forum program derived from various sources, including Dr. Maria Lowe's revelatory articles about Tougaloo College and Borinski's role there (see bibliography) and interviews with Tougaloo Nine and materials from Borinski Collection, TCC-MDAH. Also see Gabrielle Simon Edgcomb, *From Swastika to Jim Crow: Refugee Scholars at Black Colleges* (Malabar, Florida: Krieger, 1993), 117–29.

11. John Jones "Interview with George A. Owens," April 8, 1980, 39, MDAH.

12. This and the following quotes from Ed King taken from author interviews with King from 1996 and 2017, in author's possession. King would go on to participate in nearly every significant civil rights development in Mississippi after he returned to the state in early 1963 to become Tougaloo's chaplain, having been alerted by Borinski of the opening.

13. The speaker was to be Glenn Smiley, a consultant to Martin Luther King Jr. during the Montgomery bus boycott and a founder of the Congress of Racial Equality (CORE). At the time, Smiley was serving as a field secretary for the Fellowship of Reconciliation, CORE's founding organization. As a student, Ed King and his philosophy professor, Dr. Robert Bergmark, had been instrumental in organizing the lecture and securing the speaker. For more, see *CL*, March 5, 1958; *ST*, March 5, 1958; and *CL*, March 19, 1958. An additional story in *JDN*, March 6, 1958, describes a follow-up integrated meeting at Tougaloo College with

Tougaloo and Millsaps students. All stories found in Ernst Borinski Papers, T/005, box 1, folder 22, TCC-MDAH.

14. For more on the Welty visit to Tougaloo, see Suzanne Marrs, *Eudora Welty: A Biography* (New York: Harcourt, 2005), 273.

15. This sketch of Reverend Mangram's life and career is primarily derived from his obituary in the *Dallas Morning News*, March 13 and 14, 2014, as well as from the biographical note included in the "Inventory of John Mangram Papers," part of the Tougaloo College Collection in the Mississippi Digital Library, https://cdm17313.contentdm.oclc.org/digital/collection/tougaloo/id/919, Accessed July 5, 2021.

16. Vita, John D. Mangram, prepared January 2005. John D. Mangram Papers, TCA-TC. Also see John D. Mangram obituary, *Dallas Morning News*, March 13 and 14, 2014.

17. An interesting view into the NAACP's Jackson branch can be found in the Medgar Wiley and Myrlie Beasley Evers Papers housed at MDAH. Box 1, folders 1 and 2 of this collection contain the branch's Record Book, with minutes of all meetings, both of the General Membership and of the Executive Committee, for the years 1955 through 1959. Mangram was an integral part of the group's activities for each of these years.

18. See John D. Mangram Papers, TCA-TC, box 1, folder 3, Letters to Broadwater, Collins, Dixon, Lovelace, Haughton, and Smith, Jr., October 3–4, 1960. To each, Mangram wrote, "The two young people who attended the Retreat were greatly benefitted. They are much more valuable to our Chapter for having had this experience."

19. Author's interview with Reverend Ed King, August 21, 2017.

20. See letter to Honorable C. H. Humphreys Jr., June 14, 1960, item #3, SCR ID #3-12-0-69-1-1-1 and 2-1-1, accessed July 5, 2021. Sovereignty Commission Online, MDAH.

21. All letters found in box 1, folders 1–5, Mangram Collection, TCA-TC: Mangram to Rev. Oliver W. Holmes, Talladega, AL, February 3, 1960 (F-1); Mangram to Evers, Jackson, MS, April 4, 1960 (F-2); Mangram to Dr. Daniel G. Hill, Howard University, Washington, DC, March 9, 1960 (F-2); Mangram to Dr. Kenneth I. Brown, the Danforth Foundation, St. Louis, MO, April 4, 1960 and September 27, 1960 (F-3); and Mangram to D. J. Pius Barbour, Chester, PA, April 27, 1960 (F-3). Amos Brown also would count J. Pius Barbour as one of his early mentors.

22. Hollis, *March Memories*, 24.

23. Mangram to Brumback, April 22, 1961, box 1, folder 5, "Correspondence: Tougaloo Nine and Desegregation Support Letters," Mangram Collection, TCA-TC. Also available on the Mississippi Digital Archive: www.msdiglib.org.

24. The profile of Adam Dan Beittel is drawn from several sources: "Oral History Memoir of Dr. A. D. Beittel," conducted by John Quincy Adams, director, Oral History Project, Millsaps College, June 2, 1965, box 6–8, folder 16, Contemporary Mississippi Life and Viewpoints; "Interview with A. D. Beittel," conducted by Dr. John Dittmer, May 25, 1981 (copy and transcription in author's possession); "Beittel, Adam, Oral History Interview 1987," by Clifton H. Johnson, Amistad Research Center, Tulane University; and Maxine D. Jones and Joe M. Richardson, *Talladega College* (Tuscaloosa and London: University of Alabama Press, 1990), particularly the chapter "Irreconcilable Differences," 143–67. See also the as-yet-unpublished dissertation by John Gregory Speed, "A Beacon of Light: Tougaloo during the Presidency of Dr. Adam Daniel Beittel (1960–1964)" (University of Southern Mississippi, Spring 2014), downloaded from the Aquila Digital Community of USM, https://aquila.usm.edu/dissertations/244/.

25. For more on Oberlin's history and abolitionist zeal, see J. Brent Morris, *Oberlin, Hotbed of Abolitionism: College, Community and the Fight for Freedom and Equality in Antebellum America* (Chapel Hill: University of North Carolina Press, 2014).

26. Jones and Richardson, *Talladega College*, 141–67.

CHAPTER 8—COLLEGE BOUND

1. Hollis, *Back to Mississippi*, 95.

2. In addition to the author's interviews with Sawyer and Jackson, information for these stories was gleaned from the Tougaloo Alumni Facebook page that profiled both women: Sawyer on March 21, 2015, and Jackson on March 24, 2015. Recordings, transcriptions, and Facebook posts in author's possession.

3. In her retelling of this story, Edwards variously cites Registrar Dockins, Dean Branch, or the business manager, George Owens, as the administrator who called her in. This version is taken from her interview with the author.

4. A detailed history of the music program at Tougaloo, from its earliest days through the Pops Lovelace years can be found in Ben E. Bailey, *Music in the History of Tougaloo College* (Tougaloo, MS: TC, 1986), TCA-TC.

5. Bailey reports that this 902-pipe organ was replaced in the late 1950s with a Hammond electric organ—"a tragic mistake," he notes, since the Harris organ had both local and national significance. The mistake was remedied somewhat when a new pipe organ was installed in the early 2000s as part of the Woodworth Chapel's renovation. See Bailey, *Music in the History of Tougaloo College*, 14

6. Details of Lovelace's career derived from an interview he gave to Janice Kennedy for the student publication *Harambee* (n.d.), found in the Music Department file, TCA-TC. Additional details can be found in Bailey, *Music in the History of Tougaloo College*, 41–42.

7. In the *Harambee* interview, Lovelace described his most embarrassing moment: He was scolding one of his choirs, and a young choralist muttered, "Baldy," under her breath. Pops overheard it and reacted badly, saying, "Don't ever call me that again!"

8. Bailey, *Music in the History of Tougaloo College*, 41.

9. Listing of cities visited by the Tougaloo Choir taken from liner notes of Tougaloo College Choir album *To You—From Tougaloo*, circa 1966 or 1967. Lists of other tours can be found in the Music files, TCA-TC.

10. Alfred Cook comments, forty-fifth and fiftieth anniversary commemorations of the Tougaloo Nine Library Sit-In. DVD and author's transcription in author's possession.

11. Evelyn Pierce/Ameenah Omar telephone call-in to the Forty-Fifth Anniversary Commemoration of the Tougaloo Nine Library Sit-In. DVD and author's transcription in author's possession.

CHAPTER 9—COMMEMORATING A WOE-BEGOTTEN WAR

1. See Robert J. Cook, *Troubled Commission: The American Civil War Centennial, 1961–1965* (Baton Rouge: Louisiana State University Press, 2007), 26, 27.

2. Byrnes's remarks were made in April 1961, well after the commission's creation. For Byrnes's full remarks, see series 639, box 721, "South Carolina State Commission—Jan. 1963–April 1964 and Undated" folder, MCWBTS, MDAH.

3. Text of Public Law 85–305, https://www.congress.gov/85/statute/STATUTE-71/STATUTE-71-Pg626.pdf, accessed February 7, 2024.

4. The Lost Cause is a set of counterfactual claims about how and why the Civil War was fought; it lionizes the South and its leaders while demonizing the North. For more on how the Lost Cause interpretation of history developed, see David W. Blight, *Race and Reunion: The Civil War in American Memory* (Cambridge: Harvard University Press, 2001).

5. U. S. Grant III was seventy-seven when he accepted the post of chairman of the CWCC. He had had an impressive career in both military and public life. His claim to fame was his successful oversight of the Arlington Memorial Bridge Commission—ensuring the completion of the bridge's construction. Meant to symbolize the reconnection of the North and South, the bridge extends from Washington, DC, to Arlington, Virginia. The project had languished for nearly fifty years before Grant took control and saw it through to completion. See Grant III biographical sketch, record group 79, box 62, "Biographies, 1958–60," subject files, CWCC, NPS, NA. Also see *WP*, "Gen. Ulysses S. Grant III Dies," August 30, 1968, B10.

William Mumford Tuck was named after his Confederate grandfather. The son of a tobacco warehouseman, Tuck became a Harry Byrd loyalist and was elevated to lieutenant governor and then governor of Virginia before being tapped by Byrd to fill an unexpired term in the US House of Representatives in 1953. Tuck was a signatory to the Southern Manifesto, which called the *Brown v. Board of Education* a "clear abuse of judicial power" and promoted the open opposition to the implementation of school desegregation. See William Bryan Crawley Jr., *Bill Tuck: A Political Life in Harry Byrd's Virginia* (Charlottesville: University Press of Virginia, 1978).

6. For more on the reconciliationist view of the Civil War, see Blight, *Race and Reunion*, throughout, esp. 264–65. "What made possible the reconciliationist phase of the Lost Cause (1880s and beyond) is that Southerners found they could transform loss on the battlefield into a reunion on terms largely of their own choosing."

7. Tuck to Jones, June 4, 1959, Willam M. Tuck Papers, folder 5268, SCSL-W&M.

8. For Consuelo Bailey's background, see vermonthistory.org and vermonthistory explorer.com, accessed February 8, 2020.

9. The situation was not rectified until September 1961, when President Kennedy appointed African American Roy K. Davenport, special assistant to the undersecretary of the army, to the commission. See Cook, *Troubled Commission*, 139. Also see CWCC membership list, October 1961, record group 79, box 58, CWCC minutes, 12/4/1961, subject files, CWCC, NPS, NA.

10. For CWCC's overtures, see press release no. 18, July 8, 1958, record group 79, box 117, "State Commissions-MS 1958–65," subject files, CWCC, NPS, NA. Also see Capers's letter to Governor Lindsay Almond Jr. (VA), February 12, 1959, record group 71, box 22, folder 4, "Centennial Commissions: Michigan—New Jersey," series 1, correspondence and subject files, VA Civil War Commission, Library of Virginia. For more on Almond's role, see Cook, *Troubled Commission*, 43.

Karl S. Betts was a man of many talents. Early in his career, he served as publicity director for the Kansas City branch of the Redpath Chautauqua lecture circuit; later, he was a successful realtor, journalist, and investment banker. He was one of the organizers, and later president, of the DC Civil War Roundtable and helped draft the Centennial Commission legislation. See Victor Gondos Jr., "Karl Betts and the Civil War Centennial Commission," *Military Affairs* 27, no. 2, Civil War issue (Summer 1963), 49–70.

11. For Capers's profile, see mississippiencyclopedia.org entry "Capers, Charlotte" and *CL*, January 15, 1961, 14, "Capers Funeral Monday," about the death of her mother. More on Capers and her intriguing family can be found in Sherwood Willing Wise, *The Cathedral Church of St. Andrew: A Sesquicentennial History 1839–1989* (Jackson, MS: Cathedral Church of St. Andrew, 1989), 69–108. Capers's father, Rev. Dr. Walter Branham Capers, served as rector of the Cathedral from 1919 to 1946.

12. Capers quotation from minutes, MS Civil War Centennial Commission, September 10, 1959, record group 79, box 117, "State Commission-Mississippi, 1958–65," subject files, CWCC, NPS, NA.

13. Creation of MS CWCC derived from mississippiencyclopedia.org entry "Civil War Centennial." See also minutes from first meeting of the temporary commissioners: minutes, MS Civil War Centennial Commission, October 10, 1958, record group 79, box 117, "State Commission-Mississippi, 1958–65," subject files, CWCC, NPS, NA. List of original "Mississippi Centennial Commission" members can be found in the same box at the National Archives. Everett, who would be chosen as chairman of the temporary commission, had served a term as president of the Mississippi Historical Society, as had Winter.

14. Minutes, MS Civil War Centennial Commission, October 15, 1958, record group 79, box 117, "State Commission-Mississippi, 1958–65," subject files, CWCC, NPS, NA. Numbers vary depending on whose list is consulted, but there were more than 550 battles, skirmishes, raids, and other military engagements on Mississippi soil during the four years of the Civil War. Ed Bearss created a comprehensive list in his *Decision in Mississippi* (Jackson, MS: MS Commission on the War Between the States, 1962) 581—597.

15. See Capers—Betts Correspondence, record group 79, box 117, "State Commission-Mississippi, 1958–65," subject files, CWCC, NPS, NA.

16. Coleman to Hon. Ed Green, September 22, 1958, record group 79, box 117, "State Commission-Mississippi, 1958–65," subject files, CWCC, NPS, NA. At this time, the Mississippi legislature met every other year.

17. See John Knox Bettersworth and James Wesley Silver, eds., *Mississippi in the Confederacy*, 2 vols. (Jackson, MS: MDAH, 1961). Silver would later become infamous in Mississippi for his 1963 book *Mississippi: The Closed Society*, which cracked the code of the state's extreme paranoia and rigidity on racial matters.

18. For more on Florence Sillers Ogden and her influence on Mississippi society, see "Florence Sillers Ogden" entry in the mississippiencyclopedia.org.

19. Sillers Ogden to Grant III, September 20, 1958, record group 79, box 7, "Advisory Council-Mississippi, 1958–60," subject files, CWCC, NPS, NA.

20. Minutes, Mississippi CWCC, September 10, 1959, record group 79, box 117, "State Commission-Mississippi, 1958–65," subject files, CWCC, NPS, NA.

21. Roebuck background found in Roebuck to Johnson, February 20, 1964, 2, series 639, box 714, "'J'—Miscellaneous" folder, MCWBTS, MDAH. For MS Auto Club credential, see Magnuson to Roebuck, July 8, 1960, series 639, box 715, "'M'—Miscellaneous, 7/60–3/61" folder, MCWBTS, MDAH. Also see Roebuck to Farrand, June 30, 1961, series 639, box 712, "'H'-Miscellaneous, 4/60–12/61" folder, MCWBTS, MDAH.

22. Minutes, MCWCC, September 10, 1959, record group 79, box 117, "State Commission-Mississippi, 1958–65," subject files, CWCC, NPS, NA.

23. For more on the commission's linkage with Barnett's two primary goals of maintaining segregation and attracting industry, see Matthew Reonas, "Served Up on a Silver Platter:

Ross Barnett, the Tourism Industry, and Mississippi's Civil War Centennial," *The Journal of Mississippi History* 72, no. 2 (Summer 2010): 123–61.

24. Adjusting for inflation, $200,000 in 1960 would equal more than $2 million in 2024 dollars.

25. "You will remember that I was in your office in April," Roebuck to Betts, July 11, 1960, record group 79, box 117, "State Commission-Mississippi, 1958–65," subject files, CWCC, NPS, NA.

26. Roebuck to Geary (VA) et al., July 18, 1960, record group 71, box 22, folder 4, "Mississippi 1958–1961," Virginia Civil War Commission, Library of Virginia. In the MCWBTS records, there is a letter to every operating state commission within each state's subject file.

27. Mississippi was not alone in quibbling over what to call its centennial commission. Georgia, for instance, tried to bridge the divide and came up with the unwieldy *Georgia Civil War Centennial Commission Commemorating the War Between the States*. On the other hand, South Carolina just went for broke, naming its centennial governing body the *Confederate Centennial Commission*. See state commission letterhead in MCWBTS state files for Georgia and South Carolina, series 639, boxes 712 and 721, respectively, MCWBTS, MDAH. For more on the naming controversy, see Gaines M. Foster, "What's Not in a Name: The Naming of the American Civil War," *Journal of the Civil War Era*, 8, no. 3 (September 2018) 416-454.

28. Minutes, MCWBTS, May 27, 1960, series 648, box 734, MCWBTS, MDAH.

29. Minutes, MCWBTS, June 17, 1960, series 648, box 734, MCWBTS, MDAH.

30. Godwin profile derived from Reonas, *Served Up on a Silver Platter*, 138.

31. Charles Evers, *Evers* (New York and Cleveland: The World Publishing Company, 1971), 99. Evers was referring to the Citizens' Council as a whole.

32. Fulghum would eventually report that "more $44,000 went to state plants for the manufacture of uniforms and sales tax paid to the state exceeded $2,200." Fulghum to Holland, January 18, 1962, series 639, box 713, "Holland, John D.—Chairman" folder, MCWBTS, MDAH.

33. *Mississippi's Greatest Hour: A Manual for Local Observances of the Centennial of the War Between the States 1961–1964*—Civil War Centennial 1961–1965, call no. 973.76/M69m, MDAH.

34. *Mississippi in the War Between the States: A Booklet of Facts for the Information of Mississippians in Connection with the Observance of the Civil War Centennial 1961–1965*, call no. 973.76 M69mm. MDAH. "Slavery" is noted in passing in the chronology of key moments in the life of Jefferson Davis, also included in the booklet.

35. Profile of Bearss is derived from author's interview with Ed Bearss (at age ninety-six) on May 10, 2019. Also see John C. Waugh, *Edwin Cole Bearss: History's Pied Piper* (Washington, DC: Edwin C. Bearss Tribute Fund and History America Tours, 2003), 7–30.

36. Due to funding woes, Bearss and his team were unable to get enough financing to raise the sunken armored warship until 1963, and then various technical difficulties kept the vessel stuck in the mud until 1964.

37. For a sense of Godwin's business dealings with the commission, see series 639, box 712, "Godwin Advertising Agency" folder, MCWBTS, MDAH.

38. Waldrip to Roebuck, July 25, 1960, series 639, box 712, "Georgia State Director, 1/60–11/61" folder, MCWBTS, MDAH. The Confederate States Centennial Conference (CSCC)

was formed in 1958 ostensibly to coordinate regional activities during the centennial years, although a key reason was to form a political block to ensure the national commission's adherence to reconciliationist doctrine. For information about the creation of the CSCC, see Virginia Civil War Commission Papers, record group 71, box 2, "Confederate States Centennial Conference" folders, Library of Virginia. Mississippi's Gladys Slayden would play a key leadership role in this organization.

39. Snizek to Wallace, February 20, 1961, series 639, box 720, "'S' Miscellaneous, 1/61—3/62" folder, MCWBTS, MDAH. Sinclair would purchase full-page ads in *Time*, *Newsweek*, *Saturday Review*, and *National Geographic* on four separate occasions to commemorate key events of the Civil War, including the attack on Fort Sumter and the siege of Vicksburg. See attachments to Roebuck to Snizek, February 10, 1962, in the same folder.

40. Minutes, MCWBTS, September 14, 1960, 8, series 648, box 734, MCWBTS, MDAH.

41. The Northern and Midwestern states: IL, IN, IA, KS, MA, MI, MN, NH, NY, PA, RI, WI, OH, and MO. (West Virginia, inadvertently left off this list, was later added.) The Southern states: AL, AR, FL, LA, MS, NC, and SC. During the centennial, Texas decided to fund a memorial at Vicksburg. It was dedicated in November 1961. See *Mississippi in the War Between the States*, p. 11.

42. Godwin to Marlow, November 15, 1960, series 639, box 715, "'M' Miscellaneous—7/60–3/61" folder, MCWBTS, MDAH. It must have been galling two weeks later for Godwin to have to revise the date and lose the "dramatic" advantage.

43. Collier to Roebuck, November 11, 1960, and Roebuck to Collier, November 21, 1960, found in series 639, box 708, "'C' Miscellaneous—1960" folder, MCWBTS, MDAH.

44. Primos to Roebuck, November 22, 1960, series 639, box 719, "'P' Miscellaneous, 7/60–9/61" folder, MCWBTS, MDAH.

45. Minutes, MCWBTS, September 14, 1960, 1–2, series 648, box 734, MCWBTS, MDAH. See also "Firms Agree to Raise Troops for Centennial," *CL*, November 8, 1960, 1. Thompson's intervention helped turn out hundreds more volunteers for the Mississippi Greys as local banks, insurance companies, and other businesses took up the challenge. Jackson would claim twenty-five of the eighty-seven units formed. For a complete list of units (from the Aberdeen Raiders to the Yazoo Pickets), see MCWBTS Report, 1960–1962, Biennium, 11–13, call no. 973.76 M69, MDAH. A complete list of names of those who participated in the various units is included in Bearss, *Decision in Mississippi*, 541–72.

CHAPTER 10—FREEDOM'S EARLY STIRRINGS

1. *CL/JDN*, "Covering the Crossroads with Jimmy Ward," February 21, 1960, 2-D.

2. "Officials of City Air Race Issue," *CL*, March 4, 1960, 1.

3. "Tougaloo Students Get Request for Sit-Down," *CL/JDN*, March 20, 1960, 1. Also see "Courageous Negro Leadership (an Editorial)," *JDN*, March 19, 1960, 1. Evers's promotion of a boycott dovetails with the Roy Wilkins's March 16, 1960, announcement in support of a nationwide boycott of national chain stores that support segregation in the South. Wilkins called the new policy "racial self-defense." See "NAACP Calls for Boycott in Lunch-Counter Dispute," *CL*, March 17, 1960, 1.

4. See "Bills Are Introduced to Avert Sit-Downs," *CL*, March 10, 1960, 1; "House Okays Measures to Prevent 'Sit-Downs,'" *CL*, March 11, 1960, 1; and "Sit-Down Measures Rushed to Governor," *CL*, March 23, 1960, 1.

5. For more on Amos Brown and his contributions to the early Jackson movement, see his interview with David P. Cline for the Civil Rights History Project conducted in collaboration with the Smithsonian Institute and the Library of Congress on March 2, 2013, https://www.loc.gov/item/2015669159/, accessed October 9, 2021., Additional details gleaned from author's brief interview with Brown by phone on September 30, 2021. Notes in author's possession.

6. For more on Darden and his antics, see Evers-Williams and Manning, *The Autobiography of Medgar Evers*, 136 and 170–74. Also see Williams, *Medgar Evers: Mississippi Martyr*, 179–80. By the end of 1961, the Mississippi NAACP membership totaled 2,314. See "Report to MS State Conference—Membership & FFF Contributions received to date," October 29, 1962, group X, box 1478, "Membership and Freedom Fund Reports, 1962–1983, 1991" folder, undated (3 of 3), [Item number HLM-00586], NAACP Papers, LOC.

7. Myrlie Evers's comments can be found on p. 136, and the Darden/Evers correspondence with Gloster Current can be found on pp. 170–74, Evers-Williams and Manning, *The Autobiography of Medgar Evers*. Despite Darden's loss of power at the state level, he continued lead his local Meridian branch and to serve on the NAACP's national board of directors. Darden would continue to cause problems for Evers. See Evers, "Special Report: Activities of Rebellious Branch Leadership" June 15, 1962, in which Evers castigates Darden for inviting members of MLK's SCLC staff to an NAACP member meeting on the eastern side of the state in direct competition with Evers's NAACP statewide fundraising event.

8. It is important to note that one first-hand account of the development of the Tougaloo College NAACP chapter differs somewhat from Evers's timetable. Colia Liddell, a founding member of the chapter, suggests that the group was formed in the fall of 1959, though she admits that they were searching for something to do when the idea for the Easter boycott was presented to them six months later. See interview with Colia Liddell Lafayette Clark, July 17, 1974, Oral History Collection, MWC, JSU, 6. The formal charter for the Tougaloo College branch was sent from the national office in April 1960. See Wright to Evers, April 18, 1960 in "Evers, Medgar, Field Secretary, 1960" folder, group III, box C-244, NAACP Papers, LOC. A chronological listing of all sit-ins nationwide can be found at https://www.crmvet.org/docs/6004_sitin-list.pdf.

9. It is a testament to the Jones-Evers relationship that three years later, Jones would be one of three ministers leading the mile-long Evers funeral march.

10. See "Report to Mrs. Ruby Hurley from Medgar W. Evers, April 13, 1960, 'Sacrifice for Human Dignity,'" group III, box A-230, "Mississippi Pressures, Jackson, Miss. 1956–1965" folder, NAACP Papers, LOC. Also see "Medgar Evers to Gloster Current, March 15, 1960" as reported in Evers-Williams and Marable, *The Autobiography of Medgar Evers*, 172–74. In addition, see Williams, Medgar Evers, Mississippi Martyr, 180.

11. A year earlier, Amos Brown, while attending the NAACP National Convention in Cleveland, gave an interview to reporters where he criticized Mississippi's dual, separate but not equal, education system. The story made its way back to Mississippi's superintendent of schools, who refused Brown's reenrollment in Jim Hill High School to complete his senior year. It took Evers's threat of a lawsuit to get Brown reinstated onto the school's roster. See Brown, Southern Oral History Project, 9–10.

12. Press conference was reported in "No Easter Buying: Negroes Pledge Jackson Boycott," *JDN*, April 8, 1960, 1; and in "No Demonstrations: Ask Boycott by Negroes," *CL*, April 9, 1960, 1.

13. Evers reports that representatives from the wire services UPI and AP were present, as well as newscasters from the TV station WLBT. See "Report to Mrs. Ruby Hurley from Medgar W. Evers, April 13, 1960, 'Sacrifice for Human Dignity,'" group III, box A-230, "Mississippi Pressures, Jackson, Miss. 1956–1965" folder, NAACP Papers, LOC. Also see Van Landingham, "Boycott of Negroes, Jackson, Mississippi, April 10–17, 1960," SCR ID: 2-135-0-22-1-1-1, MSCP, MDAH.

14. "Bottle Hurled in Darden's Window," *CL*, April 9, 1960, 3.

15. See "Report to Mrs. Ruby Hurley from Medgar W. Evers, April 13, 1960, 'Sacrifice for Human Dignity,'" group III, box A-230, "Mississippi Pressures, Jackson, Miss. 1956–1965" folder, NAACP Papers, LOC..

16. Excerpts of Mangram's remarks are included in Evers's "Monthly Report," April 21, 1960, included in Evers-Williams and Manning, *The Autobiography of Medgar Evers*, 185–86.

17. For more on Van Landingham, see Katagiri, *The Mississippi State Sovereignty Commission*, 34 and 45.

18. This remarkable document can be found in the Sovereignty Commission online cache of documents: "Boycott of Negroes, Jackson, Mississippi, April 10–17, 1960," by Zach J. Van Landingham, April 22, 1960 (SCR ID# 2-135-0-22-1-1-1), MSCP, MDAH, accessed June 30, 2021. Printout in author's possession.

19. The *Jackson Daily News*'s Jimmy Ward appears throughout this narrative. Ward attended Millsaps College in the late 1930s and flew more than fifty B-52 combat missions during World War II for the US Army before returning to his beloved Jackson to begin his thirty-plus-year career at the paper as a photographer and reporter. In 1957, he was named editor of the paper after the sudden death of his mentor and long-time *JDN* owner and editor Fred Sullens. Both Sullens and Ward held deeply arch-segregationist and racist views, which always found their ways into the paper on a near-daily basis, often through what passed as comedy and cartoons. For more on Ward and his antics, see David R. Davies, ed., *The Press and Race: Mississippi Journalists Confront the Movement* (Jackson: University Press of Mississippi, 2001), 84–109.

20. The Tougaloo Board of Trustees minutes for all of 1960 make no mention of any suspension. If there was any such reprimand, it was slight. Mangram was retained to teach and serve as Tougaloo's chaplain for the 1960/1961 school year.

21. Evers, *For Us, the Living*, p. 150. For more on Percy Greene and his accommodationist stance, see Caryl Cooper, "Percy Greene and the *Jackson Advocate*," in David R. Davies, *The Press and Race*, 54–83. A native Jacksonian, Greene and his *Jackson Advocate* were at the vanguard of Black improvement during the 1940s, but after the *Brown* decision, his ideals of go-slow Negro progress clashed with those pushing harder for equal rights, forcing him to side more and more with the entrenched White interests for both philosophical and financial reasons. The *Jackson Daily News* carried Greene's attack on Evers as an "Editorial of Note," *JDN*, April 9, 1960, 8.

22. "Protests, Arrests Continue," *CL*, April 12, 1960, 1.

23. Projections and assessments of the campaign's effectiveness can be found in three of Evers's reports: (1) See "Report to Mrs. Ruby Hurley from Medgar W. Evers, April 13, 1960,

'Sacrifice for Human Dignity,'" group III, box A-230, "Mississippi Pressures, Jackson, Miss. 1956–1965" folder, NAACP Papers, LOC; (2) "Report to Ruby Hurley, April 19, 1960"; and (3) "Monthly Report, April 21, 1960." Reports (2) and (3) can be found in Evers-Williams and Marable, *Autobiography of Medgar Evers*, 184 and 186–87. Also see Evers's end-of-year summary newsletter: "With Liberty and Justice for All," *Autobiography of Medgar Evers*, 202–3.

24. Liddell interview, MWC, 8. See also Colia Liddell Lafayette Clark interview with author, February 16, 2015. Recording, notes, and transcript in author's possession.

25. For more, see Dr. Gilbert Mason, *Beaches, Blood, and Ballots* (Jackson: University Press of Mississippi, 2000): Mason's first meeting with Quave, 53; Mason's interaction with police chief McDonnell, 62; description of the "bloody wade-in," 65–87. See also Evers's reports on the 1960 wade-in: Evers Williams and Marable, *Autobiography of Medgar Evers*, 187–91.

26. See "Race Riot Measure Approved: House, Senate Rush Bill to Governor Barnett," *CL*, April 28, 1960, 1. The law gave police authority to stop such protests due to the *potential* for violence that nonviolent protests might spark. Such laws were overthrown by the US Supreme Court in 1965 with the *Cox v. Louisiana* case, which originated because of an arrest made during a nonviolent civil rights march in Baton Rouge in December 1961. See *Cox v. Louisiana*, https://tile.loc.gov/storage-services/service/ll/usrep/usrep379/usrep379536/usrep379536.pdf, accessed April 20, 2024.

27. The man-made beach had been developed in 1948 by the federal government, which contractually required that the beach be open to all, regardless of race. See Mason, *Beaches, Blood, and Ballots*, 54–55.

28. Evers, *For Us, the Living*, 210–11.

29. In 1958, while returning from an NAACP southeast regional meeting, Evers sat in the front of the bus at Meridian, Mississippi. He was assaulted by a White cab driver who could not abide this affront to segregationist strictures. Nevertheless, a battered Evers rode the entire way home to Jackson seated at the front of the bus. Certainly, Frazier would have heard of this incident. See "rec'd via phone from Medgar Evers, NAACP, March 13, 1958," group III, box A-115 "Medgar Evers Reports 1960–1962" folder, NAACP Papers, LOC. Also see Evers-Williams and Marable, *Autobiography of Medgar Evers*, 89, 96.

30. The story of Frazier's jailing and Evers's securing his release, with Anding in tow, is recounted in Evers's August "Monthly Report" dated August 30, 1960, found in Evers-Williams and Marable, *Autobiography of Medgar Evers*, 195–97. Meredith Anding provided details about his involvement in his October 27, 2014, interview with the author.

31. Evers, *For Us, the Living*, 234.

CHAPTER 11—A CHANGE IS GONNA COME

1. See Evers-Williams and Marable, *Autobiography of Medgar Evers*, 190–93; Re: Tougaloo PAC, 210.

2. Content of Evers's presentation is supported by recollections of Joseph Jackson, Geraldine Edwards, and others, included in author's interviews. The exact date of this meeting is known thanks to Evers's detailed travel log kept to ensure reimbursement by the national NAACP, which required meticulous expense records. See Evers's Field Travel Expense Account, October 19, 1960, group X, box 1477, "Evers, Medgar—Travel Expenses—1956–1963" folder, NAACP Papers, LOC.

3. Evers to Mason, October 18, 1960. Photographic image of letter reproduced in Mason, *Beaches, Blood, and Ballots*, 6, in photo section (emphasis added).

4. For Alfred Cook's involvement in the Student Committee for Human Dignity, see Daphne Rochelle Chamberlain, "'And a Child Shall Lead the Way': Children's Participation in the Jackson Mississippi, Black Freedom Struggle, 1946–1970" (PhD dissertation, University of Mississippi, May 2009), 102. Also See "Negro Boycott of Fair Urged," *JDN*, October 15, 1960, 7.

5. Boycott and its impact reported in Covering the Crossroads with Jimmy Ward columns, *JDN*, October 15, 1960, 7, and *JDN*, October 18, 1960, 1, as well as in "Negro Students Hint at Boycott of Fair," *CL*, October 17, 1960, 1; and "Negro Fair May Draw New Record," *CL*, October 18, 1960, 1. Also see "Record Crowds Predicted for Negro State Fair Here Next Week," *JA*, October 15, 1960, 1, and "Up and Down Farish Street," *JA*, October 15, 1960, 4.

6. Myrdal, *An American Dilemma*, 335 and 347, respectively.

7. Myrdal, *An American Dilemma*, 634.

8. For a deeper dive into the history of library sit-ins and libraries as a focal point of public life, see the works of Wayne and Shirley Wiegand, particularly *Desegregation of Public Libraries in the Jim Crow South* (Baton Rouge: Louisiana State University Press, 2018). Also see Cheryl Knott, *Not Free, Not for All: Public Libraries in the Age of Jim Crow* (Amherst: University of Massachusetts Press, 2015).

9. For a first-hand account of the Alexandria Library sit-in, see Nancy Noyes Silcox, *Samuel Wilbert Tucker: The Story of a Civil Rights Trailblazer and the 1939 Alexandria Library Sit-In* (Fairfax, VA: History4All, 2013). All charges against the original five Alexandria Library sit-in participants were finally dismissed in 2019. See https://www.alexandriava.gov/museums/history-of-the-alexandria-black-history-museum, accessed May 20, 2021.

10. See John Lewis, *Walking with the Wind* (New York: Simon and Schuster, 1998), 48.

11. The story of Wyatt Tee Walker's library protest is recounted in Wiegand and Wiegand, *The Desegregation of Public Libraries*, 82–90. Though the students at Tougaloo may not have heard of this protest, it is entirely possible that Evers and Mangram would have been aware of it and might have steered the students toward a library sit-in.

12. Cook statement to author, May 2, 2021, Tougaloo College Commencement. Notes in author's possession. The College Park Library was housed in a small space on the first floor of the College Park Auditorium, a meeting space and recreational area for the city's Black citizens. See Carrol Brinson, *Jackson/A Special Kind of Place* (Jackson: City of Jackson, 1977), 272–73.

13. Hollis, *Back to Mississippi*, 114.

14. Colia Liddell interview, MWC, 18. It is tempting to think that Evers and Mangram postponed the date of the library sit-in when the Secession Day Parade, originally scheduled for January 9, was also pushed back to late March.

15. See *Tougaloo Southern News*, January/February 1961 edition, which includes a photo of the Tougaloo "Y" delegation. Both Albert Lassiter and Donahtrus Pierce talked about the importance of the "Y" to their families.

16. Robert Carter cut his teeth on civil rights law at the NAACP's Legal Defense and Education Fund under Thurgood Marshall. He succeeded Marshall in the role of the NAACP's general counsel.

17. Besides contacting Carter, it is likely that Evers communicated verbally with his direct supervisor, Ruby Hurley, and with second-tier boss Gloster Current. Evers to Carter, March 15, 1961," group III, box A-230, "Mississippi Pressures, Jackson, MS, 1956–1965" folder, NAACP Papers, LOC.

CHAPTER 12—MISSISSIPPI PREPARES FOR A RAUCOUS CELEBRATION

1."Grant and Lee Honored as Centennial Opens," *NYT*, January 9, 1961, 1, 23; Grant telegram to Tuck found in Tuck Papers, folder 5270, "1960–Part 2, CWCC, Miscellaneous," SCSL-W&M. Grant's full remarks, which were later inserted by Tuck into the *Congressional Record*, can be found in William M. Tuck Papers, folder 5271, "1961—Part 1, CWCC, Miscellaneous," SCSL-W&M, as well as in record group 79, box 67, "Centennial Opening," subject files, CWCC, NPS, NA. In his remarks, Grant III praised his famous grandfather, closing his prepared text thus: "The great and prosperous United States of today—and we who have inherited it—owes much to the military leader who not only won the victory but also the confidence of its enemies and to the President who supervised its re-establishment under the Constitution." Tuck telegram to Grant III also resides in the same folder. His remarks at Lee Chapel (as well as his original telegram to Grant III) can be found in William M. Tuck Papers, folder 5271, "1961—Part 1, CWCC, Miscellaneous," SCSL-W&M.

2. A lengthy profile of Grant III accompanied the *Times*'s coverage in which Grant III repeats his reconciliationist views: "It is not the commemoration of a victorious war," he said about the centennial, "rather, of a nation that tested its ideals in battle and bound up its wounds." See "In Grandfather's Shadow," *NYT*, January 9, 1961, 23.

3. Several letters from Holland, Roebuck, and Wallace give various reasons as to why the date was shifted. The letter from Wallace to Quave gives the most detail. See Wallace to Quave, November 30, 1960, series 639, box 720, "Q Miscellaneous" folder, MCWBTS, MDAH. Roebuck would also find Fulghum's work shoddy, complaining of "buttons missing; buttons loose; one sleeve shorter than the other," and so on. See Roebuck to Fulghum, November 29, 1960, series 639, box 711, "F Miscellaneous, 7/1960–12/1961" folder, MCWBTS, MDAH.

4. Letters to mayors went out throughout the summer of 1960, first from Barnett (July 14),), then from Holland (July 19), and finally from Roebuck (August 4). For an example of the pitch, see Holland letter to Thompson, July 19,1960, "Dear Mayor," series 639, box 712, "H-Miscellaneous, 4/1960–12/1961" folder, MCWBTS, MDAH.

5. *Join the Mississippi Greys: A Guide for the Organization of Units of Mississippi's Centennial Military Force in Memoriam*, call no. 976.896/M678j, MDAH.

6. Numbers gleaned from *MCWBTS Biennial Report, 1960–1962*, 10, call no. 973.76/M69r, MDAH. At an early planning stage, Roebuck and the Mississippi Commission had suggested that the effort would turn out "a minimum of 100,000 men in Confederate uniforms." See "Suggested Program," series 639, box 719, "'P' Miscellaneous, undated" folder, MCWBTS, MDAH. At this same time, Roebuck was harassed by both Barnett and his son about using various friends as vendors and hiring friends to work for the commission. He successfully fended off each suggestion. See Barnett to Roebuck, August 2, 1960, series 639, box 708, "Barnett, Ross R., 6/60–6/62" folder, MCWBTS, MDAH; and Barnett Jr. to Roebuck, November 23, 1960, and Roebuck to Barnett Jr., December 5, 1960, both included in series 639, box 707, "B Miscellaneous" folder, MCWBTS, MDAH.

7. See Wallace to Quave, November 30, 1960, series 639, box 720, "Q Miscellaneous" folder, MCWBTS, MDAH.

8. Capers to Wallace, December 14, 1960, series 639, box 710, "C—Miscellaneous" folder, MCWBTS, MDAH.

9. See "Barnett Draws Parallel With 1861 Secession," *JDN*, January 9, 1961, 1. Also see "State Secession Re-Enacted in Ceremony at Old Capitol," *CL*, January 10, 1961, 1, 12.

10. Barnett statement included in "Civil War Centennial Begins" an article in the March 1961 edition of *The Bell Tel News*, a publication of the Southern Bell Telephone and Telegraph Company. See series 639, box 708, "Barnett, Ross R." folder, MCWBTS, MDAH. Just after Barnett's presentation ended, Mississippi congressman John Bell Williams rose on the floor of the US House of Representatives, Washington, DC, to introduce into the *Congressional Record* Mississippi's Ordinance of Secession. In similarly coded language, Williams, too, made the connection between 1861 and 1961, saying that "unlike a century ago, in 1961 the people of Mississippi, instead of fighting to dissolve their ties with the Constitution of the United States, are zealously and relentlessly fighting to preserve our Constitutional republic." See *Congressional Record: Proceedings and Debates of the U.S. Congress*, January 9, 1961, Eighty-Seventh Congress, 1st Session, vol. 107, part 1, bound edition, 430–31. Williams's administrative assistant sent a copy of the *Congressional Record* with the congressman's remarks, including the inserted Ordinance of Secession, to Roebuck the next day. See series 639, box 711, "'G' Miscellaneous, 1/1961–11/1961" folder, MCWBTS, MDAH.

11. Interestingly, in January 1961, a teenager from New Jersey wrote to Roebuck asking that he and a small regiment he had formed become part of the Mississippi Greys for the purpose of participating in various battle reenactments. The boy, Ronald C. Kurtz, said he had ancestors who fought in the war on the Confederate side. "Because of my kinship I have become an extensive student of the War for Confederate Independence." See Kurtz to Roebuck, January 28, 1961, and March 16, 1961, series 639, box 714, "'K' Miscellaneous" folder, MCWBTS, MDAH.

12. Roebuck to Michelson (CBS), McAndrew (NBC) and Hagerty (ABC), January 27, 1961, series 639, box 715, "'M' Miscellaneous' 7/60–3/61" folder, MCWBTS, MDAH.

13. Descriptions of Alabama's opening centennial events taken from "Oath Davis Took in '61 is Repeated," *CL/JDN*, February 19, 1961, 1, 4, and from "Montgomery Re-enacts the Inauguration of Davis," *NYT*, February 19, 1961, 50. Program of Alabama events included in February 10, 1961, letter of invitation from Governor Patterson to Roebuck, series 639, box 707, "Alabama" folder, MCWBTS, MDAH. Roebuck was reported to be too "chicken" to ride the Barnetts' small plane, and as it turned out, with good reason. A "driving rain" plagued the group's return home. See Moore to Roebuck, March 17, 1961, series 639, box 707, "Alabama" folder, MCWBTS, MDAH. Also see "Oath," *CL/JDN*, February 19, 1961, 4.

14. Barnett's entourage included his cousin and her husband from Carthage, Mayor John Holland of Vicksburg, as well as two of Barnett's secretaries. See "Oath" *CL/JDN*, February 19, 1961, 4.

15. "No State Has More to Offer," *CL/JDN*, February 19, 1961, 2-E.

16. Beauvoir brochure from 1961 found in series 639, box 707, "B Miscellaneous, 5/1961—12/1961" folder, MCWBTS, MDAH. Today Beauvoir boasts a "Jefferson Davis Presidential Library."

17. For more on the senseless slaying of Bud Strong, see Mason, *Beaches, Blood, and Ballots*, 77–78.

18. Parks wrote an account of the finding of the USS *Cairo* during two planned scuba diving attempts in late 1959. See *Helping Build Mississippi*, the official publication of the Helping Build Mississippi Club published as a public service by Mississippi Power & Light. Parks served as the program director for WJTV in Jackson. His first-person account, "Operations Cairo," can be found in the January/February 1960 edition of the magazine, 8–9 in record group 79, box 117, "State Commission, Mississippi, 1958–1965" folder, CWCC, NPS, NA.

19. Topics covered at February meeting compiled in February 25, 1961, minutes, MCWBTS, series 648, box 734, MCWBTS, MDAH. Also see Mississippi Civil War

Centennial News, Press Release #9, February 24, 1961, record group 79, box 117, "State Commission, Mississippi, 1958–1965" folder, CWCC, NPS, NA.

20. Wallace visits recounted in March 27, 1961, minutes, MCWBTS, series 648, box 734, MCWBTS, MDAH. In addition, Holland travelled to Iowa and Roebuck travelled to Wisconsin with the same mission. Barnett Proclamation, undated, found in series 639, box 708, "Barnett, Ross R." folder, MCWBTS, MDAH.

21. Betts to Roebuck, February 9, 1961, and Betts to Roebuck, March 1, 1961, series 639, box 708, "Betts, Karl S." folder, MCWBTS, MDAH.

22. Wilkins's various statements can be found in group III, box A-76, "Civil War Centennial, 1957–1962" folder, NAACP Papers, LOC. These include his memo to Presidents of Branches and State Conferences, "RE: Civil War Centennial," n.d.; and the NAACP press release "WARNS 'PRO-SOUTH' CIVIL WAR PROPAGANDA CAN SET BACK MOVEMENT TOWARD EQUALITY," 3/17/1961. The triggering event for Wilkins was the refusal to house a Black member of the New Jersey CWCC at the segregated headquarters hotel for the upcoming national CWCC's Fourth National Assembly in Charleston, South Carolina. For more, see Cook, *Troubled Commission*, 88–119. Wilkins's call to "Make it clear" led several state NAACP groups to hold teach-ins as counternarrative programming to the official state Civil War centennial commemorations, including in states as varied as South Carolina and New York. It is likely that Evers and Mangram used the same justification to launch the library sit-in as a "countermeasure" to the upcoming Mississippi Civil War centennial events.

CHAPTER 13—"WE'RE NOT SITTING STILL"

1. "Jackson Negro Speaks," *CL*, March 20, 1961, 1, 8.

2. During the James Meredith–University of Mississippi integration crisis, Barnett appeared at the packed, newly renovated stadium holding forty-six thousand football fans attending an Ole Miss game and declared, "I love Mississippi. I love her people. Our customs. I love and respect our heritage." See "On This Day in 1962," https://mississippitoday. org/2023/09/29/on-this-day-in-1962-ross-barnett-whipped-u-all-white-crowd-at-ole-miss/.

3. Evers-Williams and Marable, *The Autobiography of Medgar Evers*, 220–22. The list of demands is summarized.

4. Evers also refers to Leontyne Price in his April 20, 1961, speech at a mass meeting in response to follow-up protests after the library sit-in. See Evers-Williams and Marable, *The Autobiography of Medgar Evers*, 225–27. This reference to Price and Buck Rogers seems to be a standard paragraph dropped into his presentations at this time. Evers even referenced Price during his first locally televised appearance on May 20, 1963, when he was given equal time to rebut Mayor Thompson's defamatory statements about the NAACP in the run-up to the Jackson Woolworth's sit-in. See O'Brien, *We Shall Not Be Moved*, 111.

5. Price's achievement merited a *Time* magazine cover story just two weeks before the Tougaloo Nine library sit-in, complete with a description of downtown Laurel, Mississippi, including the Confederate soldier statue in the town square. See "Music: A Voice like a Banner Flying: Leontyne Price," *Time*, March 10, 1961.

6. Unless otherwise noted, this and other stories and quotations by Dorie Ladner are taken from author's interview, August 1, 2014. Recording and author's transcription in author's possession.

7. "Negro Messboy Gets Navy Cross at Pearl Harbor," *Chicago Tribune*, May 28, 1942, 5.

8. Unless otherwise noted, all quotations of Joyce Ladner are taken from two sources: (1) Dr. Joyce Ladner presentation, October 5, 2011, Jackson State University's "Fiftieth Celebration of the Tougaloo Nine" sponsored by the Fannie Lou Hamer Institute, and (2) Dr. Joyce Ladner presentation, "Daughters of Howard/Women of Excellence" Lecture, Howard University, April 13, 2017. Both lectures were transcribed by and are in the possession of the author.

9. The troubling story of Clyde Kennard is well known in Mississippi civil rights lore. See Dittmer, *Local People*, 79–83, and Evers-Williams and Marable, *The Autobiography of Medgar Evers*, 165, 199–201. Also see Robert Shetterfly's entry "Clyde Kennard" on his Americans Who Tell the Truth website, www.americanswhotellthetruth.org, accessed March 25, 2024.

10. Dorie Ladner recounted going to downtown Hattiesburg to conduct family business on occasion and detouring over to the Hattiesburg city jail to look up to where she imagined Kennard's cell to be while he was awaiting trial. "It was powerlessness to the nth degree," she said.

11. Jackson State history derived from JSU website, https://www.jsums.edu/about-jsu/, accessed July 14, 2022. See also Jackson State University entry in mississippiencyclopedia.org.

12. Reddix biographical sketch derived from Jacob L. Reddix, *A Voice Crying in the Wilderness: The Memoirs of Jacob L. Reddix* (Jackson: University Press of Mississippi, 1974). Also see Reddix entry in mississippiencyclopedia.org. For more on Reddix and his success with cooperatives, see Jessica Gordon Nembhard, *Collective Courage: A History of African American Cooperative Economic Thought and Practice* (University Park: Pennsylvania State University Press, 2014), 108–9, 140–41. During this period, such luminaries as W. E. B. Du Bois and Ella Baker were promoting cooperative business practices, as well.

13. Reddix, *A Voice Crying in the Wilderness*, 124.

14. Jackson State development numbers included in "Jacob Reddix" entry, mississippi encyclopedia.org.

15. Recognizing that she and her husband would be witnessing history in the coming months, Aurelia Young began keeping a diary of developments within the growing protest movement in Jackson. Unfortunately for this study, the diary begins just after the events of late March 1961. The diary is housed in the Aurelia Young Papers, TCC-MDAH.

16. Dr. Beittel in two separate interviews with historians denied knowing anything about the preparations for the library sit-in, indicating that he only found out about it while out of town. See Beittel interview with Johnson, 1987, Amistad Research Center, Tulane University, and Beittel interview with Dittmer, May 25, 1981.

17. Dorie Ladner would at times say that she was the one who recited the prayer. See Emilye Crosby, "'I Just Had a Fire!': An Interview with Dorie Ann Ladner," *The Southern Quarterly* 52, no. 1 (Fall 2014): 79–110.

CHAPTER 14—DAY 1: THE STUDENTS TAKE CHARGE

1. The G. W. Carver Library—a full service and well-appointed facility—opened in 1956 and touted its "modern" look and its "professionally trained librarians" (one of whom was a Tougaloo alum). Built in the wake of the *Brown v. Board* decision—as were many new schools for Black children—the new library was meant to prove the segregationists'

assertion that the races were treated equally in Mississippi. See "Building Meets Community Need," *CL*, April 20, 1956, 9.

2. There are varying reports about who actually called the media. Some suggest it was a Tougaloo student who had been involved in the preparations for the demonstration. Others, including reporters who received the call, said it was Evers himself. Also, some students reported being driven around to the back of the library and entering through the back door in case police were poised to stop those going through the front.

3. This account is derived from an interview Ethel Sawyer provided to researcher Elise Chernier as quoted in the Wiegands, *The Desegregation of Public Libraries in the Jim Crow South*, 148.

4. Transcript, US Court of Appeals for the Fifth Circuit, no. 19961, *Rev. L. A. Clark, et al. v. Allen C. Thompson, Mayor, et al.*, March 6, 1963. See group V, box 1174–175-5 folders "Clark v. Thompson Appeal, 1962," NAACP Papers, LOC. Includes complete transcript as well as background information, depositions, and lawyers' notes.

5. Author's interview with Bill Minor, October 9, 2014.

6. See "Nine Jailed in 'Study-In,'" *CL*, March 28, 1961, 1, and "Tougaloo Students Arrested for Entering White Library," *JDN*, March 27, 1961, 1. Although all were "smartly dressed," Geraldine recounts exactly this interchange in her many descriptions of her interaction with the police, including the "Suh" pronunciation. She recreated this interchange during her comments at the 2017 Historical Marker dedication ceremony. Audio recording and transcript in author's possession.

7. This type of mugshot took on more cultural currency when two months later, the Freedom Riders began arriving in Jackson and were promptly arrested. See Eric Etheridge, *Breach of Peace: Portraits of the 1961 Mississippi Freedom Riders* (New York: Atlas, 2008).

8. Recounted in Evers's March 29, 1961, letter to Roy Wilkins summarizing the events of March 27, 1961, and suggesting that the Tougaloo Nine be invited to the National Convention in Philadelphia. See Evers-Williams and Marable, *Autobiography of Medgar Evers*, 223–24. Bond fund contributors noted in "Trial Set for Today," *JDN*, March 29, 1961, 1.

9. Two important interviews with Beittel provide his perspective on this and other civil rights demonstrations during his tenure at Tougaloo. They are John Dittmer, "Interview with A.D. Beittel," May 5, 1981 (in author's possession), and Clifton H. Johnson, "Interview with Adam Daniel Beittel," 1987, Amistad Research Center, Tulane University.

10. Roebuck to Stockett, March 27, 1961. MCWBTS, series 639, box 720, "'S' Miscellaneous, 1/61–3/62" folder, MDAH. Robert Stockett was the grandfather of Kathryn Stockett, author of *The Help*. Mr. Stockett was concerned about liability should anything go awry with the horses in such an unusually large crowd. Also see Roebuck to Stockett, March 21, 1961, in the same folder.

11. Unless otherwise noted, reports about the events of March 28, 1961, are derived from the multipage reporting and photographs presented in *CL* and *JDN*, from March 27, 1961, to March 29, 1961. Wallace comment: "Proud Rebels Parade," *ST*, March 28, 1961, 1.

12. Quoted notations taken from a seven-page press briefing, Mississippi Civil War Centennial NEWS, n.d., found in record group 79, box 117, "State Commissions, Mississippi, 1958–1965" folder, CWCC, NPS, NA.

13. Liddell's comments taken from two interviews recorded with an interval of more than forty years: "Interview with Colia (Liddell) Lafayette (Clark)," by Dr. Afferteen Harrison,

July 17, 1974, MWC, Jackson State University, 19–21; and "Phone Interview with Colia Liddell Lafayette Clark," by the author, February 16, 2015, 17–18.

14. Cook comments, Tougaloo Nine Fiftieth Anniversary Commemoration, October 6, 2011, Woodworth Chapel, Tougaloo College. DVD and transcription in author's possession. Cook briefly reenacted the scene to entertain the crowd that night. Lassiter comments made during post ceremony remarks at the Tougaloo College Commencement ceremonies, May 2, 2021. Audio recording and transcription in author's possession.

15. Confirmation of the basic facts of what happened that evening are provided by Herbert Wright, National Youth Secretary for the NAACP. In a message to both Roy Wilkins and Gloster Current—and likely conveyed to him via Medgar Evers—Wright states that "following the arrest of the Tougaloo students, some 800 members of the student body of Jackson State College held a sympathy demonstration on their campus to protest the arrests of their fellow classmates. Doctor Jacob L. Reddix, President of Jackson State, attempted to break up the rally but was unsuccessful. He is alleged to have slapped Eunice Steward, 19 year old junior from Pas[c]agoula, Mississippi during a wild melee over the demonstrations. The students rallied from 7:30 to 9:30 p.m. and then broke up and went to their respective dormitories." Wright to Wilkins and Current, March 29, 1961, group III, box A-290, "Sit-Ins—States A-N, 1960–1965" folder, NAACP Papers, LOC. Also see *JDN* account, March 28, 1961, "President Quells Student Disorder," 1.

16. Colia Liddell quotes from interview with Colia Liddell Lafayette Clark, MWC, July 17, 1974, and phone interview by author, February 16, 2015.

CHAPTER 15—DAY 2: SECESSION DAY

1. For weather conditions in Jackson during this momentous week, see front-page stories in all three mainstream papers: "During Centennial Ceremony—Rain May Mar Parade" and "Showers Threaten Festivities," *ST*, March 27, 1961; "Secession Day—Parade Will Go On Come Rain or Shine," *JDN*, March 27, 1961; "Hail, Wind Storms Plow across State," *CL*, March 29, 1961.

2. Author's interview with Martha Bergmark, January 11, 2019.

3. 1960 Census of Population, Supplementary Reports, September 7, 1961—PC(S1)-10: *Race of the Population of the United States by States: 1960*, US Department of Commerce Bureau of the Census.

4. "Reb Yells Enliven Mammoth Parade," *JDN*, March 28, 1961, 1. Also see "Covering the Crossroads," *JDN*, March 29, 1961, 1, and the photo "Clean Up Detail," 5.

5. Minor somewhat facetiously gave primacy of place to this photo on page 2, adjacent to the chapter titled "Characters, Likely and Unlikely," in his *Eyes on Mississippi: A Fifty-Year Chronicle of Change* (Jackson: J. Prichard Morris Books, 2001), a compilation of his insightful columns during the state's most troubling years. His inscription says it all: "to all the 'little people' who helped me fathom what took place in this fathomless state in the last half-century."

6. Author's interview with Bill Minor at his home in Jackson, October 9, 2014. Author's recording and transcription in author's possession.

7. See "Reb Yells Enliven Mammoth Parade," *JDN*, March 28, 1961, 1, 4; "Giant Parade Draws Crowd to Centennial," *CL*, March 29, 1961, 1, 12; and "State's Secession Echoes

Amid Rain; Proud Rebels Parade; Heavy Rains Fail to Curb Cheering Crowd," *ST*, March 28, 1961, 1. All three papers carried large photo spreads. See also "Parade Here Kicks Off Centennial Celebration; 5,000 Will Take Part in Civil War Spectacle," *CL*, March 28, 1961, 1.

8. "Our Readers' Viewpoint—Centennial Observance Offers Opportunity for Good Will," *JDN*, March 30, 1961, 12.

9. Gladys Slayden also rode up Capitol Street in a commission convertible along with fellow commissioner Byrd Mauldin, both dressed in Confederate-era attire. Photo can be found in MCWBTS collection, series 641, box 550, folder 7, MDAH.

10. This group continues to operate. See https://hqudc.org/children-of-the-confederacy/, accessed April 19, 2024.

11. Hazel Brannon Smith's *Northside Reporter* ("Secession Day Celebration Draws Large Crowds Despite Threatening Weather," March 30, 1961) said that "an estimated 25,000–30,000 people watched." Hodding Carter's *Delta Democrat-Times* ("State 'Secedes' from Union with Mammoth Parade in Jackson," March 28, 1961) citing a UPI report, pegged the crowd at "25,000 persons."

12. The Ladner sisters provided first-hand accounts of this protest march, which was also reported in the papers: "Trial Set for Read-Ins Today," *JDN*, March 29, 1961, 1, 14; "Negroes Try Jail March in Jackson," *CL*, March 29, 1961, 1, 16; "Demonstration Curbed," *ST*, March 28, 1961, 1, 2A; and "Jackson Has Its First Sit-In Demonstrations," *JA*, April 1, 1961, 1, 8.

13. Years later in an interview for the radio series *Will the Circle Be Unbroken*, Aurelia Young, wife of civil rights attorney Jack Young, noted that students from Millsaps College had also staged a march toward the courthouse to protest the arrest of the Tougaloo Nine. Though not reported by any news outlet, Young stated that the march was turned back by the police. She also ruefully noted, "The Millsaps students were turned around without incident—the White students. The Black students were chased . . . through the city (and) sprayed with tear gas." (Interview with Aurelia Norris Young, *Will the Circle Be Unbroken*, Collection 934, box 9, folder 8, 3. Rose Library, Emory University.)

14. The Outset program is described in various local news reports: "MS 'Quits' U.S. as State Relives Past; Secession Re-enacted in Old Capitol Drama," *CL*, March 29, 1961, 1, 16; "At Old Capitol: Secession Drama Re-Enacted," *JDN*, March 29, 1961, 4; and "State's Secession Echoes Amid Rain," *ST*, March 28, 1961, 1–2.

15. Dollarhide's original script of "The Outset: A One-Act Play Depicting the Secession Convention of Mississippi" is housed at MDAH, call no. OS/812.5/D690. The script is based on the actual minutes of the Secession Convention, the original of which are also available for review at MDAH.

16. For the complete remarks, see "Jefferson Davis: Complete Text of His Speech before the Legislature of Mississippi," *NYT*, March 17, 1884, 5. Retrieved through *NYT* "TimesMachine," April 15, 2022.

17. See "'New' Old Capitol, with Museum, Opens on Tuesday," *CL/JDN*, March 19, 1961, 3A and 1F.

18. This anecdote is included in this unpublished satirical article by Charlotte Capers titled "Diary of a Museum Director." In it, Capers centered her memory on the Old Capitol Museum's Secession Day grand opening: "When the doors opened at two, approximately 5,000 men, women and children lunged through the building. Madness reigned supreme. Chains snapped, windows broke, doors rocked on their hinges." Capers (Charlotte) Papers,

Accretion, Z/U/1997.019, box 1 of 1, MDAH. Thanks to Clint Bagley, MDAH, and Professor Leigh Ann Wheeler, SUNY Binghamton, for calling my attention to this artifact.

19. "Covering the Crossroads," *JDN*, March 28, 1961, 1.

20. "Interview of Dr. A. D. Beittel by John Dittmer," May 25, 1981, 7. Transcribed by author. In an oral history given six years later, Beittel would say that he had sprung the students from jail, but this was incorrect. ("Interview with A.D. Beittel" by Clifton H. Johnson, director, Amistad Research Center, Tulane University," 1987, 5.) In an earlier oral history from 1965, much closer in time to the event itself, Beittel said, "Mr. Evers arranged for bail and got them out." ("Oral history memoir of Dr. A. D. Beittel," conducted by Dr. Gordon C. Henderson, for "Contemporary Mississippi Life and Viewpoints—1965," in John Quincy Adams Papers 1965–1994, MCA.) See also Evers's report to Roy Wilkins, March 29, 1961, in Evers-Williams and Marable, *The Autobiography of Medgar Evers*, 223–24.

21. Beittel's comments to press quoted: "President Quells Student Disorder," *JDN*, March 28, 1961, 1; "No Action Planned by College," *ST*, March 28, 1961, 2A; and "Tougaloo College Plans No Action against Sit-In Students," *JA*, April 1, 1961, 1.

22. Summary of College Hill Missionary Baptist Church Mass Meeting: "9 Negroes Face Trial Here Today," *ST*, March 29, 1961, 1; "Negroes Try Jail March in Jackson," *CL*, March 29, 1961, 1; "Trial Set Today for 'Read-Ins,'" *JDN*, March 29, 1961, 1 Also see Evers, *For Us, the Living*, 228. In his monthly report, Medgar Evers estimated the "capacity crowd" at College Hill Missionary Baptist Church to be closer to eight hundred.

23. Description of the Confederate Balls: "Centennial Events: Merry-Making Features Balls," by Pat Flynn, and "Four Brilliant Confederate Balls Climax Secession Day Activities," by Seymour Gordon, *JDN*, March 29, 1961, 15.

CHAPTER 16—DAY 3: THE TRIAL, THE DOGS, THE BEAT DOWN

1."Covering the Crossroads," *JDN*, March 29, 1961, 1. Ward's comments were, indeed, self-congratulatory as he headed the Hinds County Company of the Mississippi Greys. Other Jackson-based units included the Burt Rifles, Company K, sponsored by the Jackson Citizens' Council. See Wallace to Snowden, March 6, 1962, MCWBTS, series 639, box 721, "'S' Miscellaneous—3/62–3/64 and undated" folder, MDAH.

2. "Civil War Memorials?," *Atlanta Constitution*, April 8, 1961, 1.

3. "Affairs of State," *CL*, April 1, 1961, 1.

4. "Jackson Police on Guard," *CL*, March 30, 1961, 7.

5. The pundit was Hazel Brannon Smith. See "Through Hazel's Eyes," *NR*, April 13, 1961, 2. *Wagon Train* was a popular cowboy Western TV series.

6. For more on Whitney, as well as a Black perspective of the melee at the courthouse, see "Police Dogs Incidents Puts City in Spotlight," *JA*, April 8, 1961, 1, 6. The next day, Whitney would lose his job at the White-supported seminary because of his presence at the courthouse.

7. Various news outlets record this amalgamation of AP and UPI-filed stories, including "FBI to Study Outbreak of Violence in Jackson," *DDT*, March 30, 1961, 1.

8. Hydrick was a controversial figure in Jackson. He had a history of drunken, violent outbursts at those who crossed him. He had run-ins with law enforcement as early as the mid-1950s. He once shot at a Black man for cursing in the presence of White women. He

always carried a gun and was not afraid to use it. He was charged several times with assault (once with intent to kill) but often got off with just a fine or a suspended jail sentence. Hydrick appears in multiple, unflattering front-page articles in *The Clarion-Ledger*: "Hydrick Appeals in Liquor Case," January 20, 1953; "Hydrick Fined on Gun Charge; Given Suspended Jail Sentence," September 9, 1953; "Hydrick Jailed Here on Liquor Charge: Gets 90 Day Term in County Jail," January 5, 1954; "Wild Auto Chase Lands 2 in Jail; Gun Use Claimed," August 1, 1955; and "Hydrick Charged with Shooting," February 3, 1957.

9. Story of Tom Armstrong and Red Hydrick taken from various news reports, including Bill Minor's first-hand account, "9 Miss. Sit-In Figures Fined; Jackson Police Rout Crowd at Courthouse," *NOTP*, March 30, 1961, 18. Additional Minor quotes from author interview with Minor, October 9, 2014. Also see "Feds Order Inquiry of Clash Here," *JDN*, March 30, 1961, 1.

10. "Race Riot Measure Approved," *CL*, April 28, 1960. "The breaches would be punishable by maximums of four months in jail and a $200 fine."

11. This was the first time the 1960 "breach-of-peace" statute had been used in Mississippi. "Trial Set Today for 'Read-Ins,'" *JDN*, March 29, 1961, 1, 18; and "Feds Order Inquiry over Clash Here," *JDN*, March 30, 1961, 1, 16.

12. See Evers-Williams and Marable, *Autobiography of Medgar Evers*, 223–24. The registration packet for the NAACP annual convention had just arrived at Evers's office, putting it top of mind. See "Memorandum re: Advance Registration for the 52nd Annual Convention, Philadelphia, Pa.," March 23, 1961, series X, box 1478, "Financial File, Mississippi State Conference, 1960–1972 (1 of 2)" folder [item no. HLM-00002087], NAACP Papers, LOC.

13. See "rec'd by phone from Medgar Evers, March 28, 1961," group III, box A-230, Mississippi Pressures, "Jackson, MS, 1956–1965" folder, NAACP Papers, LOC.

14. It is through Wright's memo to Wilkins and Current that we learn that students from both Tougaloo and Jackson State had planned another sit-in for March 29, the day of the trial, at the Jackson Airport, where Wright, the NAACP Youth field secretary, would be arriving. Wright advised against this plan, suggesting instead that Evers and the students hold a mass student rally where they could call for an end to segregation and discrimination. Though likely reluctant, Evers agreed so as not to expose more students to physical danger and legal jeopardy. See "Memorandum: Herbert L. Wright to Messrs. Wilkins and Current, March 29, 1961, RE: Jackson, Mississippi Library Sit-In," group III, box A-290, "Sit-Ins, States A–N, 1960–1965" folder, NAACP Papers, LOC.

15. Text of Wilkins telegram found in group III, box A-230, Mississippi Pressures "Jackson, MS, 1956–1965" folder, NAACP Papers, LOC.

16. Quote found in "Student 'Sit-Ins' Convicted," *ST*, March 30, 1961, 1.

CHAPTER 17—REACTIONS PRO AND CON

1. Detailed stories about the weather appeared on the front page of all three Jackson dailies: "More Storm Days Forecast in State," *CL*, March 30, 1961, 1; "Wind, Hail Likely Here," *JDN*, March 30, 1961, 1; "More Rain Forecast for Jackson," *ST*, March 30, 1961, 1.

2. "Police Dogs Emphasize Law, Order," *ST*, March 30, 1961, 1. The city of Jackson would purchase its own squad of six German shepherds in July in response to the Freedom Rider "invasion." See "Six Police Dogs Will Soon Be 'Regulars' on Force Here," *JDN*, July 12, 1961, 1, 16.

3. Mitchell comments quoted from various sources: "Wire To: Honorable Robert Kennedy," March 29, 1961, group III, box A-230, "Mississippi Pressures, Jackson, MS—1956–1965" folder, NAACP Papers, LOC; "Clarence Mitchell, High NAACP Official, Sees Incidents as Call for More Civil Rights Laws," *JA*, April 8, 1961, 1; "Jackson Mayor Sets TV Appeal Tonight for Racial Quiet," *DDT*, March 31, 1961, 1. Three years would pass before any meaningful civil rights legislation was enacted at the national level.

4. "800 Negroes Hear 'Read-In' Try Praised," *JDN*, March 31, 1961, 4; "FBI Will Probe Charges in Miss.," NO*TP*, March 31, 1961, 18, sec. 3; "Probe Charges of Negroes on Jackson Police," *Daily Herald* (Biloxi), March 31, 1961; "FBI Continues Its Probe of Jackson Racial Violence," *DDT*, March 31, 1961, 1.

5. Mangram comments quoted from various sources: "Map All-Out Drive for Most Backward State," *PC*, April 8, 1961, 3, sec. 2; "Jackson Mayor Sets TV Appeal Tonight for Racial Quiet," *DDT*, March 31, 1961, 1; "Probe Charges of Negroes on Jackson Police," *Daily Herald* (Biloxi), March 31, 1961.

6. "Attempted Blackout: We Don't Want Censorship of News in Jackson," *NR*, April 6, 1961, 2.

7. "Police Halt March by Negro Students," *NYT*, March 29, 1961, 25, and "Police and Dogs Rout 100 Negroes," *NYT*, March 30, 1961, 19.

8. Local businessman Jesse Drake registered as a candidate for mayor the day after the melee at the courthouse. He would demand equal TV time after Thompson's address, claiming it was "80% politics and 20% racial issues." See "Jesse Drake Qualifies for Mayor's Race," *JDN*, March 30, 1961, 1, 16; and "Segregation Views Told by Drake in TV Talk." *JDN*, April 4, 1961.

9. "Affairs of State," *CL*, March 31, 1961, 10. Hills also derided the NAACP's meeting the previous evening: "The highlight, as we get it, was that they took up a collection."

10. Western Union telegram: "NAACP WILL DEFEND NINE," March 31, 1961, group III, box A-230, "Jackson, MS, 1956–1965" folder, NAACP Papers, LOC. A follow-up mimeographed memo containing the entire text of the telegram, along with other commentary from Wilkins, was sent to all "Branches, State Conferences, Youth Councils and College Chapters" the following week at significantly less cost. See "Memorandum to Officers" April 3, 1961, group III, box A-230, "Operation Mississippi, General—1961–1962" folder, NAACP Papers, LOC. Telegrams to Armstrong etc. found in same folder.

11. "NAACP WILL DEFEND," March 31, 1961, group III, box A-230, "Jackson, MS, 1956–1965" folder, NAACP Papers, LOC.

12. NAACP Press Release: "'Operation Mississippi' Now Working Full Force," June 9, 1961, group III, box A-230, "'Mississippi Pressures—Operation Mississippi' General, 1961–1962" folder, group III, box A-230, NAACP Papers, LOC. The commitment to public education would lead directly to the NAACP's ardent support of James Meredith's successful effort to integrate the University of Mississippi the following year.

13. Wilkins, *Standing Fast*, 1.

14. "The Education of the South," *Time*, April 7, 1961, 45; "A Police Dogs' Supremacy in Mississippi," *LIFE*, April 7, 1961, 30; "When Dogs Were Used to Break Up a Crowd," *U.S. News & World Report*, April 10, 1961, 6; "MISSISSIPPI: The Read-In," *Newsweek*, April 10, 1961, 27–28.

15. The study was called *The Audience of 5 Magazines: Size, Characteristics, Possessions, Cost Analysis* (New York: Audits and Surveys Company, 1962), 13. (The fifth magazine was *The Saturday Evening Post*.) It can be found at https://babel.hathitrust.org/cgi/

pt?id=mdp.39076006845627&seq=1, accessed October 15, 2024. The weekly readership numbers per magazine (in millions): *U.S. News & World Report*, 4.07; *Newsweek*, 7.57; *Time*, 8.95; *LIFE*, 31.14.

16. One perhaps unexpected consequence of the library sit-in was the admonition by White parents to their teenage children to stay away from the library, a place where White school-age youth gathered most nights during the school week to do homework and socialize. It had become an unsafe space according to Jeanne Luckett, who was in high school in Jackson at the time. "We weren't afraid that Black people were going to do anything to us. It was just that police were there, and that was a scary thing. . . . Our going to the library slowed down that year." This same reaction by Whites would apply to the zoo, the parks, and eventually to downtown Capitol Street as the Jackson movement shifted to more direct-action tactics. See author interview with Jeanne Luckett, June 28, 2014. Recording and transcript in author's possession.

17. "Thompson to Tell Progress, City Problems on TV Tonight," *JDN*, March 31, 1961, 4; *Today* show appearance reported in "Jackson Mayor Sets TV Appeal Tonight for Racial Quiet," *DDT*, April 1, 1961, 1.

18. "Police Dogs Incidents Puts City in Spotlight," *JA*, April 8, 1961, 1.

19. Both stories, "Mayor Right Not to Ignore Crisis" and "Race Relations Harmony Sought" appeared in *ST*, April 1, 1961, 9A. One of the two officers ejected from the force for excessive roughness was Bennie Oliver, who two years later would show up at the Jackson Woolworth's sit-in and initiate the violence against another Tougaloo-led demonstration. See O'Brien, *We Shall Not Be Moved*, pp. 124–28 for more on Oliver's role and background.

20. Marshall's comments: "U.S. Probing Violence in Mississippi," *PC*, April 8, 1961, 3. Report on Marshall's confirmation: "Senate Confirms Rights Executive," *JDN*, March 28, 1961, 1.

21. "800 Negroes Hear 'Read-In' Try Praised," *JDN*, March 31, 1961, 4.

22. Evers March 31, 1961, affidavit re: March 29, 1961, assault can be found in the FBI vault website as part 3 of the Medgar Evers file, https://vault.fbi.gov/Medgar%20Evers/Medgar%20Evers%20Part%203%20of%205/view, accessed May 12, 2022.

In this same file is information Evers shared with the FBI regarding the March 28, 1961, Jackson State uprising, which he garnered from students who were attacked. Original FBI file no. 100–428915. The March 31, 1961, redacted affidavit can also be found in Kenneth O'Reilly, *Black Americans: The FBI Files* (New York: Carroll & Graf, 1994), 132–36.

23. Wrenn affidavit can be found in Medgar Evers FBI file, part 3, https://vault.fbi.gov/Medgar%20Evers/Medgar%20Evers%20Part%203%20of%205/view, accessed May 12, 2022. A copy of the June 1961 NAACP Operation Mississippi brochure is included in group III, box A-230, "Mississippi Pressures: Operation Mississippi—General, 1961–1962" folder, NAACP Papers, LOC. Another unredacted affidavit by Rev. S. P. Johnson of Canton confirms other reports of police violence. Johnson ended up at the same doctor's office where Armstrong and Whitney were being treated. Johnson affidavit found in Medgar Evers FBI file, part 4, https://vault.fbi.gov/Medgar%20Evers/Medgar%20Evers%20Part%204/view, accessed May 12, 2022.

24. "Tom Armstrong Fails to Appear against Attacker," *JA*, April 8, 1961, 1. Hydrick would also be on hand during the Jackson Woolworth's sit-in of May 28, 1963. (He appears in the famous Fred Blackwell photograph in the upper left.) See O'Brien, *We Shall Not Be Moved*, 124–25.

25. "Solon Blasts Using Sovereignty Body as Secret Police," *DDT*, March 14, 1961, 1, and "Solons Argue over Placing Blame for First State Sit-Ins," *DDT*, March 29, 1961, 1. Also, see "Claims Sovereignty Group to Blame for Sit-Ins Here," *CL*, March 29, 1961, 16; "Sovereignty Group Blamed for 'Read-In,'" *JDN*, March 29, 1961; and "Sovereignty Commission Defended by Evans-Demonstration 'Was Coming,'" *ST*, March 29, 1961, 1.

26. "Young Legislators Assert Independence," *DDT*, March 30, 1961.

27. "Tougaloo Students Arrested for Entering White Library," *JDN*, March 27, 1961, 1, 16.

28. Hollis, *Back to Mississippi*, 134, 137.

29. Reverend Pierce's strokes seriously imperiled the family's economic stability. His condition never fully improved until years later, when Armendia Pierce helped her parents move to her new teaching post outside Erie, Pennsylvania, where Reverend Pierce began to see more competent doctors.

30. The five "inquisitors" were Bayard Van Hecke, proprietor, Jitney Jungle stores; E. C. Vernon, insurance executive; James Young, attorney; Meisburg; and Cox, Dunn and Clark attorney Charles Clark, whose office they met in and who would soon serve as special counsel to Mississippi's attorney general, Joe Patterson, for various civil rights cases, including the James Meredith integration of the University of Mississippi. (See Robert E. Luckett Jr., *Joe T. Patterson and the White South's Dilemma* [Jackson: University Press of Mississippi, 2015], 103.) In August, Meisburg resigned from the board of Tougaloo, saying that "two or three persons there have begun using it as a propaganda center for northern agitators." "Meisburg Resigns Tougaloo Post," *JDN*, August 16, 1961, 4.

31. Beittel's handwritten notes of the meeting (April 17, 1961) and copies of letters to all five individuals (April 19, 1961) can be found in the Mississippi Digital Library, www.msdiglib.org. Copies in author's possession.

32. See John Gregory Speed, "A Beacon of Light: Tougaloo during the Presidency of Dr. Adam Daniel Beittel (1960–1964)" (dissertation, University of Southern Mississippi, 2014) 161–62, which provides insight into the Beittel years at Tougaloo.

33. All referenced letters included in Mangram Papers, box 1, folder 5, "Correspondence: Tougaloo Nine and Desegregation Support Letters—1961," TCA-TC. "We are grateful for Christian leaders like you . . .," Galen Weaver and Chester Marcus to Mangram, April 11, 1961; "Rev. Mangrum—steady, imaginative . . .," from Bob James to "Dear Friends at Tougaloo," Easter Morning (April 2) 1961; "It is such faith in action . . ." from Wm Lloyd Imes to Mangram, April 21, 1961; "We are all very proud," Mangram to Imes, April 27, 1961. All letters can also be found in the Mississippi Digital Library, www.msdiglib.org. Mangram's reference to "the one dozen students" recognizes the nine who sat in plus three more who helped significantly with the planning of the event.

34. For more on SCEF, see SNCC Digital Gateway entry, https://snccdigital.org/inside-sncc/alliances-relationships/scef/, accessed March 22, 2022.

35. "There are many others . . .," Braden to Mangram, April 20, 1961, in Mangram Papers, box 1, folder 5, TCA-TC. "Our goal is to establish . . .," *The Southern Patriot* 19, no. 5 (May 1961). Copy in author's possession.

36. "Spirit Has Caught Fire, 1961," Mississippi Digital Library, John Mangram Papers Collection, https://cdm17313.contentdm.oclc.org/digital/collection/tougaloo/id/6070ai:cdm17313.contentdm.oclc.org:tougaloo, accessed June 8, 2021 (emphasis added).

CHAPTER 18—RISE UP

1. "Coed Denies Being Hit by Jackson State College President J. L. Reddix," *JA*, April 8, 1961, 1.

2. All quotes from "Mean, 'Hate-Negro' Dogs Being Trained in Pittsburgh Area," *PC*, April 15, 1961, sec. 3, 2.

3. Current to Evers, April 4, 1961, group III, box C-245, "Evers, Medgar W., 1961" folder, NAACP Papers, LOC.

4. "NAACP Rally Held at Farish Street Church Sunday," *JA*, April 15, 1961.

5. "Constitutional Government and States Rights"—An address by the Honorable Ross Barnett at the University of Mississippi on April 15, 1961. Found in series 639, box 721, "Speeches, undated" folder, MCWBTS, MDAH.

6. By 2020, nearly sixty years later, the Black population in the United States totaled less than 50 million. Black population as a percentage of total population remained relatively constant at 14.2 percent compared to 10.5 percent in 1960. The 2020 census also confirmed that the state of Mississippi had the largest percentage of Black residents at 36.6 percent, followed by Louisiana (31.4 percent) and Georgia (31.0 percent).

7. In an early form of a racial dog whistle, Barnett's "hang on" could easily been heard as "hang 'em," which makes more sense in the context of his last sentence.

8. The four students were Georgeann Washington, Doris Bracey, and Walter Jones of Jackson State College and Johnny Barbour of Campbell College. See Evers's "Monthly Report: Desegregation Activities," April 21, 1961, group III, box C-245, folder 1, NAACP Papers, LOC. Also found in Evers-Williams and Marable, *The Autobiography of Medgar Evers*, 228–30. Additional details from NAACP press release, "Ride-In Arrests Spark NAACP's March on Bias throughout Mississippi," April 22, 1961, found in group III, box A-230, "Mississippi Pressures: Operation Mississippi, General 1961–1962" folder, NAACP Papers, LOC. Also see "4 Jackson Negroes Held for Mix Try," *ST*, April 20, 1961, 1.

9. Evers remarks attached to his April 1961 "Monthly Report," in group III, box C-245, folder 1, NAACP Papers, LOC. Remarks are also reprinted in Evers-Williams and Marable, *The Autobiography of Medgar Evers*, 225–27.

10. Quoted from Evers's April 1961 "Monthly Report" found in group III, box C-245, folder 1, NAACP Papers, LOC.

11. Evers, Myrlie, *For Us, the Living*, 243.

12. "Ride-In Arrests Spark NAACP's March on Bias Throughout Mississippi," April 22, 1961, group III, box A-230, "Operation Mississippi, 1961–1962" folder, NAACP Papers, LOC.

13. The Evers interaction with Pierce is recounted in a memo from Gloster Current to Roy Wilkins and others dated April 24, 1961, titled "Operation Mississippi." Astonishingly, Current minimizes the danger to Evers of the veiled threats, instead suggesting that the police discomfort "points up the successful beginning of Operation Mississippi." This myopia on the part of Evers's superiors about the danger he was in would persist for the remainder of his life. See group III, box A-230, "Mississippi Pressures: Operation Mississippi, General 1961–1962" folder, NAACP Papers, LOC.

14. Fund-raising flier and accompanying letters found in group III, box A-230, "Mississippi Pressures: Operation Mississippi, Appeal for Funds 1961" folder, NAACP Papers, LOC.

15. The most comprehensive book about the Freedom Rides is Raymond Arsenault, *Freedom Riders: 1961 and the Struggle for Racial Justice* (New York: Oxford University Press, 2006). Also see Dittmer, *Local People*, 90–99, and Etheridge, *Breach of Peace*, esp. 19–29.

16. "Covering the Crossroads with Jimmy Ward," *JDN*, May 24 and May 25, 1961, 1.

17. "Thompson on TV; National Audience Hears State's Side," *JDN*, May 30, 1961.

18. See Current to Wilkins, June 6, 1961, group III, box A-289, "Sit Ins—General, 1961–1964" folder, NAACP Papers, LOC.

19. Hopkins was called as a witness in the *Clark v. Thompson* case, which combined the Tougaloo Nine case with various other breach-of-peace cases. For coverage of local demonstrations during this period, see "Wilkins Says NAACP Supports 'Riders' Ideals," *JDN*, June 8, 1961, 10, and "Incident at Zoo," *JDN*, June 23, 1961, 1.

20. Eddie Jean Thomas, who attempted to integrate the swimming pool, would also be called as a witness in the *Clark v. Thompson* case. For Thompson's threat to close the parks, see "Mayor Vows No Mixing," *JDN*, July 6, 1961, 1.

21. Some of the SNCC members who made Jackson their base of operation included James Bevel, Diane Nash, and Bernard Lafayette. Together they created a "Freedom House" on Rose Street, not far from Evers's NAACP offices at the Masonic Temple and close to the Jackson State campus. See Dittmer, *Local People*, 116–17.

CHAPTER 19—HISTORY MARCHES ON

1. The total for centennial advertising in various publications came to $88,490. See "Mississippi A&I Board, Centennial Ads" attachment to letter from A&I board Travel Department manager Ned O'Brien to Sidney Roebuck, January 17, 1961, series 639, box 716, "Mississippi A&I Board" folder, MCWBTS, MDAH.

2. See Deale to Roebuck, June 2, 1961, and accompanying documents, series 639, box 716, "Minnesota State Chairman" folder, MCWBTS, MDAH.

3. For more on this event, see group III, box A-139, "Fund Raising: 'Freedom Now Suite' 1961" folder, NAACP Papers, LOC.

4. Specific information about the NAACP Freedom Train comes from four documents: "The Freedom Train to Washington" urgent memorandum from Wilkins to presidents of state branches, et al., June 16, 1961; "NAACP Freedom Train" memorandum from Clarence Laws to Wilkins et al., June 29, 1961; "Delegates' Fact Sheet about the NAACP Freedom Train" (n.d.); and "This Is What the NAACP Wants Congress to Do," a list of initiatives, all found in group III, box A-12, "Freedom Train" folder, NAACP Papers, LOC.

5. Indeed, the Secret Service balked when Wilkins first requested that all of the estimated twelve hundred delegates traveling to Washington meet with the president. Instead, a smaller group of about seventy members of the NAACP leadership were vetted for the short meet and greet. See NAACP minutes, NAACP board of directors, July 11, 1961, group III, box A-26, "Board of Directors Minutes" folder, NAACP Papers, LOC. A complete list of those invited to meet with Kennedy is included in the NAACP's records of the Philadelphia convention. See group III, boxes A-12 and A-13, "1961 Annual Convention" folders, NAACP Papers, LOC.

6. Wilkins, *Standing Fast*, 284–85.

7. Wilkins' nineteen-page closing address to the 1961 NAACP annual conference can be found in group III, box A-13, "Speeches" folder, NAACP Papers, LOC.

8. Hollis, *Back to Mississippi*, 147–49.

9. This story is derived from several sources, including "Beittel Says Citizenship Aim of Sit-Ins," *JDN*, September 2, 1961, 16 (which also provided the names of the journalists on the panel), Campbell and Rogers, *Mississippi*, 198–99; and Speed, "A Beacon of Light," 183–85. It is noteworthy that activist teacher John Salter had just arrived at Tougaloo and was staying with the Beittels at the time of Dan Beittel's TV appearance. It was a bracing introduction to Mississippi for the man who would help lead the next phase of the Jackson movement. See John Salter, *Jackson, Mississippi: An American Chronicle of Struggle and Schism* (Malabar [FL]: Krieger, 1987) 6–7.

10. According to NAACP documents, the case was *Students of Tougaloo College v. City of Jackson*. See Young to Carter, March 30, 1961, found in Library of Congress History Vault, https://proquest.libguides.com/historyvault/NAACP, file "001475_006_0023_1_to_121 RCarter-JYoung Correspondence 1961–1965.pdf." For evidence of delay, see "Appeals by Nine Negroes Continued," *JDN*, April 10, 1961, 10, and "Tougaloo Group Hearing Slated," *JDN*, May 9, 1961, 7. The case got pushed to June 9, by which time the Freedom Riders had arrived, the local courts were overrun, and local reporters on the Tougaloo Nine case seem to have lost interest.

11. See "NAACP Files Suit to Desegregate Recreational Facilities in Jackson," *Mississippi Free Press*, January 20, 1962, 1. Also see "Negroes File Suit to Mix City Parks," *CL*, January 13, 1962, 1.

12. Entire transcript of *Clark v. Thompson* case found in the Library of Congress History Vault, https://proquest.libguides.com/historyvault/NAACP, files "001477_22_0001_Ck v T-App—Vol I WMAT 62.pdf" and "001477_22_0196-CvT-Appeal V-II WMAT 62.pdf."

13. A long list of continued cases from 1961 through 1964 can be found in the Library of Congress History Vault, https://proquest.libguides.com/historyvault/Npdf. AACP, file "00147_026_0347_JXN Demonstration Cases 61–66 (1).pdf." The list is attached to an NAACP petition asking the court to drop the longstanding cases, charging that they have been continued indefinitely "with the sole purpose and effect of harassing petitioner."

14. For a brief but compelling account of the Union occupations of Jackson, see Brinson, *Jackson/A Special Kind of Place*, 95–110. See also "Battle and Siege of Jackson" entry in mississippiencyclopedia.org, accessed July 22, 2022.

15. From Yonkers, New York, March 7, 1961, series 639, box 717, "New York State Chairman" folder, MCWBTS, MDAH.

16. For an in-depth look at the Jackson Woolworth's Sit-In and its impact on the local movement, as well as an exploration of the Evers assassination, see M. J. O'Brien, *We Shall Not Be Moved*. Also see Williams, *Medgar Evers: Mississippi Martyr*.

17. MS CWC *Bulletin* 11, June 19, 1961, and "A Special Rededication Day" attachment. See record group 79, box 117, "State Commissions-Mississippi, 1958–1965" folder, subject files, CWCC, NPS, NA.

18. MS CWC *Bulletin* 12, July 5, 1961. See also "Suggested Program for a Civil War Centennial Rededication Day," in record group 79, box 117, "State Commissions-Mississippi, 1958–1965" folder, subject files, CWCC, NPS, NA.

19. See *Report of the Mississippi Commission on the War Between the States (1960–1962 Biennium)*, Jackson, MS, 1962. MCWBTS Biennial Report 1960–1962, call no. 973.76/M69r, MDAH.

20. See Biddle to Everett, July 28, 1960, series 639, box 719, "PA State Chairman" folder, MCWBTS, MDAH. Technically the Battle of Gettysburg was fought from July 1 through 3; the Union victory was announced on July 4. Theoretically, it would have been possible for Civil War enthusiasts to visit both sites for their commemorations, but generally, Civil War enthusiasts picked one or the other site to visit in 1963.

21. Draft "Summary of Vicksburg Centennial," n.d., found in series 639, box 713, "Holland, John D., Chairman" folder, MCWBTS, MDAH.

22. In 1961, $300,000 was equivalent to more than $3 million in 2024.

23. Bearss's *Rebel Victory at Vicksburg* focuses on the South's adept capability of defending the "Gibraltar of the Confederacy" from Union attack during the summer of 1862. One thousand copies were printed, many of them given out at the Vicksburg centennial.

24. See "Military Park Visitations," in "Summary of Vicksburg Centennial," n.d., found in series 639, box 713, "Holland, John D., Chairman" folder, MCWBTS, MDAH.

25. Everett reported that there were one thousand participants in the parade and an estimated forty-five hundred spectators. See draft "Summary of Vicksburg Centennial" in series 639, box 713, "Holland, John D., Chairman" folder, MCWBTS, MDAH.

26. *Sixty Day Mourning Period Proclaimed for Medgar W. Evers* brochure found in NAACP Baltimore archives (prior to the archives' conveyance to the Library of Congress). Copy in author's possession. The resolution—unanimously passed at the NAACP's annual meeting on June 19, 1963, the very day that Evers was buried at Arlington National Cemetery—also called for an intensive lobbying effort during the sixty days "to support the President's Civil Rights Legislation and to cooperate with him in his constructive efforts to relieve tensions in this country." Additionally, the Baptist Convention pledged to underwrite the education of the three Evers children.

27. See Roebuck to Johnson, February 12, 1964, in series 639, box 714, "J Miscellaneous" folder, MCWBTS, MDAH.

28. Johnson inaugural address, as quoted in Katagiri, *The Mississippi Sovereignty Commission*, 143. Johnson campaigned on a staunch segregationist platform, but once inaugurated, he attempted to move his state away from the "rear-guard defense of yesterday" and toward "an all-out assault for our share of tomorrow."

29. See Roebuck to Johnson, February 11, 1964, in series 639, box 714, "J Miscellaneous" folder, MCWBTS, MDAH.

30. Roebuck to commission members, October 19, 1963, in box 718, "Notice of Commission Meetings" folder and Roebuck to Gentry, May 1, 1964, in box 712, "G Miscellaneous, 1/62–4/64" folder, series 629, MCWBTS, MDAH.

CHAPTER 20—THE FIRST TO GRADUATE

1. "Covering the Crossroads," *JDN*, June 7, 1962, 1.

2. Joyce Ladner—another one of Borinski's stars—would follow Ethel to Washington University in St. Louis a few years later. The two women would become lifelong friends.

3. Hollis, *Back to Mississippi*, 163.

CHAPTER 21—THE FOLLOW-ONS

1. At the forty-fifth anniversary gathering of the Tougaloo Nine, Evelyn Pierce—who could not attend due to ill health, but who joined via telephone hook-up—made it a point to comment on Lassiter's voice. "I just *love* to hear Albert talk," she said a bit coquettishly. "Every time Albert talked, I'd have a fit, like a starstruck little girl, because he always had that commanding voice. And, of course, when he stood up, he had a commanding presence. But that voice was out of sight!" Tougaloo Nine Forty-Fifth Anniversary Commemoration, October 14, 2006, Woodworth Chapel, Tougaloo College. DVD and transcription in author's possession.

CHAPTER 22—THE ÉMIGRÉS

1. Cook quotations pulled from transcriptions of the three Tougaloo Nine commemorations he attended: The forty-fifth anniversary gathering in October 2006, the fiftieth anniversary gathering in October 2011, and the historic marker dedication in August 2017. Recordings and transcriptions in author's possession. See also "Obituary for Mr. Alfred Lee Cook Sr" at https://www.lawrenceemoonfuneralhome.com/obituaries/Alfred-Cook-4/#!/ Obituary, accessed June 1, 2023. Copy in author's possession. The Cooks would eventually have three children, Lisa, Cynthia, and Alfred Cook Jr.

2. It was John Held who walked into the office of Sovereignty Commission head Erle Johnston in April 1964 and urged him to do something about Tougaloo president A. D. Beittel. In a now-famous memo from the Sovereignty Commission files, Johnston recounts how Held said "that if Dr. Beittel and [name redacted, likely Ed King] were fired from their positions and the administration could be turned over to more responsible hands, Tougaloo would cease to be a school of agitation and return to its prescribed function of education only." Later that month, Beittel was pushed out, though King remained. See Sovereignty Commission Record no. 1-84-0-8-1-1-1.

3. Pianist Ran Wilde accompanied Jackson on several occasions and said, "It's been my privilege to accompany some of the finest singers in the country in my career and Joseph stacks up well." "Summit Club News" 1962. Joseph Jackson Collection. Copy in author's possession.

4. For this and other details of Jackson's life after Tougaloo, the author is indebted to Gabriel San Román's beautifully rendered profile: "Mississippi Learning: Decades Later, Joseph Jackson Jr. Is Finally Embracing His Role as a Civil-Rights Hero," *OC Weekly*, June 26–July 2, 2015, 20, no. 44, 11–15. Original in owner's possession.

5. See San Roman, "Mississippi Learning," 13.

6. For more on "Medgar Evers Homecoming Celebration," see entry in mississippiencyclopedia.org.

7. Specifics of Ameenah Omar's career and family life can be found in her obituary, published in the Erie *Times-News* on June 27, 2010. Found on the Legacy.com site, https://wwww.legacy.com/us/obituaries/erietimesnews/name/ameenah-omar-obituary?n=ameenah-omar&pid+143764819. The story of Evelyn's first marriage to Al Johnson comes from author's phone interview with her sister Demathraus Pierce Perry.

8. Specifics on the life of Abdul Aziz Omar (Philbert Little) can be found in his obituary: *Detroit Free Press*, February 8, 1994, 14. For more on Omar's role in introducing his brother to the Nation of Islam, see Manning Marable, *Malcolm X: A Life of Reinvention* (New York: Viking, 2011), 75.

9. Local 4 Detroit News, "State Will Manage Highland Park's Finances," December 6, 2000, https://archive.ph/2012.07.15.093738/http://html.clickondetroit.com/det/news/stories/news-20001206-140225.html, accessed May 15, 2021.

10. It is indicative of her personal appeal that Ameenah Omar's funeral was attended by a representative of then-governor Jennifer Grandholm as well as various state congressional leaders and regional officials. "Memorial Program, Dr. Ameenah E. P. Omar," June 12, 2010. Copy in author's possession.

11. Story by Stephen M. Silverman, November 28, 2001, *New Eminem Movie: Some Like It Hot*, can be found on the *People*.com site: https://people.com/celebrity/new-eminem-movie-some-like-it-hot/, accessed June 22, 2021.

12. The story of Omar's enstoolment as Queen Mother comes from author's interview with Armendia (Pierce) Dixon. Also see *Erie Times News*, February 25, 1998, section B-1.

CHAPTER 23—THE END OF AN ERA

1. W. A. Bender, "Desegregation in the Public Schools of Mississippi," *The Journal of Negro Education* (Summer 1955): 287–92. Copy in Bender Papers, box 1, folder 19, TCA. Katagiri also writes about the Negro leaders who refused to go along with the continued segregation of schools. He puts the number at ninety. Katagiri, *The Mississippi State Sovereignty Commission*, xxxi. Bender quoted from Borinski, "Mississippi's Challenge to Tougaloo College," which appeared in the "faculty edition" of the school's newspaper that year.

2. Dedication page, *The Eaglet* 1957, TCA-TC.

3. Mangram Eulogy of William A. Bender, box 1, folder 10, William A. Bender Papers, TCA-TC.

4. Lovelace's work with the Ohio Farm Bureau is recounted on its website, ofbf.org on the blog Together with Farmers in its "Centennial Profile" section. The tribute was posted by Craig Lovelace (no relation), a writer who is compiling a one-hundred-year history of the Ohio Farm Bureau Federation. See https://ofbf.org/2019/06/05/centennial-profile-ariel-lovelace, accessed on June 26, 2021. Lovelace's work in Ohio is also mentioned in what appears to be a career summary used as an introduction of him during Tougaloo's choir tours, found in Music Division Collection, TCA-TC.

5. Profile of Mary Lovelace O'Neal: "A Painter and Social Activist with an 'Unruly Nature,'" *NYT*, March 1, 2020, C1. Also see author interview with Lovelace O'Neal, September 10, 2021. Recording in author's possession.

6. See two memos in Sovereignty Commission files related to Lovelace: "Application of Negroes for Membership in Jackson Music Association," October 24, 1964 (three pages: SCR ID #2-55-11-68-1-1-1; 2-1-1; and 3-1-1), and "Jackson Music Association," October 22, 1964 (one page: SCR ID # 2-55-11-69-1-1-1). The author of the memo, Sovereignty Commission director Erle Johnston, says that "Lovelace has not participated in any of the agitation originating at Tougaloo; in fact, he has several times expressed his opposition to such activities at the college." The fact that Lovelace applied for admittance to the JMA along with

then-Tougaloo Chaplain Ed King, one of the leaders of the 1963 Jackson movement and a continued thorn in the side of the Jackson authorities, suggests that Lovelace had a subversive streak. The others who applied, Robert Honeysucker and Fred Crump, both Tougaloo students, were admitted along with the Lovelaces despite some objections to the youths' previous antisegregation activities. King was denied admission.

7. Interview with George A. Owens by Clifton H. Johnson, November 24, 2000, 41. Amistad Research Center, Tulane University. Copy in author's possession.

8. Borinski, "Last Will and Testament" and "Certificate of Death," found in box 1, folders 28 and 29, respectively, Ernst Borinski Papers, TCC-MDAH.

9. John Mangram Papers, box 1, folders 3 and 4, TCA-TC. "Year of study," letter to Rev. Hubert H. Eaton, October 6, 1960; "plans for the future," letter to Dr. Kenneth I. Brown, November 29, 1960; "the work that I did at Yale," letter to Dr. Kenneth I. Brown, April 4, 1960. Also see "Staff Members Receive Grants," *Tougaloo Southern News*, May 1961, 3.

10. One might have hoped that such a discussion of faith and campus ministry by Mangram would have yielded some stories of his time at Tougaloo. However, the dissertation is a highly theoretical discussion of Richard Niebuhr's work and its values-centric focus for ministry and for life. Copy in author's possession.

11. Mangram's later career summarized from his two-page vita submitted to Tougaloo College in January 2005, Mangam Papers, TCA-TC. Also see Jarvis Christian College alumni magazine *The Jarvisonian*, Fall 2016, 22–23, for more information about the Mangram Ministerial Institute.

12. Mangram appreciation posted on Facebook and other online platforms by Rev. Britt, March 2014. Printout in author's possession.

13. Campbell and Rogers, *Mississippi*, 196.

14. Dittmer, *Local People*, 235–36. Also see Danielle Cerny, "Electric Keeney Acid Test," *The Brown Daily Herald*, September 21, 2004.

15. See Katagiri, *The Mississippi State Sovereignty Commission*, 154–55. Johnston had also demanded the ouster of Tougaloo chaplain Ed King, which did not happen.

16. Derived from two key interviews with George Owens: "George A. Owens Oral History with John Jones," April 8, 1980, MDAH, 25–29; and "Interview with George A. Owens by Clifton H. Johnson," November 24, 2000, 25–30, Amistad Research Center, Tulane University.

17. Reddix, *A Voice Crying in the Wilderness*, 157.

18. Margaret Walker Alexander's profile compiled from two main sources: MWC, JSU website, https://www.jsums.edu/margaretwalkercenter/margaret-walker/; and Internet Poetry Archive, http://www.ibiblio.org/ipa/poems/walker/biography.php, both accessed August 30, 2022. Excerpt from "Sonnets to the Presidents of Jackson State College" used by permission, MWC, JSU. The sonnets first appeared in published form in B. Baldwin Dansby's *A Brief History of Jackson State College: A Typical Story of the Survival of Education among Negroes in the South* (Jackson, MS: Jackson College, 1953), xvii–xix. The five sonnets were reused during the centenary celebration of Jackson State in 1974. See JSU Centennial Celebration Program, Aurelia Young Papers, box 3, folder 34, TCC-MDAH. Also see Margaret Walker Alexander, *Prophets for a New Day* (Detroit: Broadside, 1970), and "A Litany from the Dark People," from Margaret Walker Alexander, *October Journey* (Detroit: Broadside, 1973).

19. Reddix, *A Voice Crying in the Wilderness*, 163.

20. Reddix, *A Voice Crying in the Wilderness*, 222.

21. Reddix biographical summary derived from his memoir, *A Voice Crying in the Wilderness*, as well as from Jacob Reddix entry in mississippiencyclopedia.org, accessed May 30, 2022.

22. Author interview with Dorie Ladner, August 1, 2014. Recording and transcript in author's possession. "I was in Chicago when they sat in at Woolworth's," Ladner said, "otherwise, I would have been right in the middle of it."

23. Dr. Joyce Ladner, "Daughters of Howard/Women of Excellence Lecture, April 13, 2017. Recording and transcription in author's possession. The Ladner sisters are portrayed in the 2023 film *Rustin* about the legendary activist and March on Washington organizer Bayard Rustin.

24. Dorie Ladner would repeat this phrase often, including to the author when he interviewed her in 2014.

25. For a more complete description of the Jackson Woolworth's sit-in, see O'Brien, *We Shall Not Be Moved*.

26. Press release by the Veterans of the Mississippi Civil Rights Movement, "JSU Apologizes to the Ladner Sisters, Williams," n.d., includes this quotation from JSU president Mason's letter of apology. Press release in author's possession.

27. Walter Williams declined to participate in this project, just as he did for the author's *We Shall Not Be Moved*. His story has been pieced together from 1961 news reports and from the February 6, 2013, edition of *Chicago Daily Law Bulletin*. Perhaps as Williams told his surprised court colleagues when they unexpectedly discovered the local Jackson coverage of his receiving his belated diploma in 2011, "It's just, you don't go telling everybody your business."

28. James Baldwin, "Notes for *Blues*," *Blues for Mister Charlie* (New York: Dial, 1964), xv. Baldwin continued his dedication ". . . and to the memory of the dead children of Birmingham." For an insightful article about bringing the play to Broadway, see Anna Venarchik, "When Baldwin Took on the Great White Way," *NYT*, August 4, 2024, Arts and Leisure section, 7.

29. Video footage of this event can be found at https://www.youtube.com/watch?v=tS7hfUSxuvs.

30. "Biden Awards Presidential Medal of Freedom to 19, including Evers, Pelosi and Ledecky," *WP*, May 3, 2024, https://www.washingtonpost.com/politics/2024/05/03/presidential-medal-freedom-recipients-biden/, accessed September 22, 2024. For quotes from Evers family, see Mississippi Public Broadcasting story by Kobee Vance, "Medgar Wiley Evers Granted Presidential Medal of Freedom," May 14, 2024, https://www.mpbonline.org/blogs/news/medgar-wiley-evers-granted-presidential-medal-of-freedom/.

31. For outlines of Aaron Henry's consequential life, see "Aaron Henry" entry in mississippiencyclopedia.org as well as in the SNCC Digital Gateway (snccdigital.org). See also various references to Henry in Dittmer, *Local People*, and in Evers and Marable, *The Autobiography of Medgar Evers*. Also see Françoise N. Hamlin, *Crossroads at Clarksdale: The Black Freedom Struggle in the Mississippi Delta after World War II* (Chapel Hill: University of North Carolina Press, 2012).

32. Percy Greene profile drawn from the following sources: Caryl A. Cooper, "Percy Greene and the *Jackson Advocate*," in *The Press and Race*, ed. David Davies, 54–83; Julius E. Thompson, *The Black Press in Mississippi, 1865–1985* (Gainesville: University Press of Florida, 1993); and the mississippiencyclopedia.org entry "Percy Greene." His age at death was taken

from "Percy Greene," *CL*, April 19, 1977, 8, though the mississippiencyclopedia.org lists his dates as 1897 through 1977. Benjamin Jealous would serve as president and CEO of the NAACP from 2008 to 2013.

33. Profile drawn from the "Colia Liddell Lafayette Clark" entry in mississippi oencyclopedia.org; the "Colia Liddell (Lafayette)" entry in the SNCC Digital Gateway; and Civil Rights Teaching website sponsored by Teaching for Change at https://www.civilrights teaching.org/resource/colia-liddell-lafayette-clark, accessed May 15, 2024.

34. Johnny Frazier's biographical sketch based on snippets of information found online: "John Frazier," Veterans of the Civil Rights Movement website, https://www.crmvet.org/ vet/frazierj.htm; "Frazier, John," Civil Rights Digital Library, University of Georgia, https:// crdl.usg.edu/people/frazier_johnny; "Frazier, John, 1941, University of Southern Mississippi Special Collections, https://specialcollections.usm.edu/agents/people/941; and "The Black Humanist Fellowship," Unitarian Universalist Association, https://www.uua.org/re/tapestry/ adults/resistance/workshop12/182672.shtml. All accessed October 9, 2024. Also see, "Youth Night," *The Crisis Magazine*, August–September 1964, 456, and Evers Williams and Marable, *The Autobiography of Medgar Evers*, 194.

35. Summary of Brown's life derived from his interview with Southern Oral History Project conducted in collaboration with the Smithsonian Institute and the Library of Congress on March 2, 2013, https://www.loc.gov/item/2015669159/, accessed October 9, 2021. Also see *Speak Now: Memories of the Civil Rights Era*, transcript of program with Rev. Dr. Amos Brown on May 27, 2011, MDAH. Additional details and quotes gleaned from author's brief interview of Brown by phone on September 30, 2021. Notes in author's possession. Additional material taken from Brown bio on NAACP Board of Directors site, https://naacp .org/people/rev-amos-brown, accessed September 23, /2024. Printout in author's possession. Also see Mitchell Atencio, "Meet Vice President Kamala Harris' Pastor, Civil Rights Leader Amos C. Brown," *Sojourners*, July 23, 2024, https://sojo.net/articles/meet-vice-president -kamala-harris-pastor-civil-rights-leader-amos-c-brown, Accessed October 9, 2024.

CHAPTER 24—THE OLD GUARD DIES BUT NEVER SURRENDERS

1. Closing profile of Ross Barnett drawn from "Ross Robert Barnett" entry in mississippi encyclopoedia.org and from John Dittmer and John Jones, "An Interview with Ross Barnett," February 11, 1981, MDAH.

2. Roebuck to Barnett, May 30, 1963, in series 639, box 708, "Barnett, Ross R., 7/62–9/63" folder, MCWBTS, MDAH.

3. Roebuck to Johnson, February 12, 1964, in series 639, box 714, "J Miscellaneous" file, MCWBTS, MDAH.

4. See Roebuck obituary in the *Newton Record*, November 10, 1982, 1. Found online at https://www.findagrave.com/memorial/192582987/sidney-theodore-roebuck, accessed August 17, 2022.

5. For an analysis of Ward's career and influence, see David R. Davies and Judy Smith, "Jimmy Ward and the *Jackson Daily News*," in *The Press and Race*, ed. Davis, 85–110. Also see "Daily News Editor Jimmy Ward Retires," *JDN*, January 6, 1984, 1, 10.

6. Thompson was memorialized in various obituaries and editorials, including "Allen Thompson," *JDN*, October 21, 1980, 10A, and "Former Jackson Mayor Dies of Heart Attack,"

CL, October 19, 1980, A16; and "Jacksonians Pause to Remember Man They Elected Mayor 5 Times," *CL*, October 21, 1980, 1, 16. For more on Thompson on the *Today* show, see "Thompson on TV," *JDN*, May 30, 1961; for the proposed debate with Dr. King, see "Thompson Snubs Debate on Sit-In: Invited to Appear on TV with Negro," *JDN*, October 13, 1960, 1.

7. For Thompson conversation with Kennedy, see "JFK Request to Thompson was Urgent," *CL*, July 6, 1984, 1. The article was written in response to the tapes of the conversation being released by the JFK Library in 1984. For more on "Thompson's Tank," see MDAH, "Historic Resources Inventory Fact Sheet, Thompson's Tank," https://www.apps.mdah.ms.gov/Public/prop.aspx?id=2145892973&view=facts&y=1176, accessed May 14, 2024.

8. For Thompson's testimony, see *Congressional Quarterly*, February 20, 1964. On Thomson's acquiescence, see "Mayor Asks Compliance," *CL*, July 1964, 1.

9. See "Thompson Heads Body Here Seeking Freedom of Choice," *CL*, January 31, 1970.

10. See brief obituary, "Chief M. B. Pierce," *CL*, September 11, 1979, 12.

11. See Willie Mae Bradshaw, *Big Red: A Biography of the Late G. W. "Big Red" Hydrick* (New York: Vantage, 1977), 103, 198.

12. See "Jacksonian is Wounded in Fracas," *CL*, August 21, 1961, 1, 6; and "Red Hydrick Is Arrested on Assault," October 15, 1963, 10. The "intent-to-kill" assault charge went to trial, and a jury convicted Hydrick. The Mississippi Supreme Court, however, overturned the conviction on a technicality. See "Court," *CL*, March 5, 1963, 6.

13. Bradshaw, *Big Red*, 230–31.

14. Stephanie R. Rolph, *Resisting Equality: The Citizens' Council, 1954–1989* (Baton Rouge: Louisiana State University Press, 2018), 158–60. Also see mississippiencyclopedia.org entry "Mississippi Private School Association." Bill Minor quote from the Associated Press obituary of Simmons found in *Northeast Mississippi Daily Journal*, November 28, 2007.

15. Rolph, *Resisting Equality*, 165. Also see *Mississippi HISTORYNOW* site, "The Citizens' Council" entry by Stephanie R. Rolph, October 2019, https://www.mshistorynow.mdah.ms.gov/issue/the-citizens-council, accessed May 14, 2024. The page includes a photo of Simmons interviewing Smith.

16. Rolph, *Resisting Equality*, 175 and 183.

17. Rolph, *Resisting Equality*, 186. For Simmons obituary, see "William James Simmons," *CL*, November 27, 2007; also see history of Fairview Inn at https://fairviewinn.com/history-fairview-inn/, accessed May 25, 2024.

18. Quoted in Suzanne Marrs, *Eudora Welty: A Biography* (Orlando: Harcourt, 2005), 308, 312.

19. See "Charlotte Capers" entry in mississippiencyclopedia.org as well as references in Marrs, *Eudora Welty*, 269–70, 486, 517–18, 561.

20. For more on Ed Bearss and his eventful life, see John C. Waugh, *Edwin Cole Bearss: History's Pied Piper* (Washington, DC, and Dallas: Edwin C. Bearss Tribute Fund, and HistoryAmerica Tour, 2003). Also see his obituary: "Edwin Bearss, Park Service historian and Civil War authority, dies at 97, *WP*, September 29, 2020; and an appreciation: "Civil War Expert Treasured for His Tours," *WP*, October 8, 2020, B6. In addition, see author's interview with Ed Bearss, May 10, 2019, and Bearss's presentation to the Civil War Roundtable of DC, November 10, 2019. Recordings and notes in author's possession.

CHAPTER 25—COMING FULL CIRCLE

1. Wilkins's full speech can be found in group III, box A-13, "Speeches" folder, NAACP Papers, LOC.

2. Wilkins would clash publicly as well as privately numerous additional times, perhaps most notably after the assassination of Medgar Evers. See O'Brien, *We Shall Not Be Moved*, 202.

3. Wilkins, *Standing Fast*, 270.

4. For full review, see "He Had a Dream," *NYT Book Review*, August 1, 1982, 10. For *NYT* year-end listing of notable books, see *NYT Book Review*, December 5, 1982, 16.

5. For more on the Evers-Williams rise to lead the NAACP, see Evers-Williams, *Watch Me Fly* (New York: Little Brown, 1999), 249–56. Madison and Bond each, separately, described their roles in her victory to the author.

6. Myrdal, *An American Dilemma*, 4.

7. See Michael Martina and Jarrett Renshaw, "'Democracy Prevailed,' Biden says after U.S. Electoral College Confirms His Win," Reuters, December 14, 2020, https://www.reuters.com/article/world/democracy-prevailed-biden-says-after-us-electoral-college-confirms-his-win-idUSKBN28O0H1/, accessed October 23, 2024. Biden repeated the phrase "battle for the soul of America" and "battle for the soul of the nation" throughout his 2020 campaign. Also see Elizabeth Dias, "Battle for Soul of Nation," *NYT*, January 20, 2021, A12, https://www.nytimes.com/2020/10/17/us/biden-trump-soul-nation-country.html?searchResultPosition=1, accessed October 24, 2024. By the end of the campaign, candidates from both parties were using some version of this phrasing.

EPILOGUE

1. All quotes from Minor taken from author's interview with Bill Minor, October 9, 2014. Recording and transcription in author's possession. It is of interest that in early 1961 Robert Kennedy contacted Ralph McGill, editor of the *Atlanta Constitution*, asking him to compile a list of media contacts, lawyers, and other regional leaders in the South who might give the new Kennedy administration a fair shake. McGill compiled a list of nearly fifty names from nine states. McGill expressed confidence in the list with a few exceptions: "The South Carolina list is quite weak. The Mississippi list is small but both names are excellent." The only names McGill could come up with in Mississippi were Hodding Carter Jr. and Wilson "Bill" Minor. (See McGill to Kennedy [Robert], February 6, 1961, Personal Papers of Robert F. Kennedy, Attorney General's General Correspondence, box 051, "McGill, Ralph" file. John F. Kennedy Presidential Library.)

2. The next day, the hearing was rescheduled due to Hurricane Ian striking the Florida Gulf Coast.

3. Phone interview with Congressman Bennie Thompson (D-MS), September 26, 2022. Recording, notes, and transcript in author's possession.

4. Myrlie Evers, *For Us, the Living*, 235.

5. Historian Neil McMillen coined this term in referring to the Citizens' Council. See McMillen, *The Citizens' Council*, 81.

6. For more on "Seven Days of 1961," by *USA Today* reporters, see https://www.usatoday.com/story/news/nation/2021/10/19/hear-activists-who-changed-history-seven-days-1961-podcast/8511587002/, accessed October 20, 2024.

SELECTED BIBLIOGRAPHY

BOOKS

Bailey, Ben E. *Music in the History of Tougaloo College*. Tougaloo, MS: Tougaloo College, 1986.

Bearss, Edwin C. *Decision in Mississippi: Mississippi's Important Role in the War Between the States*. Jackson, MS: Mississippi Commission on the War Between the States, 1962.

Blight, David W. *Race and Reunion: The Civil War in American Memory*. Cambridge: Harvard University Press, 2001.

Brinson, Carroll. *Jackson/A Special Kind of Place*. Jackson: City of Jackson, 1977.

Campbell, Clarice T., and Oscar Allan Rogers Jr. *MISSISSIPPI: The View from Tougaloo, Second Edition*. Jackson: University Press of Mississippi, 2002.

Carter III, Hodding. *The South Strikes Back*. Garden City, NY: Doubleday, 1959.

Cook, Robert J. *Troubled Commission: The American Civil War Centennial, 1961–1965*. Baton Rouge: Louisiana State University Press, 2007.

Crespino, Joseph. *In Search of Another Country: Mississippi and the Conservative Counterrevolution*. Princeton: Princeton University Press, 2007.

Davies, David R. *The Press and Race: Mississippi Journalists Confront the Movement*. Jackson: University Press of Mississippi, 2001.

Dittmer, John. *Local People: The Struggle for Civil Rights in Mississippi*. Urbana and Chicago: University of Illinois Press, 1995.

Edgcomb, Gabrielle Simon, *From Swastika to Jim Crow: Refugee Scholars at Black Colleges*. Malabar, FL: Krieger, 1993.

Evers, Myrlie (with William Peters). *For Us, the Living*. Garden City, NY: Doubleday, 1967.

Evers-Williams, Myrlie, and Manning Marable, eds. *The Autobiography of Medgar Evers: A Hero's Life and Legacy Revealed through His Writings, Letters and Speeches*. New York: Basic Civitas Books, 2005.

Hamlin, Françoise N. *Crossroads at Clarksdale: The Black Freedom Struggle in the Mississippi Delta after World War II*. Chapel Hill: University of North Carolina Press, 2012.

Hollis, Geraldine. *Back to Mississippi*. Bloomington, IN: Xlibris, 2011.

Jackson, Walter A. *Myrdal and America's Conscience: Social Engineering and Racial Liberalism, 1938–1987*. Chapel Hill: University of North Carolina Press, 1990.

Johnston, Erle. *I Rolled with Ross! A Political Portrait*. Baton Rouge: Moran, 1980.

Johnston, Erle. *Mississippi's Defiant Years: 1953–1973*. Forest (MS): Lake Harbor, 1990.

Jones, Maxine D., and Joe M. Richardson, *Talladega College*. Tuscaloosa and London: University of Alabama Press, 1990.

Katagiri, Yasuhiro. *The Mississippi State Sovereignty Commission: Civil Rights and States Rights*. Jackson: University Press of Mississippi, 2001.

Marsh, Charles. *God's Long Summer: Stories of Faith and Civil Rights*. Princeton: Princeton University Press, 1997.

Masouka, Jitsuichi, and Preston Valien, eds. *Race Relations, Problems and Theory: Essays in Honor of Robert E. Park*. Chapel Hill: University of North Carolina Press, 1961.

McMillen, Neil R. *Dark Journey: Black Mississippians in the Age of Jim Crow*. Urbana: University of Illinois Press, 1989.

McMillen, Neil R. *The Citizens' Council: Organized Resistance to the Second Reconstruction 1954–1964*. Urbana: University of Illinois Press, 1971.

Minor, Bill. *Eyes on Mississippi: A Fifty-Year Chronicle of Change*. Jackson: J. Prichard Morris Books, 2001.

Morris, Tiyi M. *Womanpower Unlimited and the Black Freedom Struggle in Mississippi*. Athens: University of Georgia Press, 2015.

Myrdal, Gunnar. *An American Dilemma: The Negro Problem and Modern Democracy*. Single vol. ed. New York: Haper & Brothers, 1944.

O'Brien, M. J. *We Shall Not Be Moved: The Jackson Woolworth's Sit-In and the Movement It Inspired*. Jackson: University Press of Mississippi, 2013.

O'Reilly, Kenneth. *Black Americans: The FBI Files*. New York: Carroll & Graf, 1994.

Reddix, Jacob L. *A Voice Crying in the Wilderness: The Memoir of Jacob L. Reddix*. Jackson: University Press of Mississippi, 1974.

Rolph, Stephanie R. *Resisting Equality: The Citizens' Council, 1954–1989*. Baton Rouge: Louisiana State University Press, 2018.

Smith, Frank E. *Congressman from Mississippi*. New York: Random House, 1964.

Southern, David W. *Gunnar Myrdal and Black-White Relations: The Use and Abuse of "An American Dilemma" 1944–1969*. Baton Rouge: Louisiana State University Press, 1987.

Wilkie, Curtis. *DIXIE: A Personal Odyssey through Historic Events That Shaped the Modern South*. New York: Simon and Schuster, 2001.

Wilkins, Roy (with Tom Matthews). *Standing Fast*. New York: Viking, 1982.

Williams, Michael Vinson. *Medgar Evers: Mississippi Martyr*. Fayetteville: University of Arkansas Press, 2011.

Wilson, Charles E. (chair). *To Secure These Rights: The Report of the President's Committee on Civil Rights*. New York: Simon and Schuster, 1947.

JOURNAL ARTICLES

On *An American Dilemma*

Du Bois, W. E. B., and Reuter, E. B. "Review: The American Dilemma." *Phylon* 5, no. 2 (1944): 114–24.

Dunbar, Leslie W. "The Enduring American Dilemma." *Virginia Quarterly Review* 59, no. 3 (1983): 369–83.

Matzner, Egon. "Portrait: Gunnar Myrdal." *Challenge* 20, no. 2 (May/June 1977): 67–68.

Pressman, Steven. "*An American Dilemma*: Fifty Years Later." *Journal of Economic Issues* 28, no. 2 (June 1944): 577–85.

Southern, David W., "*An American Dilemma* after Fifty Years: Putting the Myrdal Study and Black-White Relations in Perspective." *The History Teacher* 28, no. 2 (February 1995): 227–53.

On Tougaloo College, Campbell College, and the Mississippi Movement

Crosby, Emilye. "'I Just Had a Fire!': An Interview with Dorie Ann Ladner." *The Southern Quarterly* 52, no. 1 (Fall 2014): 79–110.

Dittmer, John. "The Politics of the Mississippi Movement, 1954–1964." *The Civil Rights Movement in America*, ed. Charles W. Eagles. Jackson: University Press of Mississippi, 1986.

Lowe, Maria R. "An 'Oasis of Freedom' in a 'Closed Society': The Development of Tougaloo College as a Free Space in Mississippi's Civil Rights Movement, 1960 to 1964." *Journal of Historical Sociology* 20, no. 4 (December 2007). 486–520.

Lowe, Maria R. "'Sowing the Seeds of Discontent': Tougaloo College's Social Science Forums as a Prefigurative Movement Free space, 1952–1964." *Journal of Black Studies* 39, no. 6 (July 2006) 865–87.

Lowe, Maria R. "An Unseen Hand: The Role of Sociology Professor Ernst Borinski in Mississippi's Struggle for Racial Integration in the 1950s and 1960s." *Leadership* 4, no. 1 (2008): 27–47.

Williamson, Joy Ann. "Quacks, Quirks, Agitators, and Communists: Private Black Colleges and the Limits of Institutional Autonomy." *History of Higher Education Annual: 2003–2004* 23, ed. Roger L. Geiger, 49–81. New York: Routledge/Taylor & Francis, 2005.

On the Mississippi Civil War Centennial

Foster, Gaines M. "What's Not in a Name: The Naming of the American Civil War." *Journal of the Civil War Era* 8, no. 3 (September 2018) 416–54.

Gondos, Victor. "Karl S. Betts and the Civil War Centennial Commission." *Military Affairs* 27, no. 2, Civil War Issue (Summer 1963) 49–70.

Reonas, Matthew. "Served Up on a Silver Platter: Ross Barnett, the Tourism Industry, and Mississippi's Civil War Centennial." *The Journal of Mississippi History* 72, no. 2 (Summer 2010).

Warrick, Alyssa D. "Mississippi's Greatest Hour." *Southern Cultures* 19, no. 3 (Fall 2013) 95–112.

DISSERTATIONS

Chamberlain, Daphne Rochelle. "And a Child Shall Lead the Way: Children's Participation in the Jackson, Mississippi, Black Freedom Struggle, 1946–1970." University of Mississippi, May 2009.

McWhite, Sally Leigh. "Echoes of the Lost Cause: Civil War Reverberations in Mississippi from 1865 to 2001." University of Mississippi, May 2003.

Speed, John Gregory. "A Beacon of Light: Tougaloo during the Presidency of Dr. Adam Daniel Beittel (1960–1964)." University of Southern Mississippi, Spring 2014.

PERIODICALS

San Roman, Gabriel. "Mississippi Learning: Decades Later, Joseph Jackson Jr. Is Finally Embracing His Role as a Civil-Rights Hero." *OC Weekly* 20, no. 44 (June 26–July 2, 2015): 11–15.

AUTHOR'S INTERVIEWS (All recordings and transcriptions in author's possession)

Anding, Jr., Meredith. Interviews conducted in person on October 27, 2014, Grand Isle, NY, and on April 1, 2016, Brandon, MS.

Bergmark, Martha. Interview conducted in person on January 11, 2019, Washington, DC.

Bradford, James "Sammy." Interview conducted in person on June 24, 2014, Jackson, MS.

Brown, Rev. Amos. Interview conducted by phone on September 30, 2021.

Dixon, Armendia (Pierce). Interview conducted in person on October 26, 2014, in Meadville, PA.

Edwards, Geraldine. Interview conducted in person on June 27, 2014, Tougaloo College, MS.

Jackson, Janice. Interview conducted in person on September 17, 2014, Ferguson, MO.

Jackson, Jr., Joseph. Interviews conducted by phone on July 11, 2014, and on February 10, 2024; and in person on July 29, 2018, Orange County, CA.

King, Rev. Ed. Interviews conducted in person on February 9–11, 1996, and on August 21, 2017, Jackson, MS.

Ladner, Dorie. Interview conducted in person on August 1, 2014, Washington, DC.

Lassiter, Sr., Albert. Interview conducted in person on June 24, 2014, Jackson, MS.

Liddell Lafayette Clark, Colia. Interview conducted by phone on February 16, 2015.

Lovelace O'Neal, Mary. Interview conducted by phone on September 10, 2021.

Luckett, Jeanne. Interview conducted in person on June 28, 2014, Jackson, MS.

Minor, Wilson "Bill." Interview conducted in person on October 9, 2014, Jackson, MS.

Pierce Perry, Demathrus. Interview conducted by phone on May 19, 2021.

Sawyer, Ethel. Interview conducted in person on September 16, 2014, St. Louis, MO, and September 17, 2014, Ferguson, MO.

Thompson, Congressman Bennie. Interview conducted by phone on September 26, 2022.

OTHER ORAL HISTORIES

Barnett, Governor Ross R. "An Interview with Ross Barnett," conducted by John Jones and John Dittmer, February 11, 1981. MDAH.

Barnett, Governor Ross R. "Ross R. Barnett, Oral History Interview," conducted by Dennis O'Brien (no relation to author), May 6, 1969, Oral History Project, John F. Kennedy Library.

Beittel, Dr. A. D. "Beittel, Adam, Oral History Interview 1987," conducted by Clifton H. Johnson, Amistad Research Center, Tulane University.

Beittel, Dr. A. D. "Interview with A. D. Beittel," conducted by Dr. John Dittmer, May 25, 1981. (Copy of audio recording and author's transcription in author's possession.)

Beittel, Dr. A. D. "Oral History Memoir of Dr. A. D. Beittel," conducted by Gordon C. Henderson, director, Oral History Project, Millsaps College, June 2, 1965. (John Quincy Adams Papers, 1965–1994, folder 16, box 6–8, Contemporary Mississippi Life and Viewpoints, Millsaps-Wilson Library).

Bradford, James C. "James C. 'Sam' Bradford Interview," conducted by Worth Long, April 30, 1983, Civil Rights Radio Documentary Project, Southern Regional Council. Housed at Rose Manuscript Archives and Rare Book Library, Emory University.

Brown, Amos C, "Amos C. Brown Oral History Interview" conducted by David P. Cline in collaboration with the Smithsonian Institute and the Library of Congress," March 2, 2013. Video. https://www.loc.gov/item/2015669159/.

King, Jr., Rev. R. Edwin. "An Interview with Rev. R. Edwin King, Jr.," November 8, 1980, by John Jones, MDAH.

Liddell Lafayette Clark, Colia. Interview with Mrs. Colia Liddell Lafayette Clark, conducted by Dr. Alferdteen Harrison, July 17, 1974. Jackson State Oral History Project, Jackson State University. (Housed at Margaret Walker Center, JSU.)

Owens, George. "George A. Owens Oral History with John Jones," April 8, 1980, MDAH.

Owens, George. "Interview with George A. Owens by Clifton H. Johnson," November 24, 2000, Amistad Research Center, Tulane University.

Young, Aurelia Norris. "Interview with Aurelia Norris Young," conducted by Worth Long, n.d., Civil Rights Radio Documentary Project, Southern Regional Council. Housed at Rose Manuscript Archives and Rare Book Library, Emory University.

PRESENTATIONS AND PROGRAMS

Remarks by Dr. Joyce Ladner, Fiftieth Anniversary Celebration of the Tougaloo Nine, October 2011, Fannie Lou Hamer Institute, Jackson, Mississippi. Copy of DVD and author's transcription in author's possession.

Remarks by Dr. Joyce Ladner, April 13, 2017, "Daughters of Howard/Women of Excellence Lecture," Howard University. Author's audio recording and transcription in author's possession.

Tougaloo Nine Forty-Fifth Anniversary Commemoration, October 14, 2006, Woodworth Chapel, Tougaloo College (two sessions, with moderators Rev. Ed King, a.m., and Prof. Richard Johnson, p.m.). Copy of DVD and author's transcription in author's possession.

Tougaloo Nine Fiftieth Anniversary Commemoration, October 6, 2011, Woodworth Chapel, Tougaloo College (with Provost Betty Parker Smith and historian John Dittmer). Copy of DVD and author's transcription in author's possession.

Tougaloo Nine Historical Marker Unveiling Ceremony and Panel Discussion, August 17, 2017, Eudora Welty Library, Jackson, Mississippi. Author's audio recording and transcription in author's possession.

Tougaloo Nine Receipt of Honorary Doctor of Humane Letters from Tougaloo College, May 2, 2021. Postceremony remarks made by Alfred Cook, Albert Lassiter, and Geraldine Edwards Hollis. Author's audio recording and transcription in author's possession.

Tougaloo Nine Thirtieth Anniversary Program, March 27, 1991. Box 1, folder 11, TCC-MDAH.

BOOKLETS AND BROCHURES

*Mississippi in the War Between the States: A Booklet of Facts for the Information of
    Mississippians in Connection with the Observance of the Civil War Centennial—1961–1965.*
    Jackson: Mississippi Commission on the War Between the States, 1960.
*Mississippi's Greatest Hour: A Manual for local Observances of the Centennial of the War
    Between the States—1961–1965.* Jackson: Mississippi Commission on the War Between the
    States, 1960.
*Join the Mississippi Greys: A Guide for the Organization of Units of Mississippi's Centennial
    Military Force In Memoriam.* Jackson: Mississippi Commission on the War Between the
    States, 1960.

INDEX

Index subentries are arranged chronologically.

ABOUT THE AUTHOR

M. J. O'Brien is a writer and researcher who served for twenty-five years as the chief communications and public relations officer for a national not-for-profit cooperative. He is author of the award-winning *We Shall Not Be Moved: The Jackson Woolworth's Sit-In and the Movement It Inspired*, published by University Press of Mississippi.